The Story of an Underground
The Resistance of the Jews of Kovno in the Second World War

The Story of an Underground

Dov Levin and Zvie A. Brown
Translated by Jessica Setbon

gefen גפן
publishing house בית הוצאה לאור
JERUSALEM ◆ NEW YORK   Est. 1981

Cover Design: Leah Ben Avraham/Noonim Graphics
Typesetting: Raphaël Freeman, Renana Typesetting

Originally published in Hebrew by Yad Vashem, 1962

ISBN: 978-965-229-616-0

1 3 5 7 9 8 6 4 2

Gefen Publishing House Ltd.
6 Hatzvi Street
Jerusalem 94386, Israel
972-2-538-0247
orders@gefenpublishing.com

Gefen Books
11 Edison Place
Springfield, NJ 07081
516-593-1234
orders@gefenpublishing.com

www.gefenpublishing.com

Printed in Israel

Send for our free catalog

LIBRARY OF CONGRESS CATALOGING-IN-PUBLICATION DATA
Bar-On, Abraham Zvie, author.
 [Toldoteha shel mahteret. English]
 The story of an underground : the resistance of the Jews of Kovno in the Second
World War / Zvie A. Brown and Dov Levin ; translated by Jessica Setbon.
   pages cm
 Includes bibliographical references and index.
 ISBN 978-965-229-616-0 (alk. paper)
 1. Jews--Lithuania--Kaunas--History--20th century. 2. World War, 1939–1945--Underground
movements--Lithuania--Kaunas. 3. World War, 1939–1945--Jewish resistance--
Lithuania--Kaunas. 4. Kaunas (Lithuania)--Ethnic relations. 5. Lithuania--History-
-German occupation, 1941–1944. I. Levin, Dov, 1925 January 27– author. II. Title.
 DS135.L52K38213 2014
 940.53'4793--dc23
                        2014005917

*This edition is dedicated to the memory of
Idan Geffen (1990–2009), born in Israel,
great-grandson of Rabbi Tuvia Geffen from Kovno,
who died tragically while serving
in the Israel Defense Forces.*

To the memory of:

My father Moshe-Pinchas Brown from Warsaw,
my mother Rosa (Hirshkoff) from Volomin
and my sister Chava from Warsaw

My father Zvi-Hirsh Levin from Kovno,
my mother Bluma (Vigoder) from Vakshena,
and my twin sister Batya from Kovno

Who were murdered by the Nazis

CONTENTS

Foreword

I am writing this foreword in Jerusalem on Memorial Day for the Victims of the Holocaust, April 28, 2014, seventy years after the liquidation of the Kovno Ghetto. In many respects one could not think of a more appropriate day to write a foreword to Dov Levin and Zvie Brown's volume, *The Story of an Underground: The Resistance of the Jews of Kovno in the Second World War.* The book was first published in Israel in Hebrew in 1962, fifty-two years ago, one year after Eichmann was put to trial in Jerusalem, a landmark in the construction of the Israeli image of the Holocaust and the survivors.

It was the first research monograph on Jewish resistance during the Holocaust, a case study of the Kovno Ghetto, which followed a series of anthologies on ghetto life, on the resistance and on the partisans. The authors, themselves members of the underground in the ghetto and partisans in the forest, had first-hand information, and participated in some of the events described in the book.

One may ask why translate and publish a book that is fifty-two years old? The question becomes more troubling if one remembers that during those years, the documentation on the Holocaust, including Kovno, increased dramatically and became more readily available to researchers. Since the 1990s, archives in Russia and in all ex-Soviet countries that hold great archival treasures were opened to researchers, and in the last decade scholars in most countries may use the new technology of the internet and digitization to reach the archives and read documents from their desk at home. The accessibility of original documentation is getting easier as time goes by.

The response to the above question is grounded on the importance of the book in its original form despite or even because of its old age. Moreover, its conclusions are still valid and valuable to the understanding of the origins of the underground movement in the Kovno Ghetto and its activities and fighting in the forest. Additionally, the research methodology used by the authors, oral history, though novel at the time, is even more relevant today, and in recent years is implemented to a large extent by historians and social scientists.

In support of my claims one should note that to date the Kovno Ghetto as a whole has not been the subject of an academic monograph. The two important and comprehensive monographs (by Yosef Gar, published in Yiddish in 1948, and by Lieb Garfunkel, published in 1959 in Hebrew), were written by persons who were directly involved in the work of the Jewish council. Garfunkel was second to the head of the Ältestenrat and Gar was employed in the labor department. Though both monographs are detailed, well written, comprehensive and extremely important, they represent the perspective of activists in the ghetto council, which shaped the internal public life. Though these two works are different from the large numbers of memoirs and narratives of Kovno's survivors that were published during these five decades, neither of these two publications was an academic critical history. Together with the numerous memoirs, they will greatly serve the future academic research on the Kovno Ghetto.

As to other general research on the Jewish underground and Jewish resistance in occupied Europe that has been published to date, it does not include Kovno, and *The Story of an Underground* still stands at the center of research on this subject. For the informed reader Levin and Brown's book will demonstrate how the larger context of Jewish resistance sheds light on the Kovno Ghetto resistance and partisans and offers a comparative analysis.

I would therefore conclude that despite the "old age" of the volume, we may look at it as "old wine." It still serves the interested reader well, and will challenge the student to compare and ask how one should integrate the information and associate it with other phenomena of Jewish resistance in Eastern Europe.

I would like now to relate to the methodology developed in the volume. The authors demonstrated that despite being members of the underground and partisans in the forest, they were able to produce a comprehensive analysis based on solid and sound research. They devoted great effort to create a methodology that would, on the one hand, make up for the missing archival materials and, on the other, safeguard the manuscript from becoming a memoir of two scholars who lived through the experience of resistance and partisans. Aware of these potential shortcomings, they thoroughly investigated the documentation in Yad Vashem archives, including the photocopies of Gestapo files of the Kovno area and Lithuania in general, and thus were able to reconstruct much of the German approach to the Jewish council and the policy of extermination and forced labor.

But they were still short of a detailed and multivocal Jewish narrative of ghetto life, beyond their personal experience, and lacking information on the origin and formation of the underground and its relationship with the Jewish council. Therefore they decided to create a database of such narratives through testimonies of ghetto survivors from all walks of life. This would allow them to gain a broad perspective of ghetto life and enable them to focus their research on what they defined as "active resistance." They used the definition of active resistance while acknowledging other forms of resistance. The outcome was the creation of a sizable oral history and a foundation for the systematic methodology of the use of oral history in the writing of the Holocaust. This was an important contribution to the writing of the history of the Holocaust in general, not just in the case of Kovno. They proved that survivors' testimonies, often the only sources for describing events within the Jewish communities, were vital and reliable.

In this respect reading *The Story of an Underground* is not only a lesson in the history of the underground and resistance in the Kovno Ghetto, but also a lesson in the historiography of the Holocaust that aims to present the Jews as a major actor and a subject of research. The Jewish perspective is presented in the book in the broader context and in connection to the political and military developments in Lithuania and the European theater of the war.

I would like to end by a note of thanks to Dov Levin. As a colleague I enjoyed his expertise in the use of oral history. I interviewed survivors for my own research, and Levin's knowledge and experience were a great source of support.

Dalia Ofer
Jerusalem

Dr. Dalia Ofer is Professor Emeritus of Contemporary Jewry and Holocaust Studies in the Avraham Harman Institute of Contemporary Jewry and Melton School for Jewish Education at the Hebrew University of Jerusalem. She is a member of the academic committee of the Diana Zborowski Center for the Study of the Aftermath of the Holocaust in the Yad Vashem International Institute of Holocaust Studies.

Preface

Why did I want to see this book published in English over fifty years after its first publication?

It is a story of connections – connections to family and to a people's fate. Dov Levin, originally from Kovno, Lithuania, and one of the authors of this book, is my second cousin. Dov survived the Holocaust and made it to Israel in 1945. I grew up safely in the United States because my grandfather, Rabbi Tuvia Geffen, decided to leave Kovno and immigrated to the US in 1903. After Dov arrived in Israel, he wrote to his great uncle Tuvia, one of the few family members alive in the world that he knew of. As a result, the American branch of the family remained in contact with Dov throughout the years, visiting him in Israel when they traveled there. When several of my cousins immigrated to Israel, Dov and his wife Bilha were an important source of support in their new country.

I first met Dov in 1974, when I visited Israel for the first time as a teenager. Prior to that I had heard stories about him and how he had survived the Holocaust as a partisan in the forests of Lithuania. My father had a couple of Dov's books in Hebrew in our house, but even though I had learned Hebrew growing up, there was no way I could tackle the language level of academic research. So we continued to hear occasional stories of what Dov had done in the war, but never many details. On a tour of the US in 1980, Dov and Bilha visited me at my home on an old farmstead in western Massachusetts. As we took a walk through the surrounding woods Dov remarked how it reminded him of the forests in Lithuania that had been his allies.

I moved to Israel in 1982 and, like the rest of my cousins, enjoyed Dov and Bilha's hospitality and help. When I married Yaffa and we had our two children, Idan and Aynat, I made sure that we continued to visit them so that the kids would get to know them well. Dov played with them and followed their progress over the years. In 2009 we suffered the sudden loss of our son Idan while he was serving in the Israel Defense Forces. I remember that evening, when Dov called me and tried to comfort me. That broke me – this man, who had lost his entire family, including his twin sister, in the Holocaust, is consoling *me*.

For some reason I started to read Dov's books that had been published in English about the Holocaust. I continued to visit him at his home in Jerusalem, especially since his health was deteriorating. I remembered one of those books in Hebrew from my father's bookshelf, the first one that Dov authored, which was about the Jewish resistance that he had been a part of – the book that was too hard for me to read as a teenager. I ordered a copy from a rare book store, picking one that Dov had once autographed to someone. After reading it, I could "return" the book to Dov after fifty years and get a new autograph to me.

I was amazed by "The Story of an Underground." Although I thought I knew more than the average person about the history of the Holocaust, here were accounts that I had never heard before. The dramatic escape from the hell of the Ninth Fort, the resistance in the Kovno Ghetto, the life of the partisans in the forests and their struggle against the Nazis – all vividly portrayed. I decided that this book had to be made available to the world in English and received Dov's permission to organize the translation and publication. At the same time there was something else driving me: seeing the photos in the original edition of various underground and partisan fighters, as well as a photo of Dov himself as a partisan, most of whom were around the age of nineteen then and many of whom did not survive, I suddenly saw my son Idan, who was nineteen when we lost him, a fighter for his people. The circumstances then and now are of course worlds apart, but there is a direct connection between the armed Jewish resistance to the Nazis in World War II, the building of the Jewish army before the establishment of the State of Israel, and the commitment of the young people in Israel today to the security of their country and people. Dov instinctively understood what I was feeling. He readily granted me permission to dedicate this edition to Idan. When I asked him for a photo of himself to put into the book, he insisted that I also include a photo of Idan, as well as one of his good friend and co-author Zvie Brown.

So the publication of this book became not only a tribute to Dov's work, but also a memorial to my son. Due to Dov's health I took on the task of going over the translated and edited text. There were a number of points to be clarified, and while Dov was able to help with that during much of the process, I am solely responsible for any errors due to mistakes in translation or editing. My hope is that this English version will be a help to academic researchers of the Holocaust and also a readable account for interested people everywhere of how a small group of young people acted to survive in impossible and terrible circumstances.

I would like to acknowledge the following people who helped bring this project to fruition: my cousin Rabbi Dr. David Geffen of Jerusalem, who put me in touch with Gefen Publishing House (no relation to our family) and continued to encourage me and check on my progress; my cousin Sheila Wilensky, for her useful advice and continual encouragement; the publisher, Ilan Greenfield, who immediately saw the value in translating this work; Jessica Setbon, for her work on the translation; the staff at Gefen Publishing, particularly the project manager Lynn Douek and editor Ita Olesker; graphic artist Talya Shachar-Albocher, whose renderings enabled us to present clearly in English the original maps and drawings; Shalom Eilati, for his encouragement and permission to use maps from his book *Crossing the River*; Yad Vashem Archives, for the use of photos; the archivists Zvi Oren (The Ghetto Fighters' House Archives), Daniela Ozacky-Stern (Moreshet Archives), and Lyudmila Sholokhova (YIVO Institute), who helped us track down and succeed in finding practically all of the original photos and documents that appeared in the 1962 edition.

Special thanks goes to Dr. Dalia Ofer, who graciously agreed to write the foreword to this edition, explaining the relevancy of the book fifty years after it was first published.

Finally, my heartfelt gratitude to my wife Yaffa, whose helpful advice and love enabled me to find the strength to carry out this project.

Robert (Reuven) Geffen

Nir Moshe, May 2014

Introduction

The Holocaust and Jewish Resistance in Eastern Europe

The Jewish communities of Eastern Europe, which fell into the hands of the Nazi army at the beginning of the war between Germany and the Soviet Union in 1941, suffered the terrible fate of being the first victims of the "final solution" designed by Nazi leaders for the Jews of Europe. Detachments of murder specialists, called *Einsatzgruppen* ("special task forces"), marched on the heels of the German army, their first task in every conquered town being to plot against the local Jewish community, plunder their property, humiliate them before the people among whom they lived by persecution and abuse, and immediately afterwards to physically destroy them. Hundreds of Jewish communities were engulfed in this torrent of blood and destruction, and hundreds of thousands of our people met their death in this way. From the day that Hitler's troops entered a town, not many months would pass before the Jewish community was torn up by its roots and wiped off the face of the earth. It happened in Lithuania, in Latvia and Estonia, in the Ukraine and Byelorussia, and in other parts of the Soviet Union.

Here and there, however, in these broad areas of conquest, the *Einsatzgruppen* refrained from completing the total immediate annihilation of the Jewish communities. The material assets of the Jews in these places was indeed plundered and destroyed, part of the population brutally murdered – but some were left alive as a work force to serve the German war machine. In such places the occupation authorities would imprison the local Jews (or those of several districts together) in a ghetto or detention camp, impose on them a reign of terror, squeeze out every drop of muscle-power and skill, and include them in the "final solution" whenever they saw fit. Some of these ghettos and detention camps remained standing until the late stages of the war. Then, even as Hitler's hard-hit troops were withdrawing in confusion from conquered areas with heavy losses, the SS teams still managed to "complete the accounting" with their remaining tortured and humiliated slaves, killing them on the spot or deporting them to the death camps of Germany.

The fate of these Jews, however, differed in at least one respect from that of the communities which were immediately wiped out altogether by the Nazi invasion. The fatal blow descended on the latter communities as a complete surprise: they had no time to reckon with the situation, no time to grasp at any means of rescue, no time to make any organized attempt at resistance – save for hopeless acts of courage by isolated individuals at the mouth of the grave. Time *was* given to the ghetto communities, whose members were left alive for a while. Moreover, there arose in the occupied areas of Eastern Europe – here and there even in the first days of the occupation – a strong fighting underground, which quickly succeeded, not without outside help, in raising a partisan army. When they had acquired the means, the partisans knew how to undermine the mainstays of the German army's rear. Insofar as the remnants of the ghetto and camp communities were emboldened to organize an underground of their own – and insofar as they were able to withstand servitude and terror – they not only could rise up in rebellion at the hour of destruction, but they also had some prospects of breaking forth from their isolation, uniting with the general underground, and repaying their murderers with a war of fury.

There are more than a few communities that followed this path, and with the advancement of historical research on the period of the Holocaust, more such communities will surely become known. There is, in all events, no longer any doubt that the history of the Eastern European communities in the Second World War, drenched as it is with tears and blood, is also the history of resistance.

This was not a single resistance movement in the ordinary sense of the term. It was devoid of a common organizational framework; it had neither a common leadership nor headquarters beyond the reach of the Germans from which its activity could be directed, the actions of its isolated sections coordinated, or assistance offered – like the other European resistance movements in this war. Liaison among its sections in occupied Eastern Europe was scattered and partial, limited and short in range. Every Jewish underground that arose grew and organized with painful slowness, groping its way through failure, defeat, and sacrifice. Each group had to work within the limits of the ghetto or camp, to find leaders from its midst, and to crystallize its own policy toward the Germans and their accomplices. Thus its tie with the common folk: the specific features of the underground in each ghetto or camp were determined by the peculiar character of the community within which it was active.

And yet, we may speak of the resistance of the Eastern European Jews as of a single movement. In every case it was the reaction to the same, most beastly and unrestrained version of the policy of annihilation, the one which the Nazis carried out in all the occupied countries of Eastern Europe. In every case it met with the same impenetrable wall of unfounded hatred and selfish indifference from the great majority of the surrounding population. The human element on which the resistance based its activities was everywhere similar, despite differences in social and political background, since Eastern European Judaism made a deep impression on the mentality of all the Jewish inhabitants of this vast territory. We can consequently discern certain patterns in the internal development of these Jewish resistance movements, which gave them common basic characteristics and permits the historian to treat them as a unit.

In investigating the history of the Jewish resistance movements in Eastern Europe during the Second World War, the historian must take notice of both the specific aspects and the common unifying pattern. But when we ask ourselves which takes precedence, from the aspect of how to carry out the research, we see that the specific must be taken up first. So long as we are without as detailed, exact, and objective a picture as possible of every branch of the movement, in all its stages of development, in its specific problems and the special ways it tried to solve them – in all its achievements and failures – we cannot possibly understand the movement as a whole, to explain it as a single historical event or phenomenon.

This book is an attempt to provide just such a picture of a resistance movement in one community of Eastern Europe – the Jewish community of Kovno, Lithuania.

The Jewish Community of Kovno and Its Resistance Movement

In Kovno, where the waters of the Vilya flow into the broad Niemen River, the Jewish community had its beginnings about three hundred years ago. From the nineteenth century it was considered one of the most important spiritual, cultural, and organizational centers of modern Jewry. Kovno gave world Jewry such great spiritual leaders as the famous rabbi and *gaon* Yitzhak Elhanan Spektor and one of the founders of modern Hebrew literature, Abraham Mapu. On the eve of the Second World War the community numbered approximately forty thousand – one-third of the population of the entire city – and was at the height of its development and maturity. It could boast forty synagogues and institutions of religious learning, the famed Slobodka Yeshiva and a long list of smaller *yeshivot*, and a highly developed Hebrew educational system, including four Hebrew high schools. It had no less than five Jewish daily newspapers and several periodicals in both Yiddish and Hebrew. It had established various cultural and economic institutions, a social welfare service, and a public health service; all the organizations and societies known to Eastern European Jewry and political parties of all shades were represented in Kovno. Furthermore, the members of the community, the rabbis, the intelligentsia, the men of letters, and the *amkho* ("the common people") were able, after their everyday activities in crafts, trade, manufacturing, services, and the liberal professions, to find recreation and spiritual enjoyment, whether in a page of the Talmud, or in delving into Jewish moral thought, following literary pursuits, or propagating Marxism underground or the ideology of Herzl and Pinsker in the open.

All of these combined to form a dynamic and creative Jewish fabric of life, such as could be found in few places in the world. Even in 1940, when Lithuania became a Soviet Republic and Vilna its capital city, the Jewish community of Kovno lost none of its vitality. It was able to retain its qualities and creativity even in the face of the flood of new orders and policies from the Soviet authorities, who did much to destroy its national, religious, cultural, and economic lifestyles and values, yet did not hesitate to exploit its organizational experience and spiritual resources in establishing and stabilizing the new regime.

It was in the very first days of the war between Germany and the Soviet Union that the death blow was struck at the community. The Nazis included Kovno Jewry among the communities destined for total but not immediate annihilation. After the initial mass murders, in which the majority of men, women, elderly, and children of the community were executed by the SS and its Lithuanian collaborators (autumn 1941), sixteen thousand of the original forty thousand Kovno Jews survived. During the next three years, the Nazis continued to reduce the population of the Kovno community by deporting Jews periodically to places of no return, or by executions in the immediate neighborhood. Still, in the ghetto itself and its affiliated labor camps, ten thousand Jews survived – until the great Soviet offensive in the summer of 1944. Only then did the Gestapo begin the final liquidation of the ghetto. A third of those still alive met their deaths after unspeakable suffering. The rest (except for several hundred who escaped the oppressors by various means), were transported to death camps in Germany. Most of them died there of exhaustion, hunger, sickness, and physical and mental tortures. Only eight out of every hundred of those Kovno Jews who had fallen into the hands of the Nazi occupiers lived to see the day of liberation. The enemy's plans for the Jews of Kovno succeeded almost to perfection.

Yet, between the mass slaughters at the beginning of Nazi rule and the final liquidation, carried out as the thunder of Russian guns was heard from afar, this community found the strength to create a fighting underground – a resistance worthy of its name.

Our research, extending over several years, has aimed at obtaining as detailed, exact, and objective an account of that movement as possible. In so doing, we have attempted to give voice to the ideal that beat in the hearts of those slain in the smoke of underground bunkers and in the depths of the partisan forests, in the ghettos and concentration camps. We have tried to give voice to the last thoughts of those Jews of the Kovno Ghetto who dipped their fingers in their own blood to write REVENGE on the walls of their houses; those who etched their names and the anticipated date of their execution on the walls of the Ninth Fort near Kovno; those who carved the Star of David on the bark of a tree deep in the forest to mark the grave of a comrade in arms; those who wrote diaries, gathered documents, and buried them deep in the earth while the enemy's sword still flashed above their heads.

First Steps of Our Investigation

Our knowledge of the resistance movement of Kovno Jewry comes first and foremost from personal experience. We ourselves were among those imprisoned in the ghetto who joined the movement in its first stages. We were active in its ranks, aiming to forge the fighting power of the ghetto, and when the moment was ripe, we and other ghetto fighters broke out to join the ranks of the Kovno battalions of the Lithuanian Soviet Partisan Brigade, which was active in the dense forest of southeastern Lithuania and Western Byelorussia. There we lived and fought as partisans until the Soviet army liberated the area in the summer of 1944.

Naturally, our firsthand knowledge cannot be exact and exhaustive. Both in the forests and in the ghetto, the movement worked under strict conspiratorial conditions, and an intimate knowledge of its dimensions and activities was in the hands of a select few in positions of leadership and command; we were but soldiers of the ranks. After the liberation, and particularly after reaching Israel, where most of the survivors finally gathered, we were able to round out our knowledge of the history of the movement to some degree. We did this by frequent and long discussions and by studying the published material on the Kovno Ghetto. This material, however, usually devoted but slight attention to the history of the ghetto underground and events affecting it.

After summing up the information at our disposal,[1] we saw that we had by no means succeeded in getting a complete account of the movement. On the contrary, we found that the deeper we delved into the facts, the more involved the picture became. Connections emerged between events that were previously considered unrelated; it seemed that a profound mutual dependence existed between the resistance and other events in the ghetto, and the extremely complex web of relations between the ghetto movement and the Soviet partisan movement became apparent. At the same time obscure points cropped up and problems requiring additional elucidation multiplied. It became clear that without a systematic and rigorous investigation it would be impossible to obtain a historically true account of how the Jewish community of Kovno stood up for its life in its fateful hour. The opportunity to undertake such research was afforded with the promise of aid and direction from Yad Vashem.

Sources and Their Classification

The most difficult problem, as might be expected in research of this kind, was to find sources of information that were both suitable and accessible. Taking into consideration both our specific subject and aspects common to all Jewish underground movements under the Nazi regime, we decided to include three principal types of source material.

1. *Documents* on the underground organization in the Kovno Ghetto; on the "Council of Elders" (Ältestenrat) and other official ghetto institutions; on the Gestapo and other German occupation authorities in Lithuania and in the city of Kovno itself; and on the Lithuanian Soviet partisan movement and other Lithuanian underground organizations.

---

1. One of our summaries was published in volume 1 of *Sefer ha-partizanim ha-yehudim*, 1958, and the second was intended for *Sefer Yahadut Lita*, vol. 2, 1960.

2. *Personal testimonials* from surviving members and leaders of the Kovno Jewish underground; from members of the Council of Elders and its departments; from several former internees of the ghetto who were not members of the underground organizations; from the leaders of the Lithuanian Soviet Partisan Brigade (its non-Jewish members and officers); and from Germans connected in some manner with the Kovno Ghetto or with the anti-partisan war in the area of the Lithuanian Soviet Partisan Brigade in general and the Kovno battalions' activities in particular.

3. *Written memoirs* of people in the above categories, or books based on diverse sources.

We evaluated the sources according to their relevance to our investigation in the order of classification given above. That is to say, the greatest importance was attached to documents written at the time the events occurred. Least importance was attached to reports in books based on sources of doubtful reliability. On the basis of this classification we directed our efforts in collecting the relevant material.

Unfortunately, sources of the first class are extremely scarce. We could find no documents from the Kovno underground. We found out from secondary sources (personal testimonials, later publications, etc.) that such material had once existed: all the underground movements in the Kovno Ghetto did keep written accounts of events in some form or other – for example, records of their activities and information bulletins circulated among the members – and also published stenciled articles. The contents of some of these documents could be reconstructed with the aid of secondary sources. As it turned out, a great many documents from the Communist underground of the Kovno Ghetto were preserved and afterwards passed on to the Lithuanian Partisan Movement Museum in Vilna. However, all our efforts to gain access to this material were unsuccessful. We were more fortunate with material of the Lithuanian Partisan Movement. We obtained several important documents issued by the brigade command, including a description of the partisan activities (*karakteristika*) of a fighter from the Kovno Ghetto (see figures 31–32). We also obtained a diary written by one of the Jewish officers in the same brigade.

A fairly large number of documents concerning the activities of the Kovno Ältestenrat was at our disposal. However, not one of those so much as mentions the activities of any underground movement. This fact is noteworthy since it is understood from several other sources that various underground leaders in the ghetto were in contact (often very close contact) with central figures of the Ältestenrat.

Some important material for our study was discovered in the archives of the Gestapo. Chief among this was a colored map prepared by the occupation authorities in Kovno in February 1944, describing the activities of the Soviet partisans in Lithuania during that year (see Map 4). The map classifies the districts of Lithuania according to the intensity of the partisan war being waged there and the degree to which authority in the area was wrested from the Germans by the partisans. Compared with other sources (including official Soviet documents), this map is amazingly accurate and shows that the Germans were supplied with precise information on the partisans' activities and the whereabouts of their bases. The map was also used by us as an important confirmation of the reliability of the other sources of information on the Lithuanian Soviet Partisan Brigade, insofar as they impinged on the Kovno Ghetto underground.

Similar value is ascribed to documents from the Gestapo archives concerning the Communist and non-Communist underground movements in Kovno. Although this material does not deal directly with the ghetto underground, it sheds light on events and activities in which Jewish fighters were involved, and is therefore an indirect confirmation of the reliability of the other sources that aided us in reconstructing many events in the history of the ghetto underground.

Eyewitness Testimony as the Principal Source of Information in This Study

The documentary material alone was insufficient to solve all the problems raised in the initial stages of our investigation. As a result, and also because of the fact that the sources of the third class – memoirs and books – were few in number, we were obliged to concentrate our efforts on material of the second class, which includes post-factum, eyewitness testimony of participants in the actual events.

We are well aware of the limitations of this method as a means of gathering reliable information about past events. Even if it were possible to contact all the witnesses who might offer relevant testimony, and every one of them were willing and able to precisely recount everything they knew, thought, felt, saw, and heard fifteen to twenty years ago, we would still have to face the difficult and complex problem of weaving the many fragmentary and subjective reports into a coherent and objective whole. Moreover, many of the most important potential witnesses – movement leaders, active members, and secret agents – did not survive the war. Others, especially non-Jewish witnesses, are extremely difficult or even impossible to contact. Of equal importance, even the witnesses who can be reached with reasonable ease have obviously changed in the intervening years. These years cover the memory of the past like a curtain; the years inflate one event and blot out others. They lead the mind to confuse facts with opinions and evaluations arrived at later, and they sometimes distort events to the point where the testimony is of little value for our research.

Nevertheless, in this particular case there was no alternative to personal testimony. It was up to us to find an approach that would reduce the inherent limitations of our method to a minimum. In developing such an approach we made use of modern sociology with its recent experience in collecting oral data and exploiting the personal interview as a means of studying social behavior.[2]

It was necessary to ensure that the method of gathering testimony was such that a systematic cross-check of related accounts would be possible. Each account was examined not only directly, for the information it gave, but also indirectly as a means of confirming or refuting other accounts. This was achieved in three ways: (1) by restricting the matters whose description and analysis would be based on eyewitness testimony; (2) by using a single, standard questionnaire; and (3) by rigorously selecting candidates for testimonials out of all the available eyewitnesses.

The first of these measures required a redefinition of the object of our study. First, it was necessary to differentiate more strictly between events that seemed to express organized, active resistance, and events that reflected only the spontaneous, unorganized attempts of individual internees of the ghetto to avoid or escape the Nazi persecution and murder machine. Second, a sharper distinction was made between events of both the above types, and events that took place in the Kovno Ghetto that were not connected with resistance and the underground, but the description and analysis of which were indispensable for a proper understanding of the subject (for example, the news from the fronts that reached the ghetto, the relations between the Gestapo and the Ältestenrat).

---

2. On this topic, see our "Problems Relating to a Questionnaire on the Holocaust," in *Yad Vashem Studies*, no. 3, pp. 91–117.

On the basis of such considerations we determined the scope of eyewitness testimony. We decided to emphasize actions, events, and developments directly connected with the active, organized resistance, both inside and outside the ghetto. Descriptions of these matters are here based chiefly on eyewitness accounts. As to events of other types, they were only slightly dealt with in the oral evidence, and their description is based mainly on memoirs, historical summaries, and other documents previously published. Those events are themselves worthy of systematic research.

It should be stressed that in focusing the investigation on the active resistance it was by no means our intention to insult the memory of those Jews of the Kovno Ghetto who did not belong to the underground organizations and suffered the trials of their terrible fate with unswerving loyalty to their families, their torn community, and their downtrodden nation.

The Method of Collecting Testimony

The above considerations were the guiding principles both in the selection of witnesses and in the preparation of the uniform questionnaire that the witnesses would be required to complete. In all, we collected the testimony of some ninety persons. Of these, sixty-two were at one time members of underground organizations in the Kovno Ghetto. One half of that number, thirty to be precise, obtained arms, escaped from the ghetto, and actively fought the Germans and their collaborators throughout Lithuania and Byelorussia. The remaining twenty-eight witnesses were former internees of the ghetto who were not associated with the Kovno underground, members of the Ältestenrat or its various departments, members of Jewish resistance movements in other areas who had some contact with the Kovno underground, non-Jews sympathetic to the plight of our people who actively aided the underground, and others. The questionnaire contained 474 questions, divided into sections according to selected topics.

An outline of this division is as follows: (1) Data on the witness in the period just before the war, questions 1–22. (2) The ghetto and the mass murders, ques. 23–36. (3) The response: rescue, ques. 37–48. (4) The response: resistance, ques. 49–90. (5) The ghetto underground, ques. 91–127. (6) Active resistance, ques. 128–176, and the flight to the forest, ques. 177–253. (7) The Kovno partisan battalions and the Lithuanian Brigade, ques. 254–287. (8) Partisan operations:

provision and supply, ques. 288–301. (9) Sabotage operations, ques. 302–313. (10) Punishment and reprisal, ques. 314–323. (11) Partisan battles, ques. 324–351. (12) The way of life and social relations in the forests, ques. 352–411. (13) Attitudes toward the Jews, ques. 412–440. (14) Long-range raids, ques. 441–449. (15) Coming out of the forest, ques. 450–462; data on the witness from liberation day until now, ques. 463–474.

This bare outline of the questionnaire obviously indicates that most of the questions (415 out of 474) were aimed at getting information on the active resistance of Kovno Jewry during the period of Nazi occupation. The rest of the questions were for the most part not intended to enlarge our knowledge of facts. They served as a means of encouraging the witnesses, aiding their powers of recollection and removing their personal inhibitions.

The questions were carefully worded so as to keep out leading implications or hints as to a "desired" answer. For the most part they dealt with facts that the witness might know or even have experienced personally. Some of the questions referred to the witness's own emotions, expectations, and beliefs, his own motives and reasons and those of others as he understood them at the time. The answers to questions of this type were a great aid in writing the book, at times no less than the answers to "factual" questions. They helped to attain a deeper understanding of the events, to explain how they were connected to one another, and to set them in the context of the events of that time.

Obviously, the questionnaire was not completely applicable to all of the witnesses. One hundred percent of the questions could only be answered by a person who fulfilled the following conditions: he or she had been active in the organized ghetto resistance movement and afterwards made an armed escape from the ghetto and joined the Soviet partisan movement. As mentioned, not more than one-third of the entire group fulfilled these conditions. Half of the questions could be answered by another third of the witnesses; all those who had served in the ranks of the resistance movement in the ghetto, but for various reasons did not leave the ghetto later to join the partisans. The remaining third of the witnesses could answer only certain sections of the questionnaire, and at times we had to resort to an alternative questionnaire designed for such individual cases. Furthermore, even in cases where the questionnaire was applicable, it never replaced the personal conversation with the witness, but rather served as a basis for it. In other words, wherever it was technically possible to obtain personal testimonies, it was done by one or both of the authors, using the questionnaire to guide the conversation.

This was the method actually employed in the case of the seventy-nine witnesses living in Israel (thirty of the conversations were recorded by means of a dictaphone). The testimonies of the eleven witnesses living abroad were collected through correspondence. The questionnaire, or parts of it, was mailed to some of them; for a variety of reasons we refrained from doing this regarding others, who answered specific questions by mail. The response of some of the witnesses living in the Soviet Union was unexpectedly eager, and their answers helped a great deal to round out the picture.

Summary of the Contents

The first part of this book contains a short survey of the history of the Kovno community under Nazi rule, from June 1941 to July 1944. It describes the principal stages of the enslavement and liquidation policy of the Nazis and the reaction of the Jews to that policy. Particularly emphasized are the attempts at rescue and outbursts of spontaneous, unorganized resistance, which found expression in every phase of ghetto life and reached a climax in the passive resistance, en masse, to deportation to Germany with the approach of the Soviet army. The initial steps in the organization of the Jewish underground in the Kovno Ghetto are also traced in this part.

The second part describes the underground's feverish search for allies outside the ghetto, and its first costly attempts to break the ring of isolation and gain a foothold from which to fight a partisan war against the murderers. The final chapter of this part describes a daring escape by a group of fighters from the ill-famed "Fortress of Death", the Ninth Fort, where tens of thousands of Jews from Kovno and other places were executed. Those who escaped had been forced by the Nazis to cover up the traces of their crimes.

The third part of the book deals with the resistance movement as it gathered momentum and reached the height of its activities: establishing liaison with forest partisans; obtaining arms for the movement, incredibly, under the very noses of the Germans; training fighters for partisan warfare; organizing escapes from the ghetto; and bringing the fighters to the bases in the forest of the Lithuanian Soviet Partisan Brigade. The intricate web of relations between the underground movement on the one hand and the Ältestenrat and the Jewish Police on the other is described in this part, as is the active aid extended to the fighting underground by various members of the Jewish population.

The fourth part traces the history of the underground movement as its center of gravity shifted from the ghetto to the partisan forests. The partisan activities in which fighters from the Kovno Ghetto were the main participants are described here, and the process of their integration into the Soviet partisan warfare is analyzed. This part also attempts to recreate the day-to-day atmosphere in the partisan battalions and to analyze the tense relations and contrasts between the Jewish and non-Jewish fighters.

The fifth part of the book concludes the history of the underground resistance in an ever-diminishing ghetto. It also describes the last marches of the Kovno battalions from their bases in the forest to the center of the country, and their entry into the liberated town of Kovno.

In conclusion, we would like to note several issues that are related to the central topic of our book, but which we were not able to research and describe in detail. First, despite the liquidation of the ghetto and murder of the thousands of Jews who disobeyed the will of their Nazi "masters" to transport them to Germany, this did not mark the end of the history of the Kovno Jewish community. The tragic epilogue continued for almost one year in concentration camps on German soil. The cells of the Kovno Jewish underground continued to exist even under the hellish conditions of the camps. Further research is needed in order to determine the scope, extent, and history of this activity up to the day of liberation.

Second, from information available to us regarding support of the Lithuanian partisan movement by the supreme partisan command in Moscow, we discover that here as well, Kovno Jewry played a major role. A sizeable number of the paratroopers themselves were Jews, as were the technical operators at the bases that sent the paratroopers. Many of these Jews were from Kovno. A good number of them lost their lives while fulfilling military, political, and technical duties. Where contemporary Soviet literature mentions their names, it does so as Lithuanians. Their activities deserve to be researched and recorded.

Third, another sizeable topic is the Lithuanian division of the Soviet army. Most of its soldiers were Lithuanian Jews who escaped to the unoccupied areas of the Soviet Union at the beginning of the war. This division participated in many battles on the front and served as a source for recruiting dozens of paratroopers and leaders of the partisan movement in Lithuania. It has been estimated that the Lithuanian division contained the largest concentration of Jewish soldiers found in one unit and was thus the largest Jewish fighting force among all the Allied armies in the Second World War. In retrospect, it also served as a framework for cultivating the Jewish experience and nationalist Jewish spirit, as the Lithuanian youths brought with them their Hebrew culture and education. This issue also deserves particular research.

*　　*　　*

It is our pleasant duty to thank all the individuals who assisted us in this research project and in preparing the book for print. We would like to thank Dr. B. Ophir and Dr. Y. Kremish for their wise and dedicated guidance on behalf of Yad Vashem. Our deepest gratitude goes to our friends from the group of former Kovno Ghetto partisans living in Israel. Without their assistance and encouragement, it is doubtful whether we would have been able to persist in this extensive project and bring our work to conclusion. We are grateful to Dr. Y. Robinson, who supported us with his enthusiastic interest in the topic of our research, and assisted us greatly in locating valuable documentary evidence. We thank the management of Yad Vashem and its archive staff, library, and bibliographic section, who granted us their kind cooperation and permitted us the use of all necessary materials. We are especially grateful to the Yad Vashem publishing department: to Mr. Y. Buxenbaum, who labored over the style and structure of the book, and to Mr. A. Ben-David, who prepared the maps. We take this opportunity to thank them and all the others who assisted in this project.

Zvie Brown and Dov Levin
Jerusalem, Tevet 5722 (December 1961)

Key to Abbreviations Used in Footnotes

FLC   *Fun Letsten Churban: Zeitschrift far geshichte fun yiddishen leben beten nazi rezshim* [From the last extermination: Journal for the history of the Jewish people during the Nazi regime]. Edited by Yisrael Kaplan. Munich, 1–10: August 1946–December 1948.

IMT   *Trial of the Major War Criminals before the International Military Tribunal.* Nuremberg, 1947–1949.

Memoirs of MY   Memoirs of Michael Yitzhaki (Gelbtrunk). Unpublished work.

PKG   Yellin, M. and D. Galpern. *Partizaner fun kaunaser.* Y. Kissin: New York, 1951.

Trials   *Trials of War Criminals before the Nuremberg Military Tribunals.* Washington, 1946–1949.

YLHG   *Yediot beit lohamei ha-getaot al shem Itzhak Katzenelson le-more-shet ha-shoah ve-ha-mered* [Newsletter of The Ghetto Fighters' House – Itzhak Katzenelson Holocaust and Jewish Resistance Heritage Museum]. November, 1951.

YVSA   Yad Vashem archives, E/17a, E/3-4, and E/17-2.

PART I
Ravage and Horror

CHAPTER 1

Murder and Plunder

The Pogroms of the Lithuanian "Partisans"

Kovno was occupied by the Germans on June 24, 1941. From the morning of June 23 to the evening of June 24, lawlessness reigned as Kovno was dominated by nationalist Lithuanian gangs and armed criminal elements who called themselves "partisans" and "Lithuanian freedom fighters." They considered it their duty, first and foremost, to rid themselves of the Jews, "who had enslaved Lithuania to the Soviets." They rioted throughout the city, robbing and pillaging. Many Jews died at their hands during those two days. The entrance of German army units exacerbated the wave of pogroms, which reached its peak on the night of June 25 in a mass slaughter carried out in Slobodka (Vilijampole), the working-class Jewish quarter. The rioters went from house to house, massacring entire families.

Two days later, on June 27, the Lithuanian murderers conducted a public show of vengeance before a mob of curious onlookers in the city center. They brought sixty Jews to a big garage, where Germans and Lithuanians attacked them with clubs and iron rods, beating them to death. They stuffed hoses into the mouths of some and pumped water into them until their intestines burst.

The abductions and arrests of the city's Jews continued throughout the first week of the occupation. The so-called "partisans" dragged the arrested to jail, and then to the Seventh Fort[1] at the edge of the city. They gathered some ten

---

1. The authorities of Czarist Russia had earlier erected nine forts around Kovno as part of the defense system of Lithuania, which was then on the German frontier. For each fort, they built embankments, cellars for storage of weapons and ammunition, and heavy cannon emplacements. In independent Lithuania, between the two world wars, the forts served as prisons and sites for execution of political and criminal prisoners.

thousand Jews there, holding them in conditions of hunger and thirst, some out-doors and others in the fort cellars. Each day they would take out large groups of men and murder them not far from the prison courtyard. Many women were raped and shot. On July 7, the women left alive were sent home; the men, six to seven thousand in number, had all been murdered and buried in large pits dug by Russian prisoners.[2]

Up to this point, the Lithuanians had been responsible for most of the kill-ing. Although Germans participated in the pogroms at times, the occupation authorities ostensibly stood aside, "without interfering in the dispute between the Lithuanians and the Jews." But this "non-interference" was only a facade. The mass murder of the Jews of Kovno was initiated and encouraged by the German Security Service (Sicherheitsdienst – SD). At the time, however, it was more convenient for the Nazi murderers to remain in the shadows and pull the strings, preferring that the Lithuanians carry out their mission. This was clearly stated in a report sent by SS-Brigadier General Franz Walther Stahlecker,[3] commander of Einsatzgruppe A,[4] operating in the Baltic countries, to Reinhard Heydrich on October 15, 1941:

> In order to fulfill the SD missions, we had to enter the big cities together with the attacking units.... A small advance unit, with myself at the head, entered Kovno on June 25, 1941. The first activities were to catch commu-nist activists and communist material.... In addition, during the first hours after the forces entered, and with considerable difficulty, we encouraged the

2. Gar, Umkum, 33–43; Garfunkel, Kovno, 28–36; Gruenhoyz, "Churban Kovne", FLC 7:11.

3. Chief murderer of the Jews of Kovno and the Baltic states. He was a friend of Adolf Eich-mann, and when the war broke out in 1939 he was also his direct officer in SiPo. In 1940, they administrated the implementation of the Nisko Plan to establish a Jewish "reservation" (Ju-denreservat) in eastern Poland (see District Court of Jerusalem, Israel, Criminal Case 40/61, Legal Counsel vs. Adolf Eichmann, protocol of meeting 91 of July 11, 1961: 13 ff.).

4. The Einsatzgruppen (SS paramilitary mobile killing units) were comprised of four task forces (Gruppen), with three companies (Einsatzkommandos) in each task force. The task forces were known as A, B, C, and D, while the companies were numbered 1–12. Einsatzgruppe A was ac-tive in the Ostland region (Estonia, Latvia, and Lithuania) and the front regions on its border (Leningrad Front). Its companies covered the following areas: Einsatzkommando 1 operated on the front border; Einsatzkommando 2 – Estonia and Latvia; Einsatzkommando 3 – Lith-uania and Byelorussia (Ereignismeldungen UdSSR des Chefs der Sicherheitspolizei und SD, Yad Vashem archives, IM/1766/69). Editor's note: According to Raul Hilberg in The Destruction of the European Jews, the four Einsatzgruppen were responsible for the killing of 1.4 million Jews.

local anti-Semitic factors to riot against the Jews. According to orders, SD had made a final decision to solve the Jewish problem definitively and in any way possible. But it was preferable that at least at first, SD avoid performing these actions in public, because the methods used were irregular in severity, and might provoke reaction, even among German circles. Outwardly, it was preferable to show that the first deeds were performed by the local population on its own initiative, as a natural reaction to the repression the Jews had carried out against them for dozens of years, and for the recent communist terrorism.[5]

Another section of the same report states:

Partisan commander Clematis, who was expressly recruited for this action, successfully organized a pogrom according to the orders given him by our advance unit deployed in Kovno, with no outside indication that the Germans had given an order or encouragement. On the first night of the riots, the night between June 25 and 26, the Lithuanian partisans liquidated 1,500 Jews, many synagogues were set on fire or destroyed, and the Jewish quarter with about 60 houses was burned. On the following nights, 2,300 Jews were killed [*unschädlich gemacht*] in a similar manner.[6]

The cruel deeds of the "partisans" and the barbaric murders of hundreds of Jews in the streets of Kovno did provoke a response by the Wehrmacht officers in that section of the front, who found them objectionable, even considering they were committed by non-Germans. Field Marshal Wilhelm Ritter von Leeb, commander of Army Group North, ordered one of his officers, Georg von Küchler, to "avoid the reoccurrence of such events."[7] On the one hand, this was a hint to the Germans orchestrating the slaughter that the time was not yet ripe for haphazard pogroms in the city streets.[8] On the other, it indicated to the Lithuanian "parti-

---

5. Document L-180, IMT 37:672.

6. Ibid., 682.

7. The High Command case, *Law Reports of Trials of War Criminals* (London, 1948) 12:31; compare Reitlinger, 213.

8. The intention of von Leeb's order was that such clashes should not take place in public, in Kovno's main streets. Von Leeb had no intention of interfering in the authority of the *Einsatzgruppen* or to prevent the "solution to the Jewish problem" in Lithuania. The division of responsibilities between officers of German army units in the campaign in the Soviet Union,

sans" that even in the war against "their Jews," they were not their own masters, and that in this area as well they were subordinate to the Germans. "Partisan" leader Clematis, four of whose gangs "excelled" in the Slobodka massacre, disappeared entirely. His men were attached to the Einsatzkommando operating in Lithuania, where they served for an extended period under German command, liquidating Jews and communists.[9]

The murders ceased for a time, and all Kovno Jews were ordered to move into the ghetto. But on the day they entered the ghetto, the so-called partisans renewed the lawless abductions. On Thursday, August 7, they rounded up some 1,200 Jewish men and imprisoned them. About two hundred were sent back home, while the remaining Jews were taken to a site near the city and murdered. (Kovno Jews remember this destruction operation as "the *Aktzia* of the infamous Thursday.")[10] Several days later, a new disaster hit the ghetto. On August 18, a group of 534 Jews, most with higher education – teachers, lawyers, physicians, and other professionals – were taken on the pretext that educated Jews were needed for special work in the city archives. They were taken to the Fourth Fort and shot.[11]

---

and SiPo and Gestapo units advancing in their wake, was formulated in a specific agreement between the German army High Command and the RSHA (*Reichssicherheitshauptamt* – Reich Main Security Office). (See the well-known Heydrich-Wagner agreement, which was signed previously on March 26, 1941, IMT 4:375 ff.) According to this agreement, security matters were removed from the responsibility of army officers and given to the commanders of SiPo, which was established by Heinrich Himmler and Reinhard Heydrich. The term "security matters" was given a broad interpretation, on the basis of the Führer's order from early March 1941. This stated that the future war with the Soviet Union (code-named Operation Barbarossa) required complete liquidation of "Jews, Gypsies, inferior races, other antisocial elements, and communist party functionaries" in all areas of the occupation. The Keitel Order stated that "according to the Führer's directive, the Reichsführer-SS [Himmler] was given special vital duties in the final struggle between two opposing political systems. Within the outlines of this system of duties, the Reichsführer-SS will operate independently and on its own responsibility" (PS-447, IMT 26:54). Clearly, Stahlecker's activities against Kovno Jewry were based on basic orders supported by the army high command. At most, the regional army commander could request that he avoid acting in public or doing anything that might damage the Wehrmacht's reputation.
9. The second report sent by Stahlecker to Heydrich says that the Lithuanian "partisans" completely justified his faith in them, and that in his extermination companies, eight Lithuanians served for every single German soldier (PS-2273, IMT, 30:75).
10. Garfunkel, *Kovno*, 49.
11. Ibid., 56–57.

The "Actions" (*Aktionen*)

The methodical liquidation operations began some forty days after the ghetto was closed. On September 26, all inhabitants of one quarter were gathered in a square. The murderers performed a "selection," separating those who looked fit for physical labor from those who seemed unfit. The "fit" were sent home two days later, while the "unfit" – about one thousand men, women, and children – were sent to the Ninth Fort ("The Fortress of Death"), where they were murdered.[12]

On October 4, the murderers carried out another mass slaughter.[13] This time, an entire section of the ghetto, called the Small Ghetto, was liquidated.[14] Some 1,500 individuals who did not have authorizations that they were craftsmen or the families of craftsmen, were taken to the forts to be killed, and the rest were taken to the Large Ghetto. The Germans set fire to the hospital, which was in the Small Ghetto, and the sixty patients, as well as doctors and nurses, were burned alive.[15]

About three weeks later, on October 27, a notice was publicized that all inhabitants of the ghetto, without exception, had to gather at 6 A.M. the next day, October 28, in Democrats Square at the center of the ghetto, for an "inspection." At the appointed time, the ghetto inhabitants were at the site. German soldiers and Lithuanian "partisans," armed with machine guns and rifles, were posted around the square. Crowds of Lithuanians clustered on the surrounding hills at a distance. At 9 A.M., SD personnel arrived, along with SS Master Sergeant Helmut Rauca, the official in charge of Jewish affairs for the Gestapo, members of the *Stadtkommissar* (the municipal German government in Kovno), and SA Captain Fritz Jordan, the officer in charge of Jewish affairs for the German civil administration. The murderers began the selection process, which continued throughout the day until 6 P.M. Those chosen by Rauca to live were permitted to return to their homes in the ghetto. The rest – over ten thousand individuals – were taken under heavy guard to the Small Ghetto, to homes that had been

---

12. Ibid., 68.

13. Ibid., 69; Gar, *Umkum*, 67–70.

14. At first, the Kovno Ghetto was comprised of two unequal sections, separated by Paneriai St., which was not included in the ghetto. A wooden bridge connected the two sections from above.

15. Aharon Peretz, *Dem goral antkegen: reshimos fun a daktar* [Towards fate: a doctor's writings] (Haifa, 1952), 20.

emptied following the previous *Aktion*. The next morning, the guards led them on a death parade through the streets of Slobodka, past Lithuanian passersby and the remaining Jews of the ghetto, to the Ninth Fort, where enormous pits had been prepared in advance. The German and Lithuanian murderers pushed them by groups into the pits and showered them with machine-gun fire. They then poured lime over the pits and covered them with dirt. The Kovno Jews called this the "Great *Aktion*."[16]

After the Great *Aktion*, the mass murders in Kovno ceased for the next two and a half years. During that time, there were numerous individual incidents of murder, as a result of the draconian regime and the atmosphere of terror that constantly prevailed in the ghetto. Jews were shot for insufficiently submissive posture or executed for crimes such as smuggling, walking in the streets without the yellow star, purchasing a newspaper, or posting a letter. On February 4, 1943, the Germans avenged their defeat at Stalingrad by murdering some fifty Jews (the Jews called this the "Stalingrad *Aktion*").

The murders recommenced in March 1944, four months after the ghetto was transferred from the authority of the civil administration to the sole authority of the SS (the concentration camp section of the Reich Main Security Office – RSHA). At that point, the process of dividing the ghetto into small, isolated concentration camps began. One of the hallmarks of concentration camps as opposed to ghettos was that they had no designated area for children or the elderly; theirs was a "working population," in the exact Nazi understanding of this phrase. The moment that the Nazis decided to transform a ghetto into a concentration camp, the fate of the children and elderly in that ghetto was sealed. The time had come for all those children and elderly who had been saved from the previous "selections," and whom the Nazis had permitted to remain alive between the ghetto walls.[17]

But the children and the elderly were not the only obstacles on the path to complete transformation of the ghetto into a concentration camp. The entire ghetto administration, with its organizations and institutions, and most importantly the Ältestenrat ("Council of Elders")[18] and the ghetto police, had the

---

16. Gar, *Umkum*, 72 ff; Garfunkel, *Kovno*, 71 ff.

17. An exact description of this terrifying *Aktion* appears in the testimony of Dr. Aharon Peretz at Eichmann's trial in Jerusalem, meeting protocol 28 of May 4, 1961, 22 ff.

18. Kovno's *Judenrat* – see next chapter.

potential to block the effort. This was all the more relevant since the Gestapo heard rumors that the Ältestenrat's "liberal" regime and the Jewish police were fertile ground for a strong underground. This underground was suspected of connections with the Soviet partisans, smuggling people to the forest, and expulsion of Gestapo agents from the ghetto. Other suspected acts of the underground against the Reich and the Nazi regime included construction of underground hideouts, sending Jewish children to Lithuanians in the city, smuggling newspapers into the ghetto, and listening to the radio.

The Germans disbanded the Ältestenrat and decided to dispose of the children, the elderly, and the ill, as well as the police, in one blow. The first victims were the police, except for the traitors among them;[19] afterwards came the turn of the children, the elderly, and the ill. On March 27, 1944, the same day that the police were taken to the Ninth Fort, the "Fortress of Death," a large detachment, comprised of SS, Ukrainians, and Russian soldiers of General Andrei Vlasov,[20] stormed into the ghetto. With unspeakable cruelty, they dragged away children under age twelve and elderly over age fifty-five as well as the bedridden, threw them into trucks, and took them to the Ninth Fort. Some 1,800 individuals were killed in this *Aktion*.[21]

Liquidation of the Ghetto

Many contradictions, disagreements, conspiracies, and intrigues that were part of the Nazi war and murder machine led to the fact that the Kovno Ghetto lasted until the final weeks before liberation. When the Soviet armies approached Vilna, with the momentum of the powerful Vitebsk offensive, which began on June 23, 1944, the Nazis began their liquidation of the ghetto.[22] On July 6, ghetto commandant SS-Captain Wilhelm Goecke informed the "Elder of the Jews," Dr. Elkhanan Elkes, that the authorities had decided to empty the ghetto and move its inhabitants from the front to Eastern Prussia. That day, the ghetto was sur-

---

19. See detailed description in chapter 14.
20. Russian Red Army general who collaborated with the Nazis.
21. A complete description of the murders at the Ninth Fort was given by the Lithuanian director of the fort in 1941, Juozas Slesoraitis, in his testimony as the accused before a Soviet court (see *Tiesa*, 1959:119–20).
22. A complete description of the liquidation of the ghetto appears in Gar, *Umkum*, ch. 26; Garfunkel, *Kovno*, 190–7; Moshe Segelson, "Di liquidatzie un evakuatzie fun Kovner ghetta," manuscript, Landesburg, 1945; see also testimony of Leah [Lucia] Elstein-Lavon, yvsa, 19.

rounded by a chain of reinforced guard units. The next day, a curfew was imposed, and the Jews were no longer permitted to leave for jobs in the town. Those Jews who were in labor camps surrounding Kovno were brought into the ghetto.

On Saturday, July 8, the deportations began. Only a few ghetto residents willingly obeyed the order to leave, and the SS troops who came to take the Jews away had to remove them from their homes by force. Many hid in the underground shelters they had prepared, while the Germans hunted them using search dogs, blowing up suspicious locations with hand grenades and bombs. Those who were found were taken to a collection point inside the ghetto, and from there to the train station, where they were loaded onto boxcars and transported to Germany. On the way to the train station, some Jews attempted to escape, but the guards shot at them, and almost all were killed. Some even tried to escape from the train, but they were also killed.

On July 14, a special liquidation force was brought to the ghetto, and it proceeded to burn, bomb, and raze the ghetto buildings down to their foundations. Those Jews who attempted to escape their burning shelters were shot and thrown into the fire. Only a few hiding places remained safe, and ninety Jews found shelter in them until liberation.

Of the ten thousand Kovno Jews who were alive when the Nazis began liquidating the ghetto, some three thousand were killed in the ghetto, while seven thousand[23] were sent to the most brutal concentration camps in Germany, some in Bavaria, near Dachau, others in Eastern Prussia. Of these, only 2,500 survived. In Kovno and its environs, six hundred Jews survived, some in hideouts outside or inside the ghetto, others by escaping the ghetto and joining the partisans in the forests. Of the forty thousand Jews living in Kovno at the time of the Nazi occupation, thirty-seven thousand were slaughtered – ninety-two out of every hundred.

Organized Robbery

From the first days of the war, the Lithuanian "partisans" committed robbery as an inseparable part of their bloody vengeance. During the kidnappings and arrests, they stole Jewish property and made themselves at home in the Jews'

---

23. The exact numbers are unknown. See Garfunkel, Kovno, 190–97; Gar, Umkum, 270 ff., PKG, 130–32; Sudarsky et al., Lita, 1711; YLHG 21:142.

houses.[24] But the German authorities responded to the robberies with a strict prohibition; shortly following the occupation of the city, proclamations were posted in the streets: "All looters will be shot." This was intended to remind the Lithuanians that the Germans relished order, even in matters related to the Jews, and that the property of the Jews belonged to the Reich. Among the orders that the German *Stadtkommissar* issued regarding the status and obligations of the Kovno Jews was an order prohibiting the Jews from selling or giving non-Jews any of their property, including furniture and household items.[25] The unrestrained robbery stopped, but in its place came organized "legal" theft.

Establishment of the ghetto prefaced the methodical acts of robbery. Homes abandoned by Jews when they moved to the ghetto and any Jewish property that remained outside the ghetto (such as bank deposits, debts, stores, storage rooms) were "confiscated" by the authorities. Just four days after the closure of the ghetto, the Germans initiated the process of stealing Jewish property.[26] Every day for two weeks, German officers and soldiers and SD members came to the ghetto and searched the Jews' homes, taking away in their cars anything they desired. After they finished, the Ältestenrat was ordered to organize the delivery of any valuables that the Jews still possessed. Collection points were assigned inside the ghetto, and the residents were ordered to deliver all remaining property on a certain day. Ältestenrat officials were put to work sorting and classifying the property, and Jewish laborers packed it into suitcases and loaded it onto cars. In this manner, within several days the Germans stole from the Jews 75–80 percent of the property they had brought into the ghetto.[27] It is difficult to estimate the worth of the valuables stolen in the first stage of the process, during the searches, but the property stolen in the "delivery" stage is estimated at fifty million gold marks.[28]

The killing operations also provided the Germans with the opportunity

---

24. See, for example, Der Zibeter Fort [the Seventh Fort], by Yitzhak Nementchik, FLC 7:58–70. At the Ninth Fort as well, the Lithuanians who carried out the murders inherited the Jews' jewelry. For example, in late 1941, the Lithuanian commander of the fort removed rings, watches, and other items from the murdered Jews and put them in his own pockets (Hitlerine, 73).
25. Gar, *Umkum*, 46.
26. Gar, *Umkum*, chapter 9; Garfunkel, *Kovno*, 59–62.
27. Garfunkel, *Kovno*, 225.
28. Ibid., 62. This estimate is based on numbers given to the author by Ältestenrat officials who worked at the collection sites.

to steal property. They took from their victims' hands the valuables they had brought to the murder sites, and removed their clothes, before leading them to pits and murdering them. The Germans exploited this source to its fullest about two and a half years after the mass murders, during the operation for "erasing the traces."[29] They made sure to remove every item of value, such as rings and gold teeth, from the corpses destined for burning. When the ghetto survivors were deported to camps in Germany they were allowed to take some belongings with them, and many were able to hide a few valuables they had kept hidden until then. But even this last remainder of the Kovno Jews' property would eventually reach the Reich's treasury. At the transfer stations on the way to the concentration camps, the Jews were robbed down to their last items of clothing – all of their belongings were taken, and instead they were given filthy prisoners' rags.

Forced Labor

For the Gestapo officials and the *Einsatzgruppen* in Kovno, the imprisonment of the Jews in the ghetto eased the systematic implementation of the two main parts of their plan: the murders and the organized robbery. This was in accordance with the function that Heydrich, architect of the "final solution to the Jewish problem," had defined for the ghettos. But in his original plan, the large ghettos in the occupied territory to the east, including the Kovno Ghetto, had another role: to serve as a shelter for German and Western European Jews who had been deported from their homes and would be brought to the occupied areas in the east.[30] According to this plan, the local Jews in the eastern ghettos had to gradually make way for the Jews of Germany and the west – to be exact, for those fit for labor, who would be employed, as long as they lasted, in building roads, digging trenches, and other jobs of military import.[31] The local Jews were candidates for immediate destruction, aside from perhaps a few professionals who were needed for a limited period in order to operate the factories in their towns.

---

29. See chapter 6.

30. See NG-2586-J, *Trials* 13:243 ff. Most of the first shipments were brought to Riga Ghetto, where the plan was implemented almost in its entirety. The shipments that reached Kovno were defined by the murderers as worthless with regards to war potential and were directed straight to the killing sites (Reitlinger, 219 ff.; compare the conclusions of the special Soviet-Lithuanian committee for investigating Nazi crimes in the territory of the Lithuanian Republic, August 23, 1944, Kondratas, 31–32).

31. See "Report of the Wannsee Conference," NG-2586-G, *Trials* 13:210 ff.

The histories of the Kovno Ghetto and of the other large ghettos in the Ostland – Riga, Vilna, and Minsk – demonstrate that the first stages of Heydrich's plan were implemented successfully, but that the implementation was slowed or stopped after several months. The ghettos were erected, and the first destruction attempts made room in them for tens of thousands of other Jews. But the transport of Jews from the west met with difficulties.[32] The army authorities strenuously objected to using the transportation arteries in the occupied territories for needs that were not directly related to the war. By late 1941, Heydrich had succeeded in transferring to the Ostland several shipments of German Jews, but he was forced to cease this activity in early 1942.

At the same time, the fate of the Jews who remained in the eastern ghettos was sealed. As German sources reveal, the decision about what to do with them involved certain frictions between the three major German authorities that acted in the occupied Eastern territories: (1) the *Einsatzgruppen*, which was subordinate to Heinrich Himmler's office; (2) the Civil Administration, which was subordinate to Alfred Rosenberg's *Ostministerium* (OMi, East Ministry); and (3) the *Wirtshaftsstab Ost* (Economic Staff East), headed by General Georg Thomas, who administered the equipment for the German corps on the eastern front, and which was subordinate to the Wehrmacht chief of staff.

The *Einsatzgruppen* chiefs wanted the immediate destruction of the Jews who fell into the hands of the occupation army. They objected on principle that any military, political, or financial considerations should influence the process of total annihilation.

The *Ostministerium* also desired the total annihilation of the Jews in the occupied territories. In the schema of ethnic hierarchy that was supposed to be implemented in the east, formulated by Rosenberg, the Jews were not given a place at all because they were meant to be completely erased from this land.[33] But they were interested in temporary exploitation of the Jews as labor, should the process of rebuilding the occupied territories so require. In their opinion,

---

32. In the first weeks after the outbreak of the war, Russian prisoners of war served as a labor force (the Germans completely ignored international laws regarding treatment of prisoners of war). But even in the first months, the barbaric treatment meant that masses died of exhaustion, starvation, and disease. The Jews had to take their place in the important jobs. At least 165,000 Soviet prisoners died on Lithuanian soil (*Hitlerine*, 105).

33. Dallin, 277.

destruction by "selection" and closed ghettos under draconian rule were efficient ways for implementing this policy.

General Thomas of the *Wirtshaftsstab*, for whom destruction of peoples and races "was not included in the realm of his responsibilities," was interested in the Jews only to the extent they could be used, particularly for their professional knowledge, for the organization and operation of a military industry. In the first months of the occupation, he and his assistants became convinced that relying solely on non-Jewish labor would make it difficult to supply the needs of the army, ensure transportation to the front, and manufacture the necessary equipment for the army. When they became aware of the existence of the ghettos and the composition of their population – a large percentage of individuals fit for manual labor and a significant percentage of people with desirable professions – they demanded delaying the liquidation plan in order to temporarily exploit "war potential" of the ghettos to the very last drop. Because they could not expect professional labor to be carried out by people denied minimal conditions of housing, food, and clothing, they did not agree to extreme draconian treatment of those Jews who were so lucky as to be employed in their factories.[34]

There is reason to assume that the German Civil Administration of Ostland supported this demand. Although they assisted in implementing the first stages of the Heydrich plan with great enthusiasm, at this point they apparently realized that liquidation of the ghettos in the Baltic countries would cause more harm than good to their interests – in other words, to the strengthening of their authority in these areas. They also feared that it would be difficult for them to fulfill the army's demands for labor; they were especially concerned that drafting masses of locals, such as Lithuanians and Latvians, for hard labor in military installations could lead to difficulties in the relationship between the occupation authorities and the population. Further, they themselves expected to benefit from the trained Jewish labor force, which could be exploited at almost zero cost.[35]

---

34. Reitlinger, 202 ff., 235.

35. Compare Dallin, chapter 10. In Stahlecker's words, "After implementing the first major destruction operations in Lithuania and Latvia, we realized that at this stage, complete annihilation of the Jews was impractical. Most of the crafts in Lithuania and Latvia were performed by Jews, and certain professions ... were dominated almost completely by Jews. For this reason, a large portion of the Jewish craftsmen are vital, both for operating the necessary factories, reconstructing destroyed cities, and performing jobs of military importance. In any event, the factories aspire to replace the Jewish labor employed in the production process,

Thus Kovno Ghetto, after it was emptied of almost half its inhabitants, was "left alone" with one single justification for its existence: forced labor for the German war machine. All signs indicate that this decision was made around January 1942. The ghetto took on the character of a labor camp. Among the institutions of the Ältestenrat, the "Labor Office" quickly seized the most important position, and the main role of the ghetto police was to ensure that the Jews fulfilled their "labor requirement" with precision.[36] The labor requirement was first imposed on men aged fourteen to sixty (later, to sixty-five) and women aged fifteen to forty-five (later, to fifty-five, and in the final days, to sixty).

After the *Aktion* against the children, elderly, and sick, the labor requirement was applied to all ghetto residents, without exception. The men were required to perform a full week of work of six to seven days, while the women worked three days a week at the beginning, then five days. From spring 1942 until the liquidation, many ghetto residents were assigned to regular places of work, and had to come every morning to their workplace if it was inside the ghetto, or to the square beside the ghetto gate, if they worked outside. Those who did not have a regular place of work had to come early in the morning to the gate plaza and wait to be sent to a temporary workplace. Inside the ghetto, the work managers were Jewish, while at the workplaces outside the ghetto, the managers were German or Lithuanian. Armed guards of German soldiers or Lithuanian "partisans" escorted the Jewish workers to the outside workplaces.

Exploitation of the Jewish labor force was organized precisely: workplace supervisors who were interested in employing Jews contacted the *Stadtkommissar* or the German Labor Office. If their demand was authorized, it was sent to the Jewish Labor Office, which ensured that at the appointed time the required number and type of workers would be standing next to the ghetto gate. Many times, the Jewish office received no advanced notice, and the Germans – army or SS officers – would arrive directly at the ghetto gate with their soldiers and

---

particularly in the large cities. On the other hand, an operation is being performed, in cooperation with the Labor Offices, to catch Jews who are no longer fit for labor, and they are immediately executed in small operations.... In this context, we note that in certain locations, there was sizeable resistance from the local authorities to large-scale annihilation operations, but this resistance was overcome by reliance on basic orders regarding this issue (Stahlecker's report, L-180, IMT 37:688 ff.).

36. A detailed description of this chapter in the history of the Kovno Ghetto appears in Gar, 100–111, 312–44, Garfunkel, *Kovno*, 45, 83–100.

demand the number of individuals that the *Stadtkommissar* permitted them to take. Because it was not easy to find the required configuration of workers at a moment's notice, the Germans would pour out their wrath on the Jews at the gate square, with curses and beatings, and sometimes shooting. Over time, these incidents decreased as the Jewish Labor Office increased its efficiency and supervision of the ghetto population in fulfilling the labor requirement.

We may categorize the places where Jews were employed according to work conditions. The most difficult conditions were in the military installations that directly served the front, such as the airfield. At these sites, the Jews were put to work almost exclusively at exhausting physical jobs, such as paving roads, carrying heavy loads, and digging. The pressure was lethal, and most of the work supervisors were evil personalities who abused the workers and wore them down. Some six thousand Jews, both men and women, which was over one half of the ghetto's laborers, were employed in such workplaces (4,500 of them at the airfield alone).

Relatively easier conditions existed in factories that employed small details of Jewish laborers – a total of about 1,500 individuals. These were mostly factories, workshops, and warehouses in which the Jews worked as professionals. The supervision was less deadly, and in certain conditions the Jews came into contact with Lithuanians, which enabled them to obtain food.

A third type of workplace was the ghetto institutions and workshops, in which the Jews worked without the direct supervision of the Germans and Lithuanians. At its peak, the number of workers in the ghetto workshops reached 4,600 individuals, working in forty-four different departments. Organization in these workshops was exemplary, and the Germans received from them a sizeable quantity of goods, of which a significant portion went toward their personal needs and "gifts" to their superiors. Thanks to these workshops, Kovno Ghetto "enjoyed" frequent visits by important Nazis from the *Reichskommisariat*, the *Ostministerium*, and the high echelons of the SS, and at a later period – from the Wehrmacht economic staff. The local authorities would put the workshops on display as a supreme achievement of the German civil administration and evidence that the Germans could turn even the *Ostjuden* (Eastern Jews), the lowest of the low, into useful creatures.

The wages that the Jews received for their labor had no relation to the efforts they invested, either willingly or not, or to the output they produced or goods the Germans obtained from them. Throughout the ghetto's lifespan, Jewish laborers never received payment in the usual sense of the word (except for a few months at the beginning, after the great robbery operation, when the Germans paid the Ältestenrat thirty thousand marks "to divide among the airfield workers." After this, for a short period the workers received five marks per day – about the price of a half kilo [one pound] of bread). The ghetto received one collective compensation: it was exempt from taxes to the municipality and other authorities, payments for water and electricity used by the residents, and rent. Even the food rations that the Germans supplied, based on the number of residents, were handed out "for free." But these provisions, even if they had been provided regularly and precisely (which never was the case), were in fact starvation rations. This is what the ghetto residents received per person for an entire week: bread – 700 g (24.7 oz), meat – 125 g (4.4 oz), flour – 122.5 g (4.3 oz), coffee or tea substitute – 75 g (2.6 oz), and salt – 50 g (1.8 oz). Laborers were allotted a weekly supplement: bread – 700 g (24.7 oz), meat – 125 g (4.4 oz), and fat – 20 g (0.7 oz).[37]

Isolation and Humiliation –
Destruction of Communal and Cultural Life

Establishment of the ghettos in the Ostland and determination of their organizational structure – this was the "directive" that *Reichskommissar* Hinrich Lohse[38] adopted for his area of the regime. In part, this directive was based on the Nuremberg laws and on Heydrich's orders to establish the ghettos in the occupied territories, but it also showed signs of the "concept" that Lohse placed at the foundation of his government in the Ostland.[39] Although in principle Lohse was subordinate to Rosenberg, *Reichsminister* for the Occupied Eastern Territories, he preserved a certain measure of independence in the area of legislation, particularly on issues for which the *Reichsminister* had not given orders. At any rate, even if the ghettos in this region of the occupied territories had a unique

---

37. According to Gar, *Umkum*, 254.
38. Former Nazi Gauleiter (regional party leader) for Schleswig-Holstein. On July 28, 1944, as the Red Army approached Riga, he fled to Germany without obtaining prior permission. He was tried in 1948 and sentenced to ten years of forced labor, but in 1951 was released from prison for "health reasons" (Reitlinger, 219).
39. Dallin, 182 ff.

element, this did not change the basic function that the ghetto fulfilled as part of the Nazi regime. Their main intention was concentration of the Jews in one location; their complete isolation from the remainder of the population; their abject humiliation; total destruction of community, culture, and spirit; exhaustion of their physical and spiritual strength; and organization of their lives exclusively in accordance with the needs of the Nazi regime.

Kovno Ghetto was established by a directive of the Gestapo chief in Lithuania, given on July 10, 1941, and publicized by the municipal director. At first, the Jewish committee, which was appointed to carry out the move to the ghetto, was directly subordinate to the Gestapo chief, but supervision of this work was given to the chief of the Lithuanian "partisans" and the mayor.[40] When the German civil administration was established in Kovno on July 17 of that year, the ghetto was transferred to the authority of the *Stadtkommissar*,[41] thus seemingly becoming a branch of the German administration.

Kovno's *Stadtkommissar* Kramer was faithful to his *Reichskommissar*'s policy, and translated it into the language of orders and detailed instructions. A short time after the order was given for establishing the ghetto, Kramer bombarded the Jews of Kovno with a flood of orders and instructions.[42] They were ordered to wear identifying emblems on their clothing – a yellow badge in the shape of a Star of David. At first, the order specified that they had to wear the badge on their chests only, but later, they were obligated to wear it on their backs as well. They were also ordered not to walk on the sidewalks, but rather in the road on the side of the sewage canals. When they met up with German military personnel, they had to greet them by removing their head coverings and performing a submissive bow. They were forbidden to be in public places, to use public transportation or telephones, to keep radio transmitters in their homes, or to purchase periodicals.

On February 18, 1942, the ghetto Jews were ordered to hand over to the

---

40. Gar, *Umkum*, 44; Garfunkel, *Kovno*, 42 ff.

41. City director. The Kovno *Stadtkommissar* was responsible to the *Generalkommissar*, the German administrator of Lithuania, who was in turn subordinate to the *Reichskommissar*, governor of the fabricated administrative department the Germans called Ostland (this included Lithuania, Latvia, and Estonia).

42. Gar, *Umkum*, 46. These directives were publicized on the city notice boards, and in the Lithuanian daily *Į Laisvę*, no. 16, July 11, 1941, and no. 30, July 28, 1941.

authorities any books, printed material, manuscripts, or valuable certificates they may have in their possession. In this "Book *Aktion*," over one hundred thousand volumes were confiscated in the ghetto. A special team in Kovno, a branch of the "Rosenberg headquarters" wearing European uniforms, sorted the material. After sorting, everything considered valuable by Rosenberg's apprentices was sent to Germany, while the remainder was sent to the paper factory in Kovno.

On May 7, 1942, the order was given that the women in the ghetto were forbidden from getting pregnant. The punishment for this "crime" was death to mother and infant.

On August 26, all synagogues were closed, and public prayer services in the ghetto were prohibited. That day, the Jews received the order to close the education department next to the Ältestenrat and the schools that had operated in the ghetto until then. All organized educational activity, except for professional education, was severely prohibited.[43] Among the specific prohibitions applied to the ghetto that should also be recalled was the prohibition against bringing food into the ghetto, except for those items provided to the Jews by the authorities.

By no means does this include all of the prohibitions and directives that the Germans issued for the ghetto. There were many more prohibitions that applied to the Jews and were demonstrated to them at various opportunities, mostly in very bloody actions. For the intention of the Nazi "legislation" for the ghetto was to slowly but surely reduce the living space and activity of the Jew, until he was lowered to the level of a beast of burden, which received no more from its owners than its basic physiological needs, and even this to an extent that fit the specific stage in the "final solution to the Jewish problem." It should be emphasized that the organization of the ghetto was more appropriate for this purpose than was the lifestyle and organization of free citizens; nonetheless, there was more freedom in a ghetto than there was in a concentration camp, in which the prisoner was under the harsh supervision of the *kapo* day and night. Indeed, the Kovno Jews learned – as will be made clear in the following chapters – how to exploit the limited freedom of movement left to them in the ghetto in order to break or circumvent the prohibitions and draconian orders. There is no doubt that the Germans knew about the loopholes in the ghetto regime, or at least some of them.

---

43. Gar, *Umkum*, 98; according to Garfunkel, *Kovno* (127), this occurred on February 27.

Apparently, this was one of the main reasons for the annulment of this regime in fall 1943 and the breakdown of the ghetto into several work camps, which were true prison camps in the full sense of the term.[44]

---

44. See chapter 5.

CHAPTER 2

The Ghetto in Frenzy

The Jewish Representatives

The report of General Stahlecker (commander of Einsatzgruppe A), portions of which were cited above, declares:

> Immediately following the first pogroms, a Jewish committee was summoned. We told them that so far, there was no reason for the German authorities to interfere in conflicts between the Lithuanians and the Jews. One condition for the creation of normal relations was the establishment of a Jewish ghetto. When the Jewish committee voiced reservations, we explained that otherwise, there would be no way to prevent additional pogroms. With this justification, the Jews immediately expressed their willingness to do anything in order to transfer the fellows of their race without delay into the Vilijampole quarter (Slobodka), which was designated for the Jewish ghetto. This quarter was located in the triangle between the Memel River and a branch of the Memel River, and it was connected to the city of Kovno by a single bridge, which could be easily blocked.[1]

Jewish sources indicate that five individuals participated in the above discussion.[2] Gestapo chief SS-Colonel Karl Jäger (commander of Einsatzkommando 3) informed them of the decision to establish a Jewish ghetto in Slobodka, and promised that if the Jews cooperated, the murders at the fort would cease and the

---

1. L-180, IMT, 37:689.
2. Attorneys Ya'akov Goldberg and Leon (Leib) Garfunkel, physician Dr. Ephraim Rabinowitz, and Rabbis Shmuel Abba Snieg and Ya'akov Moshe Shmuckler (see Goldberg, FLC 7:34; Garfunkel, Kovno, 37 ff.).

women and children there would be returned to their homes. They replied that they were not official representatives of the Jews, and that they had to consult with their brethren. The Gestapo chief agreed to wait until the next day for an answer.

The five community leaders went to consult with Rabbi Avraham Dovber Kahana-Shapira, chief rabbi of Kovno, and with him they found a large number of Jewish leaders. Unintentionally, the meeting with the rabbi was transformed into a fateful consultation about whether or not to cooperate with the Nazis. At the time, the issue they had to decide on was limited – whether they take responsibility for a "quiet and orderly" transfer of the city's Jews to the ghetto. They were not yet confronting the problem of organization of daily life inside the ghetto. Although the community leaders were undoubtedly aware of the principle involved in the decision whether or not to cooperate with the Nazis, the immediate need swayed the balance: they decided they had to obey the Germans, hoping they would remain true to their word and return the thousands of women and children in the forts to their homes and end the pogroms. Those in favor of cooperation cited another reason as well: "Even if the city remains quiet, in today's situation it would be better for the Jews to live together, no matter what happens – even in a ghetto."[3]

From that point, the five Jews who were in contact with Jäger could view themselves as a representative group. They did not formulate their reply on their own; supporting the line they took in the negotiations with the Gestapo stood several dozen individuals who represented various groups within the Jewish population. When they returned to the Gestapo chief, they informed him that they agreed to take responsibility for transferring the Jews to the ghetto. They also dared to demand changes in the ghetto size and details of the transfer. But Jäger denied most of their requests. He announced the date of the transfer and appointed the five responsible for choosing a committee to implement the transfer. "You will determine its composition yourselves, but all of you who are sitting in my room right now are responsible to me for fulfilling my order," he said.[4]

---

3. Goldberg, FLC 7:34. Goldberg emphasizes that the decision was made "after protracted arguments." In contrast, Garfunkel writes that the meeting was "very short, with almost no arguments. It was clear to all that we had no choice but to submit to the Gestapo's new decree. There was nothing to decide, because another power – a Satanic power – had already made its decision and handed down its decree (41–42)."

4. Garfunkel, *Kovno*, 42. See also Garfunkel's testimony, YVSA, 1 ff.

In the second consultation of the same five leaders with Rabbi Shapira, the composition of the committee was determined, and an additional five members were added to the original group.[5] They decided to establish a network of assistants, because they expected that there would be a lot of work involved in the transfer of tens of thousands of Jews to the ghetto. Afterwards, on its own initiative, the committee expanded its range of responsibility beyond the "transfer" matters. At that time, the Lithuanians and Germans often kidnapped Jews for forced labor. The committee proposed that the authorities grant it responsibility for drafting Jews for labor, and the Germans accepted this proposal. From that point on, until the liquidation of the ghetto, the Jews bore responsibility for drafting labor, supervision of the fulfillment of the labor requirement that the Germans cast on the Jews, and the punishment of "slackers."

As noted, after the ghetto was established in Kovno, it passed to the authority of the German civil administration. The *Stadtkommissar*'s official responsible for the ghetto immediately ordered the replacement of the committee with a "Council of Elders" (Ältestenrat), led by a "Head Jew" (*Oberjude*). The Germans allowed the ghetto residents to elect these positions, taking no interest in the method of election. Apparently they did not care how the Ältestenrat was chosen, as long as it "proved itself" afterwards, meaning it would succeed in organizing ghetto life so that the Germans could do what they wanted for as long as they wanted; and if not, the council would be removed and replaced by another.

The committee members never imagined that the instruction that the Ältestenrat be elected by the Jews could be interpreted literally, meaning by democratic election. They thus appealed to community leaders from a number of groups.[6] This time, the meeting was large, but in fact, the agenda included only the election of the Ältestenrat head, and not the entire body. The other five members, four of whom were part of the original committee that had met with Jäger,[7]

---

5. G. Wolf, Zvi Levin, R. Roginsky, L. Rostovsky, and Naftel – according to Goldberg (FLC 38). According to Garfunkel, Kovno (54), the following also joined the committee at the same meeting: Ya'akov Goldberg, Leib Garfunkel, Rabbi Shmuel Abba Snieg, Ephraim Rabinowitz, and Michael (Misha) Koppelman. Afterwards, the following joined in an advisory capacity only: G. Wolf, L. Rostovsky, Rabbi Ya'akov Moshe Shmuckler, and Zvi Levin.

6. Garfunkel writes "from all the groups" (47), but this is an exaggeration, because these leaders were far from representing all the groups in the ghetto – if representation is even relevant here.

7. Rabbi Shmuckler was replaced by Michael (Misha) Koppelman, who immediately afterward was appointed chief of the ghetto police.

"were elected by the committee ... in accordance with opinions expressed at the meeting of community leaders."[8]

At that meeting, Dr. Elkhanan Elkes was chosen as head of the Ältestenrat, and as will become clear afterwards, there could not have been a better choice.[9]

The Ältestenrat in Action

The Ältestenrat operated under the exacting supervision of the supervisor (*Referent*) for Jewish affairs in Kovno. It received instructions from messengers from the office of the *Stadtkommissar*, or from Nazi officials who visited the ghetto. At these opportunities, the Ältestenrat would give a report of what it had done to fulfill the orders. It also submitted regular monthly reports on the activities of its institutions.

In a very short time after its establishment, the Ältestenrat succeeded in establishing an administrative system that often proved its efficiency in organizing ghetto life. This system was built on departments (or *amten* – offices, by the official German term): the ghetto police, the labor office, the office of health affairs, the office of social welfare, the statistics office, the education office, and so forth. The Ältestenrat appointed the department directors and determined the general operating procedures. Members of the Ältestenrat took turns in supervising the various departments.

In "normal times," meaning between *Aktion*s, the Ältestenrat was wholly responsible for implementation of the decrees and orders (during the *Aktion*s, the Germans themselves took responsibility). Its main concern was the issue of labor. It understood that the labor quota was, to the Germans, the sole right to existence of the ghetto inhabitants, and this rule was the main principle of its operation. This was first expressed in the organizational side: within a short time, the labor office, the operational arm of the Ältestenrat in this area, became the most important of the Ältestenrat offices. It also had the most highly developed and efficient system of operation. The other important offices – the police, the health service, the nutrition office – were mostly involved in assisting the labor office in various ways. The individuals whose characters were most suited for

---

8. Garfunkel, *Kovno*, 54.
9. Garfunkel gives a dramatic description of the election of Dr. Elkes (47 ff.).

this work were placed in this office – they were organized and decisive, and able to act "without sentiment."

Their first obligation was to give the Germans the required number of workers daily, or at least to approach this number as far as was possible. The number was all important. For this reason, the labor office kept precise statistics on all the ghetto residents who fell under the labor requirement, which meant 75–80 percent of the ghetto population. The office knew all the necessary details about all of them and received updated information on where they worked each day. The precise lists permitted the office to identify those who were evading the labor requirement and they were punished, if the heads of the institutions were interested in doing so. But the record-keeping method permitted hidden evasion: the lists were made at the workplaces according to the work certificate numbers of the workers. If the number of a certain individual appeared on one of the lists that were given each day to the labor office by the "unit chiefs" (*kolonenfirer*), the office assumed that this person had fulfilled his labor requirement for that day. Thus a person could send someone else to work in his place, with his number. Of course, only those to whom the labor requirement did not apply could serve as substitutes – in other words, young men and women under fifteen or sixteen and the elderly. But such incidents were frequent, and working instead of someone else became a source of income in the ghetto.

The Ältestenrat members and the labor office ignored these "crimes," as long as only the number of workers was important in fulfilling the labor quota, and the Germans did not make specific demands about the type of workers. But the Germans were not satisfied for long with only the number; they asked for "quality" workers who were healthy and strong, who were capable of performing difficult physical labor. The office had to ensure that in each labor unit there was a certain percentage of healthy men, and to limit or annul the hidden evasion.

During the *Aktions*

We have given a general description of the Ältestenrat's activity and its most important offices in "normal times," when the ghetto residents' worries focused on housing, work, sources of income, and other such issues. Although these areas of activity also meant difficult roles and decisions for the Ältestenrat, the main test was during the period of the *Aktions* and deportations.

This is not the place to determine whether and to what extent the behavior of the Ältestenrat in Kovno during the *Aktion*s may be viewed as cooperation or indirect assistance to fulfill the Nazi plan for extermination. We only intend to describe the quality of its behavior in this case as an extreme expression of the mode of response the Ältestenrat adopted toward Nazi policy in general. From this aspect, especially characteristic is its behavior during the terrible massacre, known in Kovno Ghetto history as the "Great *Aktion*."[10]

The first rumors of impending trouble circulated among the ghetto residents in mid-October 1941. Lithuanians who lived near the Ninth Fort said that Soviet war prisoners were preparing enormous pits at the fort, and this was a sign that a mass destruction would be carried out there soon.

On the afternoon of Sunday, October 26, Rauca, the Gestapo official for Jewish affairs, visited the Ältestenrat office and delivered this message:[11] the authorities have decided to separate laborers from non-laborers in the ghetto. For this purpose, those unfit for labor would be housed in the Small Ghetto,[12] while the laborers would remain in the Large Ghetto. Those employed at the airfield and other places of work of military importance would receive additional food rations. In the early morning of October 28, all ghetto residents would gather in Democrats Square, the largest square in the ghetto, where the selection would be performed. The Ältestenrat was to inform the ghetto population of the obligation to report, and whoever did not report would be killed.

At the same opportunity, Rauca gave instructions for implementation: the ghetto would be closed, and no one would be allowed to leave that day. The homes would remain open. Those suffering from terminal illnesses would be permitted to remain at home, but in such a case a note would be affixed to the door that a Jew remained inside. In the square, the people would organize by families in the following order: at the front, members of the Ältestenrat and the Jewish police with their families, followed by workers in the other ghetto institutions, then workers in the labor units employed in the city, and the airfield

---

10. See chapter 1; compare Gar, Umkum, 72–82; Gruenhoyz, FLC 7:17–18; Garfunkel, Kovno, 71 ff.

11. According to Gar, *Umkum*, 73. The versions in the various sources are similar but not identical.

12. This section of the ghetto had been evacuated several weeks earlier, and some of its inhabitants were executed at the Ninth Fort (see chapter 1). The Germans did not inform the Ältestenrat of the fate of these Jews, but there was hardly any room for doubt that they had all been murdered.

workers. Jewish policemen would instruct the people where to stand, and keep order during the selection.

According to the text of the order and Rauca's explanation, the Ältestenrat members had no room for doubt about the nature of the calamity threatening the ghetto. To the Germans, the Jews were nothing more than labor. If so, what other fate than death could be expected for those who were specifically classified as unfit for labor and sent outside the ghetto?

The members of the Ältestenrat faced a fateful question: Should they fulfill the order, or not? The decision was hardly an easy one. After Rauca left, they continued their meeting for many long hours. They took a short break to go home, so as not to arouse suspicion, then recommenced. Late at night, they sent a group to Rabbi Shapira to hear his opinion of how to proceed in this situation, according to *halacha* (Jewish law) and ethics. The rabbi's answer was that if the Ältestenrat had reason to hope that by fulfilling its duty they could save the ghetto, even if only part of it, they should do so.

The next morning – one day before the deadline – the Ältestenrat made an effort to obtain more exact information about the Germans' intentions. They sent a messenger to the Gestapo's confidant in Kovno, the Jew Josef Caspi-Serebrovitz.[13] They asked to meet with Rauca at once. They told Caspi-Serebrovitz to tell Rauca that the Ältestenrat was struck with fear by his order. Caspi-Serebrovitz should also try to obtain details about the decree. Caspi-Serebrovitz answered their request, and Rauca visited the ghetto a second time, again attempting to calm the Ältestenrat members, telling them "that there is no basis for these fears, that this is an administrative matter only."[14]

The Ältestenrat decided to obey the Gestapo's order. Notices in its name were pasted on the ghetto houses, with the text Rauca had demanded.[15]

The *Aktion* process and its horrifying results are described in detail in the sources mentioned above. Only the Ältestenrat and the ghetto police passed the *Aktion* without harm. In fact, the selection began only after these individuals and their families were on the "good side," the side of those permitted to live. Only then did Rauca put into practice the fatal principles of selection. The younger

---

13. See chapter 8 for a description of Caspi's role as a Gestapo agent.
14. Garfunkel, *Kovno*, 73.
15. For the text of the notice in Hebrew translation, see Garfunkel, ibid.

and healthier people, and small families with only a small number of persons unfit for labor, were sent to the good side, and all the rest – to the bad side, the side of those doomed to destruction in the Fortress of Death.

The former vice-chairman of the Ältestenrat, Leib Garfunkel, describes the group's deliberations in those fateful hours:

> We had more than a suspicion that this was a terrible decree, but Rauca said that some would be taken to another place, and then the living conditions in the ghetto would improve. We realized that he intended to deceive us.... The question was whether we ... were permitted from a Jewish viewpoint to do what Rauca was demanding, because instinctively we understood that this would mean an enormous disaster.... The question was whether to publicize this announcement – in other words, that all the Jews had to come to the square on October 28 ... or to commit sabotage: do what you want with us – we won't publicize the announcement.... The question was constantly with us: How should we behave? We sat almost the entire night, asking ourselves: What should we do? ... Finally, someone proposed that we consult with Rabbi Shapira, if whether from a Jewish point of view we were permitted.... Rauca did not ask us to perform the selection.... We understood that he would do it. It was our responsibility to announce that everyone had to appear. We consulted and weighed whether to do one thing or the other. The memory of the "Trial *Aktion*"[16] influenced us: at that time ... at the last minute, the *Aktion* was cancelled, and maybe this time it would be that way as well. But if we committed sabotage, he was liable to bring disaster on the entire ghetto. The whole time we had a principle – to save the remaining survivors, to save whom we could. We could not pursue a policy of protest – this would bring us nothing, aside from the fact that later, history would record how proud those Jews were, they refused, etc., but then we thought more about the lives of the Jews....
>
> Each of us was divided in his heart. No one voiced the opinion – only this, only sabotage; on the contrary, everyone said that logically, this was forbidden, because if we did so, we would lose the small chance we still had, and we were commanded to save what we could. What did we know? Perhaps

---

16. On September 17, 1941, the Germans began an *Aktion* in the Small Ghetto, but after the selection, it was cancelled and the Jews were sent home. This *Aktion* was called the "Trial *Aktion*" (Gar, *Umkum*, 61).

in another week or two the war would end – for all kinds of things could happen, not only miracles. In war, anything could happen, and thus we were commanded to save what we could. But if we pursued a policy of protest, we would not scare the Germans. Any resistance at all was completely out of the question in the first months. We were dejected and could not imagine any possibility of showing resistance. Surely they would destroy us.[17]

In answer to the question why they did not consult with wider circles of the public, Garfunkel replies:

There was no time to do so. Rauca came on Sunday at 12 noon, sat in the meeting until 1 or 1:30, and then of course we were left with that impression [of Rauca's appearance]. We sat and deliberated, and decided that still we had to go home, so that our relatives, the families, would not sense that something was going on here. Should they sense it, the entire ghetto would know right away. We kept it a secret more than twenty-four hours. It was impossible to tell. If we had told, it would have been terrible.... In the afternoon we returned and continued the meeting. Many from within the administration did not even know. Even the secretaries did not know. We went out to talk somewhere... and we met – I remember – all evening and all night... at night we went to Rabbi Shapira. We woke him up.... That night many [Germans] broke in to kidnap people for work at the airfield. There was shooting. We arrived at the rabbi's house at one or two A.M. – we met with him for about an hour. Then we had to go home – again so as not to arouse suspicion. The next day we sent Zvi Levin to Serebrovitz to try... we awaited an answer. At about three or four P.M., Rauca came to Goldberg with Serebrovitz, and again it took time. Then there was no technical possibility [for a broad consultation], and also because it was dangerous, it was impossible to do....

If we had to report on Tuesday at 6 A.M. already, we would have to publicize it on Monday evening at 5–6 P.M. at the latest. We had no knowledge of any underground, and no underground existed..., it was the worst period in the ghetto, there was no community organization – everyone was depressed.... [18]

---

17. Garfunkel's testimony, YVSA, 5, 8 ff.
18. Ibid.

Response of the Ghetto Masses

How did the simple Jew – as opposed to members of the Ältestenrat and its institutions on one hand, and members of underground organizations on the other – behave under the Nazi regime in Kovno Ghetto? In particular, we would like to know whether we can distinguish examples of resistance to the Nazis in the behavior and reactions of the Jewish population in the ghetto. If so, then we may view the resistance and underground movement of the Kovno Jews, whose history, methods, and achievements are described in the following chapters, not as an exceptional phenomenon of ghetto reality, but as a movement that had a broad public foundation and deep roots in the consciousness of the masses.

ATTITUDE TOWARD FORCED LABOR

The attitude of Kovno Jews to the work the Nazis forced them to perform was determined in large part by the conditions that prevailed in the first days after the outbreak of the war. In those times of nightmare and terror, kidnappings were very frequent. The Lithuanian "partisans" raced through the streets, kidnapping Jews for work. Sometimes they really intended to employ the kidnapped in jobs related to the fighting – such as removing destroyed buildings, burying the dead, digging, and loading – and when the job was finished, they were released. But in many cases, the work was accompanied by humiliation and torture, and even cruel acts of murder. Furthermore, frequently the work served as a pretext – an easy way to bring large groups of Jews to sites far from the city and butcher them. When this became known, the Jews tried as far as possible to avoid being kidnapped for work, out of fear for their lives.

When the ghetto was erected and closed, the kidnappings ended, as did the labor conscriptions that camouflaged murder preparations.[19] From then on, the Germans took care not to combine forced labor with the liquidation operations, apparently intending to convince the ghetto prisoners that working for the Reich was their only salvation. As we have seen, the Ältestenrat also did much to instill this belief.

It can be assumed that the ghetto masses understood the significance of this. Apparently, not many believed the promise that if they worked enthusiastically,

---

19. The *Aktion* against the intelligentsia (see chapter 1) was an exception to this, as it was performed immediately after closure of the ghetto.

the Nazis would let them live for an extended time. But logic told them that this promise carried a threat, which they had to relate to seriously, that if they refused to work, they would soon come to a bitter end. As long as the ghetto existed, the Jewish Labor Office did not encounter serious difficulties in supplying the Germans' demands regarding the workers, and the percentage of shirkers was negligible. The labor office did have a system of conscription and punishment, but on "quiet days," when the threat of deportation did not hang over their heads, they did not need it much, and the conscription representatives' job was relatively easy. The public carried the heavy burden, and the ghetto leaders had nothing to complain about in this area.

Undoubtedly, this is proof of the self-discipline, responsibility, and realistic approach that characterizes Lithuanian Jewry in general. But a correct evaluation of the ghetto residents' attitude to the forced labor must take into account not only the willingness to go out to work but also behavior at the workplace. Here we discover an interesting picture. As noted above, there were differences among the workplaces, in terms of the work regime and other conditions. These differences influenced the attitude to the work itself. At the places where the workers received some form of compensation for their work (a larger portion of food, leftover food for the family, a certain amount of freedom in contact with non-Jews at the workplace and outside it), the Jews worked diligently and raised their productivity level. An important example of this type of workplace – especially in the later period of the ghetto – is the ghetto workshops that produced goods for the German army, but were given a certain degree of independence in terms of administration and organization. This enabled their workers to derive benefit from their work for themselves, their families, and the underground movement.[20]

The attitude of the ghetto residents differed with regard to work in places where they were treated roughly and cruelly, and where they had no opportunity to obtain food, except for starvation rations. At these places, the Jews worked slowly, their senses frozen, and only so that their superiors would not view them as idle. Against this background, over time, a system of secret signals was developed to warn workers of impending danger during working hours.[21]

---

20. See chapter 8.

21. On this, see especially Yisrael Kaplan, *Dos folksmoyl in Nazi klem: reidenishn in getta un in katzet* [The nation in the Nazi vise: sayings in the ghetto and concentration camps], Munich, 1949.

THE BATTLE FOR SURVIVAL

It would be far from the truth to think that work was the ghetto residents' primary source of anxiety. Far more worrisome was how to support themselves and their family, for the work itself was not then a source of income. They had to fight the German regime, the goal of which was systematic starvation of the ghetto. This was a quiet but stubborn battle, and the Jews applied to it all their talents, quickness, cunning, and rich imagination. In this battle, any means was legitimate.

The main source of income for the ghetto Jews was the remaining property, movable goods and valuables that they had brought with them to the ghetto and saved from the organized robbery. The property they left in the city in the hands of the Lithuanians was mostly lost. Only a few managed to save something of it while inside the ghetto. A small addition to their property was the items – underwear, clothing, and food – that the Jews filched from the Germans' stores, whether in the ghetto workshops or in workplaces in the city.

The main problem was how to exchange this property, at the right pace and for a rate that would sustain them for as long as possible. They exchanged the goods for food or medical supplies, and eventually, for weapons and ammunition. The other main problem was how to bring the property home to the ghetto.[22] This involved dangers at every step. Commerce with non-Jews usually took place at the workplace, but because the circle of clients was limited, demand was low and the prices were very low. Thus many who were more daring tried to find customers outside the workplace, which was like walking through a minefield. They had to sneak away from their workplace and wander through the streets of the city, which were absolutely off-limits to the Jews. They were also subject to the mercy of the non-Jewish customers, who could steal their wares and turn them in to the Gestapo.

This situation led to the "nimble peddler," who would leave the ghetto along with a work unit, then remove the yellow star and sneak away from the line. All day he would deal in his wares, and toward evening he would hide among the people returning from work and reenter the ghetto with them.

Bringing food into the ghetto was a story in itself. Because of the strict prohibition against this, everyone who returned from the city underwent a rigorous

---

22. On purchasing food items and methods of smuggling them into the ghetto, see Gar, *Umkum*, 103–4, 119, 315–16.

search. There was no end to the inventiveness of the ghetto residents to hide their merchandise from the searchers. The Jewish policemen and members of the Jewish Labor Office had to stand beside the gate on the inside and help the Germans with the searches. They developed their own methods of easing the search for their fellow Jews.

Another form of scheming against the Germans was trade through the barbed-wire fence that surrounded the ghetto. This method was common at the beginning of the ghetto's existence, but later only a few daring individuals practiced it, because approaching the fence involved mortal danger. Still, Jews managed to smuggle in significant quantities of food even by this dangerous method.

THE SMOLDERING EMBER OF JEWISH CULTURE

As noted, Nazi policy for the ghetto was intended to break the Jews' spirit, to take from them every source of encouragement and comfort, and to destroy everything that bore the stamp of the Jew's creative force. The ghetto residents rose up against this plot. Sources reveal that in the life of the Kovno Ghetto, there were amazing expressions of faithfulness to Judaism and to Jewish books, of preserving the ember of human culture with the last of their strength, and even individual literary expression.[23]

Cultural life in the ghetto was highly diverse.[24] In particular, cultural activities abounded during the period of relative quiet in 1942, and reached their peak in spring 1943. Lectures were given on literature and science, and seminars, musical evenings, and concerts were offered. Other activities included sing-a-longs, plays, Hanukkah and Purim parties, Jewish memorial days, art exhibits, and school balls. One phenomenon that was widespread in the ghetto from the very first day until the liquidation was reading books, which involved very many and did not cease even after the prohibition against owning books came into effect (February 18, 1942). Individuals and groups collected books, storing them in private homes and storage rooms. Many utilized the libraries that operated in Block C

23. Here we are referring to expressions that were personal and spontaneous, as opposed to the cultural activities that were an organic part of the underground, and that are described below.
24. For details on cultural life, see Gruenhoyz, "Hurban Kovne," FLC, 8:27 ff.; Das kultur leben in Kovner getta, Sudarsky et al., Lita, 1743–56; P. Kaplan, FLC, 9:13; Y. Aliesky, FLC 9:29–30; Y. Gurwitz, (Kovner Getta-Arkester,) FLC, 9:52–59.

and other locations.[25] In addition, an attempt to commemorate the events in the ghetto was made with the methodical management of archives and diaries.[26] All these activities involved serious danger.

Religious life was characterized by devotion and spiritual inspiration.[27] Inside the ghetto, there were two synagogues, but *minyanim* (prayer quorums) were also held in private homes and public areas (workshops, hospitals), and Torah study sessions were organized. The home of the head of the Slobodka yeshiva, Rabbi Avraham Grodzensky, served as a focal point for religious life and Torah study. The sermons of the elderly *tzaddik* (pious man) acquired a reputation in the ghetto. He often spoke of the issue of *kiddush Hashem* (sanctifying God's Name) and its significance for our generation.[28]

---

25. Testimony of E. Gutman, YVSA, 3–5; Oshry, *Hurban Lita*, 87. See map of Kovno Ghetto, (Appendix III): the three large apartment buildings are marked A, B, and C.

26. Gar, Umkum, 99, 385, 400; PKG, 51, 53–56, 104; FLC, 9:13–14.

27. On this issue, see also Oshry, Hurban Lita, particularly the chapter "Das geistike leben fun di yiden in Kovner Getta" [Cultural life of the Jews in Kovno Ghetto], 104–12: "Even in those bitter, dark days, when murder and robbery were everyday occurrences, when the majority of Torah scholars and yeshiva students perished for the sanctification of God's name, when murder lay in wait for every Jew, despite everything the Jews of Kovno went to the synagogue to pray, to study Mishnah, to read Psalms, to pour out their hearts before their Father in Heaven, and to draw strength to continue living until God on High would have mercy on Israel and save us from their terrible situation." See also Garfunkel, Kovno, 257 ff.; Rabbi A. Person, Rivka Gutman: "Das Religieze leben in Kovner getta" [Religious Life in the Kovno Ghetto]," FLC 9:36–52.

28. The following incident is characteristic of the atmosphere among the *haredi* circles in the ghetto. One man relates that once he saw Rabbi Avraham Dovber Kahana-Shapira, chief rabbi of the city, sitting in the courtyard with his beard hidden in his clothes (he was the only rabbi who did not shave his beard in the ghetto). The man went to him and began a conversation on *kiddush Hashem* and resistance against the Germans. The conversation turned to two stories that were well-known in the ghetto:

It happened during the liquidation of the Jews of the Lithuanian city of Kelm. As the city's Jews were standing beside the pit, facing the barrels of the machine guns, the city's chief rabbi, Rabbi Daniel Movshovitz (head of the Kelm Beis Ha-Talmud), asked the German in charge to permit him to say a few words to his congregation. The German permitted him to speak briefly. The rabbi began to talk about the issue of *kiddush Hashem*, quietly and calmly, as if he were speaking before his students in normal times. He spoke for too long, and the German began to shout at him to finish. Then the rabbi turned to the Jews standing on the edge of the pit, and said, "We are now standing in the situation of which I was just speaking a moment ago – *kiddush Hashem*. So do not panic, we have to accept the decree quietly." Turning to the German, he said, "I have finished – you can begin." (A yeshiva student from Kelm who escaped publicized the story to Kovno Ghetto residents.)

The same feeling of devotion to cultural values drove the non-religious groups in the ghetto and found various modes of expression. In the first months of the ghetto, during the days of nightmarish fear of the *Aktions*, many parents made efforts so that their school-age children would keep up with their studies. The parents' efforts went hand in hand with the willingness and dedication of the elementary and secondary school teachers, who began to gather their students and organize instruction in private homes. This served as the basis for the establishment and activity of the education office of the Ältestenrat.[29] If the two schools the Ältestenrat established, with several hundred students, achieved a decent pedagogical level despite the extremely harsh conditions of the ghetto, then this was primarily thanks to the dedicated work of the teachers and their deep comprehension of educational needs. After the authorities closed the schools in August 1942, the initiative was again transferred to private bodies and the organized movements. Worthy of special mention was the teaching activity carried out in secret in the professional school, which continued to operate even after the closure of the ghetto school network.[30]

The refusal to be cowed by the threatening reality found concrete and sharp

---

Another event took place during the destruction of the Jews of Kaidan. The city's Jews had already been pushed into the pit, when at the last minute a Jewish butcher leaped from the pit, attacked the German officer, and bit him fatally in the windpipe. (See Oshry, *Hurban Lita*, 291.)

The man asked the rabbi: "Which one of the two incidents is preferable?" The rabbi deliberated, then said, "The path Rabbi Daniel took was most appropriate for him, but for the butcher – the second method. It would have been very strange for the two to switch their deeds. I am certain that Rabbi Daniel would also know how to do such things, but still, the path he took was fitting for him." (Testimony of Ephraim Gutman, addendum, 1–2.)

29. For details on the educational system in the ghetto, see Yisrael Kaplan, "Kovoner shul un lerershaft in umkum," FLC 9:3–23; Ya'akov Eliasky, "Di Fakshul in Kovner Getta," FLC 9:23–36; PKG, 54–55; Oshry, Hurban Lita, 110; Sudarsky et al., Lita, 1748–9; Gar, Umkum, 383–84.

30. The Nazis viewed the professional school as training laborers and craftsman for their war machine, as it taught "safe" topics like science and math, and permitted its continued operation. One of the teachers in this school recounted an incident from that period. In the curriculum, his name was mentioned as a science teacher, while in fact his subject was Jewish history. One day, the school was honored by a visit from SA officer Hermann, chief of the German Labor Office in the ghetto and responsible for supervising the professional school. The door of the teacher's classroom opened and the German appeared. The teacher was in the middle of a lecture on Josephus Flavius, but he remained calm. Almost instinctively, he began to write a mathematical formula on the blackboard and explain it in a quiet voice. The German was satisfied... (testimony of Avraham Melamed, YVSA, 2).

expression in the lyric folklore that was created in the ghetto and became wide-spread throughout it. Some thirty songs are extant today,[31] most in Yiddish. Some were preserved in writing by their authors or the authors' friends, and were published only after the war. But most became known rapidly among the ghetto masses, written on slips of paper and passed from hand to hand and from mouth to mouth. This was especially true for those songs that were sung to a known melody, or written as new versions of songs familiar to the people. About one-sixth of the songs are anonymous, but of the authors whose names are identified, only one or two were known as poets before the war. The rest were people who had never before attempted authorship. The simplicity of the songs is evident in their lack of poetic devices (in some, the only characteristics are the meter, which is sometimes weak, and the rhyme); their simple language, lively and full of expressions that were coined in the ghetto or that acquired special significance there; and their close connection to the reality of daily life.

The songs can be divided into three types, based on content: (1) songs of mourning and grief; (2) satires of ghetto life; and (3) songs expressing fury, rebellion, and vision.

Nine songs form the category of mourning and grief: "*Der 9-ter Fart*" [the Ninth Fort], "*Yiddische Brigades*" [Jewish brigades], "*In Slobadker yeshiva*" [In the Slobodka yeshiva] – all by Avraham Axelrod; "*Di Grosse Aktzia*" [The great Aktion] by Sima Yashunsky; "*Zays shoyn bald a yar avek*" [Almost a year has passed], "*Tzaros un leid*" [Trouble and suffering], "*Litvishe partizaner*" [Lithuanian partisans], "*Mir zenen bey dem drat*" [Beside the barbed wire], "*An alte yeydene klaft in tir*" [An elderly Jewess knocks on the door] – authors unknown. The songs were mostly written between 1941and 1942, near the time of the annihilation operations. Their structure is basically uniform: in the first part, which sometimes forms the majority of the song, the writer expresses his grief for the thousands of brothers and sisters who were murdered, and his horror at the acts of the murderers and their helpers. From within the description of robbery, humiliation, and murder, we detect a note of bitter criticism at the behavior of the ghetto residents before, during, and after the murders. The last verse of the song is usually highly stylized, as if the entire song was written with it in mind.

---

31. *FLC*, volumes 1–3, 7–10, see section "Fun unzer lider-zamlung"; Garfunkel, Kovno, 266–321; *PKG*, 22, 27; Gar, Umkum, 402–13.

Here the atmosphere suddenly changes, and the songwriter concludes on a note of hope, appealing furiously to the conscience of the world, or with a cry for vengeance.

For example, Sima Yashunsky concludes her song with a detailed description of the Great *Aktion*:

> Hah, world! The blood cries out to your conscience
> Blood of men and women, young and old;
> Mass graves stand at the Fort
> Alone and orphaned – until the day arrives![32]

Two songs by Axelrod have similar endings. This is the ending of the song about the Ninth Fort:

> Mothers and brothers, cease your weeping!
> Despite the wound in the heart that flows and pounds,
> Be strong of good courage, hope and wait!
> The day of vengeance will arrive, the day of vengeance and payment![33]

The ending of the song "Jewish Brigades" – a marching song, to judge by its melody – is characteristic of the hope the author guarded in his heart, as did many others in the ghetto:

> We will yet enjoy, the time will come
> For spring, victory, and light.
> We will straighten our backs, then, and sing aloud
> A new song of freedom and liberty.
> Jewish brigades,
> Brave, without the yellow star,[34]
> They march back
> To their land, their homeland.[35]

---

32. *FLC* 10:139.

33. Garfunkel, *Kovno*, 268, trans. Yehoshua Tan Pai (Shaiye Butchatsky).

34. This is the correct translation of *an lates*. Translator Tan Pai incorrectly translated this as "adorned." The intention is that the Jews marched without the badge of shame. For ghetto Jews, removal of the yellow star symbolized the day of liberation.

35. Garfunkel, *Kovno*, 272.

The second group – songs satirizing the ghetto experience – is the largest, with ten songs: *"Beym getta-toyerl brent a feyerl"* [Fire burns at the ghetto gate], *"Yalhes"* [Big shots],[36] and *"Baym toyer"* [At the gate] – by Avraham Axelrod; *"Hoycher man"* [The eminent one] and *"Der Fliefeld Arbeter"* [Airfield worker] – by Natan Markovsky; *"Nit ayer mazal"* [You have no luck] by Shaul Shenker; *"Brigades"* [Brigades] by Rachel Salkija; *"Witamin"* [Vitamin] by G. Shenker; *"Meystas lid"* ["Meystas" brigade song] by A. Zipkin; and *"Lichvod di gramen-fabrikatzie in getta"* [In honor of the ghetto rhyming industry] by Lerke Rosenblum.

Apparently, these songs were mostly written during the quiet period in the ghetto, from 1942 to 1943. Issues of housing, forced labor, and income were at the top of the ghetto resident's list of worries, and these are the main subjects of the songs. Some express a tone of bitter ridicule, condemning the organization of the Ältestenrat and the attitude of its officials toward the simple resident, the practice of favoritism, and the corruption that became widespread in many circles. In others, the basis of the song is comedy, and the author describes ghetto life with humor. Behind the barbs and critique, we catch a glimpse of the glowing faith that, thanks to agility, cunning, and endurance, "We will wear down our enemies and reach the day of redemption."

An example of lashing satire is "Brigades" by Rachel Salkija.[37] This epic poem of nine chapters and 270 lines contains fascinating and incredibly exact descriptions of the various incidents that took place every morning beside the ghetto gate when the worker units went out to work in the city. It also depicts the unique experience at the workplaces themselves, with the constant efforts of the ghetto Jews to expend minimal effort at work but maximum effort in obtaining food. The poet directs her wrath against the Jewish police and labor officials responsible for keeping order beside the gate and the *arbeitseinsatz*.[38] They had a dual responsibility: to ensure that men or women who did not belong (in other words, who were not loyal to them) did not infiltrate the preferred brigades,

36. Plural of *"yaleh,"* a nickname for those in power. On the development of this expression, see Garfunkel, *Kovno*, 88, note 7.
37. Apparently authored in 1943, sent for publication by the author and published in September 1948, FLC 9:84–92.
38. The daily quota of workers from the ghetto required by the German labor office.

and – by force or cunning – force the others, who reported that morning at this modern slave market, to go to the undesirable workplaces. Below is a dramatic description of a trick the labor officials played when the turn came for a labor unit whose members were unaware that "the work there was harder than hell." Below are the words to the song:

"Come near! Where are you? What do you sense?
I've already called thrice, *Shtabmeyor Shu!*"[39]
"Well do we hear your voice, *Rish baba,*
A little patience, the army is still incomplete
(The voice of the brigadier,[40] his hand on the list
His men in each column, four by four.)
Bring more women, without them we won't march,
The work with the bridge at the fort is hard."
"Women, excuse me… What do you say of worry?
They're a dime a dozen!" he roars,
"Any woman, to me! A good brigade!
You can score a package.[41] As for the work – fulfill your duty!"
Confusion reigns, pushing and shoving,
Forcing a way through before the volunteering daughters of Eve.
Jewish policemen adopt [the idea], confirming:
"It's a good brigade, *Shtabmeyor Shu.*"
They smile to themselves and push their hordes:
"Can't we leave already? The quota's been filled."

The poet found another target for her sharp criticism among the workers themselves: in particular members of the unit that worked in the Gestapo office. Their source of income was unique. Ever since German Jews had been brought to Kovno and murdered in the Ninth Fort, the Gestapo storehouses were filled with clothes, shoes, underwear, and other personal items. The warehouse workers

---

39. A German company that collected scrap iron in the occupied territories. Jews were employed at the Kovno branch. The workplace was infamous due to the harsh labor, rude treatment, and scarce opportunities to "score a package" (see below, note on *machen a pekel*).
40. *Brigadir* – term for work unit leader.
41. *Machen a pekel* – term for obtaining food items.

stole anything they could get their hands on, for personal use and to sell. Below is a section from this poem:

> Silently, silently, without a word
> Down there below, without a witness
> All day long they take turns
> Grab and try on, clothes, clothes.
> "How this purple dress
> Will compliment my figure.
> Another blue georgette jacket
> Enough for today, go in peace."
> Then in her place, a friend
> Spreads out the cloth of her garment
> For herself she takes wool, georgette
> And on top – a "Finette" suit.
> Erase the blood, the stain, from clothing
> (Explanations are superfluous.)
> Shoes and socks as well
> By color, a good pair
> Carrying garment upon garment on your back
> And on top of it – the yellow badge.

The tone changes when we turn our attention to the humorous songs. Here, it is as if the same issues take on a different meaning. In "*Meystas lid*," Zipkin sees the amusing side in the history of the women's unit that worked in the Kovno municipal kitchen. Movement throughout the enormous factory is intense, the labor is stressful, and the women must keep up the pace despite their plentiful worries. But all work is worthwhile, because this is a "good brigade" that provides its workers with a respectable income:

> … Hah, geese, chickens, come to the ghetto
> Hah, fowl, follow us, yes, like that.
> If meat and fat remain
> Two kilos or three, it's all the same.
> How pleasant, then, the contrasting thought
> That these chickens are still whole.

All here trussed into a binding in our panties[42]
Geese and ducks are silent here.[43]

The third type, songs of anger, rebellion, and vision, include three songs by Diskant (the father of Abba Diskant): *"Zu dem toyer"* [To the gate], *"In der yeshiva"* [In the yeshiva], and *"Ale birger fun getaland"* [All are citizens of the ghetto state]; A. Zifkin's *"Hafenung"* [Hope]; Sima Yashunsky's *"Di groye geta"* [The gray ghetto]; *"Yiddish tange"* [Jewish tango] by Reuven Zarfat; and Yitzhak Katz's *"Ha-sikrik im ha-tlai ha-zahov"* [The Sikrik with the yellow star].

Diskant's songs expressed the feelings of those circles in the ghetto that chose the path of active resistance.[44] For example, the song "To the gate"[45] expresses both vision and rebuke. The poet imagines the day of liberation, when the end comes for the regime of the Lithuanian nationalist "partisans." The uncouth, cruel "partisan" has been banished from the ghetto gate, and the poet calls for the Jews to destroy the barbed wire fence and go out free, for "the air is replete with freedom." Lithuania "will be liberated," but will the ghetto prisoners remain to live there after liberation? Not a chance.

Lithuania,[46] foreign land,
We will leave quickly
And at the border
Everyone will shake out their shoes.
Not one grain of soil should stick to our shoes
From the land of impurity;
It wrapped the shame of its disgrace
In the warm coat of a cruel enemy.
Forgive me, Father, Mother

---

42. The original, *heyzelach*, means "short pants," but in Lithuania this was also the word for women's underwear. During their work outside the ghetto, women of the Kovno Ghetto often hid food in their underwear, then smuggled it in. Tan Pai translated this word into Hebrew as "in houses," but that translation takes the sting out of the verse.

43. Based on Tan Pai's translation into Hebrew, Garfunkel, *Kovno*, 276.

44. His son, Abba Diskant, was active in the rebel movement and one of the ghetto's best partisans. The father supported the movement with his stirring songs.

45. Garfunkel, *Kovno*, 312. Based on the Hebrew translation by Ephraim Talmi.

46. In the original, the name "Lithuania" is not specifically mentioned. The verse reads: *"Un das land groys vey a genetz…"* ["And this land the size of a hiccup"].

For I will leave your ashes here forever
In the land of *didwiru zhame*[47]
Cursed with robbery and blood.
With the devastated blood of Jews
Its despicable, ephemeral existence,
So thus –
May justice appear and destroy
May it descend to rot in hell.

Yitzhak Katz's song "The Sikrik with the yellow star," the only one among those that reached us that was written in the ghetto in Hebrew,[48] is also related to the concept of rebellion. It is a direct expression of the attitudes prevalent in ghetto underground circles after the Great *Aktion*: we will no longer be led like sheep to the slaughter; in case of another *Aktion*, we will rebel, set the ghetto on fire and flee in all directions, or die where we stand, fighting the enemy.[49] The author, one of the leaders of the Irgun Brit Zion (IBZ – Covenant of Zion Organization) in the ghetto,[50] begins his song with a description of the scene of the yearned-for rebellion:

Shadows glimpse from the caves in the hills
Darkness and gloom surrounds
Suddenly a shot slices the night
Breaks through darkness around.

The ghetto burns, oh, the ghetto burns
The Jews have set it afire
Beside the gate entrance the guard was killed
The bell of the shift has rung.

In the third stanza, he brings us to the valley of death, sketching in harsh lines the horrifying scene of slaughter:

---

47. "Land of the brave" – name used for Lithuania in its national anthem.
48. Recorded by Miriam Tur-Kasneskevitz, based on her memories from the Kovno Ghetto.
49. See chapter 3, "Stages and Factors," which describes the first use of the word "resistance."
50. Died in an escape attempt from the ghetto. See chapter 14, "Continued Departure of Groups from the Ghetto."

Shots, screams, and cries of woe
Join the thunder of guns
Jews stand at pit's edge in the valley
Enemy fire rushes above their heads.

Into the pit they fall with a shriek
Father and son embracing each other
Mother clutches infant to her chest
But a bullet has pierced his innards.

The moon rises and leaks cold light
Revealing the terrifying sight
The enemy revels, standing on the hill
Delighting in the bloody scene.

Then the song returns to the uprising – the last act of bravery:

Sparks of fire gallop, and pillars of smoke
Shroud the black carpet of night
Today this will be a terrible field of slaughter
We will sanctify the night with heroism.

In the two last stanzas, the poet reflects on the historical significance of the uprising. It is nurtured by the tradition of Jewish resistance in ancient history, and redeems a debt for the coming generations – the debt of vengeance for the massacre of tens of thousands of innocent Jews.

If our lives were the basest slavery
We deliver them to die a lion cub's death
Ben-Yair[51] has taught us how to die
When the enemy conquers the city.

You coming generations, you too carry the debt
And the enemy will know vengeance

---

51. Editor's note: Reference to Eliezer Ben-Yair, leader of the rebellion against the Romans at Masada.

Then the Sikrik with the yellow star[52] will arise
And climb the high rock of Masada.

SAVING LIVES

The ghetto residents who were not members of organizations practiced two methods for saving their own lives: (1) fleeing the ghetto and hiding in a city or village, and (2) digging underground inside the ghetto. Each of these two methods involved its own particular dangers and obstacles, and those who attempted them faced a harsh struggle and indescribable suffering. Many died in the attempt, while only a few reached the day of liberation. Below are several testimonies of escape attempts from the ghetto. The first describes an unsuccessful attempt of Hasia Nadel,[53] whose husband Haim joined the partisan movement in the ghetto and fled to the forest. He planned to take his wife with him, but was unable to do so, and she tried to leave the ghetto on her own.

> A *goy* [non-Jew], an acquaintance of my husband Haim, arranged a place for me with a farmer near Tavrig. The farmer received a caracal fur coat, a leather coat, a sewing machine, bedding, undergarments, and dresses, plus sixty thousand marks in cash.... I had to graze the cows and milk them. This was in late December 1943. It was almost certain that Haim was about to go out to the forest, but at that time they said that women had no chance of doing this. We hoped that at this farmer's place, where there were no more Jews at all, I would not get caught, especially since the farmer received so many items and money....
>
> After staying with this farmer for about nine weeks, I caught a cold. I went to the doctor in the next town, disguised as a Ukrainian. At first, the doctor refused to examine me, because I had no papers, but finally he gave in and decided I had pneumonia. He gave me a note for the farmer that said I was sick. I gave him a false name for the farmer. He told me in an aside that in a certain village (the one I was staying in), at a certain farmer's (my farmer),

---

52. Editor's note: The Sikrik was another name for the Zealots, some of whom were at Masada. The poem is making a parallel between the Sikrik Ben Yair and the ghetto fighter with the yellow star.

53. For more details of this incident, see Gar, *Umkum*, 194–5; Garfunkel, *Kovno*, 166.

there was a nice Jewess, and people were saying that the farmer had informed on her to the Gestapo. The doctor even asked me to go warn her....

When I returned to the farmer's wagon, I told him that I knew he had informed on me.... The farmer was very angry at me, and threatened to throw me out of the wagon, even though I was very sick. In the evening, he ordered me to milk the cows – even though my temperature rose to 39°C [102°F]. In the meantime, I heard the chime of horse bells, and I realized it was the Gestapo.... Immediately I left the barn and ran straight into the adjacent forest.... I ran for several hours until I reached the home of the brother of the farmer who had informed on me.... From that place, there was only one way to reach Kovno – by steamship on the Nemunas [Nieman] River.... I boarded the boat. Near Kulautuva there was an inspection.... I seized the opportunity to disembark, and for 500 marks and an Omega watch I had, I asked two raft oarsmen to row me across to the other bank of the Nemunas. In the meantime, people began to shout from the boat: "Jewess!" They even shot at us, but we managed to cross the river safely.

I reached Aleksot [Aleksotas],[54] and asked for shelter from an acquaintance who was a *goy*.... But because she was also suspect already, she did not let me in. When I reached the bridge over the Vilya, I saw another inspection – and it was midnight. Suddenly, a labor brigade on its way to the ghetto appeared. At first the women shouted, "You'll bring disaster upon us!" But an elderly woman removed one of her badges and stuck it to my back. The brigadier warned me that if they counted his workers at the gate, I had to run away immediately. Luckily, the German ordered everyone to go in together.[55]

Here is the story of a family that succeeded in this manner:

In May [1943], I said, that's enough, I'm leaving the ghetto.... I spoke with my leader in the IBZ movement.[56] He was not encouraging, but he also didn't tell me not to go.... I began to put pressure on my parents to leave as well. I argued that one way or another, in the end they would kill us.... Father objected. Mother tried to sway my feelings, she said I didn't love her, that her

---

54. Suburb of Kovno.
55. Testimony of Hasia Nadel, YVSA, 4 ff.
56. See chapter 3.

life was nothing without me, that she would die without me. "Our fate will be like that of everyone else." ... The atmosphere at home was tense for several days.... Father gave me his word that we would not remain in the ghetto and that we would leave as soon as the right moment arrived; Mother would not withstand the difficulties of the journey, and he had to organize the flight so that Mother could go....

Life went back to normal, but we were living in tension, hoping that when the time came, we would go. In the meantime, in October 1943, the Germans cleared out the "Big Blocks."[57] We were left without a home.... We went to live with my uncle, my mother's brother. Nine people lived in one room, in the understanding that "today" we would leave the ghetto. Mother continued to delude herself that we would not leave. But Father ... took care of the departure, hiring a truck with a trustworthy "partisan" driver, and organizing the people – eleven of them.

We had nothing with which to fund our departure. Father brought to the group a woman who had a lot of money (and her son), and with this money they paid for the truck. Father organized the departure in the most comfortable way possible, so that we could take some belongings with us, mainly clothes, so that we could live and also give to the *goyim* [non-Jews] – only as gifts. Admittedly, the Lithuanians saved us not for any reward, but only out of human and religious feeling. The first woman we stayed with was an elderly Lithuanian woman, a cardiac patient, very religious, living with her eighteen-year-old grandson.

On December 20, we completed all the preparations. I emphasize the assistance of the police, who allowed us to leave. Yankele Verbovsky stood beside the gate, fully aware that he was placing himself in danger.[58]

They read our names one by one. The car stood alongside the

---

57. After each *Aktion*, the Germans would reduce the size of the ghetto. In October 1943, they sent 2,800 Jews from Kovno Ghetto to work in Estonia (the "Estonia Deportation"). Just after this, occupants of the Big Blocks, or large apartment buildings, were ordered to leave their homes. These residents were mostly Ältestenrat officials or individuals with other connections.

58. From the testimony of Yisrael Leibenson, YVSA, 10: "Then I organized it. There was a car with a Lithuanian driver. He was a Gestapo 'brigadier.' We paid seven thousand marks. Beside the gate – our policemen knew this – stood Yankele Verbovsky.... He took some [money], I think it was five hundred or one thousand marks."

ghetto...Verbovsky told the Germans we were going to work the night shift.... We got into the car – it was already dark.... We rode north. In the middle of the route, the car broke down.... The driver demonstrated supreme calm, fixed the breakdown, and we continued. We reached the place where the car could no longer continue – about half a kilometer from the forest near the town of Erzvilkas [Erzhvilik], 100 km north of Kovno. We paid the driver. We walked half a kilometer in the mud – it took an hour. Then we entered the forest.... Two of us approached the house to ask if we could enter. This was Shimkainiya's home. We knocked on the window, and she woke up and said to bring everyone immediately. It was Christmas. We stayed with her. The Jews that were with her welcomed us warmly, despite the extreme danger.... After some time, the group divided, because it was impossible for such a large group to remain in one place. From then on, we wandered from place to place.... We had no special hiding place – we were always in a side room....We had to be completely silent, restraining ourselves from talking, coughing, and sneezing. The barking of the dog served as a warning sign to stop all activity. If the dog failed, we were in trouble.

This happened to us once. We were eight people – two families and another woman – staying with the Shimkainiyas' sister (each did not know that the other was hiding Jews). I could no longer remain in the hiding room, and went out to the living room to take care of the baby of the youngest married son. The dog did not bark, and a neighbor walked straight into the house. At once I began to speak Russian, and pretended I was a Russian woman. I was wearing appropriate clothing in the proper style (I was wearing boots). I knew I had to remove any suspicion on his part that I was a Jew. I addressed him...I said I was waiting for the mother of the family. My face could pass, because at that time the Germans were bringing Russians to such places. The neighbor left, and I went into our room.... The youth entered and said my acting was perfect, and he hoped nothing would happen to us. Still, we decided we should look for a new hiding place. We changed places six times.

The situation was particularly critical during the period of confiscations: the Germans would search for food, and found Jews. Once, the Ukrainians were hunting for Jews. Quickly we built a double wall. The Ukrainians would enter our house, but still they did not find us. In the house was a woman who had recently given birth, but still they kept us.

Only in one place was I told to leave during danger. This is what happened: In Erzvilkas, there was a Lithuanian who was known as a Jew slayer; the locals also called him that. Earlier, he had carried out the butchery of the town Jews, and then he hunted down the survivors. He searched for them, and when he found them – he murdered them. Once he came to visit the very house where I was hiding. I was told to go out to the sparse forest near the house. I knew he would pass through the forest. I hid under a tree.... When he was directly opposite me, he shot at a bird on the tree, but he did not notice me.

We hid that way for ten months, until the Russians came.[59]

Here we should note the story of how children were rescued from the ghetto by giving them to non-Jewish families (for payment or goods). This was mainly done by the parents themselves, but was given moral and technical support by the underground organizations and leadership groups within the Jewish ghetto organizations – mainly the gate guard, as well as the management of the large workshops and the professional school, and the Jewish ghetto police, among others. These rescues were conducted throughout the existence of the Kovno Ghetto and reached their peak in late 1943 and early 1944. At that time, the Jews had heard of *Aktion*s against children in ghettos nearby, such as Shavli (Šiauliai).

Even if they found someone in the city or surrounding villages to take their children, smuggling the children out of the ghetto was fraught with complications and mortal danger. Parents who decided to follow this course tried a variety of ruses to deceive the ghetto guards. If the children were big enough, they dressed them in adult clothing, placed work permits in their hands, and put them in the rows of a labor brigade. If they were little, they gave them a shot to put them to sleep and wrapped them like packages, or other such tricks. Many of the children who were able to escape in this way to a hiding place outside the ghetto were caught when the Lithuanian neighbors informed on them, or else they were discovered during police searches. Often they were simply turned over to the Gestapo by their "benefactors," after these had squeezed the maximum possible from the parents. There were also cases in which the emotional trauma the child suffered in his hiding place forced the parents to bring him back to the ghetto.

---

59. Testimony of Sara Leibenson-Binyamini, 23 ff. Compare testimony of Yisrael Leibenson, YVSA, 10 ff.

Only a very small number of the hundreds of children who were smuggled out of the ghetto withstood the ordeals and reached liberation.[60]

Below is the story of Ella Griliks, who at age ten was smuggled from Kovno Ghetto to the city.

> One winter night, my father and mother took me to the [ghetto] gate. There was a car parked there. The Jewish policemen gave the order to push the car. At that point, I sneaked out of the ghetto with my mother. A Christian youth who was waiting for us took us to his home.... I stayed there for two days.... My mother came to me and took me to the Christian orphanage. I was there for two or three days, until they gave me to a farmer. They disguised me as a Russian girl, because I spoke Russian well. The farmer took me to the village of Taumasheve near Aukštadvaris and put me into a children's home. I worked there with the other children, peeling potatoes and in the field. The children did not know I was a Jew, but the adults did know. There were other Jewish girls at this home, younger than me. I realized this by their faces. They did not know that I was Jewish. We never talked about it.[61]

MALINAS

The testimonies we have recorded above are sufficient to prove the difficulty of escape through the ghetto gates; indeed this was not a possibility for the masses. A simpler way was to dig under the ground.[62]

The practice of building *malinas* (bunkers)[63] became popular in the Kovno

---

60. Gar's book has much material on this issue, especially 169–72, 194–95, 206–7, 341. See also Garfunkel, Kovno, 153–54. Several women underground activists invested great effort in fulfilling this mission. Their role was to search outside the ghetto for places to put the children, teach them Lithuanian and sometimes even the principles of Catholicism, and equip them with documents, appropriate clothing, and other items (see PKG, 110–12; Sefer ha-partizanim ha-yehudim 1:231–2). Regarding the assistance of the management of the large workshops and the professional school in hiding and rescuing children, see Moshe Segelson, FLC 8:56; Y. Aliesky, FLC 9:31 ff. According to PKG, over four hundred children were taken in by non-Jewish families and institutions. See also Sudarsky et al., Lita, 1703.

61. Ella Griliks, "Meine iberlebungen be'et der milhama" [What I underwent during the war], FLC 9:82–83.

62. See detail of this issue in Gar, *Umkum*, 197–200; Garfunkel, *Kovno*, 163–65.

63. *Malina* was the word that Lithuanian Jews used to describe these underground hiding places. Before the war, this word was used for hiding places built by criminals. Some suggest that the origin of this word is the Hebrew *meluna*, "lodge." Dr. Mark Meir Dvorzetsky also

Ghetto at a relatively late date, in late 1943 or early 1944. Until that point, only a small number attempted it. During the Great *Aktion*, no one had yet thought of the idea of hiding and saving themselves in this manner. Possibly, this was due to the text of the announcements published by the Ältestenrat and the reassuring rumors that were disseminated throughout the ghetto. We may assume that immediately after the *Aktion*, many reached the conclusion that it would not be so difficult to save themselves the nightmare of the selection in the square, if they had a proper hiding place. During the deportation to Riga,[64] ghetto residents had used this idea, and a large number of those whose names were on the deportation lists were not found in their homes, and thus were saved.[65] At that time, some of the residents began to prepare hideouts in the cellars, attics, or woodsheds.

Over time, the method was improved. Engineers and technicians in the ghetto added their own inventions, and underground organizations promoted this practice, until the size of the *malinas* "movement" far bypassed the size of the underground movement. By the time of the Estonia Deportation in October 1943, the ghetto already had a number of advanced *malinas*, well camouflaged, with light, water, and a sizeable stock of food. At the time of the *Aktion* against the children, elderly, and sick[66] in late March 1944, the number of such *malinas* had reached the dozens.

In the period between the Estonia Deportation and the *Aktion* against the children, elderly, and sick, a certain incident left its mark on the continuation of the *malina* project and their fate on the date of liquidation of the ghetto. In November 1943, residents became aware that one quarter of the ghetto, called "the Old City" (*Altstadt*), was to be evacuated, and Lithuanians were to be housed there. Some *malina* enthusiasts – mostly members of the underground – decided that this was the right moment to implement the concept in a manner that would ensure success. There was enough time left to construct the *malinas* before evacuation, and also, they had time to contact the Lithuanians who were to take the

---

notes: "The Polish also used this term, in conversation and proclamations." See Mark Meir Dvorzetsky, *Yerushalayim de-Lita ba-meri u-va-Shoah* [Jerusalem of Lithuania, in rebellion and Holocaust] (1951), 72. On the technique of building the *malinas*, see Dvorzetsky, 72, 76–77.

64. On 5–6 February, 1942, several hundred Jews were taken out of Kovno and sent to work in Riga. This *Aktion* was called the "First Riga *Aktion*" (Garfunkel, *Kovno*, 126–27).

65. See, for example, the testimony of Shmuel Ben Menahem (Dietz), YVSA, 4.

66. See chapter 1.

houses above the *malina*s and persuade them – with the promise of payment – to serve as contacts between the *malina* occupants and the outer world. The *malina*s also had the advantage that they would be located outside the ghetto when the time came for its liquidation. Thus several *malina*s were built in that quarter, and on evacuation day their occupants did not go into the ghetto, but rather went down into the *malina*s, with the intention of remaining there until liberation. But events did not follow the expected course.

Following is the story of one of the more advanced of these *malina*s:

> All the bunkers were in the First Quarter,[67] about fifteen all together – some belonged to the communists, some to the IBZ [Irgun Brit Zion], and some to wealthy Jews. They decided that after the area was cleared of Jews, each would ensure that the house above their *malina* would be occupied by a Lithuanian with whom they were in contact and whom they could trust. This Lithuanian would serve as a contact person, in exchange for payment. In order to construct a bunker at that location, three conditions were required: (1) money to purchase building materials and food (the calculation was that we would prepare food for six months); (2) labor to construct the bunker; (3) contact with a *goy* [non-Jew]. It was impossible for one person to have access to all three requirements, and so individuals joined into groups to build one bunker. I was part of the yeshiva group's bunker. Moshe Wolberstein also belonged to that bunker. We constructed it under an unfinished three-story house…. All of the builders were yeshiva students. There was also a place reserved for Rabbi Avraham Grodzensky.
>
> Moshe Wolberstein and I organized the labor – we recruited some thirty yeshiva students who were fit for physical labor. Our mission was not simple. We had to dig about ten meters deep, move about one hundred cubic meters of earth from one basement to another, and then up above the bunker. The main building material was planks that had to bear the weight of a layer of earth five meters thick. We cut these beams from the roof of the new cinema, which stood opposite the yeshiva…. At night we carried the beams to the unfinished house. The Jewish police was aware of this, but did nothing.

---

67. When the ghetto was established, it was divided into four administrative quarters, each with its own police station. The south quarter, which included the Jewish neighborhood of Slobodka, was called the "First Quarter."

The *malina* under the workshops – Krikszolaicoi 107

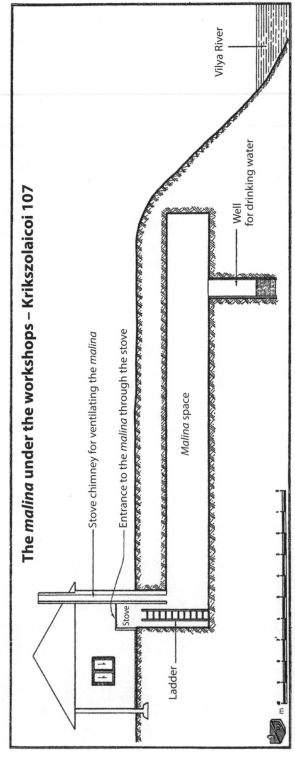

Stove chimney for ventilating the *malina*

Entrance to the *malina* through the stove

Stove

Ladder

Malina space

Well
for drinking water

Vilya River

m

This sketch was provided courtesy of engineer Zadok Eviatar (Bleiman) of Kovno, then Haifa, Yad Vashem

Sometimes they let us know that we were making too much noise. In order to solve the problem of finances, we contacted a wealthy Jew. This Jew also had contact with the Lithuanian who was supposed to go live there....

For the bunker's air supply, we chiseled through the cement of the chimney's foundation until we reached the chimney, then passed a pipe from one of the building's pillars to the chimney. We also installed electricity and connected it directly to the grid, passing through a house on the other side of the street for camouflage. The bunker had an electric stove, electric kettles, and a sufficient stock of kerosene for cooking. The problem of water supply was relatively easy to solve, because the entrance to the bunker was through a well. This was a deep well constructed of eleven cement rings. We dug a hole in the eighth ring from the top (the third ring above the waterline), and from it a short tunnel extended to the *malina's* hidden door. The *malina* itself was a room three meters wide, eight meters long, and two and a half meters high, and a bathroom. In it, we placed a Torah scroll, a library of about four hundred books, a three-month supply of biscuits, and a variety of dried legumes.

As soon as the First Quarter was evacuated, fifteen of us went down. I was commander of the *malina*, because Moshe did not come down with us at that time.... Moshe moved to the ghetto, and only after some time did he begin to act as a contact person between the ghetto and the *malina*. He would come to the First Quarter with the labor brigade doing the evacuation work, sneak away from the group, and come down to us. We had no weapons. We had no plan for resistance, because we did not think they would find us.... We had a daily schedule of reading and studying Talmud. Every day we held a *minyan* [prayer quorum]. For security reasons, we had a guard rotation twenty-four hours a day....

When we went down into the bunker, Moshe Levin gave us a radio. I managed to adjust it, and we heard the Kovno radio station. This was a holiday for us, as during the first weeks we had no connection with the outside.

One Friday night, after we had said Kiddush over the bread[68] and sat down to eat our "festive" dinner, we suddenly heard a rustling in the well. When we heard the password, we opened the door. In came a group of

---

68. Translator's note: On Friday night, observant Jews usually recite the Kiddush blessing over wine to sanctify the Sabbath. In the absence of wine, this blessing may be recited over bread.

about twelve comrades from IBZ, who we knew were hiding in a *malina* in the First Quarter. They told us of their failure: Lithuanians who worked in that area had discovered them, broke into the *malina*, and robbed them of all their valuables. They then feared that the robbers would return that night to complete the theft, and so they came to us for shelter. Of course we took them in, as a ship might take in the drowning passengers of another vessel. We sent ten of our group to help them transfer their remaining belongings from the robbed *malina*. That night, I snuck into the ghetto to hear the exact situation and decide how we should act in case of another such incident. In the ghetto, I heard there was a suspicion we had been betrayed, and that all the bunkers in the First Quarter had fallen into the trap. We decided to evacuate our bunker at once. [69]

We have reason to assume that following this failure in the evacuated quarter, news of the existence of the *malinas* in the ghetto reached the ears of the Gestapo, because during the *Aktion* against the children, elderly, and sick, the Gestapo had also begun an operation for discovering the *malinas* in the ghetto. This was an important issue in the investigation that the Gestapo officer Kittel conducted against the Jewish police when they were tortured and murdered at the Ninth Fort.[70] A few policemen broke, betrayed their comrades and the entire ghetto, and revealed to the Gestapo the location of several *malinas*.

The Germans thus knew a few months before the liquidation of the ghetto that the Jews were preparing *malinas*, and they also had enough time to learn the methods of construction, camouflage, and so forth. Naturally, this took away from the value of the *malinas* as a method of survival. Still, it was not enough to completely dissuade the builders. On the contrary, in spring 1944, the *malina* concept appealed to thousands, particularly with the beginning of the major Russian attack on the Byelorussian front and the approach of the liberation armies. In the end, however, only a small number were saved in this manner.[71]

---

69. Testimony of Shmuel Ben Menahem (Dietz), YVSA. On the discovery of the *malinas* in the First Quarter, see chapters 7 and 8.
70. See chapter 14.
71. See chapters 1 and 14.

CHAPTER 3

Birth of the Underground

Initial Stages

The period of existence and activity of the Kovno Jewish underground almost completely overlaps the period of Nazi rule in the city. The first signs of Jewish underground activity were apparent in the early days – at the latest, following the first weeks of occupation of the city by Hitler's troops. This activity did not stop for a minute throughout the existence of the ghetto, even after its liquidation and deportation of its survivors to Germany – until the liberation of these survivors by Allied armies from the East and West. According to a conservative estimation, at its peak the underground counted some eight hundred members. Over half of these were involved in preparations for active resistance, and about one third left the ghetto armed, in order to fight the Nazis face to face.

But this underground did not reach its full strength all at once; it underwent different stages of development. It was bound up in the terrible events of those days, and its birth pangs were extremely painful.

The occupation of Kovno by Nazi troops found the Jewish public in the city fragmented and bewildered. They had just gone through the tumultuous year of the Soviet regime.[1] That year, the Jewish organizations were disbanded (except, of course, for those connected to the Communist Party), Zionist newspapers were closed, and leaders of the Zionist parties were thrown in jail. Several days before the outbreak of the war, a mass "purification" was held throughout Lithuania of elements considered disloyal to the Soviet regime, and hundreds of Jewish activists were deported to Siberia. But the administrative prohibitions

---

1. Gar, *Umkum*, 26–29; Garfunkel, *Kovno*, 25–27.

and the police persecutions did not completely silence the Jewish organizations' operations. The activists who were not caught went underground and attempted to organize Zionist activity. They adapted the organizational structure of parties and youth groups to underground conditions, developed methods of disseminating news about events in the Zionist camp throughout the world, worked to prevent additional arrests, and organized assistance for prisoners and their families.

At first, the end of the Soviet regime and the sudden flight of the Red Army aroused a feeling of some relief among many activists of the Zionist underground, who did not comprehend that they had been thrown from "the frying pan into the fire." "Now we can speak Hebrew out in the open again" – these were the kind of statements Jews made at the time. But the rioting of the Lithuanian "partisans" in the streets of Kovno and their acts of abuse, robbery, and murder during the early days forced the Jewish public to open their eyes and relief was transformed into grief.

The imprisoned Jewish activists, who were then released together with the other political prisoners, were not joyful for long. The attorney Ya'akov Goldberg, for example, who later became vice chairman of the Kovno Ghetto Ältestenrat, was held in a Soviet prison and released when the Germans entered the city. The next day, he was again taken to that very same prison, this time along with his entire family.[2]

We have no evidence of attempts to organize resistance during the first days of the Germans' entry into the city, when the initiative of pogroms against the Jews was still in the hands of the Lithuanians. But we do know of acts of spontaneous defense performed by individuals at that time.[3]

During that period, there were two centers of pogroms in Kovno: the Seventh Fort and the Jewish quarter of Slobodka, and individuals performed acts of heroism in both these locations. The laborer Benzion Fein, a resident of Slobodka, used an axe to split open the head of the first rioter who broke through his door. The youth Strazh, bookkeeper for a Kovno bank, attacked one of the murderers and put out his eyes. Blacksmith Shlomo Katz and metalworker Yitzhak Friedman used their tools to fight the rioters, who were armed with rifles and

2. Ya'akov Goldberg, FLC 7:30.
3. Eglinis, 17; PKG, 12–13; Meir Leib Goldschmidt, YVSA, letter 4, 4. See also L. Kunyokhovsky, "Gut geshassen," Das Vart, 44, September 5, 1947.

submachine guns. In many apartments in which entire families were slaughtered, signs of desperate struggle by the victims were discovered afterwards. Crushed corpses of men and women were found on the apartment thresholds, courtyard gates, and basement entrances where they defended their families' hiding places with axes and iron rods. In one of these apartments, Akiva Puchert, before he died, used his finger to write the word "revenge" in blood on the wall. The Germans closed off and forbade access to some apartments that showed clear signs of struggle. Avraham Golob recounts that he and artist (Esther) Luria sneaked into the apartment of well-known Kovno Zionist activist Yatkunsky to document the state of the apartment after the pogrom.[4] Large blood stains were visible on the walls, various hard objects were scattered across the beds, furniture was overturned: "Everything bore witness that a bitter and desperate struggle was waged here."

By contrast, we do have evidence of preliminary steps to organize armed resistance during the period of the *Aktion*s. Two versions of evidence document this.

One eyewitness relates[5] that around the time of the *Aktion* in the Small Ghetto, either before or after (in late September 1941 or early October), an informal meeting was held in the ghetto of representatives of the Zionist public, in the apartment of former teacher M. Bramson, who was then serving in the ghetto as a senior police officer. Aside from the teacher, the participants included Hechalutz activist Shlomo Goldstein, Irgun Brit Zion (IBZ) member and ghetto police officer Ika Greenberg, Hashomer Hatzair member Yerachmiel Voskoboynik, Berel Cohen of the Zionist Socialist Party, ghetto police officer (and later police commander) Moshe Levin of the Revisionists, Avraham Melamed of IBZ, ghetto police officer Peretz Padison, and Dr. Haim Nachman Shapira, the well-known historian of modern Hebrew literature.

The participants all agreed that the formal explanation given for the *Aktion*s was a base deception and had no doubt that the Jews who had been sent out of the ghetto were no longer alive. They also had no illusions regarding the future of the rest of the ghetto. The *Aktion*s that had been carried out were preliminary links in the chain of destruction. The participants stood before the fateful

---

4. Testimony of Avraham Tory (Golob), YVSA, 21–22.
5. Testimony of Avraham Melamed, Proceedings of the Partisan Conference at Givat Aliya, 5.

question: How should the ghetto public react to the Nazis' deeds and plans? They considered flight from the ghetto to be pointless. The front was already too far from Kovno, the Lithuanian population was openly hostile toward the ghetto population, and most cooperated with the occupation authorities in everything related to destruction of the Jews. This was when the word "resistance" was first suggested. Ika Greenberg and Peretz Padison presented a plan for rebellion in case of a new liquidation operation. They proposed to start immediately with establishing cells to train the youth for an uprising. The command, to be composed of public leaders, would work to purchase weapons and explosives and train the cell members in their use. When the Germans arrived to implement their scheme, the ghetto would be set on fire and the armed fighters would attack the murderers. If they succeeded in overpowering them, they would break through the barbed wire fenced, and the remaining ghetto residents would flee. If the rebels did not succeed in overpowering the guards, at least they would die honorably, in a Masada-style battle.

A second witness, Avraham Golob, offers us another version of the events.[6] During the *Aktions* (Golob does not remember the exact date), his friend Dr. Eliyahu Segal and a Jew from northern Lithuania (a Yiddishist) named Zack approached him and told him that a "Committee for Self-Defense" (*Zelbastshutz-kamitent*) was organizing in the ghetto. The committee planned to purchase weapons and resist the Germans in case of a new *Aktion*. Golob agreed to join the committee. Eventually he learned that Bramson and Ika Greenberg were also committee members, and even Haim Yellin of the "leftists" was connected to it. Zack said he found a way to purchase a pistol, but he had no money. They decided to contact the head of the Ältestenrat, Dr. Elkes. Golob told Elkes that "this is important to us because we need to start defense actions." "You don't have to convince me" was Dr. Elkes's reply. Zack received the money, purchased the pistol, and brought it to the ghetto. The pistol was given to Ika Greenberg. There was also talk of organizing cells for weapons training, and it is possible that Ika Greenberg established training cells that existed for some time – apparently until early 1942.

The two versions of events are very similar. The difference between them mainly concerns the connection between this group and the Ältestenrat. The

---

6. Testimony of Avraham Tory (Golob), YVSA, 9.

issue is highly significant, but we cannot determine which version is the correct one.[7] At any rate, the plan was not implemented, and we do not know of any resistance acts from the *Aktions* period. We cannot speak of a true underground in Jewish Kovno at the time of the mass murders, which continued until late October. The entire Jewish public was mired in gloom. Those underground groups that managed to become firmly established had yet to find their way and had not yet formulated stable, clear patterns of action. Their first attempts at organization were disturbed time after time by the murders, which thinned their ranks, annihilated their best organizers, and cut off communication among the members. Only after a month or two had passed and ghetto life had returned to normal did these groups – from which the Jewish underground would rise – begin to recover from the brutal nightmare and despair, and accelerate the process of organization.

The Kovno Jewish underground had its ups and downs. We may divide the period of its existence into four parts: (1) From its inception until spring 1943: this period was characterized by organizational rift and the search for methods of realistic and efficient action. (2) Summer and fall 1943: this was a period of unity of the underground, based on a plan to establish a fighting force in the ghetto, arm it with weapons, and send it outside the walls of the ghetto to locations from which it could direct a war of vengeance against the Germans. The event that divided between this period and its predecessor was the defeat of the Germans outside Stalingrad. The turn that began then in the course of the war also offered new possibilities to the Kovno underground. (3) Winter 1943–1944, from November 1943 to March–April 1944: this was the height of the Kovno underground, in which the combat action plan was implemented. Some three hundred well-armed fighters were sent from the ghetto into the forest. (4) The last months of the ghetto and deportation to Germany, and the period of relatively weak underground activity in concentration camps in Germany.

A variety of factors, external and internal, determined the image of the underground in each period. External factors included the policy of the German

---

7. The weak point in the second version is that the witness, aside from belonging to the underground, was also involved in the Ältestenrat. It would therefore be wise to obtain authorization for the details of this version from another source, especially for the statement that the Ältestenrat gave money for purchasing the first pistol in the ghetto. We were not able to obtain such authorization from any source (compare testimony of Segal, YVSA, 1).

authorities toward Kovno Jewry, which was mainly decided by the extermination policy and also by subordinate factors, which we have noted in chapter 1. Another external factor was the level of obstinacy or flexibility of local government representatives – from Gestapo commanders and *Stadtkommissar* officials, to the German and Lithuanian police who guarded the ghetto – in fulfilling their superiors' orders. Also included in this category was the relationship of the Lithuanian population to the ghetto Jews in all its aspects, both positive and negative. These included initiation and participation in the destruction; willingness to trade in food and equipment, including weapons and ammunition; and readiness to hide Jews and assist underground members in many ways. A further external factor was the international political situation, particularly the situation on the battlefronts, which had a significant influence on the atmosphere outside the ghetto as well as on the mood inside. The status of the Lithuanian underground in Kovno and throughout Lithuania was also influential, as was the distance of Kovno from large concentrations of partisans, which were in southeast Lithuania and western Byelorussia.

Internal factors that should be noted include the status of the organized Jewish population in Kovno throughout the year of Soviet rule, particularly the underground activity of outlawed Jewish organizations. Another internal factor was the ability of Jewish organizations to adapt to new, ever-changing underground conditions. In addition, we note the economic status of the ghetto population, and the physical and emotional state of the older ghetto youth, who shouldered most of the burden of underground activity. Lastly, an internal factor was the composition of the Ältestenrat, its policy, its sense of national responsibility, and especially its relationship to the underground and its projects, which needed the assistance of ghetto institutions.

From the inception of the underground in the Kovno Ghetto, the Ältestenrat faced a number of underground camps. It was aware that they were organizing, and we are almost certain that it did nothing to prevent this. The Ältestenrat accepted the underground as an established fact. The problem the Ältestenrat apparently faced was how to support the underground in such a way that it could influence underground activity, in order that the underground not hurt the interests of the ghetto as the Ältestenrat saw these. At any rate, from the underground's point of view, the Ältestenrat did not intentionally cause any difficulties for it, and this is the case for all the underground camps.[8] But this does not mean that the relations between the Ältestenrat and the various camps were identical in all senses. Below we will outline the differences between these relationships.

A number of organizations participated in the underground, organizations of adults and of youth. Some were veteran, such as the political party organizations, while others were new, established during the ghetto period or just before, during the Soviet regime in Lithuania. The organizations can be classified into three groups: the Zionist camp, the Communists, and underground groups with no political character or direction. The Zionist camp included the following political parties: Zionist Socialists (zs); General Zionists A; General Zionists B; Mizrahi, Hapoel Hamizrahi, and the Revisionists. The following youth groups were also part of the Zionist camp: Hashomer Hatzair, Hechalutz Hatzair-Dror, Gordonia, Irgun Brit Zion (ibz – established during Soviet rule by high school students and Jewish college students in Kovno), Beitar, Tiferet Bahurim, and Tiferet Bahurim Tze'irim.

At first, the Communists were divided into several small groups, but they quickly united and established the Anti-Fascist Fighting Organization. This organization included the Komyug youth group and the children's group Pioneer. We know of four non-political groups: Zareg (*Zelbestshutz Argenizatzia* – Self-Defense Organization); *Zelbestshutz Kamitet* (Self-Defense Committee) – these two did not maintain their independence for long, the former joining the Communists and the latter joining the Zionists; Kvutzat Keidan – a small partisan group, which operated in the labor camp near Keidan, a branch of the Kovno Ghetto; and a partisan group in the labor camp in Koshedar – also a branch of the Kovno Ghetto.

The Zionist Organizations

We have noted that a Zionist underground existed in Kovno even before the Germans' arrival. We have evidence of continuous activity of the Zionist Socialist (zs) Party. The inspirational spirit behind the activists of this party, which went underground during the Soviet period, was Pesach Mashkutz. Before the war, he

---

8. Even the *pkg* Communist organization offers no clue of such difficulties, although it felt free to criticize the general policy of the Ältestenrat, in the spirit of fellow Communists.

had served as director of the party publication *Das Vart*. He maintained contact with members, organized assistance for Zionists who were persecuted by the regime, and unified the underground ranks.[9] Two activists assisted him: Isaac Serebnitzky and engineer Mendel (Menachem) Sadovsky, former secretary of the Kovno branch. These individuals also stood behind the renewal of activity during the first period of the Nazi occupation.

Preliminary efforts at organization were modest. The group of active colleagues met for discussions over tea in the home of Berel Cohen, formerly an editor of *Das Vart*. Party activists who participated in these meetings included Pesach Mashkutz, Leib Garfunkel, Isaac Serebnitzky, Herschel (Hirsch) Brick, Aharon Cohen, Dr. Kissin, Yisrael Leibenson, Meir Guttman, David Treger, and Ya'akov Rabinowitz. At first, these discussions were intended only to outline the situation. What were the Germans' true intentions regarding the ghetto? This was the question that occupied them all. The participants were thirsty for news of events outside the ghetto, in the city, on the battlefronts, and throughout the world. Attorney Garfunkel, who was an Ältestenrat member from its establishment and had news from a number of sources, and Isaac Serebnitzky, who left the ghetto regularly in his position as manager of the ghetto pharmacy, gave political analyses.

There was also a practical issue that united the group of activists and even broadened it over time: several members were appointed to positions of responsibility in ghetto institutions. We will clarify the extent to which this was a result of a deliberate "policy of appointments" by the Ältestenrat, and its significance for the relationship between it and the underground. At any rate, the holders of positions had the ability to offer their comrades real assistance in housing, workplaces, and – most importantly – a certain protection during the murders, such as by distributing labor certificates, which could sometimes save their possessors.[10]

Other Zionist parties also reorganized in a manner similar to that of zs, but in the renewal of the traditional organization frameworks, the practical issue was of greater importance than the ideological connection. On one hand, regular party members desired to preserve their personal connection with those activists

9. Menachem Ganuni (Sadovsky), "Bi-ntivei mahteret" [The paths of the underground], YLHG, 20:89.
10. Garfunkel, *Kovno*, 65–66.

who occupied important positions in the ghetto, and on the other, the activists aspired to surround themselves with members of their own parties who shared their political views, in order to bolster their position within the Ältestenrat or in the other ghetto institutions. These justifications were a significant factor in the development of the coordinating body of the Zionist underground, later known as *Merkaz Zionei Villiampole, Kovno,* or MZVK, which was a federation of the four strongest Zionist parties in the ghetto: General Zionists A and B, ZS, and the Revisionists.[11]

MATZOK

Data on the first period of activity of this alliance is not completely clear or confirmed. According to one version, it was established in April 1942; another version maintains that it was established before that date, and in April it was broadened to include the majority of the Zionist camp.[12] Still, we may assume that in spring 1942 the Zionist federation was already founded and known as MZVK or Matzok.[13] Leaders included Dr. H.N. Shapira of General Zionists A, Avraham Golob of General Zionists B, Zvi Levin of the Revisionists, and Isaac Serebnitzky of ZS. Also participating in Matzok meetings on occasion were Dr. Elkes and Attorney Garfunkel of the Ältestenrat. According to the evidence, we cannot consider them as members of the Matzok directorate, but the fact of participation of the Ältestenrat leaders in Matzok meetings is evidence of the strong connection between these two bodies.

We also know that Matzok tried to influence Ältestenrat activities and institutions and struggled for some time for the status of a "public forum" superior to these institutions.[14] The Ältestenrat was even asked to inform Matzok about every important issue and to refrain from making any important decision before discussing it with Matzok. But this was not put into practice because, first, the Ältestenrat acted under constant pressure of orders, and in many cases it had to

---

11. Testimony of S. Shapir (Frenkel), YVSA, 4.

12. Gar, *Umkum,* 397.

13. According to the testimony of Dr. Eliyahu Segal, he was the proposer of this name, and it stood for *Merkaz Zionim Vatikim be-Kovno* (Kovno Center for Veteran Zionists). According to him, the name MZVK (or *Matzok,* according to the Hebrew pronunciation) was a convenient camouflage, because it sounded like the Lithuanian last name Matzokas. Invitations to secret meetings read: "You are hereby invited to a meeting with Mr. Matzokas."

14. Testimony of Leib Garfunkel, YVSA, 19.

decide urgently and had no possibility of consulting with any public body; and second, not all Ältestenrat members were Zionists. The non-Zionists, particularly attorney Goldberg, objected to the idea of the Ältestenrat being subordinate to Matzok.[15] Still, there was coordination between the two bodies: Matzok did not make any important decisions without first consulting with the Ältestenrat leaders, and vice versa – the Ältestenrat directors tried, whenever possible, to hear the advice of the Matzok members whenever they faced important decisions.

Avraham Golob, who was first a deputy secretary of the Ältestenrat, then appointed as secretary, while at the same time serving as Matzok representative to General Zionists B, describes the birth of Matzok:

> On August 4, 1941, a meeting of activists was held at the Jewish community school on 24 Daukšos Street. It later became known as "the last meeting of the activists of Jewish Kovno." Twenty-eight activists participated in the meeting. One item was on the agenda: electing the head of the Ältestenrat, or as the Germans preferred to call it, *Oberjude*. The discussion was highly dramatic, and at its conclusion, Dr. Elkes was chosen for the fateful position. That day, three people met in another room at the school: Shlomo Goldstein, Berel Cohen, and myself. We suggested that with the establishment of the Ältestenrat, the time had come to found an alliance of the Zionists in the underground. In light of the emergency situation, we all agreed that the divisions between parties no longer had significance as they had in the past, and that now we had one mission: to preserve the pioneer-Zionist core, to maintain Zionist activism.
>
> Each of us represented a different party: Shlomo Goldstein represented Hechalutz, Berel Cohen – zs, and myself – the General Zionists. (Before the war, I had been a member of the steering committee of the General Zionists, and deputy national leader of the Lithuania Zionist youth.) We decided that the founding of the alliance would be kept secret and should not be revealed even to the activists. Each of us had the responsibility to gather his colleagues, and if we decided among us to carry out a joint operation, we would inform the colleagues through the various cells and party circles. In order to

---

15. Ibid.

encompass the entire Zionist camp, we decided to invite a representative of the Revisionists to join us. We mentioned the name of Zvi Levin, whom we knew as one of the leaders of the Revisionists in Lithuania and who had just been released from Soviet prison. We contacted him, and he immediately joined the group. The first action we carried out was to collect information about the situation. Each one of us made a commitment to make every effort to obtain information from any source, to enable us to decipher the intentions of the Germans toward us.

After we entered the ghetto, new tasks arose. First, we made lists of all our fellow Zionists in the ghetto, so that we could quickly inform them of any imminent danger. Second, we decided to warn our members against any undesirable individuals who aroused suspicion with their behavior in the ghetto or at the workplace. Third, we tried to offer moral and material support to the widows, parents, and children of our colleagues who died or went missing. And fourth, we made efforts that our colleagues, or individuals whom we trusted, worked in ghetto institutions, such as the departments of housing, welfare, and labor; police; workshops; and every other possible place. The intention of this activity was to deflect anti-social and untrustworthy elements from key positions in the ghetto, in order to uphold the spirit of public responsibility and ensure fair division of all that was and all that was not....

Mashkutz was intentionally appointed as director of the housing department; Dr. Segal of the Revisionists was appointed director of the social welfare office; Hirsch Berrick became one of the workshop directors, and Dr. Yitzhak Rabinowitz (who was unaffiliated, but we had full trust in him) – contact person in the German labor office. At first, an assimilated Jew, completely unknown to the Jewish public in Kovno, was appointed director of the police. But he also recognized Matzok and took into account its recommendations. He appointed – according to Matzok advice – several members of the Zionist parties to be senior police officers. In essence, only a few individuals in positions of importance in the ghetto had not been appointed at Matzok recommendation. This situation had significant import, not only in the various administrative departments, but also in the Ältestenrat itself. Dr. Elkes, its director, also considered himself a Matzok member, and gave his full assistance and moral support to every plan of action Matzok presented to him – both for appointments to positions in the ghetto institutions and for the pioneer underground organization.[16]

While the statement of Avraham Golob – that "in essence, only a few individuals in positions of importance in the ghetto had not been appointed at Matzok recommendation" – may be somewhat of an exaggeration, the rest of the details in his testimony seem to be very plausible, in light of the information we have from other sources regarding the activity and status of Matzok in the ghetto at later stages of development of the underground.[17]

Matzok focused their activities in two ways: (1) initiation and supervision of activities of benefit to the entire underground, and (2) aid to Zionist organizations in their independent activities. Because the underground's activities encompassed all areas of life of its members, Matzok's efforts were extremely varied – ranging from issues of housing, work, food supplements, and cultural-educational programs, to rescue and defense methods. Due to the broad influence of Matzok on ghetto institutions, it was able to give highly efficient assistance to the underground. In particular, with the help of Matzok, the Zionist underground organizations derived great benefit from the ghetto workshops. Most of their leaders were listed as workshop workers. This exempted them from forced labor outside the ghetto, and also often enabled them – with the agreement of the management – to absent themselves from their workplace and dedicate their time to underground activities. The workshops were also ideal places for clandestine meetings, especially during night shifts. Meetings held in private homes could have attracted attention.

During this period, Matzok repeatedly attempted to break the ring of isolation that the Germans imposed on the ghetto and to create ties – officially "illegal" – with the outside world, In particular, they tried to make contact with other ghettos in Shavli and Vilna. The first contact with the Shavli Ghetto was made through a man in the Kovno Ghetto who had previously worked as manager of a leather factory in Shavli. At Matzok initiative, the Ältestenrat obtained a license from the authorities to send him to Shavli to bring leather for the ghetto

---

16. Testimony of Avraham Tory (Golob), YVSA, 1–5.

17. On this issue, compare the testimony of Leib Garfunkel, YVSA, 18 ff. According to the testimonies of Y. Melamed, recording 1, and Y. Tarshish, 2, a large number of police officers in the ghetto and holders of key positions were Beitar members.

workshops. In this way, they obtained a detailed report of the fate of the Shavli community and life in that ghetto.[18]

Matzok also succeeded in making contacts with the Vilna Ghetto. A few Matzok members exchanged letters with members of their movements who were in Vilna (in 1940–1941, many Jewish leaders went from Kovno to Vilna, and when the war broke out, they were stuck there). This was extremely dangerous. At one point the Gestapo found out about the correspondence, and only with great effort was the Ältestenrat able to avoid disaster.[19]

In this manner, Avraham Golob contacted Nissan Resnick, former member of the Zionist youth leadership in Lithuania, and received the first news of the organization of the Vilna Ghetto underground and the founding of the FPO (United Partisans' Movement).[20] But the FPO exercised extreme caution in its contacts with other ghettos. Apparently, in spring 1942, Yosef Glazman, FPO leader in Vilna and former Beitar head in Lithuania, sent a young woman to Kovno to find out what was happening there.[21] This representative contacted one of the Revisionists in the Kovno Ghetto named Levin (possibly Zvi Levin). After she returned, the FPO members understood from her report that some of the leaders of the Kovno Ghetto were simultaneously working for the Gestapo, and they feared that through Kovno the Gestapo would discover the FPO. For this reason, the FPO avoided contacting the Kovno Ghetto, and Matzok did not receive any news from the FPO for several months.

At the end of summer 1942, the situation began to change. The FPO leadership found a way to send to the Kovno Ghetto the loyal and experienced envoy of the Jewish underground in Poland, Irena Adamovitz,[22] a Christian. The visit

---

18. See A. Yerushalmi, *Pinkas Shavli* (Jerusalem: Mossad Bialik and Yad Vashem, 5718), 221, 231.

19. On this topic, see A. Zilberman, FLC 10:42–47.

20. *Fareynegte Partizaner Organizatye* (FPO – United Partisans Movement) of the Vilna Ghetto, founded on January 21, 1942 (see *Sefer ha-partizanim ha-yehudim* 1:16 ff.). On the exchange of letters with the Vilna underground activists, see testimonies (YVSA) of Masha Gail-Yaron (recording 5), Nissan Reznik (1), and A. Tory (Golob) (13 ff.).

21. See testimony of Abba Kovner, YVSA, recording 1. According to testimony of Haim Lazer, the young woman's name was Krapyovnik.

22. Prior to the Second World War, Irena Adamovitz served as a senior leader in the Polish Scouts movement. She became acquainted with Hashomer Hatzair and studied the movement's educational method and ideology. Irena was so impressed by this movement's achievements and aspirations that she became one of its most enthusiastic and faithful friends. Her service

of Irena – as the movement members called her – to the ghetto marked a turning point in the Zionist underground. This is her statement about the mission:

> My mission began in June 1942, but it was decided on and preparations were
> made for it far in advance, a few weeks after the outbreak of war between
> Russia and Germany. I met often with the group from the leadership[23] and
> from Hechalutz. We received news of the sudden occupation of Lithuania
> and eastern Poland by the Germans, and of pogroms against the Jews in
> those territories, and we decided we should make contact with organization
> members there. I was given this mission and began to consult as to how to
> go about it.
>
> Quickly we thought of an idea. At that time, I was a social worker in War-
> saw. In summer 1939, before the war began between Germany and Poland,
> we performed a partially secret evacuation mission for the Polish orphans
> under our supervision who were living in various institutions in Warsaw. I
> was one of those who carried out the operation, and I then went out to the
> Vilna outlying towns (I knew them because this was my native area). I found
> appropriate places and placed the orphans there. We thought the places
> near the eastern border were safer than the center of the country, but this
> assumption was proven false. Within a few days, the Germans occupied most
> of Polish territory, while the Russians crossed the eastern border, and the
> Vilna region was entirely in their hands. Our orphans were then in a region
> that was outside the Generalgouvernement, and until summer 1941 it was
> impossible to take them back to Warsaw. At that time, when these territories
> were occupied by the Germans, the opportunity arose to carry it out, and the
> director began to take care of it right away.
>
> I welcomed this opportunity. I said to myself…I'll volunteer to travel
> to Vilna to look for our orphans, and because this mission was formal and I
> would have formal papers from the Germans, I could take care of movement
> matters relatively securely.…. For months I badgered my superiors, until the
> mission was carried out in June 1942, exactly one year after the war had be-
> gun. Movement members gave me a sum of money and a packet of letters,

---

to Hashomer Hatzair in particular, and to the Jewish underground in the ghettos in general,
places her among the most respected of the "Righteous among the Nations."
23. Meaning the national leadership of Hashomer Hatzair in Warsaw.

apparently written in Hebrew and in code – I'll never know exactly, because I did not open them. I sewed them into my clothing and went on my way.

I most feared meeting up with the Lithuanians. The local government in Vilna zone was in Lithuanian hands; I knew that they hated the Polish virulently, and I feared that if I fell into their hands, they would search my belongings and find the letters, and that would be awful. I was not so concerned for my personal safety and my life. But I was on a formal mission of the Warsaw municipality, and my papers were signed by my director. Should the Germans discover that I was assisting the Jews, and further, that I was involved with them on issues of politics, movements, and resistance, they would take vengeance on him and all connected to him. The formal mission eased my way both technically and for security, but it weighed on my conscience.... Luckily, all went well.

Once in Vilna, I began to take care of matters related to the movement mission. I entered the ghetto eight times. There I met with movement members and FPO leaders, and I confirmed the situation. A few days later, I went on my way to Kovno.... The only sign I was given in the Vilna Ghetto before my departure was that in the Jewish Banhof labor brigade (the term "labor brigade" was known to me from other ghettos), I would find a Jew named Yeshurun,[24] to whom I should give greetings from his niece in the Vilna Ghetto. I found this Jew there, after infiltrating that workplace.... I gave him the greetings, and asked him to tell the leadership in the ghetto that a Christian envoy from Vilna wanted to meet with one of them and asked for assistance in entering the ghetto. At first Yeshurun said that it was impossible to get me into the ghetto, and that if I wanted to say something to the top echelon of the ghetto, I had to tell him and he would pass it on to them.... Having no other choice, I began to tell him about the situation in the ghettos of Poland. I spoke for three hours, purposely making things complicated. I hoped he would suspect he would never be able to remember what I had said, and perhaps this would convince him to get me into the ghetto.

Indeed, this is what happened: he sent me to Kolonnenführer Roth.

---

24. Other sources indicate that Yeshurun was the leader of this labor brigade (Kolonnenführer). Roth, mentioned below, was leader of the labor brigade that was employed nearby in the soldiers' bathhouse and disinfection station.

Roth told me to put the yellow patch on my chest and back, and he put me in among his workers. We walked toward the ghetto. Next to the gate, Roth handed me over to one of the policemen, who took me to the police station (or jail),[25] which was on the ground floor of a large house.... I asked them to present me to someone from the leadership. By the time they managed to do this, darkness had fallen, and suddenly we heard a siren. Apparently the Russians were attacking Kovno from the air. A strict curfew was placed on the ghetto, and it was impossible to conceive of a meeting with someone from the underground. I sat all night in the station waiting room, frightened and hungry....

The next day, I was taken to representatives of Matzok – the coordinating committee of the Zionist parties – Hirshke [Zvi] Levin, Isaac Serebnitzky, Shlomo Goldstein, and others. We met three times, six straight hours each time. First I gave my story, then they gave me theirs. Two days later, I left the ghetto and Kovno.[26]

The meetings with Irena included all members of Matzok, as well as Ältestenrat members Garfunkel and Elkes. From her they learned about the internal life of the ghettos, and the various forms of oppression, humiliation, and internecine division that the Germans carried out in different locations. Irena spoke at length about the pioneer organizations and their important role in underground operations in many ghettos. Her story left an indelible impression on them.[27] This was the first time they had heard of the existence of a widespread underground in Polish ghettos and of indirect contact with the Land of Israel and Jewish institutions throughout the world. As one of the participants said, "She liberated us from our isolation. Until then, we had been closed up in a sack. After that, we saw ourselves as part of a large body that one day would awaken to rescue."[28]

Irena met with the Hechalutz representative, Shlomo Goldstein, and with Gita Vishkin, a veteran member of Hashomer Hatzair in the ghetto. At these meetings, Irena told the members about the pioneer movements in Poland and

---

25. In the jail next to the ghetto gate, there was a small police station for the guard police.
26. Testimony of Irena Adamovitz, YVSA, 2–10.
27. Testimony of Leib Garfunkel, YVSA, 21–22.
28. Testimony of A. Tory (Golob), YVSA, 16; compare also testimony of Eliyahu Segal.

in Vilna, and emphasized that in Kovno as well, these movements should lead the attempt at an active rebellion against the Nazis.

Her visit had a huge impact on the Zionist underground.[29] Matzok and the Zionist movements formed the opinion that they should transfer the focus of underground activities from culture and education to self-defense. If until then there had been underground groups who deluded themselves that the mass destruction of Lithuanian Jewry was only a local issue due to the war between the Germans and communism, Irena's story of the fate of Polish Jewry came as a slap in the face. Clearly, the fate of the surviving Jews of Kovno had also been decided, and the time had come to reach decisive conclusions about the character and methods of the Zionist underground.

Apparently, one of the first actions taken by Matzok leadership due to the influence of Irena's visit was organization of radio listening and the methodical distribution of the news received through this channel.[30] They decided to purchase a radio receiver and install it in a hiding place in the ghetto. They spoke with a technician who went to work outside of the ghetto; he bought a receiver in the city, took it apart, and smuggled it into the ghetto in pieces. The receiver was placed in the basement of the pharmacy managed by Matzok member Isaac Serebnitzky. Serebnitzky himself listened to the news each day in the early morning. He recorded the main items in Yiddish and distributed this report to Matzok members. The entire operation was executed in complete secrecy; only a few individuals outside the Matzok leadership knew about it (for example, Attorney Goldberg and Rabbi Snieg of the Ältestenrat knew nothing). Because there was some suspicion that people living near the pharmacy might hear the sounds coming from the basement early every morning and discover what was happening, it was decided to move them to other apartments in the ghetto.[31]

The months following Irena's visit formed a lively period in the Zionist

---

29. In fact, Irena visited the Kovno Ghetto twice. After the first visit, she went to Shavli and visited the ghetto there, and on her way back to her country she entered the Kovno Ghetto again, and updated Matzok regarding the situation of the Shavli Jews. After Irena, the Polish woman Edwige Dodzitz visited from Vilna on a similar mission (testimony of Masha Gail-Yaron, YVSA, 25–26, recording 5; Garfunkel, *Kovno*, 117).

30. The proximity of these events is indirect evidence of this. Ghetto residents listened to the radio much earlier than this (see PKG, 29; testimony of Z. Friedman, YVSA, 2; and testimony of Malka Pugatzky-Smali, YVSA, 6), but in an unorganized fashion.

31. Testimony of Leib Garfunkel, YVSA, 21–22, and his book, 117.

underground. From the testimony of Avraham Golob, we learn that during that period, Matzok decided in favor of the idea of active rebellion, and even began to act. A significant factor in this decision was pressure from "below" – from the underground Zionist movements, especially the youth movements. This change in their focus brought with it internal changes in the various organizations. But here we must first survey these organizations and the developments that took place within them up to the period we are now addressing. We will begin with the largest of the Zionist youth movements in the ghetto, which was also the first to consolidate stable patterns of underground activity.

IBZ

IBZ (Irgun Brit Zion – Covenant of Zion Organization) was "born underground." It was founded in Kovno in the summer of 1940, a few weeks after the Soviet occupation of Lithuania, as a general Zionist youth organization in the underground. Its founders were twelfth-grade students of the Kovno secular high school, some members of Hanoar Hazioni. Some time later, former members of Hamaccabi Hatzair and non-party affiliated students also joined. It was undeniably a youth organization, as most of its members were between the ages of eighteen and thirty. The head of its activities during the Soviet period was a twelfth-grader, Shimon Graz, age eighteen. According to the testimony of an individual who was closely acquainted with him,[32] Graz was a very talented young man. His worldview was a combination of Hanoar Hazioni, leftist socialist, and traditional Judaism. The main activities of this organization during the Soviet period were rescuing people who were imprisoned by the Soviets; maintaining the pioneer training camp, which previously belonged to Hanoar Hazioni and continued to operate under camouflage, even after the Soviet occupation; preparation and distribution of propaganda material; and organizing classes for teaching Hebrew and Zionism. It also clandestinely published a monthly newspaper, *Nitzotz* (Spark), which was mimeographed onto sixteen folio pages. The editor was Graz. During the Soviet period, six or seven editions were published in several hundred copies each.

After the German occupation, the IBZ members rapidly renewed their

---

32. Testimony of S. Sapir (Frenkel), YVSA, 1.

internal ties,[33] and in the first weeks of the Nazi regime, they achieved an important accomplishment: they took possession of the libraries in the city and transferred the large library of high school teacher Meir Kantorovitch, who had been deported to Siberia, to the area designated for the ghetto. This library became the foundation for the central IBZ library in the ghetto, which contained over one thousand Hebrew books. In September 1941, *Nitzotz* reappeared under the editorship of Avraham Tiktin. While its format did not change, it was no longer mimeographed but rather handwritten in several dozen copies only. In total, some thirty editions of this newspaper were published in the ghetto.[34]

IBZ member Sara Leibenson-Binyamini, twenty-six years old at the time, recounts:

> IBZ was organized in 1940. I was then placed in a small cell of Zionist activity. When the war broke out, I lost contact with the organization, because the coordinator of our cell was gone and two of my fellow cell members were deported to Russia. One cell member entered the ghetto, but I had no contact with her; I didn't think about the organization then. In fall 1941, during the *Aktion*s, a friend came to me and began to put out feelers. Slowly, she began to tell me that the organization existed inside the ghetto, and that I was a candidate to join the youngest battalion, the "Future" battalion. She said we had to wake up and not live passively, not atrophy. Despite the terrible conditions, we had to preserve our Zionism, attract youth to us as much as possible, so that they would not be carried away in the murky stream of ghetto life ... buying and selling, ethical corruption, and demoralization. She said we would get together and study history of the Land of Israel and of Zionism. This friend set up a meeting for me with her counselor, the counselor of the battalion, which numbered some fifteen to twenty people. He spoke with me several times, apparently he wanted to check whether he could trust me, especially regarding conspiracy. In those meetings, we were not yet discussing our underground in general, but just the battalion that I would join.... We

---

33. Ibid., 2 ff.

34. On the deliberations throughout the history of *Nitzotz*, and about its first editors (Shimon Graz, Haim Tiktin, Shraga Aronovitz, and Yitzhak Katz), see article by S.L., "*Le-regel zet ha*-Nitzotz *bi-dfus*" [*Nitzotz* appears in print], *Nitzotz*, Munich, July 11, 1949. Aside from this, IBZ published a journal in the ghetto, called *Shalhevet* (several issues), dedicated to the problem of resistance (Gar, *Umkum*, 397; testimony of Menachem Golan [Korlianchik], YVSA).

were told that we must not tell anyone in the ghetto about the organization, because its existence was prohibited, and we had to take extra care that the Germans would not catch us.[35]

Another member relates:

I think that it was in September 1941 that I made contact with IBZ through Haim Tiktin, who had taught me Hebrew one year earlier. Tiktin told me that an underground organization had been founded, and that its role was to organize the youth and fill the void that was created due to lack of schools and cultural life, and to plan organized resistance together with the ghetto institutions. It was defined as a Zionist youth organization. I agreed, and Tiktin set up a meeting for me with Yitzhak Shapira. He explained to me that the organization had existed since the Russian period, but that its founders had been deported to Siberia. I agreed to the proposal to join IBZ, because I was already prepared to make *aliya* to Eretz Israel. In addition, I found ideological satisfaction and occupation for my free time; I had a feeling – an illusion, actually – that we were doing important work.[36]

During that period, the time of the slaughters and *Aktions*, the structure and method of operation of this organization had not yet been formulated. As in Soviet times, it was led by a central command; this was comprised of the same individuals who had been active in renewing contact among its members. Yitzhak Shapira, mentioned above, son of the head of the directorate of Keren Kayemet Le-Yisrael (KKL) in Lithuania and an activist in Hanoar Hazioni A, directed the command's activities. He also directed it throughout the period discussed in this chapter,[37] as well as from June 1943 to February 1944 (from April 1943 to June 1943, Avraham Melamed held this position). In late 1941 or early 1942, the members decided that it was time to improve the structure of the organization and to limit the authority of the command. They decided that it would be led by a high council, which would have the authority to choose the command members, shape general guidelines for its operation, audit its activity, and even express lack

---

35. Testimony of Sara Leibenson-Binyamini, YVSA, 49.
36. Testimony of Haim (Pima) Rosenberg, YVSA, 1–2.
37. Testimony of S. Sapir (Frenkel), YVSA, 7 ff., and testimony of Masha Gail-Yaron, YVSA, 16–17 (recording 5).

of confidence in the entire command or in some of its members. The council would meet every six weeks for an all-night meeting.

During this period, IBZ was divided into five or six "battalions," each composed of three to five "platoons" of five or six members, including the platoon leader. At its height, the organization numbered 150 members, and several dozen supporters who participated in activities but were not sworn in. Aside from this, several dozen "recruits" – youths aged thirteen and fourteen – were connected with it for educational work. Some of the battalion commanders were also central command members, but the platoon commander could also be a command member. The command held three or four meetings each week, sometimes even daily, as needed. We may learn about the areas of activity and their character from the division of responsibilities: (1) command leadership, (2) general secretariat, (3) organizational issues, (4) culture and propaganda, (5) funding and finances, and (6) defense. The individual responsible for organizational issues was also director of the "battalion commander group." All issues were decided by the entire command, except for defense, which was autonomous and under the authority of the person responsible for organizational affairs, together with another command member or two (in actuality, throughout the entire ghetto period, Ika Greenberg was responsible for defense issues).

In the first months of 1942, IBZ still operated under a strict code of secrecy. Activity was carried out within the platoons only, and members were obligated to keep the details secret. But when relative stability in the ghetto was achieved, the leash was gradually loosened, and the command began to have members meet within battalions. During Passover 1943, they even considered the possibility of gathering the entire organization. At that point, they held festive parties at Passover, Hanukkah, and Purim, with over one hundred participants. But after battalion meetings were permitted, only a few cultural activities were held within this broad framework. The remaining activities – organizational contact for emergencies, mutual assistance, and of course, military or paramilitary training – were held within the platoons, with the requirement of secrecy applied.

In early 1942, a special "ideological committee" was founded by the council. It was given the job of formulating the IBZ platform.[38] The committee held some

---

38. In fact, the older group within IBZ had worked on formulating the platform earlier, as far back as the Soviet period.

forty meetings (most led by Shlomo Frenkel), and at the end of its work, they presented the platform to the members in *Nitzotz*. The platform expressed the desire to unify all the parties in the Zionist movement, an alliance that would "connect Zionist thought to Zionist action." According to Frenkel's testimony, it also included sharp criticism of the political structure of the Histadrut (Labor Federation) and its extreme partisanship, and expressed bitterness that political Zionism had not succeeded in converting the Jewish masses to the Zionist ideal of making *aliya* to Eretz Israel. It stated that Zionist policy should be a complete negation of living in the Diaspora, of the "stay put" stance,[39] and that the litmus test of every Zionist was *aliya*. The platform also took a stand in the stormy argument waged within the Zionist movement before the Second World War about the division of Eretz Israel, and identified with the call for establishing a permanent Jewish state on the basis of the partition plan. It said that the Zionist leadership must demand that the other nations draw conclusions from the terrible destruction of the Jews, and solve the Jewish problem by establishing a Jewish state in Eretz Israel. (During Hanukkah 1942, a rumor spread through the ghetto that a Jewish state had already been established.) The platform reflected a number of views on the internal problems of the Jewish community in Eretz Israel: on one hand, the pioneer vision, the Histadrut and the kibbutz movement as the best way to realize Zionism; while on the other, the demand for strict preservation of individual freedom. The platform based its socialist views on the principles of "individual socialism," and as an example, it chose "reformist socialism" of the 1930s. According to the platform, one of the organization's ideologues was A.D. Gordon.

IBZ activity focused on three main areas: culture, rescue, and defense. Cultural activity had a dual goal: education for Zionist and pioneer values, and basic Jewish education for youth. All activity was carried out in Hebrew. Members learned Jewish and Zionist history and gained knowledge of the various modes of life of the Jewish community in Eretz Israel. They also had writing lessons. Occasional tests were administered to members by platoon and battalion commanders.

The field of rescue was quite broad and included all activities held by the

---

39. This view focused on Jewish values formed in the Diaspora and the struggle for Jewish interests in their local settlement.

organization directorate – like the directorates of all other organizations – in order to offer people maximum assistance in their difficult struggle for existence in the ghetto. In days of relative quiet, help meant finding living quarters or workplaces, and encouragement of mutual assistance among members. At that time, IBZ had many young orphans left without families – refugees from outside Kovno or Lithuania who found shelter in Kovno at the beginning of the war, as well as Kovno natives who lost their families in the pogroms and massacres. These individuals had a strong tendency to join together and live cooperatively. The organization supported such incidents of mutual assistance, and gave them what help it could.[40]

Ghetto conditions forced the organization to divide into areas or "blocks" – as the members called them – in addition to the division into battalions. Each block had an apartment or two, which served as the meeting place for IBZ members, and also as living space for some of the members without families. Block A met at the Shapira brothers' home, in the large apartment buildings; Block B – at the home of Melamed the redhead, on Linkuvos Street; Block C – at the home of Avraham Rapopsky in old Slobodka; and Block D – at the home of Hannale Trotsky. They held singing parties and readings, and sometimes members came just to eat lunch or dinner together.

This was in the quiet days. But the main mission in the field of rescue fell on the shoulders of IBZ leaders during the times of decrees and pogroms, primarily during the deportation decrees, some of which affected the ghetto during the period discussed here. The leaders ensured that their members were not included in the lists of candidates for deportation, which were prepared by the Ältestenrat. However, it quickly became apparent that the deportations were not managed exactly according to the lists, and unlisted individuals could also be caught in the streets and homes in the cruel manhunts that accompanied each deportation.[41] Their first role in such conditions was to warn members of the coming disaster. For this purpose, the organization established its own information center and a system of secret signals for its members. This enabled the leadership to quickly inform them of impending events.

As noted earlier, after the first *Aktion*s the opinion emerged that should new

40. Testimony of Michael Yitzhaki (Gelbtrunk), YVSA, 6 (recording 2b).
41. Testimony of Shmuel Ben-Menachem (Dietz), YVSA, 4.

liquidation operations begin, the Jews should resist them with force. But thereafter a period of relative quiet ensued. According to the information available to
us, IBZ did not neglect the idea of defense, but the sense of urgency disappeared.

With regard to the activities in this area, the main participants were the leadership and the older membership.[42] There were two types of activities: (1) preparation of underground hideouts, or bunkers, "*malinas*" as ghetto residents called
them, and (2) purchasing weapons and training with them. The organization
began preparing *malinas* relatively early, at first for the purposes of its own institutions. In 1941, members dug a *malina* under the home of Avraham Rapopsky
(Block C) for preserving documents and the archives. A tunnel led from this
malina outside the ghetto, and later it served as a hiding place for members. By
1942 the leadership viewed building *malinas* as an important element of rescue
and defense operations, but in 1941 it was not yet a central activity and did not
involve the majority of the underground, as it would later in 1943. We have no
clear data about weapons purchase or training in the IBZ in this period. Some
testimonies state that the organization purchased two or three pistols in 1942,
aside from the pistol owned by Ika Greenberg since the ghetto's inception.[43]

> Apparently, during this period organization members even underwent pistol
> training, but we do not know how many people participated in the sessions.
> Leaving the ghetto to hide with Lithuanians was also considered a rescue
> method, and members who did so received assistance from the organization.
> But this was a solution for a few individuals only, and thus the leadership de-
> cided to exclude this matter from the organization's scope of activity.

Fleeing the ghetto to join the partisans was still not discussed during this
time. The first signs of interest in this idea appeared in late 1942–early 1943. In his
testimony, Michael Yitzhaki Gelbtrunk reports[44] that at the time, he and friends
in the organization discussed rumors heard about partisan units in the forests of
Lithuania, and expressed the opinion that they should find a way to join them.
"You are climbing up a steep wall," the friends answered. The only one willing to
listen to him was Avraham Rapopsky, a policeman in the ghetto. Rapopsky, who

---

42. Testimony Moshe Levin, YVSA, 2.
43. See, for example, the testimony of Menachem Golan (Korlianchik), YVSA, 1.
44. Testimony of Michael Yitzhaki (Gelbtrunk), YVSA, 1 (recording 2a).

was an observant Jew, stood out among IBZ members for his constant support of the concept of active resistance. Another expression of this was the IBZ *malina* dug under his home.[45] Encouraged by his conversations with Rapopsky, in early winter 1942 Gelbtrunk joined a labor brigade that went out to the Jonava region in order to work at felling trees in the forest.[46] He hoped to make connection with the partisans there. These were the initial attempts at putting out feelers for fleeing to the forests, after the change that took place in the Zionist underground following Irena's visit.

OTHER ORGANIZATIONS

Hashomer Hatzair had a special status during the Soviet period. It did not oppose the regime, but aspired to gain its support. The line that the underground party leadership decided on was if a member were questioned by the authorities or the Communist Party, they should deny the existence of an organized underground of Hashomer Hatzair. But they should by no means deny their ideological connection with the movement.[47]

The group leaders who acted in the Kovno chapter before the Soviets' arrival remained loyal to the movement, and all of them, without exception, continued to work underground. Several weeks before the outbreak of war with Germany, the Soviet security services began to trail movement activists. One was imprisoned and asked to propose to the leadership that the movement end its activities of its own free will; then no harm would come to its members. Two main reasons lay behind this special treatment on the part of the security services: (1) at first, the purge performed in that period was against "counter-revolutionaries," and the authorities did not yet place Hashomer Hatzair in that category; (2) they were aware that the best of Jewish youth in the country were members of this movement, and they hoped that over time, these youth would become enthusiastic supporters of the regime. But this was not enough to convince the leadership to change the basic party line. The only change made was organizational: secrecy

---

45. Testimony of Shmuel Ben-Menachem (Dietz), YVSA, 5–7.
46. Apparently, at the same time that Shmulik Mordkovsky made similar attempts (see below).
47. Yitzhak Vidukela, manuscript.

methods were intensified, and movement activities were permitted only in very small cells.[48]

When the war broke out, many activists from the Kovno chapter fled to the Soviet Union, and some of those who remained were murdered in the first few days by the Lithuanian "partisans." Two weeks later, a meeting was held, and this can be considered as a foundational event for the Hashomer Hatzair underground.[49] Five members participated, including Ze'ev (Vovik) Rosenblum and Yerachmiel Voskoboynik, veteran members of the central leadership, and Leo (Aryeh) Ziman and Miriam Buz, from the young members. It was decided that these five would serve as the "chapter council," and they were to organize the members, each one responsible for his own age group. They divided the members into secret cells of three each. The general feeling was that it was still early to define directions for activity, because they could not know what the Germans were planning.

Several days later, the chapter council met again. This time the meeting topic was "Our relationship to the Soviet Union and its army, which is now retreating." This was particularly important due to the issue Hashomer Hatzair had debated previously, regarding its relationship to the Soviet Union in general. The failure of the Red Army and its chaotic retreat might put their ambivalent relationship to a severe test. The attention to general problems also had another aspect: "Just at this time of overall humiliation, we needed to focus on theoretical issues, because this was the source of hope and faith, in spite of the gloomy despair. Vovik, who spoke on this issue, explored the problems deeply, and even dared to predict the strategic tactics of the Red Army. He ended with an expression of faith that the Soviet Union, and with it, the forces of progress, would soon end the war as victors."[50] Such expressions were typical of the prevalent view in Hashomer Hatzair during the passage from the Soviet period to the ghetto period, and they also offer a clue as to the future of this movement's path in the ghetto underground.

The recovery of Hashomer Hatzair after the *Aktions* was relatively late – apparently spring 1942. Organization began from below. Slowly, groups formed and

---

48. On the activities of one of these cells, led by Leo Ziman, see testimony of Leah Ackerman-Baht, YVSA, recording 1.

49. Testimony of Y. Rochman, YVSA,11. Compare *Sefer Hashomer Hatzair* (Merhavia: Sifriat Poalim, 1956), 741.

50. Miriam Buz, manuscript, 2–3.

began to meet at one of the members' homes. At first, the content of the meetings was group singing and talks about the situation in the ghetto, on the front, or throughout the world.[51] Later, the meetings included ideological discussions, and the participants even read Marxist reference books together.

Throughout the summer months of that year, connection was reestablished with some thirty members. Yerachmiel Voskoboynik, Yona Rochman, Eli Rauzuk, Leo Ziman, and Moshe Patrikansky served as the chapter council. But they felt strongly the absence of a central personality that could unite the ranks, define a path of action, and take a stand on the problems of the ghetto.[52] Hashomer Hatzair members of that time were particularly troubled by the complete disconnection from the movement centers, and lack of any hint as to their policy. The leftist tendency that strengthened among them during the Soviet regime meant that in the ghetto, these members became close to the Communist underground.

In his testimony, Yona Rochman says that during that period, Eli Rauzuk and Leo Ziman had contact with activists of the Communist underground, and they had an argument over the form of active resistance toward the Nazis. This argument was echoed in meetings between the Hashomer members, but most considered that they should examine the issue in light of specific ghetto interests and not according to wider interests, as the Communists would. This was the stance of the members at that time toward sabotage, which the Communists actively pursued (see next section). Hashomer members expressed doubt whether this was justified, because there was no proportion between the damage they would do to the Germans and the disaster it might bring upon the ghetto. In particular, they knew that the Germans used the method of collective punishment; they did not bother to find the individual who had performed the act, but took cruel revenge against the group to which the guilty party belonged.[53]

The mutual assistance among members of this movement was quite substantial. Members who left the ghetto for work brought food back to those who did not go to work, due to illness or other reasons.[54] In certain cases, Hashomer members relied on the assistance of ghetto officials who were known as

---

51. Testimony of Gita Foger-Turchin, YVSA, 1 (recording 1).
52. Pnina Sukenik, YLHG 20: 91–92; compare testimony of Y. Rochman, YVSA, 16.
53. Testimony of Y. Rochman, YVSA, 8.
54. Testimony of R. Zagay, YVSA, 2; compare also testimony of Gita Foger-Turchin, YVSA, 1.

supporters of the movement. The main assistance was removing the names of Hashomer members from the deportation lists. This apparently happened just before the second Riga *Aktion*.[55] The members justified this act: "We viewed ourselves as a pioneer Zionist movement, for which *aliya* to Eretz Israel was the main goal, and thus we thought we had more of a right to immunity."[56] However, in conversations about the situation in the ghetto, the social strata, and internal and external Ältestenrat policy, they criticized the favoritism that reigned in the ghetto institutions, apparently believing that the term "favoritism" applied only to individuals, not to organizations or movements.

After Irena's visit, there was a far-reaching change in the atmosphere of Hashomer Hatzair. In late 1942, at Hanukkah, there was a chapter meeting in the apartment of Eli Rauzuk.[57] Eli led the meeting along with Leo Ziman, and this signaled that the leadership had passed to the youth. On the agenda was the problem of defense. They decided to pursue the path of active resistance and begin preparations for self-defense and weapons training. Rauzuk was chosen to act as contact person between Hashomer Hatzair and the other underground organizations, in all things related to these activities. They also decided to return to the previous organizational structure and secretive methods of operation, and reestablished the three-member secret cells, in which resistance activity had taken place during the *Aktions* period.

At that event, a new configuration was confirmed for the chapter leadership. The following were elected: Yerachmiel Voskoboynik, Gita Vishkin, Yona Rochman, Eli Rauzuk, and Miriam Buz. This was also when the chapter began to publish a periodical called *Tochelet* (Hope).

The other pioneer youth movements in the ghetto – Hechalutz Hatzair-Dror, Gordoniya, and Netzach (Noar Zioni Halutzi) – underwent similar developments. But these groups maintained a strong connection from the beginning with the "adult" party: Zionist Socialists (zs), whose members organized during the *Aktion* period and continued their meetings afterwards. Because the party had a representative in Matzok, this gave it security and stability for the internal organization, but we cannot know to what extent Matzok influenced relations

---

55. In October 1942, 370 Jews were sent from Kovno to Riga for forced labor. This was called the "Second Riga *Aktion*" (Gar, *Umkum*, 126).

56. Testimony of Y. Rochman, yvsa, 11.

57. Pnina Sukenik, ylhg 20:91–92.

within the party. According to testimonies, at first ZS members did nothing to organize the youth.[58] Almost certainly here, as well, the initiative came from below. After the party leaders realized that the pioneer youth were making attempts to renew their organization, and that the Communists had already established an underground that was in the process of consolidation (see next section), they decided to assist in the renewed activity of these pioneer movements.

One witness describes the first meetings of these youth:

> The first person I met with was Berke (Berel) Rudman, a young man and member of Hechalutz Hatzair-Dror, who before the war had been in *hachshara* [pioneer training program] near Kovno. He began to connect me with other people. The first cell I met included: Zvi Friedman, Esther Yaffe, and David Rudnick, a member of the Gordoniya leadership, I think. We met at a meeting at Esther Yaffe's home, and there we laid the foundations for this organization. We began with information matters....
>
> This was in early 1942; I don't remember the exact date.... We had to be extremely cautious. We did not want anyone to know about our organization, and we did it under the guise of "youths holding meetings." Zvi Friedman brought us news, he was a policeman (representing the movement – as we later realized). We decided on a mode of operation, and at first – regular meetings. Each week, we met mainly in order to hear information about what was happening.[59]

We hear of the development of another group in the testimonies of Michael Glass and Rachel (Rashke) Rosenzweig. Before the war, members of this group had belonged to ZS *Studenten Farband* (Students' Union of ZS) in Kovno. The group apparently organized in late summer 1942. Yitzhak Kashiv (Kapchovsky) and Mendel Sadovsky were also members. At the time it organized, a joint meeting of several groups was held. According to Haim Gechtel, this was

> the unification meeting with ZS *Studenten Farband*. This meeting was mainly with the older members: Michke Glass; Esther Schwatz; Sheinke, Hirshke Friedman's girlfriend (I don't remember her last name); Mendel Sadovsky;

---

58. Testimony of Menachem Ganuni (Sadovsky), YVSA, 5; testimony of Yitzhak Kashiv (Kapchovsky), YVSA, 4 (recording 1).

59. Testimony of Haim Gechtel (Galin), YVSA, 8 (recording 4–5).

and Isaac Serebnitzky, who was leader of the group.... He was known as an active youth with energy and talent. I don't remember exactly how many we were all together – some fifteen to eighteen people.[60]

Rashke Rosenzweig also remembers this meeting. She mentions Berel Rudman and Shmulik Mordkovsky as participants:

I remember that we spoke about what we could do for the members, how we could save them. Berel was a member of Hechalutz. He was in *hachshara* for many years. I remember what he said at that meeting. He said that first of all, we were pioneers, and if we lived, of course our path was to Eretz Israel. In order to achieve this goal and fulfill our pioneer mission, we had to survive. For this reason we were organizing, in order to help our friends survive.[61]

After the joint meeting, activity was again held in small groups, with strict observance of secrecy rules. Michael Glass relates:

They tried many ways of maintaining the cultural level.... It helped to a certain extent, to prevent us from sinking into despair and fatalism.... Their enthusiasm was what kept people going, and perhaps we should say – their courage. People who do not believe and who are broken in spirit, cannot demonstrate, in my opinion, courage. During that period, I might have become a profiteer, if I had had the opportunity.[62]

We cannot know for certain whether at these meetings in 1942, they discussed resistance or self-defense.[63] The testimonies we have indicate that the idea of resistance was raised only in late 1942 or early 1943, and this meant organizational change. Haim Gechtel recounts (from the context of his testimony, he is clearly referring to the time period under discussion here):

One fine day they informed us that we were disbanding and switching to another organizational format. In other words, we would not lose contact with our movement, but switching to a general organization in the ghetto,

---

60. Ibid., 9 (recording 5).

61. Testimony of Rachel Rosenzweig-Levin, YVSA, 13–14 (recording 2a).

62. Testimony of Michael Glass, YVSA, 9 (recording 3).

63. "At first, we organized in order to ensure our safety within the ghetto, without a far-reaching goal" (testimony of A. Schwartz-Glass, YVSA, recording 1).

which would be called AYA (*Algemeine Yiddische Arganizatzie* or General Jewish Organization). I remember that we then divided into groups of five. In my group, I was the only one from my movement. Our meeting place was at the home of a young woman who was a Revisionist. In the first cell meetings, we were not yet acquainted…. The Revisionist woman was leader of our group of five. I recall that we talked about organizing self-defense in the ghetto…. We didn't discuss details at the time. We talked about training and obtaining weapons. This organizational framework did not last for long – I think we met two or three times. We discussed only general issues, general organization. Each group of five was attached to a region, in other words, regional groups of five.[64]

The above testimonies mention the names of Shmulik Mordkovsky, a refugee from Poland, who was active in the first meetings of these groups. Later, Mordkovsky became one of the best and most talented partisans in the ghetto. In late 1942, he was one of the first to make contact – if only for a short time – with partisans. He joined the "Tree Fellers Brigade," which was established at that time in the ghetto, and was sent by the Germans to work in the Jonava Forests. There he met a Russian widow who lived in a rickety hut at the edge of the village, near a thick forest. He gained her trust and became a friend of the family. In those days there were popular rumors of people wandering the area, who the locals called "forest people" or "partisans." Some of the peasants treated them with great sympathy, others with resentment, fearing that their presence in the area could bring disaster on the *burliokas*, the local Russian peasants, who were already suspected by the authorities as being loyal to the Soviet regime.

One day, Shmulik dared to ask the widow about the "forest people." After some hesitation, she told him that they had been wandering around in the Jondava Forest area for quite some time. At first there were two or three people, and at that time, fifteen. Most were former soldiers from the Red Army, while some were Communists, Soviet citizens who had been caught in Lithuania during the year of Soviet rule. Shmulik asked her to arrange a meeting with them. A meeting was held, and then other meetings. The "forest people" trusted Shmulik and even proposed that he join them. They told him that their forces were not

---

64. Testimony of Haim Gechtel (Galin), YVSA, 9–10 (recording 5).

great, but that they managed to obtain food for subsistence and to bolster their arms supply by attacking lone Lithuanian policemen and German soldiers. They also dreamed of partisan operations that would be worthy of the name, such as attacking transportation arteries and liberating war prisoners. "The temptation was great," Shmulik admitted to his friends. "The forest and the way of life of free fighters tugged at me as if with ropes; I was confident that the forest would accept me with love, and overnight I would become one of its faithful sons." But he rejected the enticing offer, because he viewed himself as part of the ghetto and his movement.[65]

It should be noted that Shmulik's attempt could have brought disaster on the Jewish brigade in which he worked. The German security authorities were aware of the connection between the local peasants and the partisans, and they also suspected the Jews. One afternoon, SS officers and Lithuanian soldiers under their command came to the worksite of this brigade and interrogated its members about their connections with the "bandits." But the Jews remained silent and revealed nothing. In the end, the German commander of the brigade gave the Jews a severe warning that if he discovered any contact with partisans, he would kill them all. With that, the matter was ended.

The Revisionist groups and Beitar, which operated underground during the Soviet regime, began their activity in the ghetto in a limited framework prior to the Great *Aktion*. We know of the existence of several cells that prepared "cold" weapons (knives) and "live" ones (pistols). Several activists were placed in the Jewish police in order to facilitate underground activities. After the Great *Aktion*, correspondence was carried out with Yosef Glazman of Vilna, and the policy of general resistance was delineated. Movement members waged internal arguments on this issue. They pressured Moshe Levin and Yehuda Zupovitz, who held central positions in the police, to motivate the ghetto institutions toward a more active, aggressive policy. At a later date, when cooperation among the organizations began, the Revisionists' position was expressed by the slogan "Together with all our rivals in war against the Nazis." Their representative in the Ältestenrat, Zvi Levin, filled a very important role in maintaining contact between this body and the underground leadership.[66]

---

65. Memoirs of Zvie Brown.
66. See testimony of Mordechai Karnovsky, YVSA,1; testimony of Avraham Frenkel, YVSA, 1–2; compare testimony of Yosef Melamed, YVSA, recording 1.

Finally, we will mention the independent youth group.[67] The founder of this group was Baruch Camber (Ezged), son of a wealthy family. Before the war, Camber was a member of Bnei Akiva, but he said that he left this movement because he objected to the policy of restraint in the face of Arab terrorism in Eretz Israel. His parents came from a revolutionary background. Before the October Revolution, they were members of underground revolutionary organizations of the Socialist Revolutionary Party in Russia. To them, individual terrorist tactics were the right way to undermine the regime of tyranny, particularly because it was likely to arouse sympathetic opinion throughout the state and the world. In family conversations during the *Aktions*, his parents hinted at the possibility of an underground in conditions like those in the ghetto, and at the need for daring acts of reprisal. These hints had their effect on the youth. He had the idea of organizing a group of "terrorists" in the ghetto that would carry out acts of reprisal, in order to awaken public opinion throughout the world.

At first it was no more than a fantasy, but in early 1942 he began to implement his idea. He spoke with several friends whom he trusted, and proposed that they establish a secret organization. "No one asked, targeted against whom? The problem was how to convince people that it was possible and worthwhile. . . . At the time, we were unaware of the existence of other bodies." According to him, he was joined by David Beider, Shalom Yatkunsky, Aharon Rosen (son of Rabbi Rosen), and Bube Bloomberg. They formed a group that called itself "Bar Giora." At this point, *Irgun Shmira Le-Ganim* (ISL – Garden Protection Organization) was founded,[68] in which IBZ leaders were particularly active. Members of Camber's group joined ISL, but were immediately disappointed. "Instead of weapons training and preparation for real acts, they stuffed me with philosophy." Camber raised the issue in his cell meetings. There was a bitter argument, which ended with him quitting ISL and IBZ.

But his period within the organization was not unproductive. In it, he learned the conspiracy method of organization – activity in small cells, connection between the cells – and used this lesson when he reorganized his group. This time,

---

67. Testimony of Baruch Camber (Ezged), YVSA, 2.
68. This organization was formally founded by the Ältestenrat to protect the vegetable gardens in the ghetto. In fact, it served as a Zionist educational framework for eight- to fourteen-year-olds and included some four hundred children and youth. It was headed by Dr. Haim Nachman Shapira and Dr. Yitzhak Rabinowitz (Gar, *Umkum*, 398).

he succeeded in organizing five cells, some thirty-five individuals all together, including Leibke Latz (who at one point wanted to walk to Eretz Israel), Hanne Segelson, Beider, David Schein, Aharon Reches, "Zippe" Beilis, Starovolsky, Moshe Kagan, Uri Chanoch, Haim Kunevitz, Grishke Melamed, and Izke Berman. Camber admits that these cells also "wasted time" as in the IBZ, but they also searched for ways to purchase weapons. "We told the new recruits that when the time came, we would do something." In late 1942, members of this group learned that Beitar was reorganizing in the ghetto, and that weapons training cells were operating there. They decided to join Beitar, while preserving ideological independence. In 1943, the group began to operate in the framework of Beitar.

The Communist Underground

For the Communists, the transition from the Soviet regime to Nazi occupation had a different character, for obvious reasons. The enthusiastic reception with which the large majority of the Lithuanian population welcomed the victorious Germans immediately awakened them to the danger they faced. They might expect that the fury of the Lithuanian nation, and the iron hand of the German security services, would first of all turn against the remaining Communists who had not been able to flee to the Soviet Union, and primarily target the Jewish Communists. Therefore, they immediately adopted strict secrecy measures. Every Communist tried, at least in the early days, to camouflage himself, not to be seen in the street as far as possible, and to change his address, name, and even his appearance. The precautions were taken mainly because of the Lithuanians,[69] but there was reason to be wary of Jews as well, particularly those who had a role in the ghetto institutions, and even other Jewish Communists.

Haim Yellin, for example, who was to become a leader of the Jewish Communist underground in the ghetto, almost never went outside during the initial period. He changed his name, grew a moustache, and often tied a scarf over his face to disguise himself as if he had a toothache.[70] Others who took similar steps were Dimitri Galpern, who in the pre-Soviet period was secretary of the Communist Fund for Aid to Political Prisoners at Kovno's university, and Rivka

---

69. For example, for a long time, former Komsomol member Bayle Rudashowsky feared to meet with a Lithuanian woman with whom she had worked in a factory during the Soviet regime (testimony of Bayle Rudashowsky, YVSA, recording 1).

70. PKG, 25–26.

Uriash, manager of a large weaving factory in the Soviet period. At first Haim Yellin and Dimitri Galpern did not permit themselves to meet face-to-face and made contact through Haim's father, Eliezer Yellin.

The case of Malka Pugatzky is typical. Because she was already a Communist before the war, during the Soviet regime she attained a high position in her town's local regime. Shortly before the Germans' attack on Russia, she moved to Kovno. When the war broke out, she tried to escape to Russia, but she was too late. She never returned to her room in Kovno, because she knew that she was known there. "My mother warned me … that they had already killed my brother and all the Communists. The police held my mother and sister and interrogated them as to my whereabouts. She had to give my address, and so I had to save myself and hide."[71]

Gradually, the Communists became aware that inside the ghetto they were not in as much danger as they had thought.[72] The daring among them experienced an awakening of the "party conscience," and they began to contact other members in order to organize. The first steps toward organizing a Communist underground were made with great caution and in separate groups. We have definite information about three such groups, which organized and operated in the fall and winter months of 1941.[73] The most active of these was the Shmuelov group, whose organizer, Eliyahu Shmuelov, was a veteran leader in the Communist movement. Other members of this group were Miriam (Mara) Lan, a Communist activist with an underground background, Hannah Vidlewosky, Hinde Markovitz, Pesach Shater, Haya Shmuelov, and Meir Leib Goldschmidt. Their first activities were the material support of several members, caring for children of the Pioneer Communist group when their parents were absent, and propaganda among the ghetto residents, to convince them to ignore the Germans' orders.[74]

---

71. Testimony of Malka Pugatzky-Smali, YVSA, 2 (recording 1).

72. Bayla Rudashevsky recounts that she once heard a conversation among Jewish policemen in the Jewish police quarter, that the Lithuanians were pressuring the Jewish ghetto police, and even offering them a prize, for arresting and imprisoning Jewish Communists. The Jewish police responded by mocking the Lithuanians' request (testimony of Bayla Rudashevsky, YVSA, recording 1).

73. PKG, 32 ff.; see also article by Povilas Štaras, Podvigi Komsomoltzev Litvi, Druzhba Narodov, Organ Soyuza Pisatelei SSSR 1958,10:161–70).

74. According to one testimony of a member of this group, "the main focus of the group was on defense with weapons, and this was the reason for the searches for connections in the city" (Meir Leib Goldschmidt, YVSA, letter 1:2).

Eventually, they were able to contact an anti-Fascist Lithuanian group led by Po-vilas Malinauskas, an experienced Lithuanian activist of the professional union.[75] Shmuelov joined the leadership of the group, changed his appearance so as to resemble a non-Jew as much as possible, and lived outside the ghetto in secret. The anti-Fascist group, which called itself Kova (Struggle), purchased weapons and prepared to go out to the forests. In the meantime, they conducted propaganda and information campaigns among the Lithuanian population, calling for them to ignore the Nazis' orders, refrain from joining the German army, and sabotage the German war machine.

But the group did not last long. Apparently someone informed on them, and the Germans captured them while they were in a meeting. They defended themselves with pistols but some of them fell, and the survivors – including Shmuelov – were caught and imprisoned.[76] Shmuelov was held for a long time at the Ninth Fort, and was tortured severely before he was murdered. One of the

---

75. See Tiesa, journal of the Lithuanian Communist Party, April 25, 1958, and PKG, 32. Contact with Povilas Malinauskas's group was made by three women who were sent to the city for this purpose. They were assisted by a long-time Communist activist, Janina Zichinausky. Another representative of this group, Monik (Zalman) Holzberg, found his comrade from the period of the Communist underground in independent Lithuania – the youth Romas Kulvinskas from Murava village near Kovno (A. Viršulis, Didvyriu kelias [Vilnius, 1959], 58 [hereafter, Viršulis]; Štaras, 83). As we will see below, connections with the underground center in Murava deepened with time, and it became one of the most important outside bases for the underground movement in the ghetto.

76. This information is confirmed by formal German sources. The "Report of Events" of the Nazi chief of security police from January 28, 1942, asserts: "On January 28 of this year, the security police in Kovno succeeded in destroying the terrorist group of Bolshevist activists. Einsatzkommando 3 received information that the leader of the group, Malinauskas, for whom we had been searching for some time, was holding a large meeting in a certain house [in Kovno]. Einsatzkommando forces stormed the house and waged battle with the terrorists, and finally the house was cleansed with hand grenades. Malinauskas, who defended himself with his weapon to the last minute, was shot, and another terrorist was severely wounded. We conducted a search of the house and found recently printed Communist pamphlets, explosives, pistols, and ammunition; red flags with the hammer and sickle; and other items" (Ereignismeldungen UdSSR, report 162, 10 ff.). Report 168 of February 13 adds: "Regarding the liquidation of the terrorist group, whose leader Malinauskas was shot in battle on January 28, 1942, another fifteen individuals were arrested. We suspect that they supplied the terrorists with weapons and explosives. One of them had a crate with fifty hand grenades and blasting caps (Sprengkapseln). Some of the explosive material was taken by the terrorists from a warehouse about 10 km northeast of Kovno, containing equipment left behind by the Russian army. There we found two hundred aerial bombs of 50 kg each, and thirty hand grenades of 10.5 cm caliber."

prisoners there reports that he was still there in summer 1942. He looked like a skeleton and was no longer sent out to work because he was unable to get out of bed. But his spirit was firm and his mind clear. He did not break under the brutal torture.[77]

Haim Yellin assembled another group of Communist activists and supporters of the Soviet regime.[78] Members included Dimitri Galpern, Rivka Uriash, Julia Meisel, Leah Senior, Itzik Yukhnikov, Shaul Finkel, Meir Yellin, and Shabbtai Fleishman, among others. At first, the members of this group collected news from the fronts and on the international scene, and discussed it together in light of Marxist principles. Further, they aided veteran members of the Communist movement whose health was shaky and cared for the children of absent Communists.

This group also rapidly realized the necessity of contacting Communists outside the ghetto. Haim Yellin took this mission upon himself. He did not find a Communist underground in the city, but he found a group that was comprised of several Soviet citizens, members of the party and the party apparatus, who had come to Lithuania previously in order to establish the Soviet institutions there. They had not been able to flee when the war broke out. The group also included several war prisoners who had fled from prison. This group called itself the "Red Partisans" and they planned to flee to the forests of eastern Lithuania. Yellin and his followers tried to recruit ghetto residents to this group and found some candidates. The date of departure was fixed for November 17. But in the meantime, group members outside the ghetto noticed that the Gestapo was following them and they were forced to push up the date of their departure without informing the ghetto residents. After some time, the ghetto residents learned that the group ran into a police unit, and all its members fell in battle.

A third group of active Communists in the ghetto centered around Moshe

---

77. Memoirs of Zvie Brown. Before Shmuelov was caught, he managed to obtain a pistol and several bullets for his group in the ghetto, and according to his orders, they collected a number of primitive defense implements, such as axes and benzene (Meir Leib Goldschmidt, YVSA, letter 4:6, 12). After he was caught and taken to the Ninth Fort, Shmuelov succeeded in smuggling out a short parting letter to his pregnant wife (Haya Shmuelov), in which he wrote: "I still hope we will meet, but if not – I ask this of you: take good care of the baby, and tell him about his father" (Štaras, 84, compare Viršulis, 57; Hitlerine, 328). On July 1, 1958, by order of the Presidium of the Supreme Soviet, he was granted the Order of the Patriotic War, first class.
78. PKG, 27–28.

Sherman, a member of the Communist youth group that was illegal in Smetona's Lithuania.[79] Its members included Moshe Rapp, Doba Chayat, Bashel Krepko, and Alte Boruchovitz, among others. It was supported by members of intelligentsia circles, such as the well-known Kovno music teacher and director Ya'akov Glezer and Hirsch Guttman. Members of this group conducted an energetic publicity campaign to convince ghetto residents to avoid giving the Germans their silver, gold, and other valuables. Some say that they found a sympathetic ear particularly among the profiteers, smugglers, and pillars of the ghetto underworld. Later, the Anti-Fascist Organization relied on them to purchase weapons. The Sherman group also organized a cell of Communist youth, led by Monik Holzberg, Moshe Robinson, Eliyahu Pianko, and Eliezer Zilber. At this stage they had a primitive radio receiver.[80]

As noted, the main efforts of the Communists were directed toward making contact with the Lithuanian underground – to reject the isolation and separation that the Nazis imposed, to continue the Communist activity in the spirit of "solidarity among peoples" and according to the "territorial" principle, and to avoid creating two separate areas of activity – ghetto and city each on their own. As we have seen, however, in the preliminary period attempts to make contact with the underground in the city failed.

The Anti-Fascist Organization

The Communists recovered quickly from the nightmare of the *Aktions*, and at a relatively early date, they began to formulate regular underground behavior and clarify the roles and aims of the underground. The rapid recovery of the Communists was apparently due to the tradition of underground activity that was quite well founded in the Communist movement. Ever since the inception of Communist activity, the underground was second nature to every Communist activist, and one year of Russian rule was not enough for them to forget these traditional habits. It is notable that among the Communist activists in the ghetto, not one was a member of the Lithuanian Communist leadership, despite the fact that the percentage of Jews in the Soviet regime in Lithuania was significant

---

79. Antanas Smetona, last president of Lithuania before the arrival of the Soviets.
80. According to various sources, the person responsible for disseminating the news, especially news from the front, was Moshe Robinson (testimonies [YVSA] of Grisha Sheffer, 6; Malka Pugatzky-Smali, 6; Leah Ackerman-Baht, recording 1).

(although not as high as the Nazi and nationalist Lithuanian propaganda described it). Leading the activities of these groups were young men who had joined the Communist Party in 1940–1941, but who occupied roles in the state economic system, not the party organization.

In the first months following the Great *Aktion*, the various Communist groups attempted to make contact with each other, and this led to their consolidation in one underground organization. The meeting of the unified organization took place on the night of December 31, 1941.[81] Strict precautions were followed. The meeting took place in the room of one of the activists, in a small hut at the edge of a yard covered in a thick layer of snow. Beside the gate to the yard stood two individuals whose role was to receive the arrivals according to a pre-arranged sign and to show them the way to the meeting place. The underground members entered one by one, at close intervals, and packed the small room. One of the initiators of the meeting was slightly late. This was Haim Yellin, who had just returned from the city after spending a few days there. His hair was dyed blonde, his moustache was long and pointed upwards, like a true Lithuanian.

We do not know how many participants attended this meeting, or whether they included all members of the Communist underground at that time or only some – the most active. At the end of the discussion, the participants decided to consolidate the underground groups and to establish one anti-Fascist group. At this founding meeting, they did not discuss renewal of the party activity in all forms. The main reason was apparently because the initiators of this union who did not belong to the party leadership did not consider themselves qualified for such an organizational step. They proposed that the organization call itself "Union of Activists" (*Activisten Farband*), but this name was not accepted, neither within the ranks of the organization nor outside it. Usually, it was simply known as the "Organization" (*Die Arganizatzie*), or jokingly, "The Moustache" (*Die Wanse*), hinting at Stalin's moustache.[82]

At the meeting, the goals of the Organization were defined generally by Haim Yellin: "We are not abandoning the ghetto, but our primary goal is open struggle among the ranks of the partisans."[83] They decided to begin formulating the "plat-

---

81. *PKG*, 33.
82. According to the testimony (yvsa) of Shmuel Ben-Menachem (Dietz), the organization was called "Antifa" (abbreviation for *Antifashistishe Arganizatzie*).
83. This wording appears in *PKG*, 35. We cannot know whether this text is completely authentic. The word "partisan" was actually derogatory to the ghetto residents, and referred to the

form of struggle" (*Kampfs pragram*) and the articles of the Organization and to begin the search for contact with the Lithuanian underground. They nominated a steering committee, which at first had five members, and later seven.[84]

The committee activity eventually encompassed several fields, with each committee member taking responsibility for one. Haim Yellin was elected as committee secretary and in charge of training the activists and special problems. Pesach Gordon-Stein and Moshe Sherman were appointed as responsible for the military-technical domain. Dimitri Galpern was given the responsibility for information and external relations. Mara Lan was responsible for the organizational side, while Alte Boruchovitz (Tepper) was in charge of the economic and social issues. The entire organization was divided into two brigades: the combat brigade and the support brigade. Only members who were fit for combat could join the fighting brigade; the rest formed the support brigade. All organizational activity was conducted under strict secrecy. Members were divided into cells, and members of one cell did not know what the other cells were doing. In the combat brigade, each cell had three or four members, with five to eight members per cell in the supporting brigade. In the combat brigade, every seven cells formed a "platoon," and the cell leaders were subordinate only to the platoon leader. The platoon leaders apparently received their orders directly from the committee, or from the director of the military-technical field.[85] Activities were planned on a weekly cycle (adherence to this rule was of course dependent on the objective conditions in the ghetto). On Thursday, the committee determined

---

nationalist Lithuanians. Although the word "partisan" is recalled in another context regarding the group that attempted to organize a small war against the occupier, and with which Haim Yellin was in contact (see above), they were called "Red Partisans." Quite possibly, at this foundational meeting of the fighting Communist organization, the word "partisans" was uttered only together with the word "red."

84. PKG, 37, shows a photograph of committee members Haim Yellin, Moshe Sherman, Dima Galpern, Pesach Gordon-Stein and Miriam (Mara) Lan. The caption under the photo notes that it was taken in the ghetto in summer 1942 (the yellow badge stands out on their chests), and that Alte Boruchovitz (Tepper), also a member of the committee, is not shown (see also Hitlerine, 286–87).

85. PKG (36, footnote) says, with regard to the establishment of the steering committee, that after the connection was made with the underground committee of the Communist Party in the city, the steering committee of the ghetto fighting organization operated under its direct leadership. However, this comment does not seem accurate, also in light of what this book says about the development of connections between the organization in the ghetto and the Communist underground in the city. We will discuss this further below.

the weekly plan of action. The plan was given with appropriate explanations to the platoon leaders and leaders of the support brigade. On Saturday, cell leaders conferred, and on Saturday evening and Sundays, tasks were assigned in the cells. The activities were usually carried out without delay at the beginning of the week, and they immediately reported the results to the committee through the secret channels.[86]

Several selections preserved from the Organization's "platform of struggle" are cited here in full:

> Because we live in the border region, we were the first to experience the enemy invasion. The Germans attacked the Soviet Union, and occupied Lithuania within the first week. A storm of terror struck the country. On roads, in cities, and in villages, anyone who was suspected of supporting the Soviet regime was killed. Tens of thousands of Jews were caught during their flight to Soviet cities. Hundreds and thousands of Jews were imprisoned in the Kovno forts, in synagogues, and in prisons of cities and towns, and from there taken to slaughter. Alive, wounded, and dead, they were tossed into the pits that had been dug in advance. The survivors of Lithuanian Jewry were imprisoned in concentration camps and ghettos....
>
> Along with the Soviet people, within the Jew the flame of struggle burned against the murderers of women and children. In the ghetto, the ground was laid for the organization of the Jewish masses to struggle in the rear against the occupier. Only the organizational framework was needed, which would train them and lead them to open struggle against the enemy....
>
> To organize the rebellion, to recruit those ready for battle, and to present ourselves as soon as possible in the service of the general partisan movement – this is the main goal of the anti-Fascist and partisan organization in Kovno Ghetto....
>
> Military training is given to members through talks and practical instructions in these areas: military discipline, camp life, forest life, digging bunkers,

---

86. Ibid., 38. This book also gives a detailed description of the order of a cell meeting: (1) Weekly report on the situation in politics and on the fronts; (2) reading the committee's weekly article and discussion of it; (3) military-technical instructions; (4) sabotage activity (report on missions carried out and assignment of new missions to the cell members; (5) arrangements related to mobilizing means for the organizations' needs (see also Meir Leib Goldschmidt, YVSA, letter 5, 2).

combat methods (attack, defense), structure of the units, knowledge of the rifle, pistol, hand grenade, machine gun, combating various forms of weapons (machine guns, tanks, cannon), setting fires, communications, Morse code signaling, scouting, topography (signs and maps), and military hygiene.

The problem of hiding places arose early. Due to political reasons, the members had to hide. With the progress of our activity, we have increasing numbers of documents, certificates, instruments, and weapons that we must hide. Preparation for struggle does not mean only preparing the fighter. It also means preparing the means that will enable the struggle. The items are collected and preserved in bunkers (*malinas*). Each member, or at least every cell, is responsible for preparing hiding places for goods and materials. Hiding spaces intended for larger amounts of items and for people are collective in nature and are being built according to a general plan. The hiding places for people are designated: (1) for people who are wanted for whatever reason; (2) to hide from the Germans when they are hunted for labor; (3) for secret meetings and work; and (4) as a gathering place during alarms.

In order to successfully carry out the construction work, members must obtain building materials, such as logs, planks, nails, cement, bricks, and tools. They must supply the items that should be found in every hiding place, such as barrels for water, flashlights, candles, matches, hoes, iron rods, axes, hammers, metal cutters, ropes, a minimal amount of food (biscuits), a set amount of hot noodles [code word for live weapons, e.g., firearms and explosives] and cold pasta [code for cold weapons, e.g., knives] – according to the size of the hideout and the number of people.

If we wish to make war against the enemy, we must not forget that as far as the camp that follows in the footsteps of our faithful activists and politically mature members grows, so will our achievements multiply and our chances for success increase. In these difficult conditions in which we are forced to live and fight, we cannot transform our movement into a mass movement. But from the above follows an important role for us: without recruiting the masses into our ranks, we must enlist them psychologically and educate them to join us shoulder to shoulder in our struggle against the occupier.... [87]

---

87. PKG, 25. According to this source (page 8), one copy of the platform is preserved in the museum of the Lithuanian partisan movement in Vilna (the Jewish section of the museum was dismantled in 1948 but reconstructed in 1961).

Following is the declaration that new members of the Organization had to sign:

> In the knowledge that the struggle against Fascism in all its forms is a sacred obligation, I hereby express my willingness to join the ranks of the Red Partisans as an active fighter. I hereby commit to fight the Fascist invaders indefatigably, not let them rest, disrupt the arteries of transportation, set fire to and blow up bridges, destroy train tracks, organize acts of sabotage at every opportunity and under all conditions, and assist in their execution. I hereby promise to fight without care for my health, and if needed – to give my life, until the final liberation of my homeland from the burden of occupation. I commit to be a faithful and disciplined soldier; to fulfill the orders of my commanders precisely, courageously, and immediately; to carefully preserve with the utmost secrecy the secrets I may learn and everything I find out during work; and to make sure not to violate the rules of secrecy. I am aware that for breaking discipline and revealing secrets, partisans are considered traitors and are given the death sentence.[88]

We do not know when or by whom this "platform of struggle" was written. The text in the citations above (such as the exact description of the military training and the detailed instructions for construction of underground hiding spaces) awakens suspicion whether the platform was written in this exact format at such an early date in the history of the Kovno Ghetto underground – in early 1942. These descriptions could only have been written based on accumulated experience, that is to say, not before the second half of 1942. But there is reason to assume that the consolidation of underground operation in the Organization took place earlier than the writing of the platform text, and that by early 1942, it expressed fairly clear positions in the following areas:[89]

> 1. *Reception and distribution of news from outside, including focused explanation among Organization members and supporters* – A critical step was taken in February 1942 with the installation of a five-tube radio receiver in an underground hideout (at 18 Vežėju Street). For security reasons, the receiver was

---

88. Ibid., 39–40.
89. Testimony of Malka Pugatzky-Smali, YVSA, 3–10 (recording 2-3); YLHG 20:90; testimony of Ephraim Senior (Senion), YVSA, 2; Meir Leib Goldschmidt, YVSA, letter 2.

connected to the electric current outside the ghetto and this was also a very dangerous operation. Members took turns listening to the news. Moshe Robinson supervised the operation, which meant the Organization obtained for him an exemption from the labor requirement. They mainly listened to Radio Moscow and relayed the news daily to the steering committee, which copied it and distributed it to the cells in "The Daily News" and a weekly bulletin.[90]

2. *More thorough political and ideological propaganda and placement of books for this purpose in the hiding spaces* – During the Book *Aktion* in the ghetto in February 1942, Organization members were ordered to sabotage the decree and to hide their books instead of handing them over. Further, members who were employed by the Germans in the city in confiscating the public libraries smuggled many books into the ghetto, particularly Marxist books. Organization members later collected the surviving books in one location, establishing a library for member use. The cells also arranged systematic study of the history of the Communist Party.

3. *Accumulation of cold weapons and primitive explosive and incendiary materials* – We know of many Organization missions to acquire weapons, but we do not have exact dates. We may assume that most – mainly the missions for purchasing "heavy" weapons such as rifles and machine guns – were carried out in 1943. Apparently, in 1942 the Organization was mainly occupied in collecting explosive and incendiary materials (Molotov cocktails), first aid materials, topography instruments, and so forth.

4. *Organized sabotage against German military installations* – The sabotage missions were among the main achievements of the Organization during this period. Haim David Ratner wrote the report on sabotage operations performed by the members. Below are citations from his list for 1942:[91]

III [March]. Member Pok [referring to Moshe Zimlovitz], who worked at loading grain, stuffed a shovelful of snow into each sack. As a result, a large quantity of grain rotted. IV [April]. Two hundred liters of benzene is the quota that the General Commissariat office received for one week. Our

---

90. *PKG*, 51.
91. Ibid., 42–43.

members poured this quantity into the sewage pipes at their workplace at KL [Kriggs-Lazaret – a German military hospital]. V [May]. Medicines have a special importance during war. While unloading a cargo of thousands of trays of medicines, Member S. [Mottel Stein] grabbed the crate in such a way that the Lithuanian driver who held the other end had to drop it onto the ground. VI [June]. A shipment arrived of gas masks destined for the front, and our members removed the filters from six hundred of them. VII [July]. Member M. [Moshe Milner] who was employed in the Kovno garage poured 80 percent acid and 20 percent water into the battery – the opposite of the specification. The result was double: first, the expensive acid was wasted, and second, the battery plates were corroded. Ninety-eight units have already been ruined by this. VIII [August]. Shoemaker A. [Haim Aron] and his work unit, assigned to the ghetto workshops, sanded thin the inner soles of a large quantity of boots. Within a short time, some one thousand pairs of boots were returned as unfit for use.

Members who worked at the train stations and its workshops also pursued methodical sabotage. They switched the destination signs and lists of repairs on the cars, removed screws from engines, and moved the railway signals from their correct positions. These actions disrupted the work of the stations, caused quarrels among the senior station managers, and sometimes even train crashes.[92]

According to several sources, in February 1942 several large sawmills on Jonavos Street on the banks of the Vilya were set afire and burned, with the active participation of a member of the ghetto Anti-Fascist Organization – Leib Segalov.[93]

5. *Continuation of the search for contact with the Communist underground in the city* – During this period, Organization members renewed their searches for ties with the anti-Fascist underground in the city. Several members who had the required qualities specialized in this job: an "Aryan" appearance, the

---

92. Testimony of Ephraim Senior (Senion), YVSA, 2; compare PKG, 44; Hitlerine, 285; Viršulis, 60–61, 148.

93. Meir Leib Goldschmidt, YVSA, letter 5:1; PKG, 41. See also Stahlecker's report from October 15, 1941: "In certain places, especially in Kovno, the Jews armed themselves, initiated active guerilla warfare and caused many fires" (L-180, Trials, 4:161). See also Viršulis, 43, 61.

correct Lithuanian accent, quickness, and levelheadedness. But despite the agility and dedication of the contacts, they enjoyed only partial success. The main mission – discovering the Lithuanian anti-Fascist underground – was a complete failure throughout the entire period discussed in this chapter – in other words, until spring 1943. What the contacts did manage to do was to renew old friendly relationships and to make new contacts with individual Lithuanians, workers and members of the intelligentsia who were willing to support the anti-Fascist activity guided from the ghetto. The Organization received especially practical assistance from Dr. Helen Kutorgiene, with whom Haim Yellin was in contact. She organized several hiding places in the city, distributed anti-Fascist literature, which was supplied by Yellin, and later also helped purchase weapons. Below is a characteristic citation from a conversation between this woman and Haim Yellin:

> You gave me so much courage, refreshed me, encouraged me. I feel much stronger when we are together, and I don't want you to go, even though we are both endangering our lives and our families.... Every day I watch Jews being led under my window to forced labor. Every day I write in my diary what is happening to the Jews.... Each week they come and search my house. I hide my writings. I record everything in them...death, fear, murders by day and by night – and despite it all, you keep on living and hanging on. How do you stand, despite everything? ...How do we stand, despite everything? – Yellin replies: Eventually, in historical perspective, the significance of our optimism will become clear to all.[94]

6. *Adjustment of the relationship between Organization leadership and ghetto institutions* – Relations between organization members and ghetto institutions developed in the first place on the basis of compromise – a mutual de facto recognition. In the first months after the outbreak of the war, ghetto institutions and police helped the Communist activists hide, and did nothing that might lead to their discovery.[95] Possibly, the motivation for such treatment on the part of the ghetto authorities was self-interest: they did not

---

94. PKG, 68–69. For other sections from Dr. Kutorgine's diary, describing the endurance of Kovno Jewry, see Hitlerine, 93.
95. Meir Leib Goldschmidt, YVSA, letter 1:3.

want the Germans to think that there were Communists in the ghetto. With time, the ghetto institutions became aware of the Anti-Fascist Organization, but we do not know whether or when they discovered details of the scope of its activity. In contrast, we do have knowledge of personal contact between members of the Organization steering committee and senior police officers and Ältestenrat members in the first months of 1942.[96]

According to its members, the attitude of the Anti-Fascist Organization toward the ghetto leaders was:

1. Fundamental negation of the Judenrat as "the servant of the occupier and implementer of its orders."
2. Sharp criticism of those members of the Ältestenrat and its institutions who took advantage of their position to protect themselves and their families from deportations and *Aktions* and who lived lives of luxury and profligacy.
3. Singling out of several Ältestenrat members, including Dr. Elkes, as exceptional, since they had proved their honesty and courage in fulfilling their roles as leaders of the ghetto.
4. Insertion of Organization members into ghetto institutions, to serve the needs of the Organization.[97]

As for the principled negation of Ältestenrat policy, we have no information that it was given true expression in the period discussed. The Communists accepted the authority of the Ältestenrat, but they made sure that the ghetto institutions assisted them in their activities, or at least did not hinder them. The attitude toward career-makers and scoundrels among the Ältestenrat had no practical expression, not even later, when the partisan organization had weight in the ghetto. Despite this, the Communists implemented the decision regarding insertion of their people into ghetto institutions. Organization members received positions in the ghetto police, in the labor office, and in the other institutions. Those who held these positions ensured that those who went to the city on special missions could leave and reenter the ghetto without incident, that Organization members were referred to workplaces desirable to the Organization, and that Organization activists could move around inside the ghetto even when under

96. Testimony of E. Segal, YVSA.
97. PKG, 57–58.

curfew. They also ensured that Organization members were not included on the lists of those destined for deportation. They warned their members against coming disasters and decrees and arranged comfortable workplaces for them, also from the aspect of opportunities to trade with the Lithuanians. They also utilized their positions in order to transform the members of their organization into a privileged stratum. From this aspect, there is no difference between the Anti-Fascist Organization and other underground organizations whose members worked in ghetto institutions.

We may summarize our survey of the development that began in the various ghetto underground organizations in 1942 as follows: In most of the organizations and groups – perhaps except for the Communists and the Camber group – they focused during this year on internal unification and cultural and educational activity, as well as organized rescue efforts. If the idea of resistance was raised in a certain group, it was accompanied by bitter arguments of conscience based on fear for the ghetto's fate or else only a few individuals supported it. After Irena's visit, mainly in late 1942 and early 1943, ferment was felt in almost all the organizations. Interest in problems of self-defense increased, as well as the recognition that this was the best path under the given conditions.

As a result of this foment and the influence of world events, the underground factions achieved unity of purpose, and they began to establish a joint fighting force in the ghetto.

PART II
The Awakening

CHAPTER 4

Toward Active Resistance

During the first half of 1943, several world events caused a change in the mood that prevailed in the underground circles of the Kovno Ghetto. The first of these events was the victory of the Red Army in Stalingrad.

The "intelligence service" of the ghetto underground organizations (responsible for such activities as listening to the radio, smuggling in newspapers from the city, and contact with Lithuanians and Germans who related events in the world) was already developed by early 1943, such that almost every important political or military event was known to the Jewish public soon after its occurrence. In January of that year, the ghetto Jews – and particularly the underground activists – were aware of the encirclement of massive German armies at Stalingrad and that Hitler's forces were absorbing terrible blows in that region, as well as in other parts of the eastern front. This news inspired a wave of joy among the ghetto residents. They saw the Nazis' defeats as distant signs of liberation and the beginning of the fulfillment of their greatest dream. Rumors flew from person to person and sparked open, excited conversations in homes and workplaces. The Jews received the news of the end of the Stalingrad battle with the glorious Soviet victory as something certain and expected. The very day that was declared in Germany and occupied Europe as a day of mourning over the defeat of the "undefeatable" German army became a great holiday in the ghetto.

Their joy did not go unnoticed by the Germans and they decided to take revenge on the Jews. On February 3, during the formal mourning days, some fifty people were caught and executed the next morning at the Ninth Fort.[1] This killing was known by the ghetto residents as the "Stalingrad *Aktion*." It was meant

---

1. Gar, Umkum, 135–37; Gruenhoyz, FLC 7:27.

to remind the ghetto residents of their true status, and that, regarding their own fate, the significance of the Stalingrad victory could be completely different from its significance for the course of the war in general.

The second event that influenced the underground's path was the Warsaw Ghetto Uprising, although in the Kovno Ghetto they had only scant information about it. Apparently they heard the first news of the uprising in the Warsaw Ghetto by radio. The Ältestenrat and Matzok (the underground alliance of the Zionist movements) tried to obtain additional information, and an attempt was made to renew contact with the Vilna Ghetto, assuming that at least its underground had constant contact with the underground in the Warsaw Ghetto. A Lithuanian reported that when he had been in Warsaw he saw flames rising from the ghetto quarter and heard the thunder of cannon.

Events that took place closer to Kovno also did not bode well. In March 1943 the officials responsible for the Kovno Ghetto informed the Ältestenrat that they intended to bring in five thousand Jews from the Vilna environs, following the liquidation of the ghettos in those locations. These Jews came from the towns of Oshmyan (Ašmena), Smorgon (Smurgainys), Olshan, Kreve (Krevė), Michalishok (Michališkis), and others.[2] The Ältestenrat prepared a plan to absorb them, but the Gestapo in Kovno refused to take responsibility for the Jews of the Vilna district. They said that these Jews had assisted the Soviet partisans in the forests of Vilna and that the Jews themselves were all partisans. In early April the Gestapo loaded the Jews onto railroad cars, telling them they were taking them to Kovno Ghetto. The train advanced toward Kovno but stopped along the way. The Jews were ordered to descend from the train and they were shot on the spot. Only a few were able to flee.

A small number of Jews from the Vilna district survived this massacre because, at the time, they were working on paving the Vilna–Kovno road. They were housed in a labor camp in the town of Zhezmer, and there was danger that when the work ended they would also be murdered or sent to the northern front. A small group of Jews from this camp were brought to work in Kovno. The Ältestenrat succeeded in making contact with them and discovered the danger facing the camp residents. It decided to attempt a mission to rescue them. The

---

2. Gar, Umkum, 139; Gruenhoyz, FLC 7:27; Sefer ha-partizanim ha-yehudim [Book of the Jewish partisans] (Merhavia: Ha-Kibbutz Ha-Artzi Hashomer Hatzair, 1958), 1:30.

job was given to Dr. Yitzhak Rabinowitz, who at that time represented the ghetto labor office to the German labor office. Rabinowitz was in constant contact with the supervisor of Jewish labor in the German labor office, Hermann, and on occasion managed to exploit this contact for the benefit of the ghetto. He convinced Hermann to help bring the Jews of the Zhezmer camp to the ghetto – all or most of them. The justification was that there was great demand for labor in the Kovno workplaces and that in the ghetto they were short of working hands. Hermann contacted the Gestapo in Vilna and received permission to transfer four hundred Jews from the Zhezmer camp to Kovno Ghetto. As Rabinowitz recounts in his testimony:

> We explained to Hermann that if Germans came to transfer these Jews, the Jews would not believe them. The Jews were well aware that Germans came to take Jews [out of the ghetto] only to kill them, and not for work, and so their reaction might be negative. We asked them not to send Germans to take the Jews, but only the Jewish police. Finally we obtained the license, and cars to transfer the people.... Throughout the day we brought out eight hundred Jews or more. Only a few remained. They were taken to Kovno Ghetto, where they shared the fate of the Kovno Jews. At any rate, this operation caused great upheaval in ghetto life.... The Zhezmer people, especially the youth, who came from the Vilna area, apparently had some contact with the partisans, and they already were strongly inclined toward joining the partisans. Some of them, for example those who were transferred to the labor camp in Koshedar (Kaišiadorys), made contact with the partisans. There as well, there were incidents of rebellion.[3]

From these Jews, the ghetto residents heard stories and legends about "the Soviet partisans wandering the forests of southern Lithuania and Byelorussia, terrorizing the Germans." There were many rumors of Jewish partisan groups walking the roads and villages and taking food from the peasants.

At that time, Soviet war planes began to appear in the skies above Kovno. At first these were reconnaissance flights, but then they began to bomb military targets in the city. Panic reigned among the Lithuanian population and the Germans in the city. In contrast the Jews were silent. The knowledge that the ghetto would

---

3. Testimony of Dr. Yitzhak Rabinowitz, YVSA, 14 ff. (recording 4).

not be bombed, while the Lithuanians and Germans sat in shelters in fright, was a highly significant symbol of the change that had begun in the course of events. Gestapo officials, as usual, blamed the ghetto residents for signaling the Soviet pilots. We have no hint that underground members in the ghetto intended to attempt such a thing. But at the time an incident occurred near the ghetto gate that the Germans could interpret as proof of their guilt.

As mentioned in the previous chapter, the underground organizations were then smuggling weapons into the ghetto, although in very modest amounts. Among those involved in this dangerous work was Yerachmiel Berman, a member of the Anti-Fascist Organization (AFO). He worked in the big weapons storage room at the Fifth Fort, from which a sizeable number of weapons were stolen for the AFO. One day in March 1943 Berman came across a signaling device, and he decided to smuggle it into the ghetto.[4] He stuffed the instrument into a bag full of wood, taking it with him when he returned to the ghetto with his labor unit. Unfortunately, that day the Germans conducted a strict search of those entering the ghetto, and they found the device. Berman was arrested and handed over to the Gestapo. Aware of the gravity of the situation, the ghetto leaders used all their influence to release him and brush over the entire incident. Within a few weeks Berman was returned to the ghetto.[5]

In June 1943 there was an enormous explosion in the Fifth Fort, next to Kovno, where a brigade of Jewish laborers from the ghetto worked at sorting and dismantling Soviet weapons and ammunition.[6] That explosion killed Meir Luria and Faivel Farad, members of the ghetto underground,[7] and another member,

---

4. Another source indicates that Berman did not follow AFO instructions in this case. Proof of this is that following the incident, Alter Feitelson, Berman's partner in smuggling arms into the ghetto, was ejected from the AFO due to the accusation that this was a provocation (see Feitelson, YVSA, letter 17).

5. Gar, *Umkum*, 143.

6. According to several sources, the operation was carried out on underground instructions. Every so often, the AFO would send members to the Fifth Fort for special jobs. This is documented in the testimony of Michael Gelbtrunck. One day, his organization gave him the task of working there. When he arrived, he identified himself with the code "It's fine." He was told that his role was to cough when the work manager approached, because "They're doing something there" (testimony of Michael Yitzhaki [Gelbtrunck], YVSA, 3–4, and compare *PKG*, 41).

7. On July 1, 1958, Meir Luria was posthumously decorated with the Order of the Red Banner by the Presidium of the Supreme Soviet of the Soviet Union.

Yerachmiel Siniuk, lost his hand.[8] Two German sentries at the site were also killed. The Germans' response was not late in coming, but this time they were satisfied with merely disbanding the labor brigade.

All these incidents together served as a source of agitation among the ghetto public. Discussions and arguments about the situation and the chances for the future were now held in broad forums, extending far beyond the limits of the underground, both "upward" into ghetto institutions and the Ältestenrat, and "downward" to the unaffiliated ghetto inhabitants. Two things became clear, and almost no one disputed them: the war was approaching an end and the Germans' defeat was inevitable. But on the question of what this meant for the fate of the ghetto and what the Jews should do – opinions were divided.[9] Some said that signs of an approaching end demanded intensifying the policy of restraint. They should refrain from any act that might anger the Germans and motivate them to act against the ghetto; every day passed in safety was a step toward liberation – "Let's not arouse their anger!" Others said that the time had come for action; until that point there had been no reason for it because they had no chance of success, but now it was time to act. They had to escape from the vise of the ghetto, to flee, to hide, to do something.

If the ghetto was agitated, the underground organizations were all the more so. Here the turbulence took the form of heated debate about the underground's path in the new situation. Among the Zionist youth organizations, who for a few months had been holding military training in secret cells, the argument was increasingly heard that the time had come to decide on a clear plan of action for the developing force, whether in an uprising inside the ghetto or a battle outside it. The rumors of the partisans in the Lithuanian forests fired their imagination. Since Irena's visit, Hashomer Hatzair had adopted a position supporting active rebellion, and its members searched for ways to implement this. The general excitement affected the IBZ as well, and a lively argument took place among the members.[10] The leadership was asked to reevaluate its modes of action. They said

---

8. According to the testimony of the cell secretary of the organization to which Siniuk belonged, the original plan was that the explosion would be set in a railcar after the workers had left the workplace (Meir Leib Goldschmidt, YVSA, letter 5, 1–2; see also Y. Siniuk, letter 3, 1–9).

9. Gruenhoyz, FLC 8:30.

10. Testimony of Masha Gail-Yaron, YVSA, 17 (recording 5).

there was no longer any reason to make the educational and publicity activities a priority. From then on, rescue and defense were first and foremost.

Cooperation among Underground Groups

The Communists reacted to the "new situation" by intensifying their searches for contacts with the Lithuanian underground. In the ghetto, as well, they felt the need to abandon their isolation and aspired to cooperation with underground organizations on the basis of active struggle against the occupier. There are signs that among the Communist leadership opinions were not united on this issue. This becomes clear from a description of the events that led to this cooperation.

We do not know exactly when the initiative began for cooperation between the Communists and the Zionist camp in the ghetto. Golob recounts that in the summer of 1943, Zvi Levin informed him of his meeting with Haim David Ratner and Dima Galpern of the Anti-Fascist Organization, and that the latter had proposed cooperation between their organization and Matzok.

> My opinion was negative, because I did not believe the Communists, and I thought that we must not place our members under joint command with them. During the first period of Soviet occupation,[11] I had seen many young members of the Zionist movement who joined Komsomol under the influence of the strident propaganda and promises, and mainly through repudiation of the national idea, which was presented as a disguise for imperialism. This hurt me. As an active member of the Zionist youth, I held myself responsible.[12]

The proposal was brought before the Matzok directorate and an intense debate was held, with the participation of Haim Nachman Shapira, Isaac Serebnitzky, Zvi Levin, Golob, Dr. Elkes and Attorney Garfunkel. The Ratner-Galpern proposal was as follows: (1) to unite all the fighting forces in the ghetto and place them under one command, and (2) to determine in principle that the role of the fighting force – which the two bodies would work to expand and strengthen – was not only to protect the ghetto in case of liquidation, but also to actively fight the occupier outside the ghetto limits as part of the Soviet partisan movement.

---

11. Meaning the year of the Soviet occupation of Lithuania, 1940–1941.
12. Testimony of Avraham Tory (Golob), YVSA, 37 ff.

The Matzok leadership understood that they would not fulfill their historical duty if they did not join the struggle against the occupier. Because they knew that this was not in the realm of the possible unless they joined the Soviet partisans, and this they could only achieve through the Communists, they decided that they had no other choice but to cooperate with the Anti-Fascist Organization. But the decision included one reservation: to ensure that members of the Zionist movements could maintain a nationalist ambience within the combat units, to speak Hebrew and to sing Hebrew songs.

Zvi Levin and Golob were appointed as Matzok representatives for negotiations with the members of the Anti-Fascist Organization. But before the official negotiations began, Golob made unofficial contact with Haim Yellin.[13] Yellin did not hide his opinion that "objectively, it will not be possible to maintain separate cells with different songs and ambience…and it is unimportant. The direction should be rebellion and struggle against the occupier, and everything should be subordinate to this goal." He added that for his part, he did not wish to complicate the negotiations, as he was not leading them, but "certainly, we will accomplish nothing in this manner." Golob believed Yellin more than the others, and proposed terminating the negotiations. When his proposal was rejected, he resigned from the position of Matzok representative in the negotiations, and Isaac Serebnitzky was appointed in his place.

In the early contact between the two sides, Dr. Rudolph Volsonok was very active. He was known before the war as an adept journalist, well versed in economics and politics, and even certain military matters.[14] Rumor had it that when he was young he would write essays on military topics and Russian czarist generals published them in their name. Later he served as a senior officer and military expert on the Polish general staff. Finally he settled in Kovno, where he worked for the Lithuanian government. In the ghetto he first worked as director of the airport department at the Ältestenrat labor office, then as director of the statistics office. At times he tended toward Revisionism, but in the ghetto he moved toward the leftist circles. We cannot know whether he had a recognized position there,[15] but leaders of the Anti-Fascist Organization utilized his

---

13. Ibid., 41.
14. Sudarsky et al., *Lita*, 1094–93.
15. His name is not mentioned in PKG.

proficiency in political and military matters as well as his persuasive powers in their relationships with Matzok and ghetto institutions. The two sides viewed him as coordinator of political and military information for the underground. In his analyses in this field, he surpassed all of his colleagues. Based on the sparse, fragmented news items that reached him through the sources available to the underground, he always managed to paint a comprehensive picture of the situation and to analyze it with consummate expertise. He supported the proposal for unification with enthusiasm.

When Isaac Serebnitzky joined the negotiations, the sides met again, and Ratner and Galpern announced that they accepted all of Matzok's conditions. An agreement for cooperation was formulated and a protocol recorded and signed by the four negotiators. It specified:

> The two camps – the Zionist camp and the Jewish freedom fighters (the Communists) – would organize the combat units together and avoid any separate activity. Each one of the sides would recruit its members, and they would receive training, instruction, and equipment.... There will be uniform planning for instruction and activity until going out to the forests...and we will avoid any ideological pressure or influence. The activity will be limited to struggle against the Germans and rescue, through the partisan battalions in the forests. Those who join the combat units will be required to obey the regional or local commander. During rest hours, social activity will be held freely according to the will of the members.

It also stated that "this partnership would last until the defeat of the Germans, and then each fighter will be allowed to choose his path in life, whether to remain where he is or to make *aliya* to Eretz Israel."[16]

The Communist sources lack any record of the episode of negotiations and agreement. Cooperation between the two camps is described in one of these sources:

> Various Jewish parties and organizations, bourgeois and sub-bourgeois, that were active in bourgeois Lithuania, have now renewed their activity in the

---

16. Testimony of A. Tory (Golob), YVSA, 42. The joint organization was afterward called the "Organization" (*Di arganizatzie*) or the "Fighting Organization." Its full name was *Yiddische Algemeine Kamfs-Arganizatzie* (General Jewish Fighting Organization), hereafter JFO.

ghetto underground. The top echelons of these organizations worked for an extensive period on cultural activities among their followers. Their practical activity was limited to utilizing the ghetto institutions for the interests of the organization members.... In light of the surrounding events, and under pressure of their followers, the leadership of the various parties was forced to take a stand on the day-to-day issues distressing the ghetto, and primarily toward the Anti-Fascist Organization, whose influence increased, and whose activity in the rebel movement against the occupation began to be felt increasingly among the general population, as they stirred up enthusiasm among people from various circles to join the struggle. Some of the leaders of those parties expressed their willingness to cooperate with the fighting Anti-Fascist Organization. For this purpose, a cooperative council was established. Then a committee was elected called MTK (*Militarist Technishe Kamisiye*, "Military-technical committee"), responsible for raising funds to purchase weapons. But the MTK operated for only a short time.[17]

In Golob's testimony, he does not mention the MTK committee. He does say that after the agreement a joint command of the two sides was formed, comprised of those who had signed the protocol of the agreement: Isaac Serebnitzky and Zvi Levin for Matzok, and Ratner and Dima Galpern for the Communists. "This staff headed the activity the entire time."[18]

Some identify the joint command with the institution called the "Public Committee" (*Gezelshaftlecher Kamitet*, or *Gez. Kamitet* for short).[19] Golob's testimony reveals that although there was a body in the ghetto underground called the Public Committee, this was not the same as the joint command. The Committee was not a formal institution but an instrument of action that the joint command used on occasion in order to perform various projects on behalf of the fighting force, such as raising funds, purchasing clothing and equipment, purchasing weapons and smuggling them in and out of the ghetto, recruiting instructors for weapons training from among former military personnel, assistance in organizing members of the organization in certain workplaces in the

---

17. *PKG*, 62.

18. Testimony of A. Tory (Golob), YVSA, 44. This joint command is not the same as the "Black Staff" (chapter 8).

19. Meir Leib Goldschmidt, YVSA, letters 1, 4.

city, and defending them from deportation. Depending on the character of the project, the Committee would call a meeting of appropriate individuals and the command would send one or two people to organize the project. But while the Command operation took place in complete secrecy, the Committee performed its work partially in the open, and within a much broader circle than Matzok and the Communists combined. The individuals it recruited for projects were told that they were not working on behalf of any specific party but for the "Hebrew Movement for Rebellion and Resistance against the Germans." There was almost total response to its appeals; we will discuss this further below.

We find a third version of the structure of the united underground leadership, closer to that of the Communists and different from Golob's, in the testimony of Ze'ev Friedman, director of one of the ghetto workshops, who tells that he was in constant close contact with the leadership.[20] According to his testimony, two bodies were established following the negotiations about cooperation: the Public Committee and the Coordinating Committee. The Public Committee was the higher authority. It outlined the general policy of the ghetto fighting force and covered for its activities vis-à-vis the ghetto institutions. The Coordinating Committee was responsible for planning and carrying out the operations such as those listed above.

According to Golob's testimony, the content of the agreement indicates that the cooperation related only to the issue of departure to the forests and joining the partisans. But if the agreement was signed in summer 1943, as noted above, we cannot accept this. For at the time, there was no reason to discuss an organized departure to the forests, as they had not yet made contact with the Soviet partisans. We can also not assume that Matzok members abandoned in principle the concept of defense within the ghetto in case of liquidation. The other sources indicate that from early 1943 until the deportation to Germany, the underground remained faithful to the defense idea. Further, Yellin and Galpern report a detailed program for ghetto defense that was drawn up during that period by the Anti-Fascist Organization.[21]

This plan divided the ghetto into eight defense areas. A commander was appointed for each area and two meeting points were determined – one for the

---

20. Testimony of Ze'ev Friedman, YVSA, 3.
21. PKG, 63–65.

general population, the other secret, for the combat units attached to the area. The few weapons the underground had were divided among the fighters according to their roles, while the rest of the population would be given a quantity of cold weaponry such as axes, iron rods, and knives. A secret workshop was established to prepare the equipment, with metalworkers Alter Feitelson and Yisrael Milstein appointed in charge. As soon as the Germans sent military or police units into the ghetto with the clear intention of murder on the spot or removing the inhabitants for liquidation, the ghetto Jews would immediately be called to the meeting points. Some of the combat units, especially those attached to the regions where the Germans would begin their operation, would storm the enemy with all the weapons at their disposal. The purpose of the attack was to kill as many Germans as possible, take their weapons, hold back the German units, and gain time for the combat units at the border areas of the ghetto to break through the fence and enable the population to flee. An important role was to be played by the "Incendiary Units," who would be equipped with Molotov cocktails and other incendiary materials. At the height of battle they were to set the empty houses on fire, thus sowing panic among the Germans. One of the important activities planned was to attack the ghetto guard in order to disarm it and immediately distribute the weapons among the fighters.

Yellin and Galpern attribute the preparation of the plan to the committee of their organization. Even were this so, we must assume that it was authorized by the joint command, or the MTK, as a joint defense plan of the entire underground.

At any rate, we must assume that the cooperation agreement among the factions defined the need for a fighting organization outside the ghetto, without renouncing the principle of defense within the ghetto. It also emphasized the issue of departure to the forests, although the problem of contact with the forest partisans had yet to be solved.

The Search for External Contacts

The ghetto Jews had reason to expect that the turning point in the war, signaled by the Germans' defeat at Stalingrad, would also influence the atmosphere among the Lithuanians and their relationship to the German regime. During 1942 the Lithuanians awakened from the euphoria of victory and their illusions of achieving national independence from the Nazis, "saviors of humanity from the Bolshevist nightmare." The Germans revealed no indication of establishing a Lithuanian government in the country, and all efforts of the Lithuanian nationalists in this direction were in vain. Lithuania was part of Ostland and the entire regime was in the hands of the Nazis. The Nazis also did not bother to promise the Lithuanians independence after the war.

The national Lithuanian economy was transferred to military production lines, and the German ministers ensured that the vast majority of the country's products would supply the German war machine. Labor was closely supervised, and every Lithuanian who was not useful to the local military regime could be sent to Germany or other occupied areas. The national social and cultural institutions were shut down, and every channel of influence and mass education was placed at the service of the war machine. The country was rapidly emptied of both its material and spiritual resources.

The one and only "compensation" that the Lithuanians received in exchange for their loyalty to the Nazis was – destruction of the Jews. Undoubtedly, the Lithuanian nationalists considered this a true benefit. In 1941–1942 they earned a reputation as the most diligent and expeditious Jew-murderers in all of occupied Europe. The Germans derived maximum benefit from this. But here, as well, the Lithuanians considered themselves deprived as they were not permitted to inherit the Jews' property. The Germans decided that the property of Lithuanian Jewry belonged to the German Reich. A memo sent by the Lithuanian Nationalist Party to the Reich government in Berlin reads:

> The Lithuanians believe that the Lithuanian Jews who have not yet emigrated can be successfully used as a labor force in the reconstruction of destroyed Byelorussia and Russia. The Lithuanians believe that the property of the Jews who left Lithuania[22] should be given to the Lithuanian people, although [the party] is aware that in 1941, the *gebiets kommissar* [district official] of Shavli announced to the district heads the basic law that all Jewish property belonged to the Third Reich.[23]

---

22. By "Jews who left Lithuania," the authors of this memo apparently referred to those Jews who had fled Lithuania at the beginning of the war, as well as those who were murdered by the Germans and Lithuanians up until the memo date.

23. A. Yerushalmi, *Pinkas Shavli*, 224. A proclamation of the Union of Lithuanian Freedom Fighters from April 1942: "By what right are the Germans expropriating the property of the

Indeed, the Lithuanians had no reason to be satisfied with the German regime in their country. But as long as Nazi armies held steady on the eastern front,
the Lithuanians accepted the decision humbly, while bargaining weakly about
the Jews. But after the turning point in the war, would they continue upholding
this position? Would a nationalist Lithuanian underground not arise to battle
the occupier? And if it did arise, would it be willing to join forces with the Jewish
underground?

Apparently the leaders of the Kovno Ghetto underground asked themselves
these questions. Its two factions had already gained some experience in this area.
The Jewish leaders well remembered the stone wall they faced during the mass
murders of 1941, when they approached Lithuanian personalities, members of
the intelligentsia, and begged them to intervene, to wield their influence, in order
to "preserve the honor of the Lithuanian people." Such memories certainly did
not encourage them to renew their attempts. Matzok and its supporters did succeed in making contact with several Lithuanians in the city. These Lithuanians
demonstrated some willingness to assist individuals, but they were not ready
for underground cooperation.[24] The hope that a national Lithuanian fighting
underground would arise had no basis. Even Matzok members understood that
if some sort of Lithuanian underground should arise, it would be Communist,

---

Jews and foreign citizens? This is the property of the Lithuanian people and state" (YIVO archives, OccE3b, 24–27).

24. Testimony of Dr. Eliyahu Segal. We learn something about the relationship between the
nationalist Lithuanian underground groups and the Nazi occupation regime from a statement
distributed in Kovno in early 1942, which is attributed by the German administration to the
"Christian Democrats": "Thousands of our youth are serving them [the Germans.] We would
willingly continue to assist them with weapons in hand, but they are not interested in this. They
apparently think that this type of help shows signs of authority... and therefore there is no
reason to discuss this at all. The Germans are not thinking of giving us our country, not now
and not after the war. On the contrary: the assumption is growing that they want to destroy
us as the Lithuanian people, to force us to deny our nationalism or to disperse throughout
Germany and distant Russia.... It is the sacred duty of each Lithuanian to defend the honor of
his ancestors, his country, his language, and his rights. We do not intend to incite rebellion. The
Germans are thirsty for revenge, and for every German, one hundred peace-seeking civilians
are killed. Let us fight them with the ammunition we know well from the First World War:
bribery. From those days, we know how much the Germans value bribery. Today they come
to us in fancy uniforms and smooth slogans. But in fact, hiding behind most of these uniforms
are the same egoists, materialists, and sadists...." (YIVO archives, OccE3b, 20–23).

and no one in the ghetto would be able to create ties with such a group, except for the Communist activists.

Activists of the Anti-Fascist Organization, who throughout 1942 had not stopped working in this direction, now intensified their efforts. Indeed, in March 1942 the first signs of success appeared. One of the AFO's contacts, Yasha Davidov, met a Lithuanian tailor, Vaclovas Tomasaitis. This man told him that since early 1943 there was an anti-Fascist underground organization in Kovno called the "Union for Battle against Fascism in Lithuania." Its goals were sabotage in the factories operating on behalf of the Germans, directing information campaigns among the population, and establishing partisan units for direct battle against the enemy. Davidov told the Lithuanian that in the ghetto there was also an underground organization with similar goals. Each gave his organization leadership the information he had obtained, and the two sides decided to make contact between them, taking care to observe strict security measures.[25]

We know that Haim Yellin participated in a secret celebration on May 1, sponsored by this Lithuanian Union, in the apartment of its leader, Mikas Kiaupa.[26] At the party they listened to Radio Moscow, which aired a special broadcast for International Workers' Day, and Stalin's celebratory address as the supreme commander of the Soviet armed forces. Haim Yellin participated in the party disguised as a Lithuanian who had just joined the Union. After the party a small group of members stayed to confer. Only this limited circle of the organization's activists were aware that the "new Lithuanian" introduced to the gathering as a man named Vladas was really a Jew from the ghetto. Haim Yellin described the activities of his organization under the harsh ghetto conditions, eliciting admiration from those gathered. After exchanging information, both sides reached the conclusion that their organizations shared identical goals and that there was room for close cooperation. They decided to coordinate the operations and that at least once a week representatives of both organizations would meet to arrange the joint matters.

The meetings of the representatives were carried out in the bushes on the banks of the Vilya, not far from the ghetto. Dima Galpern participated on behalf of the Jewish organization, slipping out the ghetto gate. On behalf of the

---

25. PKG, 69–70.
26. Ibid., 73.

Lithuanians – Tomasaitis, who arrived by boat from the other bank. Cooperation between the two groups was in the form of acts of sabotage, distributing local propaganda materials and material received from Moscow by air and preparing forged documents. The organization in the ghetto received from the Union the illegal local newspaper *Kova* (Struggle) and other newspapers that were sent from Moscow, *Tiesa* (Truth) and *Tarybų Lietuva* (Soviet Lithuania). Workshops in the ghetto prepared for the Union stamps and linoleum plates for printing handbills. Even the copy machine that AFO member Moshe Muselis "appropriated" from the Germans was given to the Lithuanian Union.

Later the two organizations decided to establish a partisan battalion in the Betigole (Betygala) Forest near Kovno.[27] They erected several earthen huts and placed a small amount of weaponry inside. The first to move out there were several Soviet prisoners of war who had fled from prison and hid for a while in Kovno. They were joined by a few Lithuanians sought by the Gestapo.

The battalion was given the name Pergale (Victory). The first ones prepared the base to receive a larger number of fighters from the city and the ghetto. The Jewish organization sent equipment, such as boots, combat belts, and undergarments, and also assembled a group of Jews who intended to join the battalion. But before they could do so the Gestapo discovered the base. There was a clash between the partisans and a police unit. The battalion commander and his lieutenant fell in battle, and they had to abandon the base.

The two organizations tried again to establish a partisan base in the forest beside the town of Chaykishok (Čekiškės), also near Kovno, but this attempt also came to a bitter end. Union leaders Kiaupa, Tomasaitis, and others were caught by the Gestapo. The Germans suspected cooperation between the Union and ghetto inhabitants. They tried to squeeze details from Tomasiatis's wife, tortured her brutally, and even brought her to the ghetto. She withstood the ordeal and did not give up any of the ghetto activists whom she had met. Some members of the Jewish organization were forced to "disappear" and hide in bunkers belonging to the underground, fearing their names had been turned in to the Gestapo.

Following the two failures and heavy human losses, the Union in the city disintegrated. In the ghetto, however, the AFO continued to operate and was

---

27. Ibid., 71. Štaras's article makes no mention of the Union and its connections with the Anti-Fascist Organization.

not discouraged from its aspiration to make contact with the "Lithuanian partisan movement," which at that time was more of a legend than actual fact. The leadership learned a lesson from the failures. In the meantime, information from various sources reached the ghetto underground about the presence of partisans in the forests of southeastern Lithuania, and in Kaidan and Vilkomir provinces. They decided to begin an intensive search for large partisan units in these distant regions.

This activity continued for about two months (August–September 1943).[28] Three scouting groups went out during that period. The first departed on August 5 with five fighters, who according to Yellin and Galpern[29] were among the best and bravest in the organization. The leader of the group was Yisrael Milstein, a strong young man, a metalworker by trade, and one of the first activists in the ghetto underground. With him went Bezalel Yaffe; Yasha Davidov, expert in underground communications; Moshe Slawiansky, outstanding in daring sabotage against the Germans; and Michael Teitel.[30] They were armed with pistols and hand grenades, and equipped with maps and compasses. Their goal was to search for partisans in the forests of eastern Lithuania. No news of their fate was heard for an extended period. Later it was learned that they had met up with a police unit and all fell in battle.[31]

A second group of scouts departed in late August, led by Aharon Vilenchuk. The group reached the Yezne (Jieznas) Forests but found no traces of the partisans. The scouts returned to the ghetto safely. In early September, another group of scouts departed with three members: Mordechai Lefkovitz, Mordechai Stern, and Zalman Borodavka. They were supposed to make contact with a partisan group that, according to their information, operated in the Jonava Forests under the command of a Jewish paratrooper, Leib Solomin ("Petrovitch"). They were also meant to go as far as Vilkomir province. One source[32] reveals that Solomin avoided contact with them. On the road between Jonava and Vilkomir

28. Gar, *Umkum*, 145.

29. *PKG*, 74; compare Viršulis, 63.

30. See also testimony of Eliezer Moses, YVSA, 3 (recording 1). According to this testimony, Zalman Kravitz also went as part of this group.

31. Milstein was awarded the Order of the Red Star on July 1, 1958, by order of the Presidium of the Supreme Soviet (Viršulis, 8).

32. Testimony of Malka Pugatzsky-Smali, YVSA, 19. For details on the Solomin group, see chapter 10, "The Lithuanian Underground in Action."

(Ukmerge), they came across Lithuanian police and fell in battle. At that same time individual fighters also went out on scouting expeditions: Hanne Padison reached the Jonava Forests and Hirsch Guttman went to the Garliawa-Mauručiai (Gudleve-Mavrutsh) area.

Yet these expeditions yielded no substantial results. Despite the bravery and dedication of the scouts and the numerous casualties, they were not able to make contact with the partisan movement outside the ghetto. The siege that the Germans and Lithuanians placed on the ghetto could not be broken as long as the attempts to break it were made solely by local forces.

In late summer, a change took place in this situation.[33] In September 1943 several Jews who went out to work in the city met a Lithuanian who asked about "the writer Haim Yellin" and wanted to contact him. The underground leaders in the ghetto suspected provocation and decided not to respond to the Lithuanian's demands at first. But in the meantime, the Lithuanian met Ya'akov Levi, a member of the Anti-Fascist Organization. Levi recognized the Lithuanian as a leftist and recalled that once, before the war, he had been interned with him in a detention camp where they had been sent for revolutionary activities. Although it was not certain that he had not become a traitor and a servant of the Gestapo, the underground leaders decided to take the risk and meet with him. The meeting was held on September 14. Dima Galpern went alone as a representative of the ghetto underground, but Haim Yellin and Moshe Muselis sat armed nearby, ready to react at any sign of betrayal. The Lithuanian introduced himself as Juozas Tubialis, representative of the Communist underground in Vilna. He related that he had already visited Kovno several times on missions in order to make contact with the "Lithuanian comrades," but without success. Finally he received an order to attempt contact with the Kovno underground through party activists in the ghetto and mainly through Haim Yellin.

The ghetto residents were still not sure whether they could place their full trust in a Lithuanian. Tubialis sensed this and promised to bring proof of his mission. The next day he returned from Vilna and brought with him a letter written in Yiddish, addressed to Ya'akov Levi and signed with the letter "G." Signs in the letter led them to understand that it had been written by Gesia Glezer, a known activist of the Communist underground in Lithuania from before the war, who

---

33. *PKG*, 75 ff.

went by the underground nickname of "Albina." Tubialis said that the letter was written by a woman paratrooper from Moscow and that she asked the AFO to send to Vilna "a responsible person, to receive information and instructions."

It was natural that such a difficult mission fell upon Haim Yellin: no one knew the camouflage tricks on the Aryan side as well as he did or had up-close, personal experience of the underground conditions, its achievements, and needs – both in the ghetto and in the city. He was also the best fit for the journey in terms of his character, status in the underground, and the trust accorded him by his friends. Without much hesitation, Haim dressed in the uniform of a train clerk, which he wore regularly in the city, placed his pistol in his bag, and slipped out of the ghetto. He traveled the 90 km between Kovno and Vilna without incident, and that same day met with the members of the Vilna underground and the woman paratrooper from Moscow.

We do not know the exact content of their conversation or whether they reached an agreement easily. We do know that Gesia Glezer had an earlier opportunity to become familiar with the problems of the Kovno Ghetto underground, based on the precedent of the Vilna Ghetto underground, with which she had been in contact since her parachute landing from Moscow. The information we have about her relationship and discussions with the FPO (the Vilna Ghetto partisan organization) sheds light on her approach to these problems in general and on the position she was likely to take regarding the problems of the Kovno Ghetto underground. As we discover from the testimony of Abba Kovner (commander of the FPO), Gesia Glezer brought with her clear instructions of how to direct the Communist underground and how to regulate, or try to regulate – directly or indirectly – relations between the ghetto underground organizations and the Lithuanian underground:

> I do not know firsthand exactly what mission Albina came on from Lithuanian headquarters in Moscow, but from reconstruction of the events, we can assume that the Lithuanian headquarters, which afterwards became the leadership of the Lithuanian partisan movement, sent Albina to operate in the capital and its environs. I do not know if she was the first envoy for this mission. At any rate, she was the first envoy with whom we met. She reached Vilna Ghetto, and we [apparently referring to the FPO leaders] had several meetings with her. She impressed me as being a serious, daring person. After

she familiarized herself with the problems in Vilna Ghetto (she spoke Yiddish) and saw the underground organization and was quite impressed, she left the ghetto. By the way, we had an argument with her over the problem of defense in the ghetto.... She objected to the existence of the underground inside the ghetto and argued that there was only one way [to operate] – to leave the ghetto and organize the partisan war in the forests and the underground in the city. [She said] the ghetto was only a prison, it had no national unity, and so forth.... Luckily for us, the leaders of the Vilna Communists had a more positive and nationalist attitude.... Due to that, we succeeded in convincing Albina and other Communists that it was our duty as Jewish fighters to stay with the Jewish community until its end, until the act we could perform on behalf of the Jewish community of which we were a part. She came with the clear instruction to forbid the organization of an underground inside the ghetto, only in the city, and not exclusively Jewish.... She tried to convince us to give up our activities in the ghetto. She said that anyone who was involved should be sent to a base outside the ghetto, in order to participate in the general underground operations. We convinced her that this should not be the case.[34]

Kovner continues by asserting this was not merely an issue of verbal victory. The facts also contradicted Albina's approach. Shortly before Albina's arrival paratroopers were dropped around Vilna, also sent by the Lithuanian leadership. They "did not rely on their weapons" – as Kovner expressed it – but attempted to base their activity on assistance from supportive farmers and connections within the Lithuanian population. Shortly afterward these paratroopers were caught and killed, after they were discovered in the village they had trusted. Some believe that one of the missions for which Albina was sent to Lithuania was to look for the traces of these paratroopers. She could also hear from Haim Yellin information about unsuccessful attempts and bloody failures in this matter of establishing a "united Lithuanian" underground. We do not know for certain whether Glezer learned a lesson from these facts regarding her strong belief in a "city underground" and a "united Lithuanian" underground, or whether her opinion on problems in the Kovno Ghetto underground was affected by the

---

34. Testimony of Abba Kovner, YVSA, 4 ff. (recording 2).

experience she gained in Vilna. But we find a hint in the fact that the day after Yellin's arrival in Vilna, he and Albina both went to the Rudniki Forests, where the Lithuanian partisan brigade was located. It was commanded by Jurgis – actually a Jew named Ziman – a Communist activist from Kovno.

Haim Yellin remained in the Rudniki Forests for about two weeks. In the Communist sources we find not one word about his meetings with the brigade commanders. They only state that he "received theoretical and practical training in several partisan battalions: in destroying a German garrison near Varėna and blowing up a bridge on the Merkinė River.[35] After receiving appropriate instructions for continuing operations, he returned to the ghetto." But other sources reveal that conversations between him and the commanders did take place, and they discussed issues of great importance to the fate of the Kovno underground. Apparently, in these conversations, the plan of action known as the "Augustova Plan" was decided upon. Its implementation cost the ghetto underground many lives and could also have brought destruction on the entire ghetto, due to faults in the plan itself. We will focus on this in the next chapter.

Albina's Visit to the Ghetto

It is also important to note Gesia Glezer's visit to Kovno Ghetto, a visit whose influence on the Anti-Fascist Organization was similar to the influence of Irena Adamovitz's visit on the Zionist camp in the ghetto (see chapter 3).

Gesia Glezer came to Kovno some time after Haim Yellin returned to the ghetto. Her purpose was to organize the Lithuanian Communist underground, but she also expressed the desire to become acquainted with the work of her comrades in the ghetto. Her entry into the ghetto demanded exact planning. In that period it was not particularly difficult to enter and exit the ghetto, with the help of the Jewish gatekeepers, without attracting the notice of the German or Lithuanian guards, so ghetto residents often did this. Sometimes Lithuanians from the city also entered and exited.

At the time, relations between the Jewish gatekeepers and the German and Lithuanian guards were so interdependent – thanks to a complicated system of gifts, bribery, and favors – that any special operation could be carried out relatively easily, on condition that everything was done with the knowledge and

---

35. PKG, 76, apparently referring to the Merkys River, also called the Merechanka.

agreement of the police chiefs and Jewish labor office officials. But there was always the chance that the gatekeepers might be surprised by an unplanned visit of the German higher officers. In such a case, the inspection at the gate was taken over by the guests or was under their strict supervision, and any infraction was likely to be discovered. In such cases they would search the people extremely thoroughly. Should Albina fall into the hands of such a stringent guard, undoubtedly they would find her personal pistol, from which the Soviet paratrooper refused to part, and this would endanger the entire ghetto. So on that day the atmosphere beside the gate and in the underground leadership was anxious. But everything went as planned and Albina entered smoothly.

Gesia Glezer remained in the ghetto about ten days. She spent most of her time with the Anti-Fascist Organization, but she also met with the head of the Jewish police, Moshe Levin, and with the representative of Hashomer Hatzair, who was then connected with the AFO.[36] We do not have detailed information about these meetings, but her visit was valuable for the AFO and its plans for the near future, and it had significant influence on the direction of operations of the entire ghetto underground. "Finally we have achieved what we desired from the inception, and which cost us so much in effort and victims – to stand under the direct leadership of the party for battle against the occupier."[37] In other words, after Glezer's visit to the ghetto, a fundamental change took place in the formal status of the Anti-Fascist Organization. It was recognized by an "authorized representative" of the Communist Party Central Office as part of the party, and as implementing the party line in the struggle against the Nazi enemy. It is hard to know how this fact was received by AFO members who were not Communists, of which there were a number. But for the Communist members, this was somewhat of a release from the feelings of insecurity and doubt that disturbed their "party conscience," so long as they were completely disconnected from the central office and had to decide on their course of action solely on the basis of their "Bolshevist intuition."

The change was not only formal. In meetings in which Gesia Glezer participated, the leadership formulated a plan of action for the coming weeks, which was based on the directives of the Moscow representative and received her

---

36. Testimony of Gita Foger-Turchin, YVSA, 16.
37. PKG, 78.

authorization. The general outline of the plan was the AFO would continue to cooperate with the other underground groups, using the services of the ghetto institutions, but it would bolster efforts to drive the entire underground toward immediate departure of the fighters to the forests and their attachment to the Soviet partisan movement. The practical means for implementing this mission were: (1) attempting to establish contact with Solomin's partisan unit in the Jonava Forests, with the goal of sending at least some of the ghetto fighters to its base; (2) sending several groups of trained, armed fighters from all underground organizations to the Augustova Forests – a block of forests about 130 km south of Kovno, at the shared borders of Lithuania, Poland, and Eastern Prussia – in order to found partisan bases there; (3) establishing intermediate partisan bases near Kovno, to support the journey to the distant Augustova Forests.

CHAPTER 5

The First Breakthrough

For several months in 1943, the "Augustova Plan" was the focus of activity in the ghetto underground. The changes that began at that time in the ghetto and the implied threat of new decrees influenced underground members' attitude to the plan. This was the beginning of the period known in Kovno Ghetto history as the Goecke period, after SS *Obersturmbannführer* Wilhelm Goecke. During this period, from September 1943 to July 1944, the ghetto was gradually liquidated and remaining survivors were deported to Germany, with Goecke supervising the stages of implementation.

Goecke arrived in Kovno in early September 1943. The residents of the ghetto learned that he was administering the hurried transfer of the ghetto from the domain of the German municipal commissariat, which was under the civilian occupation authorities, to that of the SS. As became clear later, this administrative move was to the SS bureau that supervised the concentration camps in Germany and German-occupied territories. Goecke did not reveal his plans for the ghetto immediately; he even took steps to gain the trust of the Ältestenrat and the ghetto inhabitants. He organized the supply of food rations to the ghetto, promised larger rations to those employed at hard labor, and moderated the inspections at the ghetto gate, as if he did not object to Jews smuggling in food when returning from their workplaces in the city.

Goecke's behavior did not match the information that the Ältestenrat gathered in various ways about his activities and attitude toward the Jews. He was known in many locations as a cruel and murderous expert in the liquidation of ghettos. The ghetto residents' suspicions about his plans grew when in mid-September they discovered that the Germans were liquidating the Vilna Ghetto. Most of those fit for physical labor were deported to Estonia to the front regions, while the weak, the old, and the children were murdered at Ponar. Several thousand remaining Jews were sent to labor camps around Vilna.

Gradually, the Ältestenrat discovered details of Goecke's plans, which led them to assume that the Kovno Ghetto was about to follow in the footsteps of the Vilna Ghetto. Goecke was too shrewd and experienced to reveal all his plans at once – that is, the deportation of a large part of the ghetto population to distant locations and destruction of those "unfit for labor." But he did not hide from the Ältestenrat the fact that the ghetto had already been declared a concentration camp (*Konzentrationslager Kauen*) and that soon most of the laborers would be sent to several large labor camps in Kovno and its environs, as the first stage in the process of dividing the ghetto into several prison camps. He told the Ältestenrat that it could determine the candidates for transfer to the labor camps.

Again the Ältestenrat faced the decision of whether to cooperate with the Nazi authorities in carrying out the plan – which undoubtedly would lead to a deterioration in ghetto conditions and showed all the signs of leading to more convenient conditions for the final liquidation – or whether it should refrain from cooperating in this case. This was not the first time the Ältestenrat faced a fateful dilemma, as during the *Aktions* period in 1941 it had not decided against cooperation. But the situation at this point was different from that in 1941. First, it was now clear – and at this point there was no longer any room for doubt – that the Nazis had a plan for the total destruction of the Jews and permitting the Jews of Kovno to live was only a temporary situation. Second, the situation on the fronts had radically changed. Then, in 1941, the Germans enjoyed one success after another, but now their armies were suffering heavy blows on all fronts, and their defeat seemed imminent. In those very days, early September 1943, the radio listeners in the ghetto received the news of the surrender of Italy and the landing of the Allied forces on the European continent. This made a great impression on the Jews.[1]

Inside the ghetto as well, the situation was vastly different than during the *Aktions* period. Before, there were only the first buds of an underground, and it barely possessed even one pistol. But in 1943, the Ältestenrat knew that the underground had established a force of several hundred fighters; it had also purchased weapons and smuggled them into the ghetto – guns, pistols, hand

---

1. Testimony of Leib Garfunkel, YVSA, 21.

grenades, and even a machine gun; and its leaders had a detailed plan to defend the ghetto when the time arrived.

Still, the Ältestenrat's decision in this case was not different from its decisions in all the previous instances. We do not know whether this question was even raised on the agenda of its meetings, or whether its acquiescence to the decree of the *Kasernierung* (literally, "quartering in barracks" or "billeting"; actually, relocation) – as Goecke called his plans – was an obvious development. We do know that eventually the Ältestenrat established this special committee – the Billeting Committee – to attend to issues related to transferring the ghetto residents to the labor camps.

In principle, the underground organizations also accepted the decree as a fait accompli. The proof is that major underground activists joined the Billeting Committee, such as Dr. Volsonok, engineer Shimon Ratner, and Moshe Levin.[2] Their participation in the committee, however, was to ensure that underground members would not be included in the lists of those designated for the labor camps. In this the underground representatives demonstrated great efficiency, as we know of only a few instances in which underground members were sent to labor camps, and these were ordinary members, not active ones.[3] This was nothing new – throughout 1943 the underground had safeguarded its members from deportation during the period of recruitment for the labor camps in Kaidan, Palemon, and Koshedar. This is apparently the reason that underground activity in these locations was weak and disconnected from the underground center in the ghetto, and sometimes the residents even refused to accept its authority.[4] The "protection" policy arose from the general strategy of safeguarding and strengthening the fighting force, and was not a goal in and of itself. Clearly, the conditions that existed inside the ghetto for strengthening the fighting force did not exist in any of the labor camps outside it.

But the underground certainly did not view the *Kasernierung* decree as the final stage. Its members realized that this was only the first step in the final, definitive liquidation of the ghetto. Developments within the underground reveal that all participant organizations shared this awareness, although not to the same

---

2. Gar, *Umkum*, 156.
3. Testimony of Ester Wolfson, YVSA, recording 1.
4. On the independent underground in Kaidan camp, see chapter 9.

extent. A concrete expression of this was the Augustova Plan and the argument that erupted surrounding it, among both the ranks and the leadership.

The Augustova Plan, which ended in total failure, was proposed to the underground by representatives of the Anti-Fascist Organization. As a member testifies:

> When we began to discuss the Augustova Plan...we come to the most miserable part of our work. Haim Yellin brought the plan to go to Augustova from the anti-Semitic Jew Ziman, formerly a teacher in the Kovno trade high school. Gershon [Henach] Ziman,[5] teacher of Yiddish language and literature, closed his ears to the painful cries of his tortured and hunted people, and replied to Haim Yellin: "Unfortunately, we can't accept Jewish fighters in the Rudniki Forests. Russians and Lithuanians – yes!" He wanted to make an exception of Haim Yellin. He made him an offer to stay and not return to the ghetto. When Haim Yellin explained to him whom he represented and who awaited him, Ziman gave him the Augustova plan, and added cynically that we had to build our own partisan base and not come to an already existing one. When Haim Yellin said we have no weapons, he replied that weapons were acquired from the Germans.[6]

Abba Kovner's testimony offers support for the assumption that the Augustova Plan came from Henach Ziman:

> It was in September 1943, after the arrival of Jurgis [Henach Ziman], the brigade commander, at his headquarters in the Rudniki [Forests]. At one of the meetings with him, I discovered Haim Yellin in his headquarters. The Augustova episode began then.... The Augustova Plan was also connected to us – the Jewish battalions [from Vilna]. We had four battalions then. At first, we saw it only as a desire to disperse the large concentration of Jews throughout this forest, which was not so convenient, but there was another plan as well – mainly political. The role of the Lithuanian brigade was purely political; it wanted to base its military activities on Lithuanian soil, surrounding its capital cities.... The brigade was not made up of Lithuanians, but its name

---

5. Ziman's first name is unclear. Some called him Gershon, others Henach. The Lithuanian sources always call him Genrikas.

6. Meir Leib Goldschmidt, YVSA, letters 1, 5.

was Lithuanian and its leadership was Lithuanian. At first, it was located in Byelorussia, in the Naroch area. When [Jurgis's] headquarters came to the Rudniki Forests, it was as if the Lithuanian brigade was relieved of responsibility for a foreign partisan area. Its plan was to establish partisan bases for the Lithuanian movement in purely Lithuanian areas … and to place a Lithuanian brigade in the Augustova area. Then Yellin arrived and most certainly told that there were units inside the ghetto that were prepared for and enthusiastic about partisan activity. At that point, apparently, the plan was authorized for establishing the base in Augustova. In retrospect, this plan was dangerous, unproven, and had not been checked thoroughly.[7]

It is difficult to know to what extent the plan's formulators believed in the possibility of its implementation, but they saw no other way. Beforehand, they attempted to make contact with the partisan base in the Jonava Forests. For this purpose, an important activist of the Anti-Fascist Organization, Mara Lan, was sent to these forests. She did not return to the ghetto, and for a long time no one knew what had become of her. Eventually, it transpired that she had joined Solomin's group, and from this we learn that Solomin had again rejected the plan to bring fighters from Kovno Ghetto to his bases. The Communists in the ghetto could not delude themselves that Solomin might change his position. The Augustova Plan then became the focal point, and it was proposed to the joint leadership of the underground.

Communist representatives in the JFO command spared no effort to sway the opinions of the other leadership members in support of the plan. Dr. Volsonok, who served as the spokesman of the Communists, played a particularly active role in this.[8] He described the Augustova Forests as an appropriate base for large partisan battalions, and recounted that a group of "expert partisans" (*spetzgruppe*) had been sent from Moscow and had parachuted into these forests in order to assist the ghetto fighters. He praised the plan highly as opening opportunities for transferring "masses of youth and adults" from the ghetto into

---

7. Testimony of Abba Kovner, YVSA, 6 (recording 2). On the other hand, it is speculated that in September 1943 Jurgis had not yet arrived in the Rudniki Forests. We know that he was there on October 4, 1943 (Mončiunskas, 165). Perhaps the witness erred in the date he gave in his testimony (September 1943), and it should be October.
8. Testimony of Yona Rochman, YVSA, 13.

the forests, and as the only real answer to Goecke's plans, whose intention was without a doubt the destruction of the remaining Jews in Kovno.

Besides the Anti-Fascist Organization, the Hashomer Hatzair members were apparently the first to support the plan. Throughout the summer of 1943, a noticeable rapprochement took place between them and the Anti-Fascist Organization. In one testimony, the witness even said that Hashomer Hatzair had joined the AFO[9] – in other words, that the two groups had united organizationally – but we have no confirmation of this from other sources. We also know that Hashomer Hatzair activists were divided regarding their stance toward the Communists. Two activists of this movement, Leo Ziman and Eli Rauzuk, who served as go-betweens with the Communists in the ghetto, did not agree on this issue. Ziman represented the "leftist" position, demanding intensified contact with them, while Rauzuk insisted on the preservation of organizational independence, with only coordination of the operations.

The majority opinion in the Hashomer Hatzair chapter seems to have followed Eli Rauzuk, and thus Rauzuk replaced Ziman as the intermediary. Yona Rochman reports: "Leo Ziman, and later Eli Rauzuk, served as intermediary between the Hashomer Hatzair chapter and the Communists,"[10] and "The Augustova idea was initiated after the Communists argued that partisans were already located there. After each meeting with the Communists, we received a report from our representatives. There were arguments between Eli and Leo. Leo was more influenced, and so we replaced Leo with Eli."[11]

The practical cooperation between the two organizations was mainly in the field of military training and purchasing military equipment. For example, Hannah Ziman was once sent to the Tot Organization brigade on Ozheshko Street to get nitroglycerine, apparently in order to construct Molotov cocktails. She was also sent there in order to contact a Hashomer Hatzair member from Poland who worked there, regarding preparation of a car for transporting underground members to Augustova.[12] Gita Foger recounts that she led a training cell of Hashomer Hatzair members, and that she received instructions from Eli Rauzuk on how to organize work in the cell and how to teach weapons use. Once she

9. Testimony of Shmuel Ben Menachem (Dietz), YVSA, 5.
10. Testimony of Yona Rochman, YVSA, 19.
11. Ibid., 17.
12. Ibid., 13.

even received a rifle bolt from him.[13] In her testimony, she does not specifically say from whom Rauzuk received the instructions and the rifle parts for training sessions. No one was allowed to know this, in order to keep the information secret. But in this context, Eli was defined as a liaison, and we know that at that time he was the liaison with the Communists.

Dov Levin reports on that same training cell:

> I contacted the partisan movement through Gita Foger, whom I knew from the Hashomer Hatzair chapter in Kovno. She got in touch with me in the summer of 1943 and connected me with the chapter. I began to go to the meeting place, which was at 63 Linkuvos Street, not far from the apartment where my family was living. At that time, regular chapter activities were being held. In the autumn, around September, Gita revealed that "there's something else here besides the chapter." She told me that we were not getting together just for entertainment. She introduced herself as my contact person. In our three-person cell, we were Batsheva Agranat, Gita Foger, and myself. I remember the day she brought a rifle bolt wrapped in the Lithuanian Fascist newspaper. She taught me how to disassemble and cock it. We also reassembled a rifle. We had written material to study, which we learned by heart. We learned practical topography, first aid, and other topics. Aside from this occupation, we were also responsible for collecting bottles and other materials, such as backpacks and sacks. Everything was done in secret. I didn't reveal it, not even to my parents or my sister. Even in the chapter, we did not speak of it.[14]

This was the position of Hashomer Hatzair during the period preceding the Augustova mission, according to the testimonies of the members. The testimony of the underground members outside Hashomer Hatzair is also interesting. Below are statements of Zionist Socialist members:

> At first, they worked together with the Communists. They coordinated their activities closely. When we proposed that they join us (meaning Eretz Israel Ha'ovedet – the Palestine Labor Movement) they were not willing to do so, but rather joined together with the Communists. This was before Augustova.

---

13. Testimony of Gita Foger-Turchin, YVSA, 3 (recording 1).
14. *YLHG* 20, 93.

There was a period I remember, when we organized and proposed that they join us.... [We proposed this] to Eli Rauzuk, I don't remember [other] names – at any rate, we had contact, but they did not agree. This aroused deep animosity in our circles toward them.[15]

The opinion of Hashomer Hatzair was that we should only consider the combat aspect of joining the partisans. Eli Rauzuk preferred this aspect to the rescue issue.... They saw it as a goal in and of itself.... We [the Zionist Socialists] saw it as rescue, or one method of rescue. [We accepted] any method for saving lives. The consideration was to rescue each person where he was.... We let the person who can fight go where the fighting was, and let the weak individual stay in his hiding place.[16]

It was no surprise that the Augustova Plan was accepted by Hashomer Hatzair members with no particular reservations. Other underground organizations, however, had reservations, which were expressed apparently in the positions of Matzok (the underground alliance of the Zionist movements) representatives on the JFO command. The most vocal opposition came from the IBZ, the Irgun Brit Zion. Although some of its rank-and-file members wanted to go out to the forests, the leadership position was negative in principle, and the arguments within the brigades and cells led to the conclusion that they would not participate in Augustova. This became the official IBZ position, but the leadership did not prevent individual members from joining those who planned to go out and even assisted them.

IBZ activists also did not view the Augustova Plan as a solution for the danger of liquidation of the ghetto. At most, several hundred youths would depart for Augustova, while the danger of liquidation threatened thousands of ghetto residents, primarily families in which the children were the primary caretakers. They did not consider the IBZ authorized to demand that its members abandon their parents, brothers, and sisters in this time of danger. The concept of battling the enemy hundreds of miles away from the ghetto among the Soviet partisans, where there was no room for Jewish national unity, was not enough to justify this. For the IBZ, the answer to Goecke's scheme would be the *malina* project – the

---

15. Testimony of Yitzhak Kashiv (Kapchovsky), YVSA, 8 (recording 2); compare testimony of Haim Gechtel (Galin), YVSA, 12 (recording 6).
16. Testimony of Menachem Ganuni (Sadovsky), YVSA, 13–14 (recording 2b).

secret underground shelters. With these, the members would not be forced to abandon their families, and the organization would accept its public responsibility for the fate of the entire ghetto.

As for the armed fighting force in the ghetto, in which the IBZ played a significant role, its position was that even now an uprising should not be planned, even though the scheme for liquidation of the ghetto was apparent. "Dying with honor is a noble slogan, but completely unrealistic, because the atmosphere in the ghetto is not supportive – the ground has not been prepared, and we have no base of support, neither inside nor out. This might be applicable to a certain group of people hiding in a place and preparing for real battle, but we do not have the right to impose [uprising] on the entire ghetto."[17] They concluded that the only way was to hide in the *malinas* during the *Aktion*. If the Germans and their accomplices discovered the *malinas*, then it would be time for armed resistance. They would have the opportunity for it, as they would store in the *malinas* the weapons smuggled into the ghetto, and during the *Aktion* distribute them among members trained in their use. Another IBZ member said in his testimony: "A sentence said in one of the meetings still rings in my ears: better to die than fight under the red flag."[18]

These were the two extreme positions – on the one hand, there were the Communists, joined by Hashomer Hatzair, and on the other, there was the IBZ leadership and groups close to them in Matzok. The opinion of the other organizations and activists was a compromise between the two extremes, as was the opinion of the underground leadership. In actuality, the Communists accepted this compromise position.

As we discover from many testimonies and the development of events, their position was approximately as follows: The fighting force in the ghetto was established so that the Jews could wage armed resistance against any attempt at destruction of the remainder of Kovno Jewry. The question was how to behave

---

17. Testimony of Masha Gail-Yaron, YVSA, 15–16 (recording 4).

18. Testimony of Moshe Levin, YVSA, 4. Moshe Kahanovitz states that "the sharp debate waged in the Vilna Ghetto – battle in the ghetto or go out to the forests – was not held in the locations with the two largest concentrations of Jews, Kovno and Minsk" (*Milhemet ha-Partizanim ha-Yehudim be-Mizrah Eiropa*" [The battle of the Jewish partisans in Eastern Europe], *Ayanot* [Tel Aviv, 5714], 87). But this was incorrect regarding the Kovno Ghetto. Zvie Brown also erred on this point in his article "*Di shlacht oiyfen breg teich*," *Zichronot fun Kavner Geta* (Memories from Kovno Ghetto), *Neyvalt*, May 19, 1950.

in the new situation that was created with Goecke's arrival and declaration of the ghetto as a concentration camp, which could only be interpreted as preparation for the final destruction of the ghetto. Between the two methods – the first, immediate initiated resistance, and the second, hiding in the *malinas* and armed resistance after discovery – the second option was preferable. But at the same time, the fighting force could be used in a third manner, namely, sending a group outside the ghetto, with the clear intention of establishing partisan bases there. There was no conflict between the positions; on the contrary, this plan eliminated the hopelessness inherent in the *malina* concept. The bases outside the ghetto would serve as the longed-for rear support in any struggle against deportation and destruction inside the ghetto, and as destinations for retreat after the last defensive battle. Establishment of such bases therefore became the urgent agenda of the ghetto underground. Of course, for these reasons, bases closer to the ghetto were preferable to those much farther away, such as in the Rudniki Forests. For purely partisan reasons, they did not dare dream of real bases near Kovno, but rather intermediate bases, which would serve as stops on the way to farther locations.

These considerations are clearly revealed in the testimonies of Beitar members. One of the Beitar activists from the ghetto recounts:

> We thought that rebellion in the Kovno Ghetto was hopeless, like the Warsaw Ghetto Revolt. Here the conditions were also unfavorable tactically. The ghetto territory was demilitarized, and the atmosphere inside and the composition of the population did not enable such an action. We also needed to collect weapons.... If the plan succeeded and we got out [of the ghetto], then we would pursue military operations from there. To us, conditions were not good for going out, tactically as well. The ghetto territory...to constitute a force that could absorb all those fleeing from the ghetto."[19]

As mentioned, the Communists' "Albina Plan" also spoke of establishment of intermediate bases around Kovno. This plan was dictated by the interests of the Communist underground in the city, not in the ghetto, and in this respect, the instructions that Albina brought with her were the same as those Solomin

---

19. Testimony of Baruch Ezged (Camber), YVSA, 5.

followed previously – namely, that under the Gestapo reign of terror no underground was possible without partisan bases nearby.

The Communists began implementing the plan right away. Apparently, during his first visit to the Rudniki Forests, Haim Yellin arranged a meeting with a Lithuanian-Russian paratrooper, Konstantin (Kostia) Radyonov, who later led the Kovno battalions in those forests.[20] The meeting seems to have been held in late September or early October 1943 in Murava, a suburb of Kovno. Earlier, Radyonov had begun to establish an underground organization there and contact was established between the Anti-Fascist Organization and the Communist underground in Murava. Soon after this, they established an intermediate partisan base. In the forest next to Murava, they built several dugouts, intended for hiding weapons and temporary accommodation for underground members. Haim Yellin and several members of his organization worked diligently to establish the base. In the forest near Zapyškis, a town about 16 km west of Kovno, they tried to establish a similar base. Members who went out for this purpose included Ya'akov Levi, Yitzhak Boruchovitz, Ya'akov Ratner, Ya'akov Holtzman, and others. But before they were able to complete their work, the Germans discovered the operation and the fighters had to abandon the area. By contrast, the Murava base lasted for some time and was very useful, both for the city underground as well as the ghetto fighters.

It was clear, however, to the leaders of the Anti-Fascist Organization in the ghetto, who were already experienced in this field, that the main bases could not be constructed around Kovno. They had little difficulty in convincing the Matzok leadership of this. Thus the JFO command decided to establish bases in the Augustova Forests. From then on, the problem was technical and organizational, and the best forces of the underground were mobilized to implement the project.

At that time, several factors were in place, which were necessary for the success of the operation. According to the evaluation of the JFO joint command, the first stage required that they send some 150 fighters to the Augustova Forests; there was no problem recruiting this number among the members of the underground organizations, who had practiced for months in the combat companies and were ready for any circumstance. Although the specific character of the

---

20. *PKG*, 83–84.

operation demanded special knowledge from its participants, the JFO command already had a staff of trainers, former military personnel, who could teach the fighters the needed information. Also the problem of leaving the ghetto was not a particular concern for the JFO command. Assistance on the part of the police and other ghetto institutions was almost assured – within certain boundaries, of course, and under strict conditions of security and secrecy.

The most difficult question was how the fighters would travel the long route from Kovno to the Augustova Forests, a distance of some 120 km, through a densely populated region. The JFO command already had experience of two types of illegal movement outside the ghetto: the roaming of the "rabbits," the nickname for Jews who sneaked out of the ghetto into the city for the purpose of smuggling or underground activities and roamed the Kovno environs, and the patrols of small groups of fighters throughout Lithuania in search of the partisans. The "rabbits" developed a clever technique for swift movement around the city, while deceiving the Germans and Lithuanian policemen. By contrast, the second type of experience, the patrols throughout Lithuania, mostly ended in tragedy. Not only did the patrols fail to achieve their goal, but their members were unable to return to the ghetto and died in skirmishes with the police and gendarmerie. For the Augustova Plan, the second type of experience was an acute warning that they should search for methods other than those of the initial patrols.

But apparently the JFO command members – particularly the Communists among them, because they were intimately familiar with the history of the first patrols – ignored this lesson. They decided that those planned for departure would receive small weapons – pistols and hand grenades – that could easily be hidden from view. They would behave like Lithuanians – they would be dressed like Lithuanian laborers or farmers, and some would carry tools. They would speak only Lithuanian among themselves and would try to limit contact with the local population, so that they would not be discovered as Jews. They would move by day, not by night, because travel by night was likely to attract attention. They would have to avoid using the weapons in their possession at all costs, until they reached their destination.

In accordance with the principles above, the JFO command decided that those leaving would move in small groups and on different roads. The command would prepare exact routes in numerous variations, and the departing fighters would have to memorize the details, so that they could advance confidently and not have to ask questions of the local people. Because the route was long and they could not assume that all the fighters would overcome the challenges of the route, they decided to send a scout group of the fastest fighters, whose job would be to take key points along the route and wait there for the remaining fighters in order to guide them. The first group would then return to the ghetto and report on the progress of the mission. This was the same idea as the intermediate bases in a different format. They apparently decided to establish bases in the Kazlu-Ruda Forests (30 km south of Kovno) and near Yezne (50 km southeast of Kovno).

These were the general outlines of the plan. The JFO command immediately set to work sketching maps and refining the details of the instructions. For this job, they recruited fighters outside their ranks, such as Ephraim Senior, who sketched maps, and Tevke (Tuvia) Pilovnik, who constructed primitive compasses in the home of Malka Pugatzky.[21]

In the meantime, preparations began in the training cells. The training sessions were adapted for the upcoming mission and their pace was intensified. Close attention was paid to studying the details of the route, so much so that one of the participants still remembered the details in his testimony:

> After the Aleksot bridge, we turn right and walk to the Murava farm. From there, we go up the path that leads to the hill, reach Mironiski village, and after walking 3 km south we reach Taborishki [Tabariškės]. From there we continue in the same direction to Girininkai, where there is a narrow railroad track. We walk along this railroad track 3 km west until we reach a canal. There we turn left and continue along the canal until it widens and joins the Pilvė River. We cross the Pilvė stream and reach the large village of Papilvis.[22]

We do not know exactly when the first advance party was formed – almost certainly in late September or early October.[23] The group numbered some twenty individuals. It was composed of volunteers from all the organizations who agreed to participate in the mission – according to a ratio decided by the JFO command.

---

21. These "compasses" were merely magnetized needles. When they were placed in a bowl of water, they pointed north and south (testimony of Malka Pugatzky-Smali, YVSA, 12, recording 4).
22. See the history of the Netzer pioneer group at Kibbutz Beit Zera, 1946 (manuscript).
23. Some believe it was formed and left the ghetto before then, in August (testimony of Michael Yitzhaki [Gelbtrunk], YVSA, 13). But this belief is not confirmed in other sources.

Some of the participants were Lazer Zodikov, Haim Gechtel (Galin), Shmulik Mordkovsky, Yankel Kaveh, Avraham Frenkel, Aharon Vilenchuk, Michael Gelbtrunk, Moshe Zimlovitz, Yosef Feuerstein, Haya Shmuelov, Shlomo Perlstein, and Leah Port.

One member of the group recounts:

> I recall that they told us about Augustova. We learned all these things from our movement representatives. This was Isaac Serebnitzky, who was our movement's representative to the JFO command. He told us, and we decided immediately who would go out in the first group. Shmulik, Yankel Kaveh, and myself – the three of us went in the first group. No one said we had to go out. They said, there is this number of places ... and we said that we were going.... We received information that contact had been made with the partisan movement. We learned that in the Augustova Forests, Soviet paratroopers would be dropped, in order to establish a new partisan base. They proposed that we organize this new base.... In the first group, we were some eighteen individuals from all the movements.... We received very few weapons. I think we had only two pistols. Every one received a knife manufactured in the ghetto, a long knife. We had three hand grenades, if I'm not mistaken, and that was all the weapons. We met at what was called a *shtaub*, a kind of headquarters. I think it was in the room of Haim David Ratner, or Haim Yellin. It was on Kriščiukaičio Street – the entire group met there, and there we received the latest information before departure. At that meeting Lazer Zodikov was appointed the group commander.[24]

To enable the group to leave the ghetto, false identification was prepared – apparently by underground members who worked in the labor office. They were identified as a labor brigade sent outside the city to fell trees. Furthermore, the manager of the small ghetto farm gave the group three carts and horses, for two reasons: first, to heighten the impression that this was a brigade of tree fellers; and second, to enable those departing to move away from Kovno more quickly. An Ältestenrat member recounts that on the part of those responsible for the ghetto, giving the carts to the group was an act that "defied all logic": they were aware of the danger that the mission posed to the entire ghetto, yet they agreed

---

24. Testimony of Haim Gechtel (Galin), YVSA, 13 (recording 6).

under "heavy pressure from the partisan leaders in the ghetto."[25] The farm manager was told that the carts would take the people no more than 5–10 km, and would be back in the ghetto by 8 A.M. (apparently the group left at dawn, at 4 or 5 A.M.). But the carts returned only in the evening. For the farm manager, and for those Ältestenrat members who were aware of the matter, this was a day of anxious anticipation. They suspected that the entire group had been caught and imprisoned, and that the plan had been discovered by the Gestapo. (The farm manager, M. Potruch, died two weeks later. According to one theory, the intense apprehension on that day was the main reason for his death.)

In the evening they learned that the first stage of the plan had succeeded. The carts continued until they reached the forest edge, about 20 km from Kovno, where they left the fighters. They then returned safely to the ghetto. The group continued on foot. A witness reports on the fate of the group:

> They took us to the forest – I can't remember the name of the forest.... The order was that on the way we would not enter into any skirmish. With our first steps as free people, of course we removed the signs of the ghetto, the yellow stars, and began to walk in the forest. Right away we almost made a mistake, because the commander Zodikov was not familiar with the map.... A few moments later, we ran into the forest warden. We were all shocked. We did not know what to do. We overcame our confusion and continued. Unfamiliarity with the map was a serious obstacle. I remember that Shmulik [Mordkovsky] came up, studied the map, and immediately began to familiarize himself with the paths and roads. He quickly became the group guide, and so we continued until evening, until we reached the railroad tracks.... Shmulik and Aharonchik Vilenchuk went out to scout the tracks. We waited for the scouts to come – in vain. Perhaps they strayed to the side and lost contact.... We did not know what to do. Arguments broke out. What could we do without a map, without scouts?.... Most of the members decided to return to the ghetto. Five people, including myself, decided to advance. We received the weapons of those returning, and parted from them.
>
> After advancing somewhat, we realized that it was difficult to find our way without a map. We saw that we had no choice – we had to return to the

---

25. Testimony of Leib Garfunkel, YVSA, 13, and his book, 170.

ghetto. This was at the 35 km mark from Kovno. We placed the weapons into food containers, dug holes, and buried the weapons next to the column with the kilometer mark, so that it would be easy to find the place. The three of us – Moshe Milner, Lazer Zodikov, and myself – tried to join a brigade of Jews from the ghetto that worked near the area, laying a cable for the German army. We were not successful. The Germans noticed us when we approached, and informed on us to the Gestapo, but they found nothing on us. We spent one night there and were sent back to the ghetto. There we discovered to our joy that all members of the group had returned.[26]

Yellin and Galpern said that some members of the first group, led by Dr. Shlomo Perlstein, continued south, looking for contact with partisans, and were killed. These details have not been confirmed.[27]

The ghetto leadership had not yet drawn conclusions about the departure and return of the advance party, when the calamity for which they had awaited with foreboding arrived: deportation to Estonia. According to the testimony of people who were members of the Ältestenrat or who worked in their institutions, the Estonia deportation was preceded by a base act of deception by Goecke toward the Ältestenrat.[28] In late September or early October, Goecke informed the Ältestenrat of his plan to establish a labor camp for 3,500 ghetto residents in the village of Eżerėlis near the town of Zapyškis (Sapizishok), some 30 km from Kovno. The Billeting Committee was charged with composing the lists of individuals who would be transferred to this camp. Preparation of the lists continued for several weeks, during which Goecke tried to give the impression that this was just a regular operation, like the establishment of the camps in Keidan and Koshedar. The Ältestenrat was apparently tempted into believing him.

On October 25, Goecke asked them to hand over the lists, still promising that the people would be sent to the labor camp in Eżerėlis. But several hours

---

26. Testimony of Haim Gechtel (Galin), YVSA, 14 (recording 6); see also protocol from the partisan's meeting at Kibbutz Yagur, 8–9, and compare testimony of Avraham Frenkel, YVSA, 3 ff.

27. One of the participants in this group, Leah Port, along with her boyfriend, Shmuel Ingel, later joined a group of fourteen Jews that wandered southern Lithuania, led by Abba Weinstein (see Abba Gefen, PORTZEI HA-MAHSOMIM [Breaking the barriers] (Tel Aviv: Yesod, 1961), 51–52.

28. Gar, *Umkum*, 157–65; Garfunkel, *Kovno*, 147–52.

after they gave him the list, news reached the ghetto that led them to conclude that the plan for a labor camp in Ežerėlis was only a façade for a terrible *Aktion* that the Germans planned to carry out the next day. We do not know whether the Ältestenrat was in contact with the leaders of the underground that evening, but from the testimonies of members of various underground organizations, we learn that the headquarters was on alert. Although they knew that no underground members were included on the lists delivered to Goecke, at that point there was no longer any reason to rely on this method of keeping members off the lists. They had reason to suspect that the Germans were preparing a large-scale *Aktion*, and the lists were merely a method of calming the Jews.

That evening, the command decided that the next morning they would put the Augustova Plan fully into action – meaning they would send to the Augstova Forests all members of the organizations who had prepared for it. If they discovered that this was indeed a mass *Aktion* and there was no way out, they would break through the ghetto fence. The remaining underground members, including the members of the command, would go down into the *malina*s and stay there until the *Aktion* died down. That night, they activated the secret alarm system, and underground members were placed on alert. Those meant to go out to the Augustova Forests were informed of the meeting point where they would gather early in the morning ready to go.

At that point, the Ältestenrat runners were occupied with another job: they placed a notice on the noticeboards that the Ältestenrat had been ordered to supply three thousand Jews for labor in Ežerėlis. Emphasizing that lists of those slated for the new camp had been prepared, the Ältestenrat requested that the ghetto inhabitants follow exactly the instructions of the Jewish ghetto police, who would come to the houses and hand out the notices for travel to Ežerėlis. The notice ended with an expression of sympathy for those whom fate determined would go to the camp, and wished them happiness in their new home....[29]

At 5 A.M., Goecke arrived in the ghetto accompanied by a large ensemble of Gestapo officials, German policemen, and Ukrainian soldiers. Security around the ghetto was reinforced, and a long convoy of freight trucks entered. The Ältestenrat members and ghetto police were called. The police had to round up the candidates for deportation alongside the trucks, together with their families.

---

29. Gar, *Umkum*, 160.

The police fulfilled the order, but apparently many on the lists hid. The roundup proceeded slowly. The Ältestenrat tried to prepare new lists, but in the afternoon the Gestapo decided to take matters into their own hands. The German and Ukrainian soldiers received the order to act, and they attacked the ghetto with indescribable fury and cruelty. Their wild rampage in the ghetto alleys continued until the evening. Some three thousand men, women, and children were packed into the trucks and sent out of the ghetto.

The underground leadership followed the events carefully throughout the day. In the morning, they received reports from the meeting points throughout the ghetto of the gathering of fighters ready to leave and join the partisans. The fighters waited for the order to depart, but the command apparently hesitated to give the order due to the police and SS forces gathered around the ghetto and inside it. The idea of immediate escape was apparently finally rejected the moment that SS and Ukrainians went into action. The underground fighters were commanded to go down to the *malina*s and dig in there, weapons ready for use. The descent into the *malina*s was carried out under the strictest secrecy.

Below is one story from the events of that day:

That night we were ordered by messengers to gather early the next morning at 36 Ariogalos Street, ready to go. Each of us had to inform another, according to a pre-arranged order. In the morning, when everyone in the ghetto was frightened and agitated and looking for a corner in which to hide, a group of young men (most with moustaches) and women stood together in one of the rooms, wearing short jackets and boots, with backpacks under their arms.... This was the first time the members of the combat units came face-to-face with their fellow fighters. There were members of the Communist organization, Revisionists, IBZ, Shomrim [Hashomer Hatzair], and ZS.... Some of us (I'm talking about the Shomrim) gathered at 27 Linkuvos Street, in the home of Yerachmiel Voskoboynik (Leo Ziman, Moshe Patrikansky, Yona Rochman, Eli Rauzuk – members of the directorate) and in the other part of the ghetto (which was disconnected from us by the "neck") at the home of Penina Sukenik. Many of the Communist leaders were there, including Haim Yellin.... When searches were conducted there, they hid in a *malina* in the courtyard and waited with loaded pistols for the Germans and Ukrainians to enter at any moment....

At about three o'clock, we received the order to go to the other side of the ghetto and gather in the basement of the large apartment building.... We said the password ... to the Jewish policeman standing there (he was also part of the organization – his name was Daniel Birger). He let us in. Downstairs, again someone checked us over carefully. It was completely dark in this basement, although electric lights flickered here and there. We went down through a square hole. A small room was revealed, with a large pile of coal. We thought this was the place, but we were wrong. We were ordered to crawl through the coal into a narrow tunnel, where two strong hands grabbed me and threw me into a dark corridor. From there I entered a small hall full of people....

I knew many faces there. Only at that moment did we realize that we had been working together for a long time, in one organization, for one goal. Strong handshakes confirmed these thoughts. Every second more friends came in, or rather, were thrown in. Then they closed the breach upstairs with coal, closed the doors, and we sat in silent anticipation.... Suddenly the *malina* commander ordered us to collect all the tobacco, cigarette papers, food, and drink. Then they distributed food and smoking rations. Holding our breaths, we sat and listened to the commotion outside. This was apparently the Ukrainians, who had surrounded the apartment block and were searching for people. We heard muffled knocking all around, the screams of women and children. We sat as if on hot coals for several hours until the clamor died down. After a while, a special messenger arrived and informed us that we could leave. The quota was filled and the people were sent out of the ghetto.[30]

Some testimonies about the underground during the Estonia *Aktion* mention weapons in the *malina*s and the decision to resist. One fighter recounts:

We received the order that everyone had to gather ... to be ready. I came, and did not leave the place. We went down there spontaneously. We saw there was no other way ... Some of us had "cold" weapons, and Haim [Yellin] had a firearm. He had a pistol. We saw it.... There were other weapons as well. There was some other crate. We talked about it. There was an order ... that as soon

---

30. *Al tekufat Augustova* [The Augustova period], memoirs of Dov Levin (manuscript), written soon after the events (September 19, 1944), 3.

as they found us – we should open fire. We should resist. We also talked about breaching the fence.... They tightened security, and no one could go out.[31]

There are signs that even outside the organized underground, which was under the leadership of the JFO command, the idea for resistance came up during the Estonia *Aktion*. One author writes:

> On that terrible day, we already knew that this was the beginning of the end. Those of us who hid in the bunkers, prepared for battle, if the Germans would discover us. If a German would come in, we would shoot him and kill him, before the Germans would manage to kill the rest of us. I myself hid in a bunker along with eighty-seven other Jews. The Jews told me that in our hideout we had weapons, and if they discovered us – we would resist. "Rabbi" – they said to me, pointing to a sack with weapons inside – "this is where the weapons are hidden. We think that the Rabbi must learn to shoot. We will no longer permit them to slaughter us like sheep."[32]

Things did not, however, reach the point of resistance. According to the information we possess, the Germans did not discover even one *malina* that day.[33] The underground leadership could count one achievement to its credit: the deportation barely touched the ranks of the underground. Reasons for this were the system of *malina*s, the information and communications network that operated smoothly, and the members' discipline and speed. But most of the members lost their parents and their brothers and sisters, who were deported to Estonia.

The underground members did not have time to contemplate their losses. They remained on alert even after the *Aktion* was over; the JFO command was about to decide when the groups would make their way to Augustova. The loss of their relatives brought the members even closer to each other. This was particularly felt in the various youth movements. Barriers between underground cells fell away. Larger groups of ten to twelve people joined together spontaneously in the empty houses, awaiting orders from the Command.

---

31. Testimony of Baruch Gofer (Grodnick), YVSA, 10 (recording 4); compare also testimony of Malka Pugatzky-Smali, YVSA, 12 (recording 4); Rivka Gordon YVSA, letter 2:5.
32. Oshry, *Hurban Lita*, 121–22.
33. For additional details about the Estonia deportation and the fate of the deported, see Gar, *Umkum*, 160 ff.; Garfunkel, *Kovno*, 149 ff.; S. Dolnitzky, "*A tag hinter shtechige draten*," in Sudarsky et al., *Lita*, 1735–42.

We went out [of the *malinas*] and were commanded to meet at 9 P.M. in the pre-arranged locations. We were completely sure that that night, we would depart. Many of us returned to our homes and found only the four walls. They took our parents and other family members. This was my situation as well – my father, mother, and twin sister were taken the night before. But we had to be ready and not cut off contact between us, because any moment could bring news.... Most of the members, from all the different organizations, slept in groups in empty houses of fellow members. We gathered at Penina's house at 9 Broliu Street. We organized ourselves in three rooms and in the kitchen (the residents had been taken that day, and all their property remained). We had plenty of food. We appointed two cooks. We slept three to a bed, or on the floor.[34]

Meanwhile, the JFO command made final preparations for sending the fighters on their way. The ghetto work assignments had been disrupted by the Estonia deportation, and the command could take advantage of the disorganization beside the ghetto gates to send out the groups, which were organized into platoons with twenty to twenty-five members in each. Each platoon had a commander, or *politruk*[35] as some called it in their testimonies, and the platoon members came from a variety of groups. The platoons were divided into cells, with three to six people in each. The fighters left the ghetto one cell at a time. According to the plan, the cells of each platoon were supposed to meet at a prearranged meeting point, a sizeable distance from Kovno. Each platoon carried equipment: a map and compass for the commander, a map for each cell leader, three to five pistols, hand grenades, a larger quantity of cold weapons (daggers, axes), and a first aid kit. Some testimonies state that the weapons were dismantled and hidden in the clothing of the carriers.

One of the members recounts in detail the story of the platoon that left the ghetto two days after the Estonia deportation:

October 28, 1943, 5:30 A.M. My brother accompanies me to the ghetto gate, where my group is supposed to meet in order to depart early in the morning.... We go out through the gate as a work unit, a group of twenty-five, with

34. *Al tekufat Augustova*, 4.
35. Testimony of Azriel Levi, YVSA, 2.

Meir Zalinger marching at the front, wearing an armband of a work brigade leader. After we pass Aleksot bridge, we divide into small cells in order to advance on different roads toward one point. In our cell – six people: Berel Gempel, Michael Gelbtrunk (Yitzhaki), Berel Levin, Meir Zalinger, Moshe Zimlovitz, and Shimon Idelson. We walk dispersed, without yellow stars.... Our cell had a special mission. At kilometer 35 on the Kovno-Marijampole road, we had to dig up additional weapons that had been hidden under the ground: four pistols and eight hand grenades.[36] Using these weapons, we had to perform an act of sabotage in the area and obtain more weapons for the other cells, whom we would see at the nearby meeting point.... When we reached kilometer 20 south of Kovno, right of the town of Gudleve (Garliawa), Lithuanians noticed us and informed on us to the authorities. Due to this informing – as we later discovered – the Savisauga unit went out after us. (Savisauga was a gang that battled the Jews and Communists. They wore black uniforms with gray stripes, and were well armed with submachine guns, pistols, and hand grenades.)...

At kilometer 23, we were surrounded by Savisauga members armed from head to toe, along with local farmers armed with iron rods and hoes. In the short skirmish, we used the weapons in our possession, and we had two victims. Berel Levin fell dead, and Meir Zalinger was severely wounded.... They took us to the town of Garliawa, a distance of 8 km. Zalinger lay on a cart in terrible pain. He was shot in the stomach. The body of nineteen year-old Berel Levin remained in the field.... We were able to destroy the documents, the small maps with the route marks, and the swastika armbands that my brother had made in the ghetto, on which was written, "In service of the German Army, Train System of Germany." These armbands were supposed to be our camouflage on the journey.... Before we reached the town, two members of another cell joined us – Alter Feitelson and Aharon Manyeskin.[37] We made the daring decision that under no circumstance would we reveal the truth. We would say that we had fled from the deportation of 3,500 people.

They brought us to the courtyard of the police in Garliawa – seven people, one of us severely wounded.... They chose an appropriate solitary

---

36. Compare testimony of Haim Gechtel (Galin), this chapter.
37. Compare Alter Feitelson, YVSA, letter 5.

confinement cell for us, and they beat us as they threw us inside. Before that, we put the wounded man in a nearby solitary cell and lay him on a hard bench. The small room was dark. We could not see each other. Through the wall we heard the moans of our companion. Our hearts broke. We began to beat on the door. We gave the guards a lot of money, shavers, soap, leather gloves, and other items, in exchange for water and light. We checked our belongings, and sewed yellow stars on our clothing. We feared a thorough search. I found a photograph of my brother among my belongings. I tore the photograph into tiny pieces and swallowed them. There was nowhere to throw them away, and I could not risk them finding it on me. An order stated that for the crime of one Jew, the entire family would be punished....

We had a short consultation and again decided: they can torture us, shoot us – the truth would remain hidden deep inside. We shook each other's hands in agreement.

6 P.M. We heard a noise in the corridor. They opened the door. They came to take us in an armored car to the Gestapo in Kovno – four Gestapo officials and a Lithuanian Gestapo agent in civilian dress, all armed. They took us to the office, shouting, humiliating us, and threatening that they would kill us all. They wrote a memo, which said that on October 26, 1943, we all fled (here they wrote our first and last names) from the shipment of 3,500 Jews who were deported to Estonia, and that we went to the workplace of the Kabel brigade that worked near Marijampole. When the "ceremony" was over, they put us in the car, weapons aimed toward us – in this manner they took us to Kovno.... The car stopped in front of the Gestapo building.... They took us into the basement and put us into solitary cells by pairs. I was in the cell with Manyeskin. There were shelves attached to the walls for sleeping, and a small table. They brought supper into the cell: coffee and fifty grams (1.7 oz) of bread. Now we had time to think. We pictured our comrades who had just fallen: Zalinger, whom the Lithuanians had murdered in such a shocking manner...[38]

Following is the testimony of the tragic end of Meir Zalinger:

---

38. "*Der emet wegen troyerik barimten 9-ten fart*" [The truth about the Ninth Fort], by Berel Gempel (memoirs), 1 ff.

Meir Zalinger lay in a pool of blood and groaned.... I lay beside him and saw him swallow the map that we had followed. After completing this task, he poured out the bottle of spirit we had received in the ghetto.... A doctor came and determined that Zalinger had been shot in the stomach. Then they commanded me and Simha [Idelson] to dig a hole near the police courtyard, and they put Zalinger inside, although he was still fully conscious. Simha asked one of the policemen to shoot Meir in the head to put an end to his torture. The policeman replied that he could not do so without an order. Zalinger understood what was going on. When he heard the reply, he asked Simha to step on his heart, maybe that would hasten death.... Weeping copiously, we covered him with earth, and I recited the *Kaddish* [mourner's prayer].[39]

The fate of the other cells that left the ghetto on that day was similar to the fate of this cell.

The news of the arrests must have reached the ghetto that evening or the next morning, but the operation was not terminated. For about one week, groups of fighters left the ghetto daily under cover, whether through the gate as a labor brigade or through the barbed wire fence. Each group had its own route, a few weapons, and medical equipment. Each faced its own obstacles, failures, threatening attitude of the population, informants, pursuits, and encounters with enemy forces.

The one platoon that was slightly more successful than others was that of Nehemiah Endlin. Some twenty individuals went out in this group, among them Shmulik Mordkovsky, Leo Ziman, Miriam Buz, Azriel Levi, Moshe Gerber, David Goldin, Miriam Idels, and Lifschitz and his wife. The platoon divided up into cells as soon as it left the ghetto, and proceeded southward. The cell that Shmulik Mordkovsky led reached Lazdijai, a town in the last third of the distance between Kovno and the Augustova Forests.[40] When they realized that searches for Jews were being carried out in the area, they decided to hide in a suitable location and wait until the searches ended. Thanks to Mordkovsky's alertness and navigational abilities, the cell found a hiding place in a farmer's attic. Two days later they again advanced, but the maps failed them, and the cell lost its way. For several days they wandered the roads until they lost contact with each other.

---

39. *Memoirs of MY*, 1:1–2.
40. Testimony of Azriel Levi, YVSA, 9.

Azriel Levi and David Goldin were caught by Lithuanian policemen, who robbed them and left them with only their shirts and pants. The policemen then took the Jews to the Marijampole prison, where they met up with other members of their platoon: Leo Ziman, Miriam Idels, Lifschitz, and others – fifteen in total.

Another cell of the same platoon was able to slip away from the pursuers. Miriam Buz recounts:

> We left through the ghetto gate with the others who were going out to work. We crossed the bridges over the Vilya and Niemen rivers safely. We advanced southwest. If the villagers did not fully trust us, whether due to the Jewish looks and ludicrous Lithuanian of my two companions, or whether due to our slightly awkward farmer's dress – they left us alone. In the middle of the first day, we discovered that the maps were leading us astray.... The canals on the map were nowhere to be found, and instead of the forests that were marked, we occasionally came across settlements. Despite this we reached a railroad track before a big forest – the meeting point with Leo's group. They did not arrive. We had no choice but to continue. The map completely misled us. We made our way to the Kovno-Marijampole road (according to our orders), and there the police discovered our tracks. We took shelter in a pit surrounded by bushes. All around us, we heard whistles and the pounding of boots. But they went back the way they had come.
>
> Evening fell and we had to make a decision. One of us got sick and began to cough. I went out to assess the situation. The farmers told me that searches had been conducted here in the last few days, and Jewish youths were caught. We had no choice but to return to the ghetto and report on our route, the maps, and the situation. Returning was no less dangerous than advancing. We walked along the road one by one, at distances of 50 meters from each other. We reached the city on foot and in farmers' carts, and slipped into the ghetto along with labor brigades returning to the ghetto. In our shared apartment, I found three of our companions ready to go. I delayed them. They warned Eli, and at a meeting with the Communist command, we decided to delay departure.[41]

The only ones of all the participants in the operation who succeeded in

---

41. *Sefer Hashomer Hatzair*, 742–43.

overcoming all the obstacles along the route and to reach the Augustova Forests were two members of this platoon: platoon commander Nehemiah Endlin and Shmulik Mordkovsky. They met near the designated section of forest, entered the forest, and even found the location near Brozhany Lake where Soviet paratroopers were supposed to be located. There was no sign of the paratroopers. Instead, the two discovered that the area was populated with Poles. When the Nazis arrived, these Poles became Volksdeutsche,[42] and were known for their exceptional loyalty to the German authorities.[43] According to another testimony,[44] the two met up with "White Poles" – Polish nationalist partisans who were under the authority of the nationalist Armia Krajowa (Home Army) command.

Endlin and Mordkovsky remained in the forest for only a short time, and when they realized that no others of their group had arrived, they returned to the ghetto. They arrived safely, and this in itself was a phenomenal partisan achievement. Later, the two became outstanding partisan guides and were among the best fighters of the Kovno battalions in the Rudniki Forests and of the entire Lithuanian brigade.

We do not know exactly how many fighters took part in the Augustova Plan. Yellin and Galpern report that over one hundred fighters left the ghetto for Augustova.[45] We have not found confirmation for this number, but apparently it is close to the truth. Other sources mention the names of forty-four fighters who participated in the journey, but undoubtedly, the names of most of the participants are not mentioned.

Among the fighters whose names are known, only eleven returned safely to the ghetto: Miriam Idels, Miriam Buz, David Goldin, Azriel Levi, Yehuda Lifschitz, Rachel Lifschitz, Eliezer Moses, Ephraim Senior, Malka Pugatzky, Yehezkel Steinberg, and Hirsch Shmuliakov. The remainder died along the way or were arrested by the Gestapo: Michael Gelbtrunk, Alter Feitelson, Abba Diskant, Moshe Gerber, Pinchas Krakinovsky, Moshe Zimlovitz, Meir Zalinger, Aharon Vilenchuk, Berel Gempel, Tuvia Pilovnik, Aharon Manyeskin, Leibel Mitzkun,

---

42. Editor's note: Volksdeutsche were registered ethnic Germans entitled to special privileges by the Nazis.

43. Alter Feitelson, YVSA, letter 11.

44. Testimony of Eliezer Moses, YVSA, 7 (recording 2). Compare also testimony of Gita Foger-Turchin, YVSA, 2 (recording 1).

45. PKG, 82.

Berel Levin, Ya'akov Strassburg, Moshe Iliyonsky, Binyamin Volovitzky, Leo Ziman, Kadish Goldfarb, Shimon Idelson, Katz, Moshe Rozhansky, Itzik Kirkel, Hanne (Hanan) Meskup, Haim Vidutzky, Velvel Schuster, Hirsch Gen, Reuven Zweigorn, and Yosef Kodos.

The fighters who were captured by the Gestapo did not all share the same fate. They were beaten cruelly and robbed by Lithuanian policemen, then interrogated and tortured by the Gestapo. But as the interrogations progressed, the decision of the Gestapo officials for each group of arrested fighters depended on a variety of circumstances: the reports of the Lithuanian policemen about the Jews were important as well as the extent to which the Gestapo believed them; the story the Jews told in their defense; and whether one of the ghetto leaders was working on their behalf.

One of the arrested fighters reports in his testimony:

When I was at the Gestapo, I prepared an excellent defense for myself. I told them that David Goldin and I had joined a labor brigade that was laying a cable. We went out to search for bread, and a Lithuanian policeman caught us, abused us and robbed us. We noticed that the Germans were impressed by this story, and one commented to his companion: "See what the Lithuanians are capable of!" To us they said, "You, we hate by law, but the Lithuanians – from the heart." We took advantage of this point in order to provoke an argument between the Germans and the witnesses, the Lithuanian policemen. We recounted in detail how they caught us, stripped us naked and robbed us, and we emphasized that this was their entire reason for catching us. It worked.... I sent greetings to Ika Greenberg through Haitovitch, the lieutenant of [Benno] Liptzer (the Gestapo's Jewish agent), and apparently thanks to this, I was given "only" fifty lashings and released.[46]

Bitter by far was the fate of the group that was caught near Garliawa and attempted to resist. One of those arrested from this group recounts:

At eleven o'clock at night, we were sent to the Gestapo in the city of Kovno. The next day we were interrogated and beaten again. We did not admit anything. The Gestapo commander, Dr. Fuchs, informed us that the next day

---

46. Testimony of Azriel Levi, YVSA, 2.

they would send us back to the Kovno Ghetto. Liptzer, the Jewish police officer who served as the Gestapo's agent in the Kovno Ghetto, was called to the Gestapo office and ordered to take us to the ghetto. At the last minute, Dr. Fuchs asked him if he could verify that these Jews were simple laborers and not partisans. Liptzer looked at us, pointed at Moshe "Pok" [Zimlovitz], and replied: I can't testify for these people, because this one is a Communist. Fuchs was furious. He took out his rubber whip from the cupboard and began to beat us viciously in the face. An hour later, we were taken to the "Yellow Prison." We were in prison for three weeks. We were held together with known criminals. We were tortured. Then we were taken to the Ninth Fort.[47]

In his memoirs, Berel Gempel provides additional details of the fate of that group:

On the morning of October 29, the well-known Gestapo official Schroeder went down into the basement. The first ones he took for interrogation were myself and my cellmate, Manyeskin. He took us up the stairs to the third floor, room 306. First Manyeskin went in, and I remained in the corridor under guard. I heard Manyeskin's screams through the wall. Half an hour later, he came out, battered and beaten, his clothes ripped, and then I went in for interrogation. Schroeder took out my wallet and found a few photographs of my parents. "Who are these?" he asked. "They are my parents," I replied. "Where are they?" "They were taken out of the ghetto on October 28, 1941, to the Ninth Fort," I answered. "How do you know?" he asked, and then he punched me in the face until the blood began to flow.... He went over to a glass cabinet, which had a number of whips hanging inside in remarkable order, and chose one of them.... He beat me fifty lashes with all his strength, until he was covered in sweat. Then he said that by law we deserved the death sentence, but because this was the first time and we were fit for labor, he would commute the sentence. They returned us to the basement and took another couple.... At 12:30 P.M. the interrogation of our group was over.... After we had been there a few days, they gathered all the Jews into one cell – number thirty-five. Here we met many companions, partisans who had been captured in various locations on their way to Augustova. We were eighteen

47. Michael Yitzhaki (Gelbtrunk), YLHG 18–19:78.

Jews.... Among the eighteen were several Jews who had been caught in the city without yellow stars.... Whenever one of us exchanges an item for bread, we divide it into eighteen portions....

Thirty-three people sat in the cell. The Lithuanians were criminals. At night, when we lay on the ground to sleep, there was no room to walk between people, so it was warmer. By day we played chess and checkers, to forget the hunger. We organized a chess tournament. Michael [Gelbtrunk] would recite "Warsaw is Burning" and other recitations.... One day we held a meeting, and decided what each one had to give of his possessions to exchange for food. In payment, we received bread, salt, and tobacco, and divided it all equally among us. By day they would take us on a walk in the courtyard for half an hour. Some of the Lithuanians who sat with us were brought recently from the Ninth Fort. They told us that all the prisoners who had been in that fort were sent to various prisons, and the fort was transferred to the Gestapo. Even the Lithuanians who were part of the fort staff were banished from it.

On the morning of November 19, the door opened, and the two jailers called out from a list the names of the six prisoners who had been brought in the first group. They ordered us to go into the office, where several Gestapo men awaited us. They took us out into the street under heavy guard, where a covered truck stood. We got into the car, and found another Jew there who was growing a beard and who had bruises around his eyes.... It was Moshe Gerber. In the front part of the truck sat nine guards, and we started moving.... Through the cracks in the covering we could see that we were crossing the bridge beside the ghetto. The truck made a turn toward the hill. When it stopped and we got off, we saw before us the Ninth Fort.[48]

As mentioned, most of the participants of the Augustova Plan were captured by the Gestapo and harshly interrogated. From the available testimonies, we gather that the fighters stood firm and did not reveal anything they were supposed to hide. Some said they had fled from the deportation to Estonia, while others asserted they had walked to the villages in order to exchange valuables for food.

---

48. Gempel, "Der emet wegen" (memoirs), 5.

It was suspected that one youth, Moshe Gerber, did not hold up, and was later even accused of betrayal. We know that Gerber was the only one on whom they found a pistol when he was arrested. Some said that because of this, he was beaten more than the others, and broke. Other said that he was not beaten at all, but rather that he cooperated with his interrogators from the outset.[49] What did Gerber reveal? There are various conjectures about this. Some say that he said he had received the pistol from a man named Bloch, apparently referring to Shimke Bloch of the Anti-Fascist Organization, who was also one of the arrested. Rumor had it that immediately after this, everyone in the ghetto with the name Bloch was arrested, but they were released due to lack of evidence. Another theory is that he revealed that the person who had helped him escape from the ghetto was Dr. Yitzhak Rabinowitz. If this had been true, undoubtedly they would have brought Rabinowitz in for interrogation, but this did not occur. Whatever the truth about Gerber's behavior while with the Gestapo – the rumor spread among the Augustova prisoners that he succumbed to the interrogators and revealed secrets about the underground – that is to say that he betrayed them. This rumor was expressed in the way the group treated Gerber in the Ninth Fort, and afterwards in the ghetto. It also weighed against him in the forest, and eventually sealed his fate.[50]

---

49. Testimony of Michael Yitzhaki (Gelbtrunk), YVSA, 17–18 (recording 4a); compare Feitelson, YVSA, letter 9.
50. See chapter 11, "Discipline."

CHAPTER 6

Escape from the Fortress of Death

From August to October 1943 there was an increasing number of signs that the defeat of Nazi Germany was imminent. In southern Europe the British and American armies advanced. The Italian government surrendered unconditionally to the Allies which meant that the entire weight of the war in the south from then on rested on the shoulders of the German army. The success of the "second front" in the south increased the chances of opening a "second front" in the west as well. On the eastern front the Nazi army was pounded by heavy blows, which undermined the German forces and brought them closer to total collapse. At the same time, the Moscow Conference was held, and its decisions emphasized the responsibility of the German government for crimes against the people of Europe – crimes that had no peer in the history of the human race.

Fear gripped the mass murderers. Although the fear of humanity's vengeance did not prevent them from continuing their mission of destroying races, they decided it would be advisable to take steps to cover their crimes so that the ongoing "production of death" would not leave any traces. As part of the plan of "erasing all traces," the mass murderers in Berlin decided to begin with a clean up operation at all the destruction sites in Eastern Europe. They ordered the opening of mass graves and the burning of the corpses of the murder victims of 1941–1943. The Kovno Gestapo received such an order in September 1943. It was first commanded to "clean up" the Ninth Fort, in which nearly seventy thousand people were killed – mostly Jews.

Responsibility for the technical implementation of the order was given to a German excavation and construction company, which had apparently gained experience in similar work in other locations.[1] Responsibility for the actual execu-

---

1. Similar work was carried out at the time at the destruction sites of Pskov, Vilna, and elsewhere.

tion of the task was given, however, to a Gestapo "special unit," Sonderkommando, commanded by *Obersturmführer* Franz Radif and his lieutenant, *Unterscharführer* Walter Velis. Two experienced police commanders from Vienna, Appel and Lichauer, were given the job of guarding the prisoners who would do the work.

The corpse-burning brigade was comprised of several categories of people. Its core was a group of ten Red Army prisoners of war – veteran prisoners in the fort – who had survived out of a group of five hundred Jewish prisoners of the Red Army. These Jewish prisoners had been separated from the Russian prisoners at the beginning of the war and brought to the fort, where they were employed as a labor force during the *Aktion*s: they dug the pits, spread lime over the corpses of the murdered, and covered the pits with earth. Although they themselves were not killed in the *Aktion*s, most did not survive for long under the cruel regime at the Fortress of Death. They wasted away slowly, some from the beatings that rained down on them at every opportunity, others from hunger, exhaustion, and disease, still others from the bullets of the SS. The few that survived until that point were apparently the strongest, the skilled laborers, and those with qualities the Germans valued. Over time another twenty-four Jewish prisoners joined this group. Other Jews slowly joined the group. One was Dr. Portnoy (first name unknown), a Jew from Kovno who did not enter the ghetto but hid with a German priest. Together they worked on writing a German-Lithuanian dictionary until they were discovered by the Gestapo. The priest's attempts to assist were not successful, and Portnoy was taken to the fort. Another was a Jewish woman who was found hiding with Lithuanians. A Jew who had converted to Christianity, Jonas Pilvinskas, had been in the fort since 1942. Rabbi Gabriel Shusterman – known to Lithuanian Jewry as the *maggid* "Ben Moshe Yedaber" – was taken to the fort from the labor camp at Koshedar.[2] This was the Gestapo's punishment for the crime of two prisoners escaping from this camp.

In addition, fifteen Jews were brought straight from the ghetto. They were taken out through the ghetto gate as if for ordinary work and instead of bringing them to their usual workplace in the city, they were taken to the fort: Yisrael Gitlin, Moshe Levin, Grisha Shalit, Shmuel Shmulevitz, Meister (first name

---

The project director was Paul Blobel, a subordinate of Eichmann. His unit bore the number 1005 (see Eichmann trial in Jerusalem, protocol of session 111, 46).

2. Oshry, *Hurban Lita*, 122–27.

unknown), Abramovitz (first name unknown), Tuvia Friedman, Mendel Kass, Schmidt (first name unknown), Kanovitz (first name unknown), and five others whose names are unknown. Two women were also brought from the ghetto to "entertain" the prisoners. In late November, twelve youths from the Augustova Plan arrived: Shimon Idelson, Michael Gelbtrunk, Berel Gempel, Moshe Gerber, Mendel Dietz, Abba Diskant, Aharon Vilenchuk, Moshe Zimlovitz, Aharon Manyeskin, Alter Feitelson, Tuvia Pilovnik, and Pinchas Krakinovsky. Along with them was a youth of sixteen, Scher, who had hidden in the forest for two years by himself. They called him "Forest Man."

Four non-Jews also joined the group: the three Korganov brothers from Kuneshkis village near Jonava, who were Lithuanians apparently of Russian origin. They said they had resisted the Germans who had come to take them to forced labor and so they were punished by the Gestapo with this work in the fort. Another member of the group was a Polish Christian physician who was accused of contact with the partisans. In total the brigade numbered seventy-two individuals.[3] One of the Jews from the ghetto and seven prisoners of war were shot in November, and sixty-four remained.

The work process was planned and organized most systematically by the Nazis, as described by one of the prisoners:

> About two hundred meters from the fort, on the right, were pits in which were buried Jews of Kovno and also those from outside Lithuania. There were Jews from Czechoslovakia – Prague and other cities; Jews from Germany – from Munich, Frankfurt-am-Main, Dusseldorf, Dresden, Cologne; and many Jews from Vienna. The pits continued down the hill. There were fourteen large pits and many smaller mass graves. Each pit was the size of a street – 100–120 meters in length, 4 meters deep, and 3 meters wide.
>
> Engineer Vasilenko[4] drove the large bulldozer.... The bulldozer removed

3. These details were taken from a number of sources, mainly from M. Eglinis, *Mirties Fortuose* (Vilna, 1957) and Memoirs of MY (Gelbtrunk). See also Kurganovas, 77 ff.

4. Kulia Vasilenko, a Russian Jewish prisoner (his real name was Yisrael Vaselnitzky), a captain in the Soviet army, 36 or 38 years old. He was born to a traditional nationalist family in the Jewish village Sadeh Menuchah in the Kherson district of Ukraine. Before the war he was a mining engineer and at the beginning he helped build fortifications in Sevastopol. He was taken prisoner on the Byelorussian front and hid his Jewish background until October 1943, when he was turned in to the Gestapo and attached to the corpse-burning group.

a half-meter layer of earth – almost down to the corpses…Sometimes the bulldozer brought up bodies and tore limbs apart.… Here there was a group that cleaned [the dirt] from above the bodies with hoes, so they could be brought up. The corpses lay in the pits in piles – men, women, and little children.… The Jews of Lithuania lay mostly naked, some in underwear, some men in pants, all barefoot. The Jews from abroad lay wearing shoes and pants, and most of the women were clothed. This was because at the time of the killings, the Jews from abroad resisted somewhat. The faces of the corpses were frozen in the expressions they had worn at the time of death: faces full of terror, mouths wide open, as if in a choked scream. The faces were black as coal. The horrible expression bore witness…that among the thousands of victims in the pits only a few died from the bullets – most were buried alive.…

Forty-two Jews were chained together.… We were divided into small groups, and each one had a different job: the "pullers" – these were eight prisoners who worked with four big hooks – long iron rods, with two handles on one end and a crooked hook on the other.… The pullers stuck the hooks into the corpses and pulled. Limbs tore from the corpses that did not move – arms, legs, heads. The whole corpses were brought up on steps that were dug into the sides of the pit. The pullers gathered the single limbs into the corner of the cleared pit. They made a pile of limbs, including legs of children wearing warm shoes.…

The pullers were given another job as well: collecting valuables. The pullers checked the corpses of the Jews from abroad, who lay clothed, looking in their pockets and other places where they might hide valuables. For the Kovno Jews who lay naked, they opened mouths and pulled out gold teeth. When they returned to the fort after work, they had to turn over the valuables to the Germans.…

When the corpses were pulled up and placed beside the pit, the "porters" would begin their work. They were equipped with stretchers. They would lift the corpses in their arms and place them on the stretchers – two corpses on one stretcher. They brought them to the bonfire and threw them on the ground. Two people worked beside the bonfire…these two placed a layer of wood in a 4 × 5 meter square. They dug narrow channels around the square, into which the fat of the corpses ran. On the layer of wood they placed seventy-five corpses.... Then one of the workers climbed on top of the pile with a hose in his hand and poured large amounts of kerosene on the corpses. The workers covered the layer of bodies with a layer of wood, then another layer of corpses, four such layers in total. Each one had seventy-five bodies, all together three hundred bodies in each pyre. At first they would light the pyre by a simple method, with benzene. Later, in December, the Germans brought special explosives for this purpose: thermite bombs. This was a bottle of explosives with a wick inside. They would place it under the bodies and light the fuse. The bomb exploded into a flame of 2000°C [3600°F], and the entire pile burst into an inferno. The pyre burned for twenty-four hours. Over time, the burning pile of bodies crumbled slightly, and then they would adjust the bonfire and throw limbs into the center. They collected the fat that dripped into the channel and poured it back onto the fire so it would burn.

The Russian prisoner Niminov stood beside the pyre.[5] ...He held a notebook and he wrote down the number of bodies that were burned. The Germans called him the *Brandmeister* [burn-master]. The workers flung the single limbs they collected in the pits onto the pyre. The *Brandmeister* had a special order from the *Sturmführer* to list every single head as a corpse....

After the whole pile was burned...nothing but a pile of charred bones remained. One worker had the job of disposing of the bones.... He had a large bin. He would grind and pulverize the bones to powder, then scatter this "flour" in all directions or mix it with earth, so that not a trace would remain.[6]

This was how they carried out the hellish job of obliterating all traces of the crimes. Two issues were at the top of the agenda for the Germans responsible for this job at the fort: (1) no outside person could ever find out about the project, and (2) the pace of the job and scale of "productivity" had to fit the demands of their superiors. These priorities determined the regime at the fort and the treatment of the prisoners. For the purpose of the first goal, a strict blackout was imposed toward the outside on everything done at the fort. Surrounding the work area, at a considerable radius, warning signs were posted that whoever

5. Michael Niminov, about sixty years old. He was said to have been a major-general in the medical service of the Red Army. He told the ghetto Jews that in his youth he had belonged to the Zionist movement. At the time, he also expressed interest in Hebrew literature.
6. Gempel, "*Der emet wegen*" (memoirs), 20.

approached the fort would be shot on sight. So that nothing would be visible from afar, broad sheets of cloth were stretched around the area.

Most important, however, was that none of the prisoners would ever leave that place. This was entirely clear to the Germans as well as the prisoners. The security arrangements were organized toward this purpose. From this aspect the status of the prisoners inside the fort was different from those outside beside the pits. Inside the fort the regime was more "liberal." The Germans apparently trusted the fort to a sizeable extent and considered it a first-class prison. Its structures gave the impression that no one could escape. The fort was dug into a high hill, and on the only wall that was visible a system of guard towers overlooked all sides and was apparently manned by experienced and trustworthy SS troops. The fort had a number of support facilities, such as workshops for repairing work tools, warehouses, and a kitchen. The prisoners who worked in these places had a certain freedom of movement, and supervision of them was not at the strictest level.

Those who worked outside also enjoyed a modicum of freedom of movement in the hours after work, when they were inside the fort. Until 8 P.M., and according to some witnesses even until 9 P.M.,[7] they were permitted to walk around in the corridor, to enter other prisoners' cells, talk, and even sing. At those times the jailers' supervision of them was apparently quite lax. At 8 P.M. (or 9 P.M.), two SS troopers entered the corridor to escort the prisoners into the cells, count them, and close the doors. One soldier would stand beside the cell door while the other entered and counted the prisoners several times. The cells were large. The cell wall facing the corridor was made of iron rods, and from the corridor one could always see what was going on inside the cell. Each cell held eight or ten prisoners, sometimes more.

By contrast, when prisoners worked outside they were under the strictest surveillance. Before they went out to work the guards chained their legs together. At first they chained them together in pairs, but later they chained them one by one (this was a sign of "liberalization"). On the way to the workplace and during work, the prisoners were surrounded by SS troops armed with machine guns and submachine guns. The guards never took their eyes off of the prisoners and counted them and recounted them endlessly. The threats, insults, and beatings

---

7. Testimony of Michael Yitzhaki (Gelbtrunk), YVSA, 20 (recording 4a).

that sometimes rained down onto the prisoners were also intended to break their spirits and banish any thought of flight or resistance.

As for ensuring suitable "productivity," the Germans used psychological methods in addition to the usual practice of beatings and oppression. At first they tried to hide from the prisoners the true nature of the mass graves. Despite the absurdity of the assertion, the police officers and high-level guests (SS generals, Gestapo officials) who visited the "factory" on occasion continued to argue that the corpses in the pits were victims of the Communist regime.[8] They also promised the prisoners at every opportunity that if they did their work faithfully, no harm would come to them; they would be transferred to similar jobs and finally be released.

Below is one prisoner's description of his first day at the fort:

They brought us into the courtyard through a small hut. We organized into one line.... It was November 19, a cloudy day, with thin, cold rain drizzling after the snow. Two Jews from the ghetto made a depressing impression as they stood in the courtyard wrapped in worn-out rags, sawing wood. They pulled the saw like the living dead. The terrible odor penetrated our nostrils, the odor of burning bodies.... The wall of the fort and the thick iron bars on its windows and the heavy iron doors imposed fear.... A short German came out in SS uniform, a Russian submachine gun across his chest, his murderous face red with drink. Shouting wildly...he commanded us to empty our pockets.... He was looking for pocket-knives, razor blades, scissors, or any hard object. Other items such as photographs and letters did not interest him, as this was the last stop – the death stop. The ceremony ended and he permitted us to enter.... In less than fifteen minutes, a German came in. He commanded us to go out to the courtyard. This was the *Polizeimeister*. We later found out that he had been a policeman in Vienna for thirty years. He was then fifty-five. Tall, with a pale face and murderous eyes, a true hangman and sadist.... He stood us in one row and gave us a lecture:

"This is a cemetery that the Russians left behind. Here they murdered civilians, Lithuanians, Eastern Germans, and members of your people. The water in the surrounding area was polluted because of it. To prevent plagues

---

8. On this, see reconstructed dialogue between an SS sentry and Yisrael Gitlin (Eglinis, 52).

we must destroy it. The bodies will be removed from the earth and burned. Nothing bad will be done to you.... The main thing is – here you must work. If you work well – I will not skimp, and you will receive good food. I will even improve the food; you will get cigarettes, even alcohol. And when you have finished the job, you will receive a special prize and be sent back to the ghetto. If you don't want to work and your productivity is low – you will feel the weight of my blow. Now," he said to us, "anyone wearing boots, take one step forward!"

I and several others stepped out of the line. He took us into a small hut next to the gate of the fort and gave each one of us a pair of wooden clogs. We were permitted to keep the boots in a locker. The *Polizeimeister* called out, "Shakhov!" A tall Jew appeared, black and with a moustache. He held a wooden crate under his armpit.... The crate was full of chains.... The *Polizeimeister* gave me the sign to place my foot on the open crate. Shakhov held one end of the chain, wrapped it around my leg and quickly closed it with a heavy ring. He did the same thing with my other leg. Several seconds later I was standing in chains.... Already we were surrounded by SS troops armed with one machine gun and submachine guns.... The gate of the fort was opened before us. We could take only short steps.... We passed through the gate in one line, one behind the other. After the gate, they counted us again.... We were dragged to a work site about 200 meters from the fort. It was very difficult for us to go that distance. The ground was wet clay, and the mud reached our ankles. The wooden clogs got lost in the mud. The chains dragged on the ground. We often slipped and fell. Finally we reached the work site. Our first impression was that we had stumbled into hell. One pit was already empty and we had to fill it with dirt. We watched as the porters passed with the stretchers, carrying bodies to the bonfire. Beyond the piles of dirt we could see the big bulldozer, which was then opening a new pit.... We worked until 4 P.M. At the sound of the whistle, the entire labor brigade – close to forty people – had to organize into two rows, one behind the other. Surrounded by the guards and the machine gunner, they counted us four or five more times. They did not take their eyes off us. We returned to the fort, taking small steps in the mud. When we got inside they took the chains off us. Our legs were dripping with blood and gave off a horrible smell.[9]

---

9. Gempel, *"Der emet wegen"* (memoirs), 11.

The *Polizeimeister*'s speech about the "good" living conditions was not mere lip service. The prisoners soon noticed that the food was improving. Sometimes they received smoking materials and liquor. They were given blankets and pillows,[10] they were permitted to take from the pits shoes and clothes that were still usable, and encouraged to "enjoy themselves" with the young Jewish women who were brought from the ghetto.

And the prisoners – how did they react to all this? It is difficult to imagine any reaction other than extreme depression and despair. In their testimonies the prisoners describe this despair and their revulsion of the work; they were disgusted not only with their oppressors, but with themselves – their own eyes that saw, their hands that obeyed them and performed the abominations, and their feet that stepped on the corpses of their families:

> Until my dying day I will never forget the horrifying feeling of that moment when I stood before the corpses of the victims. Tears filled my eyes and I completely forgot myself; I forgot that I was standing in chains, surrounded by murderers. Suddenly I felt a sharp stab in my back, and when I turned my head, an SS man shouted at me, [asking] why I wasn't starting to work.... At twelve noon they ordered us to come up from the pits for lunch. They brought the lunch to the bonfire where the corpses were burned. We recent arrivals could not eat, even though we had starved for such a long time. It was horrifying to see the Germans forcing prisoners to drink tea from the skulls of the corpses.... I said to Moshe Zimlovitz that I would commit suicide at the first opportunity.[11]

We may assume that he was not the only one with such a reaction, although this was an initial response. The prisoners remained inside this hell, adapted to it somehow, and went on living. We do not know of any suicide attempt during the work period of this brigade.

We can divide the prisoners' brigade into three groups in terms of their reactions: the twenty-four Soviet prisoners of war, the fourteen ghetto fighters, and the remaining prisoners.

---

10. Some assert that these items were supplied especially from the ghetto. Others say that these were the possessions of Jews from abroad, who had brought their belongings to the fort (testimony of Michael Yitzhaki [Gelbtrunk], YVSA, 20, recording 4a).

11. *Memoirs of MY*, 2:1.

The highest level of adaptation was among prisoners of war. Their long stay in the fort and complete isolation from the outside world; their forced participation in the *Aktions*; the suffering and the dreadful oppression, as a result of which hundreds of their comrades-in-arms died before their eyes; the hunger and disease – all these led them to a state of complete apathy and made them capable of reacting with a positive feeling toward the change for the good in their living conditions, which began with the corpse-burning at the site. "We never ate so well at the fort" – such remarks were made often by the prisoners of war. This was the "satisfaction" of humans who were completely detached from ordinary life.

Two of the prisoners were exceptions to this: "Sasha the Brigadier"[12] and Captain Vasilenko, mentioned above. The former enjoyed a special position thanks to the Germans' trust in him. He enjoyed freedom of movement within the fort, and even outside it, and better living conditions than the other prisoners. This situation might have led him to oversubmissiveness to the Germans, but also gave him independence of judgment and activity. Captain Vasilenko had recently arrived at the fort and was still at his full physical strength. His character did not permit him to submit easily to his fate. These two also played an important role in later developments, although it is difficult to know how they might have reacted had the corpse-burning brigade been composed solely of Soviet war prisoners. In their relations with the other prisoners, the prisoners of war were a tight group with predictable reactions.

The third group, consisting of miscellaneous prisoners – which included several non-Jews – had no connection to each other or to the rest of the prisoners, aside from the nightmarish labor. The rabbi and "Forest Man" tried to escape the horrific reality with incessant prayer and confessions. The ghetto Jews, brought straight from their labor brigade to the fort, apparently for no particular reason, maintained their conviction that the ghetto institutions were intervening with the Germans on their behalf. In the end, they believed, some sort of "misunderstanding" would be revealed, or else the Gestapo leaders would be convinced that they belonged in the ghetto and not there in the Ninth Fort. "For we are not partisans" – they constantly asserted. Possibly this illusion regarding the

---

12. Alexander Kheilovsky, an engineer from Moscow, from an assimilated Jewish family. He did not understand Yiddish. The Germans trusted him and appointed him as a kind of inspector of the other prisoners. At first, he was the only one permitted to move around the area of the mass graves (which was outside the fort) without leg chains.

difference between them and the rest – and the absurd hope that the Germans would correct their "mistake" – lightened the burden of terrible suffering, both emotional and physical, that was the lot of these individuals. Indeed these futile hopes deterred them from any thought of initiating activity to escape from the inferno. Furthermore their tendency to emphasize the difference between themselves and the "partisans," meaning the Jews who ended up there in their attempt to join the partisan movement, made them uncomfortable partners in any initiated operation. From this aspect, relations in the the Ninth Fort corpse-burning brigade between the almost-partisans from the ghetto and ordinary ghetto Jews faithfully reflected relations inside the ghetto between the underground movement and the large majority of ghetto inhabitants.

As for the viewpoint of the ghetto fighters, we do not know whether their reaction was uniform in all aspects. Almost certainly, differences in feeling and behavior were present here as well. But in all the testimonies on this issue one aspect stands out: refusal to accept their fate from the outset. To these young men it was clear that at heart nothing had changed and they had to continue the path of resistance.

Michael Gelbtrunk, one of the prisoners who was a ghetto fighter, writes in his memoirs:

Moshe was always full of energy. Even then he did not give up. He said to me, "We can run away from here!" I am sure that he himself did not believe it, but his words are engraved deep in my memory, and I believe that thanks to him and several others, we were saved.... What did each of us think about his end? I'll mention the fact that at the fort we adopted as our bedtime song the Russian tune: "No one will come to my grave, but when spring arrives, a bird will visit me and sing me a song." But no, we did not want to be murdered as our brothers had been! Resist and fight! Take revenge! Be freed! But how could we accomplish this? The brains of each one of us toiled. We had to do something![13]

We were together in the group: we had arrived together and we felt good together. All of our conversations were among ourselves. At first, we had no connection with the Russians. After Abba Diskant and the other fellows

13. *Memoirs of MY*, 2:6. Compare also Alter Feitelson, yvsa, letter 11: "On the first day at the fort, we had already decided to run away."

arrived, it was a little bit cheerier. We saw that we had begun to be a force inside the Ninth Fort, and we could think about serious things.[14]

Plans for Escape

The witnesses do not fully agree about the identity of the first person to initiate the escape plan or the establishment of the organization for implementing it. It is clear that the plan underwent several transformations until its successful execution.

The earliest plan was simple. "From the very first," writes Feitelson in his letter, "we discussed it among us: myself, Moshe Zimlovitz, and Shimke Idelson proposed that we remain in the courtyard after work, climb the wall, which was 6 meters high, and run away." Gelbtrunk mentions another version of this plan in his testimony: "Alter Feitelson once proposed that we run away when they brought us back from work, simply flee. Whoever got shot – got shot, and whoever succeeded in fleeing – would flee. We walked in chains, but we arranged it so that if needed, we could remove them."[15] They quickly abandoned this plan.

The second plan was more reasonable, if more daring – a classic plan of prisoners attempting to break free out of jail. According to this plan, the prisoners would attack the two SS guards who entered the corridor in the evening, kill them, and use their weapons to kill the other guards and break through the fort gates.

> Then we had an idea, and we formed a plan to act against the guards and attack them. Abba Diskant came up with the idea and formulated the plan. The idea was to attack the ones who came to lock us up at night, to do it at roll-call time, when one of the German guards stood beside the door and the other was inside the cell, counting the people. We planned that a Jew would stand beside the door holding a heavy stick. At the right moment he would strike the head of the German; at the same time we would attack the other one and kill him as well. Then we would break into the guards' room, grab the weapons, and storm the house next to the fort, where the rest of the SS lived, destroy everything, and flee to the forests. We were already certain of our victory.[16]

---

14. Testimony of Michael Yitzhaki (Gelbtrunk), YVSA, 19–20 (recording 4a).
15. Ibid., 23; Feitelson, YVSA, letter 11.
16. Testimony of Michael Yitzhaki (Gelbtrunk), YVSA, 20.

Another version of the same plan:

Now about the escape plan: our first plan was to jump the two Germans who came to us at 8 P.M., kill them, and wear their uniforms. Then we would attack the guard booth in front of the fort and flee in the truck that was parked in front of the fort every night. We already knew all the details — how many guards remained at night, how many weapons they had. We also decided on the four who would attack the guards: Shimke Idelson, myself, and two others of our group. When we evaluated the plan, we realized it was not doable.[17]

The fighters themselves ruled out the first two plans. Formulating the plans and analyzing them proved worthwhile, however, as it led to renewal of the bonds between the fighters and consolidation of their relationship on a practical level.

These plans were canceled not just for practical reasons, but also due to a sense of collective responsibility.[18] The first plans were envisioning individual escape. The fighters then realized that there was no justification or chance of success for a plan that did not include all the prisoners, or at least the majority of them. But this course involved difficulties. They had a serious suspicion that in case of any failure the ghetto Jews were likely to surrender easily to the Germans and betray the others. Communication with the Russian Jews was also difficult. The fighters had almost no contact with the "simple" Russians, while Sasha the Brigadier was too close to the Germans to be fully trusted.

Apparently the first prisoners of war to communicate with the ghetto Jews were Major Niminov and Vasilenko. Many testimonies state that they tried to approach the ghetto Jews, asked them to tell them about Jewish life before the war, and demonstrated some knowledge of Jewish history. Thanks to these friendly relations, the two were able to serve as mediators between the two groups. Gelbtrunk's testimony reveals that the connection was made as follows: the three Russian-Lithuanian brothers who shared Gelbtrunk's cell participated in the discussions of the second plan. One of them revealed the secret to the Brigadier. "He explained to us how childish we still were. First of all, we would not be able to kill all the Germans quietly. Secondly – what about the rest of the prisoners?

17. Berel Gempel, letter 1:2.
18. Alter Feitelson, YVSA, letter 11.

Would they remain silent when they saw an uprising and they remained under lock and key? No! We all had to get out of there, and not by spilling blood, because we were too weak for that."[19]

Whatever the reasons for rapprochement between the two groups – the fact is that it happened. Both sides agreed to establish a joint committee for organizing the escape of the entire corpse-burning brigade. As for the composition of the committee – again there are contradictions among the sources. Feitelson asserts that he organized the committee and that it included two representatives from each cell: Feitelson, Zimlovitz, Friedman, Vaselnitzky (Vasilenko), "and two other prisoners whose names I do not recall." In Gelbtrunk's memoirs, he writes that at first two individuals alone were given the responsibility of formulating a joint plan: Abba Diskant on behalf of the ghetto fighters, and Sasha the Brigadier.[20] A few days later they held a meeting of a larger group. Aside from these two, the participants were Mishka Estis[21] and Vasilenko representing the war prisoners, and Moshe Zimlovitz, Pinchas Krakinovsky, Alter Feitelson, and Gelbtrunk on the part of the ghetto fighters.

Aside from the difference between the two versions regarding the participants, another important difference is regarding the principle behind the committee composition. According to Feitelson, the principle was representation by cell, and the committee was also open to those who were not part of the Augustova Forests group (Friedman was not among them). By contrast Gelbtrunk emphasizes that of the ghetto Jews only "our fellows" joined the committee, meaning participants in the Augustova Plan. He also says that for an extended period the committee members were very careful not to reveal the secret of the plot to prisoners outside a limited circle, although they realized it would be revealed to all close to the time of the escape.

The committee formulated a new plan of escape, mainly based on digging a

---

19. *Memoirs of MY*, 2:6.

20. According to Eglinis's version (61–65), Sasha the Brigadier did not help initiate contact, but rather joined in afterward.

21. A Jew from Odessa, nicknamed "Brodiaga" (the Wanderer). He said of himself that he belonged to the underworld: "My father was a thief, my mother was a thief, and I was also a thief." He spent most of his life in prison. He was an officer in the navy. In the fort, he was well liked by all and encouraged the prisoners in their most difficult moments. He was skilled in many trades.

tunnel under the fort wall. According to Feitelson's testimony, the prisoners of war on the committee proposed the plan.

> The day after [the meeting], we gathered in a small cell opposite the toilet. A pile of worn out German uniforms stood there. After pushing back the pile, we chose a place where we would begin digging. It was an old well in the corner of the cell. By digging a tunnel from that point, we could go out under the fence surrounding the fort. We gave Shimke Idelson the job of digging. We took out the dirt in our pockets. Due to the threat of the Germans' sharp eyes, after that we began to pour the dirt into another well that was in the corridor. On the third day we had to give up the plan because we hit large stones from the building's foundations.[22]

The failure of the tunnel plan did not discourage the conspirators. The main thing was that they managed to keep everything secret, and no one around them – neither the rest of the prisoners nor the Germans – sensed their feverish work under the ground. For security, they covered a good part of the tunnel they had dug with dirt and continued to search for a way out.

Several days later a third plan was born. This time the plan was proposed by Sasha the Brigadier, who had become an expert in the fort's labyrinths over his years of imprisonment there. He discovered that at the end of the fort corridor, on the second floor, on a platform of iron stairs, stood a door on which a cabinet hung. The door led to a dark cell, an abandoned storeroom filled with rags and used fabrics. In this was another door covered with iron. No one knew where it led.[23]

The committee decided they should make all efforts to discover where the mysterious iron door led. Sasha proposed an original idea: he commented to the Germans that the front of the building needed cleaning and so they should collect bushes to make brooms. The Germans agreed and Sasha gave the job of collecting bushes to those individuals who were involved in the plan. They spread themselves throughout the fort and thoroughly searched the entire area. They discovered that behind that iron door was a twisting underground corridor, which exited to an area that lay within the sentries' view. At a distance of 25

22. Alter Feitelson, YVSA, letter 11; compare *Memoirs of MY*, 2:6, Eglinis, 61.
23. Eglinis, 61–65.

meters from the corridor was a tunnel full of firewood. On the other side of the tunnel was a steep slope, about 35–40 meters, which was a "blind spot" for the sentries. Across the bottom of this slope stood the 6-meter wall surrounding the entire fort, and atop the wall was a barbed wire fence.

After the committee collected this information, they determined a plan of action. They would open the first door that led to the dark, locked cell and drill a hole in the door leading to the underground corridor. Then they would remove the firewood from the tunnel and prepare a ladder with which to climb over the surrounding wall of the fort. It was clear from the outset that this was a daring and difficult plan. It demanded exact planning, recruitment of additional people to assist in preparations, imposition of iron discipline on the conspirators, and supervision of the prisoners who were not party to the plot, particularly the untrustworthy ones. The committee determined the order of operation and the division of labor and energetic preparations were begun.

The biggest obstacle was the iron door in the abandoned storehouse. They decided to try to break a passageway in it large enough for people to go through by drilling holes side by side in a circle of the right diameter. Pinchas Krakinovsky, who worked in the fort as a metalworker, took this job upon himself, and Alter Feitelson assisted him. The two would remain in the building as if ill, by "authorization" of Sasha the Brigadier. Because the Brigadier was permitted to leave only two patients per day in the building, often individuals who were truly ill had to go out to work so that these two could remain. Apparently the first door was opened by a fitted key. Feitelson stood guard in front of it, while Krakinovsky did his job without interruption inside the abandoned storeroom. He worked by the light of a small benzene lamp they prepared especially for this purpose. Using three small, old drills he "lifted" from the metal workshop, he drilled 314 holes. He completed the job three days before zero hour. His fingers were worn to the bone, and in the final days he worked with swollen hands (after escaping the fort he contracted blood poisoning).[24]

Another obstacle was the firewood in the tunnel, but they found a ruse to remove it. The *Brandmeister* (Niminov) and others who worked at the fires, as well as the kitchen workers, began to complain to the Germans that the trees brought in from outside were wet and barely caught fire. Sasha found a convenient

---

24. Kurganovas, 112–13; Viršulis, 154; Eglinis, 64–65; Štaras, 92; Alter Feitelson, YVSA, letter 12.

solution: he proposed using the dry wood from the tunnel. The *Polizeimeister* agreed on condition that removing the wood from the tunnel would not reduce the labor force. "Let them do it after work hours," replied Sasha, as if with concern for "factory interests." Several days later, on December 24, the tunnel stood completely empty. Gelbtrunk relates in his memoirs:

> That day after work, they ordered us to remove the wood. Knowing that each piece of wood we removed brought us closer to freedom, we worked with all our might. By contrast, others complained that they were at the end of their strength and did not understand the hurry. At any rate, [the Germans] would burn us as a reward.... We listened to the harsh words of our comrades in distress and were obliged to remain silent.[25]

Blacksmith Roman Shakhov fitted keys to the doors of all the cells and even greased their locks so that during the escape the doors would open easily and silently. Carpenter Mendel Kass (of the ghetto Jews' group) built a ladder for the escapees to climb the high wall. He prepared sticks that could be joined together at the last minute with strips of torn sheets.[26] They also made a screen from white sheets to use as a mobile camouflage while they would be passing from the corridor into the tunnel.

The committee also thought to prepare rations for the escapees. With the assistance of the kitchen workers they were able to accumulate food for the prisoners to take with them. They decided that everyone would flee, without exception, and if someone hesitated or refused to join the escapees, they would force him to do so. For this purpose, and in order to maintain discipline and punish offenders, they established a security unit led by Mishka "Brodiaga" Estis, whom everyone feared. Members of this unit were equipped with knives they found in the pockets of the dead. They also took measures to distract the Germans from the escape preparations. The prisoners were instructed to make a special effort to increase their "output." This pleased the Germans, who praised the corpse-burning brigade. After work the prisoners sang songs and acted cheerfully in order to conceal the covert activities.

---

25. *Memoirs of MY*, 2:7.
26. Alter Feitelson, YVSA, letter 15. According to another version, a ladder was constructed by Mishka "Brodiaga" Estis, the former navy officer, of sheets alone (*Memoirs of MY*, 2:8). Apparently this refers to a second ladder.

"Zero hour" was set for Christmas Eve. The intention was to take advantage of the holiday situation: the SS would certainly be drinking heavily that night and would be less alert. The committee decided that the prisoners would leave the cells and go out to the wall in groups of ten to twelve, with a committee member leading each group.

During the last two days, the committee members checked the entire plan in detail. They tried the keys and the ladder, went back and forth through the hole in the iron door several times, and repeated the details to each other so that everything would go as planned and they would not waste even a moment. The plotters were well aware that any extraneous movement during the escape could ruin everything. They could not make a sound; they had to control their excitement and not make a move without an order.

Escape from the Fort

Finally December 24 arrived. One of the participants describes the escape:

> Toward evening, *Hauptsturmführer* Radif lectured us, noting that to date we had performed our work satisfactorily. We should not fear, because when we finished our work there, they would transfer us to another site. There were many more such sites. He wished us a Merry Christmas and gave us all liquor. He informed us that during the two days of the holiday, we would not work. One of us translated his speech into Russian....
>
> That day we decided to tell everyone that the next night, a miracle would take place: we were escaping from the fort.... Luckily, we did not have to work that day, and the SS man came into our cells infrequently, because people were walking around crying with joy like little children. The food was almost all thrown out – no one was able to eat. Everyone washed, to remove the stench of the dead somewhat. Everyone was deliriously happy at the thought that they would be free men again. For how long? That was unimportant! For example, Major Niminov said that he knew that at his age he did not have the strength to go far. So he would wait in one place until he saw that they had discovered his traces, and then hang himself from a tree. He added, "My joy is boundless that I have the opportunity to die as a free man, and at my own hands...."
>
> That day, the prisoners at the fort formed groups of people who had

decided to go together. Most agreed that the goal should be to reach the forests; perhaps they would find partisans there and then they could fight the
murderers. The Kovno youth, except for Moshe Zimlovitz, decided to return
to the ghetto. Moshe Zimlovitz and Abke [Abba] Diskant, who represented
the group, waged an emotional debate on this.[27] Zimlovitz thought we did
not have to return to jail of our own free will – we had to take revenge. Against
this, Abke argued that, first of all, those who wanted to get to the forest could
not do so in one night, because the closest forest was 40 kilometers away.
Second – they did not know whether the partisans were there. Third, we were
not armed, and it would be easy for the Lithuanian population to kill us. On
the other hand, we had a chance of entering the ghetto, and then we could
use the assistance of the underground movement to continue our original
mission [to the forest].... All the Kovno youths were with Abke, as mentioned – maybe because they all had relatives in the ghetto and hoped to see
them. Even Moshe Zimlovitz had someone in the ghetto, his elderly mother.
But he was an idealist. Only rarely do we meet such a noble individual.

9 P.M. The guards came and informed us that they wanted us to celebrate
for another hour. We had to sing and dance. They were very pleased that we
were jolly.... Finally they ordered us to enter the cells because it was 10 P.M.
already. Quick as lightning, everyone went to their places. Each second was
like a year. They counted us and turned out the light. Everyone was silent.
From far off we heard the gate locking.... Avraham Manyeskin[28] got out of
his bed, removed several bars from the wall grating (that were sawed off previously), and was on the other side in an instant. With a fitted key he opened
all the doors. We were last. Our companions passed us rapidly, the sound
of their footsteps muffled with the blankets they had already managed to
spread over the floors and on the iron steps. Anatoly[29] was busy hanging a

---

27. Diskant, who was brought to the Ninth Fort later than the others (November 27), already
knew that the ghetto had made contact with the Rudniki Forests, and so he defended his
position forcefully. (Compare Alter Feitelson, YVSA, letter 13; Viršulis, 150–51.)
28. This should be Aharon Manyeskin; his brother Avraham was also active in the ghetto
underground, but was not in the Ninth Fort. Avraham was killed later, in a battle with the
Gestapo in the Kovno streets.
29. Anatoly Gran, a Russian Jewish prisoner, son of an important Communist activist, a
handsome fellow and talented artist. He had little connection to Judaism.

picture across the main entrance, depicting the middle finger pointed at the *Hauptsturmführer* . . .

I went down into the tunnel with my group. Others stood there to receive us. We saw young men holding sheets to hide us so they would not see us from outside. I reached the ladder. . . . I climbed the hanging ladder swiftly . . . and saw the Brodiaga in front of me lying on the snow, a knife in his mouth, warning quietly but sternly that whoever lifted his head – would be killed. And when the Brodiaga spoke – you believed him! We rolled on the snow for a few hundred meters until we were completely white with snow.[30]

The daring escape operation was a complete success. All sixty-four prisoners escaped from the fort without attracting the notice of the guards. The roads were open to them in all directions and each one was free to decide where to go. The escapees divided into four groups. Two groups, totaling more than half the prisoners – most of them Soviet prisoners of war – went toward the forests in order to look for the partisans. Of these, one group went south toward the forests on the border of Lithuania and Byelorussia, while the other went east. A third group of about ten all together, including the four women and Dr. Portnoy, scattered among the villages nearby in the hopes of finding shelter with Lithuanians. The fourth group went toward the ghetto.[31]

The various sources that relate the story of the escape indicate that the most successful were those who fled toward the ghetto, but even they did not all succeed. Of the twenty-five fugitives who fled in the direction of the ghetto, nineteen entered safely – most were "Augustova veterans." The remaining six were caught beside the barbed wire fence or next to the gate. Most of the other escapees were caught by the Gestapo in a big hunt that took place the next morning, immediately following discovery of the escape.[32]

---

30. *Memoirs of MY*, 7.

31. See article by Avraham Tory (Golob), based on the testimony of Kulia Vasilenko (Yisrael Vaselnitzky) (YLHG, 18–19:88; *Memoirs of MY*, 3:2 ff). Another source describes division of the group of escapees according to the advance plan, as follows: group 1 (fourteen people) led by Alter Feitelson planned to flee to the ghetto; group 2 (twenty people) led by Tuvia Friedman and Jonas Pilvinskas – to the city of Kovno; group 3 (twenty-seven people) led by Yisrael Vaselnitzky – to the forests of eastern Lithuania; group 4 (three people) to the Jonava region (Kurganovas, 118; compare Feitelson, YVSA, letter 13).

32. Of the sixty-four escapees, thirty-seven were caught by the Germans and shot. Six fell in battles with the partisans on Lithuanian soil. Three died of old wounds. The fate of four

As Gelbtrunk writes in his memoirs:

The group divided in half so that it would be easier to move on the roads. I led one group, Abke led the other. We began to advance toward the ghetto on side paths. By mistake we entered the courtyard of a home, where dogs welcomed us with their barking. We fled and were shot at from the courtyard. Then we decided to be closer to the road, until we saw the light next to the ghetto gate from afar. We infiltrated the ghetto through the fence next to Democrats Square. Berel Gempel went ahead to scout out the road. Moments later, he returned and informed us that guards were patrolling there. We went over to Varnių Street and began to crawl alongside Lithuanian homes. Suddenly we saw a group of people hiding behind a house.... We realized these were Abke's people.... They pointed to the German guard who stood nearby, deep in conversation with a Lithuanian prostitute. Since we were already a large group, it was dangerous to wait until the German walked away. We decided to take a chance and run toward the barbed wire fence....[33] Luckily the wire was rolled back at that point.... Like an arrow from a bow, I ran toward the apartment blocks. When I stopped, everyone was beside me....

Alter Feitelson proposed going to Haim David Ratner (he had connections with the Communists).... Feitelson knocked on the door.... When they opened it, they were confused and did not know what to do. Vasilenko asked Ratner if he had a place where we coud hide, because the house was not appropriate for us. Ratner went out and promised he would return right away and everything would be all right.... It was almost 3 A.M. and we knew that soon they would begin to hunt for us. Moments passed, and Ratner returned with Moshe Levin, ghetto police chief.... He received us with true joy, as if we were his children. Tears fell from his eyes and he said to us, "Boys,

---

remains unknown. At the time this book was written, fourteen were still alive (Kurganovas, 155). Following is the official announcement of the escape as reported in the monthly report (for December 1943) of the German security police in Lithuania: "On the evening of December 25, 1943, sixty-four prisoners fled from the Ninth Fort, who had worked here in factory 1005. Their escape was not discovered right away. When it was discovered, the hunt began at once. To date, our personnel have caught thirty-seven of the fugitives, of which five were shot in an attempt to escape (*Hitlerline*, 134).

33. Vasilenko testified that he was willing to kill the German, but the youths from the ghetto prevented him from doing so (Avraham Tory [Golob], *YLHG* 18–19:88).

you have nothing to fear. We will save you from the Gestapo. You must remain alive in order to tell the entire world what you saw with your own eyes in the Ninth Fort, what the German and Lithuanian animals are capable of doing to innocent people. You are more important than myself and my own children!" He added, "Now come, I'll hide you so carefully that even if they stand on their heads they won't be able to find you." Indeed, who could imagine that under the broken toilet in the courtyard, not far from the cemetery on Kriščiukaičio Street, the escapees from the the fort now lived, with all the amenities: electricity, heating, water, and comfortable beds.... [34] Before dawn they brought us food and clothing, since our clothes reeked and might lead the tracker dogs to discover us. They burned our clothes from the fort right away.[35] They took Pinchas Krakinovsky away to treat his swollen hands.

Vasilenko, who had joined us at the last minute, was pleased. He realized that he had done the right thing.... In the evening, guests arrived: Haim Yellin, Ika Greenberg, Moshe Levin, Padison, and Ze'ev Friedman, who was responsible for supplying our needs. They were overjoyed, especially Haim Yellin. He did not know what to do with us. They told us the latest news of interest to us: the Gestapo was in a terrible state, all the SS personnel from the fort had been arrested and also the *Hauptsturmführer*, thousands of soldiers were combing the area, searching for the fugitives. In the ghetto, it was quiet then. The guard shifts surrounding it were reinforced, and four people who tried to get inside in the morning were caught....

On the third day, several more Jews who had managed to enter the ghetto

---

34. The bunker belonged to Lipman, and stood beside the fence. Possibly, it had an opening that led outside the ghetto (testimony of Ze'ev Friedman, YVSA, 4).

35. On this, Rabbi Oshry (137–38) writes: "Suddenly Haim Yellin from the underground movement came to me, and asked me to meet with him. 'Rabbi, I must speak to Your Honor immediately. Does the Rabbi know about the escape from the Ninth Fort?' – 'I know.' – 'What should we do?' asked Yellin. 'How many of them are in the ghetto?' I asked. I knew what this meant. I was responsible for the 'disinfection area' beside the bathhouse. They had to bring the Jews immediately to the bathhouse and wash them thoroughly, to remove the smell of the dead. We also had to burn their clothes, because if we did not, the Germans would come with their tracker dogs, and then we would all be lost. This was a daring act, endangering lives. Haim said to me: 'Rabbi, does Your Honor not know what this involves?' – 'I know. I don't care. I am prepared to die while saving Jews.' I heated the bathhouse right away, at midnight. I did it myself, so that no one would know. Everything was arranged. The fugitives from the Ninth Fort bathed and put on new clothes."

with the labor brigades joined us. They brought us sad news of the others. Major-Doctor Niminov had fulfilled his vow: the day after [the escape], he killed himself. He hung himself from a tree. They told us that Rabbi Shusterman[36] had also entered the ghetto, but that his legs were frozen (later we learned that he died in the ghetto, in terrible pain).

After remaining in the *malina* for four days we were taken to an abandoned house on the edge of the ghetto, which was under the surveillance of the Jewish police. In the meantime, Gestapo chief Dr. Fuchs arrived in the ghetto and informed the police that terrible robbers were hiding in the ghetto who could be harmful to it. He therefore wanted the police to search for them and find them. The police searched for us in places where they knew they would not find us... and in the meantime we took advantage of our time and Captain Vasilenko taught us how to use weapons. That day we also wrote a "record of events" of the Ninth Fort, which we all signed. We also gave the Ältestenrat a bag of gold that we had brought from the fort.

On January 1, 1944, a guest visited us – a Lithuanian who was a leader of the Communist underground in Lithuania. We celebrated the New Year, and again we prepared for departure. But this time, the situation was completely different. We felt that the organization was functioning effectively. We received pistols (not all of us). I got a new Mauser from Ika Greenberg; it was a gift from IBZ. I cannot describe my joy.[37]

At that point, the situation in the underground had changed. The resistance movement in the Kovno Ghetto was at its height.

Below is the text of the "record of events," written and signed by the fighters who had escaped from the fort:

Record of events, Kovno, December 26, 1943.

We, the undersigned, the group of prisoners from the Ninth Fort who fled on the night between December 25 and 26 of this year: Yisrael Vaselnitzky (Vasilenko), Abba Diskant, Alter Feitelson, Michael Gelbtrunk, Pinchas Krakinovsky, Mendel Dietz, Aharon Vilenchuk, Tuvia Pilovnik, Gempel,

36. Oshry, *Hurban Lita*, 126–27.
37. *Memoirs of MY*, 3:1 ff.

Shimon Idelson, and Manyeskin – we wrote this record of events on the following issues:

1) From 1941–1942, the German command used the area surrounding the Ninth Fort to commit mass murder.

2) To cover up their crime, the German command, through the Gestapo chief in Kovno, organized the opening of the pits in which the victims of the slaughter were buried and began to burn the corpses.

3) To carry out this job, the Gestapo brought seventy-two individuals to the fort in late October–early November. Thirty-four were Soviet prisoners of war, fourteen were Jewish partisans,[38] and three were local Russians caught in an act of sabotage. Four were women – three Jews and one Pole – and seventeen were Jews from Kovno Ghetto.

4) The work was organized such that the surrounding population and others would not be aware of anything that was happening in the the Ninth Fort area. They hung signs around it at a distance of 2 kilometers, forbidding people from approaching and threatening violators with death by shooting. The workplace, an area of two to three hectares, was surrounded by a cloth fence. The people who did the work were fated never to leave the fort alive. As proof of this, one of the ghetto Jews who developed an illness in the intestine was shot on November 5, and seven prisoners-of-war – elderly and handicapped – were shot on November 13 of this year. Thus sixty-four individuals remained on the job.

5) Throughout the work, from November 1 until December 25, the day of the escape, four and a half pits were opened. Each one was 100–120 m long, 3 m wide, and 1.5 m deep. We removed from the pits some twelve thousand corpses – men, women, and children. These corpses were placed into piles of 300 corpses each and burned. The remains of the pyres (coals and bones) were ground into dust in mortars. The dust was mixed into the earth so as to leave no trace.

6) In order to prevent any possibility of escape during work, the laborers were locked in chains. They were surrounded by towers armed with machine guns. The guards were armed with submachine guns and pistols.

---

38. Referring to fighters who had been captured on their way to the Augustova Forests.

7) Among the twelve thousand corpses that were burned were seven thousand Kovno Jews.

8) The appearance of the corpses showed that first they pushed the victims into the pits and then shot them. This meant that many were buried alive – wounded or not wounded at all.

9) On the day of the escape, many pits remained that had not yet been opened. The Gestapo chiefs intended to finish the job by February 1, 1944.

[Eleven signatures]³⁹

---

39. *PKG*, 102–3.

PART III
Momentum

CHAPTER 7

The Partisan Forest Receives the Ghetto Fighters

The episode of the Fortress of Death that we recounted in the previous chapter was a short interruption in our narrative. We digressed somewhat from the Augustova story, which is where we had arrived in the narrative of the resistance movement in the Kovno Ghetto. We return now to that subject.

After the Failure

The activists in the ghetto – including the top echelons of the Anti-Fascist Organization (AFO) – all agreed that the Augustova Plan ended in failure. Heavy losses were incurred among the almost one hundred participants in the journey; at least forty young men and women fell into the hands of the Gestapo. Among them were some of the best of the underground activists. The leaders of the ghetto succeeded in saving three to five of them from the clutches of the Gestapo through intercession by intermediaries (mainly Liptzer, the Gestapo informer). There was little hope, however, that the others would survive. The objectives of the journey were not attained. Even the two who did reach the Augustova Forests with superhuman efforts returned empty-handed, as they found no trace of the partisans or their bases. Their report left no reason to believe that it would be possible for the ghetto underground on their own to set up partisan bases.

Aside from this, many feared that the underground would be exposed, with all that this implied. Because of the many arrests, the Germans might have suspected the existence of a secret organization in the ghetto that was behind those who participated in the journey. We cannot know how the Gestapo interpreted the "wanderings" of such a large number of ghetto residents moving in one direction along the roads of Lithuania or what the interrogators of the detainees were able to discover. The circumstances that led to the release of a few of the detainees were also unclear. According to Liptzer's behavior when some of the captured were sent to the fort[1] we might surmise that although the Gestapo did suspect the detainees, they were convinced that it was an ordinary escape attempt without the involvement of an underground organization. This did not apply to the Communists in the group, for whom the intermediaries were not willing to take responsibility. In any case, after a few days passed without punitive acts against the ghetto, the underground members understood that the danger had passed for the meantime. This reassured the Ältestenrat and the police, some of whom had assisted the Augustova Plan.

The reactions among the underground members were different. For them the failure aroused bitter disappointment, complaints, and even anger against the organizers of the plan. Apparently the most severe reactions came from the Zionist parties and the IBZ. They viewed the failure as confirmation of their doubts, and in their internal arguments, they placed the blame on the Anti-Fascist Organization. They asserted that the AFO leadership itself had never believed in the success of the plan but decided to try it at any cost, even if it led to sacrifices. The IBZ leaders also argued that the Communists' intentions were tainted and that this had been an attempt on their part to dupe the rest of the underground organizations into using their brave members as guinea pigs to implement the Communist Party's plan – leaving the ghetto in order to join the Soviet partisan movement. An IBZ activist recounts: "The organization leadership took advantage of the Augustova incident for negative propoganda. Their justification was that they could not trust the Communists, and that really they would mislead us regarding the sites where one could operate and also remain alive, and would use us as guinea pigs."[2]

A member of IBZ relates in vivid language: "When I returned from the road to Augustova, my rear end was quite swollen from the fifty lashes. I realized that it had been a huge bluff, especially since the organizers themselves remained behind, even though they promised that everyone would leave within a day or two."[3]

---

1. See end of chapter 5.
2. Testimony of Masha Gail (Yaron), YVSA, 27 (recording 6).
3. Testimony of Azriel Levi, YVSA, 3.

A more reasoned critique, but no less severe, came from Ika Greenberg, who had connections with IBZ:

> I told Ika Greenberg every single thing, exactly how it was [on the way to Augustova].... He said that responsibility for the whole thing had been given to a certain individual [apparently referring to Dr. Volsonok – see below], who had no idea what to do and no training.... It was more like a group leaving school, or a youth movement going on a trip.[4]

But not all IBZ members reacted in such an extreme manner:

> The failure of Augustova was due to lack of cooperation on the part of the Lithuanian population, and after such active betrayal another departure was impossible. We thought the distance to the forest was shorter. In IBZ there were arguments, but there was no opposition in principle to the departure for the forests. We emphasized that we preferred not to be under the authority of the Communists [in the forest] because we feared they would discriminate against us.[5]

The reaction among the Zionist Socialists and related youth movements was more moderate.[6] They tried to identify the real reasons for the failure. They were influenced by the fact that one of the only participants who reached the Augustova Forests and returned safely, Shmuel Mordkovsky, was a member of Hechalutz Hatzair-Dror, and he gave this movement a full report of his success. The mood in the movement was described by one of its members:

> The feeling was that there had been some mistake.... There were rumors that Dr. Volsonok had initiated this idea, and that he did not have any information.... There was no contact and there were no partisans there, but he formulated the idea that in those forests *should* be partisans, that there *had* to be partisans in those forests.... There was also another opinion that they did not go completely blindly but that there was some knowledge of partisans in the forests and possibly they were not able to find them or make

---

4. According to the testimony of Michael Yitzhaki (Gelbtrunk), YVSA, 15 (recording 3b).
5. Testimony of Shmuel Ben-Menachem (Dietz), YVSA, 5.
6. Testimony of Avraham Frankel, YVSA, 2. In Beitar circles as well, not all reacted critically. Biderman, one of the leaders of this movement, tried to explain to his companions that the failure was due to Lithuanian provocation.

contact with them. But clearly, the thing was not completely thought through. Even if the second idea was true, something did not work.[7]

It is interesting to note the opinion of a former army officer, also from a pioneer movement, who had helped train the fighters for the journey:

> I had the topographic plan of the route for their journey.... I thought they would make it through. If they walked the way they were supposed to, then they could make it to Augustova.... The training and practice were not enough. Apparently they made more mistakes and so they did not reach the end.... Two succeeded [in reaching the Augostova Forest] ... because I gave them a course on topography, a course on the use of light weapons, and then a course on scouting in enemy territory.... Even if they would have reached Augustova, they would not have succeeded at all, because there was no base there, and you can't be a partisan without weapons.... The ones they sent apparently didn't understand ... the meaning of being a partisan, how to live, what to do.... The attitude to all this was superficial.[8]

Embarrassment after the Augustova failure ran deep within Hashomer Hatzair. First, losses for this group were particularly heavy. Six of its best members were executed by the Gestapo: Leo Ziman, Moshe Iliyonsky, Leibel Mitzkun, Menachem Levin, Binyamin Volovitzky, and Ya'akov Strassburg. Second, Hashomer Hatzair activists had been staunch supporters of the Augustova Plan. They placed almost unlimited trust in the Anti-Fascist Organization, especially Dr. Volsonok, and strengthened their relationship with it during preparations for the journey and the journey itself. Apparently, aside from the close relationship among the leaders of the two organizations, a certain rapprochement also began from below. After the Estonia deportation, some Hashomer Hatzair members established a collective and went to live in the apartment of one of the members at 8 Broliu Street.[9] Members of the Anti-Fascist Organization were frequent visitors to the Hashomer collective, eating and sleeping there on occasion. We cannot know the exact extent of this closeness as regards the organizational and ideological aspects, but the fact is that from the outside, to the Zionist organization

---

7. Testimony of Yitzhak Kashiv (Kapchovsky), YVSA, 11, recording 3; see also testimony of of Menachem Ganuni (Sadovsky), YVSA, 18 (recording 3a).

8. Testimony of Zadok Eviatar (Bleiman), YVSA,19 ff. (recording 3b).

9. See history of Netzer pioneer group at Kibbutz Beit Zera, 1946 (manuscript).

members, this behavior of Hashomer Hatzair was considered a severe deviation from their Zionist principles.[10]

Not surprisingly, then, Hashomer Hatzair reacted with bitter disappointment, in the Augustova Plan in particular and in the Communist activists in general. Accusations were made that the Communists had not given the departing fighters the weapons they had set aside for this purpose.[11] Hashomer Hatzair's first reaction was to distance themselves from the Communists and renew their relationship with the Zionist camp. This is not to say that Hashomer Hatzair abandoned the position that had previously motivated them to develop a relationship with the Communists – in other words, active defense and resistance. On the contrary, the idea of reintegration into the Zionist camp was accompanied by a desire to establish a united fighting force of the pioneer movements that would act independently from the Anti-Fascist Organization. In other words, in the areas of defense and resistance this united force would not be dependent on the mistaken and hasty considerations of AFO activists.

Eli Rauzuk, Hashomer representative, contacted Mendel Sadovsky, the Zionist Socialist youth representative, with a proposal for unification, and they negotiated this issue for a while. As Sadovsky relates:

> I knew Eli Rauzuk personally.... He contacted me and suggested several ideas for establishing an independent Zionist Socialist youth movement that would act in the areas of combat and defense. Of course I told him that I could not decide on my own and that I had to bring up the idea for discussion in the party. There was no contact [between the Zionist Socialists and Hashomer Hatzair at that time]. In truth, when I brought up the idea for discussion in the party, members were divided for and against as to what extent we should strengthen our relationship with Hashomer Hatzair as they had not before found it necessary to approach the Zionist movements themselves, but were in contact with the Communists.... They did not find it necessary to contact any of our members.... But the majority opinion was that after all, they were our youth.[12,13]

---

10. Testimony of Menachem Ganuni (Sadovsky), YVSA, 19 (recording 3b).
11. Testimony of Lerke Rosenblum-Hadari, YVSA, 6 (recording 2).
12. Testimony of Menachem Ganuni (Sadovsky), YVSA, 19 (recording 3b).
13. Regarding the unification of Hashomer Hatzair and the pioneer movements, see also testimony of Haim Gechtel (Galin), YVSA, 15–16 (recording 7), and testimony of Yitzhak

This was the course of events in the Zionist camp following the failure of the Augustova Plan, and it led to the isolation of the Communists. Although the Communists were not discouraged, they were somewhat embarrassed. It was clear to them also that the journey was a mistake: the fighters had not been adequately prepared for such a long and arduous journey, and the Augustova Forests were not the ideal location to establish partisan bases, especially since the fighters had never been in the military. Anti-Fascist Organization leaders knew actually on whom to pin the blame – the commander in the Rudniki Forests and the paratrooper Albina (Gesia Glezer), who had pointed the ghetto fighters in the direction of the Augustova Forests.[14] Below is the testimony of an Anti-Fascist Organization activist:

> Albina – Gesia Glezer – gave the order not to lose time and to go to the Augustova Forests to establish a partisan base there. She promised to ask [Moscow] to parachute weapons and other supplies there. This was an unsound step on her part, and her superiors severely criticized her for it. Another reason for the failure of the Augustova Plan was the fighters' lack of experience. They walked by day, instead of by night like partisans. The weapons were inadequate. Despite this, the plan served as a test of the independent force. They learned a great deal from their mistakes.[15]

We do not know whether the small circle of Communist activists in the ghetto also recognized the fact that the plan was flawed and that Gesia Glezer was responsible. At any rate, the Communists did not reveal the true initiator of the plan to the outside, meaning the other underground organizations. They apparently saw it as an internal party issue and did not attempt to disprove the assertion that they themselves were responsible for it.[16] But on the inside, they made every effort to encourage their members and banish feelings of despair. We have a portion of the special set of orders issued by the AFO leadership following the Augustova Plan: "We must not be shocked or discouraged by the victims and the obstacles. We *must* pave new roads and we *will achieve* this. Our daring

---

Kashiv (Kapchovsky), YVSA, 9 (recording 3).

14. See chapter 4.

15. Compare also Meir Leib Goldschmidt, YVSA, letters 1, 3.

16. Compare letters of Alter Feitelson, YVSA, 9 and 11.

Bolshevist will and our indisputable decision to wage open war against the murderous occupier will ensure our success [emphasis in original]."[17]

The Dissolution of the Ghetto Begins

We have seen that the depressing results of the Augustova Plan had an effect on some organization to the problems of the resistance's approach and caused a shift in the inner composition of the underground. These internal changes, however, could not influence the situation that the entire resistance movement faced together with the other ghetto residents. The Estonia deportation was only the SS ghetto commandant Goecke's first step in implementing his fatal plan. Just after it came other operations; the liquidation process had begun.[18]

At the height of the Augustova Plan, in early November 1943, the Jews learned that the ghetto had been transformed into a concentration camp and that rapidly it would be divided into separate labor camps. The Billeting Committee received an order to prepare lists of candidates for the labor camp adjoining the airfield (formerly a Soviet prisoner-of-war camp, known as a *gefangenenlager*). The military barracks for this camp were already ready to absorb 1,500 prisoners. A similar number would be absorbed by the labor camp in Šančiai (Shants); another camp, according to the plan, was to be erected at Petrashun, 7 kilometers from Kovno, and so forth. Goecke announced specifically that within a month or two up to five thousand Jews would be sent out of the ghetto to labor camps, after which some seven to eight thousand Jews would remain in the ghetto, mainly employed in the ghetto workshops which he greatly favored. The ghetto officials would also be allowed to remain. Goecke did not hide from the ghetto leaders that along with establishment of the labor camps, the ghetto space would be reduced and its sections emptied one by one and transferred to the non-Jewish population.

At the same time, terrible news reached Kovno from the Shavli Ghetto. On November 5, 1943, the Germans carried out an *Aktion* against the children, elderly, and handicapped, murdering over eight hundred people. The Jews of Kovno recognized that this event was a side-effect of the *Kasernierung* (relocation) process. It affected the ghetto residents in two ways. First, those responsible for children made desperate attempts to send them out of the ghetto and if possible to hide

---

17. *PKG*, 83.
18. Gar, *Umkum*, 172 ff.; Garfunkel, YVSA, 154 ff. See also chapter 5.

them with Lithuanians in the city. The elderly and ill tried to obtain any kind of work position in the ghetto. Second, the strange logic of ghetto reality led many to believe that the labor camp was the lesser of two evils. They grasped at this hope as a drowning man clutches at a straw and did not object to inclusion of their names on the lists. But a large portion of the ghetto population, possibly the majority, was highly suspicious of the *Kasernierung*. They made efforts not to be included on the lists and searched for other means of escape.

This was the situation in which the underground organizations had to navigate after the failure of the Augustova Plan. The first and most urgent question was: Should they go to the labor camps or not? As we recall, the underground organizations had some choice in this matter, as its representatives sat on the Billeting Committee and they had the power to prevent inclusion of the names of their members and their families. As noted, they also took advantage of this before the Estonia deportation. Interestingly, at this point not all the organizations immediately reached the conclusion that they should avoid going out to the labor camps. Within Hashomer Hatzair, for example, in the first few days the general opinion was that it would be better for them all to go together to a labor camp. An activist in this movement writes:

> The question was presented: What should we do now? In those days, the atmosphere held a note of despair. Some proposed going out together to one of the labor camps near Kovno and wait for a miracle. . . . In the ghetto, rumor had it that they would send the people out to camps and liquidate the ghetto. So why wait? Maybe they would disperse us? It would be better for us all to go out together – and there we would see.[19]

But this was only a passing mood. In the joint leadership of the underground organizations, they weighed the issue and decided that the fighters should remain inside the ghetto and not disperse in the camps. We may assume their consideration was that the dispersal of forces would significantly weaken the underground, perhaps even completely disable it. Even if the fighters reorganized in the camps, operating conditions there would be much more difficult than in the ghetto, both for preparation for a defensive battle in case of physical liquidation and for efforts to find a way to the partisan movement outside the ghetto.

---

19. Dov Levin, *Al tekufat Augustova*, 2.

This viewpoint was accepted by all the organizations and they implemented it in the following months. From that point the underground leaders worked so that none of the fighters would be included on the lists. In this way the fighters took on the status of the "protected."

Another step that almost all the underground organizations took consistently and decisively was to cooperate on the construction of *malinas*. The Estonia deportation had proved the usefulness of the bunkers. Now they became a general operation, although not all the organizations gave the *malinas* equal status among the range of fighting and rescue methods. Members of IBZ and of the Zionist parties considered the *malinas* as the only public solution. They had entirely given up on the idea of going out to the forests to join the partisans, while hiding places outside the ghetto could be a solution for individuals only. It comes as no surprise, then, that during this period they invested almost all their energy in constructing *malinas*.[20]

The *malinas* played a particularly important role in the process of reunification of the pioneer movement in the ghetto. We described above the initiative for unification and the agreement between Hashomer Hatzair and the other pioneer movements that were related to the Zionist Socialists. The practical sign of this unification was the establishment of a joint "*kibbutz*" (collective) of these movements together, and the establishment of the *kibbutz* was closely related to construction of the joint *malina*. This process deserves a detailed description. First we will cite Dov Levin, a member of Hashomer Hatzair:

> Most of our members were left without families (after the last deportation to Estonia). Being brothers in fate and in distress, the Augustova days, the goal we all shared, and the loss of our dear companions – all these united the group even more, and we all had the strong desire to be together in any conditions. "If our fate is to be imprisoned in a labor camp, at least we'll be together." This is what many of our members said out of bitter dispair. Only a few opposed this opinion, while the rest were indifferent and did not express their views at all.
>
> One evening, the atmosphere changed due to a new plan.... It was suggested by Eli [Rauzuk], who organized matters and directed contact with

---

20. Details from the IBZ bunker story; see testimony of Moshe Levin, YVSA, 12 ff.

the ghetto organizations, the "Defense Committee," and the Communist faction.... This was the plan: for the meantime, there was no chance for our members to leave the ghetto and go out to the forests in an organized fashion. To be imprisoned in a labor camp – this was always an option. We could not take such steps hurriedly (and we ourselves had objected to this previously!). Therefore we would begin to construct a refuge we could use in an emergency, and even for an extended period of time. The site was already selected. The ghetto institutions and Zionist Socialist members promised their assistance. Member Mendel S. [Sadovsky] took it upon himself to direct the work. The members of Hechalutz Hatzair-Dror would also participate with us in the project.

His announcement rejuvenated and encouraged us. Although deep in our hearts no one placed great hope in the *malina*, still we considered it worse to sit with our arms folded and allow the current to wash us away into oblivion. Many such *malinas* were located in the First Quarter under the cellars – old ruins equipped with abundant food, electricity, radio, and other conveniences. A number of these were exposed by informants, or else their owners destroyed them after the deportation decree for this quarter.... The reason for their failure was that they lay outside the area of Jewish occupation, and up until the liquidation of the ghetto any unnecessary movement between the ghetto and the *malinas* was likely to arouse suspicion. We hoped ... that the location of our shelter would remain inside the ghetto borders until the last day, and only then would we have the opportunity to go down to the bunker and break all connections with the "upside." Until that time, we had to prepare the bunker as a long-term shelter. We approached the project energetically. The site chosen was a wooden hut containing five apartments. We built the bunker under two of them. It was located on 7 Mildos Street, and we called our apartment "7 Mildos" after the street....

The work proceeded in complete secrecy. We did the digging and earth removal at night. A chain of people would remove the buckets of sand, while the rest dug and reinforced the walls with planks and columns. We worked by the light of a weak flashlight, fearing the German patrols, which made the rounds of the ghetto. We had many disruptions: a wall collapsed (the bunker was built in sandy soil), and an oven in a home began to sink due to the empty space under its foundations. But with energetic work and dedication we overcame these setbacks. We "organized" building materials, bricks, and wood from the empty First Quarter through all kinds of ruses. We would go out there in a cart (the carter, Yosef Melamed, was also one of us), bribing the German guard at the gate. Then we removed walls from empty houses after first dismantling them. All this involved danger but luckily we were never caught.

In the meantime, the Hashomer collective moved into the rooms above [the bunker]. We took over the two apartments and lived crowded together. By day we made space in the rooms for meetings, but at night they were filled with folding beds. The atmosphere was like a kibbutz *hachshara*. Our numbers grew. Members of Dror joined and their integration was successful.

The kibbutz…at 7 Mildos numbered around twenty-five members. Our mood was much improved. The sing-along evenings and dances were resumed. We danced the "underground hora" to the harmonica notes of Yosef Rosen with enthusiasm and joy, emotions that were strangers to the ghetto experience.…

The material conditions also improved. Thanks to Mendel's dedicated efforts we often received extra food rations. Aside from this, every day two or three members would go out to the city to work and would bring food back home. The other members formally worked in the large ghetto workshops and every day "vacation" was arranged for them. They were thus able to dedicate all their time to construction of the bunker, and the work advanced quickly. At night we threw the earth out and piles of sand rose up in the area. By day we worked on the bunker interior. After building four rooms, we began to drill a well and construct a tunnel 10 meters long – an emergency exit. We also made preparations for hoarding food inside underground cupboards and crates.… The women, who numbered more than the men, worked side by side in the construction work, although it was hard labor.… The focal point of activity in the collective was our member Yerachmiel [Voskoboynik]. He managed the collective with extraordinary precision and dedication. The kitchen manager was Leah [Voskoboynik]…Dinaleh [Morovitz] and Gita [Foger] entertained us in the evenings with their singing…and when we felt down, Lerke [Rosenblum] read us her comic works.… [21]

---

21. Lerke and her mother were noted in the ghetto for their humorous works. See testimony of Lerke Rosenblum-Hadari, YVSA, recording 4.

Slowly our apartment at 7 Mildos was transformed into a meeting place for the progressive youth in the ghetto and our supporters increased daily. The ghetto police were also aware of what was going on inside the house; during their searches for shirkers and hunts for people they looked the other way.... We also held ideological discussions among ourselves and with members of the [Communist] party about the force of tomorrow – the Soviet Union. We maintained friendly relations with the rest of the ghetto parties, including the Communists, but our contact was limited to formal ties under the joint defense committee and visits of individual members to us. When construction of the bunker was almost completed, we received word of a new route to the forest and actual contact with the partisans in the Vilna forests....[22]

Following is the testimony of a Hechalutz member who was part of the collective at 7 Mildos:

The idea of digging the *malina* at 7 Mildos was not originally ours, because at that time everyone started to look for various ways to save themselves, even right away, from all kinds of *Aktion*s and other difficulties.... We were together with Hashomer Hatzair. Because we were about to receive the apartment at 7 Mildos, we said that we would dig a bunker that would serve as a hideout in times of danger, and also for an extended period.... Not all the women would be able to go out to the forest. We were already aware of the Communists' opinion that they did not want to take women....[23] We said we would dig this bunker so that people could hold out there for a certain time. Over time the idea was developed, and we thought that if the Red Army was delayed and we would have to sit there for a while, we should build it properly.... So we thought of electricity, water, a stock of food, and other details.... 7 Mildos was not the only place we dug; we also dug in Mendel Sadovsky's home before we began to dig at 7 Mildos. The diggers were myself, Shmulik [Mordkovsky], and Mendel.... That bunker was not particularly successful. From it we learned to avoid mistakes when digging at 7 Mildos....

---

22. *The history of 7 Mildos*, by Dov Levin (manuscript), 1 ff. This text was written in 1945, at the time of the author's *aliya* to the Land of Israel.

23. On the issue of the women going out to the forest, see chapter 8, "The Struggle over the Composition of the Groups."

We went there every night.... Everyone helped. The women also helped....
This bunker was designated for the movement members. Everyone felt they
had to help even if they thought they wouldn't use it. So everyone [movement
members] knew we were digging a bunker....

The leadership of the movement and of the collective were two separate
entities.... As a collective I think some twelve to fifteen people actually lived
there, and all who lived there worked; everyone brought something home.
Aside from that, we also got jobs inside the ghetto. I remember that someone
not far from us asked us to dig holes and we earned a little money. That was
our existence....

There was also a Hanukkah party in which Garfunkel participated, and he
had an argument with Eli Rauzuk.... An ideological debate about Hashomer
Hatzair...

Relations were decidedly friendly. I do not recall even one incident of a
quarrel – we were all one block. There was only one way. We shared concern
for all.... [24]

From these testimonies, as well as other testimonies of members associated
with the collective at 7 Mildos, it is apparent that this collective, especially the
work related to digging the *malina*, served as a primary unifying factor. The

---

24. Testimony of Haim Gechtel (Galin), YVSA, 19–20 (recording 8). See also Menachem Ganuni (Sadovsky), YVSA, 22–24 (recording 3b); testimony of Rachel Rosenzweig-Levin, YVSA,
15 (recording 3a); testimony of Gita Foger-Turchin, YVSA, 3–4 (recording 1); Garfunkel, *Kovno*,
259; memoirs of Esther Wolfson, 14. Following is a complete list of members of the collective
and regular visitors to the house:
MEMBERS OF THE COLLECTIVE: Yerachmiel Voskoboynik, Leah Voskoboynik, Gita Foger
and her mother, Bella Marcus and her mother [first name unknown] Zeitel, Penina Sukenik,
Zipporah Sukenik, Rachel (Koka) Rosenthal, Berel Miroslavsky and his wife and their son,
Berel Rudman, Yankel Kaveh, Haim Gechtel, Zvie Brown, Grisha Sheffer, Dov Levin, Yosef
Rosen, Baruch Grodnik, Ya'akov Sasnitzky, Esther Yaffe, (first name unknown) Nathanson,
Rashke Shmuliakov, Shmuel Mordkovsky, Leah Goldblatt, Dr. (first name unknown) Katzav.
REGULAR VISITORS TO THE APARTMENT: Shmuel Smalikov, Masha Rabinowitz, Leibel
Krebchinsky, Eli Rauzuk, Sonya Rauzuk, Miriam Idels, Lera Rosenblum, Hava Marshak,
Mendel (Menachem) Sadovsky, Michael Glass, Rivka Glass, Esther Schwatz, Yentel Schwatz,
Miriam Schwatz, Rashke Rosenzweig, Reuven Glickman, Hirsh Glickman, Yosef Melamed,
Miriam Buz, Dina Morovitz, Dina Joels, Esther (Edna) Yaffe, Leibel Konyuchovsky, Zvi
(Hirsh) Friedman and his wife, David Rudnick and his wife, Hemda Yonsevitz, Shoshanna
Strashoner, Shulamit Mashkutz, Isaac Serebnitzky, Mrs. Ziman (mother of Leo Ziman), "Zippe"
Beilis, (first name unknown) Opiter.

collective functioned to supply the needs of the members and to rescue them in times of distress. Yet from November to December 1943, the problem of defense and going out to the forests remained in the background. For members of the collective and those who regularly visited the collective apartment – the majority of the pioneer underground in the ghetto – beyond being an actual solution, the *malina* became a way to assuage their conscience; these were individuals whose entire being longed to act and fight while they were forced to sit and do nothing.

Most of the members of the collective yearned for the opportunity for real action. "Real action," in those conditions, meant the partisan forest – at least this was the understanding of fighters who overcame hesitations arising from the failure of the first real attempt to breach the ghetto walls. Was the path to the partisan forest really blocked, and even the greatest sacrifices could do nothing to change this? Was the members' blood that marked the path to the Augustova Forests spilled for nothing? These were the type of questions faced by the collective at 7 Mildos. Even the hesitant among those who visited the apartment could not help think about them, or aspire to solve them. But eventually, the way out of the dead end faced by the ghetto underground after the failure of Augustova appeared on the horizon.

The Partisan Forest Welcomes the Fighters

We have already seen that the Anti-Fascist Organization (AFO) activists did not give in to the atmosphere of despair following the Augustova failure. They did, however, admit – and this was apparently brought to the attention of the underground joint leadership – that the current situation did not offer hope for independent establishment by the ghetto fighters of partisan bases in the Augustova Forests. The testimonies also indicate that in the ghetto they began to dig *malinas* for their people and also tried to find hiding places outside the ghetto for some of their members. But this did not distract them from what they viewed as the essential matter, which was to forge a path to the forest, come what may. They were also convinced that there was no replacement for the connections formed between the AFO in the ghetto and the command of the Lithuanian brigade in Rudniki Forests. Although we saw above that the members of this command had supported the Augustova Plan, even intiated it themselves, in the meantime the plan had been evaluated on a practical level, and it is possible that the command also judged it unfounded.

We do not have exact information as to how the Anti-Fascist Organization members renewed contact with the command in the Rudniki Forests following the failure of Augustova. One source reports[25] that at that very time, a meeting was held in the Kovno suburb of Murava between Haim Yellin and the Lithuanian-Russian paratrooper Radyonov. We do know that Radyonov was then establishing a Communist underground at that location and planned to return to the forest accompanied by several local underground members in order to establish a Kovno partisan battalion. Possibly, through Radyonov, Haim Yellin was able to report to Jurgis, commander of the brigade, about the status of the ghetto fighting force following the Augustova failure and asked him to change his opinion and take a new approach to the problem of the ghetto fighters leaving for the forest.

Regardless of how the connection with the forest command was renewed, in mid-November the leaders of the Anti-Fascist Organization discovered that Jurgis had ordered the commander of the Kovno battalion, which in the meantime had been given the name "Death to the Occupiers," to accept the ghetto fighters at his bases. In addition, partisan guides had already been sent to Kovno to lead the first group of fighters from the ghetto to the Rudniki Forests.[26] We do not know exactly what Jurgis's instructions were regarding the group's composition and equipment. According to one testimony, he specifically demanded that the group should not be comprised of Jews only, but that it should also include Lithuanians and Russians. In fact, such was the actual composition of the group.[27] It was composed of some eight to ten individuals, most from the ghetto, including Eliyahu Olkin, who was appointed group leader, Moshe Upnitzky, and one woman. We do not have exact information about the group's weaponry, but almost certainly several of the fighters were armed with pistols and hand grenades. They also took a radio receiver with them from the ghetto for the battalion.

The leaders of the Anti-Fascist Organization kept the departure a deep secret. Possibly, even members of the joint command of the unified underground (the Jewish Fighting Organization, JFO) did not know about it when it happened, nor did the other organization members. The departure date was set for November 23. The fighters took the equipment and, after surmounting many obstacles,

---

25. PKG, 83.
26. Ibid., 86.
27. Letter of Meir Leib Goldschmidt, YVSA, number 1; testimony of Rivka Gordon, YVSA, 9.

slipped out of the ghetto and arrived undiscovered at the meeting point in Murava, where they were awaited by the three partisan guides. The group left at once toward the forests of southern Lithuania. The route was long and difficult and cost them in blood. Gendarme and police stations guarded almost every town, and in one skirmish Upnitzky was wounded in the arm. Two fighters brought the wounded man back to the ghetto. At one point the fighters rested in a farmer's home while one of the Russians stood guard outside. By chance Olkin went out of the house, and the Russian shot him by accident and he died. The other fighters reached the base.[28]

The bloody journey of the first group of fighters to the Rudniki Forests opened a new page in the history of the resistance movement in the Kovno Ghetto. Apparently the Soviet partisan movement was willing to accept the ghetto fighters into their ranks, thus solving one of the most difficult problems, that of which partisan bases the ghetto underground members would join. A solution was also found for another serious problem, that of the guides. It was not clear, however, whether the battalion would be willing to send guides to the ghetto whenever groups wanted to leave.

But these were not the severest problems. The first group was very small, and despite this, its path was filled with countless obstacles and sacrifices. Yet in the ghetto hundreds of fighters waited to depart. How would they overcome the challenges involved in leaving the ghetto and journeying to the forest? It was clear to the leaders of the Anti-Fascist Organization that the time had come to inform the JFO command of the new situation and to demand that it direct its resources toward the departure operation. The path had been blazed – it was time to act.

A Daring Idea – Escape in Vehicles

The representatives of the Zionist organizations in the joint leadership were very gratified to receive the news that there was a way open to the partisans. It happened in late November, at the time of the implementation of the first *Kasernierung* decree. Some 1,500 ghetto Jews were about to be sent to the Aleksot labor camp. The atmosphere in the ghetto was electric, all the more so in underground circles. The leadership still avoided revealing the news to the rank and

---

28. Testimony of Rivka Gordon, YVSA, 9; compare letter of Meir Yellin, YVSA, number 7, 3.

file, but the news reached the fighters and aroused intense excitement. Pressure from below pushed the leadership to definitive actions.

The joint leadership of the underground faced serious problems, but what disturbed it the most was how to negotiate the long road to the forests, which was riddled with obstacles. The members weighed the situation and reanalyzed the attempts of the Augustova Plan and of the first group. They concluded that on foot, only a few individuals would be able to breach the ring of security that surrounded Kovno and travel the 150–160 km to the base. For a mass departure, they had to search for other routes. Then the idea arose to transport the fighters in vehicles, at least for the first half of the way, which was the most dangerous.[29] The very idea was likely to amaze even the experienced partisan. The advantages of such a plan were obvious; this way, they could take a large group out of the ghetto at once. The operation would be performed very quickly, reducing the danger and increasing the chances of avoiding an encounter with the enemy. This was desirable both for the departing fighters and for the ghetto. Such an operation, however, would require special assistance from the ghetto institutions, encumber secrecy, and arouse the fury of the underground's opponents in the ghetto. But the advantages won out.

The first mission was, of course, to find a driver and an appropriate freight truck. Either Haim Yellin or Ya'akov Levi, or perhaps both, took this upon himself.[30] After many efforts they found a driver who agreed to transport groups of Jews from the ghetto to a location several dozens of kilometers south of Kovno. Apparently, the driver had been a member of the Communist youth organization in Lithuania (Komsomol), and he agreed to risk the trip partly for idealistic reasons and partly for money. The Public Committee funded the rental of the vehicle. The JFO command ensured that the ghetto institutions supported the operation, particularly the police and members of the Jewish labor office, who were posted beside the gate and assisted the Germans in checking those entering and leaving the ghetto.

The technical preparations were completed, and the composition of the

---

29. PKG, 87. According to other sources, this idea had already been raised before Augustova (testimony of Yona Rochman, YVSA, addition). Another plan was to renovate an old vehicle that was inside the ghetto and prepare it for emergency escape from the ghetto (testimony of Zadok Eviatar [Bleiman], YVSA, 17, recording 3b).

30. Testimony of Rivka Gordon, YVSA, 10, and her letter, number 3.

group was decided. There were seventeen individuals, from the best of the fighters, who had been outstanding in underground activities in the ghetto from its inception. They represented various groups but most were from the Anti-Fascist Organization. The leaders were Pesach Gordon-Stein, Moshe Robinson, and Moshe Sherman. The group included: Zoya Tinet, Baruch Lopiansky, Yitzhak Segal, Sarah Robinson, Monik Holzberg, Zondel Shtrom, and Eliezer Zodikov, among others.[31] A day or two before the departure date, a good-bye party was held in the apartment of the Gordon-Stein family, attended by all the departing fighters and underground activists from all the movements.[32] Excitement was high and the importance of the operation was explained.

The long-awaited day arrived, December 10. It had been agreed with the Jewish gate guards that they would make every effort to permit the vehicle to enter the ghetto without the German guards noticing "something special." Toward evening the departing fighters gathered in several secret meeting places near the gate, wearing "partisan clothes": boots and short, warm coats.[33] Most of the fighters were armed with pistols, and some had hand grenades as well. Two of the fighters – Zondel Shtrom and Eliezer Zodikov – were dressed in German army uniforms so that people would think this was a group of detainees or prisoners being escorted by German guards to their place of work.

The hour arrived, but the truck did not. After waiting several hours in vain the fighters returned to their homes. The next day the contacts in the city were summoned hastily and they investigated the incident. They found that the driver simply had not found a convenient pretext for taking the vehicle with him from his workplace. The date of departure was put off to December 14.

This time everything went as planned. The representatives of the Jewish institutions performed their jobs faithfully. The truck was allowed entry into the ghetto by the back gate on Varnių Street, the fighters boarded quickly, and the truck left the ghetto. The Germans beside the gate were told that this was a

---

31. It is difficult to ascertain the exact composition of each group. For each group we will mention the names of the fighters of whose participation we are certain. At the end of this book we give a list of all the fighters who departed from the ghetto for the forests.

32. Testimony of Rivka Gordon, YVSA, 12.

33. These coats were called *kurtkes* or *peltzlech* in Yiddish. This was the basis for the partisans' nickname in the ghetto: *di peltzlech*.

labor brigade of woodchoppers being transported to work in one of the forests near Kovno.

Haim Yellin sat alongside the driver. Not far from Kovno, the group experienced an amusing incident. Yellin knew that at a certain place, about 10 kilometers from Kovno, the guides awaited them. When they reached the site, however, they could not find the guides. They waited for an hour, but the guides still did not show up. Meanwhile, policemen and German officers were passing back and forth. Suddenly Yellin noticed two Germans leading a prisoner directly toward the truck. He ordered the driver to turn the headlights on them at full power, then jumped from the compartment. He approached the Germans, only to realize that these were not Germans and a prisoner but the three guides, who had used this ruse in order to slip out of Kovno more securely. The guides entered the vehicle, and the fighters continued on their route south.

After driving rapidly for some three hours, the truck reached its destination – the village of Onuškis (Anushishok), located in a deserted region about 90 kilometers from Kovno. Here Haim Yellin parted from the group. He returned to Kovno with the driver, and the group made its way on foot to the area of the partisans.

Escape Becomes Routine

The mission of taking the group out in the freight truck was a complete success. The risk was enormous, but worthwhile – at least in the eyes of the organizers. At the time, only a limited number of underground activists knew about the operation as well as a few ghetto institution representatives who assisted in its implementation. The methods of operation were proven efficient and the leaders of the JFO decided to continue the mission without delay. Just several days after the group's departure, the driver announced that he was willing to perform another "round" with Jews from the ghetto. In addition, the Jewish underground found out that two partisans who were in Kovno for a partisan mission planned to return to the base in a few days and could serve as guides. Thus on December 24, 1943, another group left the ghetto led by David Tepper. In the meantime, several rifles were purchased and stored in the city in order to increase the arms of the fighters from the ghetto. The motto was "Time is pressing, we must act decisively."

On December 28, another group departed, led by Hanne Kagan and Lovka

Scher. A participant describes the preparations for departure and the departure of this group:

> Just after Augustova, we began weapons training. We trained in a large group. "Tall" Moshe was there, Dudke Goldin, and others. Each group that was about to depart underwent training. Because I was supposed to go out with the first group, I trained together with them. Then when I fell ill and they did not permit me to leave with them, I trained with the second group...with light weapons, pistols.... The main trainer was Lovka Scher, who was a former soldier.... Around ten people [trained].... Then they gave us personal equipment: shoes and clothes. We fitted the boots in the storeroom of Altke Boruchovitz. One of the boots I received was longer than the other. I did not need clothing.... We did not have to pay for the departure. We were a large group – I think eighteen people. Those who went out with me included Hanne Kagan, David Tepper, [Idel] Sherman, [Fishel] Feldman, Birger, [Hanne] Padison, Lovka Scher, Leah Scher.... They told us to get ready, and we sat in a corner, far from the gate. The vehicle arrived, military, with a Lithuanian driver wearing German clothing. He was from the *polizei* [the German police in Kovno]. It was nighttime. Yankele Verbovsky [one of the Jewish labor office workers who stood beside the gate] announced, "This brigade needs to go out to work."...When we reached the gate, they arranged an electrical power failure, and we climbed onto the truck immediately. I do not know whether the police knew who was leaving – Yankele knew. Haim Yellin accompanied us as representative of the Organization. We had light weapons.... We went out to the city and stopped beside a small house – I don't recall on which street. A young woman came out,[34] as well as Sasha Bilakov[35] and someone else. It seems to me they took something else from the house as well, a long weapon I think, and then we drove off. We drove for about 75 kilometers. I think up to the area of Butrimantz. There we got out and continued on foot.... [36]

34. We assume that this was Anila Zinkovitz, mentioned in Viršulis, 183–85.
35. A Russian partisan from the Kovno battalion.
36. Testimony of Eliezer Moses, YVSA, 9 ff. (recording 3).

The electrical short circuit arranged during the departure of this group is an interesting detail that demonstrates close cooperation among various parties in the ghetto in assisting the mission. The person who carried this out relates:

> We turned off the electricity on purpose when the group passed through the gate.... The electrician in the ghetto was Belkin. The engineer [appointed by the Ältestenrat to supervise the electrical system in the ghetto] did not interfere in the practical work; it was Belkin who did it, and I worked together with him. We would climb up the electrical poles, tie, connect, transfer...The phases in the ghetto were very low, and on the Christian side the phases were strong. We would climb the poles and from the ghetto phases we would go over to those phases, even though it was completely forbidden to do that.... Belkin and I had permission to climb the electrical poles.... The order to turn off the electricity came from the gate. Someone said we had to turn it off. We knew what for. We went out and arranged it. Just as they were going out of the gate, we closed off the whole line.[37]

Members of this fourth group included: Ephraim Senior, Nehemiah Endlin and his wife, Shmulik Mordkovsky, Hayale Shmuelov, and Idke Pilovnik.[38] This group was also assisted by two Russian guides, partisans from the Kovno battalions. The group made most of the journey in a freight truck and arrived without mishap at the partisan bases. Several days after the departure of this group, the escapees from the Ninth Fort entered the ghetto, as described in the previous chapter. The JFO leaders immediately began intense efforts to compose a new (fifth) group and smuggle them into the forest.

This was an exceptionally tense time for the leaders of the underground.[39]

---

37. Testimony of Zadok Eviatar (Bleiman), YVSA, 21, recording 4a. They repeated this ruse during the departures of other groups – see the following testimony. Compare testimony of Yitzhak Kashiv (Kapchovsky), YVSA, 11 (recording 3).

38. These individuals do not recall the exact dates of their departure. In his testimony, Ephraim Senior (Senion) says that his group departed "a few days after the liquidation of the First Quarter of the ghetto." We also know that the liquidation operation took place on December 22, 1943 (compare Gar, *Umkum*, 178–79). Apparently, then, the group that left on December 28 was Senior's group.

39. According to Alter Feitelson, YVSA, letter 15, Haim Yellin did not listen to the request of the Ninth Fort escapees to delay their departure for a few more days to give them some time to rest.

But the mission was performed perfectly. Those involved became expert in the matter, and after so many "rehearsals" the technical details of the "performance" were amazingly efficient. Each person knew his role and implemented it with precision and confidence. One of the former Ninth Fort prisoners who was in this group recounts:

> On the last day, a few more individuals joined in for going out to the forest. They were pleased they were able to go out with us. Among them was Padison, the police chief; Rivka Gordon, wife of a Communist leader; Frieda Rothstein; and Alter Feitelson's wife. We were over twenty individuals all together.
>
> January 6, evening. We approached the gate in torn clothing, wearing the yellow patch on our chests and backs, but underneath our coats we held the weapons. I did not feel afraid at all. We waited near the gate until they informed us that everything was "fine." People were then returning from their workplaces, tired and dirty. The SS searched them carefully to ensure no one had smuggled in any food. Watching them all, I thought that all this was so far away from me, as if I had never experienced it. Then we heard the cry of the German police officer: Where are my Jews for Roiter Hoif?[40] We did not imagine that the German officer meant us, but the people responsible for our departure told us to approach the gate. When we were not far from the gate, there was a power outage, and the gate fell into darkness.... We ran out quickly so they would not find the weapons we were holding under our coats. We quickly got into a large freight truck, which bore a large sign that read "German police." We pulled down the cover and began to move. The window of the driver's compartment opened, and we received an order from the "German officer"[41] sitting next to the driver: "Take out the weapons. From now on, you are fighters!"[42]

Further interesting details about the departure of this fifth group and events that took place along its route are included in the testimony of one of its members:

---

40. A settlement in the Kovno environs, known as Raudondvaris in Lithuanian.
41. Haim Yellin. He was the "German" who supposedly came to the ghetto to receive the Jewish labor brigade.
42. Memoirs of Michael Yitzhaki (Gelbtrunk), Yiddish manuscript, 5.

I fled the ghetto on January 6, 1944, together with the fort escapees. Aside from them, others who left then included Friedke the gray-haired woman, Rivka the nurse, twenty-eight people all together....[43] Around three or four in the afternoon of that day, they told us to come to the meeting point. They gave us final instructions to maintain discipline and quiet near the gate.... Yankele stood there. At a certain point we heard him call: "The labor brigade for Roiter Hoif – one, two three. It returns tomorrow at six A.M." He made lots of noise. The vehicle was waiting beside the gate. Several group members were armed with pistols.... Haim Yellin sat beside the driver. It was a freight truck. We lay on barrels. The whole road to Zhezmer went smoothly. In Zhezmer, they shouted after us: "*Halt!*" The driver stepped on the gas pedal and increased his speed. We reached the train tracks where we stopped in the middle of a field. We got out of the truck, then embraced Yellin, who returned to Kovno in the freight truck. We wore the white camouflage clothes and started on the route to the partisan area. Before the train tracks, we lay on the snow for a while until the train passed. We ran across the tracks and reached a pit, where we stayed throughout the day. At night we continued.

We reached the forest through which the Merczanka River flowed. We looked for a bridge to cross the river, but in vain. We began to lose our way in the forest. Suddenly we came across a forester. The group leader recognized him as a man connected with the partisans. We told him who we were. He disappeared, and in a short time he reappeared with a group of partisans armed with submachine guns.... He took us to a bathhouse in the thick of the forest. They gave us water to drink.... We continued on the paved road. We floundered in deep snow...Finally we reached the village of Stary-Marczel. They brought us inside a barn and gave us straw with which to cover ourselves. We slept there, and the next day they brought us to the base.[44]

Ghetto Fighters as Emissaries from the Forest

After five groups of armed fighters were sent from the ghetto into the Rudniki Forests, time passed and the ghetto leadership received no clear news of their

---

43. Sometimes testimonies vary regarding such numbers. In this case, we had trouble verifying the exact number – somewhere between twenty and twenty-eight.
44. Testimony of Rivka Gordon, YVSA, 12–16.

fate. They did know that the fighters had escaped without mishap from the most dangerous area of central Lithuania – they heard this from Haim Yellin, who had escorted the groups (at least the two last ones). But they did not know how the fighters had traversed the remainder of the route, whether they had safely reached their goal, and how they were received by the Kovno battalion. Several days after the departure of the fifth group, an encoded letter was received by a trustworthy Lithuanian in Kovno from the command of the Lithuanian brigade in the Rudniki Forests. The letter stated that the groups had arrived but specified no details. The resistance movement in the ghetto was anxious, although the general atmosphere in the cells – those that knew about the departure of the groups – had turned optimistic and full of combat fervor, after the depression that had followed the Augustova Plan.

The situation changed on January 11, 1944. That evening, five fighters infil-trated the ghetto, helped by a labor brigade of Jews that returned from work in the city. The five, who had previously left the ghetto in various groups, were Ne-hemiah Endlin, Shmulik Mordkovsky, Baruch Lopiansky, Sarah Robinson, and Zondel Shtrom. These five were already recognized, trained partisans and they came to Kovno on a partisan mission. The mission was assigned to them by the brigade commander, Jurgis Ziman, himself, although they already belonged to the Kovno battalion "Death to the Occupiers." They had been sent as contacts between the party committee of the Communist underground of southern Lith-uania, which Jurgis headed, and the leaders of the Communist underground in the ghetto and in the city. They served as representatives of the partisan move-ment to the ghetto resistance and as partisan guides – to take out more groups of fighters from the ghetto and escort them to the forest, and for "special jobs" that required talented guides. For them the mission was a pleasant surprise and an opportunity to prove their salient partisan skills.

On one of the first days of January, Nehemiah Endlin was asked to report to Jurgis at his headquarters for the first time since his arrival in the forest. On the spot, the brigade commander gave him the mission and appointed him group leader. Each of the other four were given a special role aside from the general mission. The group members, armed only with pistols, went on their way imme-diately. From the very start the mission went well. In several villages on the route from the Rudniki Forests to Kovno they identified trustworthy individuals and contact people from among the poor farmers. The problems began when they reached Kovno. They were all armed but without identification. They were aware that the Germans here checked along every step of the way and that they could expect a thorough search at the ghetto gate. They knew that without partisan ingenuity, they would not make it. Following is Endlin's description of the "operation," which is mildly amusing but at the time was daring and highly dangerous:

> First of all, we took a piece of yellow cloth from a farmer and cut it into patches in the form of a Star of David. We attached them, as required, to the left side of our chests and on our backs. We enlisted a farmer with a sled and ordered him to take us to the closest place where Jews were working. Our companion Robinson approached the German soldier who was guarding the Jews and informed him that she was a nurse who had brought four sick people from the Jewish camp outside the city of Kovno. They should be taken under guard to the ghetto to be sent to the hospital. We succeeded in deceiving the German, and he put us into the labor brigade. We did not even have to work, since he thought we were ill. In the evening they brought us into the ghetto, and they did not even check us at the gate, since the Germans were afraid we would infect them.[45]

When they entered the ghetto, each of the group members contacted his organization and began to carry out his role. Endlin was the main person responsible for the group mission of contacting the Communist underground in the city.[46] The Communists in the ghetto helped him contact the underground party committee. The details of his mission are unknown, but apparently it included organizing a visit of three Communist activists, leaders of the Communist underground in Kovno, to the Rudniki Forests. These individuals were Haim Yellin, leader of the Communist Party in the ghetto; Gregory Krugliakov, a member of the Communist Party underground committee in the city;[47] and Anila Zinkovitz (her original name was Valia Pusheita),[48] leader of the Communist youth in the Kovno underground. This trip apparently had a decisive influence on relations within the underground "triangle" – the underground inside the ghetto,

---

45. According to PKG, 146.
46. Ibid., and 106.
47. From the Solomin group (see chapter 10).
48. See above, note 34.

the Communist underground in the city, and the Lithuanian partisan brigade in the Rudniki Forests.

During this visit to the brigade command, Haim Yellin was authorized as a member of the Communist Party underground committee in Kovno and received detailed instructions regarding the transfer of the ghetto fighters to the brigade bases. By all signs, at this meeting Jurgis voiced to Haim Yellin his indignation at the nature of the groups of fighters who had reached the forest from the ghetto. He asserted that the fighters' weapons were too "light" and their quantity insufficient; that a pistol was hardly useful under partisan combat conditions and that they required rifles, submachine guns, and even machine guns, as well as substantial quantities of ammunition; that the percentage of women in the groups was too high; and that the fighters' military training was insufficient. Haim Yellin and his companions remained in the forest for several days. In the meantime Endlin also arrived and he guided them on the long, arduous route back to Kovno.

Shmulik Mordkovsky also carried out the dangerous and important role during this period of escorting Albina-Glezer from Kovno to Vilna. In the ghetto he was allotted one of the fighters who had not yet been in the forest, the burly Yisrael Joels. Joels' testimony includes details about this mission:

> One day – in late 1943 or early 1944 – Haim David Ratner approached me and said I should go to Haim Yellin.... I went to Yellin, and he told me that along with Shmulik Mordkovsky I was to escort an important personality to the Rudniki Forests. At the same time he warned me: "If something happens, the last bullet is for you, because if they catch you they will torture you to the death, whether or not you tell them what you know." After I agreed to go they took us to a secret weapons cache.... A double wall opened up in front of me and I saw various types of weapons on shelves: Nagan revolvers [Russian], Parabellum [Luger] pistols, hand grenades.... I took a Nagan with thirty-plus bullets and four hand grenades. They taught me on the spot how to use these weapons. When we finished they told me, "Tomorrow morning beside the gate."
>
> My friend Bela Ackman accompanied me. I met Shmulik Mordkovsky there. We joined the [labor] brigade that was working at the Real Gymnasium [Hebrew high school], and we left with it through the Varnių Gate. We

reached the work site. They took us down to the boiler basement and we sat there until evening with nothing to do. We were told that a car from the Gebitskommisariat [high-ranking German official] would come to pick us up. The car arrived, but the driver said he could not take us that evening.... We had no choice but to return that evening to the ghetto.... When my mother saw me with the weapon, she wrung her hands and said, "Be careful, son, don't carry any family photographs, and don't reveal you have parents."... The next morning we went out again to the Real Gymnasium, and Haim Yellin joined us. At four or five in the afternoon the car came and picked us up. We arrived at Jonavos Street and the driver stopped beside the second alley. Haim Yellin got out of the car and we stayed inside. Fifteen minutes later, he returned with a woman walking in front of him. He walked behind her, his right hand stretched in front of him, covered by a sack. Under it he held a PPD submachine gun. They got into the car and we drove off. Yellin escorted us as far as Petrashun, where we stopped. Yellin gave the driver a large packet of money and a German Parabel in case of any trouble. But to us he whispered that if he got up to any "funny business," we should shoot him. After Butrimantz the snow on the road was so high that the car barely advanced. We got out and told the driver to go home.

We went together with Albina (by that time we were aware of her identity) into the house of a farmer and ordered him to hitch up a cart and take us whichever way he thought reasonable. We traveled in the cart the whole night. Shmulik Mordkovsky identified the places we passed easily and precisely, as if he had walked that route every day for years. On the way, we talked to Albina. She spoke Lithuanian and Yiddish with us. She told us she had been in the ghetto. She said that now she was carrying on her chest important documents and that if something happened and one of us was killed, the others should know to give the documents to Genis....[49]

A very long line of sleds approached us from behind. We allowed two sleds to pass us. Suddenly some of the sleds stopped and a few men jumped off and shouted, "Hands up!" We approached them and what did we see – Peretz Kliatchko, Mendke (Mendel) Dietz, and other fighters from the ghetto.

---

49. Commander of the partisan battalion whose bases were at the edge of the forest, near central Lithuania.

Their leader was a partisan whom I did not recognize (later I learned that this was Zeitzev, a platoon commander in our battalion). They were returning from a weapons acquisition operation, bringing back prized booty. The atmosphere lightened. We were then twenty people and our sense of security was boosted, but incidents awaited us on the remainder of the route.

Toward morning, we went into an isolated farmhouse for our daytime stopover. Mendel Dietz was cleaning his gun, and he accidentally let off a shot. Zeitzev fumed and shouted at him, "You hooligan! If you don't know how to use a gun, why did you come here?" We were shocked, because such a shot could give us away.... In the evening, we were all called over by the partisan who stood guard in front of the house. Apparently he had seen Germans in white camouflage cloaks passing not far from the house on skis. Quickly we all donned the camouflage cloaks (we had also been given these) and fled from the house. A volley of rifle fire rained down on us. We did not return fire. We retreated somewhere, and from there went to the forest. We were shot at again when crossing the train tracks on the way to the partisan area, but we did not fire back. We quickly entered the thick brush of the forest and reached Genis's base of "For the Homeland" battalion. Albina stayed there, while we continued until we reached Death to the Occupiers battalion. They welcomed us warmly, apparently thanks to the weapons we had brought (PPD submachine gun, three pistols, and eight hand grenades). They gave us four rest days and fed us potato pancakes, like officers.[50]

Instructions for the Ghetto Underground

Above we described the activities of Endlin and Mordkovsky as contacts and guides on missions that did not directly affect the ghetto underground. Now we will see what they, and the rest of the fighters who came to the ghetto from the forest in mid-January 1944, did for the movement inside the ghetto. As noted, they arrived as representatives of the partisan brigade to the ghetto underground and their mission was mainly educational and organizational. They were supposed to communicate the partisan reality – in all its wonders, challenges, and problems – to the underground members; describe their way of life and the combat conditions that were distinctive to the forest; provide the members

---

50. Testimony of Yisrael Joels, YVSA, 2 ff.

of the various movements with assistance, advice, and training; and aid those preparing to leave the ghetto and join the partisans. Indeed, the representatives worked wonders – their appearance made a powerful impression on the underground members.

The Jews at 7 Mildos sat crowded around Shmulik Mordkovsky for hours, thirstily drinking in his amazing stories of the partisans, of entire armies that were properly organized and armed, hidden in endless forests. Every night without rest they spread out over vast areas, blowing up German posts, derailing trains full of soldiers and equipment, freeing detainees and prisoners – and taking revenge.[51] But one detail clouded the faces of the listeners – the hints in Shmulik's descriptions of signs of anti-Semitism among the partisans.

The representatives' explanations focused on the weapons problem. Over and over they explained the partisan "arms doctrine": the pistol was an insignificant weapon – its primary value for a partisan to use it on himself, to avoid being captured alive by the enemy. In battle, the pistol was useful only on rare occasions. Therefore, they needed rifles, hand grenades, submachine guns, and even light and heavy machine guns. The Kovno battalion was still young and its weapons supply meager. If the ghetto residents did not bring the necessary weapons with them they would never reach the level of a respectable fighting unit and would suffer many losses. They had to purchase the necessary weapons, learn to use them proficiently, and bring them to the forest in good working order. In the forest there was no time for training. As soon as a fighter reached the base he became a partisan like the others, with all the accompanying rights and responsibilities. He had to know how to operate his weapon instantly, as fast as a German soldier.

Those who arrived in the forest weaponless received a cold welcome. Below is the testimony of Rivka Gordon, a fighter who reached the forest in the fifth group:

> The next day they brought us to the base. The commissar welcomed us. He separated the escapees from the Ninth Fort, and to us he said: "If Vladas [Haim Yellin's underground code name] were to arrive right now, I would shoot him on the spot. Why is he sending people here without weapons? To hide out here?" He would allow the fort escapees to remain, since they

51. Memoirs of Dov Levin and Zvie Brown; see also "Across from the Ninth Fort," *Sefer ha-partizanim ha-yehudim* 1:226–27.

had proved themselves as brave partisans, but he would send us back. I don't recall what happened after that because at the same time I learned that my husband was killed in a partisan operation and I was in shock. I only remember that they checked our packs. They took my watch off my hand, saying they needed it to buy weapons. A while later I saw my watch on the hand of Zigmund the scout. I asked him to give it back to me but he refused. I went to speak to the commissar about it. He intervened and my watch was returned.[52]

The partisan command did open the gates of its base to the ghetto fighters but set clear, difficult conditions: worthy weapons for each fighter, a relatively low maximum age limit, combat fitness and military training, a small percentage of women, and full equipment for the battalion, including medical equipment.[53] Some believe that the conditions also included the demand that a doctor from the ghetto would come but we have no confirmation of this. Neither do we know of any political conditions. We may assume that Jurgis and his companions took interest in the loyalty of the candidates for departure, regarding both collaboration with the Germans and any positions held in the ghetto institutions, and also regarding political-social views and party affiliation before the war and in the ghetto. But we do not know what instructions the representatives and Haim Yellin brought with them on this issue. We also cannot know whether the non-Communists in the JFO leadership raised the same issues specified in the founding agreement of the JFO, in which the Zionist movement members were promised political autonomy in the forest. At any rate, this matter no longer had any practical value, because the ghetto fighters reached the bases prepared for a partisan army with relatively uniform organizational characteristics and behavioral rules.

In retrospect, the members of the Zionist movements in the forest had the opportunity – albeit in a very limited way and without any formal recognition – to preserve a connection and certain symbols of their identity, such as speaking Hebrew and singing Hebrew songs.[54] But the ghetto residents apparently

---

52. Testimony of Rivka Gordon, YVSA, 15. Compare testimony of Eliezer Moses, YVSA, 12–13 (recording 4): "The meeting was miserable...because we did not have enough weapons. The commissar said that. He shouted: Why are they sending people without weapons...." See also chapter 11, "Confiscation of Belongings" and "Accepting Jews into the Battalion."
53. Meir Leib Goldschmidt, YVSA, letter 1.
54. See also chapter 11, "Entertainment."

understood that they could not make such demands of the Lithuanian brigade command, which was subordinate – especially on these issues – to the supreme partisan command in Moscow. Further, it is doubtful whether the ghetto organization was in a position to dictate any conditions to the forest partisans. On the contrary – the ghetto had to accept the conditions of the forest and make every effort to fulfill them, or else stop sending its fighters. On one specific point, however, the ghetto underground organization refused to remain silent. These were the rumors regarding incidents of anti-Semitism in the forest, which the representatives hinted at in their stories. A lively argument was waged on this point within all the organizations that considered sending members to the forest, and several times the JFO leadership was asked to address this issue in its meetings. But in the meantime, it was only a rumor, while the rest of the conditions and demands were very clear and required energetic action and maximum mobilization of resources.

The Sixth Group

In mid-January 1944 the sixth group was composed, according to the new instructions. It left the ghetto on February 5, 1944. This time Jewish guides led the group – Baruch Lopiansky, Zondel Shtrom, and Nehemiah Endlin. These guides had learned the doctrine of partisan conduct in the Kovno Death to the Occupiers battalion. A member of this sixth group writes:

> The preparations for departure took about one month.... After intensive efforts to collect money, our friends from the large workshops (that labored for the Germans) supplied the necessary clothing and boots. Our women friends shortened coats, sewed packs, and knitted socks and gloves. We underwent weapons training in the apartment of the collective...under the guidance of the assistant chief of the ghetto police, Yehuda Zupovitz. We were seven members of Hashomer Hatzair, including one woman, in a group of twenty-five people...the atmosphere was uplifting at the going-away party that was held in the collective's apartment...to which a limited circle of friends was also invited. We sat at tables set with tea and ghetto-manufactured candies, and reminisced about the chapter, the [summer]camps, and meetings. We sang all the movement songs, which were collected in a songbook belonging to our companion Yerachmiel. Eli congratulated us on behalf of the movement. The party reached its height with the festive ceremony: a red flag was raised and

the seven members made their pledge.... The words resonated like an echo from another world: "To be a faithful son to my people, my language, and my homeland, and to fight for a life of freedom, brotherhood, and justice in human society." The evening, filled with experiences, ended in song and dance.[55]

Another individual who left with this group describes the departure:

We received seven places, and we decided that the ones to leave would be Gita Foger, Yosef Rosen, Grisha [Sheffer], [Yankel] Kaveh, myself, Baruch [Grodnick], and Yankel Sesnitzky.... This was when we were already at the collective at 7 Mildos. We also trained with weapons there.... I remember the Russian rifle – we learned how to load the rifle and dismantle it. Somehow we decided who and what – I don't remember that part. They did not discuss money with me.... We received equipment from the General Organization [JFO]. I recall that we received boots, pants, and other items...everything we needed.... The departure was set several times but was not carried out. We were about to give up. We went to the gate twice, but nothing happened. The third time we left the ghetto. A few of us were equipped with weapons and we had some medical supplies. The weapons included two machine guns, several pistols, and mainly ammunition, bullets. Each of us received a few bullets. Aside from that, we also had packages of bullets meant for the base. The weapons were wrapped in blankets, because we went out as if we were a brigade going out to work outside the ghetto and it was the accepted practice that people took with them blankets to sell or to use, so they would not check it.... The clothing and equipment were mostly in good condition. Everyone received boots and clothes made in the ghetto workshops out of German uniforms.

We got into the vehicle that awaited us at the ghetto gate, and after a short ride we were in Jonavos Street, where we were given two more packages. Haim Yellin put these inside next to the driver. Haim Yellin rode with us in the driver's compartment. There was also a Lithuanian with us, an activist of the Lithuanian Communist Party. We received one rifle per person – they ordered us to load it on the spot – and final instructions on how to behave should we be attacked – we should return fire immediately.... Some members of the group wore real German clothes. One of these was Grishka, and

---

55. *"Bein ha-meitzarim," Sefer Hashomer Hatzair*, 1:744–46.

maybe Joseph. They were supposed to be German guards escorting Jews or prisoners. While driving, they stood and we sat. They stood in the corners of the truck. Sometimes they cursed in German. They had practiced how to curse well in German.

We traveled in that truck with no incidents, a distance of some 80 kilometers. The truck stopped. We were told to get out. We continued on foot.... When we got out of the truck, we were all armed. We looked like real partisans. I remember that the Lithuanian I mentioned earlier, the Communist Party activist, opened his eyes wide with surprise. He said, "I took you out bundled up, and now I see standing before me fighters."...After we got out of the truck we walked on a route that our guides apparently knew, until early morning. We reached a house that stood alone and decided to remain there during the day until we could continue. That was the plan, and this was the first lesson, that we walked by night and slept by day.... Toward evening we left. Early the next morning we reached the outskirts of the Rudniki Forests. We were all wearing clothes made from German uniforms, and we aroused suspicion among the guards of the partisan battalions who stood on the edges of the forest. They let us approach a certain distance and prepared to attack us. They thought we were Germans. Then they changed their minds and permitted the first ones to approach and asked them for the password. Of course we did not know it. They detained us, and only after much negotiation and explanation did they allow us to continue.

These were partisans from Genis's battalion. They took us to the bases, gave us a meal, and permitted us to continue. When we approached the train tracks, we encountered a group from the Vilna brigade that included Didalis (commissar of one of the Vilna battalions). [Didalis was the code name for the Jewish Soviet paratrooper Isser Schmidt.] Together we crossed the railroad tracks; I remember that we encountered shots.... After crossing the tracks Didalis gave us a speech and asked us to help the Vilna people with ammunition.... Our guides and some of the Communists in the group replied that they were forbidden to do so.... We continued in this manner until we reached our base.[56]

---

56. Testimony of Haim Gechtel (Galin), YVSA, 23 ff. (recording 9).

The Seventh and Largest Group

When the sixth group left the ghetto, tension rose in the organizations' cells. A few days after the group left Kovno, they learned that the operation had succeeded in full. The fighters journeyed the long distance with no mishaps and reached the brigade bases with all their supplies. There were no signs that the Germans had discovered anything about the operation. The leadership decided to increase the rate of departure, enlarge the groups, and augment the weapons and ammunition. They began to assemble the seventh group, the biggest and strongest of all the fighter groups to leave Kovno Ghetto for the partisans.

The composition of the group continued throughout February 1944. The ghetto conditions did not change fundamentally, although Goecke made successful efforts to calm the atmosphere after the Estonia deportation and the first *Kasernierung* decrees.[57] The economic condition of the ghetto inhabitants improved. One reason for this was the improvement of the food rations they received from the "new" German authorities under Goecke's supervision. Another reason was that Goecke was somewhat lax about the searches at the ghetto gate. Consequently barter blossomed, both inside the ghetto and between the ghetto and the Lithuanians in the city, perhaps more than during any other period of the Kovno Ghetto. Goecke, who had recently returned from an extended "home leave" (his absence from Kovno could only add to the increased calm), also convinced the Ältestenrat, and through it the ghetto residents, that in the near future the ghetto should not expect any upheavals.

The improvement in the ghetto conditions was so visible that in the labor camps in the Kovno environs a movement to return to the ghetto sprung up and people with contacts in the Ältestenrat began to petition to be sent back to the ghetto in exchange for other Jews who had not yet tasted a real prison camp. Under those conditions, it was still difficult to expect to find volunteers for the labor camp. Most of the Jews then considered the ghetto as the lesser of two evils, and perhaps even "the best of the possible solutions." Some of the Jews who had given over their children to Lithuanians even brought them back to the ghetto. Another source for the optimistic mood was the news from the fronts. The winter offensive of the Red Army forced the Germans to retreat on most parts of the

---

57. Gar, *Umkum*, 186–87.

front and to abandon – for the first time – broad areas they had occupied. In Italy, the Allied armies enjoyed victory after victory. In addition, they stepped up the bombings of industrial centers, ports, and large cities in Germany. The ghetto Jews firmly believed that liberation was very near.

These factors had a decisive influence on the reaction of those affected by the decision of the underground leadership to expand the departure movement. Reactions were different within the organizations and without. Inside the organizations the members felt a mild relaxation of the pressure to depart. There was a slight decrease in the numbers of those who were willing to exchange the "improved" conditions of the ghetto for the partisan forest, with its ordeals, demonstrations of anti-Semitism, and difficult winter conditions. This should not be understood as a renunciation of the fight against the Nazis but more as a tendency – in most cases, not entirely conscious – to delay the decisive moment, and not just for a few days or weeks. With regard to the activists, the leadership may have pursued an intentional policy to put off their departure. First, they were needed in order to organize the operation in the ghetto and the city. Second, if the "breathing period" in the ghetto ended, they would be able to leave the ghetto more easily than other organization members.

Despite this, among the unaffiliated or semi-affiliated who had some contact with the underground, the desire intensified to join the departing group. Arguments broke out among those who decided that if there were a real opportunity to escape to the partisans, they would do so without delay and not be tempted by the momentary improvements in the ghetto conditions. Thus the seventh group included some who were unaffiliated, who had recently joined the underground or renewed their contacts with it. Following is the testimony of one of this group, Zvie Brown; he describes the group's composition, its departure from the ghetto on March 3, 1944, and its journey to the forest. Brown had been connected with the Hashomer Hatzair underground in the ghetto since 1942, but throughout 1943 this connection was lessened because for most of that year he worked outside the ghetto in small labor brigades that cut wood in the forests around Kovno:

> In autumn 1943, I returned to the ghetto after this brigade, which had been working in the Jonava Forests, was reduced or disbanded. But I did not remain in the ghetto for long. When I discovered that there was a brigade

next to the town of Bavtai that was considered "good" by those in the know, I contacted Rabinowitz[58] and asked him to arrange a place for me in this brigade.... Compared to the Jonava brigade, here the regime was strict and the work difficult....

In December 1943 or January 1944, I received a note from the ghetto written by one of the members whom I had met at Hashomer Hatzair meetings in the ghetto. He wrote that I should try to come to the ghetto soon, regarding a matter of personal importance to me as well.... In the ghetto, I contacted the member who had written this note, and he took me to the apartment of the collective, at 7 Mildos. I was welcomed joyfully.... They arranged a place for me to sleep and informed me without much preparation that I was accepted into the collective "with equal rights and responsibilities." They introduced me to the collective manager Yerachmiel, and to Eli, the Hashomer Hatzair representative in the underground leadership. I told them that I had only come for one day, and Rabinowitz was guarantor for my return. They answered: "Don't worry about that. From now on, you have special protection, and no one will take you to work."

...A new world opened up before me. I simply could not believe my eyes. The atmosphere at 7 Mildos, the relationships, the conversations, everything was completely new to me. It was difficult for me to connect in my mind the first meetings in the underground, which I recalled from a year or a year and a half ago, with what I saw here: a true revolution.... The underground organization had become a ruling force in the ghetto.... I was deeply influenced by the stories of the partisan movement, with which the ghetto underground was in close contact.... A living example stood before me: Shmulik Mordkovsky. That was the first time I saw a pistol in the ghetto. I was amazed when I saw that he wore it every morning under his armpit, as if it was obvious, and as if he had been doing so for years....

I quickly found common ground with Eli and spoke to him at length about the underground in the ghetto, about the general situation on the fronts and in the international arena, and especially about the partisans in the Rudniki Forests, with whom we had contact. He told me the rumors about

---

58. Head of the German labor office in the ghetto.

anti-Semitism in the forests. (Later this was confirmed to me by Shmulik, although he did not want to expand on this topic).

In our conversations we reached the conclusion that this should not prevent him from sending people to the forest … but we would make every effort to uproot the discrimination.… We should demand that the Communists bring our protest before the partisan command in the forest … but in general, we should view the escape to the partisans, as it was carried out, as the best plan under the present conditions.…

Eli told me that a battle was being waged over the composition of the groups departing the ghetto and that the Communists always wanted to have the deciding vote on this issue. "Between us," he said, "we are fighting over places, but the real situation is that sometimes we have fewer men than the quota, but too many women.…"

One day Eli came and told me that I had been approved by the command.… From our organization [Eretz Israel Ha'ovedet] the others authorized for this group were Dov Levin (a member of the collective), Yosef Melamed, and Reuven Glickman (a frequent visitor to the house). Three weeks before the departure, we began weapons training and learning partisan tactics. The three of us from the collective's apartment went to training together, usually in the early afternoon. Only some of the departing group joined us in the training sessions, six or seven people if I recall correctly. We met the entire group only a day or two before the date of departure. The training sessions were held every day or every other day, in the Communists' apartment at 23 Mildos. This was a wooden house, similar to our house at 7 Mildos.… The house stood next to the barbed wire fence, and one wondered why they had chosen exactly this place for training.… Almost certainly under the house there was an underground bunker, and they hid the weapons we trained with in this bunker. The training sessions took place in one of the rooms in the house. The window was covered with a curtain so that from outside one could not see what was going on inside, but from the inside we could see the barbed wire fence and the guard pacing back and forth.

We mainly trained with the rifle. At first we learned the parts of the bolt without the rifle, then we learned how to hold it and aim, without the bolt. Finally we had several classes with the whole rifle. They brought a hand grenade to several meetings and explained to us how to hold the weapon properly.…

Near the time of departure, Nehemiah Endlin, the group's guide, gave classes on partisan tactics. He mainly spoke about principles of movement through enemy territory. He drilled us in how to behave in the vehicle that would take us out of the ghetto, on the route we would take on foot, and during the stops at the farmers' homes. He spoke very little about rules of partisan warfare in the forest. "You will learn that when you get there," he replied once when I asked about this.

The day of departure approached. Our excitement slowly intensified....

Several days before the departure, I was ordered to go to one of the organization's clandestine apartments, where there was a hidden storage room for clothes. I removed my worn shoes and put on a pair of boots. They were new, but it was easy to see that the upper leather had been taken from something used, a saddle or something like that.... The next day they sent me to another secret storage room, where they fitted me with a German uniform that had been died black (as I later understood – so as not to confuse the partisan guards in the forest), and two or three pairs of warm underwear. I received a short coat directly from the organization's tailor – a dark blue winter coat that was mended and shortened to the proper size.

A day or two before the departure, the entire group gathered in that same apartment at 23 Mildos. I did not know anyone besides my comrades in the organization, and those whom I had met during the training sessions.... The atmosphere was tense but festive. I think we even drank *l'chaim* and ate something. Haim David Ratner, an activist from the Anti-Fascist Organization, introduced himself (or was introduced by someone else from the leadership) as group leader. He immediately took the floor and made a flowery political speech on the roles imposed on us as partisans and – he emphasized – as "Soviet partisans." "We are not fleeing the ghetto for the forest in order to save our skins; we are joining the major body of the Soviet fighters in the enemy's rear, in order to make our contribution in blood to the sacred war against German and international Fascism. We will fight the Nazi beast until our last breath, we will faithfully carry out the orders of our commanders, representatives of the Soviet regime in the occupied territories, and we will prove we are worthy of the name partisan."

I clearly distinguished that his speech was in the Communist spirit, and that this did not exactly reflect the feelings of the non-Communists in the departing group. I asked to speak and responded to his speech. I said that we were joining the Soviet partisans, and would fulfill faithfully and honestly what the partisans imposed on us, but we would never forget, not even for one moment, that we did this as *Jews*, as people who left the *Jewish* Kovno Ghetto in order to avenge the blood of our brothers and sisters, mothers and fathers, who were murdered for being Jews, and in order to reinstate the honor of our people, who were led to slaughter....

I am not certain whether my words pleased Haim David Ratner and Nehemiah Endlin, but I felt that most of the gathering identified with me, including some who came from the Anti-Fascist Organization. Members of the collective responded to my speech with great satisfaction.

Finally the long-awaited day arrived. At 4 P.M., the three of us parted from the group at the collective's apartment. Emotions ran high. "See you *ba'aretz* – in the land [of Israel]" – these were the last words, and our hearts throbbed.... We walked toward the group's meeting point. One by one we entered a ruined building at the center of the ghetto.... Each one received a military belt – a broad German belt with leather shoulder straps that crossed on the chest and back – and four pouches, each with five rifle bullets. Most of the group also received hand grenades, two per person.... After dark...we again gathered next to one of the houses, not far from the back gate of the ghetto on Varnių Street. The vehicle that would take us was supposed to arrive at the gate at 7:00.... Then we saw it, approaching the gate. We left our hiding places and stood in the gate square.... At the last minute, the group was given important baggage: several large bundles. On the outside, bright red bedding; on the inside, two machine guns and several rifles.

The Germans were busy searching the labor brigades that were returning from the city. From within the group of Jewish gate guards, we heard the cry "*Babtai!*" This was supposed to mean that they had come to take the brigade going out to work in Babtai. One of the Germans...examined us with a quick glance.... He gave the sign and the Jewish policemen began to urge us with earsplitting shouts to exit the gate quickly. In an instant we were beside the vehicle. I saw two German soldiers standing in the corners next to the back. For an instant I shuddered, but then I realized that they were two group members dressed up as Germans....[59]

We were off.... The group leader gave the order to remove the yellow

---

59. One was Katriel Koblenz, and the other was apparently Yosef Melamed.

patches and hide them carefully.... The vehicle crossed the Niemen River bridge and went down left to Jonavos Street. It stopped beside one of the alleys. Endlin and two of our group[60] got out, and a few minutes later they returned with full sacks on their shoulders. These were the remainder of the weapons that completed the group's armaments....

Finally we left Kovno.... We began to accelerate and move southeast.... Each one received his weapons.... "Load weapons!" ordered the group leader. I withdrew five bullets from one of the pouches. I had mastered that.... Rifle loaded, I am a real partisan....[61]

Another member of this group describes the continuation of the route in his testimony:

After traveling for some two hours and after passing several villages and towns, we stopped. The vehicle returned to Kovno. We entered a nearby village, obtained carts, and placed the packages inside them.... I was appointed to be one of the group's scouts. Yisrael Goldblatt also joined the scout group. We also recruited local guides in the villages we passed.

With such guides, we usually only asked them to show us the way to the next village. There we would release him, with a warning that if he told anyone he saw partisans – he was risking his life.... In one village we made our only day stop on the way to the partisan bases. We placed a curfew on one house, forbidding the occupants to leave, and whoever came in from outside had to stay in the house until we left. We stood guard inside. Each of us sat next to the window beside the door for an hour and watched the traffic.[62]

After three days of walking at night and stopping during the day, the group, with all its weapons and equipment, safely reached the bases of the Kovno battalions. This group was the largest of the groups that departed the ghetto. As most of the participants testify, it was composed of twenty-eight individuals, aside from two guides (Nehemiah Endlin and Yisrael Goldblatt) and included eight

---

60. One was Michael Pasternak. See his testimony, YVSA, 1.

61. Testimony of Zvie Brown; compare *Sefer ha-partizanim ha-yehudim* 1:230–31.

62. Testimony of Yehuda Lifschitz, YVSA, 6. Regarding the departure of this group, see also testimony of Malka Pugatzky-Smali, YVSA, 17 (recording 5); testimony of Haim Nadel, YVSA, 2.

women. We know the names of twenty-one: Feige Abramovitz, Yehoshua Ant-
zel, Shlomo Baron, Zvie Brown, Mordechai Brick, Kalman Goldstein, Reuven
Glickman, Haim Wolbe, Feige Weiner, Sheine Levi, Dov Levin, Yehuda Lifschitz,
Yosef Melamed, Haim Nadel, David Sandler, Michael Pasternak, Malka Pugatzky,
Tuvia Friedman, Katriel Koblenz, Berel Kott, and Itta Shulman. They were apparently armed with three machine guns – two Russian and one Czechoslovakian
Bren – two or three Russian automatic rifles, nineteen regular rifles, some Russian and some German, a large amount of ammunition (according to one source
4,500 bullets),[63] several dozen hand grenades, and several pistols.[64] The group
took from the ghetto a sizeable quantity of medicines and medical equipment
for the base clinic, and essential food items such as sugar and fat.

From the aspects of weaponry and equipment, the fighters' discipline and
training, the exemplary organization at all stages of the journey, and the skilled
guides, this group was the crowning achievement of the Jewish Fighting Organization in sending people from the ghetto out to the forest. It was more successful
than all the preceding groups and, unfortunately, more successful than those that
came after it as well.

---

63. *PKG*, 108–9.

64. In his article (*FLC* 10:17), Mottel Brick gives different numbers. He says the group totaled
thirty-two members. "Ten received one submachine gun each. Fifteen had rifles, and seven had
machine guns." Submachine guns are not mentioned in any other testimony. Possibly Brick is
referring to automatic rifles, but the group had no more than three of these. As for machine
guns, it is almost certain that they had no more than three. But each machine gun was given
to two fighters, so that there were six machine gunners in this group – this is apparently the
source of Brick's error.

CHAPTER 8

The Preparations Behind the Departures to the Forest

After blazing a path from the ghetto to the forest, the underground faced difficult organizational problems. The forest partisans instructed the JFO (Jewish Fighting Organization) to equip and arm all those sent out to the forest with everything needed for a combat unit. Thus the JFO had to find funding sources and make contact with those who could supply the equipment they needed – steps involving countless dangers. Furthermore, assembling the groups was not an easy task.

Weapons

The weapons acquisition enterprise was undoubtedly the most important project of the JFO, but also the most dangerous. Ghetto residents were well aware that the Nazis considered weapons possession by a Jew to be an offense of the highest order, all the more so training and use of weapons by Jews. These "crimes" mandated the most brutal collective punishments. The threat of punishment did not deter the fighting organization, but compelled them to exercise utmost caution. These threats, however, instilled mortal fear in the ghetto population.

Only once did the entire ghetto, both its populace and institutions, experience the terror of the punishment for possession and use of a weapon against a German. This incident involved a Jew named Nahum Meck, who tried to slip away from the ghetto on November 15, 1942, through a barbed wire fence, intending to escape from Lithuania to somewhere abroad. Meck stumbled across a German during his escape attempt, pulled out his pistol, and fired several bullets.

Meck did not hit anyone but was caught by the German and then handed over to the Gestapo.[1]

The German mass-murderers deemed this an opportune moment to teach the ghetto Jews a "lesson." They arrested several members of the Ältestenrat and ordered the ghetto police to immediately arrest twenty Jews as hostages. Finally, they commanded the police to prepare a gallows in the center of the ghetto, congregate all the Jews there, and publicly hang Meck. This act of intimidation bore fruit; many of the ghetto's Jews were appalled and shaken at the very fact that a Jew dared to possess a firearm in the ghetto. The underground concluded that the secrecy and caution surrounding the arms-procurement enterprise must be applied not only to the Germans but also to the ghetto Jews outside the organization. The following description of the weapons enterprise proves that the weapons-buyers in the Kovno Ghetto passed the test of public responsibility while carefully exploiting every opportunity for arming and equipping the underground.

The story of the arms-procurement enterprise may be divided into three stages. The first stage extended from the beginning of the ghetto until the end of 1942 or beginning of 1943; the second stage – all of 1943; and the third stage began in the interval we are discussing here, January–February 1944 until the liquidation of the ghetto.

In the first stage the operation was very limited, so that we cannot truly speak of an "enterprise" per se. In this period the acquisition of a pistol and ammunition, and bringing them into the ghetto, was viewed even by the underground – including the Communists – as an extraordinary achievement, almost a miracle. We have no exact data about the quantity of weapons that the underground possessed during this period. The IBZ evidently acquired no more than three or four pistols during this time.[2] We should not assume that the Communists were much more successful in their pursuit of weapons, although according to some testimonies[3] the Communist cells had already in 1941 begun to assemble Molotov cocktails, primitive bombs, and pistols. Later on a weapons workshop

---

1. For more details about the Meck episode, see Gar, *Umkum*, 130–33, and Garfunkel, *Kovno*, 135–38.

2. See chapter 3, IBZ; testimony of Haim (Fima) Rosenberg, YVSA, 10; and compare to testimony of Avraham Melamed, Proceedings of the Partisan Conference at Givat Aliya.

3. Testimony of Malka Pugatzky-Smali, YVSA, 4 (recording 2); compare testimony of Ephraim Senior (Senion) and testimony of Bayla Rodashevsky, YVSA, recording 1.

was installed on 4 Broliu Street, in two small storerooms close to Hanne Kagan's apartment. It was nicknamed "Krupp Weapons Factory" and the following people worked there: Haim Vidutzky, Moshe Megidovitz, Alter Feitelson, Alter Rashkovitz, and Yisrael Milstein. These workers repaired and produced live weapons, cold weaponry (daggers and axes), and detonators for the saboteurs. Milstein was a metalworker in one of the ghetto's workshops and took advantage of his workplace after hours for the same goal.

Systematic activity began, evidently, during the Stalingrad victory period or afterward, close to the establishment of the JFO. The main weapons pipeline at this stage was still stealing weapons from places of work or purchasing arms with money.

The ghetto Jews worked in various places in the city that had weapons storehouses or workshops for fixing weapons. The JFO began to send their people to work at these sites, and after a period of careful surveillance they began smuggling weapons parts into the ghetto. Sometimes they even brought in whole weapons. The techniques for smuggling arms were then no different from those used for smuggling food (in which they scored many successes). Ruses like hiding butter in soup jugs with false bottoms and sausages in hollow logs were used by the fighters for smuggling arms. Sara Rubinson, Liba Schwartz, Gita Abramson, Malka Pugatzky, and Rachel Katz worked in the military hospital, housed in Kovno's Russian academic high school. The soldiers who were brought to the hospital from the front lines were too wounded and sick to properly guard their weapons, so the girls would steal pistols and ammunition from them, then hide them in jugs with false bottoms and smuggle these into the ghetto.[4]

The underground members who worked in the Fifth Fort smuggled rifle parts out of the fort's tremendous weapons storeroom[5] in hollow logs specially prepared by Leib (Lovka) Scher. As time progressed, they dared to smuggle whole rifles. It must be noted that none of the methods of subterfuge could be relied upon alone without the help of the Jewish guards at the ghetto gates. The German and Lithuanian inspectors near the gate gradually discovered all the hiding places, and even the most agile smugglers were sometimes foiled. It was infinitely easier to pass through inspection safely if one of the Jewish guards helped. The

---

4. Testimony of Malka Pugatzky-Smali, YVSA, 39; PKG, 46.
5. Testimony of Yisrael Joels, YVSA, 2.

Jewish guards would let people into the ghetto without inspection, and even if one of the other inspectors started to check a smuggler, the Jewish guard would try to take an active part in the inspection and divert the inspector's attention from the hiding places. Only once did the smuggling effort of a military item fail; it was when Yerachmiel Berman, who worked at the Fifth Fort, tried to smuggle a flare gun.[6] In contrast, scores of these kinds of operations were successful due to the cleverness, agility, and courage of both the fighters and the Jewish gate guards.

The following quote, about "lifting" weapons and ammunition from the stores that remained in the Fifth Fort from the Soviet era was related by a witness who was later active in the ghetto's secret weapons workshop:

> It happened around the end of April 1942.[7] The city [of Kovno] underground organization failed and Shmuelov was arrested. The ghetto's underground organization was dispersed. A small circle of Komsomol [Communist youth group] activists congregated in the home of Tevke [Tuvia] Pilovnik: Tevke, myself, Vilenchuk, Shalit, and Monik (Zalman) Holzberg. Monik told us about the events above, and added that Haim Yellin said we could do whatever we wanted, "Walk, run, fly…"
>
> The decision: Whatever happened, we had to supply ourselves with arms; then we would think about what else could be done. Either leave the ghetto or, in the case of an *Aktion*, fight and die on the spot. But it was not as simple as that. Where would we obtain firearms? The only place is the Fifth Fort. That's where the weapons storerooms are. Every day people are taken to go work there. Thus we have to bring firearms from there; if not to receive them [from the outside], then to steal them. Who should be the ones to go? They propose my name. I demand an assistant. We agree that Grishke [Grisha] Shalit will join me. I remember it as if it happened today. When I came home and told my sister, I'm going tomorrow to the Fifth Fort, she burst into tears.

---

6. See beginning of chapter 4 and note 4 there.

7. Evidently the witness was in error about the timing of the events described here. Shmuelov was arrested earlier, and the explosion in the Fifth Fort mentioned here, actually took place in July 1943. (See beginning of chapter 4, and notes 6–8 there.)

"Do you want to kill yourself before your time? There was an explosion there today and someone lost his hand there."[8]

The next day, and I'm standing at the courtyard [meeting area for the labor brigades]. All the other [labor] brigades have left already. They are looking for people to work in the Fifth Fort. The time – after 8:00. Grishke Shalit is together with me. When the people are taken [for work], we move. The Fifth Fort is opposite the train station, on a high hill. A path that is parallel to "Ramp 2" leads there; what an amazing place! Storerooms, storerooms, and fortifications. The workplace is called the Army Ordnance Office (*Feldzeug-Dienststelle*). Our job is to collect the various weapons and sort them. We are to dismantle the rusty weapons and then load the sorted portion on the [railway] cars and send them off.

On the first day – beatings. I am working like a horse and looking for an opportunity to go into one of the storerooms. At noon Grishke and I slip away to the large bomb storeroom. Grishke stands guard near the door. What can we take from here? Bombs – no. But after all, we have to do something. So I remove the screws from the detonators and start to remove long bags of dynamite. The dynamite will be useful in the ghetto while the bombs won't explode when they fall. Our yield is rather meager: about twenty bags of dynamite. The risks are tremendous and the result small. After filling our breast-pockets with dynamite we return safely to the ghetto.

The situation of the underground organization in the ghetto begins to stabilize. The work continues. I suggest bringing members to the Fifth Fort brigade in an organized fashion. Berkman is appointed brigade chief, and I – his deputy. The organization provides about 20 percent of the brigade laborers. A rifle was transferred from the fort to the ghetto and it was used for training exercises. Eltka Tepper brought that rifle to the ghetto in some firewood. I suggest that we switch to more active work, to organize the transfer of live weapons - hand grenades, bullets. But we encounter opposition; our leadership does not agree. The reason: if someone gets caught, we endanger the entire ghetto. The risk is too great. An argument ensues – yes, no; no, yes. I decide to make it a fait accompli: I talk to Yerachmiel Berman. I bring the first four hand grenades and hand them over to Yerachmiel. This act really

---

8. This refers to Y. Siniuk's injury (see chapter 4, ibid.).

solidifies our relationship. He agrees to my position and transfers bullets, bandages, and other materials to the ghetto.[9]

The option of purchasing weapons for money poses different difficulties and dangers. By the second half of 1943, corruption had spread in the ranks of the German army units stationed in Lithuania, as well as among their Lithuanian helpers. There were quite a few among them who were willing to negotiate deals for firearms so that they could enjoy the rich life. Of course, betrayal was always a concern. The Kovno Ghetto underground was lucky in that they did not experience even one incident of betrayal. Nevertheless, they exercised extreme caution.[10]

Ya'akov Levi,[11] member of the Anti-Fascist Organization, was a courageous and deft arms buyer. He looked like a typical Lithuanian farmer: short in stature, bent over, with a walking stick in his hand, a pipe between his lips, and a long mustache curled upwards. The German guards would never have imagined asking him for documents, but just in case he was equipped with a forged identity card under the name of Antanas Gudauskas. Levi went to the city countless times without the yellow badge and organized the most daring weapon deals. Malka Pugatzky says the following about an important arms deal that was carried out in this period:

> The work in the cells was as follows: preparation for departure for the forest, first aid, training outside in use of weapons, and the main thing – purchasing "heavy weapons," rifles. I participated in the purchase of a rifle, which as far as I know was the first to be smuggled into the ghetto. It happened liked this: Rochele [Rachel] Katz, my friend who belonged to our organization in the ghetto, made contact with a Lithuanian who had sold to her earlier. He sold her a German rifle for five thousand marks. He dismantled it into parts; the two of us hid the parts in wood bundles and brought them into the ghetto. When Dimka [Dima Galpern] saw the rifle, he was astonished and didn't understand how we had succeeded in smuggling such booty into the

---

9. Alter Feitelson, YVSA, letter 15.

10. Dvora Friedman used this method to acquire weapon parts for the organization; the parts were later assembled in the ghetto by the organization's weapons experts (testimony of Michael Yitzhaki [Gelbtrunk], YVSA, 11).

11. *PKG*, 46.

ghetto. That same Lithuanian served afterwards as our liaison in large-scale arms deals that the movement made with other Lithuanians and even with Germans – all in the name of "business."[12]

After the way to the Rudniki Forests was opened, the weapons acquisition enterprise entered its third, decisive stage. Now the fighters could no longer manage with the two "regular" acquisition procedures described above, although these had been significantly perfected and expanded. The time had come for daring procurement operations, with the objective of arming the JFO in increasingly large steps in order to satisfy (also with regard to the pace of acquisition) the demands of the Lithuanian partisan brigade command.

These operations were facilitated by the new system the organization adopted for storing arms. Previously, weapons were smuggled into the ghetto and then stored in special *malinas*, arms caches. Understandably, weapons would be smuggled into the ghetto as long as the JFO's plans were mainly for self-defense and links with the underground in the city were weak. But things changed at the end of 1943 regarding both factors. The center of gravity shifted to plans for sending the fighters, or a large proportion of them, to the forests, while contacts with the underground people in town became ever closer. Furthermore, quantities of heavy weapons and long weapons increased to the point that attempts to smuggle them into the ghetto would have been extremely difficult and entail great risk. Therefore it was decided that most of the arms that were purchased would not be brought into the ghetto at all but instead hidden in the city, and a group departing for the forest would pick up the firearms on their way. There was such a weapons cache in Murava[13] at the beginning. The cache became unusable at the beginning of 1944, after Communist underground activists were caught by the Gestapo there and tortured to death. (Among those who were arrested and executed was the old man Jagofla Radyonov, father of the commander of the Kovno partisan battalion Death to the Occupiers, Konstatin Smirnov Radyonov.)[14] By January 1944, arms caches at the disposal of the ghetto organization were installed on 53 Jonavas Street in the home of Lithuanian Communist Pyotr Trofimov and with Maria Leschinsky, on Ragucio Street in Slobodka.

---

12. Testimony of Malka Pugatzky-Smali, YVSA, 6.
13. PKG 47, see photo.
14. Ibid., 107.

The first large-scale acquisitions operation was carried out on the eve of the Olkin group departure for the forest, on November 15, 1943. The departure point for this action was still the partisan's intermediate base in Murava. The target was the home of the forest warden in the Koshedar region, a man known in his area for his hostile attitude to the village population and for his service to the German authorities.[15] The underground members discovered that in his watch house in the thick forest, the forest warden had a very respectable arms and ammunition storeroom.[16] The following activists took part in the operation, among others: Eliyahu (Elia) Olkin, Eliezer (Lazer) Klebansky, Yisrael Berenstein, and Meir Teinovitz. They walked over 30 kilometers in one night; when they reached the watch house they immediately surrounded it and severed the phone lines that connected the warden with the outside world. They stormed the house in a surprise attack, quickly overcame the warden and his assistants, and killed them with gunfire before taking over the arms storeroom. Before sunrise the fighters had returned with their precious booty, which included rifles, pistols, and ammunition as well as a radio set. They took it all to the base in Murava.

Another large-scale acquisitions operation took place in mid-January 1944 in the arms storeroom of Kovno's military hospital in the very hub of the city, on 28 Vitoto Boulevard.[17] A brigade of Jews from the ghetto worked there; underground members were sent there with the others and they systematically tracked the storeroom's guard duty roster and inspection routines. Then they prepared a detailed plan of the facilities and even prepared a key to the storeroom door. One night, the go-ahead signal was given for the operation. A squad of adept fighters (that included Yitzhak Miklishansky, Mendel Moskovitz, and Geguzhinsky) slipped out of the ghetto, infiltrated the cemetery that adjoined the hospital, and waited there until midnight, camouflaged by the high piles of snow. When all was quiet and everything had sunk into darkness, two of them wearing white camouflage cloaks dashed out to the storeroom gate. They opened it with the key and quickly each person took a full sack of rifles and ammunition. As they left the storeroom with the sacks on their backs they almost ran into the sentry. But at the last minute they jumped into a pit together with their valuable booty

15. Ibid., 84–85.
16. According to Meir Teinovitz; see his letter, YVSA, no. 1.
17. PKG, 107. Also compare recollections of Miriam Buz, and Viršulis, 61–62.

and the sentry did not notice them. A few minutes later the three were sitting in a car that awaited them not far from the hospital. The weapons were brought safely to their hiding place on Jonavas Street. An interesting detail: the military hospital stood opposite the Gestapo building in Kovno.

Another operation, similar in technique and results, was carried out in the arms storeroom of the German *Flak* (anti-aircraft guns) workshop in Kovno. The preparatory work was done by members of the labor brigade employed there, prisoners of the Aleksot work camp. Benzion Preiss was the liaison between them and the ghetto underground. The following activists took part in the operation: Yitzhak Miklishansky, Mendel Moskovitz, and Ya'akov (Yankel) Levi.

In the early stages, procurement activities took place within the individual underground organizations, with the assistance of people from the ghetto institutions. For example, we know that Moshe Levin, commander of the Jewish police, was one of the most enthusiastic supporters of the JFO and was the Beitar commander in the ghetto. Levin initiated acquisition activities and, in fact, directed them. At first Beitar members acquired and smuggled the weapons and even stored them in Beitar's *malinas*. Later on, individuals outside of Beitar were involved in these activities, and ultimately these were all integrated into the overall acquisition enterprise of the JFO. One of the Beitar weapons purchasers writes the following in his testimony:

> I supplied arms for the underground organizations, as I was a member of a Beitar cell. I made contacts with a Lithuanian police officer who lived opposite the Inkaras factory. I would slip out of the ghetto and go to his house. At first we traded in foodstuffs, but when a strong link formed between us I began to sound him out regarding weapons for the underground organizations, which were preparing to leave the ghetto and depart for the forests. I reported to Beitar commander Zvi Levin (may God avenge his blood)[18] and informed him about the possibility of acquiring arms for Beitar.... Levin appointed me as liaison between the command and the person responsible for Beitar's

---

18. Evidently, the reference is to Moshe Levin. While Zvi Levin was a Revisionist, he was not a Beitar commander; he lives to this very day in the Soviet Union. In Yehuda Tarshish's same testimony, Zvi Levin is mentioned as a police commander who was imprisoned in the Ninth Fort with all the other policemen, then executed. It is clear beyond any doubt, that the reference here is to Moshe Levin.

bunker, where the firearms were stored, and also told me to strengthen my relationship with the Lithuanian officer. Within a short period I brought at least twelve Czech and Russian rifles and they were transferred directly to Beitar. In all I brought in over twenty Nagan revolvers. I paid in cash for the firearms; the Beitar command in the ghetto gave me the cash.

I would slip out of the ghetto at the gate, with the help of Beitar police-men who knew about my job and my objectives. In the city I would remove the yellow badge, then arrive this way to the rendezvous sites. I would find my way unassisted back to the ghetto under cover of darkness to where the Beitar liaisons would wait for me. They identified me according to a password and other signs that had been agreed upon in advance. As time went on, and while cooperating with other underground organizations, I was asked to pro-cure weapons for them as well. I agreed after receiving permission from the Beitar command, which cooperated with all the organizations. I also brought weapons to the Communists and was in touch with Yellin and Ratner.

Later on, I made contact with the Lithuanian manager of the post of-fice near the ghetto. Here, too, I obtained weapons, especially ammunition. Within a short period of time I got my hands on several boxes of ammunition that included bullets for various weapons. The boxes were brought in via the fence on Kriščiukaičio Street.[19]

Over time, individuals outside the organizations were included in the acqui-sitions enterprise. These were mainly people known as war profiteers or "fence traders" ("*tsamnikes*" in ghetto terminology) due to their great expertise in smuggling merchandise into the ghetto. Their services were advantageous but also involved risks to ghetto security.[20] Beitar members also made connections with one of the fence-trader groups. We read about this in the testimony of one of the former fence traders:

Back in the spring of 1942, after I was dismissed from the fire brigade in the ghetto, I began to "work" near the fence exchanging clothes for foodstuffs. My business developed substantially. We developed good relations with the

19. Testimony of Yehuda Tarshish, YVSA, 1 ff. For more information about Beitar acquisition activities, see also testimony of Michael Katz, YVSA, 1.
20. See the episode of robbers in the ghetto, at the end of this chapter.

goyim who lived on the other side of the fence, solely of a business nature. The business brought profits because at that time the order was that no foodstuffs could enter through the ghetto gate.

The day after the decree we were invited (myself and my associate) to the ghetto police headquarters, where we were ordered by [police commander] Moshe Levin not to raise the prices of the foodstuffs that we sell the ghetto residents. We received a list of maximum prices for the foodstuffs, as well as another list of items without restrictions (cigarettes, liquor). He promised us that if we would follow these instructions, they would not harm us in the ghetto or force us to work. On the next day – and afterwards, every single night – they came to check the items, whether they were sold and to whom. A few days later, we were again summoned to the police headquarters and rebuked severely for not bringing potatoes into the ghetto for a few days (it was not worth our while). After we promised to bring in twenty-five to forty sacks of potatoes every night, they left us alone. We kept our promise. This whole inspection process kept on until they again began to bring foodstuffs through the gate. I had four partners (Shimon Schneider, Mendel Schneider, David Klinovsky, and one more).

About six months later (the end of 1942 or the beginning of 1943), friends approached me and said that they knew of a way to escape to the partisans. Immediately I agreed to go. After some time I received word that "organized *goyim*" – emissaries from the Red Partisans – would wait for us at a specific location on the far bank of the Vilya (the river that crosses Kovno). We took a boat and rowed to that spot several times (we did not take firearms with us), but no one came to take us and we gave up.

It became very clear from this whole story that there were partisans in Lithuania. Immediately I began to be concerned about a personal firearm for protection, just in case I should ever need it. It was not especially difficult for me to get hold of a weapon because I had contacts with *goyim* with whom I had business dealings. I think that was in the spring of 1943. I had the opportunity to buy a pistol from one of the *goyim* I knew. It was a 9 mm Parabellum. I paid nine hundred marks for it. Afterwards, I occasionally bought pistols and sold them to private people in the ghetto.

In the summer of 1943, the ghetto police conducted a search in my house. They put me in prison for twenty-three days. During this time they tried to tempt me by using various methods so that I would reveal where I got my firearm. The policeman who guarded me, Nachum Marish, even offered to escape together with me from the ghetto. Once, Menashe (Menashke) Sapozhnikov entered my cell – evidently he was an undercover policeman [he was a member of the Anti-Fascist Organization, in the "Black Staff"][21] and tried to coax me to hand over my weapon, saying that if I did, they would immediately free me from jail. I didn't respond. Another day, someone who called himself "De Gaulle" [Moshe Levin] came to me and clearly hinted that I should continue bringing firearms into the ghetto, but that he wanted me to know to whom I should hand over the weapons. Two days after they released me, Mordechai Michles found me. He came to me with a proposal, to sell him weapons at full price. After I turned him down out of self-respect (I was angry that they had held me in prison), he delivered the bombshell: He had come on behalf of "De Gaulle," who proposed that I purchase a firearm for him and bring it to his house. I agreed to this on principle.

After some time, Michles introduced me to a fellow named Meir Neustadt[22] in order to conduct the transaction. I was asked to bring a "sample" pistol to the meeting. To be on the safe side, I put two pistols in my pocket; one of them I took out for Neustadt to inspect and the other one I kept, loaded, in my pocket (I was still very worried). Neustadt explained to me that under current circumstances, pistols were no longer necessary; they now required rifles and submachine guns (this was after the Estonia deportation). I promised to obtain "long" weapons for him. On his part, Neustadt promised that if I would bring him weapons without making a profit, he would include me on the list of those who could depart for the forest whenever they wanted. Neustadt was then acting as the representative of the organization in charge of departures for the forest.

The next day, I immediately left the ghetto and went to my suppliers. I ordered a rifle from one of them. They promised me that I could receive it at the same spot, a day later. When I came the next day, I was very surprised to see two Jews from the ghetto with my supplier (whose name was Adolf).

---

21. See the end of this chapter.

22. According to the testimony of Michael Katz, YVSA, 3, Neustadt was in charge of acquisition activities in the Beitar command in the ghetto. Communist sources also cite him as a faithful assistant in bringing weapons into the ghetto (compare to PKG, 46).

The two men included a former policeman from the ghetto police and Meir Teinovitz,[23] someone I had known from my youth. It turned out that they had also come to buy rifles. They came on behalf of Haim Yellin. When I saw that the competition between us might increase the price, I proposed to Teinovitz that we buy the rifle together. He agreed and we closed the deal. It was a new Czech rifle with forty bullets. We paid two thousand marks for it. We received hasty but thorough instructions from the supplier on how to use it. In order not to arouse attention, we dismantled the weapon – I took the bolt and Teinovitz took the barrel – and we returned to the ghetto. Yankele Verbovsky had to help us enter the ghetto through the fifth gate (the Varniu Gate).

We waited half an hour while lying under the transformer not far from the gate, but there was no one to bring us in. I left Teinovitz with the rifle and I went in alone via the bridge to sort things out. Meanwhile, Yankele Verbovsky arrived and brought Teinovitz in. I looked for Teinovitz afterwards in the ghetto, so that we could together hand over the "merchandise" to its final owner, but I did not find him. I had no choice but to go to "De Gaulle" without the rifle and tell him the whole story. He reassured me and explained that it made no difference; the important thing was that the weapon was in trustworthy hands. But I was not satisfied and asked that they show me the rifle. They brought me to a small house in the ghetto; that's where I found Haim Yellin (that was the first time I met him), Menashke Sapozhnikov, and Haim David Ratner. That's when I understood that this was a joint matter, and that Menashke Sapozhnikov was also "in the know."

After this incident I would purchase three or four rifles each week from different suppliers, including Adolf. In total, I brought between twelve and fifteen rifles to the ghetto. My suppliers lived near the Inkaras rubber factory and the Guma factory.[24] At the suppliers' house, I would put the rifle on my body, the bolt into my pants, and the stock on my back. Afterwards I would walk like a lame hunchback. I always kept a loaded pistol in my pocket and I was prepared to open fire on anyone who would stop me. I had an order not to get caught alive by the Germans ... so I used to sneak into the Guma

---

23. Compare letter of Meir Teinovitz, YVSA, no. 2.
24. Compare testimony of Yehuda Tarshish, YVSA, 2.

factory. The head of the Jewish labor brigade that worked in that factory used to give me his room (he knew I was providing weapons for the ghetto). He would set guards outside, then help me organize the rifle in a plausible manner so that I could get to the ghetto safely. I put a sack full of potatoes on the [rifle] "hump" and marched in the middle of the column. Near the gate, Yankele Verbovsky made sure I got through the gate without being checked.

I used to bring the contraband weapons directly to the home of M. Levin.... This process continued for about two months (around November–December 1943) without a hitch. In January 1944, something happened that could have tripped me up. At the time I was working together with Shlomo Baron, who also worked for Haim Yellin. That day we didn't have rifles, but a large quantity of bullets. We decided to enter via the gate. When we approached, I heard somebody call "*Halt*." I turned around and saw a guard from the Hungarian SS who was watching the fence. I tried to bribe him, but without success.... The guard decided to bring me to the headquarters.... After we had gone about a hundred meters, I felt that no one was walking behind us. I turned my head back and saw the guards standing and arguing. We could have tried to escape, but I chose another path: I approached them again, and this time succeeded in bribing them with 250 marks. This way, I ensured contact with them in the future as well. When I got home, however, I decided that the time had come for me to leave the ghetto for good. I contacted Meir Neustadt and asked him to keep his pledge to me. He agreed immediately and promised that I would depart [to the forest] with the next group.[25]

Military Training

As far back as the secret meeting held in M. Bramson's apartment at the end of 1941, one of the stated goals of the emerging resistance movement was to "teach the youth to use weapons."[26] Some of the participants of that meeting became the first instructors; these were former military officers: M. Bramson, I. (Ika) Greenberg, and Peretz Padison. Real activity began only after the Great *Aktion*

---

25. Testimony of Yehuda Lifschitz, YVSA, 1 ff. For more information about this episode, see also Meir Teinovitz, YVSA, letter no. 1.
26. See beginning of chapter 3; testimony of Avraham Melamed, Proceedings of the Partisan Conference at Givat Aliya, 4.

and especially at the beginning of 1942, for example in the Communist circles.[27] In the IBZ, "defense" was taught as a subject along with other classes such as history and literature. Special efforts were made to constantly update and refine the communications system, including numerous practice drills.[28] Several sources verify that pistol-training was carried out in the large pits of Democrats Square, in November 1942.[29] One of the instructors was policeman A. (Avraham) Rapopsky. The nature of the training drill depended on the resistance plans – protecting the ghetto, street fighting, or departures for the forest – on the necessity for total secrecy, and on the number and types of weapons available; the number of instructors who could teach the subject were taken into account for the particular purpose.

In the first stage (until spring 1943), a training system evolved that focused on establishing an intelligence network, a method for transmitting news and information, the recruitment process, and a way of disseminating initial information in the use of short weapons (pistols), including practical drills.

As departures for the forest and partisan bases became the focus, the goal of training began to shift to prepare for warfare outside the ghetto. The training methods and scope changed accordingly. In the summer of 1943, the training included military discipline; field-craft; living conditions in the forest; building dugouts; combat tactics (attack, defense, retreat, and storming the enemy); the make-up of combat units; familiarity with the rifle, pistol, grenade, and machine gun; fighting against specific weapons (machine gun, tank, cannon); arson; sabotage; communication signaling; reconnaissance; basic topography; creating primitive weapons and their use (knives, Molotov cocktails); and an intensive first-aid course.[30]

Training was conducted in cells of three or four. The cell commander would instruct his group according to written material he received from his superiors. One of the first training groups was led by Zadok Bleiman, who had served

---

27. Testimony of Pugatzky-Smali, YVSA, 4 and 6 (recording 2, 3).

28. Testimony of Haim Rosenberg, YVSA, 10.

29. Testimony of Moshe Levin, YVSA, 2; testimony of Menachem Golan (Korlianchik), YVSA, 1.

30. PKG, 88–89. First-aid courses were given by Dr. A. Berman, Dr. R. Kaplan (a woman), Dr. Aharon Peretz, Dr. Feldman, and other physicians in the ghetto; Sudarsky et al., Lita, 1913; Peretz, 46.

before the war as the only Jewish instructor in the Lithuanian Army's basic training camp. Bleiman's group was comprised of Leo Ziman, Eli Rauzuk, Moshe Levin, and Yona Rochman. The group used to train in the early morning hours, before the members left for forced labor.[31]

Slowly but surely, a staff of instructors began to form, most of whom had served in the army. The staff included Ika Greenberg, Yehuda (Yudel) Zupovitz, Haim (Dor) David Ratner, Zadok Bleiman, Haim Wolbe, Michael Pasternak, Lovka Scher, and others. When the first representatives from the forest arrived in the ghetto with their demand for "long" weapons, training was then concentrated on the rifle, its parts, and usage. The pace quickened and *malinas* were allocated to this objective.[32] The best instructors were mobilized for intensive training of the groups departing for the forest, and these trained one to three weeks before their departure.[33]

Sources of Funding

The weapons acquired during partisan operations, such as the operation against the forest warden or the break-in at the German storehouse, naturally did not involve large outlays of money. But weapons bought with money presented a huge challenge to the underground with regard to how to finance the purchases. Suppliers often demanded fantastic sums for each pistol, grenade, and bullet – even more for the "long" and "heavy" weapons such as rifles and machine guns. The suppliers also faced serious inconvenience and danger in purchasing these weapons and hiding or camouflaging them. Other activities connected to departures for the forest that also required money, thus aggravating the funding problems, were hiring drivers and vehicles and bribing the Germans at the gate. In addition, the fighters had to be equipped with combat belts with pouches, boots, and clothes suitable for the life of fighting in the forests. The partisan command required that the groups also bring with them "non-personal" equipment for

---

31. Testimony of Zadok (Eviatar) Bleiman, YVSA, 12–14 (recording 2b).

32. The weapons to be used for training were given for safekeeping to Rivka Gordon, who was given the nickname "the conspiracy lady." She would distribute them according to the list given to her (Rivka Gordon, letter 2).

33. Aside from the ghetto instructors who mainly taught the use of weapons, the guides themselves taught field-craft, partisan tactics, and the unwritten rules of the forest, as they learned from personal experience.

general use, such as medicines, radios, and printing and duplication machines. The underground therefore adopted every possible method of raising money, including the most unusual and dangerous ones. Even methods that had been rejected in earlier periods as unacceptable became indispensable to the success of the mission.

The JFO relied on two types of funding methods at the height of activity: individual and public. Individual funding meant that every candidate for departure to the forest was required to pay a certain sum of money to the underground fund for "purchasing weapons and equipment." It seems – though we have no exact data on this – that all members of movements that were represented on the joint command of the JFO paid an equal amount. Candidates who were not from these movements paid according to their financial state, usually much more than the sum demanded of the "affiliated ones."[34] If unaffiliated candidates could not pay the required sum, they could not join the partisans; by contrast, if a member of a movement did not have the required sum, the movement would pay the difference.[35] According to the information in our hands, movement members were required to pay two thousand marks.[36] Most of those leaving the ghetto would sell valuables – clothes, underwear, even furniture – in order to obtain the required sum. If the candidate was a lone individual and left property behind in the ghetto, the property was transferred to the ownership of the JFO.[37]

Public modes of raising money were diverse. The simplest way was to launch an appeal for money and collection of warm clothes among the underground

34. Most probably, the "nonaffiliated" candidates (who paid a higher sum to be included in departures for the forest) also represented a small percentage of the total number that left for the forests. An example of someone in this category is Haim Nadel. He purchased a Parabellum pistol from a Lithuanian in exchange for two leather coats and a feather quilt that were worth 5,000 marks. He handed the money to Yerachmiel Berman, one of the activists of the Anti-Fascist Organization. Only then did they agree to add him to a training-group preparing for a departure for the forest. A large proportion of the "nonaffiliated" candidates were "fence traders": these were allowed to join a forest-group without payment, as a "prize for their dangerous service."

35. Testimony of Haim (Galin) Gechtel, YVSA, 22 (recording 8); testimony of Malka Pugatzky-Smali, YVSA, 16–17 (recording 5); testimony of Eliezer Moses, YVSA, 10 (recording 3); Berel Kott, letter 2.

36. (Editor's note: then about $800, the equivalent of $11,500 in 2013.) Testimony of Gita Foger-Turchin, YVSA, 16; testimony of Baruch Grodnick (Gofer), YVSA, 10–11 (recording 3).

37. Testimony of Ephraim Senior (Senion), YVSA, 1; testimony of Grisha Sheffer, YVSA, 13 (recording 4).

members as well as among the wealthy Jews who could be counted on as dependable accomplices. In practice, this was carried out by the Public Committee which the JFO had established for this purpose. Some of the people who took an active part in this were Shulamit Rabinowitz, Mendel Sadovsky, and Yudel Zupovitz.[38] The needs of the underground, however, greatly exceeded the amount that could be obtained by regular activities such as collections from a public whose more financially privileged members tended to be of questionable morality and of weaker social fabric (such as fence traders, profiteers, owners of ghetto stores).[39]

Under these circumstances, there was no choice but to resort to less refined but more efficient methods. The well-to-do people were charged with payment quotas ("contributions") that were collected either by cordial means or by force.[40] Eventually, a special committee of activists was formed that collected the quota payments. This committee was called the Black Staff, and consisted of Yerachmiel Berman, Menashe Sapozhnikov, Lipman, and Danke Birger (a former boxer). The activities of the Black Staff were shrouded in secrecy. Its members were all affiliated with the Anti-Fascist Organization, but we assume that they operated under the supervision of the JFO joint command,[41] at least to a certain extent. Below are some details regarding Beitar's financing techniques in the ghetto, over different time periods:

> The organization financed its activities as outlined below: (A) When the Jews entered the ghetto, the Germans ordered them to hand over all their gold, valuables, and foreign currency. A unit of Beitar members infiltrated the storage place where these valuables – which had been robbed from the Jews – were kept. The Beitar group confiscated a large sum of money and gold coins, then hid it in a secret place. Shortly afterwards, they removed

---

38. *Toldot Mildos* 7, 4; testimony of Shulamit Rabinowitz, YVSA, 10 (recording 12); testimony of Menachem Sadovsky (Ganuni) 21 (recording 3b); testimony of Zvi Brick, YVSA, 2; also see chapter 4.

39. For information about the ghetto economy and sources of livelihood in the ghetto, see Gar, *Umkum*, 120–21, and Garfunkel, *Kovno*, 230.

40. Testimony of Y. Lifshitz, YVSA, 2; see also Garfunkel, *Kovno*, 173.

41. Testimony of Yisrael Joels, YVSA, 2; the members of the Black Staff forced him to steal medicines from the hospital attic (see also testimony of Eliezer Moses, YVSA, 4, recording 1). Menashe Sapoznikov was also connected to the criminal department of the ghetto police (Gar, *Umkum*, 141).

the treasure and used it for purchasing weapons and for building bunkers. (B) In 1943 there was a mass escape of Jewish prisoners from the Ninth Fort, including Beitar member Aharon Manyeskin, who later fell in an operation in the forests. Manyeskin, may God avenge his blood, brought a small bag of gold with him from the Fort, and gave it to the Beitar command.[42] (C) Police Commander Moshe Levin (may God avenge his blood), also the Beitar commander, occasionally used to transfer large sums of money to Beitar in order to purchase weapons.[43]

Yet what the individual organizations managed to scrape together was sparse compared to what the unified JFO achieved, especially after it secured the assistance of the ghetto institutions. In fact, this assistance was considerable. The workshop managers excelled in this, evidently with either the express or tacit agreement of the Ältestenrat. During the Goecke period, the German authorities paid special attention to the workshops. On various occasions, Goecke himself would emphasize his interest in the fine achievements of the ghetto enterprises and wouldn't take his eyes off of them. The workshop facilities were expanded to employ additional workers, and orders multiplied from German institutions. Of course, this activity meant the storehouses were continuously restocked with raw materials and finished products. During this time, over a period of about six months, the workshop managers did not flinch from arranging secret and well-organized supplies of German military equipment of all kinds for the JFO – combat belts with pouches, boots, uniforms, underwear. They were all too aware of the dangers this involved for the workshop employees in specific, and the ghetto in general. This entire saga, one of the outstanding achievements in the annals of the Kovno Ghetto resistance movement, is revealed in all its details in the memoirs of the workshops' manager Moshe Segelson. He penned these remembrances immediately after his liberation from the Landsberg concentration camp in Germany:

> One morning in August 1943, my friend Zvi Levin entered my office in the ghetto workshops. Levin was one of the close associates of the Ältestenrat in Kovno. He said that he had something very urgent to discuss with me....

---

42. See end of chapter 6.
43. Testimony of Michael Katz, YVSA, 2 ff.

"What we will discuss now must remain a total secret," he said. "I think that you already know about the new movement.... All the factions, from left to right, have been united. Our goal is to organize an armed mass, and its role will be war against the bloodthirsty enemy.... What we want from you is – first, to provide clothing to outfit the men and women as needed; second, to help collect money among the workshop employees."...

I decided to talk to Dr. Elkes.... I explained to him that we could easily fall into a trap. This involved large quantities of products and I feared betrayal. It could be discovered that items are missing from the workshops' storehouse. When all is said and done, it can't be kept completely secret; the items need to be produced. Perhaps, God forbid, the Germans will catch one of the fighters and find that his equipment is from the workshops, or some such scenario. He stopped me and said, "I have thought about it a lot. I've taken into consideration all the dangers and obstacles, but we must not allow these to prevent the rescue of some of our young brothers and sisters. We all need to be willing to risk our lives.... This is the upright path[44] that we must take. I accept all the responsibility on my conscience. This is only for the benefit of the surviving remnant of the Jews of Lithuania, and for the benefit of the entire Jewish nation. We must take advantage of every option for resistance, especially with regard to a struggle for our honor."...

I met with Levin at the prearranged time. I told him about my talk with Dr. Elkes. My answer was positive. We agreed that the first order would be transmitted to me in the coming days.... I decided that the first person to whom I would reveal the secret would be Berel Friedman. He was in charge of the storehouses. He was a good Jew and a faithful friend and would certainly help.... I didn't have to use much persuasion.... We consulted together on how to carry out the assignment.... We decided to reveal the secret plan to the following: Yehuda Schwartz (workshop directorate member, work foreman), Haim Kagan (workshop directorate member, responsible for supply of raw materials), Herschel (Hirsch) Brick (workshop directorate member, manager of the personnel department), Dr. Altman (worker committee chairman, worked in the shoemaker's workshop), Troyfberg (head

---

44. In Yiddish, the *virdikste*.

accountant of the workshops), and Zarmbak (manager of the first tailoring department).

About two days later, a meeting was held at my house with Zvi Levin and Haim Yellin. They brought me the first order for forty people. They gave me a list of necessary items for each person: a military coat, jacket and pants, pair of boots (with double soles), a combat belt with two pouches, backpack, canteen, hat, a side bag, sweater, two pairs of wool underwear, three pairs of wool socks, a pair of wool gloves, and three handkerchiefs.... They informed me that by the end of the year, we had to take into consideration three to five hundred people departing for the forest.... They gave me ten to twelve days to prepare the first shipment.... We decided that the contact person would be Meir Greenberg, the barber.

The following day, I consulted with Friedman.... We worked out an action plan. The work would, of course, be done at night, when the Germans were absent from the workshops. That night we held consultations with several comrades, who had to begin work immediately.... The devotion and self-sacrifice evinced by each of the workers was truly astounding. They all viewed it as an honor to cooperate and lend a hand.

A few days before the deadline, everything was ready, more or less. I notified Zvi Levin. He told me with great sorrow that the delivery would have to be postponed for a few days. There were problems in acquiring weapons, and the means of transport was also amiss.

About two weeks later I received news that the weapons had been purchased, but the issue of transportation was still problematic. They had to send the people by foot....[45] The shipment would leave in another four days. The equipment had to be taken out of the workshops.... Nineteen packed sacks. We decided that the following night, two reliable policemen would be placed near Gate B [of the workshops]. Melamdovitz, police officer of the workshops, would stand guard. Meir Greenberg would receive the equipment and place it in the *malina* on 3 Staliu Street, close to the workshops. Outside the workshops, the operation would be conducted personally by ghetto police commander Moshe Levin.

---

45. This most probably refers to the first group, whose exit point was the intermediate base in Murava.

Nine P.M. A dark night. Everyone is at their posts. The guards are going through inspection. I supervise the movement inside the workshops. Berel Friedman hands over the equipment. Meir Greenberg, two policemen, and another three or four young people receive it.

Everyone is nervous, tension fills the air. We look like thieves during their first burglary, thieves who are not yet accustomed to this line of work.... I remember that a month or two after that night, a fellow with a sack full of equipment smuggled from the workshops was almost caught by the *Unterscharführer* Fifiger, yet we were not as frightened as now [on the first night].... The procedure went remarkably well – the entire operation took less than two hours.

After the first successful shipment the work pace speeded up.... We recruited additional workers to prepare shipments.... The workshops provided the necessary equipment. Also, significant sums of money were collected among workshop employees. A special workers' committee was organized, headed by Dr. Altman, that prepared the orders, collected money, and distributed the work between the various departments. The volume was large, and due to the urgency of the matter we were forced to do the work even during the day shifts. Weapons were repaired and assembled during the night shifts in the metalwork department by a staff of experts, under the supervision of manager Engineer Mula Fein. Professionals from many spheres were found...

A certain amount of anarchy began to be felt in the workshops. Everyone knew that the workshops were the main supply source for the partisans,[46] and some exploited it for their personal interests.

One Sunday morning, the door of my house opened and two members of the administration entered, Yehuda Schwartz and Nikolai Gimlantzky, both agitated and pale. They told me that fifty pairs of boots had disappeared and that the ones who had ordered the boots – the German *Schutzpolizei* – were coming the next morning to take them. They had investigated the incident without result. Someone had used a customized key to remove the boots

---

46. This is an exaggeration. Even at its height, only a small circle of activists knew about the workshop supply mission.

from the storehouse. Cohen-Zedek, the bookkeeper of the shoemaker's workshop, had verified the shipment on Saturday.

I contacted the manager of the shoe workshop. He was white as snow and his whole body trembled. New boots – they are coming to get them tomorrow. What to do?

The managers suspected that the boots had been taken for the partisans. I negated this claim. The partisans had promised me that nothing would be taken without the knowledge of the administration. I called the workshop police and the police who had done guard duty the previous night showed up. They had not seen a thing. I alerted Ratner and Zvi Levin and explained to them the danger we faced if those boots were not ready for delivery the next day. Yesterday, on Saturday, we had notified the *Schutzpolizei* that they were ready.

Ratner and Levin were horrified. They promised me that they had not ordered anyone to take boots. Why would we do this? We receive everything we ask for. We summoned Moshe Levin, commander of the ghetto police. He promised to investigate the matter. He would also ensure that the boots would not be smuggled through the ghetto gate to the city. But what to do now? How do we extricate ourselves from this dangerous situation? There was no more material with which to make up the loss. And even if there was – how could we make fifty pairs of boots in one day?

We convened an emergency meeting of the directorate. Friedman raised the idea that the leather used for the uppers, located in the patching department, might be appropriate. There was enough of the hard leather. Now the problem remained how to make those boots by tomorrow morning. The managers of the shoe factory, together with Dr. Altman, assumed the task of organizing the necessary workers – shoemakers and stitchers (Sunday was the day of rest) – and the boots would be made.

By twelve o'clock, about forty workers were sitting and working energetically. I and the entire workshop administration were also there. We had to make sure that everything went like clockwork. At 3 A.M. Monday morning – the boots were ready. At nine, they were packed up in the Germans' truck. To this very day, I do not know who took those boots. [47]

---

47. *The partisan movement in the Kovno ghetto* (Yiddish manuscript), by Moshe Segelson (Landsberg: September 1945), 1–6. For more information about the equipment supplied by the

The Struggle over the Composition of the Groups

As the possibilities for departing the ghetto for the forest increased, a struggle was waged among the various movements in the ghetto over the composition of the groups. Formally, this was an issue that fell under the authority of the JFO leadership. But in truth, the Communist leaders in the ghetto tried to force their opinions on the unified leadership of the JFO. The fight was fierce as each side tried to play its strongest cards; the Communists undoubtedly had the strongest. They dominated relations with the partisan brigade and they had the longest experience in weapons acquisition; consequently, of all the ghetto organizations, they had the largest quantity of weapons, both inside the ghetto and outside. They also had the best chances for acquiring weapons in the future. Last but not least – all hopes for being liberated from the German yoke were necessarily dependent on the victory of the Red Army. The Communists, therefore, tried to use their position of strength to dictate "policy" to the underground leadership concerning the make-up of the groups departing for the forests, allocation of functions within the groups, and more. This was manifested most severely in the issue of the inclusion of women in the forest groups. This problem was not pressing to all the movements; Beitar, for example, had almost no women as members in the ghetto.[48] By contrast, for Hashomer Hatzair this was a serious problem. This organization was comprised mainly of women, as the male fighters had died during the Augustova Plan; almost all of these women strongly desired to join the partisan fighters. There were even some women who left their hiding places with Lithuanian priests in the city, hoping their turn would come to depart for the forest.

Each time one of the movement representatives in the JFO leadership suggested a woman as a candidate for going to the forest, the Communists opposed it. They argued that the partisan command "expressly forbade" bringing women into the forest. This did not prevent them from assertively demanding that their own women be included, rationalizing that these candidates were the wives of fighters already in the forest and that their husbands had received special

---

workshops to those departing for the forest, see also the testimony of Ze'ev Friedman, YVSA, 1–3. At the margins of his testimony, his father Berel Friedman also recalls the incident of the stolen boots that threatened to bring disaster on the entire enterprise.
48. Testimony of Baruch Ezged (Camber), YVSA, 9.

permission to bring them.[49] Only one woman from among the Zionist pioneer movements was authorized to join the forest group, as compared to seven Communist women in one group, the sixth group. Several testimonies indeed indicate that the command center of the Kovno battalions opposed the inclusion of women. Once the decision was made, however, to circumvent this order it applied to all the fighting women who expressed a desire to join the partisans and were eligible on conditions of age and health.[50]

Another point on which the representatives of the Communists demanded the exclusive right of decision was regarding the command of the groups going to the forest. They forcefully demanded that the commanders of all the groups be drawn from their ranks and this was granted to them. This was ostensibly unimportant, because the appointment was a temporary one, only in effect until the group reached the base. Yet in reality it was deeply significant because the Communist command left its mark on the atmosphere that prevailed in the group and on the way in which the members viewed their exit to the forests. These commanders, despite their brief and temporary period of command, succeeded in blurring the unique Jewish nature of the departure operation. Instead they emphasized the "general" side of the ghetto fighters joining the partisans.

We see this in the testimony of one of the fighters, who departed from the ghetto in the sixth group:

> The Communists took great advantage of the fact that all contact [with the partisans] went through their hands. They seemed omnipotent. The most salient fact is that they sent as few women from other movements as possible. By contrast, a woman who belonged to the ranks of the Communists and wanted to leave the ghetto – left, while we were very limited in this. From our united group at Mildos 7 – that included members of the Hashomer Hatzair, Dror, Nezah, and Gordonia movements – only one woman was allowed to leave for the partisans. Regarding the rest [of the women] – they

---

49. Testimony of Grisha (Zvi) Sheffer, YVSA, 11–12 (recording 3).

50. For information about inclusion of women in the forest groups, see testimony of Yona Rochman, YVSA, 20; "Annals of Augustova," 6; testimony of Malka Pugatzky-Smali, YVSA, 14–15 (recording 5); testimony of Yona Rosen, YVSA, 13 (recording 3); testimony of Gita Foger-Turchin, YVSA, 7 (recording 2); testimony of Y. Kashiv (Kapchovsky), YVSA, 12 (recording 3).

kept postponing and postponing. That was the most prominent issue. Aside from that, of course, were secret matters that we couldn't enter into.

I would say that there was no discrimination in distributing weapons during departures for the forest. If there were enough weapons, they gave them out equally. They also distributed equipment equally. But in every group that left for the forest, the Communists always took the command.... My theory is that, if not for the fact that the Communists needed help from the ghetto institutions, they never would have made contact with us at all.... Evidently they lacked several things and could not manage without them.... The fact is that the Ältestenrat knew about these activities and the police assisted in our departure [from the ghetto]. Those of us who left the ghetto are witnesses to it. All the functionaries who stood by the gate, they knew and kept silent. Even more so, they even assisted with this whole affair. My assumption is that the Communists also needed that help...no less than anyone else.[51]

In other words, while the connection to the partisan movement was the strong card in the hands of the Communist leaders, the relationship with certain individuals in the Ältestenrat and especially the ghetto police was a card in the hands of the non-Communist leadership. The result was the decision that the composition of each forest group was determined by a set ratio – each movement represented in the JFO command received a certain number of places. After this decision was reached in principle, the subject of dispute was the actual numerical composition of the ratio – how many places each movement would receive. Each representative fought to increase his proportion of the ratio.

Some testimonies indicate that the demands of the movement representative did not always match the readiness of its members to depart for the forest. Thus the movements were not always able to fill the quotas they had fought for in the JFO command. This was because sometimes not enough people were ready to leave, or there was not enough money to fund the members who were to leave, or other impediments.[52] One issue that deterred fighters from departing for the forest was the claim that there was anti-Semitism in the partisan forest, that the

---

51. Testimony of Haim Gechtel (Galin), YVSA, 18 (recording 7).
52. Ibid., 19. Three Beitar members decided against leaving the ghetto at the last minute due to family reasons; much displeasure from within Beitar ranks was expressed at this decision

Russian partisans hated their Jewish comrades-in-arms and that they did not hesitate to murder the Jews at opportune moments.[53] A similar atmosphere prevailed in Beitar circles, even though a relatively higher number of Beitar members were willing to depart for the forest than members of other movements (according to a few testimonies, this number was significantly higher). Regarding the assertion of partisan anti-Semitism, the opinion prevailed in Beitar circles that the partisans held special hatred for the Revisionist Zionists.

In the Mildos 7 circles, there was less hesitation. Although the information about anti-Semitism agitated them, it was not enough to undermine their basically positive attitude toward joining the partisans. The prevailing opinion was that the JFO leadership should pressure the ghetto Communists that when they arrive in the forest, they should appeal to the partisan brigade command, demanding vigorously that they uproot all discrimination, and perhaps even threaten them with cessation of consignments of fighters.[54] The consignments should not actually be halted, even if the appeal had no effect, and even if the rumors of anti-Semitism in the forest had substance. While this was the prevailing opinion within Mildos 7, possibly the rumors of anti-Semitism affected the personal considerations of individual Mildos 7 members when they were offered the chance of joining a forest group.

Members of the Anti-Fascist Organization understandably showed no signs of vacillation or hesitation at this point in time. The constant indoctrination to depart for the forests to join the partisans bore fruit. No one in these circles expressed opposition to the move or doubts regarding the "Jewish aspect" of the affair. The Communists interpreted any reports of anti-Semitism among the partisans either as propaganda of the "reactionaries" in the ghetto, as inaccurate description of justifiable facts, or as an exaggeration of isolated, unusual incidents. The non-Communists in the Anti-Fascist Organization evidently chose to swallow the bitter pill without making a public response. In any event, the entire group spoke out unanimously against any claim or argument based on the rationale of anti-Semitism.

This was the background for recriminations hurled among the various

(testimony of Yosef Melamed, YVSA, recording 1; also compare M.L. Goldschmidt, YVSA, letter 1, and testimony of Mordechai Karnovsky, YVSA, 1).

53. Testimony of Haim (Fima) Rosenberg, YVSA, 9.

54. Testimony of Zvie Brown.

movements. The Hashomer Hatzair members and the Communists argued that the Revisionists did not take advantage of their quota, switched their candidates, and for monetary gain sold their places to the highest bidders among the "non-affiliated," while Hashomer Hatzair fighters waited for places. The exact same accusation was cast against the Communists – that they sold places to the non-affiliated and took money in exchange for weapons that did not cost them a penny.[55]

In truth, the number of non-affiliated individuals in the forest groups was very small. The forest departure plan involved activities so dangerous that the underground leadership could rely only on individuals who received approval from one of the movements, and the movements did not dare approve someone from outside their ranks. There may, however, have been other underlying reasons. Many of the fighters viewed the forest departure option as a privilege that people outside the underground did not deserve. It was analogous to the protection underground members received from deportations, *Aktion*s, and other misfortunes. There was a mixture among the affiliated individuals of shared ideals, combat readiness, and also the dim self-interest typical of persecuted victims.

Two types of non-affiliated individuals found their way to the underground with great effort, at the high point of departures for the forest. The first type was the fence-traders and profiteers, who were allowed to join the forest groups as compensation for their dangerous, daring services to the underground in arms acquisition operations. The partnership of the underground with elements like these was indeed necessary but on occasion it proved disastrous for the ghetto, including the underground. In some cases the underground was forced to deal severely with these elements; we will discuss this further below.

The other types of non-affiliates who joined the departures for the forest were usually simple folk who had never been involved in civic activities before, but who had means. One of them tells his story:

> One day I asked David Markovsky what I could do to avoid dying like a lamb to somehow save my life with dignity. He answered, there is the option of joining the partisans.... So he had me meet Haim Yellin, who received me hospitably. I told him that he should give me the chance of dying honorably....

---

55. According to testimony of Ze'ev Friedman, YVSA, 3, and Michael Katz, YVSA, 6.

Yellin said to me, "I need fellows like you." Afterwards they set me up in a meeting with Menashke Sapozhnikov and Yerachmiel Berman. I received an ultimatum: "Bring weapons, then you'll go to the forest." I listened and did as they said. I obtained a Parabellum from a *goy* in exchange for two leather jackets and a feather quilt (it cost me a total of 50,000 rubles). I brought the gun to Yerachmiel'ke and they attached me to a group that was undergoing weapons training. We practiced on a machine gun. At first they trained me, afterwards when they saw that I was better at it than they were, they appointed me to be an instructor (I had served in the Lithuanian army).[56]

Order of the Departures for the Forest

The struggle over the composition of the groups was persistent and accompanied by mutual recriminations. This did not, however, affect the organizational aspects of the forest groups operation according to the "new procedures" – the latest instructions from the partisan brigade command that were first received by the Jewish guides and afterwards by Haim Yellin.[57]

After the candidate list was finalized, all associated parties were set in motion and all efforts were made to ensure exemplary organization of the departures, provide the best possible training and equipping of the candidates, and – most importantly – provide maximal firepower for each group.

After the JFO leadership acquired experience during the initial months with sending groups in vehicles, it was then able to define standard procedures and plan each departure of a group to the forest down to the last detail. On the basis of the sources at our disposal, we can reconstruct the stages of the departure process, as follows:

1. Determination of the specific candidates within the various underground movements who are to join the forest groups – whether voluntarily or by movement decision and obligation.
2. Interviews with the candidate to ascertain his/her physical fitness, reasons for joining the forest partisans, and options for his/her funding.
3. Approval of the JFO command for each candidate.

---

56. Testimony of Haim Nadel, YVSA, 1 ff.
57. There was a break of about a month between the fifth and sixth groups, while only a week or two separated the earlier groups.

4. Accelerated military-partisan drills in small groups (squads) for two or three weeks before the departure date.

5. Military drills in the platoon framework and meeting the rest of the candidates; memorizing instructions for the trip and partisan tactics; study of practical Russian terms.

6. Farewell departure parties within the candidate's movement, as well as for each group as a whole.

7. Sending standby announcements to the group members, concentrating all the candidates in a secret place in the ghetto, and checking the candidates' requisite personal item kits. The compulsory kit for a man was comprised of riding pants or regular army pants, boots, a warm hat with ear-flaps, a short warm coat, a combat belt with pouches, a backpack, three pairs of socks, two pairs of warm underwear, sheets or a cloak for camouflage, and several sandwiches.

8. Distribution of weapons ("short" weapons) and the ammunition that the group took with it from the ghetto, inspection of the candidates' personal weapons, and distribution of the shared equipment of the group (such as medical supplies).

9. Appointing group members to various tasks or positions and giving final instructions for the trip (smoking was prohibited, talking was severely limited, and speaking Yiddish was absolutely prohibited).

10. Assembling the group near the ghetto gate.

11. Exiting via the gate as a regular work brigade (including removing their hats in submission to the German sentry).

12. Mounting the truck and loading the equipment, including some of the long weapons, usually wrapped up in blankets.

13. The order of sitting in the vehicle: the guide sat near the driver; two to four fighters dressed in German field-police uniforms sat in the back section of the vehicle, which was covered with a tarpaulin; the group's commander sat in the front of the car; and the rest – according to a predetermined order.

14. After driving for some distance, the order was given to remove the yellow star. One of the group collected them and destroyed them ("Now you are partisans").

15. Short stop in the city, usually on Jonavos Street, to load the rest of the "long" and "heavy" weapons, then distribution of the weapons within the vehicle.

16. Loading five bullets in the rifle barrels.
17. Leaving the vehicle (75–90 kilometers from Kovno), donning the camouflage cloaks, and deploying in single file according to the predetermined order: guide, front defense, main line, rear-guard; marching according to this order.

Security Problems in the Ghetto

The security problem in the ghetto grew more serious as the forest departure project expanded. It was a known fact that the Gestapo tracked every forbidden activity in the ghetto and fear of traitors and informers was constant. The first question was who might be trying to harm the underground from the inside? Who might be a traitor? This issue demanded meticulous trailing of suspects and vigorous action against actual traitors.[58] A constant state of alertness had to be maintained toward individuals outside the ghetto who had contact with the underground – such as weapons traders, drivers, and the like – as well as vis-à-vis the ghetto residents. Although we know very little about the precautions taken in the city, we can assume that JFO activists received the assistance of the city's Communist underground with regard to security issues.

In the ghetto itself, there were several categories of people that those who worried about security had to be concerned about. First and foremost were the Ältestenrat and officials of ghetto institutions such as the Jewish police and the labor office. Various instances have already been cited in which the Ältestenrat institutions helped the JFO: near the ghetto gate, at workplaces in the ghetto and the city, in the Billeting Committee, and in the ghetto's workshops and prison. Whenever and wherever the underground needed vital assistance and the ghetto institutions could help, they did so willingly and promptly.[59] The police chiefs paid dearly for this assistance,[60] and the Ältestenrat members almost shared the same fate. But this does not mean that the entire Ältestenrat as a whole offered unqualified support for the JFO, agreed ahead of time to all its activities, or linked

---

58. See the episode regarding the elimination of looters at the end of this chapter.
59. For information about assistance even within the ghetto's prison, see testimonies of Haim Nadel, YVSA, 2, and Grisha Sheffer, YVSA, 10–11 who were released from the prison due to the intervention of the JFO. Also compare testimonies of Menachem Sadovsky (Ganuni), YVSA, 16, 25 (recording 3a and 3b); Yitzhak Rabinovitz, YVSA, 19–20 (recording 5); Michael Yitzhaki (Gelbtrunk), YVSA, 28; Gita Foger-Turchin, YVSA, 6 (recording 2); Michael Katz, YVSA, 4.
60. See chapter 14, the story of the murder of the ghetto policemen in the Ninth Fort.

their destiny to that of the organization, in such a way as to expect that when put to the test they would take responsibility for the JFO's actions.

In analyzing the relationship between the Ältestenrat and the JFO, we must distinguish between the Ältestenrat's official policy as an institution and the outlooks of its individual members, including those who held key leadership positions. We cannot say that the offical policy of the Ältestenrat was to support the JFO. Almost certainly, the issue of contact with the underground was never placed on the agenda and the ghetto leaders certainly never reached a decision on the matter. Moreover, one well-founded view is that for a long period, attorney (Ya'akov) Goldberg was unaware of the activities of the JFO and the help that the ghetto institutions extended to it. When he discovered this, from sources unconnected with the Ältestenrat, he became very angry and resigned in protest from his job as head of the Jewish labor office (the reason being, evidently, that the clerks in his office covered up for the underground members without his knowledge).[61]

It was not the Ältestenrat as an institution, therefore, that supported the JFO, but rather some of its members. This position was, in large part, due to the influence of Dr. Elkes, who was perhaps the JFO's strongest supporter on the Ältestenrat. In addition to the fact that he was the official chairman of the Ältestenrat, he also enjoyed great prestige in the eyes of all the ghetto institutional directors. Evidently, Dr. Elkes's personal sympathetic stance toward the underground was viewed by the institutions' officials as evidence that he took ultimate responsibility for the JFO, thus absolving them of doubts of conscience and partly dissipating their fear of possible results. In truth, when the Ältestenrat was disbanded, Dr. Elkes begged his colleagues to go underground or flee the ghetto, and he alone would bear responsibility for the Ältestenrat's activities.[62] Those officials who helped the JFO – either on their own initiative or ostensibly as part of their job – wanted to know as little as possible about the underground and partisan-related activities in the ghetto, so that if they fell into Gestapo hands and were subjected to torture they would have no information to reveal.[63]

61. Testimony of Moshe Segelson, 24.

62. Garfunkel, *Kovno*, 185.

63. Testimony of Yitzhak Rabinovitz, YVSA, 19–20 (recording 5). According to the testimony of Ältestenrat secretary Leah (Lucia) Elstein-Lavon (14), she did not know details about underground activities in the ghetto. Artist Esther Luria, who was involved in the ghetto's

In summary, a complex relationship prevailed between the underground leadership on the one hand, and the Ältestenrat and ghetto institutions on the other. The underground leadership made every effort to maintain smooth relations with the Ältestenrat and prove that they were cautious in everything they did, out of a great sense of responsibility for the fate of the ghetto. While they tried to make the most of all forms of assistance on the part of the ghetto institutions, the underground leadership was careful to send their own people to perform the more sensitive or dangerous activities. The fewer people who knew about the underground and its activities – the better. In other words, underground rules of secrecy prevailed in contacts between the JFO and the ghetto institutions. When a member of the Ältestenrat or ghetto institution was asked for help with a certain operation, he was told only the very minimum necessary. Thus, no one in the Ältestenrat or ghetto institutions knew of the exact magnitude of the fighting force in the ghetto, the meeting places and contact people in the city, the weapons caches and the quantity of arms and ammunition in the ghetto, and the secret apartments, as well as other such information.[64]

However, at the height of the departure of the fighting groups to the forests, the JFO faced a dilemma: either completely forgo the "new" forest groups mission or ease the secrecy rules. This was because low-level officials and policemen had to be involved in the forest groups operation, despite the danger of possible disclosure. The JFO decided to take the risk.

In addition, the JFO had to beware of other elements in the ghetto besides the Ältestenrat that could compromise the secrecy of their actions. Clearly, the Gestapo would not rely on the loyalty of the Ältestenrat but would try to infiltrate overt and covert agents into the ghetto. The JFO was on the lookout for these hostile elements, and when needed, adopted countermeasures, usually with great effectiveness.

---

public life, also testifies that "I don't know much about the underground activities in the ghetto. They were conducted with great secrecy. I knew that groups of armed youths left frequently for the forest" (Memoirs of Esther Luria, Yad Vashem archives, 03/637, p. 137).

64. Below is a list of secret apartments of the JFO and its branches. These served as secret meeting places, weapons caches, and sites for weapons training, listening to news on the radio, conducting secret trials of traitors, and carrying out the verdict: 3 Kriščiukaičio, 95 Kriščiukaičio, 36 Ariogalos, 4 Broliu, 8 Broliu, 10 Broliu, 24 Ješiboto, Bloc C, 18 Vežėju, 27 Puodžiu, 8 Linkmenu, 10 Vidurinė, 7 Mildos, 11 Mildos, 23 Mildos, 3 Našlaičiu, 9 Griniaus, 32 Griniaus, 18 Bajoru, 8 Mėsininku, 10 Vitauto, 24 Gimbuto.

Throughout the period of ghetto Kovno's existence, the Gestapo operated two overt agents: Caspi-Serebrovitz and Benno Liptzer. Caspi-Serebrovitz was one of only two Jews in Kovno given permission to remain in the city after the establishment of the ghetto (the other was a well-known Jewish doctor). From the very beginning of the Nazi regime, Serebrovitz was a Gestapo agent. Although he frequently meddled in ghetto life, informed on others, and created strife between the Ältestenrat and German authorities, we have no evidence that he attempted to expose the underground in the ghetto. He continued his nefarious dealings in Kovno until the summer of 1942, when his higher-ups transferred him to Vilna and murdered him.[65]

The second overt agent, Benno Liptzer, was far more dangerous than his predecessor – to the ghetto in general and to the JFO in particular.[66] Liptzer spent all his time in the ghetto and had the opportunity to keep close track of what was happening around him. He occasionally used his connections with Gestapo officials to assist individuals caught for offenses such as trade with the Lithuanians and smuggling foodstuffs into the ghetto (sometimes he did this at the expense of other Jews). This way, he earned the reputation among the simple folk in the ghetto as a "rescuer of Jews," a "benefactor and savior." This status made it easier for him to spy on "hostile elements" in the ghetto, which was part of his activities for the Gestapo. Liptzer's behavior in the Gestapo during the investigation of the Augustova prisoners affair is documented above; as a result of his actions, an entire group of fighters was sent to the Ninth Fort.[67]

---

65. See Gar, *Umkum*, 113, 114, 286; Garfunkel, *Kovno*, 51, 62, 72, 73, 120. Testimony to Serebrovitz's personality is found in his speech in the ghetto to the Ältestenrat officials, as recorded in outline form by one person. The document is in the Golob collection at Yad Vashem. In his book, Gar records an interesting detail about Serebrovitz (114): "Before the war, Caspi had felt close to the Revisionist movement. He tried to convince his superiors in the Gestapo that the Revisionist faction of Achimeir, who called itself 'against the stream,' was unmistakably anti-British and sympathetic to Hitler and the Axis countries. In this way he wanted to make himself look important to the Germans and acquire their trust. This matter came to light accidentally, when a package of letters sent from the Kovno Ghetto to Vilna fell into Nazi hands (see chapter 3). Caspi, who investigated the matter, wanted to protect his Revisionist friends, who sent letters to Yosef Glazman in Vilna. These letters also fell into the hands of the Gestapo." According to Garfunkel, Serebovitz was murdered in 1943, but Gar's date of summer 1942 is much more reasonable.

66. Gar, Umkum, 89, 114, 211; Garfunkel, Kovno, 137, 179, 187, 244–45; PKG, 115–16. Also see testimony of SS officer Hermann, 8–9 (Yad Vashem Archives, Munich collection 585/694).

67. See chapter 5, footnote 46.

Another act is testimony to Liptzer's special "interest" in the partisans. In late 1943 or early 1944,[68] a labor brigade of Jews from villages in the Vilna area was working on Ozheshko Street in Kovno. At that time, it became known in the Kovno Ghetto that Jews in the Vilna environs were active in the partisan movement. Liptzer visited the workplace of that brigade and investigated those workers in the presence of the Germans (and in the German language), on their "secret intentions of running away to the partisans."

The leaders of the JFO knew that Liptzer was keeping close track of the ghetto underground, and it was almost certain that he had already collected the information he needed. So far there were no signs that he had transmitted the information to the Gestapo, but it was assumed that when the time came he would not flinch at doing so. Eliminating Liptzer in the ghetto would not have been especially difficult and could have been done without the Germans being able to find his traces. But during the days of the height of the underground's activity, Liptzer's status became official; he was appointed by the Gestapo as inspector for the ghetto police. Thus the underground leaders were concerned that should Liptzer be eliminated, his disappearance would bring in its wake brutal German reprisals against the ghetto.

The JFO decided to adopt a different tactic to solve the problem. In the late period of the ghetto, January–February 1944, Liptzer indicated that he was willing to act as a double agent – that is, to betray his Gestapo superiors so as to ensure his future after the imminent liberation and German defeat. Therefore, the JFO decided to cautiously offer him "collaboration." According to testimonies in our possession, this mission was assigned to two people: Dr. Volsonok and a woman named Bayla, known in the ghetto as Liptzer's mistress.[69] According to one version, Liptzer agreed to help the underground and even passed several tests. But his "collaboration" did not last long. The ghetto was rocked by harsh events: the Children's *Aktion*, destruction of the high echelons of the police, liquidation of the Ältestenrat, and last but not least, Liptzer's appointment as commander of the *Ordnungsdienst*, which replaced both the police and Ältestenrat. His duties included hunting down Jews attempting to flee the ghetto and spying on all un-

---

68. Testimony of Binyamin Bakst, YVSA, 1.
69. Meir Leib Goldschmidt, YVSA, letter 2; testimony of Hasia Nadel, YVSA, 10; testimony of Moshe Segelson, YVSA, 23.

derground activities. There is reason to suspect that close to these events Liptzer passed on all the knowledge he had about the underground and that this betrayal was one of the decisive factors in the transpiring of events.[70]

The underground did ferret out two undercover Gestapo agents in the ghetto. The first incident occurred in the summer of 1942.[71] The Anti-Fascist Organization had a spy in the Saugumas, the Lithuanian-Nazi security service in Kovno. One day this agent obtained a letter sent by a Jew, "F," from the ghetto to the Saugumas with a list of the heads of the Anti-Fascist Organization ("F" was a member of the organization). "F" was interrogated and when he admitted that he was connected to the Saugumas, he was executed in the ghetto. Thanks to the alertness of the agent, the letter never reached the Saugumas.

The second incident took place at the beginning of 1944. A ghetto resident by the name of Fein (about twenty-five years old) used to slip out of the ghetto to trade and smuggle foodstuffs. One day he was caught in the act in the city, brought to the Gestapo, then immediately released and returned to the ghetto. His speedy return from the Gestapo aroused suspicion and the heads of the JFO ordered that he be followed. Several times Fein was summoned to appear alone before Gestapo officer Kittel, during Kittel's surprise visits to the ghetto. During one visit, high-ranking Jewish police officer Yehuda Zupovitz (who was in contact with the JFO command) eavesdropped on a conversation between Kittel and his agent. Kittel asked for information about who in the ghetto still had valuables, gold, weapons, and other "forbidden items." Another undocumented story about Fein holds that he once joined a vehicle transporting the fighters to the forest, but jumped off in the middle of the drive. After enough proofs were assembled against him, Fein was arrested on some pretext by the ghetto police and handed over to the JFO. The JFO leaders also asked Dr. Elkes for his opinion about issuing a death verdict against the traitor. Elkes answered that a verdict is something for the judges to decide, but asked that the accused not be convicted unless he admitted to his guilt. Indeed, Fein admitted under interrogation that he had committed to deliver, or actually delivered, information to Kittel about the ghetto and the underground. A death verdict was handed down, and Fein was shot in one of the organization's *malina*s. Hanne Kagan was one of the judges.

---

70. Gar, *Umkum*, 116.
71. *FLC* 10:7. We have no verification of this incident from other sources.

While the verdict was being carried out, several young people stood nearby and knocked on tin barrels, to muffle the sound of the gunshots.[72]

Another incident of a different type, to which the underground was indirectly connected, forced the JFO to pass severe judgment. In early January 1944, five young men armed with pistols stormed into the apartment of Feivush (a ghetto resident) and demanded money from him, ostensibly for the JFO purchasing fund. When he refused, they shot him. Feivush's screams alerted the tenants of the adjacent apartment, Eliezer Antopitzky and his wife. The robbers shot them as well and killed them on the spot. Feivush was found drenched in blood and died a few hours later. Before he died, he managed to inform the others of the names of the murderers and the circumstances of their attack on him. They were profiteers who had worked for the JFO in acquiring weapons and equipment. The underground court issued a death verdict against them, which was carried out.[73]

The organization also issued and carried out a death verdict against an official in the ghetto's housing department, Monya Levin, after proving he had assisted Lithuanians in uncovering several *malina*s in the First Quarter of the ghetto so that they could loot them.[74]

The JFO command was in charge of the organization's security issues, but it established a special department to carry out its security-related decisions and orders. This department was known as the Black Staff, in the ghetto and even outside it, and was also the liaison between the JFO Command and the profiteers who were acquiring arms. The organization's highest echelons viewed the Black Staff's existence as an unavoidable necessity, especially with the heightened demand for large quantities of weapons and ammunition as a result of the new orders received from the forest partisans. Nevertheless, the JFO leaders kept their eye on the Black Staff's activities and methods; when the latter had achieved power in the ghetto, they sometimes allowed themselves to act irresponsibly. Thus the JFO chiefs sometimes found it necessary to censure them strictly to keep them in line.[75]

---

72. *FLC* 10:7; *PKG*, 93 ff.; memoirs of Zvie Brown, from stories he heard in the forest.

73. *FLC* 10:8; Meir Teinovitz, YVSA, letter 2. According to Gar, Umkum (p. 196), there were about 10 "political" murders in the ghetto.

74. Gruenhoyz, *FLC*, no. 8, 27–28; Gar, Umkum, 196. Compare to Garfunkel, Kovno, 165. Also see chapter 2, "Malinas."

75. Meir Leib Goldschmidt, YVSA, letter 1; Meir Yellin, YVSA, letter 6; see Gordon, letter 2, and Yisrael Joels, letter 2.

CHAPTER 9

The Resistance Movement in the Labor Camps

In the January–March 1944 time period, labor camps already existed in several suburbs of the city, such as Aleksot and Shanz, as well as in places more distant from Kovno, such as Koshedar, Keidan, Raudondvaris, and Palemon. The residents of these camps were transferred to there from the Kovno Ghetto. The work and regimens differed among the camps, and the prisoners suffered the most in the camps in the suburbs of Kovno. These were under the supervision of the stringent Goecke, the SS commandant of the ghetto, who imposed the brutal regime of a detention camp on these labor camps.

By contrast, life in the Keidan and Koshedar labor camps, which had existed well before the others, was somewhat less brutal. Although the prisoners were also forced to work at harsh labor in these camps (digging and loading gravel, constructing military airfields), the supervisors allowed the Jews to leave the camp during their free time and make contact with local farmers, "only for trade" as they were told. Evidently the main reason for this liberal treatment were the benefits the Germans received from this commerce.

Both types of camps contained underground activists, but the situation was unique in each location. So long as communication existed between the camps and the central ghetto, the JFO command attempted to make contact, as did the underground cells in the camps. These attempts were only rarely successful, for a simple reason: during the *Kasernierung* period, the ghetto organizations adopted the express, consistent tactic of working to prevent transfer of underground members to the labor camps. Thus very few underground members were sent to the camps, and the ghetto organizations made ceaseless efforts to exchange those few activists with other Jews. Nevertheless quite a few people in the camps were aroused to adopt resistance activities, acquire firearms, and search for contact with the partisans outside the camps. For example, individuals who organized in the Shanz labor camp succeeded in stealing significant amounts of ammunition and army uniforms from the military storehouses in which they worked. They then transferred their "booty" to the central ghetto. (Moshe Kaltinovsky and Gordon headed this operation.)[1]

The conditions in the camps located in provincial towns were more suited to underground activity. We know about such activities in two camps, Koshedar and Keidan.[2] The Koshedar people managed to make contact with the Genis battalions in the Rudniki Forests, and after Genis agreed to accept the camp's activists to its bases, an escape operation of about forty prisoners was organized in one day. The group was headed by Shimon Kaviskin, Sivirsky, Abba Leibowitz, Grisha Joels, Wolf Miasnick, and Yosef Burkan. Although we don't know how many of the escapees brought firearms with them into the forest, based on what we know of the codes of the Rudniki brigade, the escapees had to have weapons in order to be admitted to the partisan bases. Below is the story of one of the escapees:

> I came to Koshedar at the end of 1943.... In the camp was a group of Jewish fellows from the town of Smorgon (Smurgainys) and its environs, who worked at woodcutting. Once they went into a farmer's home and found partisans who had stopped there for the day. As usual in such cases, the Jews were ushered into a room and not allowed to leave. They explained to the partisans that if they did not return to the camp, the rest of the Jews would suffer [be punished]. The partisans suggested killing the Germans and taking the entire group of Jews to the forest. The Jews decided to organize the rest of the camp (about three hundred people) and maintain contact with the partisans.
>
> After they returned to the camp, these fellows began whispering among

---

1. *PKG*, 124.

2. We know that in the Palemon camp, five people planned on fleeing to the forest, including Prizinger (testimony of Esther Wolfson, yvsa, recording 1). Underground groups also were active in Aleksot, Shanz, and later on, in Ponevezh (Panevėžys) camp as well (also see *PKG*, 123–24).

themselves, but refused to reveal anything to me. (I sensed that something was about to happen in the camp.)

One day I was working in arranging straw; ostensibly I was the work foreman. When I was about to move on to the second group near the railroad tracks, I noticed that the Jews there were surrounded by Germans. I discovered that people were missing. It turned out that the missing laborers were the members of the group that had been in touch with the partisans and meanwhile had received the order to flee the camp and join the partisans. I understood that there would be big trouble.

I stood up and searched for a break in the fence so that I could escape. Several people gathered around me, including Miasnick and Sivirsky. I told them, "Better to be shot from behind than from the front." ... They followed me and after running about 200 meters, they [the guards] started shooting at us. While running in zigzags, we ran into a ditch 3 meters wide. I crossed it, but the fellows behind me fell into the water.... I escaped to Zhezmer...and continued running another 7 kilometers without resting.

I hid in the attic of a village bathhouse. From there I saw a German leading several Jews. I crouched there for three or four hours, and suddenly heard approaching steps and voices speaking in Yiddish. I saw friends from the camp, including Shimon Kaviskin and Abba (Abka) Leibowitz from Shavli (Šiauliai). They called me to join them, and we walked toward the forest.

It turned out that a group of eight people had succeeded in meeting the partisans.... We knew that we could make contact with the partisans via a certain forest warden, and it was true: he had a note for us from the partisans telling us to wait, that they would come for us in another day or two.

We remained (we were twenty-two people) near the forest warden in the woods between Zhezmer and Koshedar. That was most probably in February, 1944.... One day, the forest warden came and knocked three times on a tree; that was the prearranged signal. The message was that they would come to take us at 1 A.M. And that's what happened; two Jews came, sent by the partisans to take us a distance of 70 kilometers. When they had brought us to the assigned place, the two would also be accepted by the partisans.

The two Jews led us for about 60 kilometers, and then the partisans came to take us. Our meeting with them was pleasant. Again we walked, for about 40–50 kilometers this time, until we reached the Genis base. They distributed arms to everyone and created the "Free Lithuania" unit. The commander was Russian. We remained in that unit until Vilna was liberated.

After we fled Koshedar, the Germans liquidated that camp and transported the Jews to the Kazlu-Ruda camp.[3]

We have much information about resistance and underground activities in the Keidan camp. The first Jews from the Kovno Ghetto, about forty people, were transported to the Keidan camp before the end of 1942, where they were forced to work at digging gravel. At one point, many of the laborers were sent back to the ghetto, leaving only ten people in the camp. This smaller group was able to soften the camp commanders, and the strict work schedule was eased. The Jews in the labor brigade took advantage of this – first of all to create barter connections with the farmers in the area and to circulate around the villages. But later on they began to sabotage German work projects and property, search for escape routes, and attempt to make contact with the partisans. One of the labor brigade members tells the following story:

> We started to organize sabotage projects in March. We loaded gravel into the railcars beyond the allowed capacities, and then we closed the doors improperly, breaking the sides of the cars so that the gravel would spill out on the way.... We poured [gravel] between the axles and sabotaged the air brakes.... We wanted to sabotage something, to accomplish something. Of course, we made sure the Germans would not notice what we did. If, for example, we filled the car beyond its limits, the station master thought that we were very diligent. "My people" – he would say – "are good workers." ... So we didn't have to fear anyone.... And we all did it together.
>
> My intentions [in searching for partisans] ... were not just to join them on my own, but to organize more people who would form a unit capable of fighting.... If I only was worried about myself, I wouldn't have had to search far; by that time I had already managed to acquire many friends among the *goyim* who invited me stay with them, to hide. But I wanted to save the others as well.[4]

---

3. Testimony of Grisha Joels, YVSA, 2–4.
4. Testimony of Yosef Gertner, YVSA, 1 (recording 1).

From the rest of this testimony, as well as from other testimonies,[5] we learn that the main goal of the resistance in this camp was to ensure the escape of as many prisoners as possible to the forest. At the end of 1943, a ghetto labor camp was established in Keidan with two hundred or more laborers, and the "gravel brigade" was brought to this camp. A group of activists who had contacts with the farmers in the region became the dynamic nucleus of the resistance movement in the large camp.[6] These activists were Yosef Gertner, Kirka Solsky, Haim Borstein, Ya'akov Micha Burstein, Aryeh Rafeika, and Bialostotzky. It did not take long for other groups of fellow prisoners to form around this initial group, accepting its authority and making preparations to escape. The activity was conducted in secret. Only the leaders knew what was going on in the entire camp and would meet secretly to make their plans, while the other groups' members knew only about their particular group.

Among the activists, Yosef Gertner was an expert in night hiking. He was acquainted with every road and path within a radius of many kilometers, and was in close touch with farmers who assisted in activities against the authorities. Through these farmers, Gertner succeeded in tracking down the partisans who circulated in the region's forests. His testimony includes interesting details about his first encounter with the head of a roving partisan group:

> I heard rumors that an actual Soviet paratrooper[7] was roving around our area. This paratrooper – so I was told – was the organizer of the partisan movement in the districts of Keidan, Ponevezh, and Vilkomir. I really wanted to meet this partisan and talk to him. One woman whom I used to visit, a *goy*, organized a meeting for me.... His condition for meeting with me was that we should sit [in such a way] that I would not see his face.
>
> My main request was for arms. All our hopes were – weapons. We knew that we could not accomplish anything with our bare hands alone. So my first question was whether he could lend me a weapon. I emphasize: lend. If we could have one firearm, we could get more. I received a definitive answer: "The partisan acquires his weapon with his blood." I asked him another question.... If they wanted to destroy us all and we wanted to escape, where

5. Testimony of Ya'akov Micha Borstein, YVSA, 4 ff.
6. Testimony of Bayla Rudashvesky, YVSA, recording 1.
7. For more information about the paratrooper incident, see chapter 10.

could we flee in order to meet him? His answer was, "As long as you remain [alive] in the camp, I am afraid of you [as you might lead the Nazis to me]. If you escape, you will find us." . . . Now I posed a third question. "Look, you won't lend us a weapon, and you won't tell us where to find you, so what are we to do? Help us. If, for example, I go to the camp and they catch me and take me to be killed, what should I do?" He answered, "Attack the guards and fight them." That is how the conversation ended.[8]

Although this first attempt to connect to the partisans failed, the camp's activists did not give up hope. They focused their efforts on acquiring weapons, aware that they could not escape without them. Meanwhile, several young women were working permanently in the military hospital in Keidan. One of the camp's group leaders was Rivka Levitt, known for her bravery, and she recruited some of the hospital workers to the weapons procurement effort.

Our girls, Malka'le and Bronke, worked in the military hospital and succeeded in "organizing" something. They didn't return to the camp every night to sleep; sometimes they slept in the hospital. That's how they became friendly with the wounded German soldiers and managed to get a 7.65 mm Mauser from them. Bronke was a rather charming girl and evidently one of the Germans fell in love with her; she asked for a weapon for self-defense and even received it. . . . That same German afterwards gave her another firearm. . . . A few days later (March 1944?), we got via Malka'le another 7.65 mm Mauser and three bullets. Afterwards we received a German 9 mm Parabellum, two magazines, and forty-five bullets, plus another eighty-four bullets for a German rifle. Later on we bought a 1936 Russian rifle and fifty bullets. We also managed to buy a Russian Nagant [revolver] and three bullets. . . . This means that we already had a small amount of arms. We stored the pistols in the camp, but we gave the rifle to a *goy* to hold for us. . . . We could not practice using the weapons, there was no way.[9]

On the one hand, the activists felt more secure when they acquired firearms. On the other hand, this created a certain amount of tension between the activists and the rest of the camp prisoners. One of the activists, Aryeh Rafieka, was a

8. Testimony of Yosef Gertner, YVSA, 4–5 (recording 1–2).
9. Ibid., 15–17 (recording 4).

policeman, which made it easier for them to camouflage their activities and plans. However, the Jewish camp director, Lehman, opposed the "escape plot" when he heard about it. He made sure that the German threats of severe collective punishments for any escape attempt struck deeply into the hearts of the prisoners. It was thus necessary to maintain secrecy even from them.

The activists intensified their efforts in making contact with persons outside the camp who could assist them. One of the German soldiers who gave a pistol and ammunition to the young women also expressed his willingness to join the escape to the forest. Gertner states:

> I opposed this for several reasons.... I couldn't rely on him ... but most of all, something else worried me. Suppose we took him ... how could we protect him from the Russians? ... Our girls became friendly with a second German soldier. Afterwards we found out that he was actually a Jew ... who forged his documents and became a German, enlisted, and was mobilized to the German regular army. There he was wounded and brought to a hospital. He promised to give us weapons. He also waged propaganda efforts against the Germans, even among the soldiers.... Evidently someone informed on him because they suddenly transferred him somewhere else and his fate is unknown.[10]

The activists also tried to make contact with the Communist underground, as there were rumors that this underground was active at the time (spring 1944) in the Keidan district. The prisoner Miriam Fein made the first contact by becoming friendly with a Lithuanian named Adlobas, who told the underground members who was the underground leader in Keidan and even promised to set up a meeting. The activists placed all their hopes on these contacts; they felt that the Lithuanian underground might be able to help them more than isolated partisans in the forests of the district. A meeting was held and evidently they decided to keep in touch, but someone informed to the Germans. As a result, the entire Keidan underground with its leader were imprisoned, along with Aldobas. Thus the resistance organization in the camp was isolated again. At first the camp, activists lived in fear of suffering the same fate as the Lithuanian underground

---

10. Ibid., 15 (recording 4).

members, but their fears were proved wrong. Both the leader of the Keidan underground and Aldobas knew not to reveal secrets.

The Keidan camp activists also had the opportunity to collaborate with the ghetto underground. We do not know how the initial contacts were made, but by fall of 1943, the heads of the JFO in the ghetto were aware of the Keidan camp underground and assisted with guidance and materials. There are conflicting sources regarding the nature of the contact between the groups. According to one source,[11] the Anti-Fascist Organization had contact with its people in the Keidan camp "from the first day," that is, August 1943. The AFO people received political informational material and instructions on how to operate. This source even says that "the members inflicted as much harm on the Germans as they could. Rivka Levi[12] and Alter Sadinsky, who headed the operation, made contact with the small partisan group (under the command of Vasilenko) that operated in the Keidan forests."

These facts, while correct, only refer to a small part of the camp underground. As we see from testimonies quoted above, while Rivka Levitt belonged to the circle of activists, she was not the leader; her group should not be identified with the entire underground, which was broader and less factional in nature. It seems to be true, however, that within the broader underground framework, Rivka and her group had their own specific viewpoints. This led to severe differences of opinion later on, during the escape, and to schisms in the group after the escape itself. The source above also completely ignores an interesting incident in the relations between the camp underground and and the JFO: the liaison sent from the organization to the Keidan underground. Gertner relates the following:

> One day, a representative from Kovno Ghetto was sent to the Keidan camp. He told us that the ghetto knew all about us, and that the ghetto underground had sent him as an advisor or liaison. His name was Sheinovitz (?)...He told us about the ghetto underground and the contacts with the partisans. We were proud that we already had a connection with the Vilna forests.[13] Then we planned, together with Sheinovitz, to send three of our people who knew their way around the forests near Keidan to return to the Kovno Ghetto.

---

11. *PKG*, 124.

12. This evidently should be "Levitt." Sadinsky is not mentioned in the other testimonies.

13. This is a reference to the Rudniki Forests.

From the ghetto, they would be sent to the Vilna forests, and then we would establish communication from Keidan to Vilna.... We were ready to begin the operation when the ghetto police force was arrested, so the whole plan was cancelled.... As time went on, we discovered that this Sheinovitz only wanted to take advantage of us [and have us do the work], but not take action himself. At one of our meetings he said that there were rumors of partisans in the Raseiniai Forests,[14] and he proposed that we should go there to make contact with them. Of course such a plan involves great dangers, he said, maybe even dangers we would not be able to overcome. I said to Sheinovitz that I did not agree. But he insisted. So I said, okay, let's go – I volunteer to do it on the condition that you come with me. But he didn't want to go. We saw that he wanted others to endanger themselves, but without risk to himself. So we ended our contact with him and banished him from our underground.[15]

The plans sent from the ghetto, therefore, were not successful. But the underground camp activists did not give up, and after great effort they established contact with the partisans in the Keidan forests.

They called themselves the "Red Partisans, Group A."... The commander's name was Petke, and the *politruk* [political commissar in charge of inculcating ideology in fighters] – Yashke. The unit was divided into smaller groups.... Most of them were Ukrainian, and that raised doubts among us.... Maybe they were sent by the Gestapo? Maybe they wanted to get us into trouble? We set up a meeting in the forest. Haim'ke Borstein and I hid nearby, to see if they were setting a trap for us. Petke and Yashke arrived at the spot. We learned that they really were partisans. We said that we would all join them on Thursday next week, at night.... Then we began to hold our own meetings about how to escape.[16]

The escape plot began to materialize, but differences of opinion arose. Some of the activists, including Kirka Solsky and Rivka Levitt, wanted to escape as

---

14. Jewish survivors hid in the dense forests of the Raseiniai district. Jews who escaped from the Kovno Ghetto joined them and formed a partisan group with a respectable supply of weapons. In August 1944 they were uncovered by the retreating German army (Garfunkel, *Kovno*, 167).
15. His testimony, YVSA, 12–13 (recording 3).
16. Testimony of Yosef Gertner, YVSA, 17 (recording 4).

soon as possible, according to the agreement with the partisan chiefs in the forest. Others, led by Yosef Gertner, were not enthusiastic about joining the partisan unit; they felt that this would lead to complete subordination to the authority of the Russian or Ukrainian commanders. They argued the following points:

> Our interests and those of the partisans are not identical. They are totally free, while our mission is not only war against the Germans but also, and perhaps first of all, to save Jews – to save the lives of the people in the camp from which we are fleeing. We feel that saving one Jew is more important than killing a hundred Germans. That means that we must retain our independence even after our escape. We will use their help but not accept their authority. There is enough room in the forest for separate units.[17]

Although the disagreement among the activists did not hold back the escape preparations, lack of unity among the organizers adversely affected discipline within the groups and efficient execution of the plan.

The plan was delayed once, and when it was carried out the next day the news had spread around the camp – making the prospects for its complete success unlikely. Although a state of emergency was declared in the camp, some individuals succeeded in escaping. Four women and one man were caught while trying to flee and were turned over to the Gestapo.[18] Rivka Levitt's mother was also arrested. The Jewish camp director played a negative role in these arrests.[19]

Yosef Gertner describes the unfortunate episode in detail in his testimony, below:

> Then we started to have meetings to discuss how to escape.... Everyone wanted to spare his friend. But we still had to take circumstances into account. For example, there was the problem about when to flee – during the day from work, or at night from the actual camp. Opinions were divided. Kirka Solsky and Ya'akov Micha [Borstein] argued against escaping during the workday because the women who worked at the farm would not be able

---

17. Ibid., 25–26 (recording 6).

18. The following prisoners were shot by the Gestapo: sisters Sheina and Breina Blustein, Ethel Karlin, and Sonia Levi. Their behavior when being led to execution was exemplary (see PKG, 124; and testimony of Bayla Rodashevsky, YVSA, recording 1).

19. Testimony of Yosef Gertner, YVSA, 20 ff. (recording 5); testimony of Ya'akov Micha Borstein, YVSA, 5; testimony of Bayla Rodashevsky, YVSA, recording 1.

to escape from work. Therefore, we would have to flee from the camp at night. I thought otherwise; better one intact hand than an entire decayed body. But I never made myself the final arbiter; in matters of life and death, there is no final arbiter. Everyone voted, and the majority decided to escape at night. I saw great danger in that, but I had no other solution. I was uncomfortable setting myself apart from the rest of the group....

That was on May 11, 1944. We were ready. We were supposed to leave the camp at midnight.... As I mentioned, we had Rivka'le Levitt, and her mother was in the camp as well.... The mother began to make preparations without our knowledge and without taking the proper precautions. In the camp's courtyard stood a large Finnish hut erected two weeks earlier. The woman took a basket and placed sandwiches, an alarm clock, and all kinds of small things in that basket, which she left in the Finnish hut. Her consideration was that when she would flee at night from her hut...she would pass the yard and take her basket from the Finnish hut on her way. But she was wrong...I knew that people informed on us to the Germans and told them that a group was organizing an escape. Besides that, something else was suspicious to me: I knew that usually at this late hour everyone was sleeping already. But this time everyone [those not part of the organized group] pretended to be asleep, while every once in a while they would lift their heads and look around. It was also strange that one of the Germans who guarded us was now walking around our hallway....

This had never happened before. So I went into the police room, where I saw Ya'akov Micha Borstein, Aryeh Rafeika, and Kirka Solsky. This was what I saw: a clock lay on the table and Kirka Solsky was sitting there, his hands on his head, looking at the clock. The others were lying on the beds with wet towels on their heads.... I asked Solsky, "Why are you staring at the clock?" So he said, "What do you mean? It is already eleven [o'clock] and in another hour, we have to run."...I told them, "Fools, you didn't listen to me and now go out into the hallway and see what happened." They went and realized that escape was out of the question for now. We decided not to flee and that we would postpone the escape.... We notified our people.

And then what happened? Rivka Levitt's mother had left the basket in the yard, and she went to bring it from the Finnish hut. But then they heard our footsteps. When someone appeared in the camp courtyard, the guard started to shoot. So she abandoned the basket and ran into her room. They didn't catch her, but they found the basket and all the items there with the alarm clock, and recognized that it belonged to her.... And if Rivka's mother [is involved] – then Rivka Levitt must be connected, and if Rivka Levitt – then we are all connected; the whole [plan] was discovered....

We were in such a state that the next morning we couldn't say one word to each other. So we couldn't consult to decide what to do...we went out to work. That day we were sent to do urgent labor – unloading boards for constructing huts. Even though we worked next to each other we couldn't talk because the Germans, and even the Jews, didn't take their eyes off of us. We waited impatiently for Haim'ke [Borstein] to return: he had been sent to the forest partisans to inform them of the timing of our escape and organize our reception. We were concerned about failure on that end as well.

At 6 P.M., Haim'ke appeared. He passed by each one of us and whispered, "We must escape." That's when things went crazy among us, because we didn't know what to do. Everything that had been organized and planned was turned upside-down. I myself, for example, didn't want to escape because I wasn't sure that the rest knew about it. If I ran away [alone] then the others would suffer for it. It seemed to me the others also held this opinion. But what happened was that I saw Solsky take off. If he's running away, I thought, there's no point in remaining here, it doesn't matter either way anymore. I gave the signal to Fania Rosh and Lonka Velikolud, who according to the plan were supposed to escape with me. We picked the right moment, and slipped away from the camp. We crossed the train tracks and entered the Babenai Forest.[20]

20. Testimony of Yosef Gertner, YVSA, 18–24 (recording 5–6).

PART IV
War of Revenge

CHAPTER 10

The Birth of the Kovno Battalions

When the first groups of fighters arrived from the Kovno Ghetto to the Rudniki Forests (November–December 1943), the Kovno battalion that received them was still only the nucleus of a partisan battalion. It contained only two or three Soviet paratroopers, including battalion commander Konstatin Smirnov Radyonov, and a fairly small group of Russian and Ukrainian Red Army soldiers and officers who had escaped from German captivity. They had operated as roving partisans in Lithuanian forests until they joined the bases in the Rudniki Forests. Such was the composition of the Kovno battalion at the time; however, that battalion was only a small part of the "Lithuanian Partisan Brigade" and this brigade, as well as the Lithuanian partisan movement, already had a rather long history.

The Lithuanian partisan movement was a branch of the Soviet partisan movement. This branch operated under harsh conditions, especially in its early stages, for two main reasons:

(1) Before the war, the Communist movement had been weak and not deeply rooted in the Lithuanian people. The short period of Soviet rule – only a year – was not enough to enlarge its influence, and large portions of the Lithuanian nation opposed the Soviets and welcomed their expulsion.

(2) Lithuania was completely conquered within a few days, immediately at the beginning of the war. The Communists had no time to make plans and lay the groundwork for an underground.

The news of the German invasion of Lithuania came as a complete surprise to the heads of the Soviet regime in Lithuania. Before they were able to recover, the capital city of Kovno – only about 60 kilometers from the border – was under threat of conquest. Early signs of rebellion had already begun to appear in many places. There was nothing left for them to do except immediately evacuate the Communist Party members and government apparatchiks from Lithuania, sending them to the interior of the Soviet Union. The evacuation began on the evening after the invasion and was conducted on all of the roads and routes bound for the East.[1] Tens of thousands of civilians, many of them Jews, also fled to the Soviet Union's interior. They represented the entire spectrum of society: farmers and ordinary laborers, the educated elite and government functionaries, high- and low-level officials, veteran party members and members of the Lithuanian Soviet regime. The large majority concentrated in the Ivanovo district in the cities of Gorki and Yaroslavl. They were placed under the governance of the local Soviet authorities and the heads of the Lithuanian Soviet regime. These authorities made every effort to recruit as many Lithuanian evacuees as possible for the war against the Nazi invader and also for the struggle for the "expulsion of the Fascist invaders from the Lithuanian homeland."

From the start, this mobilization had two objectives: First, the establishment of a regular Lithuanian division within the Red Army[2] and the preparation of a nucleus of operatives who would be parachuted into occupied Lithuania to organize and direct a fighting Lithuanian Soviet underground. The second goal involved recruiting individuals of a special sort: unceasingly loyal to the Soviet regime and the Communist Party, brave, and expert in underground principles and partisan warfare. Clearly they would have to operate under the most difficult underground conditions. The highest echelons in Moscow and the heads of the Soviet regime in Lithuania both viewed the partisan war as the main role of the Lithuanian Communist Party, and therefore they appointed Antanas Sniečkus, then secretary-general of the Central Committee of the Lithuanian Communist Party, to head this effort. Sniečkus was a central figure during the period of the Soviet regime in Lithuania.

---

1. For more information about the evacuation, see Kutka, 6 ff., also Bilevičius, 37–43. Regarding Kovno alone, on Sunday night, in the early morning hours of June 23, 1941, about five hundred Komsomol people left the city (Viršulis, 15, 28–30), but many were forced to return.

2. For a survey of the factors and causes involved in the establishment of the Lithuanian division, and the makeup and significance of the Jewish fighters in its midst, see the article by Y. Litvak, "The Lithuanian Division" (the largest concentration of Jewish fighters in the second World War), *Gesher*, October 1960.

A Fighting Underground Organized from Above

On July 3, 1941, Stalin delivered a now-famous speech that included a section on partisan war behind the enemy lines.[3] The sources at our disposal indicate that this speech, or directives based on it, served as Snieckus's guidelines in his mission to establish a Lithuanian Communist underground "from above."

On October 10, 1941, Snieckus, as chief of staff of the Lithuanian partisan movement, called on the entire Lithuanian nation in Nazi-occupied territory to resist the occupation authorities in every possible way. He called for establishment of committees for the war against the occupier. He enjoined the public to attack German army units and their headquarters, sabotage transportation arteries and supply lines, cut communications lines, blow up bridges and railways, destroy the provisions and weapons storehouses of the German army, and assist the partisans.[4]

We do not know if Snieckus's call for insurrection reached his target audience or to what extent it affected them. His target audience was the Lithuanian nation, but especially the Lithuanian Communists and Soviet apparatchiks in Lithuania who did not escape to the Soviet Union. We know of two underground Communist groups that operated in Kovno in the fall and winter months of 1941, with whom the ghetto Communists were in contact. The first was a group of apparatchiks, some of whom were Soviet citizens, who arrived from the Soviet Union during the Soviet regime in order to direct the new regime; the second group was composed of Lithuanian Communists headed by Povilas Malinauskas.[5] Both groups shared the same objective of partisan warfare against the occupier, but both failed very quickly, mainly due to the hostile and treasonous attitudes of the Lithuanian population. Both groups were liquidated by the Gestapo.

Snieckus and his colleagues did not limit themselves to proclamations alone. Around the same time, they began to recruit candidates to be parachuted into

---

3. "In regions seized by the enemy, we must establish partisan battalions of cavalry, foot soldiers, and saboteurs to fight the military units of the enemy, to kindle a partisan war on every single site. These units must blow up bridges and roads, disrupt wired and wireless communications, set forests on fire, and burn down storehouses and camps. We must create unbearable conditions for the enemy and all his lackeys in the occupied territories, to pursue and destroy them at every turn, to thwart their every action." See Telpuchovski, *Otcherki*, 137.

4. *PKG*, 30; Viršulis, 59.

5. See chapter 3.

Lithuania. Special partisan-training courses were organized for the veteran Lithuanian Communists and Communist youth that had been evacuated to the Soviet Union.[6] These courses varied in length from three days to six weeks.[7] The candidates learned how to jump from airplanes and the art of sabotage: blowing up train tracks and bridges, derailing moving trains, sabotaging airfields and other military objectives. They also learned principles of behavior in the enemy-occupied areas: acquiring German-authorized documents, contacting Communists, gaining the trust of the population, recruiting liaisons and intelligence experts. Finally, they learned topography and intelligence. Special schools trained wireless operators and experts in sabotage for instructing underground members as well as editors and printers of underground newspapers.

Inserting underground operatives into Lithuanian territory evidently began in the fall of 1941. The first mission we know of involved a group of three people headed by Central Committee member Itzik Meskup, a Jew who went by the nom-de-guerre Adomas.[8] Meskup was accompanied by Skleris and Vidzyunas; they, too, were members of the central institutions of the Lithuanian Communist Party.[9] The theory is that they infiltrated the German rear via the front lines and then headed toward the Rakishok (Rokiškis) district. The group was lost close to the infiltration site, and its fate was unknown. Sniečkus and his colleagues were evidently very worried about the lost group and parachuted several groups into Lithuania during 1942 with instructions to look for them. But all efforts came to naught,[10] and only after the war's end information was received that the paratroopers died in a battle against superior enemy forces.

The first group of operatives that enjoyed at least partial success parachuted into the Skarboczian Forests at the beginning of summer 1942 and landed near

---

6. Kutka, 5.

7. Dixon, 72–73.

8. Itzik (Yitzhak) Meskup, born in 1907, became a member of the illegal Central Committee of the Lithuanian Communist Party in 1935. He was known for his activities in the general strike in Kovno in 1936 (see A. Medonis, ed., *Kaunas* [Kovno, 1960], 32, 48).

9. Viršulis, 77.

10. The following appears in the Einsatzgruppen reports of February 27, 1942: "In Vilna, certain famous people from the Bolshevik era were arrested – they had just returned from the Soviet Union. Some of the prisoners had operated in the Jonai and Babtai forests, and were armed by the person who had been head of the Babtai regional council" (1M/1769, Yad Vashem Archives, no. 172, *Ereignismeldungen*). However, according to Bilevičius (113), the arrival of the group was later than the date appearing on the report (March 1943).

the town of Baltoji Vokė, about 15 kilometers southwest of Vilna.[11] Evidently this group's main mission was gathering intelligence, and it mostly collected military information. It brought a transmitter and maintained direct contact with Moscow for a while. Toward the end of the summer, Zvi Rosinovitz from the Vilna ghetto, a member of the FPO fighting organization, met one of the members of this group. The paratroopers were surprised to hear that a fighting organization existed in the ghetto, but at first were wary of tightening ties with Rosinovitz. Finally they found a way to cooperate, mainly in the sphere of intelligence. FPO members who performed forced labor for the Germans at convenient observation sites in Vilna and its environs began to systematically collect information on military movement, train arrivals and departures, the nature of the train cargo, and military targets in the territory. They gave this material to the paratroopers, who sent detailed reports to Moscow via their transmitter.

The connection with Moscow eventually ended, however, and the paratroopers were not able to restore it. Meanwhile, informers revealed their hideout to the Gestapo. One day the paratroopers found themselves surrounded by a powerful police unit, and after an intense battle they were all killed. The unwarranted trust in the rural population among whom they had found shelter was their undoing[12]

Later, groups parachuting into occupied Lithuanian territory grew in number. According to one Soviet source, no less than twelve fighter groups infiltrated the country, for a total of 126 "party, Komsomol, and council operatives."[13] A significant number of these operatives were Jews.[14] In May 1942, a group of

---

11. Avraham Sutzkever, *Fun Vilner Geta*, 166; compare *Sefer ha-partizanim ha-yehudim* 1:26; M.M. Dvorzetsky, *Yerushalayim de-Lita ba-meri u-va-Shoah* [Jerusalem of Lithuania, in rebellion and Holocaust] (1951), 371.

12. Compare to testimony of Abba Kovner, YVSA, 125–26.

13. Viršulis, 77. Until the end of 1942, a total of about two hundred paratroopers and infiltrators through the front lines were inserted into Lithuanian territory (*Hitlerine*, 263). Two Lithuanian operatives that infiltrated Lithuania at the same time, in order to operate in their hometown of Kovno, were uncovered by the Germans after a short time; they were shot in the Ninth Fort (Viršulis, 37–39). Soviet parachuting endeavors in this time period also appear in *Einsatzgruppen* reports, numbered 182, 183, 190, 191 (IM/1769, YVSA, *Ereignismeldungen*).

14. Aside from the names mentioned above – Genrik Ziman (Jurgis), Gesia Glezer (Albina), Leib Solomin-Petrovitch, and Itzik Meskup (Meskupas-Adomas), we know of the following names from available sources: Israel Itzkovitz, Roshiel (or Yekutiel) Elyashiv, Alter Kleiner, Isser Schmidt (Didialis), David Gutterman (Drotas), Shmuel Iskin (Lalis), Michael Konisky, Uriah Shuster, Michael Markovsky, Daniel Tauter, Misha Karetsky, Shammai (Siyumka) Jacobson, Haim Klebansky, Mina Marshak, M. Moses, Yadovitz, Avraham Yuslovitz, Mania

operatives was dropped into Lithuania and made it to Kovno in order to carry out a special mission of the Soviet military command.[15] In July and August 1942, more members parachuted into Lithuania: Afoninas, former first secretary of the Communist Party in the Trok (Trakai) district (known by his Lithuanian nickname, Petras), parachuted into the Trok district. He was accompanied by Fyodor Pushakov (Genis), T. Monciuskas (Shzoyrbelis), and others. Later, this group headed the partisan brigade command under Genis, in the Rudniki Forests.[16] The "Zigmus" group, with P. Kutka, landed successfully in the Virzhunai Forests in the Utena district. Afterwards, this group established the "Audra" partisan company. A strong group under Solomin was parachuted to the Turženai forests, not far from Pirmasis-Budas village in the environs of Kovno-Jonava. Solomin had been appointed first secretary of the Underground Party Committee for the city and district of Kovno.[17]

The Lithuanian Underground in Action

The material we have access to allows us to examine the instructions given to the partisans before parachuting and to evaluate the extent of their operational successes.[18] We have more detailed material on two groups: Solomin's group and Kutka's group.

Leib Solomin ("Petrovitch") was appointed in August 1942 by the Central Lithuanian Communist Party as "secretary of the Underground Party Committee for the city and district of Kovno." Solomin parachuted from an airplane

---

Barenblatt, David Markovsky, Yeshayahu Markovsky, Yosef Pik. We also know the names of the following members of the high command of the Lithuanian Partisan Movement: Eliyahu Bilvitz (in charge of the transmission station and parachuting of the groups to Lithuanian territory) and Luba Kronick.

15. Viršulis, 89.

16. The Genis brigade, called the "First Troki Brigade Named for the Great Lithuanian Prince Vytautas," established the following four battalions: For the Homeland, Free Lithuania, The Victory, and The Liberator. Dozens of Jewish youths from the Kovno Ghetto joined the ranks of these partisan fighters, including those who escaped from the Koshedar labor camp (see Mončiunskas, 23, 305; also see chapter 9).

17. That year saw an increase in the number of Soviet partisan units operating in Lithuanian territory, to a total of thirty-six (*Hitlerine*, 260).

18. See Apyvala, 123–24, a speech given by Shumuskas (Kazimir) to the commanders of the partisan battalions, about the military and political objectives of the Lithuanian partisan movement.

together with a group of young Lithuanian Communists to the Turzhenar Forest, 30 kilometers southwest of Kovno.[19] The drop was successful; the paratroopers brought with them weapons, food, and equipment, including a radio transmitter, and they established a partisan base in the forest near Jonava. The group had a twofold mission: "regular" partisan operations (blowing up trains, freeing prisoners-of-war and political prisoners, gathering intelligence), as well as establishing a Communist and general anti-Fascist underground in the Kovno city and district along with strengthening the already existing underground organizations.

Both missions were successful, although not equally. Under Solomin's command, a partisan battalion called "For a Soviet Lithuania" was established. An underground Komsomol (Communist youth group) committee was organized in Kovno that was subordinate to Solomin and Gregory Krugliakov; the latter was also the secretary of the municipal and regional party committee. Solomin's partisans operated under relatively favorable conditions. The rural population of the Jonava district villages was almost all Russian, and they had always been strongly influenced by the Communists. Most of these Russians were "Staroveri" (Old Believers), members of a Russian religious sect known for their stubborn nature. When the Germans invaded, the ultra-nationalistic Lithuanians took revenge against these Russians in massacres that touched almost every home. But the Russians were not subdued by the atrocities perpetrated on them by the Lithuanians. On the contrary, they rejoiced at every opportunity for revenge, and they willingly assisted the partisans – even the more so as some of the paratroopers had grown up in the area and their families lived nearby. The following story serves to demonstrate the strong ties between them.

In the spring of 1943, the command of the "For a Soviet Lithuania" battalion decided that the time had come for more serious partisan activity – to blow up a train carrying German military equipment. Solomin himself commanded the operation. At the time, the Germans already knew that Solomin was commander of partisan activities in the Jonava district, and they went to great effort to track him down and capture him. They put up posters with his picture in all the local

---

19. According to the description of Povilas Štaras, one of the participants of this mission and a former secretary of the Municipal Party Underground Committee of the Communist Party, *Podvigi Komsomoltzev Litvi, Druzhba Narodov, Organ Soyuza Pisatelei SSSR* 1958, 10:161–70.

communities, promising a bounty of sixty thousand marks for the "chief of the gang of bandits."

Solomin and his operatives were making the necessary preparations for the sabotage operation when, unfortunately, the explosives blew up prematurely and Solomin was severely injured in the blast. Evidently it was not possible to bring the wounded man to the partisan base. But Krugliakov, who participated in the same operation, had family who lived not far from the explosion site. The partisans decided to take the risk and place the wounded man in the Krugliakov home. Although only Krugliakov's elderly father remained at home, he did not hesitate to accept the dangerous role of hiding the injured man and nursing him. The elderly man hid Solomin in the cellar of his house and carefully camouflaged the entrance. Government officials began to suspect him and started to follow him. Once the Germans burst into the house, searched, but did not find anything. After they left, the elderly man thought that the danger had passed and opened the entrance to the cellar. He was preparing to bring the wounded partisan to his room when loud knocks were heard again on the door. Maintaining his composure, the old man closed the entrance to the cellar, heaped sacks and barrels against it, then went to open the door to Lithuanian policemen assisting the Germans in their manhunt.

The old man's delay aroused the suspicions of the police and they searched the house thoroughly, including the barrels and sacks covering the opening of the cellar. But in his cunning, the man had left food, such as meat and fat, "hidden" under the barrels and sacks. Technically these were illegal and were supposed to be reported to the authorities. When the policeman found this contraband, they thought they had discovered the reason for the delay and did not search any further. The old man then won over the policemen by wining and dining them from his stock. They spent about two hours in his house, not knowing that under the floor of the room lay the man whose head was valued at sixty thousand marks.

Solomin's group in Kovno faced harsher conditions, though they were able to score some successes nonetheless. Solomin sent two Lithuanian youths – Štaras and Urbanavičius – to Kovno after they were parachuted into the country. They lived with a simple Lithuanian woman whose house served them as a refuge as well as a base for underground operations. The woman also introduced them to people in the city who were faithful to the Soviet regime. About ten youths participated in the first meeting, at which they expressed their willingness "to do everything necessary." At that meeting the attendees elected the municipal committee of the Komsomol and determined the rules of secrecy and the plan of action for the initial weeks. In anticipation of the October Revolution holiday, the Komsomol municipal committee glued posters on the walls of Kovno houses. At night, on the eve of the holiday, they hung a red flag on the roof of Kovno's railway station with the inscription "Death to the German Occupiers."

This daring act had two results. On the one hand, it enabled the paratroopers to uncover the existence of several underground Communist groups in the city; on the other hand, it aroused the ire of the Gestapo heads, who conducted a manhunt for the underground activists. The leaders of the operation, Štaras, Urbanavičius, and Petrauskas realized that they had to leave the city, although they probably knew that their absence would paralyze all underground activity. Before leaving the city they managed to clash with the police and kill seven policemen; then they arrived safely at the partisan base in the Jonava Forests. They returned to Kovno in April 1943, after the turning point in the course of the war.

Below is an excerpt from the memoirs of the Audra company commander, who describes some of the difficulties encountered by the paratroopers in this period:

> On August 6 (1942) they told us to prepare ourselves for takeoff the following night.... We brought packages of handbills from Moscow. Our intentions were to distribute them among trustworthy, loyal people.... At our first meeting of the party's regional committee, we decided not to start an active war against the occupier until we could rehabilitate the party's organization in the district...and until we renewed the connections with the "Great Motherland" [the Russian interior], and until we received explosives. It was inconceivable to imagine fighting against the enemy face-to-face, also because of lack of arms. We had one submachine gun, a few grenades, and each of us had a pistol. So far we had not succeeded in obtaining more arms.... We were charged with establishing a partisan intelligence network in our arena. We postponed this mission as well, until after we strengthened our ties with the local residents.[20]

20. Kutka, 10 ff. This group also included a Jew from Kovno named Shammai Jacobson.

A fairly long time was needed for these missions of "strengthening ties with the local residents" and "rehabilitating the party organization" in the Communist underground and the Lithuanian partisan movement. Real partisan activities only began in the summer of 1943; these activities included sabotaging train tracks and military objectives and blowing up storerooms.[21]

The Kovno Ghetto underground began to hear of the existence of partisan groups in the second half of 1942. In the spring of 1943, the ghetto attempted to contact these groups but none of these efforts bore fruit. Undoubtedly one of the reasons for this failure was the weakness of these groups, which were forced to follow very strict secrecy policies and avoid all contact with "external agents."[22]

The Lithuanian Partisan Brigade

In fall 1942, Sniečkus, his colleagues, and the general partisan command in Moscow realized that there was little chance that the small underground groups scattered throughout occupied Lithuania would be able to unite and establish a bonafide partisan movement. Therefore, they adopted a different course. It was decided that the nucleus of the Lithuanian partisan brigade would not be established in Lithuania itself, but in one of the Byelorussian "partisan areas" adjacent to Lithuanian borders. There, the first units would organize themselves and consolidate a command staff. After the initial organization period, they would look for ways to move the partisan bases westward, into Lithuanian territory.

On November 26, 1942, the Central Committee of the Lithuanian Communist Party founded the "operative group" that would form the foundation for the future Lithuanian partisan brigade.[23] The group numbered about forty people, including members of the Central Committee, officers from the Lithuanian division, activists with underground experience, and brave young men who received

---

21. According to an incomplete assessment, the Soviet partisans in Lithuania derailed 364 trains from the train tracks, destroyed about 300 locomotives and more than 2,000 railway cars, eliminated about eighteen garrison forces and killed about 10,000 enemy soldiers and officers (Mončiunskas, 350; compare the Declaration of the Lithuanian Soviet Government and the Central Committee of the Lithuanian Communist Party on the Fifth Anniversary of the founding of the Lithuanian Soviet Socialist Republic, *Einikeit* (183) 71, July 21, 1945).

22. See chapter 4. Also compare to the details of contact with partisan groups in the environs of Keidan; see chapter 9.

23. Viršulis, 89; compare to Mončiunskas, 165; *Hitlerine*, 264; *Sefer ha-partizanim ha-yehudim* 1:182.

extensive partisan training. Kazimir was appointed as the commander of the unit. Kazimir, whose original name was Motius Shumauskas, was a Politburo member of the Lithuanian Central Committee and former mayor of Vilna under the Soviet regime. His deputy was a Kovno-born Jew, (Genrik) Jurgis Ziman.[24] The group was well equipped with the latest types of weapons, the best partisan equipment, and devices for underground operations.

On April 23, 1943, they landed in gliders at an airfield of the Byelorussian Partisan Movement in the Begomel Forests.[25] After rest and preparations, the group made its way over 100 kilometers while waging battles with the enemy, until they reached the Kazian Forests in June 1943. There they found strong bases of the Byelorussian Partisan Movement. These forests had been the frontier regions of Poland until the outbreak of the Second World War. They are part of a large forest block extending from the Naroch lake region in the south to Polotsk in the north, and from the old border between Poland and the Soviet Union in the east, to the old border between Lithuania and Poland, and beyond in the west.

The unit set up its operative base in this forest, among the Byelorussian battalions, and began to organize. Its priority was to gather and unite the Lithuanian partisans in these forests, both those who had belonged to non-Lithuanian units as well as the independent roving units. Most of these partisans were Lithuanian Soviet apparatchiks who had not succeeded in escaping to the Soviet Union. They were forced to leave their homes in the face of Nazi terror and the hostile treatment of the population toward anyone who supported Soviet rule. Youths from nearby communities also joined this newly formed brigade, which called itself "Zalgiris" (the Green Forest). Most were Lithuanian, but some were Byelorussians who were impressed by the great firepower of this force.

The brigade especially attracted Jews in these forests. Until the arrival of the

---

24. Ziman's military and political status rose over time until his subordination to Shumauskas was in name only. On December 25, 1943, the operative group of the Central Lithuanian Communist Party was divided into separate northern and southern units. Shumauskas was appointed head of the Northern Committee, while Ziman became head of the Southern Committee, which encompassed the districts of southern Lithuania including the Rudniki Forests, Augustova, and Kazlu-Ruda (Mončiunskas, 165; Viršulis, 181–82).

25. An accident occurred during these landings in which several people were killed and Ziman himself was wounded, but he refused to be returned by special airplane back to Russia for medical treatment. An earlier attempt (February 1943) to cross the front lines near the town of Cholm failed (see Bilevičius, 105–112, compare to Apyvala, 99; *Hitlerine*, 264).

Lithuanian unit from Moscow, the Jewish fighters had tasted anti-Semitism and hostility on the part of the non-Jewish partisans, including their commanders. The Lithuanian unit brought with it from "the Great Motherland" a different spirit. From its very inception, Jews were treated with the fullest trust and respect by the members of the Lithuanian unit, news that quickly spread throughout the partisan forest. Within a short time, many Jews joined the Lithuanian unit and even acquired command posts.[26]

The unit finished its initial, organizational phase in the summer months of 1943 and then split into two. Some of the members, headed by Kazimir, remained in place and formed two partisan battalions,[27] while the rest of the group, headed by Jurgis, moved their bases to the Naroch Forests, closer to the Vilna environs. These forests were a way station for Jurgis and his group before their final move to the Rudniki Forests, where they later established the permanent bases of the brigade.[28]

The Lithuanian Brigade in the Rudniki Forests

This region, called Rudnitzka Forests in Polish and Russian, is a block of thick forests surrounding the town of Rudniki.[29] This block extends over a territory of about 2,400 square kilometers; its quadrangular shape has a width of about 40 kilometers and length of 60. Its northern flank extends to within 15 kilometers of Vilna, and its southern edge – to the same distance from the city of Lida. Inside the forest are small bare areas with villages and towns, connected to one another by dozens of paths and lanes. Four transportation arteries cross the forest: two railways and two roads that connect Vilna with Lida and with Grodno. Extensive areas are covered by dense forest and in many places the sunlight cannot penetrate the tangled branches, even in the middle of the day. The area is covered with bogs and lakes with islands. These islands, ideal sites for partisans, could only be accessed by a small number of dry paths.

---

26. *Sefer ha-partizanim ha-yehudim* 1:182.

27. For more information about the fate of these battalions and of the Jews in them, see ibid., 183–96.

28. For information about the Naroch episode, the Jewish fighters in these forests, the Jewish "Revenge" battalion, and Jurgis's policy toward the Jewish fighters, see *Sefer ha-partizanim ha-yehudim*, 73–105; also see S. Ahavya (Lubetkin), Yosef Glazman, Tel Aviv, 1947.

29. Lazer, 223–24. Compare to Mončiunskas, 24–25, 149.

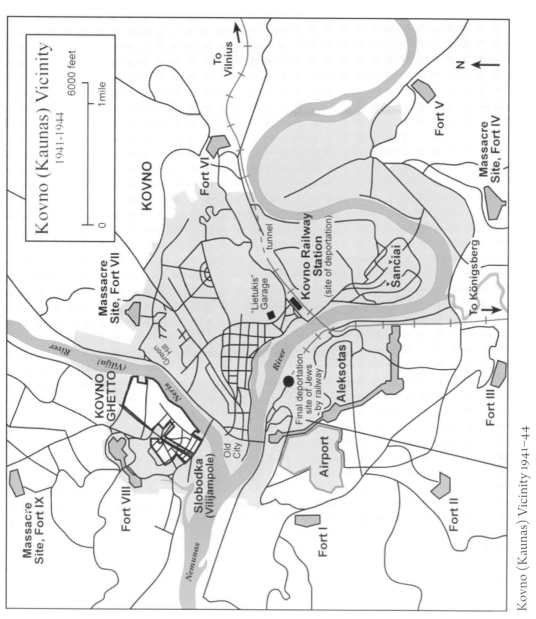

MAP 1. Map taken from Crossing the River, Shalom Eilati. Printed with permission of the University of Alabama Press

Kovno (Kaunas) Vicinity 1941–44

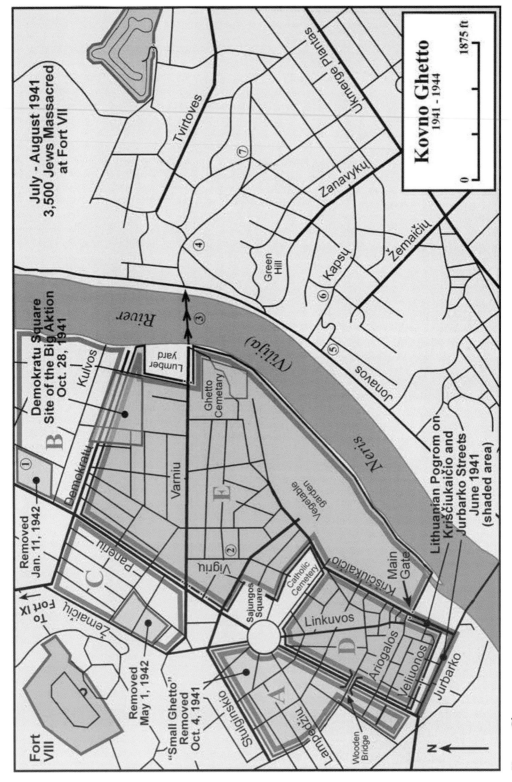

MAP 2. Map taken from Crossing the River, Shalom Eilati. Printed with permission of the University of Alabama Press

Kovno Ghetto 1941–44

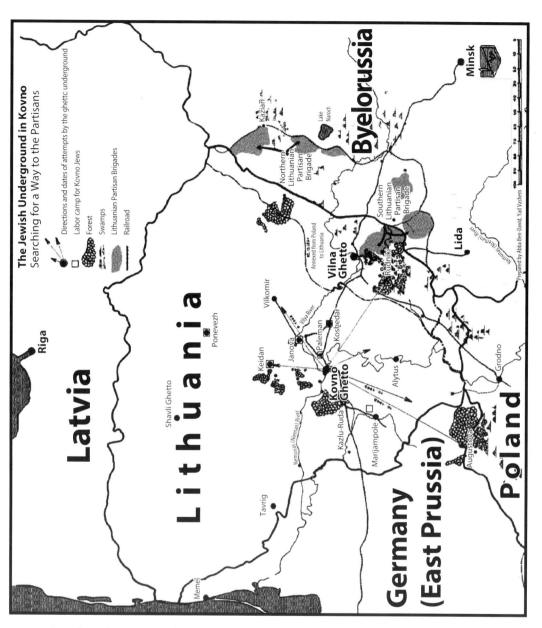

MAP 3. Searching for a Way to the Partisans

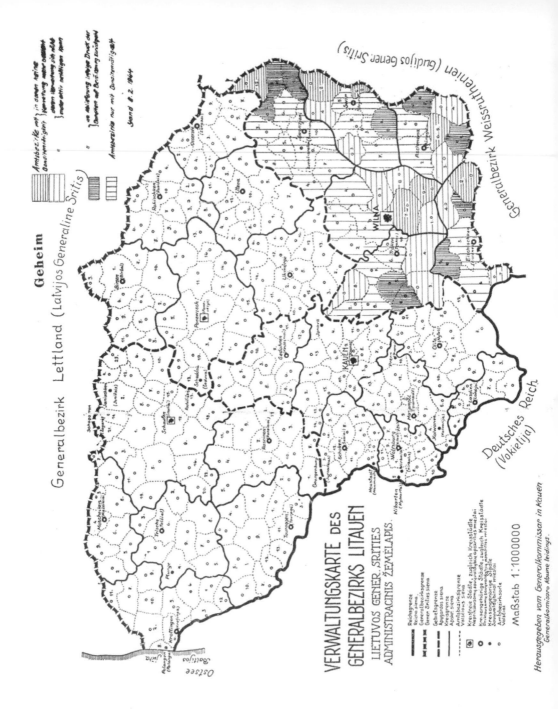

MAP 4. German map depicting the status of partisan activity in southeast Lithuania in February 1944. The areas no longer under German rule are marked with narrow horizontal lines; where the German administration had been suppressed – broad horizontal lines; where partisan pressure undermined collection of the mandatory payments from the population – narrow vertical lines; areas of partisan activity – broad vertical lines. The map was prepared in the office of the German General Commissar for Lithuania in Kovno.

The Berlin Collection, RG 215 Folder OCCE 3ba-17 Maps (2 copies) of Generalbesirk Litauen, showing partisan activities, 2/44   (Courtesy YIVO Institute for Jewish Research)

MAP 5. **Penetration of the Partisans into Lithuania and Offensive of the Red Army in July 1944**

Numbered lines:
1. Direction of penetration of the Death to the Occupiers combat company.
2. Direction of penetration of Forward battalion.
3. Direction of penetration of Vladas Baronas battalion.
4. Direction of penetration of the select unit.

The dates beside cities indicate the day of liberation by the Red Army. Kovno was occupied two weeks after Koshedar, Alytus, and Grodno, and during those fateful fourteen days, the Nazis liquidated the ghetto (see chapter 14, "Last Days of the Kovno Ghetto").

FIGURE 1. *Yidden nekume!* [Jews, revenge!] Writing on the wall in apartment of a Jewish family that was murdered in the Slobodka pogrom in June 1941. (Courtesy of Yad Vashem)

FIGURE 2. Last letter of Haim Tiktin, a leader of the Zionist resistance in Kovno Ghetto. (Courtesy of Yad Vashem)

The letter reads:

> "To the rescued IBZ members. Part of the archive is in the hiding place of Y.S. (the hiding place was reconstructed [?] in the room with the well). A second part is with the belongings of Dr. Shapira, located in the waste pit next to the storage shed opposite the exit from this basement, on the left (facing in that direction), in the trash container placed inside it. Aside from this, you will find the archive in the place known to you! I am writing this in the morning, at the beginning of a day which is apparently the beginning of our end. Which? – Our will: revenge against the enemy-beast; for you, and for the remainder of the Hebrew nation – total rescue, redemption in the land of our forefathers. – Masha! Menachem! You, who walked the path of rescue, and you, who walked the path of revenge, raise the IBZ flag, the flag of unity of the remnant of the nation!"
>
> In the name of the IBZ command, Haim Yigaeli (Tiktin)

FIGURE 3. Irgun Brit Zion youth group in the ghetto (Courtesy of Yad Vashem)

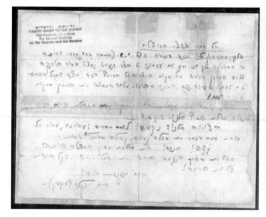

FIGURE 4. Committee of the Anti-Fascist Organization in the ghetto. From right to left: Dima Galpern, Miriam (Mara) Lan, Haim Yellin, Moshe Sherman, Pesach Gordon-Stein. (Courtesy of Yad Vashem)

FIGURE 6. Haim Yellin, commander of the Jewish Fighting Organization of Kovno (Courtesy of Yad Vashem)

FIGURE 5. Haim Yellin and Moshe Moselis during weapons training in a secret apartment (Ghetto Fighters' House Museum/Photo Archive)

FIGURE 7. Haim Yellin and Haim David Ratner, a military trainer in the JFO, at a secret meeting place on the banks of the Vilya River (Courtesy of Yad Vashem)

FIGURE 8. Abba Diskant, among those who fled from the Ninth Fort, scout, and partisan guide. Fell in skirmish with police forces. (Ghetto Fighters' House Museum/Photo Archive)

FIGURE 9. Shmuel Mordkovsky, activist, scout, and partisan guide. Fell in battle at Zhalvi village. (Ghetto Fighters' House Museum/Photo Archive)

FIGURE 10. Yisrael Milstein, scout. Fell in skirmish with police forces. (Ghetto Fighters' House Museum/Photo Archive)

FIGURE 11. Yosef Feuerstein, partisan. Fell during a sabotage mission near Tarok. (Ghetto Fighters' House Museum/Photo Archive)

FIGURE 12. Rachel Katz, member of the JFO. Smuggled weapons into the ghetto and rescued children. Fell in the line of duty. (Courtesy of Yad Vashem)

FIGURE 13. Menachem (Nyunka) Levin, member of the Jewish Fighting Organization (JFO). Fell in the Augustova Plan.(Ghetto Fighters' House Museum/Photo Archive)

FIGURE 14. Leib Gempel, one of the first fighters who escaped from the ghetto to join the forest partisans. Fell in combat in Kalitance (Kalitonys) village. (Ghetto Fighters' House Museum/Photo Archive)

FIGURE 15. Elchanan Segelson, youth member of the JFO. Fell in Israel's War of Independence. (Ghetto Fighters' House Museum/Photo Archive)

FIGURE 16. Members of the JFO (right to left): David Goldin (died in the forest), Alter Feitelson, Yisrael Goldblatt (Courtesy of Yad Vashem)

FIGURE 18. Arms smugglers of the JFO: Yehuda Lifschitz (right) and Shlomo Baron (center), bandaged in the ghetto prison. The third person (left) is unidentified. (Ghetto Fighters' House Museum/Photo Archive)

FIGURE 17. Nehemiah Endlin, one of the foremost partisan scouts and guides in the Southern Lithuanian Partisan Brigade. (From *The Truth and Nothing But The Truth*, Alex Faitelson)

FIGURE 19. Meir Luria, member of the JFO. Killed during a sabotage operation at the Fifth Fort. (Ghetto Fighters' House Museum/Photo Archive)

FIGURE 20. Eliyahu Shmuelov, one of the first members of the JFO (Ghetto Fighters' House Museum/Photo Archive)

FIGURE 21. The Ninth Fort, the Fortress of Death. General view. (Courtesy of Yad Vashem)

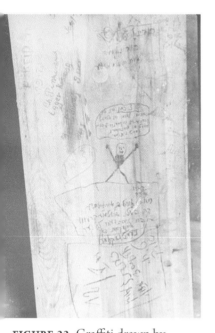

FIGURE 22. Graffiti drawn by Jews sentenced to death, on the walls of a cell in the Ninth Fort (United States Holocaust Memorial Museum).

FIGURE 23. A group of men from among the escapees from the Ninth Fort in Kovno, visiting there immediately after the war. In the photo: Mendel Dietz (front row, on the left), Tuvia Friedman (front row, center), Pinchas Krakinovsky (front row, right) Yisrael Vaselnitzky (Vasilenko) (upper row, left) Alter – Alter Feitelson (upper row, second from the left), Aharon Vilenchuk (upper row, second from the right), and A. Meister (upper row, on the right). (Ghetto Fighters' House Museum/Photo Archive)

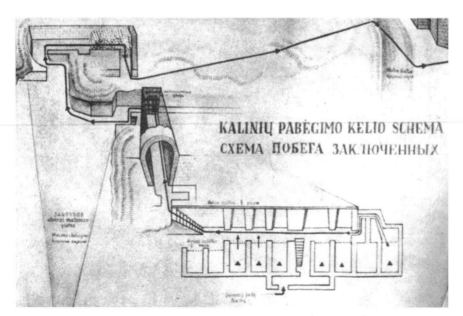

FIGURE 24. Sketch of the escape operation from the Ninth Fort (chapter 6). The long arrow shows the path of the escapees: from the cells to the first floor corridor; up the stairs to the second floor corridor leading to the iron door they had breached; through the courtyard, which was in the sentry's range of sight; through the tunnel that had been cleared of wood; out the inner courtyard; down the steep slope; by ladder up the wall. (Courtesy of the Kaunas Ninth Fort Museum).

FIGURE 26. Gesia Glezer (Albina), paratrooper, contact between the Kovno Ghetto underground and the headquarters of the Soviet partisan movement in Lithuania. She fell in a clash with Gestapo forces in Vilna. (Ghetto Fighters' House Museum/Photo Archive)

FIGURE 25. Itzik Meskup (Adomas), one of the first Soviet paratroopers in Lithuania. He fought the Germans in east Lithuania and his traces were lost. (Ghetto Fighters' House Museum/Photo Archive)

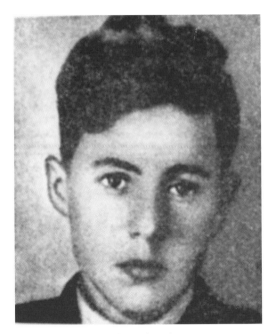

FIGURE 27. Michael Markovsky, paratrooper. He fell in battle. (Ghetto Fighters' House Museum/Photo Archive)

FIGURE 28. Shammai (Syomka) Jacobson, paratrooper and radio operator. He fell in battle with the Germans in east Lithuania. (Ghetto Fighters' House Museum/Photo Archive)

FIGURE 29. Group of partisans from the Kovno battalions, with their weapons. Standing (right to left): Itzik Yuchnikov, Aharon Gafanovitz, David Tepper, Shimon Bloch, Berel Kott, Kalman Goldstein, Yerachmiel Berman. Kneeling: Yaakov Ratner. (Moreshet Archive, Mordechai Anielevich Memorial)

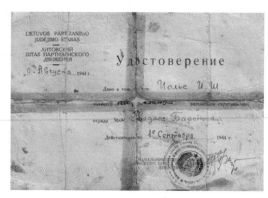

FIGURE 30. Certificate of the partisan command. (Moreshet Archive, Mordechai Anielevich Memorial)

TEXT OF THE CERTIFICATE:

"Headquarters of the Lithuanian Partisan Movement"

Authorization   August 9, 1944

This is to authorize that soldier Joels Y. S. was a partisan in the Vladas Baronas Lithuanian Partisan Battalion. This authorization is valid until September 1, 1944.

Director of the Personnel Branch of the Headquarters of the Lithuanian Partisan Movement.

FIGURES 31–32. This is a partisan letter of commendation for fighter Yisrael Joels. (Moreshet Archive, Mordechai Anielevich Memorial)

IN ENGLISH TRANSLATION:

Letter of Commendation / Characteristics / of Comrade Joels Israel, son of Shabbtai, partisan member of Vladas Baronas battalion.

During his stay in the battalion, Comrade Joels often participated in the battalion's combat missions, such as: attacks on enemy outposts in the villages of Žagarinė, Rudnick, and Večioriškiai; burning the bridge over the Marisa River; supplying weapons to the battalion. He took part in clashes with the police and an attack on the police station in Visia. He was wounded. For most of his time in the battalion, he served in the combined reconnaissance unit (of the three [Kovno] battalions). As one of the best scouts of the battalion, Comrade Joels excelled as a brave and resourceful partisan, fearless and disciplined. He willingly accepted and carried out every special reconnaissance mission assigned to him.

Battalion Commander Semyonov, Battalion Commissar Balkin.

FIGURE 33. Partisans from the Kovno Ghetto in the Rudniki Forest. Right to left: Aharon Gafanovitz, Leib Zietzv, Rivka (Alteke) Tepper, Moshe Sherman, Berl Stern, Rivka Bloch, Eliezer Zilber, Yaakov Ratner, Esther Shtrom, Shimon Bloch, Zondel (Zonia) Shtrom, Michael Lipkovitz, Yehuda (Yudel) Eidelman, Shlomo Broyer, Yitzchak (Itzik)Yuchnikov, David Tepper. (Courtesy of Yad Vashem)

FIGURE 34. A group of former Jewish partisans beside the graves of their comrades-in-arms in Kovno (1958)

RIGHT TO LEFT, SEATED: David Tepper, unidentified, Monik Holzberg, Zondel Shtrom, next three unidentified, Masha Endlin, Nehemiah Endlin, Mendel Dietz, Aharon Gafanovitz, Yaakov Ratner, Aharon Vilenchuk, Moshe Sherman

STANDING: Alter Feitelson, Berel Stern, Peretz Kliatchko, Rivka (Altke) Tepper, Sara Robinson, Moshe Robinson, Moshe Upnitzky, Dr. Helen Kutorgiene, Miriam Joels, Yisrael Vasselnitzky (Vasilenko), Isser Schmidt, unidentified, Yisrael Joels, Yisrael Goldblatt, Sima Yashunsky, Eliezer Zilber, Eidel Pilovnik, Lovka Scher, Rivka Kagan, Esther Shtrom, Meister, Leah Scher, unidentified, Dima Galpern, next two unidentified, Tuvia Friedman, Shulamit Lerman, Berkovitz (From *The Truth and Nothing But The Truth*, Alex Faitelson)

FIGURE 35. A group of former partisans from the Kovno Ghetto living in Israel (photographed at Yagur in 1954)

RIGHT TO LEFT: Michael Yitzhaki (Gelbtrunk), Yosef Melamed, Zvie A. Brown, Yosef Rosen, Penina (Sukenik) Gofer, Zvi (Grisha) Shefer, Ephraim Senion (Senior), Baruch Gofer (Grodnik)

STANDING IN FRONT: Gita Foger (Courtesy of Yad Vashem)

FIGURE 36. A gathering held in Israel of former members of the Zionist pioneering movements in the Kovno Ghetto who were part of the Mildos 7 collective . (Photographed in Caesarea in 1990).

Left to right: Tsadok Bleiman – Evyatar, Yona Rochman, Rachel Rosenzwaig – Levin, Grisha Shaeffer, Dov Levin, Avivit Rudnik – Kashiv, Michael Glas, Hinda Akerman – Katsanovski, Reuven Levitan, Dina Murevich – Galeen, Yitzhak Kopchevski – Kashiv, Yosef Melamed, Ester Shevts – Glas (Ghetto Fighters' House Museum/Photo Archive)

The population of the Rudniki Forest villages and towns was mixed, with Poles, Lithuanians, and a Byelorussian minority. The relations between different ethnic groups were sometimes hostile, depending on the circumstances. The Germans attempted to capitalize on these tensions and granted preferential treatment to the Lithuanians over the other groups. For this reason, the Lithuanians were very loyal to the Germans, at least during the first two years of the Nazi occupation. It was no wonder that the Lithuanians were usually hostile to the Soviet partisans.

The Poles, meanwhile, yearned for the rebirth of their independent Polish state, and they established White Polish partisan units. Although the professed objective of these units was war against the Nazi occupier, in effect these units protected the Polish farmers and landowners from the Lithuanians as well as as from the Soviet partisans. Usually the Poles remained inside their villages but would leave the villages occasionally to conduct "special operations" – that is, conduct raids throughout the forest region with which they were so familiar. They tried to maintain their military power in case it would be needed during critical periods of regional changes of government. The most unfortunate ones in this area were the Byelorussians, who suffered on all sides. They were also the most loyal to the Soviet partisans.

In the early years, the Germans maintained small forces in the area, but these grew in direct proportion to the strengthening of the partisan units in the forest. The German garrisons in this area in the summer of 1943 included the garrison in the Rudniki town, which numbered several hundred soldiers, mainly German, Lithuanian, and some others. The garrison in Olkeniki town numbered about two hundred soldiers. A small garrison was located in the town on the Vilna-Lida road. A garrison of Lithuanian soldiers was posted in Raveliai village, where the Germans maintained a prison next to the garrison. In addition, a garrison was located in Večioriškiai, near an anti-partisan spy school for Russian youths affiliated with the Andrei Vlasov group.[30] There were other garrisons as well. All of these garrisons prevented the Rudniki forest block from becoming overt partisan

---

30. Andrei Vlasov, a Soviet general, defected to the German side and set up an army of Soviet prisoners-of-war; they fought against the Red Army and the Soviet partisans. For more information about Vlasov and his deeds, see Dallin, 553–86.

territory, and served as springboards for German search-and-destroy operations against the partisans.

Jurgis acted very cautiously when he moved his bases to the Rudniki Forests. His choice of these forests for the permanent seat of the brigade was based on two main considerations. First, the geographic conditions were well suited to partisan bases, even large units. Second, the entire area was in Lithuanian territory, in close proximity to Lithuania's new capital city of Vilna. However, Jurgis and his staff were unfamiliar with this vast forest region, which in late summer 1943 was almost devoid of people. Only one small group of experienced Russian partisans (*spetzgruppe*) operated in this area. They were parachuted here under the leadership of Mishka Elko, a Soviet army captain, for special operations. Jurgis may have known, from Moscow, that this group was stationed in Rudniki. Although they succeeded in their special operations, it could not be deduced from this what the chances were of locating a large partisan brigade there. Therefore he could not rely on them to establish a foothold for his bases; instead, he did it on his own.

Jurgis's contact with the Rudniki Forests evidently began at the beginning of August 1943,[31] when he was still in Naroch. One of the heads of the Communist underground, who used the name Petras and had served as secretary of the Communist Party in the Trok district, was hiding from the Germans in the Rudniki villages and forests. Petras sent a messenger to Naroch with preliminary information for Jurgis about the Rudniki area, as well as giving him special signs on how to find him. Based on this, Jurgis sent the first vanguard group in August to the Rudniki Forests.[32] There were nine people in the group: four paratroopers from Moscow and five Jews from the Jewish partisan group "Revenge"; this group had already existed for some time in the Naroch Forests.[33]

Petras lived up to expectations. He came to the meeting place and helped familiarize the group with their surroundings and find an appropriate place in the forest to set up their first base. In the early weeks, the group tried as much

---

31. Lazer, 224 ff.

32. Testimony of Abba Kovner, yvsa, 8 (recording 3).

33. The names of the five were Haim Lazer from Rakishok in Lithuania, Sashke and Haim Meltzer, Gershon Gitelzon from Vilna, and Lovke from Globoki (compare to testimony of Haim Lazer, yvsa, letter 1). According to Mončiunskas (148), the paratroopers Navodomsky, Nikitin, and Krulikauskas were part of this vanguard group.

as possible not to attract attention from the Germans. After a short while the group began to grow. It was joined by several Russian paratroopers who had arrived in the area a year earlier but failed in their attempts to organize a partisan unit, barely managing to stay alive. Youths from nearby villages also found their way to the base.

As the unit grew, so did the problem of adequate arms and ammunition. The brigade command wanted to transfer to the base as many weapons and and as much ammunition as possible, but the supply route was long – about 150 kilometers. Since the partisans had to hike the distance by foot and in secrecy, they could not carry much with them. Therefore, besides purchasing food and recruiting members, a top priority was weapons acquisition operations. The partisans tried to acquire firearms and ammunition mainly from the local farmers who had collected and hidden weapons as booty when the Polish army fell in 1939 and during the Red Army's hasty retreat in 1941.

After a few weeks two more groups arrived from the Naroch Forests. At this point the unit in Rudniki numbered about sixty members, mostly Lithuanians, with ten Jews and a few Russians. The head of the unit was a veteran Communist, a paratrooper named Gabris, who became Jurgis's deputy. The unit's activity evolved into a proper course of partisan combat, while they anticipated the arrival of the brigade, with its permanent command, from Naroch.

Meanwhile, the Rudniki Forests began to fill up with new fighters, mainly from the Vilna Ghetto. In April 1943, a group of eight[34] fighters arrived from Vilna under the leadership of Dov (Borke) Friedman of Beitar. This group did not last long in the forest and dispersed after four of its members, including Friedman himself, fell in a battle against the Germans. At the beginning of September, a second group arrived with twenty-five members of the Yechiel company.[35] In the middle of September, two more groups from the Vilna Ghetto joined, and the unit of Jewish fighters grew to about 70 people. Their weapons were relatively limited: a small number of rifles,[36] one pistol per person, and grenades. The

---

34. Lazer, 230. Also compare to *Sefer ha-partizanim ha-yehudim* 1:58.

35. For more information about the Yechiel company in the Vilna Ghetto, see Dvorzetsky, *Yerushalayim de-Lita*, 199 ff.

36. According to *Sefer ha-partizanim ha-yehudim*, 1:58 – six rifles; according to Lazer, 244 – seventeen rifles.

unit established temporary bases deep in the forest, around 2 kilometers from Gabris's unit.

At first, the members of this unit did not consider joining Gabris's unit and then merging into the Lithuanian brigade, to be established after Jurgis's arrival. Instead, they were attracted to Captain Elko's group of veteran partisans. One of the Vilna fighters was personally acquainted from before the war with the captain's reconnaissance officer, Batia, and through him they were able to contact Elko himself. But the captain rejected the plea of accepting the entire Jewish unit. He was willing to accept only those who he found fit for partisan combat, and only a third of the unit fulfilled these requirements. Consequently the Jews rejected this proposal, except for isolated members who joined Elko's unit on their own.

At the end of September 1943, a group of FPO (United Partisan Movement, the combined fighting underground of the Vilna Ghetto) members reached the forest from Vilna. They were headed by Abba Kovner and Hina Borovska, from the FPO command. The "newcomers" joined the "veterans," even though the so-called newcomers had belonged to different fighting organizations in the ghetto. As soon as they arrived, however, a disagreement arose in the joint camp about the future of the Jewish unit. The veterans were in favor of an independent unit that would continue to maintain contact with Captain Elko's unit. By contrast, the newcomers (the FPO members) wanted the status of a separate Jewish unit to be recognized by the leadership of the Lithuanian partisan movement as part of the Lithuanian brigade that soon planned to move to camp in the Rudniki Forests.

We do not know exactly what the decision was and how the organization and command of the Jewish unit was determined. The sources are contradictory and obscure on this point,[37] but the fact is that the Jewish camp accepted the authority of the Lithuanian brigade command. In the future this fact was to determine

---

37. According to Lazer (244–46), the FPO heads imposed their will on the Jewish camp regarding the forms of organization and command composition; they were assisted in this by Gabris's intervention. The camp was divided into three separate battalions, and the FPO members were appointed as commanders. The previous commanders were either appointed as deputy commanders or barred from command altogether. According to Ruzhke Korczak (*Sefer ha-partizanim ha-yehudim*, 1:60–62), Gabris temporarily appointed Abba Kovner as "commander of the Jewish partisans" and Hina Borovska as "political commissar." Gabris's appointments were intended to be temporary until "the arrival of the brigade general command."

the fate of the unit and of all the Vilna units. It also affected the power structure in the partisan area of the Rudniki Forests.

Jurgis arrived in the Rudniki Forests to a "ready-made" brigade. Unlike other partisan brigade commanders he was not forced to to build up his unit in a long continuous effort starting from a small nucleus. When Jurgis moved to the Rudniki Forests in October 1943, the units under his command already numbered hundreds of armed fighters. Jurgis's fighters were also equipped with wireless transmitters and radios and had established contacts with urban centers nearby. Nevertheless, Jurgis worked intensively to expand and enlarge his brigade even more. The political circumstances of the period (between fall 1943 and early summer 1944) were conducive to his goals, as those were the days of the great Red Army offensive on the Vitebsk front [in Byelorussia].

In this short time period, Jurgis's unit grew quickly. When he arrived in Rudniki there were four battalions: Gabris's battalion, originally called "Adam Mickiewicz," consisting of about a hundred or more fighters, and three Vilna battalions (The Avenger, To Victory, and Death to the Fascists). To these, five more battalions were added: three that were mainly comprised of Kovno Ghetto fighters (Death to the Occupiers, Vladas Baronas, and Forward); one Vilna battalion, Struggle; and a Lithuanian battalion, comprised of residents of local villages, called "Perkunas" (Lithuanian for "thunder"). Meanwhile, Genis had also set up his bases in the Rudniki Forests and brought with him four battalions (the First Troki Brigade). By the spring of 1944, the number of fighters had reached about 1,200, about half of whom were Jews. Jurgis's authority had spread over the entire Rudniki Forests block.

Death to the Occupiers Battalion and Its Branches

Prior to Jurgis's arrival in the Rudniki Forests in October 1943, no Kovno battalion had existed there and, evidently, the provisional brigade leadership had no intentions of establishing such a battalion. Therefore, when Haim Yellin visited the Rudniki Forests with paratrooper Albina-Glezer in September 1943, he was advised to send the Kovno Ghetto fighters to the Augustova Forests. That plan failed, as described previously, as did all attempts to establish partisan bases in

---

The source does not indicate who decided to divide the camp into three battalions and who determined the entire command composition.

Fighting Units of the Southern Lithuanian Soviet Partisan Brigades mentioned in "The Story of an Underground"

Jurgis (Ziman) – commander of Southern Lithuanian brigades from Jan. 1944

Base: Rudniki Forests

approximately 1200 fighters (spring, 1944), 50% were Jews

First Trakai (Troki) Brigade	Kovna Brigade	Vilna Brigade	Other Units
Brigade commander: Genis	Brigade commander: Radyonov	First brigade commander was Abba Kovner	**Adam Mitzayuits** battalion (Rudniki area) commander: Gabris
			For a Soviet Lithuania battalion (Jonava area, later Rudniki) commander: Petrovich (Solomin)
4 battalions:	**3 battalions:**	**4 battalions:**	
1. For the Homeland	1. Death to the Occupiers (commander – Radyonov)	1. The Avenger (commander – Abba Kovner)	**Perkunas** battalion (Rudniki area)
2. Free Lithuania	2. Forward (commander – Zeike)	2. To Victory	**Kochargin detachment** (Kazluv-Ruda area) commander: Yerachmiel Berman
3. The Victory	3. Vladas Baronas (commander – Semyonov)	3. Death to the Fascists	**Audra Detachment** (Keidan area) commander: Kutka
4. The Liberator		4. Struggle	**Elko's spetzgruppe** (Rudniki area)
		(Revenge – Jewish battalion that was disbanded in 1942)	**Group A** (Keidan area) commander: Petke
			Group B (Keidan area) commander: Yosef Gertner

the Kovno environs, whether temporary or permanent. Even Solomin, who succeeded in setting up a partisan unit based in the Jonava Forests about 30 kilometers northeast of Kovno, was forced to abandon the site in early winter of 1943–1944. Solomin took his partisans and withdrew eastward to the Lithuanian brigade bases in the Rudniki Forests.

Evidently, these facts on the ground convinced Jurgis that Kovno partisan battalions should not be established near Kovno but in the Rudniki Forests, where conditions were much more suitable and favorable for their survival. Only when conditions improved – after the battalion became established, organized, and properly armed in Rudniki – could they be moved westward, closer to their native Kovno district. About a month after arriving in the Rudniki Forests, Jurgis proposed to the paratrooper Konstatin Smirnov Radyonov to establish a partisan battalion from the Kovno people that would be part of the Lithuanian brigade. For this purpose, Radyonov went to Murava, his city of birth near Kovno, to set up a Communist underground and also recruit fighters to his battalion. It was during this time that he met Haim Yellin, as mentioned above.[38]

Radyonov returned to the Rudniki Forests in early November to establish his base there. The camp extended over about ten dunams (2.5 acres) in the center of the forest, about 22 kilometers south of Vilna, 500 meters from the Kopana Road,[39] and adjoining the Merchanka River.

The core of the battalion, called "Death to the Occupiers," was comprised of twenty to thirty fighters. This group included a handful of Russian prisoners who had escaped from prisoner-of-war camps and had tasted the life of roving partisan fighters; four paratroopers, including Jewish paratrooper Misha (Mishka) Karetsky, who had lived in Kovno before the war; and two Jews from Byelorussia: Misha Meirov, a daring partisan who later excelled in blowing up railways and met his death while blowing up his sixth railway,[40] and Leib Zeitzev, resident of a tiny town in west Byelorussia. Among the first people to join the battalion was Russian prisoner-of-war Davidov, who was appointed political commissar of the battalion.

While the partisans in this core group were on a high level and well suited to the demands of partisan warfare, they were too few and had insufficient weapons and equipment to constitute a real partisan unit that could stand alone. The order of the day was to expand this small unit by accepting new fighters into the group. Since they could not place much hope on recruiting people through the city of Kovno's Lithuanian underground, the logical entity to approach was the JFO, the fighting organization in the Kovno Ghetto. Consequently the departure of the Jewish fighters from the ghetto to the Kovno battalion base was of vital

---

38. Editor's note: According to the authors, Radyonov had met earlier with Haim Yellin (see ch. 5) and then again in November after the failure of the Augustova Plan (see ch. 7).

39. Polish for "paved road." This road was paved by the Polish authorities for the convenience of high-ranking Polish dignitaries, such as Marshal Pilsudski, who came to this area frequently in order to conduct hunts.

40. *PKG*, 136.

necessity not only to the underground in the ghetto, but to the establishment of the Kovno battalion itself. Within a few months, the Kovno battalion was transformed from a tiny nucleus, an insignificant part of Jurgis's brigade, to one of the strongest partisan units in terms of manpower, equipment, and weapons, not just in the Rudniki Forests, but in all of south Lithuania.

This process of the growth of the battalion was hardly simple. Although the first groups arriving from the ghetto brought with them valuable equipment, their arms, consisting mainly of pistols and grenades, did not add much strength to the battalion: the battalion was in need of rifles, submachine guns, and machine guns. This aroused the ire of the core group, and the anti-Semites among them loudly cursed and defamed the Jews. They argued that the ghetto Jews had come to the forest to save their skins, not to fight. For a period, the Jewish fighters were employed in the backbreaking work of constructing trenches and dugouts in the camp's swampy land and were denied the opportunity to adjust to the partisan life of combat. They were given smaller portions of food than the others, even in comparison to the meager portions of the "veterans." Most of them felt that they were purposely assigned to this inferior status of "hewers of wood and water carriers" (providing menial labor), and they greatly resented it.[41]

The situation improved somewhat after veteran Jewish fighters of the Kovno battalion intervened on their behalf, as did fighters from other battalions. But the situation did not change significantly until the Jewish Fighting Organization in the ghetto radically changed its methods of weapons acquisition and arming the forest groups. When the groups began to arrive armed with rifles, machine guns, and large quantities of ammunition, the anti-Semites could argue no more. The door was opened for Jews of combat readiness to participate in partisan missions.

The battalion's expansion and increase in combat strength led to a process of internal reorganization and consolidation. After the arrival of a particularly large group of fighters from the ghetto – the group that included the Ninth Fort escapees – the command decided to create a new battalion called "Vladas Baronas" (after a Lithuanian Communist who was hung together with his two

41. Testimony of Rivka Gordon, YVSA, 21 ff; testimony of Abba Kovner, YVSA, 13–14 (recording 5). For more information about the attitude to Jews in general in the partisan brigades, see chapter 11.

compatriots by Lithuanian Fascists in Kovno, in December 1941). The new battalion was formed on January 11, 1944. Karp Ivanov, an officer in the Red Army (who called himself Semyonov), was appointed as battalion commander. Misha Balkin, a Jewish officer in the Red Army, was appointed as political commissar. The new battalion built its camp a distance of several hundred meters from the Death to the Occupiers camp.

Another round of reorganization was mandated after the arrival of two additional groups in February and March. On March 13, 1944, a third battalion was formed, called "Forward"; this battalion also set up its base not far from the Death to the Occupiers battalion. Captain Zeike was appointed commander of the new battalion, and Haim David Ratner of the Kovno Ghetto was appointed political commissar.

In this way, three Kovno battalions grew out of the one original Kovno battalion, thus constituting one brigade. Radyonov remained commander of the entire brigade, and the Death to the Occupiers headquarters now served as brigade headquarters as well. Aside from the headquarters, there were other bodies and facilities that served all three battalions of the brigade, including the reconnaisance platoon, the bakery, the bathhouse, and the Main Guard (that was stationed on the crossroads between the three camps).

Structure of the Death to the Occupiers Battalion

The fighting force of the battalion was divided into three units: (1) reconnaissance, (2) the combat company, and (3) the quartermaster platoon or *khozvazvod*.

> Boris Lisauskas organized the reconnaissance unit and he was its first commander. The members of this unit spent most of their time outside the base in the nearby villages. Lisuskas situated his first base in Stary-Marczel, which turned into a kind of partisan village. Lisuskas's contacts and informers met with him in Stary-Marczel, and he extended his intelligence network from the village over the entire surroundings. The following were also members of the unit: Yisrael Joels, Shimon Bloch, the paratrooper Ruta, the Pole Zigmund, and for a short while Sarah Robinson. The unit was armed with submachine guns and pistols.[42] The intelligence information collected by the

---

42. Testimony of Yisrael Joels, YVSA, 6.

reconnaissance unit was intended mainly for tactical use by the battalion and partly for use by the brigade.[43]

The combat company numbered thirty to forty fighters; it had a lot of firepower and high operative ability. This unit was designated for combat operations and missions such as combat patrols and ambushes on the roads, attacks on garrisons, reprisal operations, and detonations. Its first commander was Mishka Trushin, a former lieutenant in the Russian army who had escaped from a prisoner-of-war camp. After his death, aviation officer Stephan Kulikov was appointed in his place; Kulikuv's nickname was "Lyuchik" (pilot). This company contained the best fighters of the battalion, who possessed excellent combat skills and military experience. Some of the squad commanders of the combat company were from the Kovno Ghetto: Baruch Lopiansky, Peretz Padison, and Shlomo Abramovitz. The other Jewish members of the company were David Sandler, Shlomo Baron, Pesach Wolbe, Haim Wolbe, Hanne Padison, Haim Gechtel (Galin), Ya'akov Sesnitzky, Yankel (Ya'akov) Birger, Idke Pilovnik, Aharon Vilenchuk, Hirsch Shmuliakov, Kalman Goldstein, Reuven Glickman, Yosef Rosen, Yitzhak Nemzer, Yehuda Lifschitz, Yisrael Goldblatt, Zundel and Leibel Strom, David Tepper, and Eliezer Zodikov.

The quartermaster platoon included the staff of regular service providers in the camp, and also supplied manpower for internal, irregular functions such as guard duty. Members of this platoon were armed with rifles, and the platoon owned two machine guns as well. Besides its duties within the base, the platoon was mostly involved in requisition and obtaining supplies (within a 40–60 kilometer range of the base). The unit's commander, for the majority of the time, was Ukrainian officer Prosilenko, a former lieutenant in the Russian army who escaped from war captivity. Although this platoon mainly carried out maintenance duties, it was capable, with the addition of personnel from other units, of quickly transforming itself into a combat-ready unit with adequate firepower for combat and sabotage missions. There was always some of the platoon outside the

---

43. Special cells circulated in the forest to collect material for Moscow's military and political needs. These cells engaged in wiretapping, spying, and collecting incriminating material against traitors and collaborators. Such a cell spent an extended period of time within the Death to the Occupiers camp, but only a few people knew the nature of their work. This cell was also known by the name of "The Easterners" (meaning, from Russia).

camp participating in sabotage or other partisan missions. In order to make maximum use of personnel, individual partisans were typically charged with several tasks and functions. For example, after a grueling workday, the cook was often required to do guard-duty or go out on an all night arms acquisition operation.

Wounded fighters recuperating from injuries or illnesses were sometimes temporarily assigned to this platoon, as were partisans who were resting up after especially exhausting missions outside the camp. Since the non-Jewish fighters in the battalion were mainly former military men or stalwart farmers from the surroundings, it was only natural that the quartermaster platoon was almost completely made up of Kovno Ghetto fighters alone. A partial list of its Kovno members includes Yosef Melamed, Monik Holzberg, Berel Kott, Bayla Ganlin, Berel Gempel, Sarah Gempel, Malka Pugatzky Senior, Ephraim Senior, Dov Levin, Zvie Brown, Eliyahu Kass, Rachel Lopiansky, Sarah Gordon, Gita Foger, Feige Abramovitz, Mira Weiner, Feige Weiner, Jan Sperling, Tuvia Friedman, Yisrael Zig, Lovke Scher, Leah Scher, Itzik Yukhnikov, Yehoshua Antzel, Hanne Kagan, Meir Teinovitz, and Haya Shmuelov.

Services

The battalion supplied the following services: the battalion office, medical clinic, kitchen, bakery and flour mill, weapons workshop, horse stable, shoemaker's workshop, sewing workshop, barbershop, laundry, and bathhouse.

BATTALION OFFICE

Haya Shmuelov, wife of one of the first members of the Communist underground in the Kovno Ghetto, worked as the battalion command clerk until liberation day. Sometimes she was assisted by Sarah Robinson. Ephraim Senior sometimes worked on preparation of tactical maps of the battalion's zone of operation. Zvie Brown occasionally translated explanatory material such as leaflets and posters intended for the Polish population.

MEDICAL CLINIC

At first it was staffed with only one medic, Anya from Moscow. Its medical stock was very limited. The situation improved greatly when the Kovno Ghetto fighters joined the battalion; they brought with them large quantities of medicines, bandages, and medical equipment. They also brought reinforcement to the medical staff: surgical nurse Rivka Epstein[44] and registered nurse Zoya Tinet. When the battalion split into two, Epstein and Tinet were transferred to the new units. Anya remained with Death to the Occupiers and Gita Foger joined her as medic, remaining in this role until liberation.

In early 1944 the clinic was housed in a special dugout with room for eight people, and sick and severely wounded patients were treated there. The choice of medicines available was very limited. Much use was made of a German antiseptic called Prontosan. There were many jokes in the forest about this "wonder drug," which was dispensed for a variety of ailments, from food-poisoning to the common cold, and many other aches and pains. For external wounds, tincture of iodine was used, Kali antiseptic, and a yellow ointment called Revenol.[45] In difficult cases they would alert the doctor, Dr. Shlomo Gorfinkel, from the Vilna base. He would arrive on horseback, armed with a small suitcase of medical instruments.[46]

KITCHEN

Initially the "kitchen" was only a bonfire in a pit, over which they would place the pot, and kitchen duties were performed in a rotation system. As the battalion grew, the kitchen was transformed into a respectable institution. It was housed under a well-camouflaged shed and was equipped with half a dozen kettles, pots, and assorted kitchen equipment, which had been plundered in raids. This kitchen was used for the following functions: cooking three meals a day for the headquarters staff and the fighters in the camp, preparing field rations for partisans on missions outside the camp, and preparing special warm meals for those returning from missions. The chief chef was Berel Gempel, a butcher by profession;[47] his assistants were Rivka Gordon, Sarah Gempel, and Rachel Lopiansky. If there were available personnel in the camp, the kitchen would draft two or three of them for kitchen tasks such as drawing water and cutting trees for firewood. Eliyahu Kass was a carpenter who worked at felling trees and also did carpentry work in the camp, from renovating and fixing the dugouts to preparing

---

44. Before the war, she worked in Kovno's Jewish hospital Bikur Cholim and acquired much experience in complicated surgeries.
45. Testimony of Gita Foger-Turchin, YVSA, 8–9 (recording 3).
46. Dr. Gorfinkel died in a bombardment in Jerusalem during Israel's War of Independence. For additional details about him, see *Sefer ha-partizanim ha-yehudim*, 1: 54 and 121 ff.
47. Berel Gimpel, YVSA, letter 2.

coffins for the battalion's casualties. These were buried in the cemetery at the outskirts of the camp, not far from the entrance adjacent to the Main Guard.

BAKERY AND FLOUR MILL

The shortage of bread was a bothersome problem in the battalion. It was hard to obtain sufficient quantities of bread during requisition operations because the farmers did not bake large quantities in one batch. It was also forbidden, according to the partisan code, to take away farmers' baked bread if it was used only for personal consumption and not for sale. There was therefore only enough bread for headquarters staff and certain privileged individuals. Sacks of flour and grain were brought to the base, but these rotted in the storeroom.

The problem was partially solved in the spring of 1944 when the base acquired the tools and devices needed to set up a primitive bakery. Some time later simple millstones were found – and a flour mill was born. From then on, the fighters ground the grain into flour themselves. Yitzhak Nemzer, the combat company's machine-gunner, baked large, tasty loaves of bread from the flour. The flour mill and bakery served not only the three Kovno battalions but other partisan units as well. These partisans would bring sacks of flour and grain from all parts of the forest region and receive baked bread in return. The flour mill and bakery greatly decreased the dependence of the battalion and the entire Kovno brigade on basic foodstuffs from external sources. Thus, there was less need for acquisition operations, freeing more people for actual partisan warfare.

WEAPONS WORKSHOP

This provided a most important service, as the chief concern of the battalion fighters was for weapons and their procurement. But most of the weapons that were acquired, especially from the nearby residents, were old and broken. Consequently, at the beginning of 1944, a part-time weapons workshop was founded. Lovka Scher, the gunsmith, had gained experience in this field from his time in the Lithuanian army. But he was able to perform this work only in his "spare time," that is, between partisan missions outside the camp.

HORSE STABLE

The stable provided the basis for partisan transportation, because the horse was the only means of transportation available – and even that was reserved for special circumstances. For example, horses were available to battalion commanders, to regular partisans carrying out functions that required speed (such as evacuating wounded fighters), for reconnaissance patrols, and for liaison between the battalion and the brigade. The five or six horses in the stable were acquired from local farmers.[48] Meir Teinovitz assumed responsibility for the stable and harness equipment until liberation.[49]

SHOEMAKER'S WORKSHOP

The lack of vehicles on one hand and the swampy forest soil on the other meant that great attention had to be paid to the health of the fighters' feet and to providing sturdy shoes for them. Thus a shoemaker's workshop was founded and run by Baruch Grodnick in his spare time – between partisan missions. Grodnick also created holsters for pistols, pouches for rifle bullets, and other leather goods. The younger brother of Radyonov (the brigade commander), who left his hometown of Murava to join the base, assisted Grodnick in his shoemaking work.

SEWING WORKSHOP

A sewing machine that was "borrowed" in one of the missions became the basis for a sewing workshop. Tailors Tuvia Friedman and Yisrael Zig operated the workshop in their "spare time." They sewed military shirts and pants for the command staff and sometimes for the other fighters as well. When shipments of weapons and equipment arrived from Moscow, the tailors used the white silk sheets of the parachutes to sew shirts and underwear. These items were sorely needed on the base in the final months before liberation, when the prohibition against looting personal items became stricter.[50]

BARBERSHOP

The barber shop was run by Idke Pilovnik, a hairdresser by profession, who had an excellent reputation in the forest as a courageous warrior and regular participant in combat operations (as a member of the combat company). She worked in

---

48. One of the horses was given the same name as its former owner, Jurgelevitch. He was a farmer from Marczel who was an informer; as a result, the partisans burned his house down (see ch. 12).

49. For a short period of time (March 1944), Teinovitz served as part of the combat company as per his request. Yosef Melamed replaced him in the stable; he had been a wagon-driver in the Kovno ghetto.

50. Testimony of Malka Pugatzky-Smali, YVSA, 28 (recording 8).

her spare time at shaving and cutting the fighters' hair. Her equipment consisted of a stool, scissors, and a razor.

LAUNDRY

An important hygienic service was the laundry. A partisan who wanted to wash his underwear would give them to Bayla Ganlin (she was nicknamed "Katyusha"). Due to pains in her legs, Ganlin was unable to participate in acquisition operations, and she readily accepted the role of laundress in addition to her other service functions such as milking the cows and serving food to the sick.

BATHHOUSE

Last but not least, the bathhouse (sweathouse) was most important in maintaining the good health, as well as the good spirits, of the battalion fighters. Before it existed, the war against lice was difficult. The fighters and their commanders would sit around the campfire and, despite the bitter cold, take off their clothes; they would sit and pick out the lice while singing together. Then Itzik Yukhnikov built a sweathouse in a special dugout at the edge of the camp. Although it was a rather primitive facility – a pile of stones was heated up with fire, and large jugs of water were poured over them, producing thick vapors – it would rejuvenate every partisan returning from a long, exhausting mission. The cloud of boiling steam also disinfected their clothes. Itzik Yukhnikov continued to maintain this "institution" and over time, other people learned to operate it in rotation. The bathhouse was operative about twice a week and also served the other two Kovno battalions.

Most of these services were established at a rather late stage in the battalion's development. In its early period, extremely poor housing and food conditions prevailed on the Rudniki base. Yet the services that developed later were not at the expense of combat activities. Those who performed the services participated in partisan missions like the other fighters.

Camp Order

The constant encirclement by the Germans, the proximity of the German garrisons, the existence of White Poles in the forest, and the many espionage agents among the local population were all reasons that obligated the battalion command to maintain the camp in a state of perpetual alert to guard it from sudden attack. It was forbidden to put down your weapon for even a moment. Even during sleep, the rifle or submachine gun had to be close to the partison's sleeping body. The partisan could remove only his shoes while sleeping – no other articles of clothing.

The camp's readiness was based on a complex guarding system that consisted of four types of guard duty: Main Guard, Inner Camp Guard, Concealed Guard, and Patrol. Violating the rules of guard duty was considered a very severe offense, and one who did so was liable to incur the death penalty.

The Main Guard involved three people stationed on the only path leading into the camp, to prevent the entrance of unwanted persons. It stood twenty-four hours a day, with no changing of the guards during the 24-hour shifts.

The Inner Camp Guard was stationed at nighttime only (6–8 hours in the winter, 5–6 hours in the summer). The objective of this guard duty was to avert infiltration of outsiders from all sides and acts of traitors. This guard switched every hour. The camp's duty officer (usually a platoon or squad commander) would inspect the Main Guard and the Inner Guard.

The Concealed Guard was comprised of two members. Its objective was observation of the village of Žagarinė at the edge of the forest, a problematic area very close to the camp. Enemy forces would occasionally camp there or pass through, so it was a place from which trouble could erupt at any moment. The guards would assume their observation-site before sunrise, then leave only after darkness so that no one could see them arrive or leave. A reconnaissance squad was in charge of inspecting this guard duty.

The Patrol was positioned at the other edge of the camp, near the bathhouse, and was initiated in late spring 1944 due to the increased danger of surprise attacks and roundups by the Germans. The Patrol's hours were from 3 A.M. to 6 a.m, and its role was to secure that section of the camp's border near deep swampland (at the beginning, they had felt that entrance from that side was highly unlikely due to the terrain). This guard duty was inspected by the duty officer. Once, the duty officer discovered that one of the two guards was fast asleep. The fellow was sentenced to death, but then pardoned.

Below is the daily schedule of the camp on "regular days":[51]

---

51. The schedule varied according to the season (length of the day).

03:30	Wake-up call for the Concealed Guard
04:00	Concealed Guard assumes position
05:00	Wake-up call for kitchen workers
06:00	End of Inner Camp watch
06:30	Wake-up call for the entire camp
07:00–08:00	Breakfast
08:00	Morning roll-call, distribution of work roster
08:00–13:00	Work
13:00–14:00	Lunch
14:00–18:00	Continuation of work
18:00–19:00	Supper; news bulletin of Moscow Radio is publicized
19:00	Evening roll-call for the guard-duty teams, official announcements, stationing of the Main Guard, rotation
19:00–22:00	Free time, entertainment
21:00	Concealed Guard returns and submits its report to the duty officer
22:00	Lights out, sleep

CHAPTER 11

Way of Life and Social Relations in the Partisan Units

Nutrition

The menu of the Kovno battalions was monotonous because the supply of food-stuffs was completely dependent on what the partisans succeeded in acquiring in their supply missions; variety was not to be heard of.[1] For long periods the battalion would subsist on tasteless soup two or three times a day; the soup was made of meat and water, or dark flour cooked in water without fat or salt. The partisans quickly became sick of this drab menu, which also caused their health to deteriorate. Most of the fighters suffered from diarrhea, gum disease (from scurvy), and skin abscesses.

Small quantities of salt, bread, and potatoes were obtained through much effort and sacrifice in acquisition operations. These "delicacies" were given only to the sick, the command staff, and fighters who enjoyed special status.[2] Anton Bondor, the camp's sergeant major (*starshina*), who was responsible for the services and work in the camp, was empowered to confer this privilege on people.[3]

---

1. Rivka Gordon, one of the long-time cooks in the camp, describes the meal menus in her testimony: "…In the morning there was porridge made out of barley…. Lunch – again, the same porridge with meat, without bread or anything else. In contrast, Leah Senior used to cook real meals for the headquarters staff: she fried meatballs and cooked soup. They also received bread and potatoes. Sometimes she would take food to headquarters even at midnight" (testimony of Rivka Gordon, YVSA, 22).
2. Yisrael Joels and Shmuel Mordkovsky were also served the food of the command staff (*kom-sastab*), when they brought Albina to the base (testimony of Yisrael Joels, YVSA, 5).
3. "Bondor gives jellied calves' feet (*gleeber* in Yiddish) to the Russian prisoners-of-war here" (testimony of Rivka Gordon, YVSA, 24). In certain cases, Bondor chose Jewish fighters for

This, of course, caused much jealousy and resentment. The food shortage was such that those involved in acquisition missions would "put aside" for their own use some of the "luxury" foodstuffs, such as bread, eggs, butter, and onions. When they returned to the camp, they would gather secretly to have a meal together. The commissar would ferret out these private campfires and reprimand the participants.[4]

A significant improvement in the bread, meat, and milk supplies transpired in the spring of 1944. A large quantity of cattle was brought to the camp and the storehouse was completely filled with preserved meat. Thereafter, the partisans decided to keep a herd of cows in the camp and take them to pasture every day. The cows proved to be doubly beneficial: they produced dozens of liters of fresh milk every day for the sick partisans and the command staff, and constituted a live reserve of meat for the lean times. As a result of this improvement, the private campfires ceased almost completely; they then only somewhat existed in the Main Guard and Concealed Guard. The poor health of the Kovno Ghetto fighters, which originated from the malnutrition they had suffered in the ghetto, then significantly improved. Nevertheless, they continued to suffer from boils and scurvy. Some individuals were tempted to overeat when the opportunity arose,[5] and in one case this had tragic consequences.[6]

When the camp was first established, the fighters would receive their food portions in pots or various odd utensils, and each person would find himself a place to sit and eat. Eventually the camp acquired tables and benches, and a "dining room" was created under a canopy near the kitchen. Plates and cutlery also made their appearance, and meals began to assume a "civilized" appearance.[7]

---

food privileges, "those whom he watched out for" (testimony of Michael Pasternak, YVSA, 3).

4. Testimony of Haim Gechtel (Galin), YVSA, 32; compare to Lazer, 50.

5. Testimony of Eliezer Moses, YVSA, 21 (recording 6); testimony of Baruch Gofer (Grodnick), YVSA, 29 (recording 8). These examples were probably why it was said in the forest: "Jews die because of cream, Russians – because of vodka."

6. Machine gunner Yehoshua Antzel once gorged on excessive quantities of meat when he was on Concealed Guard. He was attacked by terrible pains and had to be transported by wagon to the clinic on the base. There he suffered from excruciating pain for several days before he died.

7. The Russian fighters described as "civilized" anything that had a shred of normal life to it, belonging to days of peace.

Clothing

As in every society, when it came to clothing, the partisans also liked to dress in style. They had no uniforms and no organized supply of clothing or shoes; each person's attire was according to his own initiative. The result was a wide variety of clothes, shoes, and hats. At the battalion's roll calls, German flight uniforms mingled with German police uniforms, rustic sheep-fur coats, civilian leather coats, faded Soviet prisoner-of-war uniforms, and short coats produced in the Kovno Ghetto. Hats were also just as diversified; Cossack-style *"papakhis"* competed with civilian bowlers, *"kaskets,"* and caps from the German, Russian, and Lithuanian armies. The one trademark feature that distinguished the Kovno battalion fighters was a badge featuring a red star on a round red background, which decorated all the hats.

The Kovno Ghetto fighters, who arrived meticulously dressed, stood out from the others. Most of these fighters had been equipped before their departure to the forest with proper boots, fur hats, leather belts, and pouches for bullets hung on two leather belts crossed over the chest. They also had pistol holsters and side-packs.

This advantage in clothing and equipment provided fertile ground for barter, a pastime that was rife in the forest. It was also the pretext for concealed and unconcealed envy on the part of the less well dressed among the veteran partisans. Over time, these advantages dissipated due to the effects of the climate and the numerous missions that took their toll on the clothing and equipment of the Kovno Ghetto fighters. These fighters were eventually forced to renew their equipment according to the usual forest methods: during both acquisition and battle operations, each partisan would take whatever he wanted from the farmers' houses and from enemy booty.[8] The partisans' term for this kind of acquisition was *bombyozhka* ("the bomb"), and it was tolerated by the command staff due to the lack of an alternative.[9] The practice gave some of the fighters the incentive to participate in as many sorties as possible, in order to replace worn-out clothing or gain possession of a small pistol, for example, merely for decoration.[10]

---

8. Over time, this practice became so routine that instead of washing their underwear, the fighters would engage in sorties in order to exchange their soiled underwear for new, clean ones from the farmers (testimony of Michael Yitzhaki (Gelbtrunk), YVSA, 47, recording 7b).
9. On the way to the Naliboki forests, the partisans surrounded the village and forced the farmers to exchange boots with them (testimony of Yosef Rosen, YVSA, 22, recording 5).
10. Partisan groups used to make special trips to Lithuania in order to "dress" (ibid.).

Clothing symbolized the individual's status and raised his worth in the eyes of others. To many, a true partisan dressed as follows: the fighter's chest was decorated with two criss-crossing bandoliers; an impressive-looking pistol hung from his belt; he wore riding-pants, shiny boots, and sported a submachine gun on his arm. Indeed this type of dress was adopted by the officers, commissars, members of the command staff, and veteran partisans[11] while the rest of the fighters emulated them. The presence of women in the base was also a reason for the male fighters to dress up.

There was, officially speaking, not much discipline regarding personal appearance. Nevertheless, at the daily roll calls, almost all the fighters appeared shaven and dressed in a more or less orderly fashion.[12] Evidently public opinion played a large part in this practice, as it did in other issues.[13]

Housing

Accommodations were relatively satisfactory. The partisans slept in *zemlyankas* (dugouts) that were constructed in the following manner.[14] First, they would dig a pit in the form of a rectangle: 50 meters long, 4–5 meters wide, and about 1.5 meters deep. At the bottom, they dug a deep ditch of about half a meter to serve as a passageway between the sleeping areas. They supported the walls with poles and across the poles they hung curtains made of white parachute material. They cushioned the sleeping-areas with poles, then straw piled on top. They covered the long pit with a roof that extended a bit above the ground, and then camouflaged the roof with branches and moss. They installed doors on both sides of the passage and constructed a window in the roof for ventilation. They stuck nails into the walls above the beds for the partisans to hang their clothes and personal items.

Some of the dugouts even boasted primitive heaters for warmth and for drying clothes and shoes. The snow that covered the dugouts also served to keep in the heat. Due to the crowded conditions and the dampness of the swampy ground, the dugouts tended to be mildewy and stifling inside. They therefore kept both doors open in the summer for ventilation, making it more comfortable,

---

11. Testimony of Gita Foger-Turchin, YVSA, 17.
12. Testimonies of Eliezer Moses, YVSA, 21 (recording 6), and Yosef Rosen, YVSA, 25 (recording 6).
13. Testimony of Grisha Sheffer, YVSA, 36 (recording 9).
14. Compare to Lazer, 295–96.

but allowing mosquitoes from the nearby bogs to enter freely and disturb the people trying to sleep.

There were two reasons why the partisans could enjoy the relative "comfort" of the *zemlyankas*. First, due to the relative security granted to them by the natural conditions in the Rudniki Forests (impassable swamps, dense forest thickets), the Kovno battalions camped in the same place for an extended period of time. Second, the site provided unlimited amounts of building material. The dugouts were a pleasant surprise for those who came from the Kovno Ghetto. "In fact, we worried that it would be far worse," relates one of the first fighters to reach Rudniki in December 1943.[15] "At least we found a dugout there, and it was warm in the dugout. I didn't think we'd have even a dugout to sleep in. I imagined open forests without anything at all. But when we found the dugout, and there was even something to eat on the January 1 festivities – that made a big impression on us!"

The dugout sleeping arrangement in the Death to the Occupiers battalion was organized according to the combat and administrative units. In the other two battalions, all the fighters – including the command staff and the women – slept in one big dugout. There were mainly objective reasons for this difference: the Death to the Occupiers battalion was larger than the others and contained the major functionaries of all three battalions. It is also true, however, that the Death to the Occupiers battalion was characterized by social differentiation and the aloofness maintained between the different standings,[16] as opposed to a greater sense of cooperation and team spirit that prevailed in the other two battalions.

Hygiene

Hygiene and cleanliness in the camp were severe problems. Even those fighters who were careful to wash regularly[17] and change their underwear were not spared the curse of infections and scabies, and especially not of the plague of

---

15. Testimony of Eliezer Moses, YVSA, 15 (recording 4).

16. The dugout was the only private, intimate space on the base, especially during winter nights and rainfall. Often, close relationships were formed between fighters in the same dugout, more than anywhere else in the base.

17. The fastidious among the fighters would get up early to wash in the pure waters of the Merechanka River. The rest made do with perfunctory washups in the muddy waters of the base's well.

lice.[18] Lice swarmed in the straw they slept on, on the walls, in the blankets, and in the clothes of one's neighbor. Many of the fighters slept in their clothes, and the crowded dugouts meant that people were forced to sleep close to one another. True, access to the nearby Merechanka River and the improvised "steambath" brought some relief. Still, the lice scourge accompanied the fighters until their last day in the forest.[19] The women were somewhat of an exception, as they spent most of their time on the base and were able to be more meticulous in their hygiene.[20] The married men whose wives lived on the base also benefited. One of the hardest trials of life in the forest for the Kovno Ghetto fighters was adjusting to the lack of hygiene in the camp.[21]

Smoking

The ghetto fighters brought with them supplies of tobacco and thin paper for rolling cigarettes; this was enough to suffice for several weeks. When they ran out of tobacco, they were forced to supply themselves with this staple from the farmers during a sortie or from enemy casualties. When luck ran out, they did what everyone else did – they begged and explored every opportunity to obtain cigarette butts from others. The liaisons from the city and the village also supplied tobacco to those who could pay. Another tobacco source was the friendly farmers from Stary-Marczel, Vishnicza, and other villages. Only a few fighters in certain units – such as the scouts and special-operations units – had access to these sources.

Within the forest itself, money had no value, and the Kovno fighters who brought money with them from the ghetto could use it on rare occasions only. Most of their money remained in their pockets until liberation. Therefore, a barter trade developed around tobacco for other necessities, including ammunition for pistols.[22] Once, they received a delivery by parachute, containing a quantity

---

18. The members of the fifth group to leave the ghetto picked up lice on their very first stop on the way to the base, in Genis's battalion (testimony of Grisha Sheffer, YVSA, 16, recording 4).
19. Testimony of Gita Foger-Turchin, YVSA, 17.
20. "I was among the first to boil the laundry" (testimony of Malka Pugatzky-Smali, YVSA, 27). Bayla Ganlin ("Katyusha") sometimes used to wash clothes for the fellows too, but her clients had to provide her with soap as that was a very scarce item.
21. By contrast, the Russians were more accustomed to harsh conditions, especially those who escaped from the prisoner-of-war camps.
22. Testimony of Yosef Rosen, YVSA, 30 (recording 7).

of chocolates and Camel cigarettes; each fighter received a small amount of chocolate and two cigarettes. The smokers willingly forfeited their chocolate to swap it for these aromatic cigarettes.

Discipline

Besides the commissar's speech that greeted the groups of fighters when they arrived from the ghetto and the various catchphrases that the commissar would utter during roll calls and such, the partisans were never taught the foundations of the partisan movement, its norms, regulations, and rules of judgment. This does not mean that no such regulations, norms, and customs existed in the forest; on the contrary, they did exist, and their moral and practical validity were absolute. They were never, however, systematically consolidated and summarized in the form of standing orders that encompassed all situations encountered by the partisan, whether in the forest or outside it.

The forest conditions and partisan combat frequently led to situations in which small details, even individual fighters, acted alone. The pre-sortie instructions and directions given to a fighter were not always sufficient, and he sometimes had to make decisions when faced with unanticipated situations. These were decisions that determined the fate of the mission, even the fate of his life. Meticulous caution, careful calculation of each step and movement, control over impulses, and calm, logical discretion were required by the fighter no less than combat skills and courage. Therefore, in addition to memorizing orders and suggestions from his commanders and peers, as well as the technical instructions regarding the mission, the partisan had to know how to apply all of these to various and diverse situations in which he found himself.

Thus, the "law of the forest" was an unwritten constitution. Little was publicized in the form of orders; most was transferred orally from person to person, from the veteran fighter to the new recruit. It was consolidated through daily experience and by learning from mistakes, which in the best case would end with a reprimand, and in the worst case, with death or even a death verdict.[23] Since every minute of the fighter's life in the forest was conducted, as it were, in a state

---

23. For an example of a death sentence, see chapter 13, page 372–373, regarding the commander Seryozha. Outstanding partisans died as a result of scorning safety rules, including combat company commander Mishka Trushin and his companions, and experienced saboteurs Jurka and his companions (see chapter 13).

of crisis, he was forced to strictly regulate his behavior accordingly – even though no one taught him how he should act. He needed much inner discipline and willingness to forfeit his personal convenience. He needed to control himself in satisfying his desires, including food and drink, which not infrequently brought disaster down on the incautious.

Most of the young, inexperienced ghetto fighters found it hard to accustom themselves to the rigorous demands of the forest, and many suffered until they acquired the vital traits of a partisan. One such example was the young fighter Jan Sperling. Once in midday, when he stood on Main Guard duty at the entrance to the battalion, he saw a group of armed people in German uniforms approaching the base. The young fellow did not wait for them to come close enough for him to identify them by password, as mandated by standing orders, but lost his head and panicked. He fired one shot in the air and started to run in panic toward the base, shouting, "Germans!" Everyone present on the base grabbed their weapons and ran toward the Main Guard – and there stood a new group of partisans, wearing German uniforms. Jan Sperling was severely reprimanded and accused of cowardice and of causing panic. In the partisan dictionary these were very grave accusations; those so accused were likely to be treated with contempt and mistrust.

In another incident, a new recruit who had arrived recently from the ghetto lost contact with the other fighters during a supply operation. He found himself alone at night, and in desperation, he began shouting "Hello!" in every direction. His shouts resonated through the silence of the night and sounded to the fighters like German cries; some of them even considered shooting in the direction of the voices. Fortunately, veteran fighter Eliezer Zodikov realized what had happened and averted a certain tragedy.

The conditions that prevailed in the forest necessitated meticulous implementation of standing orders and severe punishment for anyone transgressing them. However, the lack of a legal system and well-defined rules of judgment led to lack of uniformity in the punishments administered in the various units.[24] Commanders of all ranks had almost unlimited authority regarding the discipline

---

24. In Captain Elko's battalion, a Jewish fighter, B. Toker, was executed for sleeping while on guard duty. The same punishment was inflicted on another Jewish fighter, M. Epstein, for losing his rifle (Lazer, 296–97).

of their fighters; this sometimes led to arbitrary decisions that bordered on mal-treatment and abuse. In addition, the objective conditions left little room for variety in the forms of punishment. Imprisonment, for example, was used only rarely, and the confinement dugout only served as a place for holding prisoners until trial. Usually, transgressions fell into two categories, based on the severity of the act. The punishments for minor transgressions were additional rounds of guard duty for a few days or public reprimands. Punishment for severe transgressions could even be execution by shooting.

Below are some examples of transgressions and their punishments, as related by Michael Pasternak:

> One night when I was the duty officer, I inspected the Guard, and to my surprise I came across the sentry, a young Russian fellow, lying flat on his back, fast asleep. I removed the bolt from his rifle.... The next morning the fellow went to eat breakfast as usual, without telling anyone that the bolt was missing from his rifle. After the meal came roll-call time, and the sergeant major checked the weapons as he did every day. When he reached this fellow, he asked him about the missing bolt. The boy started to stutter. I pulled out the bolt from my pocket and proved what had happened the previous night. The fellow was punished by having to stand days and nights near the stream outside the camp, without a weapon, and half-naked.[25]

In another case, Y.M. was caught in the early morning hours by duty officer Tarasov while sleeping on guard duty in the bathhouse. Tarasov reported the matter to the command staff. Y.M. was accused of negligence and during a special roll call, his judgment was announced – death by shooting. The sentence was immediately transmuted to a severe rebuke.

One issue that disturbed the fighters in general, and the Jewish fighters in particular, was the fear of falling alive into enemy hands. This was not only a personal concern, but a very important security problem for the command. The Germans were always on the alert for reliable information regarding the locations of partisan forces and their strength. To this end, they tried to catch live partisans. Those captured were tortured brutally by the Germans to divulge information.[26]

---

25. Testimony of Michael Pasternak, YVSA, 5.
26. The Germans disseminated special orders regarding treatment of Jewish partisans. A related news item was publicized in the *Davar* newspaper (no. 5347, February 21, 1943), about a

Whether or not the poor fellows revealed anything to their captors or withstood the ordeal and revealed nothing, they were executed. Sometimes the execution was performed in public, in order to intimidate the populace. Therefore the partisan fighters received severe orders never to abandon their wounded comrades, nor even those killed.[27] Instead they were required to do whatever possible, including committing suicide at the last moment, to avoid being taken prisoner. In the partisan reality, the last bullet was always reserved not for the enemy, but for the fighter himself. Therefore, those fighters armed with weapons that could not be used for suicide – such as machine gunners, anti-tank gun operators, and mortar operators – were also equipped with pistols. Tremendous courage and emotional strength was required by the fighters who were forced to kill themselves, or by the comrades who assisted them.

In one incident, Moshe Milner and Sifroni Orlov found themselves surrounded by a superior enemy force in the environs of Novy-Marczel. The Jewish fighter, Milner, covered the retreat of his comrade, who had important information for the base. Milner remained alone and fought back against his attackers, until he ran out of ammunition. Then he shot the last bullet into his own body.[28] Similarly, Tania (Teibele) Vinishesky also killed herself, when she remained the last out of sixteen members of the blocking platoon in the Večioriškiai battle.[29]

Sometimes tragic situations ensued when fighters were forced to kill their wounded comrades so that they would not fall into German hands alive. This

---

telegram received from Kuibyshev, the location of the Jewish Anti-Fascist Committee in the USSR during part of the war: "I found out from a Soviet aviator who made an emergency landing behind German lines and succeeded in escaping that the German authorities in the occupied territories have publicized the following order: Jews caught while armed, or those that are known to participate in partisan activity, should not be shot or hung. Rather, they must receive more severe punishments. These Jews undergo the cruelest forms of torture, such as being thrown to the dogs. After they die, their bodies are given to special factories to create various forms of soap and fertilizer." Evidence to support this information appears in *Davar* (no. 5343), stating that the incident above took place in Nowo-Święciany (Švenčionėliai) (around 58 kilometers from Vilna), and that the order was printed in German, Polish, and Lithuanian, following the capture of Jewish partisans who sabotaged a train. But this news item has not been verified anywhere else.

27. Testimony of Gita Foger-Turchin, YVSA, 9–10 (recording 3).
28. Testimony of Grisha Sheffer, YVSA, 19 (recording 5), and compare to PKG, 144.
29. See chapter 13.

was the fate of David Goldin,[30] who was wounded at the base by a bullet that was accidentally discharged from the rifle of his comrade, Moshe Reichman. Goldin underwent surgery, and one leg was amputated. Unfortunately, the Germans conducted a manhunt at the same time in the Rudniki Forests, and the partisans were forced to leave for a period. The commissar was afraid that the wounded Goldin would fall into the hands of the enemy, so he ordered Goldin's death.[31] This incident severely shook the fighters, especially the Jewish fighters, but it is impossible to know if this command was an expression of the commissar's malicious intent or if it was absolutely necessary under the circumstances.[32]

The common belief in the forest was that a Jewish fighter should never give himself up alive to the enemy. The Jewish fighters overwhelmingly defended this view, although there were those who disagreed. One incident, however, served to refute this position. At the end of December 1943, a unit of the Death to the Occupiers battalion encountered an enemy ambush while crossing a frozen river. Due to the darkness and confusion, two fighters – Yitzhak Segal and Masha Endlin[33] – fell into the hands of the enemy. Neither of them had weapons. Under interrogation, they both denied any connection with the partisans. They succeeded in convincing their interrogators that they were Jews from the Vilna Ghetto being led to work when they encountered a group of partisans, who proceeded to rob them. The Germans took the two partisans to Vilna and released

---

30. David Goldin was the son of a rabbi from a small town. He graduated from a Hebrew academic high school in Kovno and ended up in the ghetto there. He participated in the Augustova Plan, was caught and freed. He was one of the first to join the partisans in the Rudniki Forests.

31. Testimony of Grisha Sheffer, YVSA, 18 (recording 5); testimony of Baruch Gofer (Grodnick), YVSA, 33 (recording 9); testimony of Haim Gechtel (Galin), YVSA, 46 (recording 15); testimony of Yisrael Joels, YVSA, letter 3.

32. "You cannot blame anyone for not taking him when we left the base. There is no other precedent of taking with them someone in that kind of condition" (testimony of Haim Galin [Gechtel], YVSA, 46, recording 15). "We were very angry and complained about it, but you can't consider it anti-Semitism. I think that something could definitely have been done to keep him alive and not do what they did" (testimony of Grisha Sheffer, YVSA, 18, recording 5). A similar incident took place with a Lithuanian fighter named Dragonas, in the Vladas Baronas battalion in south Lithuania. After Dragonas was severely wounded, his officer, Naktis (also a Lithuanian), approached him, covered the wounded man's face with a handkerchief, and shot him (testimony of Michael Yitzhaki [Gelbtrunk]).

33. The wife of Nechemiah Endlin.

them into the ghetto. Masha Endlin managed to make her way back to the Kovno Ghetto,[34] while Yitzhak Segal's fate remains unknown.[35]

In cases such as these, it was very hard to convince the partisan command that the Germans freed the fighters without getting anything in exchange. Past experience, and the strictest caution necessary in any contact with the enemy, required them to be suspicious of any explanation.[36] A suspicion of this sort brought about the tragic death of the fighter Moshe Gerber. As described earlier,[37] when the Gestapo seized Moshe Gerber during the Augostova Plan they beat him viciously because they found a pistol on him.[38] Stubborn rumors spread through the ghetto that he had not withstood the severe torture and had divulged certain details regarding the Augustova Plan. This distrust first arose when Gerber was imprisoned together with other comrades to the Augostova Plan.[39] One of the Ninth Fort prisoners describes below the hostile treatment received by Gerber from his comrades, even in the horrific prison:

> In the evening after work, when I entered my cell to eat supper, I noticed that Aronchik[40] was telling the others something and they were all worked up, especially Moshke "Puk" [Zimlovitz].[41] They told me that ostensibly, Gerber had revealed [the existence of] the [Anti-Fascist] Organization.... Gerber himself was not there at the time. Puk demanded that Gerber be eliminated. The situation was becoming critical. I calmed them down and forbade them from saying anything about this in Gerber's presence. I explained to them

---

34. Nehemiah Endlin met his wife in the Kazlu-Ruda forests, which she had managed to reach from the Kovno Ghetto at the same time as the Forward battalion.

35. *PKG*, 144–45; Rivka Gordon, letter 1, as well as her testimony on October 8, 1959, at Tel Yitzhak.

36. For example, the well-known liaison of the Vilna battalions, Vitke Kampner, was interrogated at length by Special Department head Stankevitz after she managed to slip away from Lithuanian police arrest and returned to the forest. Stankevitz only believed her story with great difficulty (*Sefer ha-partizanim ha-yehudim* 1:122).

37. See end of chapter 5.

38. The sentries in the Ninth Fort called Gerber "the man with the pistol" (Alter Feitelson, YVSA, letter 3).

39. Even during the Augustova Plan and before the arrest, tensions were high between Gerber and the other group members because of Gerber's unfriendly behavior (testimony of A. Levi, YVSA, p. 2).

40. This nickname refers to Aharon Vilenchuk.

41. This nickname refers to Moshe Zimlovitz.

that in our situation, while we were planning the escape, we could not throw him out of our group as this would perhaps drive him to do something stupid. I myself doubted that he had turned traitor. Finally I said that I accepted responsibility for him, I would bring him to the ghetto to the authority of the Organization [AFO], and they would decide his fate. That was enough to calm the fellows down.[42]

Gerber was among the escapees who were lucky enough to reach the Kovno Ghetto. We assume that discussions and investigations were held regarding his guilt. We do not know what the conclusions were, but the fact is that Gerber was sent to the Rudniki Forests in the Fifth Group.[43]

One of the Fifth Group members relates the following:

He [Gerber] was attached to the group that I was in. The plan was to eliminate him on the way and not bring him to the partisans at all. But since N[e-hemiah] Endlin was "busy" on the way, he decided to bring Gerber to the forest and there hand him over to the command. Gerber had family in the ghetto, and perhaps they didn't want to get into trouble with the family, or something like that.[44] As soon as we got to the forest, he was arrested. I must say that the person behind this whole affair, maybe even the major factor both in the ghetto and the forest [for Gerber's incrimination], was Shimon Bloch. As I said earlier, Shimon had also been caught by the Gestapo, and according to one of the versions of the story, Gerber said that they had left for the forest from Bloch's house.[45]

---

42. Alter Feitelson, YVSA, letter 9.

43. Gerber was sent with the fifth group and not with the group that included most of the Ninth Fort escapees (the fourth group). A possible explanation is that discussions continued to be held regarding Gerber's fate in the ghetto underground circles.

44. We also find this explanation in the words of Berel Gempel (letter 2), "They put him [Gerber] on trial in the ghetto, and they [his family] threatened that if anything should happen to him, they would inform on them to the Gestapo; therefore, they sent him to the forest" (see also Yisrael Joels, YVSA, letter 4).

45. Testimony of Grisha Sheffer, YVSA, 8–9 (recording 2). A rather strange fact emerges here with regard to Shimon and his wife, Rivka Bloch, whom Gerber supposedly informed on: they were freed from the Gestapo, while Gerber himself was sent to the Ninth Fort. This suspicious fact appears in several sources, albeit worded slightly differently (Meir Leib Goldschmidt, YVSA, letter 2; Joels, YVSA, letter 4; Alter Feitelson, YVSA, letter 13; and others). At least five

A companion who shared the same fate in the Ninth Fort says the following in conclusion:

> He announced that we could testify. But when they came to ask us, we said, How can we testify, when we weren't with him [during the interrogation]? And that was the end of the story. They didn't demand anything else from us. They accused him of being an informer, that he informed on the organization and everything. They didn't even officially conduct a trial. They just kept him under arrest in the dugout in which he lived, and afterwards they took him from there and sentenced him to death and then killed him. We weren't present when they shot him, but as far as I know, Bloch was the one to shoot him. That's what they said.[46]

Gerber's death was, in all opinions, the epilogue to a purely internal affair[47] in the ghetto's underground. Like other underground organizations, it was not spared the dilemmas of traitors and provocateurs, real and imagined.[48]

Drunkenness

"Intoxication is the enemy's ally" – this was the slogan used without much success in attempts to eradicate the plague of drunkenness that spread among the partisans. A second slogan used to counteract the first one was, "Without half a liter – it just won't work." No combat mission could succeed without liquor, and no festive meal worth its name could lack the bitter brew. Without *samogon*,[49]

---

reliable witnesses raise doubts regarding Gerber's guilt. By contrast, Berel Gempel writes (letter 2), "I am sure that he informed on us."

46. Testimony of Michael Yitzhaki (Gelbtrunk), YVSA, 32–33 (recording 6A). Also see Alter Feitelson, YVSA, letter 13. According to other sources, the death sentence was executed by "Little Boris."

47. The testimonies emphasize the fact that with regard to Gerber, the Russian battalion command played only a secondary role. "In this affair, the Jews had a bigger part than the non-Jews" (testimony of Haim Galin [Gechtel], YVSA, 45, recording 15); "This was not about anti-Semitism" (testimony of Grisha Sheffer, YVSA, 8, recording 2); "The whole thing came from Simke [Shimon] Bloch, but the trial could have been conducted differently" (testimony of Malka Pugatzky-Smali, YVSA, 14, recording 5).

48. Compare this to the affair surrounding the execution of Natan Ring and his friends for similar accusations in the Vilna battalions (Lazer, 281–84; *Sefer ha-partizanim ha-yehudim*1:113–14).

49. This is the name given to the homemade alcohol produced by primitive means that was widespread in this period.

no victory was complete. These were the two extreme views regarding liquor consumption in the forest.

From the military-organizational perspective, excessive drinking represented an erosion of discipline, which endangered the missions and caused loss of personnel and expensive weapons.[50] But drinking also filled a strong emotional need as an outlet for the extreme tension in forest life, allowing one to temporarily put aside his difficult present and uncertain future, a future that usually contained bitter surprises. Thus, the partisan command was well aware that drinking was a phenomenon that could not be totally eradicated, only restrained.[51]

Intoxication was also present in the Kovno battalions and was the subject of admonishment and discussion, especially when it was the cause of tragedies. Public opinion was in a tumult after the fall of Mishka Trushin,[52] commander of the combat company, and fighters Volodya (known by his nickname "Chigan") and Katya (the battalion commander's next of kin). At any rate it can be stated that even those Jewish fighters who acquired the drinking habit[53] did not reach the pathological addiction level of their Russian compatriots. They learned to drink alcohol out of the desire to fit in with the others and adopt the "approved" forest lifestyle.[54]

The Women

The Kovno battalions included about forty young women, of which thirty-five were Jewish women from the Kovno Ghetto. For various reasons, including

---

50. On occasion, alcoholic partisans would barter their ammunition for liquor (testimony of B. Gofer [Grodnik], YVSA, 18, recording 5).

51. Even command members tended to drink, and not always discreetly. When Sniečkus would accompany the paratroopers to the airplanes he would tell them, "Beware of women and *samogon*" (Kutka, 210). Sometimes they were forced to put problem drinkers on trial. But even in such cases, they hesitated to carry out the full letter of the law, and usually limited themselves to severe public reprimands or conditional death sentences (Mončiunskas, 230).

52. This officer had a reputation for excessive drinking. Despite his personal courage and exemplary combat leadership, the fighters were wary of going on missions with him (testimony of Eliezer Moses, YVSA, 18, recording 5).

53. Even at the farewell parties organized by the JFO, large quantities of *samogon* were served to the comrades leaving for the forests; this was among the various things that Nehemiah Endlin taught them to prepare them for life in the forests. Endlin himself was an expert drinker and was an example and symbol to the others.

54. When the combat company was in Lithuania it became customary for them to drink before each meal; this "custom" became obligatory (testimony of Haim Gechtel [Galin], YVSA, 35).

their limitations in physical strength, only a very small number of women were allowed to come to the forest from the ghetto, and only after an exacting selection process. The selection criterion included familial relationship with fighters who were in the forest already or due to depart soon, and seniority in the underground or the Communist Party.[55]

The limitation on the number of women allowed to join the partisans was despite the fact that the young women became well integrated into the battalion and contributed greatly to vital services, such as the kitchen and medical services.[56] They also participated in combat missions or quasi-combat missions, such as supply operations, guard duty, and special duties. The fact that they were few in number left its mark on their status among the partisans. They tried hard to blur their special standing in contrast to the rest of the male fighters. They tried to resemble the men in their clothing[57] and weapons and to participate in missions, not just the service branches. Most of the fighters, however, and especially those who had escaped from prisoner-of-war camps and lived as bachelors for extended time periods, viewed them as women, first and foremost.[58] There were many male partisans, especially the distinguished fighters among them and members of the command, who tried to court the young women and bring them gifts from the spoils of their missions.

Besides the obvious natural reasons for responding to these overtures, there was also the fact that from the day they arrived at the base, the ghetto fighters made every effort to become socially integrated. They felt it vital to remove all barriers between them and their non-Jewish comrades-in-arms as an important precondition to being successfully integrated in the partisan ranks. Many of the young women felt, therefore, that if they did not respond to or completely reject these "suitors," this would adversely affect the friendly atmosphere they desired and would be interpreted as nationalistic segregation and expression of prejudice

---

55. One striking example of the "party activity" criterion is embodied in the fact that Ulya Senior was brought to the forest even though her poor health did not even allow her to work in the camp's services. In fact, after a few months she passed away from her illness. Among those who pushed for bringing her to the forest were several well-known Communists, including brigade commissar Gabris, who remembered her past underground activities for the party.

56. Testimony of Baruch Gofer (Grodnick), YVSA, 26; PKG, 142.

57. Almost all of the women wore riding pants and boots.

58. One of the assertions raised in the camp was that the role of women in the camp should be to satisfy the sexual desires of the men (*Sefer ha-partizanim ha-yehudim* 1:127).

toward a specific ethnic group. Generally the relationships between the Jewish young women and the male fighters did not overstep accepted boundaries. Only in rare cases did these relationships arouse the resentment of the young men from the ghetto.[59]

Over half of the Jewish women were married when they arrived in the forest. The presence of families in this dynamic military framework was unusual in many ways. The command was forced to accept this fact, but they also tried, systematically and consistently, to cover up any overt signs of the existence of these couples. They limited family life with rules for separate living quarters; they placed limitations on the length of visits to the women's quarters,[60] and even split up families, transferring one member of a couple to another battalion.[61] The couples could not live with these rules and were often forced to meet secretly, which only intensified the tensions involved. The command was aware of the tensions, and once the commissar even devoted a lecture to this matter. He told them that in one of the battalions several women had become pregnant. Then the Germans conducted a roundup and the men were forced to shoot the pregnant women, lest they fall into German hands.[62] This was his way of justifying the aforementioned policies.

Nevertheless, in certain ways the couples fared better than the single men,[63] with regard to such things as laundry and repair of clothing. It should be noted that out of eighteen couples in the Kovno battalions, there was only one incident of divorce.[64]

In general we conclude that the presence of the women in the forest was, on the one hand, a source of crises in the relations between the fighters, and

---

59. Testimony of Haim Gechtel (Galin), YVSA, 36 (recording 12).

60. The visit was permitted during the daytime only, for a limited period.

61. Haim David Ratner's wife was transferred to another battalion, while he was sent to Byelorussia, then to Kazlu-Ruda.

62. Testimony of Rivka Gordon, YVSA, 26. In the Kovno battalions there was only one pregnancy (compare testimony of Malka Pugatzky-Smali, YVSA, 29, recording 9). All the couples were Jews; this element added to the tension between Jews and non-Jews.

63. Testimony of Baruch Gofer (Grodnick), YVSA, 21–23, (recording 6); testimony of Michael Yitzhaki (Gelbtrunk), YVSA, 44–45 (recording 7B); testimony of Malka Pugatzky-Smali, YVSA, 27 (recording 8).

64. Testimony of Pugatzky, YVSA, ibid. The divorce ceremony was conducted in front of the commissar. After liberation the couple remarried. Among the numerous fatal casualties among the ghetto fighters were five married men. Their wives remained in the forest as widows.

between the fighters and the command.[65] But on the other hand, the women had a positive, refreshing effect on the grey, monotonous daily life. Due to the presence of the women, the men were more careful about their clothing and external appearance in general and, to a lesser extent, about their style of speaking, which was usually filled with curses and obscenities.

Entertainment

The partisans endured unremitting tension, strict discipline, and the nagging worry that the day would come when they would not return from a mission alive. All this led to a strong need to release tension, to "live the day" and "enjoy life as long as we are alive." The more time the fighter spent outside the base, the more he needed entertainment and a way to unwind when he returned. Since the operations were so intensive, there was limited recreational time in the base between them.[66] Yet fighters enjoyed different types of recreation, each according to his own personality. One enjoyed drinking with his close friends – another, an undisturbed meeting with his wife. One preferred to sink into sweet sleep, while another enjoyed making the rounds of the dugouts, telling his tale to his comrades and hearing others' heroic acts as well. One took advantage of every opportunity to visit friends in neighboring battalions, while his comrade liked to sit near the campfire and enjoy communal singing.

In fact, most of the fighters present in the base on any given evening and not on duty participated in communal singing around the campfire. Over time, those fighters with good voices stood out[67] and were encouraged to express themselves in song. The social atmosphere was harmonious, cohesive, and even uplifting. A Jewish fighter in Rudniki describes the campfire milieu: "In the twilight hours we would get together around the campfire, our eyes riveted on the flickering flame, song bursting from every throat.... We start with Russian songs, then when our hearts open somewhat, we switch to Yiddish. Finally, we burst forth with Hebrew songs that touch our very heartstrings."[68]

---

65. There is a theory that the friction caused by the presence of the Jewish women was the real impetus for the murder of Jan Sperling by his commander, Sashka Baliakov (see chapter 13, p. 370).

66. Testimony of Grisha Sheffer, YVSA, 17 (recording 5).

67. Among them were Sima Yashunsky, Gita Foger, Michael Gelbtrunk, and Yisrael Goldblatt.

68. Lazer, 327. Among the most popular Hebrew songs in the forest, sung even by the Russian fighters, were "Hey, Harmonica, Play for Me" and "Burning Fire Surrounds Me." The Zionist

Over time, the campfire at the center of the camp became one of the most important social institutions on the base. It was a place of direct contact between the fighters and the command staff. The commander and the commissar took part in many conversations around the campfire that ostensibly began spontaneously and addressed social, organizational, and disciplinary issues in the camp. The commissar knew how to exploit each conversation to lecture the soldiers and demand alertness, preparation, and true loyalty on the part of the fighters.[69]

Other opportunities for directing the fighters' spare time toward educational and political channels were the Soviet holidays that were officially celebrated in the forest. The major holidays in the Kovno battalions were the January 14 holiday, the Red Army holiday (February 23), and International Women's Day (March 3). Above all was the First of May,[70] which was preceded by intensive preparations. It was celebrated with great splendor, and representatives of the neighboring battalions were invited.

Usually the holiday opened with a dress parade, at which the commissar delivered a speech pertaining to current events. Citations and awards of excellence were bestowed on worthy fighters.[71] On that day, only absolutely necessary work was performed in the camp. The partisans gathered in groups, dressed in their best clothes and sporting boots polished with pig fat in honor of the festival. The height of the day was a festive meal, prepared and planned over several weeks.[72] Every single fighter without exception received his share of *samogon*, this time officially. The copious drinking at the meal left many drunk and sometimes caused incidents. Afterwards the celebrants would split up into small groups, some for communal singing[73] and some for dancing.[74]

---

group Hashomrim (from the Mildos 7 collective) brought these songs with them from the ghetto.

69. Testimony of Haim Gechtel (Galin), YVSA, 31.

70. For security reasons, this festival was postponed to May 3.

71. In the First of May festivities, forty-nine Jewish fighters received citations and awards of excellence (Berel Gempel, YVSA, letter 3; also PKG, 154).

72. Testimony of Malka Pugatzky-Smali, YVSA, 30 (recording 9).

73. The Hashomrim group, together with Michael Gelbtrunk from 1BZ, Yosef Feuerstein from Beitar, and others, created a tradition of getting together on every holiday to sing Hebrew songs, accompanied by Yosef Rosen's harmonica (testimonies of Gita Foger-Turchin, 12, recording 4 and Michael Yitzhaki [Gelbtrunk], 36, recording 6B, YVSA).

74. Eventually even a dance floor was installed from boards that were brought from one of the villages (testimony of Haim Gechtel (Galin), YVSA, 27).

There were very few organized cultural activities. The literature that arrived in parachuted deliveries was mainly political and was meant to be distributed to underground activists in the city and to the general population.[75] Most of the fighters had no interest in the written word; the vast majority did not see a newspaper, let alone a book, the entire time they were in the forest. Even fewer had a need for pen and paper, except for the questionnaires and life histories that the fighters were required to fill out for their commanders in their first days in the forest.[76]

Status among the Partisans

The military "standings" in regular armies are determined from above – that is, by the official rank of the soldier. In the partisan battalions, however, there were other factors that differentiated between individuals and between groups. One of these factors was the type of operations in which a fighter participated or specialized. While all partisan activities were significant, more importance was attributed to operations that directly inflicted harm on the enemy. These included sabotage operations and attacks on German forces. In contrast, other activities, such as supply operations and camp services, were not as well respected in the forest. This value system greatly affected the appraisal of each member of the battalion. The more often an individual took an active part in important military operations, the higher his value in the eyes of others and of himself – and vice versa. This led to the following social "standings," in descending order:

Perpetrators of sabotage and special operations behind enemy lines: Most of these were outstanding commandos, fearless and bold, surrounded by a halo of heroism. Thus they were arrogant and demanded special privileges. When they were in camp, they were not given responsibilities such as guard duty and work rotations. Frequently, the commanders of sabotage squads and other operations were drawn from their ranks. The camp's standing orders did not seem to apply

---

75. The literature delivered to the camp included a short course on the history of the Communist Party and the newspapers Taribu-Lietuva and Tiasa, as well as the progressive Polish press (also see PKG, 142). Almost every evening the news bulletin from the Soviet Union Tass Agency was disseminated. Since not all the ghetto fighters could read Russian, a summary of the news was given orally in Yiddish.

76. Jewish fighter Yosef Feuerstein wrote a diary until the day he was killed (testimony of Haim Lazer, YVSA, 5, and testimony of Avraham Frenkel, YVSA, 3).

to them. The only authority they accepted was that of the camp commander, who was actually dependent on them in many ways. Almost all of them carried pistols as their personal weapons.

Guides and scouts: These also received special treatment due to their military functions. They performed special, secret operations that gave them status outside the base as authorized spokesmen and representatives of the partisan command. The mystery that surrounded them also raised their value in others' eyes. The guides were mainly Jews from the Kovno Ghetto. While the scouts continued their activities throughout the entire existence of the battalions, the activities of the guides greatly decreased due to the course of events in the ghetto; they were eventually transferred to other functions.

Combat personnel: These constituted the strike force of the combat companies. They exhibited excellent combat abilities and almost all were veteran military men,[77] among them those who had been officers. When they spent time on the base, they were sometimes attached to acquisition and supply operations.

Supply personnel: Most of their activities centered on supply and acquisitions. Between operations they were employed in headquarters functions, in guard duty, and services. They also took part in sabotage operations, but not in major roles.

Services personnel: These worked permanently in the services section, usually because of their age or problematic health. They rarely participated in operations and campaigns outside the base, and then only in emergencies.

Communist Party members: Communist Party members enjoyed a special status. The Kovno battalions included a party cell with about twelve members (eight of them were Kovno Ghetto people), and a Komsomol cell of thirty-five members (twenty-eight of them were from the ghetto). They held closed meetings in which they discussed how to improve the fighters' combat abilities and increase the level of their political awareness. Their function was to assist the command in carrying out their orders in all spheres, to explain the importance of these orders to the fighters, and to point out flaws. Some of them were appointed as internal intelligence, in order to monitor what was happening in the camp, to listen in on conversations conducted between comrades-in-arms, and to inform on them to the Officer in Charge of Special Matters, who was also a party member. The work

---

77. Except for several Kovno Ghetto fighters.

of these informers was not secret; their comrades, who called them "squealers," disapproved of them and tried to keep their distance from them.[78]

Party affiliation was an important factor in the appointment of commanders,[79] but most commanders were not members of the party.[80] In any event, the Kovno battalions had very little party activity. The party cell, which was mostly Jewish, did not address the major social problems on the base. They ignored actions or policies, such as discrimination against the Jews, that overshadowed the combat achievements and were in direct contradiction to Communist doctrine.[81] Also many of the party members were disappointed at the treatment of the Jews.[82]

Fighters earned special respect as a result of other factors, such as an individual's past, personal characteristics, and talents. The paratroopers, for example, received special treatment and admiration, as they appeared as representatives of the free "Great Motherland." A certain amount of respect, albeit less, was also reserved for the underground activists and key functionaries. As for the Russian prisoners-of-war, their military ranks were not always enough to earn them an appropriate position. Their status was generally dependent on the initiative they displayed in escaping from the prisoner-of-war camp and their seniority in the partisan battalion. The prisoners who escaped from the prisoner-of-war camps at a later period, in the last few months before the liberation of Lithuania by the Soviet Army, were not received as favorably. There were many signs that

---

78. Testimony of Pugatzky-Smali, YVSA, 18 (recording 6), and 31–32 (recording 9).

79. The political factor was what decided the appointment of Haim David Ratner as commissar of Forward battalion, as well as the status of David Tepper as acting commissar of the combat company (testimony of Haim Galin [Gechtel], YVSA, 30, recording 12; testimony of Haim Lazer, 2).

80. The following were members of the Communist Party: the camp commander, the commissar, the comander of the Special Department, and Petrovitch the paratrooper (Leib Solomin).

81. We know, for example, of serious steps taken by Jewish party members regarding the murder of Mishka Karetsky (see ch. 11, footnote 93). When Malka Pugatzky approached party member Moshe Sherman, asking him to do something, his answer was "Let it go" (testimony of Malka Pugatzky-Smali, YVSA, 32). On the other hand, PKG emphasizes the contribution of the Communist Party to nurturing brotherhood among the nationalities. "The party's organization creates an atmosphere of real international friendship" (143).

82. The courageous guide Abba Diskant, one of the initiators of the Ninth Fort escape and a Komsomol member during the ghetto period, said, "We are slaves to the Red partisans" (testimony of Michael Yitzhaki [Gelbtrunk], YVSA, 42–43).

indicated that these POWs fled to the forest in order to clear their reputations for not escaping earlier or even for collaborating with their captors.[83]

Those with positive personal characteristics also garnered respect. First and foremost were the courageous. Partisans tried with all their might to overcome their fears, lest they be branded with the terrible epithet of "coward," which would result in a wretched status and contempt in everyone's eyes.[84]

Less important, but not insignificant, among beneficial personal characteristics were social skills, such as the ability to strike up conversations with others or gladden others with jokes, tall tales, recitations, and even measured amounts of obscenities. Partisans also earned appreciation for singing or playing an instrument around the campfire, in the dugout, or even during an exhausting march.[85]

Of course, the status of an individual in partisan society was not determined schematically but by a combination of the various factors. For example, a paratrooper who was rumored to be a coward[86] was respected less than a prisoner-of-war who had proven himself in critical moments. Similarly, the respect afforded to a person who previously had held an important role in the Communist underground[87] decreased dramatically in the forest when he was negligent and careless in his personal appearance or in carrying out various tasks.

Under partisan conditions, the individual was always transparent before the eyes of the surrounding society. He could not hide his characteristics and shortcomings. Most of the time, he was subject to concealed and unconcealed scrutiny that determined his place in the society.

Groups within the Battalions

Over time, two major groups crystallized in the Kovno battalions: the Jews and the non-Jews. Each group had its own distinguishing features, and to a certain

---

83. Testimony of Baruch Gofer (Grodnick), YVSA, 340.

84. Testimony of Malka Pugatzky-Smali, YVSA, 31.

85. Yosef Rosen excelled in playing the harmonica and was often asked by his friends to play in the base and on the way to combat operations. The commander of the combat company, Mishka Trushin, tried to take Rosen with him on all his marches (testimony of J. Rosen, YVSA, 29, recording 5).

86. One example of this is the Lithuanian paratrooper "Ruta" (testimony of Rivka Gordon, YVSA, 29).

87. One example of this is Moshe Robinson, a long-standing Komsomol member who was active during the Smetona regime period in Lithuania and during the ghetto period as well.

extent the members of each group shared a sense of "us" versus "them" towards the other group. The numerical ratio of the two changed over time; at the beginning, the Jews were a small minority, but they became the overwhelming majority after the arrival of the Kovno Ghetto fighters. The situation changed again after April 1944 when on the one hand, Jews ceased leaving the ghetto to join the partisans, and on the other, large numbers of Russian prisoners-of-war reached the forest.

Most members of the non-Jewish group were army veterans, including officers. The vast majority were Russians – that is, Red Army soldiers who escaped from prisoner-of-war camps. Some were Russian paratroopers, and the remaining were villagers from the environs and a few Lithuanian policemen. Almost all were single men between the ages of twenty and thirty. All were Russian-speakers, and some also had good command of the Lithuanian and Polish languages, and even of Yiddish.[88] Most of the paratroopers and POWs had not known each other before they met in the battalion. Except for the paratroopers and a small number of the POWs who had joined the partisan ranks out of an inner conviction, most of the POWs did so for personal reasons and a combination of calculations and circumstance. The most prominent reason was the desire to prove their loyalty to the Soviet regime before the day when the Germans would be expelled from the region.

Within the non-Jewish group was a unified, cohesive sub-group of fighters (including one woman) who hailed from Byelorussia, and were thus nicknamed "Vastocheniki" (the Easterners). They were involved in espionage and in collecting secret material. They enjoyed a measure of autonomy within the battalion and were even assigned separate living-quarters.

The Jewish group was completely different from its non-Jewish counterpart. It numbered about two hundred people[89] from among the three Kovno battal-

---

88. This group included several Jews, including paratrooper Petrovitch (Leib Solomin) and Nikolai Vasilenko (Yisrael Vasselnitzky) from the Ninth Fort escapees, and squad commander Leib Zeitzev from Nowo-Święciany (testimony of Eliezer Moses, 15, YVSA, recording 4). One of the non-Jewish fighters who spoke and understood Yiddish was the elderly Polish fighter Vicenti Markovitz, nicknamed "Batka," who had picked up Yiddish from his interactions with Jews in Vilna before the war.

89. According to Rachi Ben Eliezer (Yerachmiel Berman), FLC 10:6, about 280 fighters were sent from the Kovno Ghetto to the Rudniki Forests, including eighty women. This version was also accepted by Garfunkel in his book (171). We think that this number is exaggerated,

ions. They all came from the Kovno Ghetto and included about forty women; eighteen couples who went to the forest together; and three married men and three married women whose spouses remained in the ghetto. The vast majority arrived in the forest in organized groups of twenty to thirty members in vehicles (except for the first group), between November 17, 1943, and March 29, 1944 (the day after the Children's *Aktion* and the elimination of the Jewish police force). Only a small minority arrived as individuals or in small groups.[90] Most were very young, usually between twenty and twenty-five years of age. There were only twenty Jewish fighters who were above the age of twenty-five. All the Jewish fighters had at least an elementary-school education, and thirty-five of them had graduated academic high school (Jewish or Hebrew). The overwhelming majority spoke Yiddish among themselves, and some also had command of the Russian language. About twelve of them were members of the Communist Party and about twenty-eight were Komsomol members.

In contrast to the non-Jewish fighters, only fifteen Jews had served in the Lithuanian army, including one officer.[91] Most of the rest were young and had not yet done army service. The older ones among them had no affinity to the military and had been far removed from the world of war, weapons, and fighting. Only about thirty of the fighters had taken part in the Augustova Plan before they joined the forest partisans. Almost all the fighters had been city dwellers, and the forest and village environs were foreign to them. Since they came from the same place and also belonged to the same organization (the JFO), most of them were acquainted with one another from the ghetto period or even earlier periods as coworkers, fellow party activists, fellow students, or from playing sports together. About twenty-five of them were relatives (not including by marriage). Their departure to the Rudniki Forests was the fruit of JFO's extended planning, intensive efforts, and bitter struggles in the Kovno Ghetto.

In the hearts of the Jewish partisans from the Kovno Ghetto burned a strong

---

except if it includes partisans in other frameworks than the Kovno battalions. No complete list of Jewish fighters in the Kovno battalions was ever found.

90. For example, Zivia Kapit took the train to Rudniki and walked by foot from there to the base. Shmuel Rosen arrived in a similar manner.

91. Peretz Padison was a Jewish officer who had served in Lithuania's War of Independence and later as a police officer in the ghetto. For a while he was the sergeant major of the partisan camp (the Death to the Occupiers battalion). Padison's son Hanne was also in the battalion.

desire to avenge the Jewish people and their families and relatives who had been murdered by the enemy. In addition, they were cognizant of the fact that being a partisan was their last honorable option and only chance for saving their lives, and also perhaps the lives of their family members and the ghetto residents in general. It was clear to them that the Jewish partisan did not have the option of "saving his own skin" at the price of treason or collaboration with the enemy.

The "Jewish Problem" in the Forest

The issue of discrimination and anti-Semitism toward the Jewish partisans in the forests is a theme that appears over and over in Jewish partisan literature. The problems involved in conducting a proper analysis of this issue are, first, that few documents relate to this issue, and second, that the opposing, non-Jewish side cannot be researched. Our only sources come from testimonies of the Jews. This gives much cause for concern of a lack of objectivity on the part of the witnesses, not in the description of the facts but in the way the facts are interpreted. Often the facts could be viewed in two ways. For example, it is a fact that few Jews were promoted to the command level of the Kovno battalions. Even those few who attained command positions only reached the level of squad commander. One explanation for this might be anti-Semitism, while another is that there were no Jews there with the requisite leadership skills.

The same goes regarding other acts or deeds that might appear as intentional discrimination, but could be the result of objective conditions. We usually find two opposing viewpoints in the literature. There are those that see the Jewish partisan in the forest as a particular case of "the Jews among the Gentiles." They view the attitude toward the Jewish partisans in the forest as an extension of the hatred expressed by non-Jews toward the Jews for generations, especially in Eastern Europe. This hatred was greatly exacerbated by specific elements, such as the Nazi propaganda and the portrayed linkage of Jews to the negative aspects of the Communist regime. Others deny this claim and say that the Jewish experience among the partisans was in no way special. They claim that there were fewer *facts* of discrimination and more *feelings* of discrimination, that in most cases there was an explanation for the particular incident that had no connection to anti-Semitism, and that the Jews were overly sensitive in their appraisal of these occurrences.

Undoubtedly both views above are extreme and generalize too much. In any case, we have numerous testimonies full of complaints of anti-Semitism, discrimination, and injustice. The fighters claim that expressions of anti-Semitism emanated not just from fellow partisans but from the command headed by Commissar Davidov. They claim that the latter adopted this point of view and encouraged anti-Jewish occurrences by the example he set with his own behavior. One of the witnesses states: "It can be said that the commissar set the anti-Semitic tone. I can say that those who came [from prisoner-of-war camps] did not dare make anti-Semitic statements until they got wind of the situation; in other words until they got to know the commissar and heard him."[92]

On the other hand, none of the non-Jews dared to openly present himself as an anti-Semite or incite others toward anti-Semitism. Moreover, the former members of Zionist movements maintained contact among themselves in the forest. We can assume that this was known to the command, and if there had been an intention to harm the Jews it would have been possible to use this as an excuse to harass them. We have no evidence of this. Also, we find serious charges against Jewish commanders who harmed Jews.

In any case, we bring below several accusations that were made against the partisan command of the Kovno battalions.

MURDER AND MANSLAUGHTER

This severe accusation against the battalion command relates to the deaths of the Jewish fighters Mishka Karetsky (a paratrooper)[93] and Jan Sperling.[94] The charge is that after the fact, nothing was done to punish the murderers.[95]

Another, more general accusation focuses mainly on the commissar and the intensive military policy that led to the deaths of tens of Jewish fighters out of criminal negligence. The most prominent examples in this category were sending

---

92. Testimony of Haim Gechtel (Galin), YVSA, 45.

93. Komsomol member paratrooper Mishka Karetsky and Moshe Robinson complained to brigade headquarters about the treatment of the Jews in the Death to the Occupiers battalion. It was widely believed in the forest that this was the reason that Karetzky was murdered by his non-Jewish comrades during a combat mission. See testimony of Rivka Gordon, YVSA, 25–26; testimony of Baruch Gofer (Grodnick), YVSA, 31–32, recording 9; and Berel Gempel, YVSA, letter 2.

94. See chapter 13, p. 376.

95. The murderers of Jan Sperling, Sasha Baliakov, and Mishka Karetsky's comrades were also never brought to trial. After the war the father of Karetsky demanded a reopening of the case, but without results (Testimony of R. Gordon, YVSA, 26–27).

Jewish partisans to a military operation without weapons[96] or with inoperative or ineffective weapons. The Jews also cite the indifference and inaction of the commander who made no move to punish Seryozha, commander of the blocking unit, after the debacle in the Večioriškiai battle.[97] Seryozha was finally convicted and shot, due to the pressure of public opinion and the involvement of elements outside the battalion. Even then, members of the command complained that "Russian commanders are shot because of the Jews."

In two cases, however, the charge of anti-Semitism on the part of the command is not supported by the evidence: the killing of the severely wounded David Goldin[98] and the execution of Moshe Gerber.[99] Although there were rumors in the partisan base that put the blame for these incidents on the command, according to what has been found among the testimonies we cannot concur with this view that the command was indeed responsible. The general impression of the Moshe Gerber affair is that the initiative for his execution came from the Jewish group of fighters, rather than from the command.

CONFISCATION OF BELONGINGS

Although the JFO sent equipment with their fighters (such as a radio, a sunprint device, and medical supplies) to be delivered to the Death to the Occupiers command,[100] when the ghetto fighters reached the forest they were thoroughly searched and various belongings were confiscated. It would have been possible for this not to have aroused indignation if it had not been accompanied by actions that gave to the confiscations the appearance of discrimination, abuse, and deceit.

When the fourth group of ghetto fighters arrived in the forest, for example, they were frowned at because they did not bring gold from the ghetto for the

---

96. This phenomenon was prevalent especially in the first period, when the weapons supply was very limited (testimony of Eliezer Moses, YVSA, 14, recording 4). Regarding instances of stripping Jewish partisans of their weapons and then abandoning them to their fate, compare Salomon M. Schwartz, *Ha-antishemiyut ba-brit ha-mo'atzot*, trans. A. Dromi (Tel Aviv: Assaf, 5713/1953), 87–140; Yechiel Gerntstein, *Yehudi ba-ya'ar* (Moreshet: Tel Aviv, 5715), 120; Kahanovitz, 193.

97. See chapter 13.

98. See above, Discipline.

99. Ibid.

100. *PKG*, 133.

purchase of weapons.[101] Rivka Gordon's watch was taken away from her, ostensibly to exchange for weapons, but after a few days she discovered the watch on the wrist of one of the non-Jewish scouts. Gordon protested vociferously until the watch was returned.[102] Michael Gelbtrunk's pistol, which he had received from Ika Greenberg after Gelbtrunk's escape from the Ninth Fort, was taken from him and given to the female Russian fighter Katya.[103] Also, in the initial period when basic food items were scarce on the base, the fighters sent on food-acquisition operations to the farmers were subject to searches when they returned, to ensure that they did not put aside food for themselves.

The confiscation of personal items mainly affected the Jews, because the Russian prisoner-of-war escapees arrived with no possessions and so nothing could be taken from them. The humiliating "inspections" after acquisition operations also applied mainly to the Jews because the vast majority of the participants in these missions were fighters from the ghetto. Therefore the Jews received the impression that these actions were directed especially against them, out of anti-Semitism. The Jewish fighters were certainly influenced by the memories of the humiliating inspections and confiscations they underwent in the ghetto by the Germans.[104]

ACCEPTING JEWS INTO THE BATTALION

The stringent conditions and limitations placed on the acceptance of fighters from the ghetto into the partisans ("long" weapons, equipment, limited age group) were accepted by the JFO as objective requirements of the military reality in the forest.[105] Nevertheless, in the hearts of many members of the underground in the Kovno Ghetto, as well as of the fighters who succeeded to break through to the forest, was the hope that the Jewish partisans would serve as the vanguard for masses of ghetto youths and that their camps would be a source of salvation for the ghetto .

But the Jewish fighters in the forest learned over time that the stringent

---

101. Testimony of Michael Yitzhaki (Gelbtrunk), YVSA, 31.

102. Testimony of Rivka Gordon, YVSA, 18.

103. Testimony of Michael Yitzhaki (Gelbtrunk), YVSA, 35 (recording 6B).

104. Some of them said bluntly, "This is exactly like the searches near the ghetto gate" (testimony of Eliezer Moses, YVSA, 21, recording 6).

105. For details regarding the directives given by the forest emissaries to the ghetto, see chapter 7, "Orders for the Ghetto Underground."

conditions imposed on the Kovno Ghetto fighters did not apply to non-Jews. Day after day, they saw how the Russian POWs joined the base and were accepted warmly and willingly, almost without preconditions. Sometimes there were arguments on this issue,[106] but they did not change the situation. When the last organized group came from the ghetto, they brought with them the bad news of the recent *Aktion* directed against the children and elderly, and about the new regime in the ghetto.[107] That was when everyone understood that the ghetto gates were irrevocably locked and the last hopes for more ghetto Jews to join them were ended. Add to their sorrow the fact that at exactly this time the flow of Russian POWs turned into a veritable flood – and the Jewish guides were given the task of bringing these POWs to the base. The Jewish fighters could not help feeling that opportunities were left unexploited, and they largely blamed the command for their role in blocking the stream of young people who yearned to leave the ghetto. There is no doubt that the brigade command had political and military rationales for their policy regarding the composition of the battalions and their appearance in the public eye.[108] The ghetto fighters, however, who were sensitive to the fate of their friends and surviving family in the ghetto, viewed this policy as severe discrimination, with the most fatal results.

EXCESSIVE STRINGENCY

As indicated above, the partisan law was never consolidated or summarized in standing orders. Prohibitions were loosely defined, and enforcement of the rules depended on the individual commanders, the situation, and the status of the law-breakers. Many prohibitions were not applied at all to the fighters that constituted the battalion's elite forces.[109] But for the Jewish fighters, most of whom were on the lower rungs of the social ladder, the discipline demanded was very strict, in many cases excessively so. At the same time the command staff either ignored or expressed a forgiving attitude to the violations of non-Jewish fighters.

---

106. Testimony of Yosef Rosen, YVSA, 27–29 (recording 6).

107. See chapter 14.

108. For more information about the national policy of the Soviet partisan movement, see Avraham Zvie Brown, "*Ha-partisan ha-yehudi bi-tnuat ha-partizanim ha-sovyietit*," Yad Vashem 4:169–89, 5720/1960.

109. Some examples are the Vastochniki group, the senior command staff, and other fighters who were close to the command staff.

Dov Levin describes the following incident in which he almost lost his life, an incident that the Jewish fighters viewed as blatant discrimination:

> In one of the supply operations I participated in, I also searched for soap and tobacco. A young Russian woman accompanied me.... This woman was looking for items of clothing, especially silk stockings. When we returned to the base, we were interrogated about our actions by the commander of the "Special Department." ... With him was Kostia, the commander of my battalion, and Solomin-Petrovitch was also present.... Kostia asked me if I had stolen gold. I answered him that gold didn't interest me, that I had left gold in the ghetto of my own accord. Then Petrovitch the Jew intervened and asked if I had participated in combat missions. I answered him that I had already participated in five combat missions. Nevertheless, he accused me and treated me more negatively than the *goyim* who interrogated me. The *goy* commander was more moderate than he. I relied on the young Russian woman who had been with me, but to no avail.... Petrovitch said to me, "Those who don't benefit from words, will benefit from bullets."
>
> A few days later, while I was on guard duty, I was summoned to a roll call. About 70 percent of the participants were Jews. The elderly chief of headquarters, a former teacher, presided over the roll call. I was ordered to step forward, together with Yosef Melamed and Sarah Gempel. The commander read aloud an order in which we were accused of robbing the civilian population and thus souring our relations with them.... Sarah Gempel was accused of stealing silk stockings. Yosef Melamed was accused for once falling asleep during guard duty. The young Russian woman who had looted together with me was not even mentioned. According to the directive, the three of us were sentenced to death by shooting. The commander stopped reading the order. Tremendous tension filled the air. After a short pause, he added that because we had earlier excelled in combat operations, our death sentence was commuted to a severe reprimand.[110]

This incident and many others like it, although they ended well, left a deep impact and caused distress in the Jewish group, and strengthened the feeling among them of double standards. Nevertheless, we should not conclude that

---

110. Testimony of Dov Levin, YVSA, 49.

persecution was the lot of all the Jewish fighters. A major factor was the ability of the fighters to adapt themselves to the strict demands. The disciplinary incidents mainly took place among those Jewish fighters who, for all kinds of reasons, were negligent in their jobs. As a result, they became targets of excessively strict discipline by the command staff. One of the better fighters says the following:

> You could say that the treatment of the Jews was not good. On the other hand, I never felt offended myself because I always behaved all right. Regarding the Jewish comrades, I have to say that many of them were negligent in their jobs and neglected themselves, thus providing a pretext for others to try to harm them.[111]

Another fighter from the combat company states this a bit differently: "Whoever was really a hundred percent, they couldn't say anything against him. If someone was good-for-nothing, they blamed it on his being Jewish, even though there were also *goyim* who were good-for-nothing. But then they didn't ascribe it to their nationality."[112]

The excessive strictness imposed on the Jewish fighters dampened the atmosphere in the Jewish group and left a bitter taste in the mouths of even those Jews who were not personally affected. Generalizations were particularly offensive: expressions like "the Jews are cowards" as voiced by the cowardly commander Seryozha, in his attempt to cover up his own failure, or "I will throw you [women] out of here like dogs," as said by the commissar in reaction to a dispute between two female fighters, one Jewish and one non-Jewish, referring to all the Jewish women who were in the same position.[113] These are some examples of the prevailing attitudes of systematic generalizations toward the Jews.

Up to now, we have quoted the words of the members of the Kovno battalions themselves. Since they were involved directly there is reason to suspect that their point of view was somewhat subjective. Therefore it is of great interest to

---

111. Testimony of Michael Pasternak, yvsa, 3.
112. Testimony of Haim (Galin) Gechtel, yvsa, 45 (recording 15). In another place, however, this witness tells about a severe reprimand he received from the commissar, when he brought milk from the village to his sick friend (ibid., 32, recording 11). Also, the Jewish fighters became very upset when their renowned guide, Nehemiah Endlin, was given a menial task immediately after he returned exhausted from an extensive mission. The Jews tended to view this as an intentional offense (testimony of Michael Pasternak, yvsa, 3).
113. Testimony of Malka Pugatzky-Smali, yvsa, 26 (recording 8).

examine the impressions of fighters from other units, who were able to view the situation in the Kovno battalions from a more impartial perspective. They were also able to compare the circumstances in the Kovno battalions to their own units.

Haim Lazer, one of the first Jews in the Rudniki Forests, describes the situation of the Kovno Ghetto fighters as follows:

> From their very first days, the fellows from Kovno felt that by leaving the ghetto for the forest, they had gone from the frying pan into the fire. The Lithuanian command behaved toward the Jews with unconcealed hatred, and dozens of unnecessary victims fell as a result of these commanders, who squandered no opportunity to embitter the lives of the Jews. Excellent fellows found their way to the forest, despite the difficulties and dangers, and were ready to sacrifice everything in battle to avenge the spilled blood of their brothers. Yet these same fighters were tortured under the yoke of Lithuanian hooligans, with no one to come to their aid.[114]

Grisha Joels, a ghetto Kovno fighter who served in Genis's battalion, testifies: "When I came to visit the Death to the Occupiers battalion, I saw how the Jewish comrades there were extremely oppressed."[115]

Vitka Kempner, female commander of the reconnaissance unit of the Jewish Vilna battalion The Avenger, had contact with the Death to the Occupiers scouts and even visited the battalion. She says as follows:

> I mainly met with Boris, commander of their reconaissance unit. He was an out-and-out anti-Semite.[116] ... Once I was in the company of the scouts, as they had invited me to visit them in their battalion. I was taken aback at the way the Jews there looked. We who were in a Jewish national battalion didn't know discrimination as Jews. Therefore I was very surprised to see the Jewish partisans sitting almost alone.... Afterwards someone explained to me that in that place, they lived according to groups carrying out specific func-

---

114. Lazer, 252.
115. Testimony of G. Joels, YVSA, 4. Joels was among those who had escaped from the Koshedar camp. He went to the Death to the Occupiers battalion to visit his brother Yisrael, a scout.
116. Another source provides a different view of this commander. "The fighters who just now arrived from the ghetto sense the friendly assistance extended to them as they take their first steps in the ranks of the partisans" (PKG, 143–44).

tions. In our eyes, that was unacceptable. And afterwards, when we met the partisans, I saw how most of the Jews were placed in service-related [work] groups. That left a very difficult impression on me...because that's not the way it was with us.[117]

Finally, we bring the testimony of Abba Kovner, commander of the brigade of the Vilna Jewish battalions. His status enabled him to pay closer attention to the overall issues of the Jewish partisans in the Rudniki Forests.

> Despite these two facts – the existence of the Jewish fighting camp, and the fact that the political command was headed by a Jew [Jurgis] –...anti-Semitism sent shock waves even throughout our forest. Mainly, the depressing atmosphere that prevailed among the Lithuanian battalions and the Soviet paratrooper battalion in our vicinity (of Captain Elko) left a deep impression on us. We even sent words of protest on this issue to Moscow.
>
> The bleak situation of our comrades in the Lithuanian battalions left an especially deep impression on us. We discovered this from meetings with the Jewish partisans. We also expressed our protest to Jurgis. I remember that one of the commanders of the Lithuanian battalions said to the villagers, in the presence of our partisans, that he was willing to sell one whole Jew for a sack of flour. That was Commissar Davidov.... In meetings with the Jewish partisans, they asked several times to be transferred to another camp, to the Jewish brigade. We saw certain missions that were dangerous and not well planned. They specifically sent Jews on these missions, and to overtly dangerous Lithuanian areas. We saw special intent in this, and the victims that fell are proof of it – these types of missions, as well as expressions of anti-Semitism of the commissar and commander of the battalions...[118]

Solidarity among the Jews

Feelings of discrimination among the Jews led Jewish fighters to develop a deep solidarity among themselves and tighten their relationships with one another. This solidarity assumed various guises, such as festive receptions organized by

117. Testimony of V. Kempner (pp. 16–17 of Abba Kovner's testimony, YVSA, recording 7).
118. Testimony of Abba Kovner, YVSA, 12–14 (recording 4, 5).

the veteran Jewish fighters for the newcomers arriving from the ghetto[119] and participation in burial ceremonies of their comrades in the cemetery on the base.[120] There was also mutual aid among the Jews, especially with regards to food and items of clothing, and particularly for their sick and wounded compatriots who needed items considered luxuries, such as tea, sugar, and milk.[121]

Another evidence of national solidarity among Jewish fighters was their universal use of the Yiddish language when they spoke among themselves. This led to constant friction with the command echelon that, for all kinds of reasons, viewed this unfavorably.[122] The Jews even created new Yiddish terms or code words for important phenomenon or people in their forest-world.[123] The ability to converse in Yiddish gave the Jews a certain feeling of security.

Within the overall Jewish group were smaller subgroups of people whose close ties with the ghetto continued on in the forest. One example of this is the Shomrim Zionist group, which had belonged to the 7 Mildos pioneering collective in the ghetto. Although this group contained only eleven members,

---

119. Haim Yellin was received in admiration by the Jewish fighters on his second visit to the forest. According to one source he was not allowed to enter the base, and the Jewish fighters went to meet him outside the camp (testimony of Eliezer Moses, YVSA, 29, recording 8). But according to another source, Haim Yellin was allowed into the base but was not permitted to meet with the Jewish fighters, due to the fear that they would complain to him about the harsh treatment they received (testimony of Rivka Gordon, YVSA, 18).

120. At the funeral of machine-gunner Yehoshua Antzel, no non-Jewish fighter took part. This greatly stirred up his Jewish comrades. Dr. Garfunkel, the Jewish doctor of the Vilna battalions, had to intervene to prevent a serious incident. Only the commissar participated in the funeral by virtue of his job, and he delivered a short eulogy.

121. Testimony of Rivka Gordon, YVSA, 21.

122. Solomin-Petrovitch explicitly told the Jewish fighters that speaking in Yiddish aroused the antagonism of the non-Jews. But that does not mean that he reacted similarly to those who spoke Lithuanian (testimony of Grisha Sheffer, YVSA, 34; testimony of Malka Pugatzky-Smali, YVSA, 19, recording 6).

123. The fighters "Judaized" several Russian words by adding a Jewish ending or making other changes. For example, based on the word *bombyozhka* (bomb; in code, spoils), they created the verb *bambiran* (to take booty). They also used nicknames for certain people. The commander was called "the big ape" or "the conceited Motke"; the commissar was "the little ape" or "the evil Haman." The camp's sergeant major was nicknamed *samech* (the Hebrew letter for his rank); Boris the scout commander was *beit* (first Hebrew letter of his name). Sometimes when they knew that the guards were Jews, they dispensed with the customary password and instead would answer with the words of the Hebrew prayer *Shema Yisrael* (testimony of Haim Galin [Gechtel], YVSA, 34).

they stood out in the close affinity maintained between them. They tried to stay together whenever possible; they helped one another and initiated sing-a-longs and folk dancing in the evenings that attracted large groups of Jews and non-Jews.[124] Even the Communists among the Jewish fighters approved of these activities.[125]

The Shomrim also kept in contact with members of the Hashomer Hatzair movement in the other Lithuanian battalions. These meetings between the Shomrim in the Lithuanian battalions were occasional at first but became regular over time, and specific liaisons were designated from the different battalions. A special letter written in Hebrew was received from the Hashomer Hatzair movement. This letter, which was circulated secretly from hand to hand, described the annals of the uprisings in Polish ghettos. This letter hinted, for the first time, of the need to organize a large-scale illegal immigration movement to Eretz Israel after liberation. During the departure from the forest, they even prepared a plan for continued cooperation.

Below is a description of the very consequential first meeting between Abba Kovner, commander of the Vilna Jewish brigade, and three members of the Shomrim group from the Death to the Occupiers battalion:

> We were aware of the existence of a Vilna battalion containing members of the [Hashomer Hatzair] movement, we knew Abba Kovner's name, and we searched for all kinds of ways to make contact.... I remember that once we stood, the three of us, on Main Guard duty: Dov Levin, Zvie Brown, and myself, and along came a man riding on a horse. He announced his name and immediately we hinted to one another that the opportune moment had arrived. I said, Friends, I am going to bring food, and you stay here and delay him.... I'll go slow, and you will have time to talk. And that's what we did. I went to notify [the others] and Zvie and Dov got into a conversation with Abba, and that's when we set up contact between us.... Soon a group of women was sent to [visit] us. Two young women came to us, Dina and Heska. I think that they also brought us soap. They came simply to get acquainted

---

124. Testimonies (YVSA) of Eliezer Moses, 19 (recording 5); Malka Pugatzky-Smali, 30 (recording 9); Baruch Gofer (Grodnick), 19, 22, 31 (recordings 5, 6); Yosef Rosen, 25 (recording 6); Haim Gechtel (Galin), 31–32 (recording 11).
125. Testimony of Grisha Sheffer, YVSA, 37 (recording 9).

with the other members. After that, we arranged for Baruch Grodnick to begin to visit them.[126]

Abba Kovner describes that fateful encounter in the description below, in which he also summarizes its political and social importance:

> The first meeting is a little shadowy in my memory. It was held with the first ones who came from Lithuania to our forest. But I remember the official meeting. I wanted the command to know about it as well, because any connection like that was suspect, and they also followed and investigated us.... I remember one visit. I rode on a horse to their camp's Main Guard. It was our luck that, at the time, the Main Guard was manned by several Jewish comrades. The entire Main Guard had only Jews. In this Main Guard I found Grishka Sheffer,[127] Haim Gechtel, and Dov Levin, and I remember that it was a very encouraging meeting for both sides.... But even back at that meeting, the comrades told me about their situation and their worries about the future. Afterwards we kept contact with the Jews in the forest, as much as possible, mainly with members of the movement....
>
> We also composed an official letter. Its content dealt with the history of our struggle in the ghetto, the lessons to be learned from this struggle, ideas of what we must do in the forest, and definition of our goals after liberation. The letter was secretly passed from hand to hand, and even smuggled into the Kovno camp.[128] ... I also remember that as we prepared ourselves for the [Russian] conquest of Vilna and our exit from the forest, we ensured that instructions were sent to our people, wherever they may be, regarding what to do when they returned to their former places of residence after liberation.... By the way, to ensure that our contact would not be left up to chance, we appointed liaisons. On our side it was Rozhka, on your side it was Baruch. And I must note that in the annals of all the partisan units that I was familiar with in the entire partisan movement – such liaisons were very rare.[129]

---

126. Testimony of Haim Gechtel (Galin), YVSA, 33 (recording 11–12).
127. This is a mistake; it should be Zvie Brown.
128. One copy of this official letter is in Israel, in the Hashomer Hatzair archives on Kibbutz Merchavya. Its photocopy is in Yad Vashem Archives, Jerusalem. The content of the letter is quoted in *Sefer Hashomer Hatzair* 1:641–43.
129. Testimony of Abba Kovner, YVSA, 14–15 (recording 5).

Indeed, by virtue of these liaisons, the foundations were created for a serious emigration enterprise to Eretz Israel from Kovno and Vilna, after these two cities were liberated by the Soviet Army.

Similar to the Shomrim group, the Ninth Fort escapees also cultivated close ties among their group and even a certain amount of mutual aid.

While these two groups were social in nature, they lacked an organizational structure. By contrast, the Komsomol group was organizational in nature, but for many reasons, and mainly due to their great disillusionment with the conditions in the forest,[130] its members refrained from having too many conversations together. This was to avoid the painful question that they all faced, but were unable to answer.[131] Evidently they admired, and also envied, the social lifestyle of the Shomrim group and frequently tried to become friendly with them.[132]

The Connection with the Jewish World

The fact that the partisan camp of the Kovno Ghetto fighters was situated in a remote corner of a forest, effectively under siege conditions, did not cause them to be cut off from Jewish populations. To a certain extent, the partisan base served as a relay station between the remnants of the ghetto Jews, who feared their annihilation on a daily basis, and Jewish populations in Lithuania and Byelorussia. Mainly, however, they maintained contact with the large Jewish population in the Soviet Union.

Communications with the ghetto were maintained continuously until May 1944 via the groups that came to the forest from Kovno and via the emissaries and guides sent by the forest to the ghetto. Families and friends of the fighters in Kovno took every opportunity to send their loved ones verbal regards, small written notes, and important staples such as tobacco, saccharine, and sweets. This served to deepen the fighters' connections to their homes, families, and friends who remained "there."

Thanks to the aerial connection to Moscow, the fighters received regards from Lithuanian Jews whom no one imagined had managed to escape [to Russia] at the last minute. Jewish paratroopers – Isser Schmidt (Didialis), Mishka Karetsky,

---

130. Editor's note: Their disillusionment was primarily due to the anti-Semitism they experienced there.
131. Testimony of Malka Pugatzky-Smali, YVSA, 31 (recording 9).
132. Testimony of Baruch Gofer (Grodnick), YVSA, 19 (recording 5).

and others – notified the fighters about young Jews from Kovno fighting in the Lithuanian division of the Red Army. The surprising news was passed on to the ghetto via the emissaries.[133]

On the other hand, material of great historic interest was systematically transmitted to Moscow from the Kovno Ghetto, mainly material relating to Nazi crimes. Some of it reached the hands of the Jewish Anti-Fascist Committee, which publicized the material.[134] Sometimes Jewish parents in Russia recognized their children in pictures taken in the Kovno Ghetto and transferred by air to Moscow.[135] Other documents included authentic material on the atrocities conducted in Kovno's Ninth Fort, a copy of the memorandum composed by the Ninth Fort escapees, and other reports on Lithuanian Jewry. After reaching Moscow, the material filtered to other Jewish centers in the world, including (Eretz) Israel.[136]

---

133. Testimony of Grisha Sheffer, YVSA, 16–17 (recording 4).

134. The Jewish Anti-Fascist Committee held public assemblies in several Russian cities that included the participation of Jewish poets from the Vilna Ghetto (who were flown from Vilna to Moscow), in which they reported on the Nazi atrocities perpetrated in Lithuania. (*Einikite* [Unity, the bulletin of the Jewish Anti-Fascist Committee in the USSR], no. 37 (58), Dec 16, 1943).

135. PKG, 55.

136. Information about Lithuanian Jewry under Nazi occupation most probably arrived from Soviet sources only in the fall of 1943, and even then it was highly imprecise. For example, a Lithuanian partisan who was in Moscow at the time said that no Jews at all remained in Lithuania (*Davar*, newspaper of Eretz Israel Workers, no. 5566, October 28, 1943). Abba Kovner wrote an announcement to world Jewry (at Jurgis's request) beginning with the introduction, "To the Jews of Eretz Israel, New York, and Moscow." We do not know if this announcement reached its destination, although we do know that a poem Kovner wrote in the forest, and sent together with the announcement in the same mail bundle, was printed in *Haaretz* (testimony of Abba Kovner, YVSA, 12, recording 4).

CHAPTER 12

Supply and Defense Activities

Arms Acquisition

A regular army battalion receives its needs from the supply bases, but the Death to the Occupiers battalion, like all other partisan battalions, had to obtain its own provisions, equipment, and armaments. This was extremely difficult in the first days. The weapons problem was particularly severe. Sometimes they had to borrow guns from a neighboring battalion and return them after use. The arrival of the first ghetto fighters did not solve this problem, and some of them were left weaponless or else received only short weapons (sawed-off rifles[1] or pistols). As one of the Jewish partisans relates:

> In the early period, we might say for about a month and a half, there was a great shortage. Once I went on an operation and I was given a rifle and a total of two bullets. When I returned from the operation and one of the bullets was missing, I had to report as to where this bullet went.... Only a very few of us had weapons, and at first there were no personal weapons at all. For each operation, the commander of that operation would give a weapon to whomever he saw fit.... We had weapons only for the operations. If we returned for a day or two to rest and another group went out on an operation, we would give them the weapons.[2]

---

1. A rifle whose barrel is sawed off close to the bolt, thus its popular nickname in Russian, *otrez,* "cut." Because the barrel was sawed off, it was easier for Russian prisoners to steal these from the German weapons storehouses and carry them under their coats without detection. Of course, its accuracy was poor.
2. Testimony of Michael Yitzhaki (Gelbtrunk), YVSA, 35 (recording 6b).

In the first six months of the battalion's existence, until Moscow began to parachute in mass quantities of weapons, the main source for obtaining arms was the surrounding villages, both nearby and more distant ones. The inhabitants had hidden weapons that they had collected at the beginning of the war from battlefields and defeated army units. Many of them also had weapons that the occupation authorities had distributed to the village population to use against robber bands, especially against partisans that threatened the authorities. The partisans used many methods to obtain these weapons from the villagers – promises, threats, and sometimes force.

> They did not give up [their weapons] willingly, only under threat.... Sometimes we used to beat them, and if someone knew about weapons, he would inform on his neighbors.... The first time out, we acquired a large quantity of weapons. A large group of us went, about twenty people.... But we went practically without weapons, only with pistols.... I think this was the first operation. We came to a house and the non-Jew did not want to open up. I think that he [Zeitzev][3] carried an automatic weapon. At any rate, he came, burst through the window, fired, and began to shout: "Machine gunner, ready!"...The *goy* was terrified and handed over his weapon...two rifles, and bullets. Later this *goy* told us that he had more weapons, and we received fifteen rifles in total.[4]

Even after the firepower of the battalion improved with weapons brought by the sixth group of ghetto fighters, acquisition operations remained necessary. The methods, however, became more sophisticated: instead of collecting individual rifles from a particular farmer, they began to remove weapons systematically from villages that had received them from the regime through official channels. In many cases, the very fact of entering the village with a sizeable force was enough to convince the farmers to hand over their weapons, as one of the participants in such an operation relates:

> They gathered our battalion and several others and we walked to a Lithuanian

---

3. Leib Zeitzev, a resident of Nowo-Święciany, was well acquainted with the villages in the environs, and was particularly outstanding in acquisition operations. He was a squad leader, and one of the most experienced Jewish commanders in the battalion.
4. Testimony of Eliezer Moses, YVSA, 14 (recording 4).

village that had received weapons from the Lithuanians. We surrounded the village and they were forced to bring us the weapons. Then we really obtained a large quantity of weapons.... There was no resistance – we surprised them, and only their machine gunner managed to flee.[5]

Because the fighters of the Death to the Occupiers battalion passed through the village of Strelzy when they went out on marches and missions, the Germans had armed the inhabitants and placed ambushes at the entrances to the village. Without resorting to violence, a group from the battalion succeeded in convincing the villagers to give the German weapons to the partisans.[6] When the battalion discovered that in the village of Aukštadvaris (Visoki Dvor) policemen and wealthy farmers had weapons, a group of partisans led by Baruch Lopiansky went there, took the weapons, and brought them to the base.[7]

Another group performed a similar operation under the command of Leib Zeitzev, in the Lithuanian village of Juodkaimis (Yodkaimis), near Onuškis (Anushishok).[8] The Lithuanians in the village, including the local nationalist leader, hid in a basement but were killed with hand grenades thrown inside. The spoils from this operation were fourteen rifles, three automatic rifles, one machine gun, four thousand bullets, flare guns, a radio transmitter, and other military equipment.

But all this was still not enough. The Death to the Occupiers battalion, along with the neighboring battalions, awaited weapons promised months ago by Moscow. The weapons were to be dropped by parachute but their arrival was delayed. Finally the brigade command was informed that the weapons shipment designated for its units had been parachuted into the Naliboki Forests (200 kilometers east of the Rudniki Forests, in Byelorussia).[9] A group of partisans, mostly from the Vilna battalions, was sent to collect it. Most of them, however, were killed along the difficult route by gangs of White Poles.

In late March 1944, a group was again formed for the purpose of bringing the weapons from Naliboki, with representatives from all the battalions in the

---

5. Testimony of Grisha Sheffer, YVSA, 22 (recording 6).
6. *PKG*, 135.
7. Ibid.
8. Ibid., 136. Apparently, most of the group's members were Kovno Ghetto fighters.
9. See *Sefer ha-partizanim ha-yehudim* 1:145.

RudnikiForests. It had twenty-five fighters, including sixteen Jews, six from Kovno: Eliezer Moses, Alter Feitelson, Fishka Feldman, Yankel Kaveh, Yosef Rosen, and Idel Sherman.

Following is a description of the journey as recounted by Yosef Rosen:

> They brought me to the commissar, and he informed me that they had de-cided to send me and another person in a joint group to Naliboki, where we were supposed to receive arms for this battalion. First of all, they took all of our good weapons, and gave us sawed-offs. We were lucky. The others got pistols…I think each of us received fifty bullets. The explanation was that we were going to bring back automatic weapons, and that we could leave the inferior weapons in Naliboki.[10]
>
> Because we did not know the way and our weapons were so poor, the group commander decided there was no point in sending us alone. At the first opportunity, we joined a large, well-armed company of some 150 fighters from the "Morozov" battalion. We walked by night, of course, and by day we "slept" in one of the villages we found along the way. One day we slept in a small village at the edge of the forest. In the afternoon, a farmer came to the village carrying a letter to "the partisan leader." The letter was written in Polish and signed by AK,[11] and it gave the ultimatum to put down the weapons and hand over the Jews to them. Only if the partisans accepted these conditions would they be permitted to leave the area. The letter also said that the village was surrounded by hundreds of White Poles. The commander did not hesitate for long. He soon called us to order and we started on our way even before darkness, contrary to the usual partisan procedure. The farmer who brought us the letter served as our guide. He was told that if he betrayed us and failed to rescue us from the siege – he would die. The farmer performed his job faithfully. We managed to break out of the village. Rifle and machine gun fire rained down on us from all sides.… The Morozov fighters had a mortar and they put it into action. It hit several groups of Poles, causing panic.
>
> In the meantime, we advanced rapidly eastward…until we reached the

---

10. The testimony below is taken from the witness's manuscript, *Sefer Yehudei Lita*, 50–53.
11. AK is an abbreviation for Armia Krajowa (National Army), the Polish nationalist underground ("White Poles"). According to another source, these were White Russians (compare testimony of Eliezer Moses, YVSA, 22, recording 6).

Naliboki Forests.... We advanced into the forest and reached the town of Bakshty.[12] We were surprised to find an entire town in the occupied territories that was under a true Soviet regime.... The Morozov people did not see fit to bring us into their bases but ordered the commanders in the nearby villages to board us with the farmers. Our commander went to the brigade command, to where General Platon [Vasily Yefimovich Chernyshev] was located. There he was told that although weapons had arrived for the Lithuanian partisans, they had been divided up on the spot among partisans who needed them.... Should additional airplanes arrive, the general asserted, we would also receive our portion, but in the meantime we would have to guard the airport and carry out routine partisan duties.

We knew that we would be waiting there in vain and so we decided to return immediately to the base. But how could we return alone with such poor weapons? We had no choice but to wait until the companies of the large battalions in the area entered into Lithuania [from western Byelorussia], and then we would join them.[13] In the meantime, we wandered from village to village, dependent on the villagers' generosity for bread. The rumor spread among the local fighters that the Jews did not want to fight, and that they were eating the bread of the hapless farmers. At that time, a drunken Ukrainian officer took my fine German ammunition belt that I had brought with me from the ghetto, along with the bullets. We complained about him to the Jewish commissar of the battalion, who promised to attend to the matter. But a while later we found out that the commissar was mysteriously shot while riding a horse alone in protected territory in the partisan region.

On that day we met for the first time a group of Jews from Bielski's battalion.[14] They were sleeping in the village after returning from a mission. They brought food and drink, and we spent the night together singing and dancing (we even danced the hora!). That was the first we heard about the

---

12. They journeyed this entire distance in two days and two nights (Eliezer Moses, YVSA, 23, recording 7).

13. Compare testimony of Yosef Rosen, YVSA, 32 (recording 7), and testimony of Eliezer Moses, ibid.

14. Editor's note: Tuvia Bilski and his brothers organized an independent Jewish partisan group in the formerly Polish area of western Byelorussia. The group, which also included many noncombatants, reached a total of 1,200 people. When the Soviet partisans organized in their area they became part of Platon's brigade.

large groups of Jews in Bielski's and Zorin's battalions.[15] In the sorrowful state we were in at that point we were prepared to join them at once. But we did not want to undermine the entire company because of us, and so we gave up the idea and only asked permission from our commander to celebrate May 1 with the Jewish battalion. We received permission, and went to Bielski. They welcomed us warmly....

I will never forget the experience of the May 1 party, which took place en masse in a large wooden hall. Jewish partisan children danced the well-known folkdance *sherele*. My eyes and those of my comrades-in-arms filled with tears. The entire group made a deep impression on us: six to eight hundred Jews of all ages, men and women, an enormous group; aside from this, the battalion of Jews from Minsk (four hundred people), including many youth, boys and girls.[16]

Finally we decided, the six Jews from the Rudniki battalions, to join one of the large Jewish battalions.[17] At first we remained in Bielski's brigade[18] but soon we transferred to Zorin's brigade. We received good rifles and became part of their group.[19]

---

15. Jewish commanders of two partisan battalions, most of whose fighters were Jews. Editor's note: Shalom Zorin escaped from the Minsk Ghetto and organized a Jewish partisan group that also accepted noncombatants. The Zorin group reached a total of 800 people.

16. On the emotional meeting between the escapees from Kovno Ghetto, who had a rich Jewish background, and the Jewish youth from Minsk, educated under the Komsomol from a young age, see testimony of Yosef Rosen, YVSA, 35 (recording 8). For additional details on the experience of the Jewish youth and children in the partisan camps under Zorin, see Leib Katzovitch: "*Di wald-shul bey di Minsker partizaner,*" *Einikeit* 99 (211), September 25, 1945.

17. This decision was made after stormy arguments among the six. While some of them said they should return, if only for reasons of discipline and responsibility, the others raised the emotional justification that they wanted to remain among Jews in a positive atmosphere (testimony of Yosef Rosen, YVSA, 33, recording 7). At least one of them did return to the Rudniki Forest base. "They thought I would never return, that perhaps I had been killed" (testimony of Eliezer Moses, YVSA, 23–24, recording 7).

18. "With this, Bielski, commander of the Jewish brigade, proved his Jewish solidarity and great decisiveness.... He said: I am always willing to receive Jews.... We told him that there was anti-Semitism [in the Kovno battalions]. Then he said: After the war I'll be willing to argue with them. But now, I'll accept you if you want" (testimony of Yosef Rosen, YVSA, 33, recording 8).

19. Testimony of Yosef Rosen, YVSA, 30 ff. (recording 7); compare also *Memoirs of Yosef Rosen,* manuscript, 1955, and testimony of Eliezer Moses, 22–24. After the liberation of Lithuania, several of these men met with the battalion commander, Konstatin Radyonov. He took no action but limited himself to barbed comments.

In effect, the journey to the Naliboki Forests was in vain, because only a few weeks after the mission had left a parachute drop operation was implemented at full intensity in the Rudniki Forests themselves. The nights of waiting for the weapons drop at the "airfield" were an opportunity to meet Jews from the others battalions in the area. Jews from Kovno met with Jews from Vilna and friendships were formed. One eyewitness offers a description of a weapons drop:

> Through the wireless we were promised that the central command was about to drop weapons in our forests. For this purpose, we were given the job of preparing an area where weapons could be dropped by parachute. The designated area was covered with low brush. We lit a bonfire arranged in the form of a "T." This was the agreed sign for the drop. Partisans who were off duty from operations or guard duty were ordered to spread throughout the forest to collect the dropped weapons. Often we arrived at the drop point in commotion and elation, but the airplanes were delayed, whether due to the poor weather conditions or enemy fire that blocked their path.
>
> I remember that night clearly. We sat around the bonfires, tense with anticipation. Suddenly, from afar, we heard the dim sound of motors approaching. The clatter of the airplanes filled the forest. The fires blazed and everyone rushed over the broad expanse designated for the drop. The three airplanes flew low, flashing friendly signals. They disappeared, then appeared again and dropped the load of heavy sacks. The fighters collected the sacks, their faces glowing with joy, and loaded them on carts. Most of the parachutes fell nearby but some were dropped far off, and we had to comb the forest until the early hours of the morning. The bundles, about 2 meters long, were wrapped well in sacks of khaki cloth padded with cotton.. Unfortunately, some of the parachutes didn't open and the armaments arrived ruined and unfit for use. Some were repaired in the unit workshops. Comics made use of these weapons, and said that the rifles with the crooked barrels would be given to the cowards, who shot backwards. The drop included anti-tank rifles, mortars, machine guns, sniper rifles, silencers, submachine guns of the latest model, various types of ammunition, explosives, British cigarettes, medicines, and blood plasma.[20]

---

20. Selection from the record "In the Ghetto and the Forest," by Zvi Shefer (*Sefer ha-partizanim ha-yehudim*, 2:528–29).

The supplies were distributed among the units according to their combat activities.

Supplies

The partisans generally relied on two sources for supplies: (1) German food stores, or farms and estates managed by German settlers; and (2) local farmers in the surrounding area. Sources of the first type were particularly rare in the Rudniki Forest area, and so the partisans were forced to rely on the farmers alone, whose situation in this area was quite poor. This led to a conflict with the political goals of the Lithuanian partisan movement. On the one hand, they had to make allies of the farmers, to convert them into supporters of the Soviet regime and use them as intelligence agents. But on the other hand, they needed their agricultural produce and animals.

This was a serious weak point in the relationship of the fighters with their villager neighbors, who were willing to give up hidden weapons but would never agree to the theft of the fruits of their labor, not even for the most important goals.[21] They were unable to distinguish between the German officials and the partisan groups, both of which came to take what they held most dear. These economic activities led the farmers to despise the partisans. They found an ally in the German regime, which continued its propaganda against the "Red Bandits" and also armed the farmers and organized them in defense units against the partisans.[22]

So as not to overdo their demands, the leadership gave the fighters rules for behavior with the farmers and guidelines about what they could and could not take from them. A fighter from the Forward battalion relates: "Our instructions were not to impoverish the farmers. Our behavior had to be fair.... If a farmer had two cows, we took one cow. If he had only one cow – we did not take it. If he had a few pigs, we would take some, but we always left some. In most of the

---

21. When referring to the partisans, they often used the term "bandits," or even "dear bandits." Their hatred was especially vitriolic toward Jewish fighters (see also Lazer, 240, and Apyvala, 110).

22. The German authorities fanned the farmers' hatred and adopted a number of measures to discredit the partisans in the eyes of the population. For example, the Germans encouraged gangs of bandits to rob the farmers and present themselves as Red Partisans. In these cases, the partisan command did not hesitate to fight these gangs and return the booty to the farmers (Mončiunskas, 121).

operations in which I participated, we complied with this practice and order." [23]
The fighters were also forbidden to take from the farmers items or food for themselves, as one of the women fighters recounts: "At first we asked for a great deal. Then it was forbidden.... At first we would take blankets; later it was forbidden to touch them. This was an order from above, that we must not take them." [24]

At the beginning they were not particularly careful about obeying this order. But the approach of the front and, along with this, the strengthening of the policy of friendship with the farmers – citizens of the future Lithuanian republic – led to stricter supervision on this issue and even severe punishments for those who broke the prohibition.

For a certain time, they followed the procedure popular in the villages of Byelorussia of giving the farmers written "receipts" for their items. [25] The purpose of the "receipts" was twofold: to serve as an alibi for the farmers when the German officials came to demand a certain percentage of their produce, according to the laws of the occupation regime; and to partially assuage the farmer's feeling of discrimination and involve him in supporting the representatives of the Soviet Army, who would repay them when the time came.

But these methods of placation were not enough to change the farmers' opinions. They did not accept the partisans showing up to requisition their produce and resorted to the most extreme means of resistance, even calling on German forces to drive out the unwanted guests. Only rarely were the partisans able to perform a supply operation without interference. Therefore every supply operation was planned and organized with the same standards of caution, stringency, and security of any other military operation, and even more so. Unlike other combat actions, which were performed with speed and the element of surprise, a supply mission lasted much longer. In addition, on the way back the convoy was an easy target as it crawled slowly with its heavy load. The main weak points were the river crossings; sometimes these sites became bloody battlefields and they had to abandon the booty and flee. There was no room for surprise here, because the farmers constantly anticipated these operations. Supply operations, therefore, were performed by a relatively large force (fifteen to twenty-five fighters) with

23. Testimony of Grisha Sheffer, YVSA, 19 (recording 6).
24. Testimony of Gita Foger-Turchin, YVSA, 10 (recording 3).
25. Compare testimonies of Baruch Gofer (Grodnick), YVSA, 16 (recording 5), and Yosef Rosen, YVSA, 31 (recording 7).

impressive weapons, mainly for deterrence. Treatment of farmers had to be fair, yet aggressive and strict.

Following is a typical description of a supply operation, in which almost all the participants were fighters from the Kovno Ghetto:

> After each one checked his weapon, we left the base. We were twenty-five fighters, most from the ghetto, divided into five squads with a leader for each one. . . . The route to the site of the operation, decided in advance by the command based on various considerations, was long. We did not usually conduct acquisition operations in the nearby villages, first of all because most of them were "friendly villages," and second because at any rate there was nothing left there to take. As a result of the operations conducted there in the past, most of the farmers had nothing left beyond the protected minimum (one cow, one pig, produce for food, seeds). Each time we had to go farther away from the base and penetrate deep into open enemy territory, which raised the level of risk and transformed each acquisition operation into a combat or semi-combat operation. The group was heavily armed: four machine guns, six or seven submachine guns, and the rest – rifles. Almost everyone had two or three hand grenades as well.
>
> We reached the designated village around midnight, after walking rapidly some 25 kilometers. The village was sunk deep in sleep. We surrounded it silently. In the middle of the village was a junction of four dirt roads. At the head of each of these roads we placed two people with a machine gun. The rest of the squads spread out among the houses. Dogs barked and lights began to flicker in the windows, signaling the beginning of the operation.
>
> When the door was opened, a strong odor of village food and dense air reached our nostrils as a Lithuanian farmer appeared in a long nightgown. "Get dressed and quietly open the stable, the pigpen, and the barn. We've come to take supplies for the unit," my partner hurled at the shocked farmer, half-asleep.
>
> "Are you partisans? But just yesterday some were here. They took everything from me, not even one sack of flour is left. Go to the neighbor. . . ."
>
> "We'll see. Or have you already managed to hide your goods and put them aside for the Germans? Hurry up!" As he spoke, he gave the farmer a slight push with his rifle. Wonder of wonders: the farmer changed his demeanor immediately, as if touched by a magic wand, and he appeared to wake up. He

began to run back and forth energetically. He opened the barn, where three cows dozed peacefully, took us into the pigpen and allowed us to choose the fattest of his pigs, and took out several sacks of flour from the storehouse.

"Enough, enough, now harness your horse and cart; in the meantime we'll manage with your pig. You'll get the horse and cart back tomorrow afternoon, and one day the Soviet authorities will pay you back double for the supplies." I stayed in order to help the owner bring up several sacks of flour from the storehouse, and my companion disappeared into the pigpen. The pen gate closed, and a few minutes later a muffled shot was heard – he "managed" with the pig....

About an hour after midnight, all the squads were ready. Full carts clattered over the village paths, all in one direction – to the meeting point. The machine gunners were collected from their positions, and the entire group began the journey back to the base. We still had a long, dangerous road ahead of us, twice as dangerous as the way coming. Previously, we had been empty and light. We could advance cautiously and we were not so afraid of a clash with the enemy. But now things were more complicated. We were burdened by heavy baggage, leading half a dozen cows, driving carts that made an infuriating, bone-penetrating noise.

We arrived at the most dangerous juncture: a river 20 meters wide, and we had no choice but to cross it at one of the shallow points. We barely managed to push our cows into the water when suddenly the horses startled. What was going on? In his rush, one of the partisans did not notice that the farmer had harnessed a giant stallion. When the stallion got a whiff of the fresh water with several mares crowding around him, its desire was kindled. It emitted a powerful neigh that echoed throughout the forest, uprighted the cart, and swiftly attacked one of the targets of its desire. The situation began to be serious. This equine allure could reveal our presence in the forest and bring upon us serious trouble. Quickly we released the stallion from its trappings and with sticks drove it back toward the village. We divided the load from the cart among the other carts and crossed the river safely. We journeyed the rest of the route without incident and at dawn entered the area of our brigade. The unit storehouses were again filled with meat, potatoes, flour, and other supplies.... [26]

---

26. *Sefer ha-partizanim ha-yehudim* 1:241–43.

Over time, the partisans learned to choose their supply sources so as to avoid clashes with an entire village. They did so, for example, in the "Flour Operation" at the mill near Rudnia (Rudmye). Extended surveillance by the battalion scouts enabled them to determine on which days the mill stores were full of ground flour. At that point partisans were sent to take the flour, before the stock was again depleted.[27]

We should also mention the "Sugar Operation," a coincidental opportunity. Fighters who had gone out on a special mission came across a convoy of carts carrying large quantities of sugar. They overtook the convoy, brought reinforcements from the forest, and took the sugar to the base. This item, which lasted for many days, improved the battalion's nourishment and was also used for barter.[28]

Intelligence

Intelligence operations, mainly carried out by the reconnaissance units, required the assistance of the surrounding population. For this reason, the partisans had to create friendly relationships with the residents of the nearby villages and choose from among them appropriate individuals for various supporting roles.[29] These were all called "contacts," but their jobs varied according to their abilities and level of trustworthiness. Some supplied military information about activities within their villages; others served as guides. At a higher level were individuals who were sent to German army camps as laborers, or to other places where the partisans did not have access, in order to survey troop movements or check results of battles and sabotage.[30] The highly trustworthy were appointed as "main contacts," and they independently managed intelligence networks among their acquaintances. Others were "significant contacts," who operated systematically and broadly. They were subordinate to the central intelligence staff of the brigade.[31]

The process of strengthening relations with the farmers and recruiting

---

27. Testimony of Grisha Sheffer, YVSA, 20 (recording 5); testimony of Yosef Rosen, YVSA, 20 (recording 4).

28. Mottel Brick, FLC 10:17–18; testimony of Yosef Rosen, YVSA, 19.

29. Kutka, 67.

30. *Sefer ha-partizanim ha-yehudim* 1:109.

31. Compare Hannan Maggid's description of the Jewish reconnaissance unit in the Revenge partisan battalion (*Davar* 6303, April 15, 1946).

contacts was slow and arduous. It demanded patience, tact, and a thorough understanding of the mentality of the local population. Time and again, a Lithuanian farmer living among Poles would agree to collaborate after Lithuanian-speaking scouts convinced him that cooperation with the partisans supported his patriotic aspirations. This was also the case with Byelorussian farmers, Poles, and other nationalities. Aside from the psychological treatment and promises for the future, some of the contacts received material compensation, in goods or money, according to the importance of the information they supplied.[32] Contact with farmers was made with extreme caution and complete secrecy, to avoid arousing the interest of the neighbors. On the other hand, the partisans took measures to prevent these contacts from betraying their operators. One of these measures was using the security of family members as a guarantee of loyalty.

The intelligence unit of the Kovno battalions, under the command of Boris Lisauskas, set up headquarters in the nearby village of Stary-Marczel, in the home of a veteran contact, the farmer Jurgelevitch. They also had intelligence agents in the villages of Žagarinė, Inklariskis, Vishnicza, and others.

But until an information network was established and contacts were found, the unit members themselves collected material first-hand, with all the danger involved. In one of these operations, fighter Moshe Milner of Kovno Ghetto was killed. When returning to base with his partner, the Russian Sifroni Orlov, after obtaining the required information, they fell into a German ambush near Novy-Marczel. Under cover of Milner's fire, his partner fled with the information and brought it to the base. The Germans surrounded Milner, and to avoid falling into their hands alive, he shot himself with his last remaining bullet.[33]

Some time later, the unit's commander was killed by the Germans in the home of contact Jurgelevitch.[34] Boris the scout (nicknamed "Little" Boris) was appointed to replace him.

Punishments

Together with the bloody war against the German forces, the partisans waged a fierce struggle against collaborators. At first they warned them and pressured

---

32. Compare *Sefer ha-partizanim ha-yehudim* 1:109.
33. PKG, 144; Meir Leib Goldschmidt, YVSA, letter 7.
34. With regard to the punishments meted out in retaliation, see below.

them to recant;[35] if this didn't work, they used extreme measures of reprisal so that all "would observe and be forewarned." For example, they captured in Dainava village the infamous Polish agent Boleslav Utzkoronis, who organized the farmers against the partisans. He was taken to the Vilna base camp and sentenced to death.[36]

Sometimes they had no choice but to place collective responsibility on a group of farmers or on entire villages. A clear example of collective punishment was the case of Koniuchy village.

The Lithuanian village of Koniuchy, which numbered three hundred inhabitants, was located 30 kilometers from the base of the Kovno battalions. It collaborated closely and systematically with the Germans and with Plechavičius's people.[37] Its inhabitants even actively attacked partisan units that passed close to the village, and tortured to death those whom they captured alive. The village itself was well fortified with defense excavations, sniper positions, and lookout towers. The villagers were warned several times but they still did not cease their hostile activities.

The brigade command decided to attack the village with a sizeable force and completely destroy it, to serve as a harsh lesson for other villagers. The Lithuanian Shilas, a partisan commander, succeeded in infiltrating the village disguised as an officer of a Plechavičius unit who had come to investigate the village's preparedness. Indeed, he checked the village defense system, surveyed the points of weakness, and returned with a detailed report for the brigade command.[38]

At Jurgis's orders, a collective force was recruited with representatives from all the battalions. It was composed of 150 people,[39] twenty-five from the Kovno battalions. At midnight the force reached the entrance to the village, and after a

---

35. For the text of the proclamation read to collaborators, see Kutka, 271.
36. Lazer, 303–4.
37. The largest and most important Lithuanian formation was established by the Germans in Lithuania from locals. These were the "local units" (*Vietines Rinktines*) under the command of the Lithuanian general Povilas Plechavičius, also known by the populace as "Plechavičius's people." Their role was (1) war against the partisans; (2) purification of Lithuania from pro-Soviet elements; and (3) repression of elements that expressed dissatisfaction with the regime of the collaborator General Petras Kubiliūnas.
38. *Sefer ha-partizanim ha-yehudim* 1:123.
39. According to *Sefer ha-partizanim ha-yehudim*, ibid. According to other sources – 120 fighters, including forty to fifty Jews (compare Lazer, 306).

short battle, the partisans crushed the fierce resistance of the Koniuchy inhabitants. Many began to flee from the village, but they were destroyed by ambush
units. Following the battle, the entire village was set afire. Toward morning, all
that remained of this sizeable village was a pile of ash. Only a few were able to
flee. The operation was mainly characterized by cruel hand-to-hand combat
and merciless aggression, and outstanding fighters were David Tepper, Ya'akov
(Yankel) Ratner, Pesach Wolbe, Lazer Zodikov, Leib Zeitzev, and other fighters
from Kovno Ghetto who were the first to storm the village.[40]

This punishment mission, whose scope and manner of performance were
unprecedented in the history of the Lithuanian brigade, had many repercussions.
The occupation authorities were quick to describe the cruelty of the "bandits" in
detail. Many of the fighters were also surprised at the form of the operation and
its cruelty.[41] But the local farmers came to their own conclusions. Their attacks
against passing partisans ceased, ties with the Germans loosened, and several
villages, including Setrelzy, handed over their weapons to the partisans.

Another, smaller operation for collective punishment was carried out by the
Death to the Occupiers battalion on its own initiative. It took place in March
1944, after the Germans had attacked the commander of the intelligence unit,
Boris Lisauskas, mortally wounding him. The attack took place in the home of
the farmer Jurgelevitch, and there was no doubt that he was the one who had
betrayed Lisauskas. As one of the fighters relates:

> We maintained a defense unit in this village of ours. It was Stary-Marczel....
> Boris went out there and sent the unit home.... He stayed with his *goyishe*
> woman.... Apparently, the Germans wanted to catch him alive. She seems
> to have convinced him there was no more need [for the unit], and they [her
> parents] contacted [the Germans] and told them there were no more parti-
> sans in the village and they could surprise him.... When he heard the shots,
> he managed to escape, and then they wounded him in the stomach.... The
> *vastochniks* routed the Germans, and we ran after them, but it was too late.[42]

---

40. *PKG*, 134.

41. Compare *Sefer ha-partizanim ha-yehudim* 1:124.

42. Testimony of Grisha Sheffer, YVSA, 23 (recording 6). See also testimony of Haim Gechtel
(Galin), YVSA, 37 (recording 12).

Boris died of his wounds and was buried at the base with military honors. That day, the partisans discovered that it was indeed an act of treachery. They decided on a reprisal action. That evening the battalion again made preparations and went out to Stary-Marczel to exact payment from the traitor's family. The entire family was killed. Their property was loaded onto a cart that had also belonged to Jurgelevitch and was brought to the base. The house was destroyed and stood empty until the liberation. The only memorial to the family was the noble horse that brought the bounty cart to the base, and from that day on it was called by the name of Jurgelevitch.[43]

Although this was a cruel act, the feeling of the participants was that this was a necessary evil. A participant who was a ghetto fighter asserts: "I do not know if there was any reason to think much about such things. They deserved this punishment...and there was no other way."[44]

For the Jewish fighters, the punishment missions were also a kind of revenge against murderers of Jews. The partisans' enemies and the collaborators were all anti-Semites, and most of them had participated in the murder of their Jewish neighbors. As the Jewish partisan Michael Gelbtrunk recounts:

> In one place there was a farmer whom we trusted. He gave us information, but I was completely certain that he was collaborating against the Jews. I even found several Torah parchments decorating the walls of his house. Others said that he killed Jews in the neighboring village and in all those places. At any rate, the Russians did not allow us to harm him, because he was necessary to them and was in contact with the partisans.[45] But usually, when we arrived at some village and found out that a certain farmer collaborated and killed Jews or Russians, then there was only one retribution, both for the Jews and for the Russians.... That is what we did to one *goy* – we beat him so badly that I'm sure he died...because some people reported that he had recounted how he had participated in an operation [against Jews].[46]

---

43. Compare PKG, 144.

44. Testimony of Baruch Gofer (Grodnick), YVSA, 25 (recording 7).

45. Often the Jewish partisans were accused of having an overdeveloped sense of vengeance, which aroused the fury of the village population (compare *Sefer ha-partizanim ha-yehudim* 1:124).

46. Testimony of Michael Yitzhaki (Gelbtrunk), YVSA, 36 (recording 6b).

Just as the punishment missions were sometimes extremely cruel in administering collective punishment, there were also incidents of vengeance against individuals that shared the same cruelty and character of collective responsibility. As Gelbtrunk describes:

> There was one family whose son served in the Polish police in Trok (Trakai).... We came to the parents and informed them that the son must report [to us]. If not, we would pay him back.... He did not appear, so we burned down the house with his father and mother inside.

CHAPTER 13

Partisan Missions

Combat Operations

One of the strategies used by the Germans against the partisans was the establishment of a network of garrisons in key locations, most in the heart of partisan territory.[1] These garrisons were comprised of a nucleus of military staff trained in combat against the partisans (*Jagdkommando* – "hunting units") along with supporting units of collaborators from the local population. Their role was to stop the partisan activity in the area and send rapid assistance to villages and other places attacked by the partisans. They served as bases for punitive expeditions and for training agents from the local population to infiltrate the partisan camps. They also provided shelter for collaborators who feared partisan revenge.

The Germans maintained several such garrisons in the Rudniki Forests, particularly in the village of Večioriškiai, about 10 kilometers from the base. It was stuck like a bone in the throat of the Kovno brigade territory and was a constant threat.

In February 1944, the partisans learned of increased movement of Germans in the village of Žagarinė, just a few kilometers from the Kovno brigade base. A small force of partisans under the command of Boris Lisauskas surprised the Germans, who had begun to establish themselves in this village, and frightened them away. Simultaneously, they carried out a sabotage operation at the barracks where the German forces were billeted (inside the village school). They

---

1. For more information on the counter measures that the Germans implemented systematically and extensively in the occupied areas of the USSR, see Dixon, chs. 6–7; Viršulis, 163; *Hitlerine*, 302.

set the water tower on fire and blew up the train station and two engines that were parked there. They also dismantled many kilometers of the railroad track.[2]

The second garrison that threatened the partisans was located in the village of Večioriškiai. It had several sawmills, as well as storehouses for the wood products from the area and factories for building huts for the German army. The village also served as an important junction, as a narrow gauge railroad track and the Vilna-Grodno road passed through it. A system of fortifications and military posts were set up there, overlooking the surrounding area. Barbed wire fences, foxholes, and other installations prevented any approach to this post. The military unit camped here was composed of German officer staff, several Lithuanian companies, and twenty-five Russian POWs who were in a special training school for anti-partisan espionage. Agents and collaborators from the local population also came here between missions in order to receive instructions and equipment and to report on their activities.[3]

As long as the three Kovno battalions were weak with regard to personnel and weapons, they circumvented Večioriškiai when going out on sabotage and acquisition operations and avoided entering its environs. But after the battalions grew with the arrival of groups from the Kovno Ghetto, the situation changed. First, the limited area in which they had operated until that point was insufficient for their supply needs. Second, their strength had increased to such an extent[4] that they could take on this irritant and completely destroy it. This was essential, because they feared that the Germans would use it as a base for anti-partisan operations as well as for general pursuit of them.

The partisan headquarters decided to attack Večioriškiai and began careful planning and preparation. They sent scouts to survey the emplacements from up close and interrogate local residents. Weapons were repaired and carefully inspected. On April 9, 1944, the "ready" order was given to fighters of the three battalions that were at the base at that time (about 180 people). The Forward battalion commander, Captain Zeika, was appointed commander of the operation.

The fighters left the base in a column at approximately one hour before midnight on the first night of Passover. They carried about one hundred rifles of

---

2. Testimony of Yisrael Joels, YVSA, 8; compare PKG, 135.
3. According to information that reached the battalion intelligence unit, the agent Jurgelevitch (see chapter 12) received his orders from this location.
4. In the meantime, they had received parachute drops of weapons.

all types, fifty submachine guns, twelve machine guns, one anti-tank rifle, and one light mortar. A squad of scouts was in the lead, assisted by a young Russian named Petushkov, a former prisoner-of-war who was well acquainted with the area of the objective.[5]

When they arrived at the forest, they organized in a nearby grove and the force divided into three parts.[6] The attack force, under the command of Captain Mishka Trushin, was responsible for destroying the two main facilities at the post. Its first target was the house of the German officers of the *forschutz-kommando* (border patrol), a two-story building with green shutters that stood on a hill in the center of the camp. The second target was the guard building and several huts and smaller buildings occupied by the regional forest manager and the school for anti-partisan espionage.

The sabotage platoon, under the command of Mikhail Shatchipkov, was responsible for completely destroying the enemy facilities: the railroad track, the telephone and wireless, the tar factory, huts, and the equipment warehouses in the camp.

The blocking force, under the command of Lieutenant Seryozha, was to spread out alongside the road to Jašiūnai, from where they expected reinforcements to arrive for the besieged enemy.[7]

Michael Pasternak, formerly a military instructor for the JFO in the Kovno Ghetto, describes the battle in his testimony:

> In this operation, I served as a machine gunner; my number two was Zamke Brenner. Before the attack I lay along with the other fighters of the attack force close to the barbed wire fence of the garrison, across from the large two-story house with the green shutters. The plan was to use a rifle with a silencer

---

5. Petushkov was captured in late March 1944 by fighters Yankel Birger and Dov Levin while on their way to the "Concealed Guard." He was wearing a German uniform and armed with a rifle. He was accepted into the Death to the Occupiers battalion. After the war, information was obtained that he had completed the German espionage school in Večioriškiai, but for various reasons had deserted. A Soviet military tribunal found him guilty of treason and sentenced him to death.

6. Compare testimony of Yisrael Joels, YVSA, 8, and PKG, 148.

7. According to another source, this force was also supposed to attack the guard building (Michael Yitzhaki [Gelbtrunk], YLGH 21:140).

to "take down" the sentry who guarded the front of the house.[8] The sentry sensed the rustle, and we did not manage to surprise the Germans. He fired, awakening the Germans, who began to rain down on us rapid machine-gun fire from the windows of the big house on the hill. Then Mishka Trushin, commander of the attack force, gave the order to break through the fence and make a frontal attack on the house.... I advanced with the machine gun along with the others through the hole in the fence.... As ordered, I reached the left side of the big house, where I took up my position. In the meantime, the other fighters had suppressed the fire coming from the house.... The Germans who were still alive fled to a bunker and continued to fire at us from there, while we fired back at them.[9]

One of the fighters describes the seizure of the officers' house:

We approached the officers' house from the left. We stopped before reaching the barbed wire fence. Another commander was supposed to begin the attack. We were supposed to wait and enter the battle at the decisive moment. When we reached the barbed wire fence, a distance of 30 meters from the house, we lay on the ground and began to cut the wire. Moments later, the battle flared up. The shots came from our right. We saw machine-gun fire coming from the front of the house. Trushin gave the order to advance. We burst into the yard and took positions on the left, about 15 meters from the building. We began to shoot. The Germans did not return fire from the windows of the house. Then Trushin ordered us to storm the building.

I began to run. I ran behind my direct commander, Mishka "the cripple." He threw a hand grenade at the house, but it did not explode. Then he ordered me to throw another grenade. I threw it into the window. We heard the explosion. But no shots came from the house. Then we were ordered to charge inside.

I entered through the back door. On the balcony I found an abandoned machine gun. It was still red-hot. Inside the house we met up with our fighters. I watched them escort out of the building the family of the forest keeper,

8. The job of eliminating the sentry was given to sniper Shapiznikov, who had the "Voroshilov sniper" honorary badge, awarded for top sniper skill.
9. Testimony of Michael Pasternak, YVSA, 4. Compare Michael Yitzhaki (Gelbtrunk), YLGH 21:140; testimony of Yisrael Joels, YVSA, 8; PKG, 148.

who was in the service of the Germans, and several German officers. We found ammunition and rifles in the building. We also took food and blankets. Finally we were ordered to set the building on fire.[10]

Outstanding fighters in the hand-to-hand battle inside the house were Zondel Shtrom, Yudel Eidelman, Hanne Padison, Shlomo Abramovitz, and Baruch Lopiansky. Lopiansky jumped into an open window from which machine-gun fire was spewing, and crushed the skull of the gunner with the butt of his rifle.[11] During the attack, Kalman Goldstein was wounded in the thigh.[12]

While four squads led by their commanders (Hirsch Shmuliakov, Peretz Padison, Eliezer Zodikov, and Shimon Bloch) attacked and neutralized the remaining enemy forces in the huts, the sabotage unit under the command of Mikhail Shatchipkov successfully performed its role unhindered. Most of the installations in the area and environs, including the fuel tanks, were set on fire. Still, some of the German forces managed to flee to Rudniki.

The error was that before the attack the partisans did not cut off the telephone lines, and the Germans apparently were able to call Jašiūnai and demand reinforcements.[13] This hastened the end of the operation, and with the first rays of dawn the partisans began to depart. The attacking force began to return toward the base, with spoils of weapons, equipment, personal supplies, and German prisoners. But the blocking force, under the command of Lieutenant Seryozha, was delayed – it lay in ambush on the road to Jašiūnai in order to prevent the arrival of German reinforcements.

> We moved away rapidly on paths leading to the forest. From afar we saw the building go up in flames. Soon after, we reached the group meeting place, and we heard the echo of shots.... We wondered: What happened? Where were the shots coming from? When we reached the spot, we found that our blocking force was missing, as well as several scouts that were with Captain Zeika, whose job was to maintain contact among the companies. We waited

---

10. Testimony of Zvie Brown, YLHG 21:138–39.
11. PKG, 149.
12. Testimony of Yisrael Joels, YVSA, 8.
13. Ibid.

for them, but they did not come. The whole time we heard the echoes of shots from afar. We understood that something was not right.[14]

At that moment a fierce battle was being waged between uneven forces – the blocking unit and a powerful German force that had arrived from far off in vehicles. The advantages in forces and firepower of the enemy, which now fought on favorable terms and in daylight, decided the battle.[15]

According to farmers in the area who were interrogated afterwards by the general reconnaissance unit and the search detail of the Vladas Baronas battalion, the members of the blocking force fought valiantly, and when they had used up their bullets, they threw hand grenades. Fighter Tania (Teibele) Vinishesky, wounded in the arm and the last one left alive, raised her hands in response to the Germans' call to surrender. She allowed them to approach, and when four Germans came to take her prisoner, she pulled out a grenade and exploded together with them. Farmers buried their corpses in a mass grave.[16]

The partisans later discovered that the commander, Seryozha, had abandoned his unit before the battle and hid with his girlfriend Pola deep in the forest. Because he feared a military tribunal, he attempted to prepare an alibi. He thus reported to Captain Zeika, commander of the operation, and declared that the Jews in his unit were spreading fear among the fighters and refusing to obey his orders. The captain ordered him to return immediately to duty, but Seryozha did not obey this order and went back to hide in the forest.[17]

When the news reached the base, deep mourning and unconcealed anger at Seryozha's behavior reigned. The fighters demanded that he be tried. But Commissar Davidov attempted to cover up the incident. He said, "Perhaps there is a basis to his assertion. We know that you are not military people." The matter

---

14. Zvie Brown, YLHG 21:138.

15. Thirteen of the sixteen members of this unit who were killed were Jews from the Kovno Ghetto, most from the Vladas Baronas battalion. Their names: Simha Idelson, Aharon Manyeskin (an escapee from the Ninth Fort), Lola Eckman, Shlomo Birger, Haim Berman, Yankel Holtzman, Yitzhak Volk, Mottel Taratatzky, Ya'akov Sisnitzky, David Sendler, Yuka Fabrovsky, Moshe Reichman, and Zalman Kravitz.

16. Testimony of Yisrael Joels, YVSA, 9; see also record of Michael Yitzhaki (Gelbtrunk), YLHG 21:140; PKG, 150.

17. Testimonies of Haim Gechtel (Galin), YVSA, 46 (recording 15); Malka Pugatzky-Smali, YVSA, 24 (recording 7). Zvie Brown, YLHG 21:139.

reached Jurgis, chief commander of the Lithuanian partisans.[18] Jurgis appointed Commissar Misha Balkin, a Jew from Moscow, as investigative judge. The investigation lasted for two days, after which Seryozha was convicted and shot. The site where the sentence was carried out was called "Traitors' Swamp."[19]

Although the partisans were used to fighters dying on an almost daily basis, the relatively large number of dead and the circumstances of the incident left an impression on the battalion, mainly on the Jewish fighters, for a long time. One fighter describes his concrete expression of this feeling: "After the operation in Večioriškiai, in which we lost sixteen partisans, including Yankel [Sisnitzky], I remember that I could not stop thinking about it.... For a long time I walked around in pain. The next day I stood beside a tree and carved his name on it with a Star of David."[20]

But despite the tragic circumstances and the substantial damage caused to the spirit of the fighters in the battalion, in general the operation was a victory for the partisans: the force at the village post had been eliminated, and the Germans no longer maintained regular troops there.

The third garrison that threatened the partisans was located in the town of Rudniki, in the heart of the Rudniki Forests. This district capital had several installations of military importance, such as a train station and railroad junction, the bridge over the Merechanka River, the district telephone exchange, and factories for explosives and tar. In addition, this town served as an administrative center for the German authorities in the area. For tactical and other reasons a frontal attack on Rudniki was not possible, and at that time they decided on limited harassment actions in several stages.

In the first stage, the combat company of Death to the Occupiers battalion was ordered to blow up the train station and render it completely useless, so that the town's local forces would be cut off from sources of reinforcements. This

18. This incident had a strong reverberation throughout the partisan forest. The Jewish command of the Vilna battalions raised it before the central command of the brigade (testimony of Abba Kovner, YVSA, 14).

19. Testimony of Baruch Gofer (Grodnik), YVSA, 26–27 (recording 7); Malka Pugatzky-Smali, YVSA, 24 (recording 7): Gita Foger-Turchin, YVSA, 11 (recordings 3–4); Haim Gechtel (Galin), YVSA, 37 (recording 15). See also Zvie Brown, YLHG 21:139.

20. Testimony of Haim Gechtel (Galin), YVSA, 33 (recording 11); compare his record "Zecht-zen un einer" (Sixteen plus one) in Dror, the movement newspaper in German, April 30, 1947, 12 (8):11.

would make the next operations easier. According to the operation plan, the attack force was to storm the train station. Simultaneously, it would blow up a freight train that was about to reach the station and in which two mines had been placed.

Due to a technical fault, only one mine blew up under the engine, and several cars rolled off the tracks. The train was stopped, but the Germans took up positions behind the cars and the engine and opened heavy fire. The two machine gunners, Haim Wolbe and Zondel Shtrom, charged the German machine gunner, who was shooting constantly from behind the armored engine. As they approached the engine, the machine gun Wolbe was holding jammed, and he was fatally wounded by enemy fire. Fighters Yankel Birger[21] and Batka[22] rushed to his aid, drawing most of the enemy fire to themselves. Within a few moments, Birger and Batka were both killed by machine-gun fire, and Zondel Shtrom was the only one left. But during the time these four kept the Germans occupied, the other partisans surrounded the enemy and lay down a formidable crossfire. The Germans panicked. Most of them were wounded by partisan fire. A few managed to escape, and seven surrendered, while an anti-tank machine gun, twenty rifles, and thousands of bullets were taken as spoil.

Despite the relative success the partisans enjoyed in this battle, they still had not achieved the goal that the command had set for the mission – destruction of the train station.

The second stage of the operation was initiated just before May 1, 1944, this time with the participation of the three battalions. The partisans approached the town of Rudniki from three directions, and the blocking unit, which included Shechne (Shraga) Shilin, mined the roads to prevent reinforcements from reaching the Germans. Fighters Peretz Kliatchko, Frieda Rothstein, and Rachel Lifschitz crawled undetected to the new bridge over the Merechanka River and blew it up along with the German guards on top of it. When they heard the massive explosion, the other fighters burst out from all around and attacked the garrison with cries of "Hoora!" Heavy fire forced Germans to stay in their

---

21. Before this mission, Yankel Birger, whose cousin Shlomo Birger died in the Večioriškiai battle, begged to be transferred to the combat company in order to avenge his cousin's death (PKG, 151-52).

22. "Father" in Russian. This was the nickname of partisan Vicenti Markovitz, due to his relatively advanced age of sixty.

positions.[23] Those who attempted to break out from the barracks were wounded by the sharpshooting of Aharon Vilenchuk and Moshe and Sarah Robinson, who took up positions across from its doors.

While the Germans were pinned down in their positions, the sabotage units performed their mission. One team, including Berel Stern and Shlomo Breuer, blew up the telephone exchange; a second team, which included Katriel Koblenz and Hanne Padison, set the tar factory on fire; and the third team blew up the railroad track. Throughout the entire operation, the fighters suffered no losses. On the holiday of May 1, celebrated with great festivity in the camp, an atmosphere of victory and great satisfaction prevailed. Indeed, the town of Rudniki ceased to be a threat to the partisans.[24]

Sabotage

Sabotage of the German military machine was considered to be the greatest achievement of the partisan operations. The sabotage activities brought no material benefit to the units, unlike other operations, such as acquisition, supply, punishment, and "preventive combat," which ensured the battalions their continued existence and relative security. Furthermore, they brought in their wake harsh reprisals by the Germans and widely spread manhunts.[25] Still, ideological factors meant that the sabotage operations became the ambition and badge of honor, both of the partisan organization and of each individual. Battalions and brigades competed among themselves for their achievements in this area. Every self-respecting partisan tried to participate actively in as many sabotage operations as possible and to earn the title "Derailer of X Number of Enemy Trains."

The goals and forms of sabotage were varied. For example, the partisans disrupted enemy transportation in many ways, such as dismantling railroad tracks or mining them, or through roadblocks or ambushes; they sabotaged

---

23. Machine gunner Michael Pasternak and his "number two," Natan Issacson, emptied seventeen bullet cartridges – an enormous amount in forest conditions (PKG, 154).
24. Rudniki was occupied by partisan forces in early July 1944, with the liberation of Vilna by the Soviet army. For details, see chapter 15.
25. The Germans carried out three harsh manhunts against the Lithuanian brigade in the Rudniki Forests. The first was on September 9, 1943; the second in late winter 1944, in which Kovno Ghetto fighter David Goldin tragically lost his life (see chapter 11, "Rules of Conduct"); and the third in June 1944. For a description of the temporary evacuation of partisan forces, see Lazer, 354–55.

communications by sawing telegraph and telephone poles or blowing them up, or destroying the telephone exchanges. The method chosen depended on the equipment needed – explosives or incendiary material; on the supporting weapons and number of personnel trained in their use; and on other conditions such as distance of the target from the effective range of the enemy, or dependence on the schedule of a complex operation of a different character. As described above, several sabotage acts were carried out together with acquisition operations, destruction of garrisons, and other missions.

Sabotage operations could be performed under certain conditions, the most important being that the partisan unit was well established from the standpoint of supplies and relative security.[26] But this does not mean that each partisan unit waited until it reached its full strength, and meanwhile completely avoided participation in any type of sabotage. For example, Death to the Occupiers battalion performed several sabotage missions against enemy trains when it was still a small, weak group. Misha Meirov, one of its first members, derailed five trains in the course of three months, and was killed during the sixth attempt.[27] As the battalion established itself and grew stronger, so did the number of sabotage missions increase. Finally, they became the central activities of the battalion and dictated extensive organizational and geographical changes. The Kovno battalions were rightly called "fighting battalions" in that they demonstrated superior combat ability and an intensity of sabotage activities that sometimes even endangered its fighters beyond the acceptable levels.[28]

Because the sabotage squads were out of touch with the base and disconnected from the daily organizational framework for long periods, during missions they operated as independent units and their commanders were given the broadest authority. Often a certain commander exploited his sole authority in an extreme manner, without the possibility of appealing to his superiors. For example, on one mission the commander of the sabotage squad, Sasha Baliakov, shot Jan Sperling for cowardice, in front of his companions Yehuda Birger and

---

26. An important issue that influenced the frequency of sabotage operations was the quantity of "*tol*" explosive (the Russian equivalent of TNT) that the partisans had. In the beginning, they suffered from a shortage of this expensive material in all the partisan battalions. The shortage was filled by the parachute drops of weapons, ammunition, and equipment (Lazer, 328).

27. PKG, 136.

28. PKG, 136–40; see also Sudarsky et al., Lita, 1914.

Aharon Vilenchuk, who were unable to assist him. On occasion, negligent behavior of the commander or part of the sabotage team endangered the mission and its participants.

At first, the fighters from Kovno Ghetto were beginners in this field, as their military training usually did not extend beyond short, concentrated courses in underground conditions. Even for those few who had served in the military, the technique and tactics of sabotage were a new reality they had not yet experienced. So in the beginning, they had subordinate positions in the sabotage units, while their officers and the fighters who held the principle jobs were Russians – paratroopers or escaped prisoners-of-war, or veteran, experienced partisans. Over time, many of the ghetto fighters became experts in this new profession, and several even reached a high level, achieving success and attaining command status in the sabotage squads. Theirs were considered superior exploits, as most of these sabotage plots were carried out far away from the base, even in central Lithuania, a threatening and dangerous area. Almost every Jewish fighter participated in sabotage acts.[29]

The first ghetto fighter to sabotage and derail a train transporting soldiers and military equipment was Lazer Zodikov. For this purpose he went to the Vievis station (80 kilometers west of the base). He derailed two more trains in that area, as well as a shipment of gasoline tanks to the front. Baruch Lopiansky successfully blew up the Vilya-Vievis railroad track four times and died while commanding a sabotage detail that was on its way to blow up the Koshedar station. The scout Shimon Bloch and his comrade Moshe Potchkarnik detonated four explosions. Two of these were over 100 kilometers west of the base. The first was on the Kovno-Koshedar line, near Pravieniškės, while the second was near Gaizhuna, on the Kovno-Jonava line.

Below is the description by a Jew from the Kovno Ghetto who participated in a sabotage operation in March 1944, near Kovno:

Five of us participated in the operation: three Russians – Jurka, Igor, and

---

29. The Jewish women were included in this. Among them, outstanding achievers included Tania Vinishesky, Idke Pilovnik, Haya Shmuelov, and Frieda Rothstein (PKG, 137). Rivka Gordon demanded to join a mission after she learned of the death of her husband, Gordon-Stein, in a German ambush by Kalitanz. But Captain Zeika refused her. At any rate, in June 1944, she joined a sabotage mission with Berel Kott, Dov Levin, and Mishka the Moscovite (testimony of Rivka Gordon, YVSA, 23 ff.).

Vaska; Brick; and myself. The job given us was relatively complex. First we had to set off two explosions. For this purpose, at base we were given two charges of "*tol*" explosives [TNT] of 15 kilograms each. After the explosions, Jurka and Igor were supposed to make their way to the city of Kovno, make contact with the Lithuanian underground, and receive instructions for continuing the mission.... Our squad was properly armed: three submachine guns, two rifles, three pistols, seven hand grenades, and a lot of ammunition....

We began our journey.... For the time being, we advanced through the forest in the partisan area. The route was still relatively safe. But we had to pass through many bogs and drainage canals, and the *tol* weighed us down heavily. The job of carrying the baggage fell to only three fighters, because Igor was still recovering after a severe wound to the lungs, while Jurka, as commander, had to be free to move.... In the evening we left the partisan area....

All night long we walked. Before dawn we entered a farmer's house for our daytime "rest stop." We chose a house from which we could observe the surrounding area. After thoroughly checking the house, the courtyard, and the farmer's family, we informed them that we were Red Partisans and had come to stay with them all day until evening. Throughout our stay, the members of the household were forbidden from leaving the area; if neighbors came, they would also have to remain in the house until evening.... The house was thus under a strict curfew.

Toward evening we released the neighbors who were "guests" and warned those present that if anyone informed the police or the Germans of our presence, his life was in danger and his property would be set on fire....

The next night, we advanced quickly, as we had ordered one of the farmers to harness his cart and drive us in the right direction.... Four days later, we were about 30 kilometers from Kovno. Until that point we had journeyed peacefully, with no incidents or conflicts. The Lithuanian farmers with whom we stayed welcomed us politely.... Our heavy armaments inspired both their respect and fear....

During one daytime rest stop, an awkward incident occurred, caused by the strong tendency of the Russian partisans to get drunk. We were staying with an affluent Lithuanian farmer, for whom Vaska had worked previously when he was a prisoner-of-war. It was Sunday.... The household members organized a splendid welcome for us.... We all ate and drank well, but Jurka and Igor in particular drank copiously. They drank until they lost their senses and began to rage through the house, ignoring our pleas. Suddenly they opened the door wide, walked out of the house, and began to walk openly on the village road, shouting, singing, and going wild. They aimed their weapons and even wanted to shoot. Vaska and the head of the household went out to them and begged them to return to the house before they brought disaster on everyone.

The drunks did return to the house, but continued their rampage. Suddenly Igor came up to me, pushed the barrel of his pistol against my temple, and began to scream: "Don't move, don't move, I'll shoot you!"...Deterred by my calm expression, the drunk lowered his weapon from my forehead. But the incident was not yet over. Jurka and Igor continued to go wild, and suddenly a hail of bullets escaped from one of the cocked submachine guns in their hands. The daughter of the farmer, a five-year-old girl, was severely wounded in the leg. Only then did their frenzy cease. Their shouts were replaced by the wails of the household and Igor's childish weeping as he tried to apologize to the family. Jurka immediately sobered up and began to treat the wounded girl. He ordered them to hitch up a cart at once, and gave almost all of his money to the farmer so he could take his daughter to the hospital.... After the farmer and the wounded girl left, darkness fell, and our squad went on its way.

After some time, we noticed that we were near the site of the operation. The railroad track passed near us.... We approached in order to bury the explosives under the railroad ties. Jurka ordered one of us to remain in the rear and take up a position so he could observe the whole area.... Two of us remained in place...and the remaining two began to move along the track, one on the right, the other on the left. At 50 meters from the site of the operation, each of them lay down.... If the guards appeared, the fighters had orders to shoot them at once.

After the [explosive] device was installed, they attached a rope over 100 meters long and stretched it toward the forest, and we all met up there.... Everything was ready, and we began the uncomfortable waiting for the train's arrival.... The train did not appear. In the distant east, the sky began to lighten, and there was no reason to remain in place. We dismantled the explosive device, leaving no traces, and crept back to the house of a local farmer.... We learned important details about the train's movement from the family, and we could also watch from the windows of the house what was happening on the track. That day, as if to purposely anger us, trains passed us by one after another, all going eastward toward Vilna.

The next night we did not have to wait for long. At almost the same moment that we put the explosive device in place, a long freight train appeared on the horizon. We understood from the engine's heavy puffing that it was fully loaded. We waited until the middle cars went over the mine, then Jurka pulled hard on the rope. A powerful explosion deafened our ears, throwing several cars into the air.... We retreated as quickly as possible...

We decided to wait for a day, and carry out the second explosion on the second night.... We entered an isolated house, behind which was a steep incline to the channel of a small stream. Dense brush grew along the stream's banks. This was a good place to hide.... Once again, Igor and Jurka searched for drink, and in the afternoon Vaska was sent to bring vodka from one of the neighbors....

Soon afterwards, we heard single shots, and then our house was hit with heavy fire.... A dum-dum bullet smashed through the wall, and several fragments hit my leg.... To retreat through the regular entrance would have been suicide. The firing was aimed, as in similar cases, toward the front door. Jurka... ordered us to move the things that were blocking the back door, and when he made sure that the enemy fire was not directed to that side, he gave the order: "Follow me!" We all jumped to the fence... and slid one after another down to the streambed.... We ran up the stream for 2 kilometers until we reached a small grove.... There we remembered that our precious explosive – the *tol* – was back inside the attacked house. Of course there was no way to remove it from there, and so we had to give up on the second explosion....[30]

In another incident, the commander of the operation got drunk and threatened to shoot his subordinates. Young fighter Haim Berman worked up his

---

30. Testimony of Ephraim Senior (Senion).

courage and killed him, with the tacit agreement of the other squad members, all Russians. He was tried and sentenced to death. The sentence was reduced on condition that Berman prove himself on another sabotage mission.[31]

He went out with his companions on the mission. At the beginning they encountered an enemy ambush, and the fighters dispersed. Berman, who was carrying the explosives on his back, was separated from the others. While searching for them, he met a Jewish partisan, Moshe Spanenflieg, who had also been separated from his unit. The two decided to execute the explosion on their own. After approaching the track and laying the mine, they hid in a nearby grove, holding the pull-string and awaiting the arrival of the expected train. The noise of a nearby explosion informed them that this train had already been blown up on another section of the track by a sabotage team from another battalion.

Intent on their goal, the two Jewish fighters waited in place for several days until the Germans repaired the track and the movement of trains was renewed. They then blew up the first train to reinstate service on that line. After an absence of some ten days,[32] they returned safely to their bases.

Once, after a successful explosion of a two-engine train, the retreating saboteurs met up with a German guard force. In the ensuing battle, ghetto fighter Ya'akov (Yankel) Ratner was wounded with grenade shrapnel in his leg and arm, and he fell bleeding among the bushes. His pursuers discovered him and approached to take him prisoner. Ratner allowed them to get close, then opened fire and threw two grenades at them. Several Germans were wounded, and the rest retreated and stopped searching for him, due to the darkness of which the Germans were deathly afraid. With his remaining strength, Ratner reached a farmer's hut, and collapsed unconscious across the doorsill. Partisans who passed through the village the next day took him to their battalion ("For Soviet Lithuania," commanded by Solomin-Petrovitch), where he recuperated until he was able to return to his own battalion.[33]

Following is a detailed description by Michael Yitzhaki (Gelbtrunk), one of three Kovno Ghetto fighters who were part of a sabotage team that operated far from its base:

---

31. Testimony of Eliezer Moses, YVSA, 13 (recording 4). According to PKG 138, the reason for his trial was theft.
32. Haim Berman died shortly afterward in the battle of Večioriškiai.
33. PKG, 137.

Vievis is a junction about 70–80 kilometers from the Rudniki Forests. Our mission was to blow up a train with its cargo, and on the way back to saw down the telephone posts. We had two weeks to perform the mission. One day in March we went out, a group of seven people, including three Jews: Yosef Feuerstein (a Polish refugee who came to the forest from the Kovno Ghetto), Frieda Rothstein, and myself. Mishka "the Orderly" was appointed our commander – a Russian from Moscow, a medic by profession.... We waited in a village nearby [to Vievis] until dark, then went out on our mission. We lay *tol* explosive bricks at two places and pulled the strings over the embankment. At around 8:30, we heard the rattling of the train. Frieda pulled one string, I pulled the other. The sound of the explosion thundered through the air. We rushed to escape. Only a few lone shots chased us. The next day, we discovered from farmers in the area that this was a military freight train taking domestic animals and machines to the front.

We returned by a different route. The next night we entered the village, took some twenty Lithuanian farmers out to the road, and ordered them to saw all the posts for 1.5 kilometers. Toward morning we released them and fled.

We had four more days. The commander proposed that we spend them in a village near Trok (Trakai). He knew the inhabitants from previous missions, and he had friends and allies there.

We went into a house. A village dance was going on, and it was full of young men and women. We placed a curfew on them all: no one could enter or leave. A Lithuanian from a neighboring village, fiancé of one of the village girls, was in the house. The girl begged the commander to free her fiancé. He had to return to work on his farm, and she would guarantee his silence. The commander gave in to her and released the Lithuanian. Taking Yosef Feuerstein with him, the commander went to the village shoemaker to have his boots repaired and left me in charge.

I told my people not to let go of their weapons. But the *goyim* did not obey me. We were taking our afternoon siesta, when a hail of bullets showered the house from three sides. Everyone in the house fled to the basement, while after them ran the three *goyish* partisans in our group. Frieda and I grabbed our weapons and jumped outside. We began to run on the path leading to the forest. The shots followed us. After a while, Frieda fell, out of breath: "I can't go on, I'm exhausted. You run by yourself. ..." I tried to encourage her, to convince her to get up. But she remained on the ground. I continued running and entered the forest.

I walked by myself, without knowing where I was going. ... I decided to hurry to a village and check my location.

I knocked on the door of the first hut. A *goy* came out with a flashlight. ... I asked the *goy* what he knew about military or police movements in the area, and whether he had heard of partisans in the area. The *goy* answered that he knew nothing, but that he would take me to another farmer who knew everything. He only asked that I refrain from mentioning his name. He led me to a rickety wooden hut. I knocked repeatedly until the door opened and the owner shone a lighted match in my face. When I asked him, he answered that he knew nothing. I realized he thought I was a policeman working for the Germans. I began to pressure him to talk and said I was a partisan. Only after I showed him tangible evidence that I was a Jew did his doubts fade. He turned to the hut and called in Polish, "Hannah, come out, there's a Jew here!"

The rags on top of the oven moved, and from underneath appeared a frightened woman with unkempt hair ... I conversed with her. Her entire family of six was living inside a bunker, properly camouflaged and set up in the thick of the forest. They were from Trok, former grain merchants, and they had connections from back then with the Polish forest warden. The warden's brother was an officer in the German police in Trok, and served as a contact for the partisans. Later we discovered that this officer was a Communist, and he was sent by his party for this mission.

These two brothers had declared that part of the forest as forbidden for entry, for felling trees, and other activities. The bunker was set up in that area. They supplied the hidden Jews with the best food available, without taking any payment. When the bunker inhabitants heard the shots, they thought they were aimed at them, and they fled. This Hannah was ailing in her legs, and she escaped to the farmer's house.

The farmer led me to the forest warden. There I was told that my commander and another of my companions were alive, and the next day they would take me to them. They then instructed me to go to the forest, a distance of 4 kilometers. When I reached a ruined building, I was to knock three times and say he had sent me. I went. When I entered the ruin, I found a woman with three children and a crazy old lady. The house was poor and neglected, the crazy woman shouted all night long. . . .

I was exhausted. I sat on a bench, leaned against the wall, and fell asleep. At daybreak, I felt someone shaking my arm. The woman stood before me, breathless with fear: "Police. . . ." I grabbed my weapon and bolted outside. After going several hundred meters without hearing a shot, I stopped and turned back. From afar, I noticed a man standing and waving at me. I recognized my commander and went back.

It turned out that he and Feuerstein had reached the forest warden, and had stayed in the bunker all night long with the Jewish family.

They took me with them. In the bunker, I breathed a sigh of relief. It was hidden among the roots of a tree with a broad canopy, and it was difficult to make out. The inhabitants of the bunker prepared a tub of hot water for me, and I bathed and recovered my strength.

We continued on our way – the commander, Feuerstein, and myself – and reached the railroad tracks. The partisan region began on the other side. Dawn was breaking. Mishka sent me to investigate the crossing. I approached the tracks and saw no one. But from our experience, we knew that this was often a site of trouble. I begged our commander to wait until dark and cross the tracks at night. Mishka insisted. We had just crossed the tracks and had begun to walk through the forest when shots were fired at us. Feuerstein was hit in the leg. I put him on my shoulders and advanced towards the edge of the forest. Feuerstein started to cry out from pain. The bullets continued to whistle around us. A second bullet hit the wounded man's head, and he was silenced. I lay his body on the ground, took his weapon, and followed my commander.

When we reached the forest edge, we discovered an ambush of the German guards of the railroad track. The commander sensed them first, grabbed my shoulder and threw me to the ground. We began to retreat under a hail of fire. I was wounded in the leg, and fell down. The commander thought I had been killed – he left me alone and ran off. I continued for about 200 meters more, then lay in the snow and fell asleep.

Scouts on a mission from another battalion found me, took me to their base, and gave me medical assistance. When I returned to the battalion, I found my commander, and Frieda, who was safe and sound. She had hid among some planks piled under an awning. The Germans lost her traces and passed beside her.[34]

Some sabotage missions cost the battalion a high price in blood. One evening in late May, the following daily report was posted at the base:

Report no. 37. To Death to the Occupiers partisan battalion:

1. While carrying out a combat mission, a unit of six people under commander Comrade Lopiansky, was attacked by Hitlerite bandits in one of the houses of Zhalvi village.[35] After a tenacious battle, the unit perished.
2. Comrade Lopiansky Boris Shliomovitz,[36] born 1921, was an outstanding partisan. He has been nominated for a government medal for his exceptional performance in many battles.
3. Other brave partisans who were faithful to our homeland: partisans Mordkovsky Samuil Yankelevitz, born 1922; Zodikov Lazer Yakovlevitz, born 1916; Goldberg Matis Romanovitz, born 1922; Abramovitz Shlomo Haimovitz, born 1914; Miklishansky (Itzkotis) Itzik, born 1923. Eternal praise for the fallen heroes!

Battalion Commander Smirnov Radyonov.[37]

Following is the story. On its way to a sabotage mission targeting the Koshedar train station, the squad made a daytime stop in the village of Zhalvi. Despite the precautionary measures taken, a village resident escaped from the curfew and informed the Germans that partisans were in the village. German forces rushed to the village in cars and an armored vehicle. They surrounded the house where the fighters were staying and waged a brutal battle against them. The attackers suffered heavy losses, and even the armored vehicle was damaged by grenades;

---

34. Michael Yitzhaki (Gelbtrunk), "Ba-gedud ha-partizani mavet la-kovshim," YLHG 18–19: 81–79.
35. A Lithuanian village through which the ghetto fighters passed on their way to the forests.
36. The names are written in the traditional Russian order: last name, first name, and patronymic. Editor's note: Boris is most certainly Baruch Lopiansky.
37. PKG, 155.

but in the end the six were overcome and fell. The Germans hung their corpses, and inscribed on the hanging post: "The Jews are bandits."[38]

Political and Liaison Activities

As we have seen above, development of positive relations with the local population was very important to the partisans, mainly for reasons of utility. But over time they began to consider it a goal in and of itself. The partisans took upon themselves the job of distributing propaganda among the population. This was authorized and encouraged by the headquarters of the Lithuanian partisan movement in Moscow, who gave clear instructions and sent propaganda material (newspapers and handbills) in Lithuanian in the parachute drops. Furthermore, at the initiative of the brigade command a small printing press in the "Free Lithuania" battalion was set up by Yisrael Gitlin, a Kovno resident who was among the Ninth Fort escapees. Some of the informational material that was printed there was distributed by battalion fighters on their journeys throughout Lithuania. Among the Kovno Ghetto fighters involved in this were outstanding liaisons Nehemiah Endlin, Itzik Miklishansky (partisan nickname Itzkotis), and Yankel Levi (underground nickname Antanas Gudauskas). One fighter relates:

> An overburdened cart advanced toward Kovno. Nehemiah Endlin walked a few hundred paces in front of it, his submachine gun ready for action. Yankel Levi walked behind the cart. Baruch-Itzik Miklishansky sat on top. A farmer held the reigns of the horse. From the outside, it was hard to make out that inside the wagon were hidden a radio transmitter, batteries and accumulators, and eight magnetic mines. The literature they carried was unloaded in the villages along the way, for distribution among the populace.[39]

Most of the activities of this type were performed in the course of other operations that were the main focus. In this way, the guides Zondel Shtrom, Sarah Robinson, Baruch Lopiansky, and Shmulik Mordkovsky, who were sent to Kovno for other reasons, were able to conduct propaganda campaigns among the villagers they met along the way, even transforming them into contacts. The

---

38. PKG adds (155): "This slogan did not remain as originally written for long. Someone erased the word 'Jews' and wrote 'Germans' instead, thus giving the slogan the correct meaning: 'The Germans are bandits.'"

39. PKG, 147.

combat company, which performed distinctly combat missions, distributed Soviet propaganda literature and Lithuanian newspapers to the Lithuanian population.[40] In several instances, they even distributed among Lithuanian farmers
domestic animals they had taken from German farms.

Haim David Ratner, commissar of Forward battalion, was sent on a party mission to Byelorussia.[41] When Forward battalion moved to Lithuania, he operated,
according to Communist Party orders, in villages in southeast Lithuania.[42] He
died on this mission, along with his companion Yankel Levi, several days before
the arrival of the Red Army.

Because the use of communications devices was extremely limited, for various reasons including security, the job of communication was also given to the
partisans themselves. Communication among partisan units, and between the
partisans and anti-Nazi underground centers in cities (including ghettos) and
villages was carried out by special messengers. These also served as escorts and
guides for underground members on their way to the forest or to the site of
their mission. Only experienced fighters who were especially trustworthy and
brave were chosen for these roles. They had expert knowledge of the roads and
paths and were able to keep their missions secret even if they fell into enemy
hands. Most were the same Jewish guides who had traveled from the forest to
the ghetto several times[43] – Abba Diskant, Tuvia Pilovnik, Baruch Lopiansky,
Zondel Shtrom, Yisrael Goldblatt, Sarah Robinson, Nehemiah Endlin, and
Shmulik Mordkovsky. The last two in this list were given the positions of highest
responsibility.

Nehemiah Endlin, who successfully led several groups of fighters from the
ghetto to the forest, also escorted important members of the underground on

---

40. Two Lithuanian newspapers, which appeared in 1940 in Lithuania during the Soviet regime,
continued to be published during the war years in Moscow. From there, they were sent to
Lithuania by various routes.

41. His role as commissar lasted only a few days. Within the brigade, rumor had it that the
purpose of this mission was to remove him from that high position (testimony of Michael
Pasternak, YVSA, 2).

42. Testimony of Grisha Sheffer, YVSA, 35 (recording 9).

43. After the Germans discovered the partisan base in Murava, the ghetto became the substitute
for this base. Fighters who stayed there included Tuvia Pilovnik and Yitzhak Boruchovitz together with their Russian companion Orlov, and they received full assistance from the ghetto
underground (PKG, 106).

their way from the forest to Kovno and back. Eventually, he was appointed chief liaison of the brigade headquarters to the underground in the city of Kovno.

We have already described Shmulik Mordkovsky's success in several missions. In the forest the partisans immediately identified his special qualities appropriate for reconnaissance, escort, and liaison. His outstanding ability to sense danger, his agility in finding his way in the most complex situations, and his quiet, calm nature earned him special status among the fighters, and as soon as he arrived in the forest he began to serve on special missions. Aside from his missions to Kovno, he was given the responsibility of escorting brigade commander Genis to Byelorussia. Because he was naturally secretive and quiet, we have no details of his other roles, and most of them remain unknown to this day.

A friend relates:

> He also performed several important services for the brigade command.... He told me how he moved the "com-brig"[44] to the east. As long as the commander was walking with him, he felt safe. He sent Shmulik ... to Kovno with a letter for the Lithuanian Communist Party.... Aside from this, he was one of the first to take groups out from Kovno and lead them into the forest.
>
> In the forest, he was valued, but he did not find his place. He did not feel fulfilled with ordinary service.... He was always looking for special roles, but these were not given to him within the base.... Many times he told me that he was going to ask to be sent on some operations. Even then, for that mission, when he went out with the six, he did so voluntarily. I recall that he told me happily, "Finally I'm getting away from the base, I'm going to do something." ...
>
> Before the first evacuation,[45] his special operations ended. Then he walked around like a sleepwalker; he felt he had nothing to do. He went out with everyone on missions, but since he had already tasted more important roles, he did not feel right doing anything else. He always aspired to something special. I think the people on the base did not know him so well,

---

44. Brigade commander Jurgis.

45. Editor's note: Refers to the retreat of the partisan forces to escape the German manhunts, mentioned above in note 25.

because he spent very little time there. In addition, he was modest, he didn't talk about the things he did.... They were secret.[46]

Of course, the most vital connection for the Jewish fighters was their contact with the ghetto. We should note that even after regular contact with the besieged ghetto was disrupted, the fighters who had escaped the ghetto did not stop trying to infiltrate inside and find out what was going on between its walls. When the combat company was near Vilkomir, a young woman was sent especially to Kovno to bring back a report on the situation inside the ghetto.[47] A similar initiative was taken by the command of Forward battalion when it was near Kazlu-Ruda.

Freeing Prisoners and Prisoners-of-War

As mentioned, with partisan encouragement, some forty Jews were able to escape the labor camp at Koshedar. Contact with partisans near the labor camp at Keidan was also a factor that encouraged the escape of underground activists from that camp.[48] Partisans also penetrated the infamous concentration camp at Pravieniškės, where underground members and individuals convicted of disloyalty to the Nazi regime worked at forced labor. In a planned, daring operation, the partisans liberated some of its prisoners.[49] These prisoners then joined the partisan brigades, leading to a substantial increase in manpower for the partisan movement and the underground. But even more importantly this act had political significance. The news of the freeing of prisoners-of-war, forced laborers, and detainees spread among the population, exaggerated several times over, and this encouraged every prisoner-of-war and detainee to attempt escape or at least to anticipate being freed from the outside.

Similar actions were carried out in prisoner-of-war camps. Of course, preference was given to those prisoners who had proved willingness to escape on their own initiative. The partisans arranged the time of escape, awaited them, and brought them to their battalions. In April 1944, Nehemiah Endlin was asked to collect Red Army officers in the forests of east Lithuania; they had been

---

46. Testimony of Haim Gechtel (Galin), YVSA, 49–50 (recording 16).
47. Testimony of Haim Gechtel (Galin), ibid.
48. See chapter 9.
49. Štaras, 75–76.

wandering in the forests for many days without contact with regular partisans. Endlin returned to the brigade command with twenty-nine officers who had escaped from military prison, and the majority of them joined the partisans.

That same month, members of Forward battalion broke into the prison at Raveliai (one kilometer from the village of Večioriškiai), and after overpowering the guards and warders, they released thirty-nine Lithuanian prisoners, some of whom joined the ranks of their liberators. Below are the details of this operation from one of the twelve infiltrators who penetrated the fortified building, while the entire battalion entrenched itself around it to secure their safety:

> Our company was ordered to attack the prison beside a certain village where a German garrison was encamped. The prison was guarded by ten Lithuanian policemen. This prison held Poles and Lithuanians who refused to go to Germany. Our job was to gain control of the site, free the prisoners, and take the weapons from the guards. The entire company was called up for this mission. From the company, twelve individuals were chosen to wear German uniforms and carry German weapons. Their role was to break into the guards' living quarters and kill them.
>
> At dawn we went out on the mission. The disguised squad emerged from the forest and advanced at a German-style march. The others went to ambushes and security positions in case German reinforcements were called. The squad was supposed to act quietly and decisively. According to the information we received, the guard usually changed in the early morning hours. We planned the break-in. Two fighters were to take control of the entrance. Two other fighters remained outside for cover. The guards' living quarters was protected by a wall 1.5 meters high. According to the plan, my job was to enter the room while giving orders in German. The mission went well up until the entrance into the hall. Suddenly our commander broke into one of the side rooms and yelled in Russian, "*Ruki veirch!*" [Hands up]. Then we had no choice but to burst through all the doors and take over the rooms by force.
>
> A Ukrainian fighter and I stormed a locked door. In another room, partisan Kostia met up with rifle fire. Everyone opened fire. My Ukrainian companion and I killed a few Lithuanians. We took the jail manager prisoner. The security company burst into the jail and freed the prisoners. They were

given the option of joining us or fleeing. Most fled. We took Kostia's body out of the house and dug a grave in the forest. After taking the weapons and equipment, we set the entire house on fire.[50]

The combat company, which began with thirty-five members, doubled the number of fighters[51] after a prisoner-of-war camp near the village of Pa'aglezai was liberated.[52]

Miscellaneous Missions

Aside from the activities mentioned above, which were almost routine and usually planned in advance, the partisans also implemented ad hoc operations as needed. For example, in May 1944, when they discovered that a tank unit was about to pass through the forest, the entire battalion was called up and went out to face the armored column from within special defense trenches dug hastily for this purpose.[53] Another time, on reaching the forest, a member of the Lithuanian underground from the city of Kovno was wounded in the leg and remained in Genis's partisan camp across the road. Six members of Death to the Occupiers battalion were sent to bring him on a stretcher through the treacherous bogs that stood on both sides of the Vilna-Lida road.[54] A third example was when the chemical needed to charge the transmitting equipment batteries had run out, they sent Yosef Rosen together with Polish fighter Shora to Shora's village to obtain the important substance.[55] Various roles were also given to the fighters in arranging matters with the farmers after supply missions, such as returning the carts and horses. Aside from implementing the appropriate security and

50. Zvi Shefer, "Ba-geto u-va-ya'ar," Sefer ha-partizanim ha-yehudim, 2:528; compare testimony of Grisha Shefer, YVSA, 24–25; Štaras, 106–7; Hitlerine, 323; also testimony of David Yachas.

51. At final count, the combat company numbered over one hundred individuals. After liberation, an investigation was conducted into the loyalty of the various new members. Many of them were tried for the crime of cooperation with the enemy (testimony of Haim Gechtel [Galin], YVSA, 41, recording 14).

52. According to PKG, 156. By contrast, another source (testimony of Haim Gechtel [Galin], ibid.) reports that the prisoners were given an excellent opportunity to flee from their prison, but they hesitated, and negotiations with them continued for a week.

53. Testimony of Eliezer Moses, YVSA, 24 (recording 7).

54. Ibid., 20–21 (recording 6).

55. Testimony of Yosef Rosen, YVSA, 21 (recording 5).

precautionary measures, the detail that led the column also bore responsibility for the safety of the cargo.[56]

The partisans also conducted operations of a general character together with the other battalions, in accordance with the instructions of the brigade command. For example, as detailed above, a joint company was sent to Byelorussia to receive ammunition cargo designated for the Lithuanian brigade.[57] Responsibility was divided among all the battalions in the forest for making arrangements to receive the weapons drop at the brigade "air field," including supplying gasoline for the signal bonfires, placing units to secure the site, and dismantling the cargo. Responsibility was also shared among the battalions with regard to the search units, whose job was to look for parachutes that strayed from the designated site and rescue paratroopers who landed in the thick of the forests and in the swamps.[58]

As the front approached Lithuania, the activities of the White Poles intensified in the Rudniki Forests as well, even becoming a serious threat to the supply lines of the Lithuanian brigade. Their provocation reached its height when they took control of the village of Pupishkis and turned it into their regular base. Along with retaliation operations against them,[59] the brigade command responded to a proposal to negotiate for a cease-fire. Representatives of both sides came to the meeting escorted by armed forces. Fighters from Death to the Occupiers battalion formed part of the brigade's joint company, which took up positions nearby. Several such meetings were held, but the sides did not reach an agreement.[60]

Long-Range Raids

The permanent base of the three Kovno battalions, with its organization, facilities, and services, gave the fighters a feeling of security – even relative

---

56. For a description of mishaps and technical problems in returning the vehicles to the farmers, see testimony of Haim Gechtel (Galin), YVSA, 29.

57. See chapter 12, "Weapons Acquisition."

58. Once a paratrooper/radio operator landed at the wrong location and became entangled in the branches of a tall tree, where she remained until she was rescued (see Mončiunskas, 275).

59. Punishment operations were carried out in one village that served as a base for the White Poles. Two Polish officers who had been taken prisoner in a previous battle were executed (Lazer, 361).

60. *Sefer ha-partizanim ha-yehudim* 1:256. According to another source, the partisans used cunning tactics to attack the White Poles and dismantle their weapons (ibid., 141). On relations with the White Poles close to liberation, see chapter 15.

comfort – between operations. In contrast to these advantages, which were amplified as the services improved, one shortcoming stood out and it was felt increasingly over time. This was the distance of the base from where the operations took place.

In summer 1944, the focal point of combat activities for these battalions moved to central Lithuania. In large part, this was caused by the fact that the area of operations of the Lithuanian brigade had become too crowded due to the proliferation of battalions and their increasing strength. By that time, very little room for operation remained for the Kovno battalions in the Rudniki Forest area.[61] As mentioned, in most of the military operations performed especially by the Kovno battalions, the objective was far from the base, on Lithuanian soil,[62] west of the Vilna-Grodno railroad track. The route was very difficult, consumed precious time, and involved serious dangers.[63] Aside from this, the summer offensive of the Soviet military in the Vitebsk sector raised problems related to the status and role of the Lithuanian brigade in general. The rapid advance of the Red Army was liable to transform the Rudniki Forests area into the front, while the partisans' role was to operate in the rear.

In light of these factors, the partisans decided to transfer most of the strength of the Kovno battalions to south and west Lithuania, where they had important roles and an expansive field of activity. In essence, this was a kind of renewal of the Augustova Plan, which had been assigned to the Kovno Ghetto fighters but did not succeed due to inexperience and inadequate planning. At short intervals, four large units abandoned the base in the Rudniki Forests and moved to Lithuania: the Death to the Occupiers combat company, the Vladas Baronas battalion, Forward battalion, and a select unit of the Death to the Occupiers battalion under the command of Kostia (battalion commander Radyonov).[64]

---

61. The movement of trains on the Vilna-Lida and Vilna-Grodno lines was severely reduced, almost completely stopped (Mončiunskas, 265). On the "scarcity of work" that began to be felt in the Rudniki Forests in the sabotage areas, see also testimony of Baruch Gofer (Grodnick), YVSA, 16–18.

62. Editor's note: The Rudniki area was part of the Vilna region that was under Polish rule from 1920 and was annexed to Lithuania in 1939, hence the author's referrals to Rudniki as if it were outside of Lithuania. See D. Levin, *The Litvaks* (Jerusalem: Yad Vashem, 2000), 114.

63. Crossing the railroad tracks was particularly dangerous. Dozens of fighters lost their lives there on returning from daring sabotage operations inside Lithuania. Among those killed at that site was the noted saboteur Jurka, described above in this chapter, under "Sabotage."

64. Several other units also moved. One was led by brigade commander Jurgis, and his place in the forest was filled by Commissar Gabris. The Vilna battalions remained in the Rudniki

The combat company, the strike force of the Death to the Occupiers battalion, was given the responsibility for incursions into Lithuanian territory in the Vilkomir area. It was given four to six weeks for this purpose. On the day it left the base, May 25, 1944, the company had thirty-five fighters, including seven Jews: David Tepper, Zondel Shtrom, Leibel Shtrom, Yisrael Goldblatt, Yitzhak Nemzer, Yehuda Lifschitz, and Haim Gechtel.

Following is a description of the company's expedition:

> Our officer was "the Pilot,"[65] a partisan who served at the beginning of the war as a pilot in the Red Army. He was taken prisoner by the Germans and fled to the forests.... We were ordered to perform a daring raid through Lithuania to the Vilkomir area, which had yet to feel the might of the Soviet partisans. Our goals were sabotage of enemy installations, agitating the population against the Germans, and vengeance against collaborators. We Jews added another role for ourselves: vengeance against murderers of Jews.
>
> We were well armed with submachine guns, rifles, and light machine guns, and we took a large amount of *tol* [TNT] with us. From the beginning we carried out several small sabotage operations, and we felt that an atmosphere of tension and anger prevailed among the Lithuanian population and regime. After we entered central Lithuania and carried out several successful ambushes of small German army units,[66] the rumor spread among the villages that a Soviet army had arrived. Entire units of the Savisauga[67] followed us and tried to make contact with us and give us their weapons, as a sign that they were abandoning the Germans and surrendering to the Soviet regime. A few even asked to join our ranks in order to battle the Germans. A few days later, we had collected so many armaments that we had to destroy them along the way, so that they would not fall into German hands.
>
> By contrast, some Savisauga units dared to chase us and attack us. Once

---

Forests, apparently in order to ensure that the territory would not be conquered by the White Poles.

65. *Lyetchik* in Russian. His name was Stephan Kulikov. He joined the battalion with the Solomin group, from the Jonava Forests. He was appointed commander of the combat company after its first commander, Mishka Trushin, was killed.

66. Near the village of Paglezhai, the Jewish partisans attacked and burned a military trailer-truck carrying eight German soldiers and a full load of armaments (PKG, 150).

67. Savisauga ("self-defense") was the name for Lithuanian local defense units that were founded by the Germans. For details of Lithuanian units established by the Germans, see Vicas, 27 ff.

we stayed in a small village for a rest day. In the middle of the day, the farmers informed us that a Lithuanian unit had arrived and was trying to surround us. At the last minute, we hurried into a grove next to the village, took up defense positions, and prepared a "welcome" for the Lithuanians. They had some fifty members in their unit, armed from head to toe. But we remained calm. We allowed them to approach as far as the grove, and then we began to fire all the weapons we had in the company. Our firepower was so strong and surprising that the Lithuanians scattered in panic, leaving behind many dead and wounded. After that, the surrounding population believed that a powerful Soviet unit several hundred strong had landed in their region. From then on, members of the Lithuanian "defense army" did not dare attack us, and we were able to perform our mission with more security.

Our first task was to set fire to the giant grain storehouses in the Vilkomir region, which were under the control of the German army. This successful mission was the idea of one of our fighters, Yitzhak Nemzer, a Jew who had lived in the region until the beginning of the war and came from a family of bakers and grain merchants. We advanced into the center of the Vilkomir region, and began to carry out systematic sabotage and operations to purge the area of enemy elements.[68] First of all, we blew up the narrow gauge Vilkomir-Ponevezh railroad track at several points,[69] taking it out of service. We placed ambushes on the roads and destroyed several German army units. We also rounded up and killed thirteen Lithuanian policemen from a few villages[70] who, according to the locals[71] had participated in the murder of the Jews of Jonava.[72]

In contrast to the atmosphere in the permanent battalion base, the combat

---

68. This included setting fire to a factory for alcohol and tar (testimony of Haim Gechtel [Galin], YVSA, 42, recording 14).

69. According to another source, this was the Vilkomir-Jonava line (PKG, 156).

70. Among the prisoners was the commander of the Vilkomir province police force, the officer Katurka.

71. On this issue, the Russian population in the area, called Starovei, was particularly helpful. They had suffered deeply from Lithuanian attacks (see also chapter 10, "The Lithuanian Underground in Action").

72. Haim Gechtel (Galin), from an essay in Sefer yehudei Lita 2. Compare Galin's complete testimony, YVSA, 41–45 (recording 14).

company enjoyed a spirit of tolerance between the Jewish and Russian fighters.[73] The company commander even extended special treatment to his Jewish subordinates,[74] especially veteran fighter David Tepper, and consulted with him before important decisions. Under his influence, a messenger was sent to investigate the situation in the Kovno Ghetto. The Jewish fighters also tried in many ways to find Jews who had survived the murders and might be hiding and to have them join the company. But during the entire period of their foray, they found not one Jew.

In late April 1944, the entire Vladas Baronas battalion, many of whose members fell in the battle of Večioriškiai, was ordered to move to southern Lithuania and establish a new base there. Of the twenty-two members who set out, thirteen were Jews. These included Yitzhak Lifschitz, Mendel Dietz, Peretz Kliatchko, Yisrael Gitlin, Aharon Gafanovitz, Shechne Shilin, Michael Gelbtrunk, Yisrael Joels, and three women fighters: Rachel Lifschitz, Frieda Rothstein, and Zoya Tinet. Battalion commander Semyonov led the march together with Commissar Misha Balkin (a Jew from Saratov) and Sergeant-Major Ivan Krugliakov (nicknamed "Diadia Vania").

The battalion had just left the edges of the forest toward the west, when it was engaged in fierce battle by a Savisauga unit lying in ambush near the town of Olkeniki.

A Jewish fighter relates:

> On the second day after our departure ... we were 80 kilometers west of the base. We stayed in a small grove for our daytime rest stop. ... Suddenly bullets flew at us from all sides of the forest. Apparently the attackers were Lithuanians from the Savisauga units. They surrounded the grove and were about to charge us with a force several times stronger than ours. We had to break through the siege so quickly that the enemy almost did not notice, because

---

73. The exception was one commander who aggravated the Jewish fighters. Several days before the arrival of the Soviet army, they discovered that he was collaborating with the Germans, and the "Pilot" commanded that he be shot to death.

74. According to the testimony of Haim Gechtel (Galin) (YVSA, 49, recording 16), the "Pilot" said to him: "I have to protect you [Jews] – there are only a few of you, and you have to return alive." According to another source (testimony of Yehuda Lifschitz, YVSA, 7), once, when intoxicated, the "Pilot" explained that every Jew was precious to him, because when the Soviet army would arrive and there would be no Jews in his company, they would take it for a band of robbers.

we were wearing a variety of uniforms (including Lithuanian ones). When we broke through to their rear, they were certain that we were Lithuanian reinforcements that had arrived for them. They broke out in cries of joy to welcome us. We permitted them to approach us to a distance of 10 meters, and then we broke into fire with all the weapons at our disposal. Some sixty of the enemy were hit. We continued to attack while they were confused, and in a hand-to-hand fight we broke their resistance. We took fifteen prisoners and several dozen rifles. None of us were harmed.

We continued on our route until we reached the Vainiunai Forests near Alytus, where we met with Jurgis.... Jurgis ordered us to go to Augustova and from there to send a liaison to Kazlu-Ruda in order to check the site.[75] When we arrived in Augustova, Misha Balkin and Kazis went out to the Kazlu-Ruda Forests to search for contact with the partisans, so that our entire battalion could transfer there. Because according to what we were told, Augustova was supposed to be only a temporary base.... Relations between us and the Lithuanian partisans were good.[76] ... Among the operations we performed, I recall blowing up the police building in the town of Veisiejai.... [77]

The Jewish fighters of this battalion also longed to find fellow Jews near their area of activity. The battalion's reconnaissance commander relates in his testimony:

When we discovered that there were Polish partisans in the area...we decided to contact them. I went with the command staff, and we found out that they were Red Polish partisans. They invited us to their base, and they had only a few women there. I saw a young Jewish girl...from the Grodno region. She told me that there had been many Jews there, and they had had weapons. Then they met with the Poles. The Poles took the Jews with them, but a few days later, they took the Jews' weapons, abandoned them, and took only her, because one of the Polish *goyim* fell in love with her. Later they

---

75. Scouts from the ghetto were also sent there in order to search for contact with the partisans. See chapter 14.

76. At the base, the Vladas Baronas battalion was also known for good relations between the command and the Jewish fighters.

77. Testimony of Yisrael Joels, YVSA, 6–7.

discovered that all the Jews had been caught by the police, and they had all been executed....

Once at night I was walking by myself, and I met up with a man. I suspected...that he was one of the Ukrainians that served in the army.... But after I shouted for him to throw down his weapon, I saw that he had thrown down a stick. I approached him until I could see who he was, and I saw it was a man wearing rags.... After a few moments of conversation with him in Polish, I saw that he was a Jew, a young man of seventeen or eighteen.... When he saw that I was a Jew...he went down on his knees and began to kiss my legs, and he became completely hysterical. After I gave him a drink, he told me that whole families had been in the area for three years, and they lived by going out at night to obtain food, each time a different young person.... Because they knew the farmers well and did not trust them, they stole what was left in the pigsty and other places. I took the address of the place where they were staying and said, "I'll talk to the commander. I can't take you with me right away." He also did not want to go with me immediately, because he was responsible for his family. There were elderly people in his family, and he also had younger brothers and a sister. We concluded that I would speak with the commander, and if he agreed, we would come and get all the families.

When I returned, I first spoke with Semyonov, and with Naktis, and they both agreed that they were willing to accept the young men, but the elderly would remain where they were and we would arrange their food. I went back there with another member of my group.... I offered them the proposal I had been given, but the youths objected. On the one hand, I saw that they wanted to come, but on the other hand, they bore the responsibility for their parents and families. They were some forty or fifty people, together with the elderly and the children. They were living in terrible conditions, in filth, without clothing. They wore sacks tied with ropes, and they were covered with sores. They could wash, but they had not one piece of soap. Soap was difficult to purchase. I had not known about their situation, and I had not brought any with me. At that time, we had plenty of supplies. I simply forgot, I did not think to take such things with me.[78]

---

78. Testimony of Michael Yitzhaki (Gelbtrunk), yvsa, 38–39 (recording 7a).

These meetings were not continued, because a few days later the Germans began their retreat, and the fighters went out every night to mine the roads or attack convoys. There was no possibility of visiting those Jews, and the contact with them ended.

The Forward battalion left its base in May 1944 for the Kazlu-Ruda Forests (south of Kovno). This battalion, led by Captain Zeika, Commissar Solomin-Petrovitch,[79] and Sergeant-Major Anton Bondor, numbered some sixty fighters. About half of them were Jews, including Shlomo Breuer, Katriel Koblenz, Haim Nadel, Shimon Bloch, Rivka Bloch (German), Grisha Sheffer, Rivka Epstein, Moshe Brabo, Michael Pasternak, Zamke Brenner, Reuven Glickman, Lazer Zilber, Sima Yashunsky, Yankel Levi, Shulamit Lerman, Haim David Ratner, and Berel Stern. The guide was Nehemiah Endlin, whose wonderful sense of direction rescued the battalion on more than one occasion when in dire straits. Aside from the commanders, none of the battalion members knew the final goal of the journey.

Due to the length and difficulty of the route and the aggression of the Lithuanian population, the fighters were under strict orders to avoid confrontations and battles and to make every effort to reach their destination as swiftly as possible.

The following testimony of Grisha Sheffer describes events on this journey:

Before departure, Rozhka[80] came to say good-bye in the name of the movement. She told me that one of my roles was to search for contact with movement members. She knew we were leaving, but not in which direction.... We did not know the final location either.... For several days we could not cross the railroad tracks, because the guard was augmented. There were Germans everywhere ... until courage overcame cowardice, and we broke through and crossed the tracks.[81]

We kept walking according to the usual method and moved southwest. Toward evening we would approach a village, prepare our supplies for the following day, take a guide, and he would lead us.... He was with us the whole

---

79. He replaced Haim-David Ratner in this position.
80. Ruzhke Korczak, an FPO activist in Vilna and a partisan in the first Vilna battalion. She served as the contact with the Hashomer Hatzair members in the forest.
81. Crossing the railroad tracks was carried out near Rūdiškės, which was under heavy German guard, and so the Germans did not expect partisans there at all. The decision to cross at this site was the result of Nehemiah Endlin's planning.

time, night and day, until we left the area around his village. Then we would release him and enter a new village, and repeat the routine....

One evening we went out according to the usual procedure. We entered a village, took a guide, and equipped ourselves.... At night we advanced and walked through a field of grain. At the edge flowed a small river. Beyond it was open territory.... Suddenly fire poured from the nearby hills. We hit the ground, awaiting the commanders' orders. But for some reason, no orders were given. We waited, tensed, sensing that the squads had lost contact. At this moment when we felt things were falling apart, one Jewish partisan took the initiative to operate the machine gun.[82] This was an encouraging sign, and after him the other weapons opened a volley of fire. The order went from squad to squad to attack and take over the grove, which was about 500 meters from us.... During the attack, the groups became mixed up. The headquarters commander erred and went in another direction, and the forces reorganized only when we reached the grove. There we dug a grave for a woman fighter who fell, and we moved the wounded to a nearby village....

According to the direction in which we were walking, we understood that we were still moving southwest and that we had to cross the Nemunas at a certain point.... Apparently the Germans were following our journey. As mentioned, usually we left at night, by dawn reached a small grove, and slept there.... Once Moshe Brabo fell asleep and was unnoticed. We left for the forest, and he was left behind. We began to get organized for guarding and we noticed that Moshe Brabo was missing. We began to search for him.... For this reason we did not cross at the ford...we made a big detour north and journeyed the whole night. Farmers took our battalion across in boats.[83] We then heard a rumor that a German ambush awaited us beside the ford.... Moshe awoke and did not know what to do. He went to a farmer nearby...and there our scout found him. He asked the farmer to take him over the Nemunas at a certain place...Brabo received a very severe rebuke, and his life was also in jeopardy. The punishment for such a case was death, but somehow he got out of it and explained himself, and we may admit that

---

82. This was the machine gunner Michael Pasternak, who excelled in his combat role many times.

83. Near the villages of Kruonis and Darsūniškis (PKG, 158).

his folly served us well, because we made that detour and did not cross at the ford. [84]

Even after crossing the Nemunas, dangerous ambushes awaited the battalion.[85] While the partisan force was moving along a secondary road, with thick forest on one side and bushes on the other, suddenly a hail of bullets flew at them from the direction of the bushes. The fighters lay down in place and returned heavy fire toward the bushes. The enemy fire completely stopped, and the fighters prepared to leap into the bushes to destroy the ambush and secure the continuation of their journey. But Nehemiah Endlin, the guide, surprised them with the animated order, "Back! Run after me!" Astonished, everyone obeyed his order. After running several hundred meters, Endlin stopped them in a protected place. At that moment, some five hundred German soldiers in light vehicles burst from the bushes and retreated in confusion in the opposite direction. Based on the partisans' firepower and their surprise rapid retreat, the Germans thought that a powerful force was about to attack them, and so they retreated in disarray. Were it not for Endlin's intuition, the battalion would have been destroyed by the ambush force, which was much more powerful.

Endlin's good judgment also served the battalion well when they crossed the Kovno-Marijampole railroad track. The Germans guarded this vital transportation artery twenty-four hours a day. The heavy guard was mainly in place at night, when the partisans usually operated, while during the day the Germans made do with one sentry every 200 meters. The command accepted Endlin's daring proposal to cross the track in daylight, at 10 A.M. Of course, the Germans never expected such an operation at that hour, and the entire force crossed safely and reached the new base in the Kazlu-Ruda Forests, having journeyed 230 kilometers. Grisha Sheffer continues his narrative of the journey:

> We reached a certain location about 35 kilometers southwest of Kovno, and made it our base. There we built huts, not the usual dirt dugouts, and we slept inside them.[86] It was in a real swamp.... We also found partisans there from

---

84. Testimony of Grisha Sheffer, YVSA, 26 ff. (recording 7). Compare testimony of Haim Nadel, 6 and testimony of David Yachas.

85. PKG 158–59.

86. At this site, it was not worthwhile for the partisans to build dugouts because the forests were thin and insecure, and they knew they might have to abandon the area at any given moment

a Lithuanian battalion.... Then we also had our meetings with the saboteurs. The Red Army parachuted the saboteurs down to us. They wore uniforms of the Red Army.... There was a sad incident.... The saboteurs were well armed, and he [our commander] thought that the Germans had sent them. So we blew them away, we killed half of them.[87]...Afterwards another three platoons of them arrived. They were the forward scouts.... They said that each time they were dropped, then collected, and again dropped. We had a transmitter and we were in contact with Moscow.... Lately we also heard all the news on the radio.... Our main role was to sit on the roads and railroad tracks, and to give detailed reports on the movement of vehicles, and this made a difference.... Several days later there were sorties of airplanes that bombed the roads and train tracks about which we had reported.... Jews wandered those forests.... They expressed their desire to join the partisans.... I told them I would put them in contact with my commissar. The commissar was a Jew.[88] I knew he was a Jew, and I tried to speak to him to have them join. Later he did bring them in, not to our company but to a Lithuanian one.[89]

The farmers were astonished to see Jewish fighters. It was hard for them to believe. But they did not hide their hatred, even when the Red Army approached.... They were surprised to see us....

As for the commissar – we had an argument with him once. We were

---

(see also testimony of Michael Pasternak, YVSA, 5).

87. Their commander was also seriously wounded and brought to the battalion base for treatment. After liberation, Captain Zeika, commander of Forward battalion, was tried for this. He was transferred to the front in the punishment brigades and fell in battle (testimony of Haim Nadel, YVSA, 6; compare testimony of Grisha Sheffer, YVSA, 34; PKG, 157).

88. Referring to Solomin Petrovitch.

89. Michael Pasternak describes a similar incident in his testimony. "Once I found a Jewish youth from Kovno, who had fled from a certain camp and was wandering alone on the path. I convinced the commanders to take him into the battalion, and thus he was saved from certain death, because alone and without arms he would have gotten lost" (testimony of Michael Pasternak, YVSA, 5). Apparently, permitting Jews to join the battalion was a rare occurrence. "The condition for acceptance of Jews was – they had to bring weapons. Apparently many Jews were lost because of this demand" (ibid.). Indeed, dozens of Jews who fled the camps and transports to Germany wandered around these regions. Most were murdered by Lithuanians and Germans. The Soviet partisans in Lithuania refused to accept them into their units and even threatened them, telling them to leave the area (testimony of Raphael Hollel, YVSA, 3–4. Compare Abba Gefen, *Portzei ha-mahsomim* [Tel Aviv, 1961], 43).

talking in Yiddish, and he asked why we were speaking Yiddish, because it led to jealousy and hatred....

Clothing caused a certain problem for us. Clearly we could not use the same clothes as before. We had arrived in the forest in the winter, and our clothes were not always practical, especially those boots, which were not appropriate for the damp.... At one opportunity I told my commander that I had to exchange my boots. He authorized it, and I went into a farmer's house and took a pair of shoes....

As summer approached, we began to remove our winter clothing, and it was easier for us. I participated in an operation for freeing a prison and took the policemen's clothing for myself.... I was almost accidentally killed due to this clothing by saboteurs in Kazlu-Ruda....

When the weapons drops arrived, they sewed underwear and undershirts for us from the parachute cloth.... Some also received pants made from this khaki.[90]

---

90. Testimony of Grisha Sheffer, YVSA, 30–33 (recording 8).

PART V
The Final Days

CHAPTER 14

Last Days of the Kovno Ghetto

With the departure of the seventh group of fighters from the Kovno Ghetto on March 3, 1944, the exploits of the Jewish Fighting Organization reached their peak in terms of organization and scope. Preparations for sending additional groups continued. Their accumulated experience and success granted the organization's activists some measure of confidence and even led to a certain routine.

But this "golden era" for the underground did not last for long. It ended with the *Aktion* against the Jewish police (March 27, 1944), which was first in a series of calamities suffered by the Kovno Ghetto and the Jewish Fighting Organization at the hands of the Germans, as preparation for the liquidation of the ghetto in mid-July 1944.

Within only twenty days, the Gestapo struck the ghetto with a number of blows. At least three of these – the Police *Aktion*, the arrest of the Ältestenrat, and the ambush of the vehicle of those leaving for the forest – directly damaged the underground, crushing it to such an extent that it never recovered. With the abolishment of the police and the Ältestenrat, the underground was left without vital sources of aid, while the ambush obliterated an important element of the leadership and also disrupted the connection with the outside.

The fact that these operations came close on one another's heels, and the targeted objective was different for each, leaves us to conclude that these were not random occurrences but a series of operations that were carefully planned by the Gestapo leaders in Kovno.[1] Using agents and spies within the ghetto and without, the Gestapo had for a long while been tracking activities in the ghetto,

---

1. Proof of this are the topics of interrogation of the Jewish police in the Ninth Fort, and the fact that most of the Jewish policemen who were executed were connected with underground circles (see below).

particularly the departure of Jews to the forest. Although several informers in the service of the Germans were discovered and killed, there may have been others. Further, as we have mentioned above, following the expansion of the movement's activities and its successes, the level of secrecy declined. The Germans were undoubtedly able to put together one detail after another until they ascertained the existence of an underground in the ghetto.[2]

Liquidation of the Ghetto Police

On March 27, 1944, the Jewish policemen were ordered to report for a special roll call at the square in front of the ghetto headquarters, ostensibly for civil defense training. From August 1941, when the ghetto police was founded at German order, until the date of the roll call, the institution of the ghetto police stood firm and the Germans did not harm it or its members, even during the *Aktion*s. In addition, the policemen's families enjoyed a certain immunity during troubles such as deportations. It was thus not unusual that the 140 policemen, including commanders, officers, and sergeants, turned out for the roll call, polished and shining, and harboring no suspicions. There the seven band players were separated from the rest of the group, while the others were surrounded by armed guards and taken immediately to the Ninth Fort. Simultaneously, one of the most horrifying *Aktion*s was carried out in the ghetto – the roundup of the children and elderly, which lasted for two days.[3]

One Jewish policeman, who was sent back to the ghetto after two days, describes their interrogation:[4]

> At the fort they divided the policemen into three cells. They called the commander, Moshe Levin, for interrogation immediately. He was returned to

---

2. Gestapo officer Kittel, who was responsible for investigative operations, was known for his wealth of experience in revealing undergrounds in the Vilna Ghetto and elsewhere.

3. See chapter 1. For details of this frightening *Aktion*, see Moshe Segelson, "*Di groyzame aktzia fun kinder un alte in geta kauna; a capital fun meine zichronot,*" Landsberg a.n. lach, October 1945, manuscript, 1–20.

4. Testimony of Hirsch Neuburger, YVSA, 21–25. According to this source, several policemen wanted to attack the German sentry who was in the vehicle with them. But their commander, Moshe Levin, also in the vehicle, prevented them from doing so because this could mean trouble for the ghetto. He calmed them, saying that in his opinion only the commanders were in danger but the regular policemen would not suffer. As they approached the fort, several policemen tried to jump from the vehicle and flee, but they were shot and killed by the guards.

the cell after half an hour. He said they had threatened to kill him, and they beat him, because they wanted to get information from him about the hiding places in the ghetto, the partisans, and weapons.... He answered that that they should not expect to get any information from him, and they might as well kill him, because one way or another he did not expect to leave the place alive.[5] That day he was again called for interrogation, from which he did not return. A few days later I recognized his clothing and the clothes of policemen Sasha Zilberkweit and H. [Hirsch] Levin, who were shot on the way to the fort....

The vice-commander, Yehuda Zupovitz, was also brought in for interrogation, as was the police inspector, Ika Greenberg. They were asked for information about the ghetto and beaten murderously.[6] They were told that the SD had obtained information from Jews (informers) that the police were directing revolutionary activity, that in the ghetto there were organizations which were undergoing military training and that they had weapons, and that groups were going out to the partisans in the local forests.[7] They also blamed the police for collecting documentary material and photographs.... The SD had precise knowledge of a photographer in the ghetto, Hirsch Kadushin (Kadish), and that he had a large collection of photographs.... They

---

5. According to other sources, Moshe Levin stood proudly before the interrogation table. The interrogators asked him, why did the police aid in the construction of the bunkers? He answered: "Is it possible for the bunkers in the ghetto to endanger the victory of the German people?" (Rachel Salkija, "3 yar in kavner geta," YVSA, 03/633, 25).

6. The handsome Yehuda Zupovitz, when he was returned to his cell after the first interrogation, looked like a broken old man, and his friends barely recognized him. "Our young lives are lost," he said to his companions. "Let us die as heroes and not reveal the bunkers in which thousands of innocent children are hiding. Let us have a clear conscience before we die." He then sat down among his friends and sang his favorite song, "I am surrounded by a blazing fire" (ibid., 26).

7. According to Garfunkel, Kovno (177), they interrogated the policemen on three issues: the disappearance of a Jewish Gestapo agent (Fein, who was killed by the underground [see end of chapter 8]); the location of the Jews' hiding places for silver, gold, and other valuables; and the location of the malinas in the ghetto. But other sources confirm Neuburger's testimony that one of the important topics of interrogation that the Gestapo stressed was police assistance to the partisan movement. For example, once Goecke said to the ghetto workshops manager, Moshe Segelson, regarding the Jewish police: "They have purchased weapons, organized partisan gangs, and sent them to the forest, in order to fight us. They have also built bunkers and carried out murders inside them" (Segelson, Di groyzame aktzia, 19–20; compare Gar, Umkum, 206).

searched for him in the ghetto, but somehow he had been able to miraculously disappear.[8]

When they brought Zupovitz and Greenberg back to the cell, they had
been severely beaten and were bleeding profusely. Zupovitz's skull was broken. But the SD interrogators got nothing out of them. They remained stubbornly silent.[9]

As mentioned, the policemen were jailed in three cells located in different wings of the fort. The first cell held the commanders, the headquarters
staff, and another ten policemen. The other two cells held the remaining
policemen, some forty-five men in each cell. Gestapo officer Kittel, who
had commanded the *Aktion*, visited the policemen several times a day and
demanded that they reveal all the ghetto secrets. He was especially interested
in the bunkers and promised to release everyone who revealed some sort of
hideout in the ghetto.

The cell in which I was jailed together with the headquarters staff was far
from the other two cells. We decided to remain stubbornly silent and not to
give away our brothers in the ghetto, no matter what happened. They threatened to shoot us but nothing helped – we did not give in.

This was not the case in one of the other two cells, where there were weak
individuals. They were frightened by the threats and believed the promises
of release. Some ten policemen from this cell…accompanied Kittel and
showed him some bunkers in which children were hiding.[10] Then we found

---

8. For details about the activities of this photographer in the ghetto, see article by M. Gra-
nowski, "*Der held mit der kamera,*" in *Dos fraje Vort*, Feldafing, December 12, 1945. Kadushin
was able to save a large part of his collection, which went to the United States. (Editor's note:
In 1982, the photographer donated his collection of some 2,000 photo negatives taken in the
Kovno Ghetto from 1942–1944, as well as approximately 1,000 photographs from the Displaced
Persons Camp at Landsberg, Germany from 1945–1946, to Beit Hatfutsot, the Museum of the
Jewish People in Tel Aviv. His photos can also be seen at the US Holocaust Memorial Museum
and the Yad Vashem database.)

9. Several days later, Gestapo staff hinted to Ältestenrat members about the stubborn silence
of Moshe Levin and his companions (see testimony of Leah [Lucia] Elstein-Lavon, YVSA,
9–10, recording 2).

10. They included Benzion Zhamaitis, Shlachter, Epstein, Levin, Rabinowitz, Ushpitz, and
Sergei (see testimony of Yankele Verbovsky, YVSA). According to Garfunkel, *Kovno* (177),
the informers did not understand the significance of their act. When they were taken from
the ghetto in the morning, there were as yet no signs of the Children's *Aktion*, and so "they

out that in the ghetto the most horrifying *Aktion* of all was being carried out, the Children's *Aktion*.

They kept us in the fort for four days, until Thursday (March 30). On the last day, Kittel again came in with a machine gun and threatened to shoot us all if we continued to maintain silence. He also said that our friends from the other cells would be released because they had revealed some hideouts.... He gave us another fifteen minutes to consider. We in the cell did not know that in the other two cells only a few individuals had informed, and we believed Kittel when he said that our friends in the other cells had informed. Our spirits were very depressed, but we carried out our determined decision – we kept silent. I recall...in those difficult moments, we heard the decisive voice of Ika Greenberg, who said, "Friends, our time will soon arrive...hold strong with honor until your last breaths! Do not give our hangman a reason to laugh and mock us. Do not fear death!" After he spoke, a deathly silence reigned. We parted from each other with glances and promised each other to remain proud sons of our people. Our firm decision was to remain silent – and we remained silent.

The fifteen minutes that Kittel granted us to consider our decision passed. But he did not return to our cell. Several hours later, he entered the fort and called out names of policemen. They were taken out of the cells and released.

Thirty-three policemen[11] remained in the fort and were murdered. These

---

had reason to think that there were no people in the shelters." Further, in some of the shelters about which they informed, their own families were hiding.

11. According to Gar, *Umkum*, 216, and Garfunkel, *Kovno*, 183, about forty policemen were executed. Following is the list of thirty-nine policemen who were executed, compiled from a number of sources: Moshe Levin, captain of the ghetto police; Yehuda Zupovitz, his second-in-command; Ika Greenberg, ghetto police inspector; Dr. Ya'akov Shapira, commander of the Second Quarter; Panimunsky, commander of the Third Quarter; Eliezer Bukanz, his second-in-command; Haim Robinson, commander of the unit for special issues; Lula Aronovsky, commander of the gate guard; Sasha Zilberkweit, secretary of the criminal division; Ya'akov Abramson, secretary of the prison; Avraham Finkelstein, secretary of the Second Quarter; Titushkin, facilities manager; Attorney Zack, judge-investigator; Senior Constable Yehuda Aronovsky; Senior Constable Meir Zupovitz; Senior Constable Reuven Zeltzer; Senior Constable Kaboles; Senior Constable Korachinsky; Senior Constable Kalowarisky; and policemen: Zvi Abramson, Moshe Axelrod, Lonia Berman, Shlomo Gavaronsky, Yitzhak Dembin, Vershabovsky, Wolf Wolfovitz, Ika Zilberman, Tamshe, Gutel Ter, Lonya Yablonsky, Hirsch Levin, Lev, Haim Levner, David Linkovsky, Benzion Klotz, Mottel Krakinovsky, Hennick Rod, Hanne Rosenthal, and Eliezer Shulman.

included all the officers, the entire headquarters staff, and several regular policemen. When we went out free, we found out that aside from our cell, there was one other cell of heroes who were not influenced by Kittel's promises and positive words, and they remained silent. The informers were in one cell only. When we returned to the ghetto, we learned the details of the great destruction. In two days (March 27 and 28) some two thousand children and elderly had been taken from the ghetto. (Almost all of the informers among the police died in the camps, where they were shunned by their fellows. After the liberation, some of them – Arenstam, Ushpitz, and others – were sentenced by the Russians to ten to fifteen years of imprisonment.)

After the policemen returned to the ghetto, the police was disbanded, and in its stead the *Ordnungsdienst* was appointed. It was comprised of the informers from the fort and several dozen youth, led by the de facto commander T. Arenstam. The *Ordnungsdienst* was a tool of the commandant [Goecke].

Even after the bloody slaughter of the top echelons of the police and the disbanding of this institution, the Gestapo still did not fully achieve its goal in discovering the details of the underground in the ghetto.[12] The reason for this was the proud steadfastness of the police officers and active members who were involved in assisting the underground. Word spread of the conduct of Moshe Levin, Ika Greenberg, Yehuda Zupovitz, and their companions. Their names were spoken with admiration by the ghetto residents, who until that day had little love for the police, as they were unaware of its activities behind the scenes.[13]

The Death of Haim Yellin

Haim Yellin was at the top of the list of ghetto Jews who were wanted by the Gestapo. This was due to his status during the period of the Soviet regime, and also due to his many, varied roles in the ghetto underground. He was representative of the Communists in the leadership of the JFO, the main contact with the underground in the city, the authorized representative for negotiations with the

---

12. In a conversation with Moshe Segelson, Goecke boasted that in the hideouts, the Gestapo discovered sixteen rifles, twelve pistols, several hand grenades, and even a machine gun (Segelson, Di groyzame aktzia, 19; compare PKG, 116).

13. Testimony of Yitzhak Kashiv (Kapchovsky), YVSA, 15 (recording 4); compare Gar, Umkum, 306.

partisan command in the Rudniki Forests, and in charge of purchasing weapons and transport from the ghetto to the forests. Yellin followed strict precautions and secrecy procedures, yet several factors made it easier for his pursuers to follow him: He had many personal contacts as a talented writer and scion of a well-known family, whose home was a meeting place for literary and cultural personalities. In addition, the tasks he took upon himself (especially outside the ghetto) meant he became known to a large and varied public, both in the ghetto and in the city.

On March 31, 1944, immediately after the Children's *Aktion*, Yellin managed to send out another group to the Rudniki Forests. As opposed to the previous occasions, this time the participants slipped through holes in the fence one by one, except for four who were unsuccessful. Those who succeeded got into a vehicle that awaited them nearby. This eighth group included a number of central activists of the JFO, including Altke Tepper, responsible for medical care and supplies; the experienced liaison Yankel Levi; weapons purchaser Yitzhak Miklishansky; and liaison Shulamit Lerman.[14] The guides were Nehemiah Endlin and Baruch Lopiansky, who brought the Jews safely to the Death to the Occupiers base.

On April 5, 1944, Haim Yellin went into the city in order to procure transport for an armed group of about thirty fighters that was about to leave for the forest.[15] These people were already outside the ghetto at various locations, some of them at 18 Pudziu Street, in the home of Christian contact Ulia. They were at full readiness, awaiting the signal from Haim Yellin and the driver who was supposed to arrive at 4 P.M.

When the driver was delayed, one of the young women was sent to find out what happened. She was told that the driver had been arrested. The fighters dispersed throughout attics in the neighborhood, which had previously been the ghetto's First Quarter but had been cleared of its Jewish residents shortly before. They waited there for instructions from Haim Yellin. They decided that if Lithuanian policemen arrived and discovered them, they would open fire. The fighters

---

14. Meir Yellin, YVSA, letter 11; compare PKG, 117–19; FLC 10:8.

15. This group included activists from a number of groups: Dima Galpern, Yerachmiel Berman, Menashe Sapozhnikov and his wife, Leah Kizel, Branke "Cossack" and her sister, Meir Yellin, Zadok Bleiman, Mendel Sadovsky, and Aharon Manyeskin, among others. They had around twenty weapons. Testimony of Zadok Eviatar (Bleiman), YVSA, 24, recording 4; compare PKG, 119.

passed the night in this manner, and the next day they still awaited a signal from Yellin, who continued his efforts to find another driver.

But that day, when Haim Yellin reached the corner of Daukanto Street and Laisvės Alėja ("Freedom") Avenue, near the Trikolit dry cleaner, where he was about to meet the driver, a Lithuanian police agent jumped out at him and ordered him to raise his hands. Yellin shot at the agent and hit his hand.[16] At the sound of the shots, passersby rushed to the site, and Yellin slipped away. He jumped over the fence into a courtyard on Kęstučio Street and ran along that street until he reached Maironio Street, with police and German soldiers running after him. With the last bullets in his pistol, he shot a German major and Lithuanian captain who tried to stop him. He slipped into a courtyard and found a hideout in an abandoned basement. For several hours, his pursuers combed the area using search dogs, until they found him in his hiding place, bleeding copiously. He had slit his throat and wrists with a razor blade. None other than the Gestapo commander himself, Kittel, arrived at the site and ordered that Yellin be taken to the Gestapo. There they worked to restore him to a condition in which he would be able to provide information.

There are several conflicting versions of Yellin's death.[17] What we do know for certain is that Yellin died while imprisoned by the Gestapo, and that despite their efforts, his jailers were not able to obtain any information from him about the ghetto in general or the underground in particular.[18]

The circumstances of his death had severe repercussions in the ghetto and the Lithuanian Communist Party underground, which had been about to appoint

---

16. According to Gar, *Umkum*, 226, Yellin killed the agent.

17. See R. Berman, FLC 10:10; Gar, Umkum, 227; PKG, 120; and testimonies (YVSA) of Zadok Eviatar (Bleiman), 26 (recording 4b); Menachem Sadovsky (Ganuni), 25 (recording 4a); Z. Friedman, 5; Meir Yellin, letter 4; and Hasia Nadel, 8.

18. Benno Liptzer reported that he saw Yellin in the Gestapo building (see Moshe Segelson, *Partizaner Bavegung*, 5). According to the rumors in the ghetto, the Gestapo tortured Yellin with the most cruel methods, and "cut off parts of his body one by one" (testimony of Haim Nadel, YVSA, 8). Another witness reports that he heard from a Christian woman that Yellin was held in the Gestapo prison hospital for an extended period. She said he identified himself as a paratrooper, so as not to involve the ghetto in his matter. "The fact was that none of the people who worked around him on underground matters, whether close or distant, were arrested after his capture" (Meir Leib Goldschmidt, YVSA, letter 3; compare Moshe Segelson, *Partizaner Bavegung*, 5).

him as second secretary of the city committee in Kovno.[19] Members of the underground and many ghetto inhabitants mourned him and mentioned his name with an admiration accorded to very few people in the Kovno Ghetto.[20]

The Ambush on the Riverbank

Even after the death of Yellin, who had been the efficient organizer of the departures to the forest, the JFO command continued to attempt additional departures. But aside from the enormous difficulties due to the atmosphere of terror and Gestapo undercover activities inside the ghetto, they faced a severe problem of transportation. The JFO's contact with Pyotr Trofimov, an activist in the city underground who had assisted them by finding trustworthy drivers, ended with the death of Haim Yellin. Still, with the greatest of efforts, JFO activists succeeded in finding a driver with an appropriate vehicle who was willing to transport Jews for a respectable sum. He was told that the Jews were going out to hide in a village.

Saturday night, April 14, 1944, twelve people departed the ghetto in a vehicle.[21] Among them was partisan Abba Diskant, who was in the ghetto at that time and served as the group's guide.

The next day, Meir Marshak, one of those who had been in the vehicle, returned to the ghetto and related what had happened the previous night to the vehicle and its occupants:

---

19. The formal order for this appointment was brought to the Communist Party branch in Kovno by a messenger from the forest in the name of the Central Committee. But by the time the messenger reached Kovno, Yellin was no longer alive (PKG, 121). When his death became known, the Lithuanian underground published mourning notices for him (testimony of Haim Nadel, YVSA, 8).

20. On July 2, 1945, the Presidium of the Supreme Soviet granted Haim Yellin the Order of the Patriotic War, first class, posthumously (see *Tiesa* from July 2, 1945). For an article honoring the first anniversary of Yellin's death, by Meir Yellin, see *Einikeit* 21:133, March 24, 1945. See also L. Shauss, "Oyf di khurves fun kavner geta," *Einikeit* 33:93, August 17, 1944.

21. This group was comprised of JFO activists. Aside from Avraham Manyeskin of the Revisionists, most were from the Communist groups: Yerachmiel Berman, Menashe Sapozhnikov (members of the "Black Staff"), Shaul Finkel (responsible for the JFO weapons storehouse), Liba Schwartz, Rivka Uriash (one of the outstanding liaisons with the city), engineer Shimon Ratner (active head of the command after Yellin's death), brothers Moshe and Meir Marshak, and Yosef Shapira and his wife. Military trainer Zadok Bleiman was also supposed to join this group, but he hesitated at the last minute due to doubts about the driver's loyalty (testimony of Zadok Eviatar [Bleiman], YVSA, 24).

The car arrived at the designated time next to the ghetto gate. We sat inside and everything went as planned. Just outside the gate, several other members joined us, wearing military uniforms. Engineer Ratner was in charge of the departure. He sat in front with the driver. After we crossed the bridge, the car suddenly stopped on Jonavos Street [on the banks of the Vilya River], and the Lithuanian driver announced that the engine was not working properly and he had to get out to check it. The expression on his face was suspicious. We all pulled out our pistols. Just as the driver got out of the vehicle, shots showered down at us. The first to shoot back was Ratner, and he shot first at the contemptible driver....[22] We also fired back and tried to get out of the vehicle. The intensity of the shooting toward us increased. When I jumped out of the car, I noticed that Ratner and several other companions were no longer alive. I lay on the ground. The Germans were already close to us and their bullets rained down on us from all directions. We continued to fight back. I saw a German fall.... [23] My big brother, who was near me, was fatally wounded by a bullet. I began to run while shooting behind me. Another member fell beside me, wounded in the head. I shot him, so that he would not be captured alive, and I managed to get away.[24]

In this battle with the Gestapo, several Germans and a Lithuanian citizen, a chance passerby, were killed, aside from the Lithuanian driver. Of the twelve in the car, who fought with pistols alone,[25] eight were killed. Aside from Marshak, Abba Diskant, Rivka Uriash, and Yerachmiel Berman survived and returned to the ghetto.

This vehicle that was attacked was the ninth and last of the groups that the JFO sent out to the forest.

---

22. According to a different source (PKG, 126), Abba Diskant was the one who sat beside the driver and shot him. In FLC 10:11, Yerachmiel Berman said that he did it.

23. This was the Gestapo man Villi. Before the war, he lived in the Kovno suburb of Shanz. During the ghetto period, he earned a reputation for beating Jews in the Gestapo prison (PKG, 126; compare FLC, 10:11).

24. This testimony is cited from Segelson, *Partizaner Bavegung*, 7–8.

25. Apparently several rifles and a machine gun were packed in the vehicle, but due to the surprise attack, the fighters were not able to operate them in time (Zvie Brown, *Di shlacht oiyfen breg teich*, Neyvalt, May 14, 1950).

Decrees and Obstacles

The last days of the ghetto (March 27 to July 7, 1944) proved the extent to which the various types of underground activity were dependent on the general situation in the ghetto, or to be more precise, on the stability of the ghetto institutions.

We have seen how during the period of "relative quiet," when both the Germans and large circles in the ghetto considered the status of the Ältestenrat and its institutions as firm and legitimate, the underground movement flourished and attained significant achievements. To a certain extent, it was also able to direct the policy of these institutions. Once the original police organization was dispersed and its best officers murdered – and in its stead the Germans established the *Ordnungsdienst*, whose main members were traitors and informers – and even the Ältestenrat ceased to exist, the public-organizational support of the underground was in large part destroyed. Aside from the crushing blows dealt to it by the Germans, the underground was forced to operate under the reality of hostile institutions and in an atmosphere of suspicion and surveillance that these supervisory "institutions" created among the masses. This left its mark on the underground, both from an organizational aspect as well as from an ideological-ethical aspect. Another cause for this was the loss of its central figures, who died or were forced to go into hiding. Instead of an atmosphere of drive and careful planning based on responsibility and concern for the masses, the mood was one of evacuation (departure of the leaders and activists) and spontaneous activity. In large part, the underground still derived its vitality from the "golden age" and the tradition of joint operation of activists from different circles. Continuing to send people out of the ghetto under the new conditions tempted fate and the decrees, and it demanded energy and supreme sacrifice.

Due to the efforts of Dr. Elkes, who for reasons difficult to explain was permitted to continue in his role of representing the ghetto Jews, the public nationalist foundations that determined the character of the ghetto institutions were not completely demolished. With determination and daring, he continued to gather around him the remaining public figures, both those who were removed from their positions by the Germans and those who still held key positions, and he consulted with them on every fateful decision.[26] Until the last minute, he sup-

---

26. For example, until this point, Moshe Segelson, the manager of the ghetto factories, had operated behind the scenes. But during this period, he stood out for his assistance in equipping those departing for the forest (see chapter 8, "Sources of Funding").

ported the underground movement, and with his continued influence he tried to assist it and the rescue attempts of individuals and masses.

Along with the direct operations against the underground mentioned above, a flood of well-planned decrees and restrictions hit the entire ghetto, which was still in shock from the Children's *Aktion*.[27]

On April 4, the Ältestenrat members and heads of its departments were detained for failing to fulfill the German order to apprehend Ältestenrat member Zvi Levin and labor office representative Shimon Ratner. These individuals were part of the JFO leadership, and when they realized they were being followed, they went into hiding.

The eleven detainees were taken by Kittel to the Ninth Fort and placed into a dark cell. After a day of interrogation accompanied by threats,[28] nine of them were sent back to the ghetto, including Dr. Elkes. Ya'akov Goldberg and Leib Garfunkel were detained at the fort. Dr. Elkes had given the detainees cyanide in the ghetto,[29] and after the Germans discovered it, they began to interrogate them cruelly. They focused their tortures especially on Garfunkel.[30] They demanded to know who in the ghetto was responsible for smuggling people out to the partisans in the forest and the locations of the ghetto weapons storehouse, Zvi Levin's hideout, and the hiding place for the Ältestenrat's treasure of "millions." Under the most severe torture, he divulged details of the remaining twenty thousand marks in the hands of the Ältestenrat. Thanks to the utmost efforts of Dr. Elkes and his companions, Ya'akov Goldberg and then Leib Garfunkel were sent back to the ghetto, beaten and wounded. The Ältestenrat was dispersed and Dr. Elkes was appointed "Elder Jew," which at that point became a position in name only, devoid of responsibility.

---

27. For details of the decrees, see Gar, Umkum, 220–25; PKG, 125; Garfunkel, Kovno, 184–89.
28. Among other issues, they were interrogated about connections with the partisans and hiding places in the ghetto (testimony of Leah [Lucia] Elstein-Lavon, YVSA, 13, recording 3).
29. When Dr. Elkes realized what he and his companions would soon face, he met with Goldberg and Garfunkel and proposed that they hide. They refused to do so and leave him to his fate. He then gave them the poison, and each promised the other that if they were investigated, they would reveal nothing.... When Dr. Elkes was released from the fort and heard that Garfunkel was tortured, he feared that Garfunkel would attempt suicide. He shared this suspicion with Benno Liptzer, who apparently told the Germans about the hidden poison (Garfunkel, Kovno, 185).
30. Ibid., 187.

In the Kovno concentration camp, as it was then called, the SS and the Gestapo ruled with the assistance of the *Ordnungsdienst*, which they established in place of the Jewish ghetto police. This new institution, comprised of fifty people, answered to the sole authority of concentration camp commander Goecke and the Gestapo. It was headed by Benno Liptzer, T. Arenstam,[31] and several other policemen who had cooperated with the Germans during the Children's *Aktion* and were particularly hated by the Jews. From that point, everyone had to be wary of the *Ordnungsdienst* – underground members as well as ordinary Jews who planned to escape from the ghetto or to smuggle out their children. Far from assisting the rescue operations, the *Ordnungsdienst* actively hindered them.[32]

In this period, the security surrounding the ghetto gate was intensified, and the armed escorts of the labor brigades was increased to one sentry for every five or six Jews. Twice daily the Jews had to submit an exact report of all the residents in ghetto houses. Personal accountability for every missing Jew was held by members of his family, the head of the block of apartments where he lived, and the leader of the labor brigade in which he worked. The decree of collective responsibility undermined mutual trust and intensified suspicion among ghetto residents. In order to track every activity of escape or rescue, whether organized or unorganized, the Germans brought in German criminals in the role of *kapo* to supervise all activity at the labor sites.

An activist at JFO headquarters describes the atmosphere of despair that reigned in the organization at that time:

> The most difficult period in the ghetto struggle began following the Children's *Aktion* and after the best of the policemen were shot. Spies and traitorous dogs began to swarm throughout the ghetto, such as Benzion Zhamaitis and others. By contrast, connections among the organizations were strengthened and they became a unified family.... Every member's home became a shared base. But unfortunately, we were already living in a cage from which we could not break out. The Organization [JFO] suffered one failure after

---

31. The Germans appointed Liptzer as head of the *Ordnungsdienst*, but in actuality T. Arenstam commanded the unit. Previously, as vice-commander of the gate guards, he became known for his coarse, cruel behavior toward Jews at the ghetto gate.

32. Testimonies of Yitzhak Kashiv (Kapchovsky), 13 (recording 4); Moshe Segelson, 13; compare PKG, 125; Garfunkel, Kovno, 189.

another. The city[33] showed very little interest, or none at all, in ghetto events. We received no weapons and could not obtain even the smallest amount. When they agreed to give us weapons, it was already too late.[34]

They had not yet had time to reorganize the work of the command staff, whose best members had been killed (such as Moshe Levin, Haim Yellin, and Shimon Ratner), or were forced to disappear (such as Zvi Levin and Isaac Serebnitzky),[35] when serious problems arose that had to be solved as quickly as possible. For example, in the space of one night Beitar members were forced to abandon the weapons cache in Moshe Levin's courtyard after they were warned that the Germans were about to conduct a search there.[36] They also had to urgently hide and smuggle out individuals who were hunted by the Germans.

After Dima Galpern and Dr. Rudolph Volsonok became leaders of the Communist organization,[37] other groups no longer accorded it the same authority as when Haim Yellin had stood at the helm. Yellin had based his activity on mutual respect and firm trust. In the Communist groups, friction arose on the issue of giving preference to certain people in the limited methods of rescue and departure that were still possible. For example, the wives of the partisans whose husbands were sent to the forest in the organization's groups asserted that they had special eligibility for places in the few *malina*s that were still fit for use in case of emergency.[38] Members of the Black Staff also took unwarranted initiative in committing robbery and murder, while the JFO was unable to control it or bring it under its authority.[39]

Ties also loosened among the members of the Zionist workers' parties (Hashomer Hatzair, Zionist Socialists, Gordonia), most of whom were at the 7 Mildos collective. After their *malina* was discovered during the Children's *Aktion*, there was no reason to rely on it any more. Young women with the appropriate

---

33. Referring to the Communist underground in the city of Kovno.
34. Meir Leib Goldschmidt, YVSA, letter 1.
35. Other JFO activists also avoided being seen on the streets at that time (testimony of Zadok Eviatar [Bleiman], YVSA, 27, recording 5a).
36. Testimony of Baruch Camber (Ezged), YVSA, 6.
37. After the death of Haim Yellin, engineer Shimon Ratner replaced him for a short period.
38. Testimony of Haim Nadel, YVSA, 7.
39. One of their murder victims was jewelry merchant A. Rudnick (Testimony of A.G., YVSA, 35; see also end of chapter 8).

looks (such as Miriam Buz, Penina Sukenik, Rachel (Koka) Rosenthal, and Rachel Zagai) were placed in Lithuanian homes outside the ghetto by Dr. Kissin, with the active assistance of Reverend Paukshetis.[40] But for the others, there was no chance for organized departure from the ghetto. Although the members continued to meet, they did so out of habit.[41] In essence social life at Mildos waned. All organized activity ceased and the members were given freedom of operation to save themselves and their families. This was the case for the other organizations as well, especially those that suffered heavy losses of life among the leadership. For example, activities of the Revisionist organization were extremely limited, and the center of influence moved to its youth membership, which still survived at that point.[42]

But while the underground movement experienced severe crises in the Kovno central concentration camp (formerly the ghetto), underground groups were gaining strength in detention camps near the city, which had been established previously under the *Kasernierung* framework. Some of them were even able to establish secret contact with the ghetto, collect weapons, and even assist the JFO command in the central camp.[43] Possibly this was due to their lengthy experience in the camps and talent for adapting to conditions, which had not changed greatly from the first day of their arrival. The transition from relatively comfortable conditions in the ghetto to the concentration camp atmosphere was long behind them, while in the ghetto, the change had been made only recently and in a sudden and drastic manner.

The JFO command in the ghetto, to the extent that it continued to operate then, was assisted by these branches more than it was able to assist them. Aside from general instructions to prepare escape groups and a covert arrangement with the ghetto hospital physicians, who extended the hospitalization of members brought from the branch camps, ostensibly for recuperation, we have no knowledge of any other assistance.

---

40. For details of this rescue operation, see testimony of Dr. P. Kissin, YVSA, 2–3 (recording 3).

41. Testimony of Dina Morovitz, YVSA, 3; Menachem Sadovsky (Ganuni), YVSA, 28.

42. Testimony of Baurch Camber (Ezged), YVSA, 6.

43. A group of underground activists at Shanz camp (including Moshe Kaltinovsky and Gordon) supplied bullets and army uniforms to the central JFO command in the ghetto. Other groups also operated at the camps at Aleksot (Dr. Eliezer Zilber, Benzion Preiss, and Shmuel Zeidelson), Palemon, Koshedar, and Keidan. On activity in the last two camps, see chapter 9.

Continued Departure of Groups from the Ghetto

At that time, some 150 JFO activists were living inside the ghetto area, and they were the first in line to depart for the forests. The composition of the final groups – the eighth, the group about to depart on the day Haim Yellin was killed (April 6, 1944), and the group that was ambushed by the Germans on the banks of the Vilya on April 14, 1944 – demonstrates the definite trend of sending out activists from all groups.[44] This was mainly due to the anticipated persecutions of the Germans and the *Ordnungsdienst*, and also due to the feeling that possibilities for continued activity in the ghetto were minimal. Out of fear for actions against the JFO, the remaining supply of weapons was removed and transferred to the city with the assistance of JFO members Moshe Konyuchovsky and Nina Finkelstein, who worked in the Silva factory.

After the departure of the eighth group, contact with the Rudniki Forests was cut off. Only a few individuals who were assisted by the JFO were able to sneak through the ghetto fence and reach the base of the Kovno battalions.[45] Partisans Abba Diskant and Tuvia Pilovnik, who came to the ghetto on a mission, were given the role of renewing contact with the forest. Reuven Gorgal and Menachem Rubin accompanied them.[46] Some 30 kilometers east of Kovno, the group was attacked by police, and its members fell in battle.[47]

Due to this misfortune and the knowledge that the Kovno battalions from Rudniki Forest were moving west, the underground leadership decided to search for contact with partisan groups in forests nearer Kovno, particularly the Kazlu-Ruda Forests.[48] Scouts were again sent in numerous directions. For example, Benzion Preiss, Avraham Rosen, and Shafransky went out to the Zeimai region intending to contact a *spetzgruppe* (expert partisans from Moscow), but with

---

44. Compare FLC 10:8.

45. Some of the few who succeeded in reaching the Rudniki Forests during that period were Shmuel Rosen, Shika Vershabovsky, Fania Zilberman, and Zivia Kapit. Among those who died along the way were Isaac Vlodovsky and Leib Gilman (Meir Yellin, YVSA, letter 11). According to Yerachmiel Berman, on May 14, 1944, a group of twelve left the ghetto on foot to Murava, guided by Abba Diskant. From there, a non-Jewish guide took them to the Rudniki Forests (FLC 10:10).

46. Menachem Rubin, an IBZ member, purchased a pistol on his own and received his organization's authorization to go out to the forest (testimony of Fima Rosenberg, YVSA, 12).

47. According to a Lithuanian source, Tuvia Pilovnik was identified after death as one of the escapees from the Ninth Fort. His body was taken there and burned (Štaras, 95).

48. Testimony of Zvi Friedman, YVSA, 5.

no results. The plans to establish bases near Kovno were also revived. A small group of Beitar youth – Baruch Camber, Haim Kunevitz, Uri Chanoch, and B. Blumkin – planned to breach the fence and go out to the Vershevis region, but the failure of Yitzhak Katz, who was shot in a similar breakout attempt, discouraged them from doing so. At the time, the numerous sentries guarded the fence perimeter like hawks, and many JFO members were shot trying to slip into the city on missions. Among those killed were Rachel Katz, Sonia Goldschmidt, Sheina Wachter, Rivka Uriash, Leah Kizel, Bela Ackman, Henach Segalovitz, Itzik Kirkel, and Ronia Rosenthal.[49] A special cell was established, under the command of Pesach Shater and Yosef Michles, to specialize in breaking through the fence and transferring people outside the ghetto. But people were still killed during the passage.

The attempts at contact with the Kazlu-Ruda Forests had positive results. Initiators of this effort were sisters Ira (Irena) and Lola Berman, who lived as nuns in the town of Garliawa, and visited the ghetto on occasion.[50] In late April 1944, they gave information that Soviet paratroopers were in the Kazlu-Ruda Forests, and that conditions there would support establishment of a base for the ghetto fighters. A group of four, guided by Ira, reached the forest safely. On May 4, Ira returned to the ghetto and took with her two others, Yerachmiel Berman and Shmuel Dietz.[51] On the way, Ira fell into an ambush of the Lithuanian police, while her two companions safely reached a small partisan unit that was in the organizational stage. In June, Shmuel Dietz was sent to the ghetto to bring out new fighters. The third group of eight individuals also met up with an ambush, and aside from Dietz, all were killed.

Below is Dietz's story of the second and third groups:

On Saturday we went out through the fence, myself and Rachmilke Berman. Irka was waiting with Maria Leschinsky,[52] who was living in her home. I had

---

49. Meir Yellin, YVSA, letter 11; testimony of Malka Pugatzky-Smali, YVSA, 35-6 (recording 10).
50. For a description of meetings and conversations with the two sisters and details of their personalities, see memoirs of Esther Luria (YVSA, 03/637, page 131).
51. Shmuel Dietz was a member of the religious section of the IBZ. After the Children's *Aktion*, with the knowledge of the IBZ, he contacted the Communists (who still had certain connections with the "outside"), in order to join the groups of fighters who went out to Kazlu-Ruda.
52. Maria Leschinsky was one of the most trustworthy Christian contacts who assisted the ghetto organization. Her husband was murdered by the Germans for anti-Nazi activity. She lived near the ghetto (compare *PKG*, 128, and Hitlerine, 291).

two pistols, one of which I had obtained from the Communists with money I received in exchange for a sewing machine. Rachmilke did not have a pistol. In case of an incident that took place near the ghetto, within 100 meters of the fence, our orders were not to return fire.... We slept in the Christian cemetery....

On Sunday morning we went out to the Christian woman, and Irena Berman was there. She had a small pistol, and Yerachmiel took the Parabellum. We went on our way. The two of them walked together and I walked behind, as a precaution. That day, a *goy* recognized Yerachmiel and shouted, "Jews!" The three of us jumped into a boat and crossed to the other side [of the Nemunas].... We hid in one of the groves and waited about an hour until we verified that no one was pursuing us. We began to walk on an unpaved road in the direction of Garliawa.... In one of the villages, we passed next to a house, and a boy of about five or seven years old stood and shouted, "Robber!" I noticed that this house had a telephone. After walking for another 2 kilometers, a Lithuanian with a bicycle overtook us. He stopped the bicycle next to a telephone pole, as if to put air in the tire, but I noticed he was watching the two who walked in front....

According to an agreed sign between us (whistle), they got off the road and waited for me among the bushes on the side of the road. I told them about the incident, and we realized that it was very serious. Because there was nowhere we could flee, we organized a perimeter defense and waited for what was to come. Yerachmiel was the commander. For an hour nothing happened. We continued to progress toward Garliawa, and when we crossed the railroad tracks we saw an unusual group of armed people at the far end of the village. When we arrived at a point 500 meters from Garliawa, we were attacked with heavy rifle fire.

We fled in retreat and returned to the railroad tracks. On the way, Yerachmiel lost the compass. We ran 5 kilometers through the forest and did not know how to get out. Further on our route we found an unpaved road and continued until we entered the village of Papilvis on the Pilvė River. We wanted to know where we were, so Irena decided to take a risk and approached the first farmer she saw on the road. She introduced herself as a student who was out for a hike and asked the way to our destination. The *goy* showed us the way, but after we had gone another 500 meters, he overtook us on his bicycle and apologized for pointing us in the wrong direction. We went with him, and when we passed his house again his wife and son were standing there and they invited us to spend the night with them, because darkness was falling. His name was Antanas Konzaitis, and he was the forest warden. We had no choice. We entered his house with the approach "Respect him, but suspect him." We divided the night into three shifts, and each of us was awake [for one of them].

After we lay down to sleep, the neighbors came to call him because a wild animal was ruining the field. We saw him take a hunting rifle and go out with them. We let off our safety locks and waited for what was coming. After a while, he returned and went to sleep. We calmed down and continued our watches. In the morning, after we had eaten, he hitched up his cart and took us to the main road. He did not take a penny, despite our remonstrations.

From there we continued walking on the roadside according to the same arrangement (I walked 500 meters behind the others). When we reached 7 kilometers before the village where we were supposed to make contact with the partisans, and where Lola Berman, Irena's sister, was staying, a truck carrying Lithuanian policemen overtook us, stopping when it pulled alongside the two who went first. At that moment I saw that Rachmilke pulled out the pistol and shot at them. After a struggle, they caught Irka, and Rachmilke fled to the side of the road. I was afraid they would search the forest where Rachmilke escaped, and I fled to the other side of the road, and went several kilometers into the forest. I waited three hours, and when I concluded they were not searching for me, I went back to the main road and continued walking until I reached the village of Pazeliai.

I knew we were supposed to meet in the fifth house on the left side of the road. But when I reached the village, I saw that there were two entrances, and two houses. I waited a while in order to determine the correct house. Suddenly a young Lithuanian woman of around seventeen left the village. She looked at me and asked if I knew an actor named Berman. I understood that she was looking for me. She led me into the nearby grove.... In the grove I met up with Yerachmiel Berman, who told me he had fled and arrived by a side road.... When darkness fell, we went to the home of the contact, where several Russian partisans awaited us along with Irka's sister Lola. We decided to send a messenger to Marijampole in order to see what we could do for Irena. We slept in that house.

Then we were taken to a nearby forest, several kilometers from Kazlu-Ruda. There I met up with Meir Zilber. The partisans did not want to keep him. They said he could not be a partisan. There were several other Jews there who had arrived before us in an unorganized fashion. I was there for about one month. M. Pechkis,[53] who had been a police officer during the Soviet occupation, was the commander. We were still in the stage of organization, and so we did not have real operations yet. We obtained food in the area. One day, I received an order from Pechkis to return to the ghetto to bring other people. They sent Meir Zilber with me so that he would return to the ghetto.[54] Beforehand, they took his personal weapon.

We left in the morning. We continued on the main road and walked with the railroad tracks. We were not far from the road where we had met up with the bicycle rider. We saw a new carriage approaching with a man in uniform. Meir said to me, "That's one of the forest wardens," but I realized it was a police officer. By that point, he was already too close, and there was no point in avoiding him. He stopped beside us, pulled out his pistol, and asked, where are you going? I answered that we were going to our relatives in the village. He said, wait! The moment he jumped from the carriage, I pulled out my pistol and pulled the trigger. I heard only the click of the hammer, but no more – the bullet was useless. When the police officer saw the pistol, he decided to retreat. Because my pistol did not work, I turned around and we both fled into the nearby grove. When we entered the grove, I lost Meir Zilber, and to this day I do not know what happened to him. I searched for him, because he was without a weapon (I had six bullets), but in vain. On the map I saw that further in the grove I could exit onto the main road – I had a sun map [made by holding a map in front of the sun and tracing the image on a piece of paper]. When I reached the road, a hail of bullets hit me, and

53. Compare PKG, 127.
54. Banishing a fighter from the ranks of the partisans and sending him back to a location that was under German supervision is extremely puzzling, particularly from the security aspect. We have found no similar case in the history of the Kovno battalions. PKG ignores this incident, mentioning only that Meir Zilber died (ibid., 127).

I heard "There he is!" in Lithuanian. I crawled back, bullets whistling over my heard. After 200 meters, I crawled into a trench and camouflaged myself with branches. I changed a bullet in the pistol and waited.

The police combed the forest, and one of the policemen passed about 4 meters from me. I noticed he was walking as if forced to do so, as if he was saying, "You won't touch me and I won't touch you." I followed him with the barrel of my pistol until he disappeared from my sight.

After that, I reached Maria Leschinsky, and she signaled the ghetto.[55] At night, I went back into the ghetto. They told me they would inform me as to when they would give me more people – this was several weeks before the liquidation of the ghetto. I went to the Communists' bunker near their headquarters, which was beside the Christian cemetery on Broliu Street. On the way I met up with *Ordnungsdienst* officers Arenstam and Grossman. They wanted to catch me, but I slipped away. One day, I received a message to return to headquarters, and they gave me eight more people.... As opposed to previously, at that point the orders were to walk only at night. We also had more weapons.

The route at night was very difficult to navigate. We operated according to the known system: in each village we took someone and he escorted us to the next village. In one village, after we took one of the *goyim*, someone apparently alerted the local police. We heard people running, and they shouted in Lithuanian, "Hands up!" Because they ambushed us, we spontaneously scattered in a grain field.... I heard alternating shots, and to this day, I do not know what happened to the other fellows. For two days I lay in the grain, as I knew they were searching for us in the area. I had a pistol and a pair of tefillin [prayer phylacteries] – before I left, I had a fight with Dimka Galpern, who did not allow me to take tefillin or a watch with Hebrew letters – but I took the tefillin anyway.

I decided not to return to the partisans, but rather to go to Papilvis, to that same farmer, Antanas Konzaitis. I called him outside, and told him the whole truth. He said that he already knew [who I was] at our first meeting, because

---

55. The underground had a prearranged system of signals with this contact. The color of the clothes she hung in her window, which was clearly visible inside the ghetto, served as a signal. In addition, every day she would deliver letters from the city into the ghetto and back, by tying the letter to a stone that was thrown over the fence (compare PKG, 128).

I was wearing boots and tight riding pants, and the pistol in my pocket protruded. One of the reasons I decided not to return to the partisan unit was that they were not willing to bring my sister and my three-year-old brother out to the forest. But this *goy* promised to take them out of the ghetto. He brought me to the forest that he guarded and put me in a hiding place he had made in order to conceal the meat and grain from the Germans. One week later, he went to the ghetto and contacted the Lape factory. From there he notified my sister that [she and my brother] should prepare, and that in another week someone would come to get them. When he returned two weeks later, the ghetto was in flames.[56]

During this period, the underground made several more attempts at organized departure to the forests. A small group, which included Zadok Bleiman, Aryeh Rafeika, Reichman, Intriligator, and others, managed to depart through the fence. With the assistance of farmers who had connections with the partisans, they reached the Josvainiai Forests. They stayed with farmers and over time acquired weapons and built a secret bunker. They wandered the forest in the region until the Soviet army arrived.[57] Several dozen Jews from the ghetto, some armed, reached the forests near Jurburg and hid in a bunker there. Due to a tragic incident, the bunker was discovered by the Germans. The Jews resisted, but were killed.[58]

Another group of Zionist Socialists planned to transport people to southern Lithuania to the Kopczewe (Kapčiamestis) region. A representative even spoke with a Lithuanian car owner in the city about driving them there, but the Lithuanian refused, and the idea never progressed beyond the planning stage.[59] Similar results were obtained by other organized groups that included JFO members who made daring plans to leave the ghetto.

Although the departure plans were at the top of the agenda of the JFO command, other operations were also carried out on occasion. On the day of the Children's *Aktion*, some of the activists from the Communist groups, including Frieda Lan, Sonia Berger, Rachel Katz, and Hasia Nadel, hid children in sacks in

---

56. Testimony of Shmuel Ben-Menachem (Dietz), YVSA, 14–24.
57. Testimony of Zadok Eviatar (Bleiman), YVSA, 24–25 (recording 4b).
58. Gar, *Umkum*, 194.
59. Testimony of Menachem Sadovsky (Ganuni), YVSA, 9 (recording 2a).

attics, thus saving sixty children.[60] An industry for forging stamps and certificates also developed,[61] for those going into the city.

The Final Hours and Desperate Rescue Attempts

In the first days of July 1944, Goecke informed Dr. Elkes that the ghetto was to be liquidated and its residents evacuated to East Prussia for labor. This news influenced the ghetto masses like the release of a tightly wound spring. All their potential energy and will to live were directed toward two avenues: feverish construction of *malina*s and mass escape from the ghetto. On July 7, 1944, Goecke announced the beginning of the actual evacuation. That night, many Jews were killed in the attempt to cross the ghetto fence.[62] The next day, thousands of Jews dug in inside *malina*s and basements, steadfast in their decision not to report for deportation to Germany, no matter what. The Soviet army had already reached the gates of Vilna, and this encouraged the "rebels."[63] Even after they realized that after the occupation of Vilna, the Russians did not advance toward Kovno but rather toward Grodno,[64] thousands of Jews still refused to leave the *malina*s.[65]

Within the confusion and turmoil that reigned in the ghetto after the announcement of the evacuation, the feeling grew, even among members of the organized underground, that there was no longer anyone who could be relied upon

---

60. Testimony of Hasia Nadel, YVSA, 9.

61. Testimony of Yitzhak Kashiv (Kapchovsky), YVSA, 14 (recording 4); Menachem Sadovsky (Ganuni), YVSA, 8 (recording 2a).

62. In several cases, the SS sentries agreed to take bribes and permit Jews to smuggle through the fence at night, but when passing, the sentries fired at the Jews and murdered dozens (including Eliezer Yellin, father of Haim). This trap was planned by Goecke's assistant, SS Sharfuhrer Pilgram. The next day, he boasted of this deed in front of his Jewish secretary. Testimony of Leah [Lucia] Elstein-Lavon, YVSA, 18 (recording 4); compare Gar, *Umkum*, 234; Moshe Segelson, *Di liquidatzie*, 12.

63. A popular saying in those days was, "*Di geule afen naz un der halaf afen haldz*" (Redemption is in front of our noses and the knife is at our necks; Gar, *Umkum*, 231).

64. On June 22, 1944, the Russians began the Vitebsk attack, and by July 7 they had reached Vilna. They occupied the city on July 13. Then it was Kovno's turn. But strategic justifications pushed the Red Army to pass over Kovno for the moment and to chase the enemy in other directions. In large part, this decision decided the fate of the Kovno Jews, who were sent to Germany at that very time. The Red Army occupied the city of Kovno on July 31.

65. For details on the evacuation and the sending of several shipments to Germany, see Moshe Segelson, *Di liquidatzie*, 13–18. See also testimony of Leah [Lucia] Elstein-Lavon, YVSA, 19 (recording 4).

and that anyone who could save himself should do so.[66] Indeed, this feeling was close to the truth. The underground command no longer existed in its previous framework. Several activists from the groups that were close to the previous command joined its remaining members, uniting around Dr. Volsonok and others.

The reality in which these few activists had to act was chilling. The ghetto was surrounded by three rows of police forces of all types (SS and Gestapo units from Kovno, *Schutzpolizei* from Vienna, *Ordnungspolizei* from Riga, an SS company from Hungary, and even firefighters from Kovno). They were armed with automatic weapons, hand grenades, and containers of gasoline. The hunt inside the ghetto had begun, and hundreds of Jews were locked in pens in preparation for transport to Germany. The remainder wandered in search of any kind of shelter inside houses, in basements, and in hastily prepared *malinas*. The opinion that solidified among the activists was to refuse to follow the deportation decree. "The significance of deportation for the Jews," asserted Dr. Volsonok to Moshe Segelson, manager of the workshops, "is complete liquidation, as in the Ninth Fort. We must not agree to this, and therefore we must take every step in order to prevent implementation of the decree."[67]

As a first step, the JFO declared "ready" status and ordered its members to gather at the meeting places. They publicized a message to the ghetto masses: "No one should go to the transports! Better to die here than more slavery!"[68] Numerous plans arose, some concrete, some fantastic, but in all the aspect of protest outweighed the practical side. For example, Eli Rauzuk, of the 7 Mildos Street group, proposed that the Jews throw sand in the Germans' eyes as they were deported from the ghetto, so that some would manage to flee.[69] Another proposal was that the Jews should lay on the ground, thus demonstrating their resistance, and making deportation more difficult for the Germans.[70] Other groups discussed setting the ghetto on fire.[71]

Finally, they agreed on a plan to dig a tunnel 30 meters long from 2 Broliu

---

66. Testimony of Michael Glass, YVSA, 8 (recording 2); testimony of Yitzhak Kashiv (Kapchovsky), YVSA, 13 (recording 4).

67. Moshe Segelson, *Di liquidatzie*, 5.

68. This slogan was apparently distributed in a limited number of handmade copies.

69. Testimony of Michael Glass, YVSA, 7 (recording 2).

70. Testimony of Yitzhak Rabinovitz, YVSA, 23 (recording 6).

71. Testimony of Esther Schwatz-Glass, YVSA, recording 4.

Street to Kriščiukaičio Street, alongside the Christian cemetery, and there connect it to a large sewage pipe that continued in the direction of an area where
Lithuanians lived.[72] Because this section of Kriščiukaičio Street was already
outside the fence, the Jews hoped that through the tunnel people could escape
outside the ghetto without arousing the sentries' notice, and after reaching the
city members of the underground there would assist them. In order to purchase
weapons for the escapees they even made a collection from among those who
labored in the ghetto workshops. The workers there donated four thousand
marks and many jewelry items.[73] The tunnel was dug in secret, in continuous
shifts and under the direction of the best engineers and technicians in the ghetto,
including engineer Yitzhak (Julian) Familiar, B. Kapit, and M. Rapopsky. They
removed the sand in small bags, even in their pockets. But when the diggers
reached close to the manhole in the middle of Kriščiukaičio Street, the sandy
soil collapsed, blocking the tunnel and burying the hopes and plans of the underground for organized escape.[74] Following is the story of one of the engineers
who supervised the undertaking:

> The entrance to the tunnel had to be from a house inside the ghetto, whose
> entrance was I think from Baiuru Street, and the exit was at Kriščiukaičio
> Street, outside the ghetto borders.
>
> Engineer Tola Rosenblum, if I'm not mistaken, prepared the static calcu-
> lations. The tunnel had to be built solidly, and we had to place supports at a
> distance of every few meters. In many places, we had to construct additional
> reinforcements.
>
> The work took place in shifts, continuously. All the engineers and tech-
> nicians volunteered to help, as did builders and various ordinary individuals.

---

72. As opposed to the Vilna Ghetto, which was in the city center, Kovno Ghetto was established
in an undeveloped suburb that did not have a sewage system. In the Vilna Ghetto, therefore, it
was easier to use the sewage pipes for escape during the liquidation of the ghetto.

73. The initiator of the collection was the workshops manager Moshe Segelson, with the
support of Dr. Elkes and his companions. Dr. Altman, chairman of the workshops workers'
committee, together with the director of the mutual aid fund, who had previously endangered
their lives to help equip those departing for the forests, placed the workers' fund, which at
that time contained eight thousand marks, at the disposal of the collection (Moshe Segelson,
Di liquidatzie, 5–7).

74. Meir Leib Goldschmit, YVSA, letter 5; compare testimony of Menachem Sadovsky (Ganuni),
YVSA, 10 (recording 2a), and PKG, 130.

We all worked in extremely difficult conditions. People from the labor brigades, who sometimes managed to bring in all sorts of foodstuffs from outside, began to bring in planks and cement instead of food. They carried heavy beams for several kilometers and brought in cement in small bags and in their pockets. The most difficult problem was taking out the earth we dug. To avoid arousing suspicion and preserve secrecy, as at that time many Germans and German *kapos* were circulating in the ghetto, we had to remove the earth in small bags and pockets. We had to dispose of it far from the construction site and scatter it so that it would not arouse suspicion and no one would realize [what was going on].

The work progressed well, in a race against time. We knew that the end of the ghetto was approaching. We began to collect money to purchase weapons for those who would leave the ghetto through the tunnel and would have to fight with weapon in hand.

Although this feverish activity was performed by a large number of individuals, the project was carried out in complete secrecy. The people worked with such dedication and intense energy, it was hard to believe that they had already worked a full day or night at harsh, exhausting labor outside the ghetto and had walked several kilometers to work and back.

The earth that was dug in constructing the tunnel was scattered in lots and courtyards in the ghetto with such expertise that no one could suspect that something was going on.

After we went outside the ghetto borders, when the tunnel was almost complete and reached Krisčiukaičio Street, we reached a layer of sandy soil. It began to pour into the tunnel, covering the last section. In the meantime the evacuation of the ghetto had begun, and there was no time to repair the unexpected damage.[75]

Along with the activities of the underground, another unusual attempt was made to frustrate the Germans' plot for complete evacuation of the remaining Kovno Jews. It was a daring act, bordering on suicide, initiated and carried out by Dr. Elkes himself. He requested a special meeting with Goecke, the infamous ghetto destroyer, and proposed that he ignore the order for liquidation of the

---

75. Engineer Yitzhak (Julian) Familiar, YVSA, letter 2.

ghetto. The rescue of Kovno Jewry would stand in his favor on the fast-approaching judgment day and save him from the severe punishment he could expect from the Soviet authorities, who were soon to arrive.[76]

Dr. Elkes listed for Goecke the Nazi's crimes in Kovno and elsewhere. Using ethical, humane, and material justifications, he tried to convince the SS officer to accept his proposal. Goecke's facial expression and movements revealed that Dr. Elkes succeeded in reaching the sensitive points of his personality and in disturbing him powerfully. But in Goecke's psychological struggle, the SS officer in him was victorious. Gnashing his teeth and stamping his feet, he declared, "I am an officer of the Waffen SS. I will not do such a thing."

For five days, from July 10–15, 1944, the SS search units raged through the ghetto in pursuit of Jews who were hiding. In the last days, those who were caught were no longer sent to Germany – they were shot or thrown into the flames of the burning houses. Many buildings were blown up with the inhabitants inside.[77]

Underground members and activists were among those who were pulled from their hiding places. After the failure of the tunnel, their spirit was broken. Even Dr. Volsonok, who a few days earlier was one of the strongest opponents of the evacuation, left his hideout and decided to join the transports to Germany.[78]

In the words of someone who was close to the Communists and the JFO

---

76. A detailed description of this meeting and the content of the conversation is given in the memoirs of Moshe Segelson, who was present during the entire meeting (see Segelson, *Di liquidatzie*, 10–12; compare also testimony of Avraham Melamed, YVSA, 7).

77. In the bunker where Hirsch Zedack and his family hid, a note was found on a slip of paper; Zedack apparently wrote it in the last moments of his life, on July 15, 1944. In it, he describes the experience of being trapped during the moments of destruction: "They hunted us like animals. For seven days, we hid from our pursuers in the attic, with no water and in terrible heat. Then they threw hand grenades at us and set the entire building on fire. We managed to reach the basement while the building above us burned. Many people had already perished inside.... We are the last to remain alive.... May your life goal be to avenge our lives." The entire text of the note is found in PKG, 7; compare Davar, December 10, 1944.

78. Among those deported to Germany were Dima Galpern, a leader of the Communists and a close assistant to Haim Yellin. Dr. Volsonok was sent to Dachau and survived. After the liberation, he published a newspaper in the Landsberg displaced person's camp. The Yiddish paper, *Landsberger Lager Cajtung*, was written in Latin letters. While in the camp, he also published a series of interesting articles, and became a supporter of Zionism. He died in Munich following an illness, on December 31, 1945. On his life and work, see the obituary of Dr. Gruenhoyz in *Landsberger Lager Cajtung*, 1:13, January 8, 1946; see also *Das Freye Vart*, 17, January 25, 1946; *Unzer Veg*, 14, January 4, 1946.

leadership, we find an expression of this feeling of impotence and the rationale for the lack of action:

> The community activists all lay in the *malina*, because we had no other option. During the liquidation, we had not even one pistol.[79] The partisan groups had taken the weapons with them, and whatever we had purchased recently was kept outside the ghetto, due to the German spies who were lately in the ghetto. We had no weapons inside the ghetto. At one point, the city [Communist] organization had promised to attack the ghetto from outside in case the Germans stormed the ghetto. But the city organization did nothing. Inside the ghetto, the murderers went wild and burned people alive. They discovered our basement after the entire ghetto was already up in flames. For one week we lay there, with no air, food, or water. They brought us into the hut almost unconscious.... Afterward, we found ourselves in the Stutthof concentration camp, and then in Dachau. We remained alive due to our communal struggle, which we waged even in concentration camp conditions.[80] The communal life we lived there saved us from hunger and disease.[81]

Many factors (such as lack of weapons, the loss of the leadership, the atmosphere in the ghetto in the last one hundred days, and the absence of assistance from outside) led to the fact that the "ghetto defense plan," which had been so extensively discussed by the various underground groups, was not implemented. The plan had never been cancelled, even during the height of success of sending people out to the forest. From the available material we find that this plan was neglected in the final period and not given any importance.[82] The explanation that most of the witnesses give is the untenable strategic situation in the ghetto,

---

79. We know that some individuals who went down to the malinas had weapons. For example, several pistols in Block C were not discovered (testimony of Ephraim Gutman, YVSA, 27, recording 7; Oshry, Hurban Lita, 363). Several youths who were sent to Germany also had weapons. Yisrael Kopliansky used his weapon to cover escapees who broke out of a train car as it transported them to Germany (PKG, 132; compare Esther Luria, YVSA, 03/637, 206; Gruenhoyz, FLC, 8. 36; Gar, Umkum, 247).

80. Continuous underground activity continued under the exceptional conditions of the concentration camps in Germany. A newspaper, *Nitzotz*, appeared on occasion, and lectures and other cultural activities were held (testimony of Avraham Melamed, YVSA, 1; Gar, *Umkum*, 251 ff.; Garfunkel, *Kovno*, 259).

81. Meir Leib Goldschmidt, YVSA, letter 1.

82. Testimony of Zvi Friedman, YVSA, 4.

particularly after the evacuation of the First Quarter (old Slobodka), which according to the plan should have been the center of the resistance. In one testimony, we read:

> We never gave up on the plan for defending the ghetto, but...from the practical aspect it was impossible to carry out, for the following reasons: (1) We never knew when the total liquidation of the ghetto would take place so that we could decide to take this last step; and (2) the strategic situation in the ghetto was such that the Germans could easily divide us into small groups, and we would not be able to communicate with each other. The only serious concentration was in Slobodka – the wooden houses on the street of the yeshiva and similar structures. The moment the Germans cut off this section, it was difficult to discuss armed resistance, because from then on, there was an empty area between one house and the next that was in sight of the German guards. This was proven in the Children's *Aktion*, when contact between one meeting place and another was completely impossible.
>
> The ghetto defense plan was mainly based on the "combat units." They were supposed to break through the fence in Valoanos Alley, set the houses on fire on the Aryan side, and cause confusion among the enemy attackers, who would find themselves between the flames of the burning houses and the fire of the weapons in the hands of the ghetto defenders. Apparently the experienced Goecke and Kittel realized this, and so they removed the Jews from this area and pushed them closer to the river on one side and the empty fields on the other.[83]

Others offered this explanation in various forms, and with a certain tone of justification.[84] It is difficult to know if this explanation is after the fact, or if these

---

83. Meir Leib Goldschmidt, YVSA, letter 1. In 1941, when deciding on the location of the ghetto, the Germans took into account the strategic position of the site, which was connected to the city by only one bridge that could be blocked. See also testimonies of Menachem Sadovsky (Ganuni), YVSA, 10 (recording 2a); Zadok Eviatar (Bleiman), YVSA, 7 (recording 1b); S. Rabinovitz, YVSA, 10; Rivka Gordon, YVSA, letter 2.

84. The authors of PKG (116) go so far as to praise the JFO's astuteness in resisting the Germans' provocation to engage them in open warfare.

were the real considerations at the time. In any case, the fact is that at the time of destruction of the ghetto, there was no armed resistance,[85] nor was there any true attempt to organize the ghetto masses into an uprising.

---

85. In one instance, a group of Jews who had been hiding in a burning basement ran outside. The Germans were about to throw them back into the flames, when one Jew, Haim Schneider, attacked a German and struggled with him until he choked him. Haim Schneider survived (testimony of Yankele Verbovsky, YVSA, 4).

CHAPTER 15

Liberation

The final order for liquidation was given on July 8, 1944, and the Kovno Jews stood helpless before it. The last ghetto residents, those who were not burned in the flames or choked by the smoke that filled the *malinas*, basements, and hideouts, were transported by vehicle or led on foot toward Germany. At the same time, their partisan brothers and sisters marched along the forest paths, toward their hometown, with only a few dozen kilometers separating their march of freedom from the ghetto prisoners' march of annihilation.

At the Main Base

With the departure of the best fighting forces of the Kovno battalions to southwest Lithuania, the atmosphere at the base was one of calm and expectation. The new weapons stock, the full food stores, and the warm weather imbued a positive spirit in the respite after the spring months, which had been full of activity. From that point, the military operations consisted mainly of regular patrols and disruption of the nearby enemy transportation lines. The Germans acted with extreme caution, to the point that they ceased use of the vulnerable railroad tracks.

The fighters utilized the lull for organizing and repairing their personal equipment in order to adapt it to the warm weather. But in mid-June 1944, the short period of calm and the relative quiet at the base came to an end, and several unusual phenomena hinted at the decisive moment that was about to arrive.

Each day, dozens of Soviet prisoners-of-war knocked on the gates of the base. They had been utilized by the Germans as a supporting army and fled to the partisans with their uniforms and weapons, begging to be accepted into the ranks of the fighters. Most were of Asian origin and barely spoke Russian. Lacking clear procedures for what to do with them, the partisans ordered them to complete questionnaires and write their biographies in detail. In the meantime, they were accepted into the battalion in a limited fashion. They became the target of ridicule and derision by the experienced fighters, who viewed them as last-minute arrivals who only wished to enjoy "the world to come" and be forgiven by the Soviet regime for cooperating with the Germans.[1]

The Germans feared an upcoming offensive on the western Byelorussian front, and so they gathered huge forces in order to destroy once and for all the partisan units in the Rudniki Forests, which were likely to disrupt their vital supply lines and possibly even their routes of retreat. According to the intelligence reports, the Germans were about to search the forest with the support of artillery, tanks, and airplanes. The enemy airplanes flew low and circled above the forest, attempting to locate the partisan camps. The brigade command did not hesitate but immediately evacuated the bases, gathered the battalions near the village of Salki, and drew up a detailed plan for rapid splitting of the groups and breaking through the siege. After two days of tense anticipation, the Germans broke off the siege, due to the urgent need to transfer reinforcements to shaky sections of the front.[2]

Even after the battalions returned to their locations, enemy airplanes continued the search for them. Therefore the Death to the Occupiers battalion carefully camouflaged its structures and installations, under the supervision of the commissar.[3]

At that time, the White Poles also intensified their activity. On one hand, they tried with all their might to "create" facts on the ground by occupying villages and towns that were evacuated by the Germans. On the other hand, they used "diplomatic" channels to push the Red Army to include them in the occupation of Vilna and the surrounding region, as soon as this was decided.

On June 20, 1944, three days before the Russians began the Vitebsk offensive, the partisan camps along the front were ordered to blow up the enemy railroad

---

1. Testimony of Pugatzky-Smali, YVSA, 33–34 (recording 4). During the exit from the forest, many of these "partisans" were executed by shooting, following the indication of the Soviet Army command, for the crime of collaboration with the Germans. See also *Sefer ha-partizanim ha-yehudim* 1:156.

2. Lazer, 354; PKG, 160.

3. One of the orders was that the women were forbidden from wearing colorful clothes, especially headscarves.

tracks. That night, in over one thousand attacks, hundreds of kilometers of tracks were rendered useless. A sabotage unit from the Death to the Occupiers battalion also participated.[4]

At this point, the fourth unit of the Death to the Occupiers camp went out toward Lithuania, under the command of battalion commander Konstatin Smirnov Radyonov himself. The unit was comprised of some twenty individuals, including four Jewish fighters. Three of these were Eliezer Moses, Aharon Vilenchuk, and Mira Weiner. But the unexpected success of the Red Army offensive disrupted the unit's schedule, and they had no time to operate. In the end, they met up with Red Army units and returned to base.[5]

The Last Operation: Conquering Rudniki

In late June, the Germans began urgent evacuation of their posts in the entire region. In the ensuing vacuum, the Lithuanian partisan brigade and the White Poles competed for control. Usually, the first to arrive in a particular place took over. But sometimes both sides had control in one location, and then clashes were difficult to avoid.

This was the case in the important district capital of Rudniki after the Germans departed. Aside from the proximity of this town to the Death to the Occupiers battalion, which suffered greatly from the German garrison posted there, the partisan command was also motivated by the prestige of conquering Rudniki.[6] But when a battalion unit reached the town, powerful White Polish forces were already at its gates. The two groups exchanged fire, and fighter Yisrael Zig was fatally wounded. Due to the greater strength of the White Polish force the partisans were about to retreat, when suddenly reinforcements from Gabris's battalion arrived, and the sides began negotiations.

In the meantime, fighters of the Vilna Jewish battalion The Avenger also arrived. They decided to ignore the negotiations and storm Rudniki at any price, especially when they learned that the White Poles were willing to make

---

4. *Sefer ha-partizanim ha-yehudim* 1:153 and 2:627; compare Dixon, 57, 83.
5. Testimony of Eliezer Moses, YVSA, 24–26 (recording 7).
6. Previous attempts of the battalion to take control of Rudniki ended in only partial success (see chapter 13, "Combat Missions").

an agreement with the partisans, on condition that no Jews were among them.[7] After The Avenger fighters penetrated the town, the Poles left the town without bloodshed. Only then, the remaining partisan units entered, including the Death to the Occupiers group, and took control of the entire town. They raised red flags on the buildings, and after a mass meeting of the local residents the fighters returned to their bases, leaving only patrol shifts.[8]

For the Death to the Occupiers fighters, the joy of victory was diminished by the death of Yisrael Zig. He was the last casualty of the battalion in the Rudniki Forests.

The Journey to Vilna

In early July 1944, the partisans were heartened by the distant thunder of cannons – whose echoes intensified with each passing day – more than they were by all the bulletins of the front's approach. Anticipation of the exciting moment when they would meet up with the Soviet army was shared by all, bringing together even those who differed. Battalion commanders maintained constant contact with the brigade command, awaiting orders.

On the evening of July 7, the awaited-for command was given to all the units in the forest:[9] "The undefeated Red Army has conquered Novo Vileika and is advancing in heavy battles toward Vilna, capital of the Lithuanian Republic. The supreme partisan command, together with the Red Army headquarters, orders the Lithuanian partisan brigade in the Rudniki Forests to conquer the capital of Vilna together with the victorious Red Army."

The news quickly spread through the forest. Only a handful of the Jewish fighters closed their eyes on that last night in the forest and did not join in with the spontaneous celebrations – whether with song, dance, drink, or shots in the air. For the Jewish fighters, who were swept up in the general excitement, this celebratory night was also a time of soul searching and emotional crisis. In the testimony of one, we find expression of the difficult feelings of parting from the dense forests of Rudniki:

---

7. Testimony of Abba Kovner, YVSA, 16 (recording 6). See also *Sefer ha-partizanim ha-yehudim* 1:153.
8. PKG, 160.
9. From *Sefer ha-partizanim ha-yehudim* 1:155; see also Mončiunskas, 335.

The atmosphere was spirited…. Everyone was happy. Everyone slept outside. But the Jews could not wholeheartedly accept liberation. Each one did his own soul searching. Where would he go, who would he find, after all the news [from the ghetto]…. The other fighters could accept it joyously, for they would return home as heroes and meet their families there – but the situation of the Jewish fighter was different. He also saw the end, but still, it was not the end. He anticipated more very difficult situations.[10]

On the morning of July 8, 1944, as feverish preparations began for the journey to liberate Vilna, Ruzhke Korczak, the Jewish woman fighter from the Vilna battalions, stole into the camp. In secret, she gave the members of the Zionist pioneer movements the contact orders for the coming days, after the liberation, and sneaked out to deliver her message to the other units.

The partisans ate their last breakfast at the base and readied everything for departure. The order was to leave personal items and clothing and to take only weapons and ammunition. About twenty people, most of them wounded and ill, remained in the camp under the command of squad leader Hanne Kagan and under the medical supervision of medic Anya and nurse Gita Foger.[11] They were to join the departing group in a week or two, when the others established themselves in liberated Vilna.

All the battalions of the brigade organized for the march on the Kopana Road. For the first time, the column advanced in military order, flags waving in front. The villagers came out to welcome the "bandits" of yesterday with bread and milk. The White Poles also stood at the roadsides and especially marvelled at the sight of the women fighters shouldering weapons. The White Poles were marching toward Vilna as well, mainly for the purpose of political demonstration. Lacking exact instructions of how to act toward them, the brigade command ignored them until they could made radio contact with the forward command of the Soviet army.

Occupation of "The Jerusalem of Lithuania"

On July 10, after the partisan column crossed the Baltoji-Vokė River, it made the first direct contact with reconnaissance units of the Soviet Army.

---

10. Testimony of Baruch Gofer (Grodnick), YVSA, 35 (recording 9).
11. Testimony of Gita Foger-Turchin, YVSA, 13 (recording 4).

At the southeast entrance to the outskirts of Vilna, the brigade was given special support roles:[12] in the street battles that took place, especially near Aušros Vartai;[13] in mopping up remnants of the enemy in the neighborhoods; and at a later stage, in police[14] and patrol activities[15] and in extinguishing fires in the city, which was completely occupied on July 13.[16] The Death to the Occupiers battalion was split up into operational squads for carrying out all of these assignments.

A fighter describes his impressions of the meeting with the Soviet Army and describes the events of one of the operational squads over the course of about five days:

> We were already 20 kilometers from Vilna. An undertone of anticipation and awakening passed through the camp. All eyes focused on the section of the road where rumor had it that the first Red Army soldiers would appear....
>
> Here is the first Soviet tank crewman. He is dusty and sooty, but smiling and waving at us. We are filled with elation, and many of us run to embrace him. More soldiers arrive, on foot and in vehicles. An animated conversation develops; they give us *makhorka* [Russian for a very potent variety of tobacco], and we exchange compliments. Eyes search, looking for something in the faces of the soldiers, and the glance rests on pale faces and teary eyes. "Your nationality?" asks one of us. Indeed, it is a Jewish soldier from a small town in Lithuania. He had fled from it in 1941 and has been serving for the

---

12. PKG, 160. The role of the partisan battalions in occupying Vilna is described in detail in the history of the Lithuanian division (Mončiunskas, 342).

13. Meaning the Gate of Dawn, a Vilna city gate. In this area, a company of German paratroopers barricaded itself in one of the homes known as "the White House." They held out for three days, their fire commanding the surrounding streets.

14. The Kovno female fighter Beila Ganlin ("Katyusha"), acting as traffic policewoman at the entrance to Vilna, let in the first civilian vehicle, which was carrying the members of the Lithuanian government and the chairman of the Supreme Soviet of the Lithuanian Soviet Socialist Republic, Justas Paleckis (PKG, 161).

15. The ghetto fighter patrols caught several Germans who were disguised as civilians, including an important spy. The military security authorities singled out this operation for special distinction (testimony of Eliezer Moses, YVSA, 27, recording 8).

16. The last battle in Vilna took place near Gediminas Hill. When the Red Army flag was raised on top of Gediminas' Tower atop the hill, the battles ended, and the army continued its offensive to the southwest. From then on, the partisans mainly performed mopping up and search operations among threatening elements that remained in the city.

past three years in the army. He still hopes to find someone from his family and asks us about the chances. We shake our heads and remain silent. Someone sobs. He removes his personal pack from his shoulders and divides its entire contents among us. "Take, my dear friends, to your health!" We shake hands, and he enters the car and disappears on the horizon.

With heavy hearts, we continue on our way to Vilna. We can see the suburbs, in which bitter battles were being waged. The Vilna fighters try to guess where the enemy was dug in, and where they would send us as reinforcements. None of us Kovno residents knew the city.

Mara Lan, myself, and Tarasov were ordered to see a Soviet officer, and he gave us a security mission. Our job was to take a position at a junction and stop everyone who entered the city. We also had to follow suspicious types and hand them over to the patrols of the military police. We performed this job with enthusiasm for forty-eight hours straight. Some of those we stopped were German soldiers disguised in civilian clothing.... They were deathly afraid and begged for their lives. Who knows how many Jews they murdered? I could not calm down. At the war prisoners' collection point, I was promised they would get what they deserved.

On occasion, Red Army officers came to visit us. They were mainly interested in the information we obtained from civilians about weapons caches and mines that the Germans had left.

A Pole stands before us, a short man with a white metal eagle on his hat, apparently a White Pole or a supporter. He is agitated and frightened. He says that all his life he has helped the Jews in Vilna and can even give us proof of this. An army officer asks him, "What's that badge on your hat?" Instead of answering, he rushes to remove the insignia and is about to crush it in his hands. "Where is your self-respect?" the officer roars at him. "We don't remove a badge! I'm willing to fight for my badge," here he points a finger at the five-pointed star on his own hat, "and even sacrifice my life." The humiliated Pole replaces the badge and asks us to leave him alone. I object. We order him to sit on the ground until we gather a few more detainees so that we can take them together to the collection point.

Meanwhile, the battles continued. The heavy bombardment of the artillery and the air force took place before our eyes. They barely agreed to allocate us a few battle rations. We began to get tired of the job. How I longed at that moment to be together with the others. Most certainly, they were in the city center, participating in the street battles.

The new job we were given was not particularly captivating either – guarding the food warehouses of the German army and the SS (on Pohulyanka Street) from robbery and theft. The civilian population caused no problems. You had only to raise your voice or your weapon, and they raised their hands and put everything back in place. Most of the thieves were Red Army soldiers, with no differentiation of position or rank. They would climb up the wall and jump off, carrying on their backs a crate of high-quality wine that the Germans had left behind.

The partisans did not tolerate this business and shot in the air to warn them, but in vain. "You wouldn't dare shoot me for a few miserable bottles, which at any rate will be enjoyed only by the militiamen in the rear?" asserts a "Guardia" soldier with fervor. While in the act, he opens his shirt in one movement and reveals his bared chest: "Shoot me if you are capable!" Then a major arrives, his chest decorated with medals. He says he is embarrassed to argue with us and thereby make us shoot, even in the air, all because of a sip. It's unbecoming to him. He sighs, "Please let me in. I'll drink on the spot and leave!" He ceremoniously gives his word, the word of a Soviet officer.

We had no particular interest in preventing fighters from enjoying themselves as they desired. Our arguments with them were only for the sake of propriety. Worse was the issue with the drunks, who had no limit. Some of them lay stretched out on the ground, raging at the top of their lungs. Among their ranting and blather, I made out the well-known saying, "Strike the Jews and save Russia." My ears rung. I did not want to believe. With the help of several partisans, we dragged the hero of drivel from the room and threw him outside. I was shocked, trying to reconstruct his muttering. Was it a mistake? ...

I asked for permission to visit our new base in the city center on Didzioji Street. It was formerly a young children's home, named after Adam Mickiewicz. Our battalion gathered there.

The fighters were focused on two main roles: carrying out the death sentence for collaborators with the enemy, and seizing public or private property that had been stolen by the populace. Tuvia Friedman stood beside the gate of the institution and stopped every Lithuanian or Pole who passed by in the street who was carrying a bundle.

Throughout the day, a large stock of various items that had been confiscated by the sentries accumulated in the room. In the evening we held parties. My job was to bring the wine and delicacies from the SS storehouses I guarded. This time, everyone drank. To hide our inner turmoil, we told jokes and sang. Others told about events of the day.... One recounted: Today I led a Tatar to execution three times for collaborating with the Germans. Just when I was about to carry out the sentence, I received the order to return downstairs so he could be interrogated again. The man apparently had his suspicions, but did not attempt to flee, just spoke to me with his slanted eyes. I thought I would go nuts. The third time, they hinted that the sentence was final.... Another related: During a search operation in the street, I found a woman without papers. I had already said to bring her to the detainee collection point for interrogation, when I heard her murmuring in Yiddish, "*Oy vey iz zu mir*" (Woe is me). I barely managed to get it out of her that she was Jewish. After months of nightmarish persecution, she was still afraid to reveal her identity. Another told about a meeting with his cousin, one of the few female survivors of the Vilna Ghetto, who was hidden for a long time in the city archive by a Lithuanian, a righteous gentile.

It was a day filled with events and impressions, but mainly we wondered: When would we get to Kovno, and who would we find there? This question allowed us no rest, and it was hard to fall asleep.[17]

Dissolution of the Death to the Occupiers Battalion

The operational units that acted in the city completed their role. The battalion began to take on a civilian character. Military discipline loosened, and no one paid much notice. Berel Kott was wounded in the eye, hand, and leg by a hand grenade that exploded by itself while he was drowsing. His comrades-in-arms took him to the nearest hospital, unconscious and bleeding copiously.[18] Throughout the day, lacking concrete purpose, the fighters wandered the streets searching

---

17. Memoirs of Dov Levin, manuscript, 13–17; also compare Mončiunskas, 336.

18. Kott was in military hospitals for eight months and underwent five operations. He was transferred to Moscow and then returned to Vilna. He eventually went to the United States (compare *Davar*, no. 6098, August 25, 1945).

for relatives and acquaintances among those returning from the Soviet Union. Surprising reunions on the street became a daily occurrence. Many Jews came out of their hiding places. Jewish soldiers and clerks who had succeeded in flee- ing into Russia arrived. All voiced the same question: Do you know my relative, such-and-such? Tears of joy intermingled with tears of despair. The writer Ilia Ehrenburg also arrived. He had his photo taken with the Jewish fighters and showed great interest in their stories.[19] By special order, the Jewish fighters gave in their weapons, which they had obtained with great efforts in the Kovno Ghetto. A female fighter gave expression to the feeling of isolation and helplessness after turning in the weapons:

> We walked around with a very heavy feeling.... As long as I was a partisan carrying a weapon and did not know whether I would survive, I did not think about this day. When we gave in the weapons and saw the streets and the destruction they had done to us – it was a very difficult feeling. We were truly terrified.[20]

To the fighters, turning in the weapons symbolized the loss of the defined status that had given them a certain measure of security and a feeling of belong- ing to a framework. While most of the non-Jewish fighters were able to return to their homes for good or for temporary leave,[21] the fighters from Kovno Ghetto still viewed themselves as temporarily in Vilna. Each day they followed the news from the front. The Red Army's extended encampment before Kovno worried them. Meanwhile, representatives of government, institutions, the military, and the police constantly pressured the battalion command to supply appropriate personnel for special roles and to operate the civilian services. Usually, the Kovno Jews agreed to these proposals. The occupation of the city was no comfort for them, as their families had already perished before they went to the forests. Some of them were drafted into the militia. Those who knew languages and

19. Compare Ilia Ehrenburg, "*Der weg kein deitschland*," *Einikeit* 30 (90), July 27, 1944.
20. Testimony of Malka Pugatzky-Smali, YVSA, 34 (recording 10).
21. For example, Commissar Davidov was able to get away to Moscow immediately following the liberation of Kovno. Apparently, he anticipated a reaction to his behavior in the forest toward the Jewish fighters. Indeed, some of the Jewish fighters plotted to take revenge at an appropriate opportunity (testimony of Eliezer Moses, YVSA, 21, recording 6).

had the appropriate education were given translation jobs in the military and civilian security agencies (NKVD). Others were accepted to posts in economic institutions.

Kostia, the battalion commander, parted from those who left. Aside from a formal certificate of partisanship, he gave many fighters a certificate of achievement, which they could use as a recommendation in future endeavors. To those who joined the militia, he gave the best weapons, and to stables manager Meir Teinovitz, he gave his noble horse.

Those who did not take on a position or arrangement stayed together in apartments in the city, waiting for the road to Kovno to open. Most had families and hoped they might find someone in the city, or else they were married women whose husbands were still involved in the raids in southwest Lithuania, and they had no word from them.

All sat with their bags packed, awaiting a sign from the west.

In the Naliboki Forests

Because Byelorussia had been seized by the Russians at the onset of the Vitebsk offensive, the many partisan camps in the Naliboki Forests were the first to be liberated, before their comrades in the Rudniki Forests and the forests of Lithuania.

As mentioned, four Jews from the Kovno Ghetto were there: Alter Feitelson, Yankel Kaveh, Idel Sherman, and Yosef Rosen. They had joined the Jewish battalions in the Naliboki Forests. On June 21, two days before the major attack began, Alter Feitelson participated in attacking the German garrison at Molodczena as part of the battalion of Major Shostakovitz. Yankel Kaveh took part in the large demolition operation of train tracks described above, in which all the partisan units were involved.[22]

Rosen describes the exit from the forests and meeting with the Red Army:

> The last days were terrible. At night there were shots.... The commander was severely wounded. They put the wounded on carts and went toward Minsk. There was only one route. We went to the road, and suddenly we saw soldiers from afar. At first we thought they were Germans, but then we realized this

---

22. *PKG*, 159–60.

was a Red Army reconnaissance company. They made speeches and gave us compliments. We continued with the carts, and we met many soldiers on the way.... We met a Jew, a tall officer, and he told us that the next day he would send a column of forty empty cars to Minsk. This was a mistake on our part, because we had carts and horses. We left everything there, got into the cars, and went to Minsk. There we wandered around hungry, because there was nothing to eat.[23]

Alone in a foreign city that was completely devastated, with no information on their companions in the Rudniki Forests, or of the situation in the ghetto, the four joined the regular army so they could advance with the columns that were attacking toward Lithuania.[24]

In the Keidan Forests

In the forests of Lithuania, hundreds of Jews waited expectantly for the arrival of the Soviet army. Among them were some twenty armed men and women who had fled from the labor camp near Keidan and wandered the surrounding forests.[25] Members of this group, which called itself "B Group," mainly focused on their own survival and relied on the assistance of Lithuanian contacts in order to avoid the Germans who tried to destroy them.

On July 9, 1944, the Germans destroyed the remains of the Keidan labor camp and sent its forty Jewish laborers back to the Kovno Ghetto in order to transfer them together with the ghetto Jews to concentration camps in Germany. At this point, the B Group began special operations, influenced by the approach of the Soviet Army. The leader of this group relates:

We entered a certain place, where P.S. typed handbills on a typewriter, calling the village residents to rebel against the Germans. This was on July 15, 1944. We also typed certificates for ourselves. We feared that when we were liberated and had no communication, who knows how we would stand before a Russian soldier – would he believe anything? ... So they would not say,

---

23. Testimony of Yosef Rosen, YVSA, 36–37 (recording 8).
24. In one of the enemy shellings, Yankel Kaveh was killed on the third Byelorussian front, where he served as translator on the staff of a field unit.
25. See chapter 9.

"How did you survive?" at least we had to have something. I still have such a certificate. . . .

Then the days came when the front grew closer and closer. There was no value in maintaining contact with Keidan. We didn't have any explosives or many weapons with which we could rise up and carry out some sort of action against the Germans. So we had one concern alone . . . how to get through this spot. We could already hear the shooting from the front. For seven days we were hiding in the forest and all the bullets from both sides were flying over our heads. We couldn't stick out our noses to do anything. . . .

I think it was back on July 6 when we said among ourselves that we would not stand for more than three [more] months. Then we did not know exactly what the situation was. . . . The front was stalled about 4 kilometers from us, and we could not move forward or backward. Sometimes we heard that Germans came maybe about 50 meters from us. They did not see us. There were about fifty or sixty of them. They set up positions and cannons, and we heard voices: "Fire 150!" What was "fire 150"? Quite simply, 150 meters, and we were in the middle. All the *goyim* fled from their homes. Our *goy*, as he fled, he came up to us and wept: Who knows what will happen to you? Whatever happens to all the non-Jews is what will happen to us, he said, but what will happen with you? And he wept. A *goy* like that. We might say, the righteous man of the generation.

On July 29, around 10 P.M., we heard Russian songs, and then we knew we were liberated. But we also knew that we were at the front. We could not go out at night, even to the Russians, and so we waited until the next day, July 30, and then we went to the Russian headquarters. Of course, they treated us like they treated everyone else. They were amazed that we were some of the first partisans in Lithuania they met. They took all our weapons. . . . The captain said, "You are liberated, you don't need weapons now. . . ." Then after a few days of wandering around at the orders of Russian headquarters . . . we came to Keidan. There we met up with Rivka Levitt, who was with Petke,[26]

---

26. Petke was the captain of partisan group A, which also had several Jews who had escaped from the Keidan labor camp, including Kira Solsky and Rivka Levitt (see chapter 9, p. 271).

with Avramele (Avraham) Weiner, Grishke (Grisha) Berman and his father, Fania Visselitzky and other companions. Everyone had something to tell.... [27]

The Combat Company

In mid-June, the combat company (of Death to the Occupiers battalion) marked the forty-fifth day of its departure from the base for the sortie into Lithuanian territory. According to the instructions received by its command before the departure, at this point the company should have returned to the base. But the Vitebsk offensive and the German evacuation that preceded it disrupted the schedule, and so an envoy of three fighters was sent back to the base to ask for additional instructions. But before they fulfilled their mission the company found itself among retreating German forces, and return to the base was no longer an option.

A veteran fighter of this company describes its intensive activity in the last weeks, the dramatic meeting with the Red Army on July 24, and its festive entrance into the liberated city of Vilkomir.

> We acquired a radio receiver, and we carried it with us everywhere. We heard about a strong Russian offensive. The offensive took on large proportions, and the advance of the Red Army was right beside us. When the time came for us to return ... we thought that if we started back, we might be battered between the two forces.
>
> We didn't receive any orders. We had no contact with the base or any other body that could direct us. When we reached a distance of 15–20 kilometers west of Vilkomir ... we began to sense the retreat of the German forces. We saw that the front was approaching – they stretched cables and dug positions. We were actually surrounded by the Germans....
>
> We did not let them rest – we sabotaged their telephone cable, cutting it about every 200 meters. We attacked by day, and already controlled the area. We went out on the roads by day. Then the Lithuanian collaborators and policemen began to flee to Germany. We caused them losses.... We were lucky and always evaded the Germans. We would go by, and they wouldn't notice us.... On July 24, we met up with the Red Army, not far from Vilkomir,

---

27. Testimony of Yosef Gertner, YVSA, 40 (recording 10).

near the town of Širvintos, where we operated the whole time. On the last night before we met the Red Army, we went out for an ambush and attacked a German column. During this attack, we heard Russian conversation. We already thought that perhaps we had attacked the Red Army. Later we found out that we had not erred. These were Russians who had collaborated with the Germans, and they were taking up the rear. They walked with all kinds of items they were transporting on carts. We realized that we had gone to the right address.

I think that during its stay in Lithuania, the combat company performed many operations. I cannot list all the operations now.[28] At any rate, during the conquest of Vilkomir the Red Army honored us at a festive parade there, for our role in assisting the conquest. They commended us. We stood in the military parade with everyone else. Some of us had badges. We obtained some clothing from the soldiers whom we had met and took off all remainders of German clothing, because by then it was dangerous to walk around in German clothing. It aroused suspicion, and every Russian soldier who carried a weapon could kill from afar.[29]

The Vladas Baronas Battalion

The Vladas Baronas battalion was situated in the bogs of south Lithuania, far from the scene of events in the liberation of Lithuania, and thus experienced it later.

One of its fighters describes the final period in this battalion:

The Germans began a noticeable retreat, and we went out every night to place mines on the roads or to attack convoys.[30]

Our meeting with the Red Army was very dramatic, because they shelled us. This was due to a mistake of our commanders, because the Germans had also entered the forests but we did not know this. That night, our group returned from a mission of acquiring food, and some of them were wearing

---

28. One highly important operation carried out by the combat company during this period was the demolition of a bridge near Vilkomir and destruction of two enemy tanks and a large number of convoys in retreat from the front (PKG, 157).

29. Testimony of Haim Gechtel (Galin), YVSA, 42–44 (recording 14).

30. During the German retreat, saboteurs Peretz Kliatchko, Yisrael Joels, Mendel Dietz, Yehuda Lifschitz, and Shraga Shilin blew up the bridge on the Kapčiamiestis–Grodno road and another bridge over the Marisa River (PKG, 156).

German uniforms. They crossed a bridge and apparently Red Army scouts noticed them, and the area began to be shelled intensively.... The shelling continued for about an hour. Finally two people who knew how to swim well were ordered to cross the Nemunas. They crossed at the risk of being killed, as they were shot at. When they reached the other side, the shelling stopped. We began to go over to the Russian side, and met the Russian army.

They received us with excitement.... We were free for seven days; we did nothing. We were very bored and asked for some kind of task or to participate in the battles, because the front was in the same place. The Germans based themselves on the other side of the Nemunas, and the German bombers destroyed any erect bridge. But apparently the army command had ordered not to take us for work yet. We also did not receive food, but each of us received privately from the Russian soldiers, who gave willingly and divided their food with us. After a week there were many inspections among the partisans. All those who had joined us recently, or who had been in prison and fled and came to us, or who formerly served in the German army – all these were taken for the army. Many of those who had served in the German army were taken immediately to punishment companies.... They took the Jews to search for Germans. We did it with great enthusiasm and caught a large number of Germans... Then they began to send us back north and printed all kinds of partisan certificates for us.[31]

"Forward" Fighters Enter Kovno

For about ten weeks, the Forward battalion operated under the command of Captain Zeika in the Kazlu-Ruda Forests. When the front approached, they discovered the importance of moving the partisan battalions to this area. Several vital transportation lines used by the Germans and their supporters during their retreat passed through this area (the Minsk–Vilna–Kovno–Königsberg–Berlin railroad line, and the Leningrad–Dvinsk–Kovno–Königsberg road). From the temporary bases in these forests, the partisan battalions dealt harsh blows against the retreating columns, with no serious attempt on the part of the Germans to defend themselves.[32]

---

31. Testimony of Michael Yitzhaki (Gelbtrunk), YVSA, 40–41.
32. One of the senior Lithuanian officials who collaborated with the Nazis, who was caught in such circumstances, was Y. Matulavicus, head of Saugumas, the Lithuanian security police

Aside from the Forward battalion and several Lithuanian partisan groups, a group of fighters from the Kovno Ghetto also operated in this region. They called themselves "Kochargin"[33] and worked together with the Soviet paratrooper units there.

The Forward fighters continuously disrupted the Kovno–Marijampole railroad line, set up roadblocks on the roads, and disturbed the retreat of the German forces on the Nemunas River. Squad commander Shimon Bloch and his squad established their base on the banks of the river, near the town of Seredžius. From there they destroyed German armored vehicles that tried to cross the river.[34]

In the last weeks, Forward battalion had very close contact with Red Army paratrooper and reconnaissance units. Together they sent the Soviet air force exact details of strategic enemy targets to be bombed. In the last days, fighters Haim David Ratner and Yankel Levi were killed on their way to a special political task given to them by the Communist Party.[35]

After the meeting with the Red Army, the Forward fighters marched to Kovno. As opposed to the sixty fighters in the battalion when it left the base in the Rudniki Forests, 137 fighters entered the newly liberated city of Kovno. They were led by Nehemiah Endlin, the guide who had led the battalion in all of its journeys.

Below is a description of the experiences of the Forward fighters in the final period, and their entry into liberated Kovno:

> We would go out for roadblocks and ambushes, and the Germans would run alone, because only individuals and individual vehicles could cross the forest. They would try to break out through the forest, apparently because other places were blocked or crowded and they wanted to go quickly, and here we would "welcome" them.[36] What was interesting was that we received weap-

---

(FLC 10:12–15). Shimon Bloch's squad also caught four Gestapo members in civilian dress who had fled from Vilna (PKG, 161).

33. These included Benzion Preiss, Lola and Irena Berman, Avraham Rosen, Shmuel Dietz, and others (PKG, 127, 129). According to unconfirmed reports, Yerachmiel Berman was commander of this group (FLC 10:12).

34. PKG, 159.

35. Ibid., 161. See ch. 13, p. xxx.

36. Systematic mining of the roads was carried out by fighters Shika Vershabovsky, Berel Stern, and Pesach Sadovsky. They were particularly expert in trapping tanks using a special mining mechanism called the "mousetrap" (PKG, 162).

ons then that were parachuted to us from the Rudniki Forests. We received the famous mortar that we had used in the Rudniki Forests....

We already knew that the Russians were advancing, not just from the radio but also because of the explosions, because they bombed the roads and the railroad tracks, as we instructed them. They bombed right over our heads. In addition, the thunder of the cannons grew closer, and this also indicated the approach of the front.... One day, we saw the Russians ... so we packed all our belongings. We had received more weapons that were dropped. We took carts and went out of the forest toward Kovno.... We met up with the Red Army and the meeting was friendly. They did not make a powerful impression, but rather were very friendly. We walked along and we had interesting meetings. A Soviet soldier was riding and he asked, "Who are you?" I answered, "Jews." He hit me on the head with his whip. We wanted to get back at him, but he took off, and the Russians intervened and would not allow us.

Later when we approached Kovno, we sat down to rest. A dark youth with a moustache approached us and began to speak Yiddish to me. A youth who had grown up in the Soviet Union, but still he felt some need to speak Yiddish. The bridge was demolished, and we waited for a few hours until they took us over in the ferry, and we entered Kovno in formation, singing.[37]

---

37. Testimony of Grisha Sheffer, YVSA, 33–34 (recording 8).

APPENDIX I

Members of the Resistance Movement in the Kovno Ghetto

Individuals who left the ghetto armed and went to the forests are marked with one asterisk.

Individuals who fell in action are marked with two asterisks.

This list has been compiled from several sources, and therefore cannot be considered complete.

Abramovitz, Feige Leah*
Abramovitz, Shlomo**
Abramson, Gittel
Abramson, Zvi
Ackerman, Hinde
Ackerman, Leah
Agranat, Batsheva
Alexandrovitch, Haim
Antupitzky, Rachel
Antzel, Yehoshua**
Arenson, Moshe
Aron, Haim
Aronovitz, Haim
Aronovitz, Shraga
Aronovsky, Lola
Aronovsky, Yehuda

Axelrod, Aryeh*
Axelrod, Moshe
Bak, Hirschel
Barishnik, Aryeh
Barishnik, Haim
Baron, Dina
Baron, Shlomo*
Beilis
Beilis, Yehuda
Berabin, Heine
Berabo, Hannah
Berabo, Moshe*
Berenboim, Mania
Berger, Rachel
Berger, Sonia
Bergman, Abrasha
Berlovitz, Sheina

Berman, Grisha*
Berman, Haim**
Berman, Ira**
Berman, Lola*
Berman, Rachel
Berman, Yerachmiel*
Bernstein, Yisrael
Bider, David
Biderman, Yehuda
Binyaminovitz, Feivel*
Birger, Daniel
Birger, Shlomo**
Birger, Ya'akov**
Birger, Yudel*
Birger, Ze'ev
Bleiman (Eviatar), Zadok*

Bloch, Rivka*
Bloch, Shimon*
Blumberg, Bobka
Blumenthal
Blustein, Breina**
Blustein, Sheina**
Borkan, Yosef*
Borodavka, Zalman**
Borstein, Haim
Borstein, Haviva
Borstein, Michael
Borstein, Ya'akov
Micha
Boruchovitz, Alte*
Boruchovitz, Yitzhak**
Bramson, M.
Brauns, Yasha
Brenner, Zamke*
Breuer, Shlomo*
Brick, Mott*
Brick, Zvi*
Brown, Zvie*
Broyda, Breina
Bruchson, Leah
Bruchson, Nechamah
Bruchson, Shlomo
Bukanz, Eliezer
Buz, Miriam*
Camber (Ezged),
Baruch
Chodosh, Yosef**
Dabogovsky, Moshe
Davidov, Yasha**
Davidovitz, Hanoch
Dembin, Rita

Dembin, Yitzhak
Dietz (Ben-Menachem),
Shmuel*
Dietz, Mendel*
Diskant, Abba**
Diskant, Rivka*
Donne, Reuven
Dubiansky*
Eckman, Bela
Eckman, Lola**
Eidelman, Yudel*
Endlin, Masha*
Endlin, Nehemiah*
Epstein-Kagan, Rivka*
Erdy, Sofia
Fabrovsky, Yokel**
Familiar, Julian
Familiar, Miriam
Fein, Leibel
Feitelson, Alter*
Feldman, Asher*
Feldman, Fishel*
Feuerstein, Yosef**
Finkel, Shaul**
Finkelstein, Nina*
Foger-Turchin, Gita*
Freizinger, Leib
Freizinger, Noah*
Frenkel (Shapir),
Shlomo
Frenkel, Avraham*
Friedman (Golan),
Esther
Friedman, Hirsch
Friedman, Masha

Friedman, Tuvia*
Friedman, Yehoshua
Friedman, Ze'ev
Gail (Rabinowitz),
Miriam
Gail (Spector), Esther
Gail (Yaron), Masha
Gail, Isser
Galpern, Dimitri
(Dima)
Ganlin, Bayla
(Katyusha)*
Gatz, Yehudit
Gavaronsky, Shlomo
Gechtel (Galin), Haim*
Gafanovitz, Aharon*
Gelbtrunk (Yitzhaki),
Michael*
Gempel, Berel*
Gempel, Leib**
Gempel, Sarah*
Gen, Hirsch**
Gerber, Moshe*
Gertner, Yosef*
Gibraltar, Raphael
Gibraltar, Shlomo
Gilman, Leib**
Gitlin, Yisrael*
Glass, Michael
Glass, Rivka
Glezer, Ya'akov
Glickman, Hirsch
Glickman, Reuven*
Golach, Rosa
Goldberg, Matias**

Goldblatt (Katzav),
  Leah
Goldblatt, Yisrael*
Goldin, Aryeh
Goldin, David**
Goldman (cngineer)
Goldshmidt, Meir
  Leib
Goldshmidt, Osnat
Goldshmidt, Sonia**
Goldstein, Kalman*
Goldstein, Mottel
Goldstein, Shlomo
Golob (Tory),
  Avraham
Gordon, Rivka*
Gordon-Stein,
  Pesach**
Gorgal, Reuven**
Gotfarstein, Frieda
Gotfarstein, Malka
Gottstein
Graz, Shimon
Gratzotis, Moshe
Green, Mendel*
Greenberg, Hannah
Greenberg, Ika
Greenberg, Meir
Greenstein (Kaplan),
  Leah
Grodnick (Gopher),
  Baruch*
Grossman, Bunke
Guttman, Hirsch*
Hanoch, Uri

Harness, Eliyahu
Hass, Eliyah**
Hass, Mendel
Hayat, Doba
Hayatin
Hodess, Sheina
Holtzman, Yankel*
Holzberg, Monik*
Idels, Miriam*
Idelson, Shimon**
Iliyonsky, Moshe**
Ipp, Aryeh
Isaacson, Natan*
Jaffe (Ziegler), Esther
Jaffe, Bezalel**
Jaffe, Shimon
Joels, Dina*
Joels, Grisha*
Joels, Yisrael*
Kagan, Aryeh
Kagan, Berel
Kagan, Ethel
Kagan, Haim
Kagan, Hanne*
Kagan, Yisrael
Kalfus, David
Kaltinovsky, Moshe
Kaminsky (Shapir),
  Mina
Kapit, Beba
Kapit, Zivia*
Karlin, Ethel**
Karnovsky, Mordechai
Karnovsky, Pesia

Kashiv (Kapchowsky),
  Yitzhak
Katz, Mottel
Katz, Rachel**
Katz, Rivka
Katz, Yitzhak**
Katz, Zipporah
Katzav, Dr.
Kaveh, Yankel**
Kelzon, Lola
Kirkel, Itzik**
Kizel, Leah*
Kliatchko, Peretz*
Klibansky, Lazer**
Klotz, Benzion
Koblenz, Katriel*
Koldovsky, Yosef
Kolodiansky, Haim
Kolombus, Henni
Kolotnitzko, Frieda*
Konyuchovsky, Leibel*
Konyuchovsky, Moshe
Kopliansky, Yisrael**
Koppelman, Yankel
Korlianchik
Korlianchik (Golan),
  Menachem
Kott, Berel*
Krakinovsky,
  Mordechai (Mottel)
Krakinovsky, Pinchas*
Kravitz, Zalman**
Krebchinsky, Leibel
Krepko, Batya
Kveskin, Shimon*

Lan, Haim
Lan, Mera*
Latz, Leib
Lazerson
Leibenson (Binyamini),
  Sarah
Leibenson, Yisrael
Leibovitz, Abba*
Lerman, Shulamit*
Lev
Levi, Azriel*
Levi, Rivka*
Levi, Sheina*
Levi, Sonia
Levi, Yankel**
Leviatan, A.
Leviatan, Reuven
Levin Hirsch
Levin, Avraham*
Levin, Berel**
Levin, Dov*
Levin, Menachem
  (Nyonka)**
Levin, Moshe
Levin, Moshe ("De
  Gaulle")
Levin, Zvi
Levner
Lifschitz, Itzik*
Lifschitz, Rachel*
Lifschitz, Yehuda*
Linkovsky, David
Linkovsky, Hannah
Lipkovitz**

Lopiansky (Gempel),
  Rachel*
Lopiansky, Baruch**
Luria, Batya
Luria, Meir**
Man, Frieda
Manyeskin, Aharon**
Manyeskin, Avraham**
Marcus, Bilhah
Mariampoler, Moshe**
Marish, Nachum
Markovsky, David
Markovsky, Hannah
Marshak, Hava
Marshak, Meir*
Marshak, Moshe**
Mashkutz, Shulamit
Maskhkutz, Pesach
Mazover, Bilhah
Megidovitz, Moshe*
Meisel, Olia**
Melamed
Melamed, Avraham
Melamed, Grisha
Melamed, Yosef
Melamed, Yosef*
Melnick, Avraham
Meshi, Henia
Meskup, Hanne*
Messenblum, Mania
Miasnik, Wolf*
Michles, Yosef
Miklishansky, Itzik
  (Itzkotis)**
Milner, Moshe*

Milner, Moshe**
Milstein, Yisrael**
Mirmelstein, Yosef
Miroslavsky, Berel
Miroslavsky, Dvora
Mitzkun, Leibel
Mordkovsky, Shmuel**
Moselis, Moshe
Moses, Eliezer*
Moses, Mark
Moskovitz, Leib
Moskovitz, Mendel
Murevitz, Dina
Nadel, Haim*
Nadel, Hasia
Nathanson, Avraham
Nathanson, Yitzhak*
Neumark, Leeah
Neustadt, Meir
Novidelsky, Hasia
Nudinsky, Ya'akov
Nussenbaum, Yosef
Olkin, Eliyahu**
Opiter
Padison, Hanne*
Padison, Peretz*
Farad, Faivel**
Pasternak, Michael*
Patrikansky, Moshe
Perlman, Yitzhak
Perlstein, Shlomo**
Pianko, Eliyahu
Pilovnik, Ida*
Pilovnik, Tuvia**
Port, Leah*

Preiss, Benzion*
Puchkarnik, Moshe*
Pugatzky-Smali,
　Malka*
Pumpiansky, Yitzhak
Rabinovitz, Mania
Rabinovitz, Yankel
Rafeika*
Rafeika, Aryeh*
Rapopsky, Avraham
Rapopsky, Leah
Rashkovitz, Alter
Ratner, Haim David**
Ratner, Shimon**
Ratner, Yankel*
Rauzuk, Eliyahu
Rauzuk, Sonia
Reches, Eliyahu
Reichman, Moshe**
Reiss, Clara
Relsky, Moshe
Robinson, Haim
Robinson, Moshe*
Robinson, Sarah*
Rochman, Yona
Rogol, Miriam
Rogol, Rivka
Ronder*
Rosen, Shmuel*
Rosen, Yosef*
Rosenberg, Fima
Rosenblum, Lera
Rosenblum, Vovik
Rosenthal, Rachel
　(Koka)

Rosenthal, Ronia
Rosenzweig (Levin),
　Rachel
Rosh, Fania
Rothstein, Frieda*
Rozhansky, Moshe**
Rubin, Menachem**
Rudashevsky, Bayla
Rudman, Berel
Rudnick, Avraham
Rudnick, David
Rutenberg, Ephraim
Sadinsky, Alter
Sadovsky (Ganuni),
　Mendel*
Sadovsky, Pesach*
Sandler, David**
Sapoznikov, Menashe**
Schein, David
Schein, Hannah
Scher, Leah*
Scher, Leib (Lovka)*
Schuster, Velvel**
Schwartz, Liba**
Schwatz (Glass),
　Esther
Schwatz, Miriam
Schwatz, Yentel
Segalov, Leib
Segalovitch
Segel, Eliyahu
Segel, Yitzhak**
Segelson, Aryeh
Segelson, Elchanan
Segelson, Moshe

Senior, Ephraim*
Senior, Leah*
Shalit, Grisha
Shapira, Dr. Haim
　Nachman
Shapira, Haim
Shapira, Tamara
Shapira, Tirza
Shapira, Ya'akov
Shapira, Yitzhak
Shapira, Yosef
Shapransky
Shater, Ida
Shater, Pesach
Shavelson, Wolf*
Sheffer, Grisha (Zvi)*
Sheffer, Malka
Sheikovitz*
Sherman, Idel**
Sherman, Moshe*
Shilin, Shechne*
Shmerkovitz
Shmoshkovitz
Shmuelov, Eliyahu**
Shmuelov, Haya
Shmulevitz, Shmuel
Shmuliakov, Hirsch*
Shmuliakov,
　Menashke
Shmuliakov, Shmuel
Shov
Shulman, Eliezer
Shulman, Itta*
Siderer, Feivel
Siniuk, Yerachmiel

Sisnitzky, Ya'akov**
Skatch, B.
Smilg, Ida
Soloviansky, Moshe**
Solsky, Kira**
Sperling, Jan**
Srebnitzky, Isaac
Staravolsky, Moshe
Staravolsky, Sarah
Stashoner, Shoshanna
Steinberg, Yehezkel
Stern, Berel*
Stern, Mottel*
Strassburg, Ya'akov**
Strelitz, Esther*
Strom, Esther*
Strom, Fina
Strom, Leibel*
Strom, Zundel*
Sukenik (Gopher),
    Penina
Sukenik, Shulamit
Svirsky, Haim
Tabachnik, Aharon*
Tamshe
Tarataisky, Obsei**
Tarshish, Hannah
Tarshish, Yehuda*
Teinovitz, Meir*
Teitel, Michael**
Tepper, David*
Tiktin, Haim

Tinet, Zoya*
Tinovsky, Yitzhak
Trotzky, Hannah
Tur-Kasneskevitz,
    Miriam
Upnitzky, Moshe*
Uriash, Rivka
Velikolud, Luba*
Vershabovsky, Shika*
Vidlewosky, Itzik
Vidutzky, Haim*
Vilenchuk, Aharon*
Vinik, Yosef
Viniuk, Hillel
Vizgordinsky, Yudel
Vizgordinsky, Zila
Volk, David**
Volk, Yudel
Volsonok, Rudolph
Voskoboynik, Leah
Voskoboynik,
    Yerachmiel
Wechter, Sheina*
Weiner (Joels), Fania*
Weiner (Joels), Mira*
Weiner, Yankel*
Weinter, Itzik**
Wolbe, Haim**
Wolbe, Pesach*
Wolberstein, Moshe
Wolovitzky,
    Binyamin**
Yachas, David*

Yashunska (Feitelson),
    Sima*
Yatkunsky, Haim
Yellin, Eliezer
Yellin, Haim**
Yellin, Meir
Yochnikov, Itzik*
Yonasevitz, Hemda
Zagai, Rachel
Zakova, Sarah
Zalinger, Meir**
Zanovsky, Esther
Zarfat, Fania
Zarfat, Reuven
Zessler, Berel
Zidelson, Shmuel*
Zig, Yisrael**
Zilber, Avraham
Zilber, Eliezer*
Zilber, Fania*
Zilber, Meir**
Zilberman, Ika
Ziman, Leo**
Zimelevitz, Moshe**
Zimmerman, Lucia*
Zimun (Rochman),
    Hannah
Zimun, Shoshana
Zipkin, Zipke*
Zodikov, Lazer**
Zupovitz, Yehuda
    (Yudel)
Zweigorn, Reuven**

APPENDIX II

Index of Witnesses

The witness material is preserved in the Yad Vashem archives, collections E/17a, E/3-4, and E/17-2.

The witnesses whose names are marked with an asterisk completed their testimony after arriving in Israel. (Editor's note: Some of the unstarred witnesses from outside of Israel eventually emigrated to Israel, after 1970, where they publicized their personal accounts.)

In Israel

Ackerman (Baht), Leah

Bakst, Binyamin

Birger, Ze'ev

Blatt, Arie

Bleiman, Zadok (Eviatar)

Borstein, Ya'akov Micha

Brown, Zvie

Camber (Ezged), Baruch

Dietz (Ben Menachem), Shmuel

Elstein (Lavon), Leah

Familiar, Yitzhak (Julian)

Foger-Turchin, Gita

Frankel (Shapir), Shlomo

Frankel, Avraham

Friedman, Ze'ev

Gail, Masha (Yaron)

Garfunkel, Leib

Gechtel (Galin), Haim

Gelbtrunk (Yitzhaki), Michael

Gertner, Yosef

Glass, Michael

Golob (Tory), Avraham

Grodnik (Gopher), Baruch

Guttman, Ephraim

Hollel (Halak), Raphael

Joels, Zvi (Grisha)

Kapchovsky (Kashiv), Yitzhak

Karnovsky, Mordechai

Kasneskevitz (Tur), Miriam

Katz, Michael

Kempner (Kovner), Vitka

Kissin, Pesia

Kovner, Abba

Kronik (Geller), Luba

Kurlianchik (Golan), Menachem

Lazer (Litai), Haim

Leibenson (Binyamini) Sarah

Leibenson, Yisrael

Levi, Azriel

Levin (Rosenzweig)

Levin, Dov

Levin, Moshe

Lifschitz, Yehuda

Lippman, Moshiya

Mariner, Hillel

Melamed, Avraham

Melamed, Yosef (Lehavot Ha-Bashan)

Melamed, Yosef (Tel Aviv)

Morovitz (Galin), Dina

Moses, Eliezer

Nadel, Haim

Pugatzsky-Smali, Malka

Rabinowitz, Shulamit

Rabinowitz, Yitzhak

Resnick, Nissan

Rochman, Yona

Rosen, Yosef

Rosenberg, Fima

Rosenblum (Hadari), Lara

Rudashevsky, Bayla

Sadovsky (Ganuni), Menachem

Schwatz (Glass), Esther

Segelson, Moshe

Senior (Senion), Ephraim

Sheffer, Zvi (Grisha)

Shpitz, Yitzhak

Siniuk, Yerachmiel

Sukenik (Gofer), Penina

Sutzkever, Avraham

Tarshish, Yehuda

Trigonov (Traeger), Yehoshua

Wolfson, Esther

Yachas, David

Zagai, Rachel

Zimun (Rochman), Hannah

Outside of Israel

Adamovitz, Irena*

Cohen, Berel

Feitelson, Alter

Gempel, Berel

Goldschmidt, Meir Leib*

Joels, Yisrael*

Kott, Berel

Pasternak, Michael*

Stein-Garbazavska, Rivka*

Stern, Berel

Teinovitz (Tanner), Meir

Yellin, Meir

Map of Kovno Ghetto

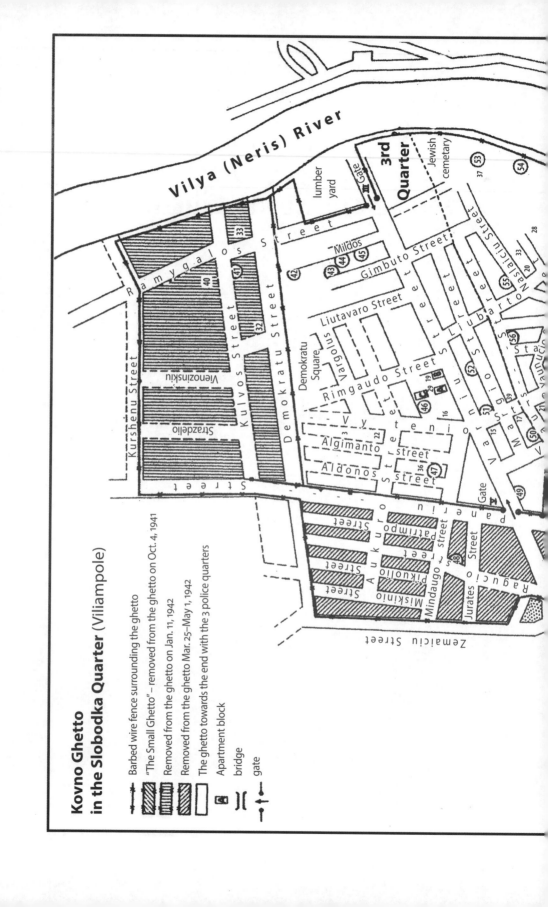

Kovno Ghetto
in the Slobodka Quarter (Viliampole)

Barbed wire fence surrounding the ghetto

"The Small Ghetto" – removed from the ghetto on Oct. 4, 1941

Removed from the ghetto on Jan. 11, 1942

Removed from the ghetto Mar. 25–May 1, 1942

The ghetto towards the end with the 3 police quarters

Apartment block

bridge

gate

Vilya (Neris) River

3rd Quarter

Jewish cemetery

lumber yard

Ramygalos Street

Kurshenu Street

Kulvos Street

Demokratu Street

Vienozinskiu

Strazdelio

Mildos

Gimbuto Street

Liutavaro Street

Demokratu Square

Vargolus

Rimgaudo Street

Algimanto street

Aldono Street

Stuburto Street

Liubarto Street

Naslaiciu Street

Stati

Vaunuciu

Vytenio Street

Varnio Street

Maistu

Panerin

Aukuro Street

Patrimpo Street

Pikuolio street

Mindaugo street

Miskinio Street

Jurates Street

Ragucio Street

Zemaiciu Street

Gate

Gate

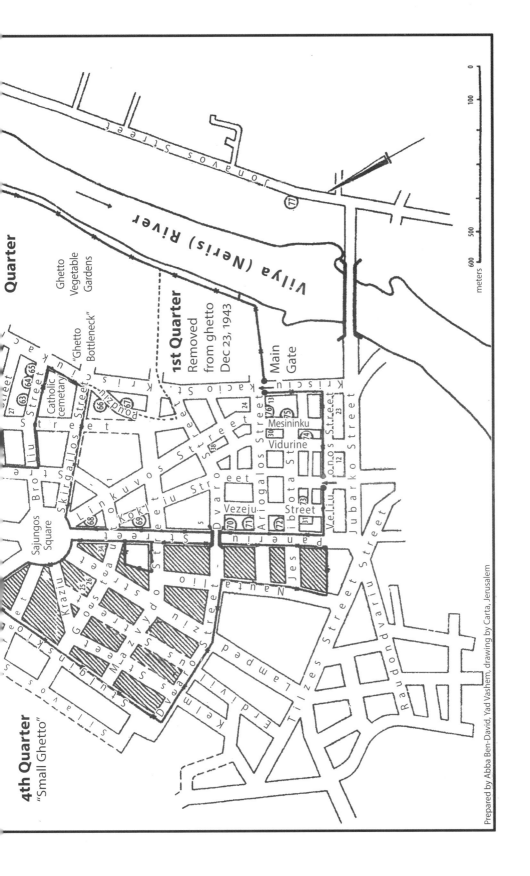

Quarter

Ghetto
Vegetable
Gardens

"Ghetto
Bottleneck"

1st Quarter

Removed
from ghetto
Dec 23, 1943

Vilya (Neris) River

Jonavos Street

77

Main
Gate

Catholic
cemetery

27

63 64 65

66

67

24

Street

Brolu Street
Skirgailos Street
Linkuvos Street
Kokliu Street

Poznu Street

Krisciu Street

Kacio Street

Dvaro Street

38

26 13

30

75

74

23

Mesininku

Vidurine

Street

Jonos Street

12

31

Vezeju Street

70 71

72

73

Jubarko Street

4th Quarter
"Small Ghetto"

Sajungos
Square

68 69

34

35 26

Kraziu Street
Goast Street
Mazoji Dvaro Street
Sjdivil Street

Stulginskio Street
Kelm Street
Erdivili Street

Paneriu - Nautelio Street

Jeso Street

Veliu Street

Arogalos Street
Ribota Street

Lampedu Street

Tilzes Street

Raudondvariu Street

Jubarko Street

Prepared by Abba Ben-David, Yad Vashem, drawing by Carta, Jerusalem

0
100
500
600

meters

SLOBODKA-VILIJAMPOLE QUARTER

This map was prepared based on three previous maps: a schematic map of the Jewish Historical Committee, formerly in Munich (published in *Fun Letzen Hurban* 9 [1948] and preserved in the original at the Yad Vashem archives); and two maps – one in Yiddish, the other in Lithuanian – in the archive "Slobodka Ghetto 1942," prepared in the ghetto (ed. Avraham Golob [Tory], drawn by P. Gadiel), and in the possession of Avraham Tory, Tel Aviv.

Map Key:

1　Jewish police, First Quarter (Old City, cut off from the rest of the ghetto and the Jews evacuated from this area in December, 1943); transportation department; mill
2　Jewish police, Second Quarter
3　Jewish police, Third Quarter
4　Jewish police, Fourth Quarter (in the Small Ghetto, cut off from the ghetto on October 4, 1941)
5　Bridge between the Small Ghetto and the Large Ghetto
6　Site of passage that was begun but blocked after the first reduction in the size of the ghetto.

I, II, III, IV, V – five ghetto gates.

12　German guard
13　German guard
14　German guard; pharmacy nearby

Ghetto institutions

15　Ältestenrat office; Jewish Labor Office, Nutrition Department, Maintenance Department
16　Statistics Department
17　Drawing and sketching workshop; Police Criminal Department
18　Center of Ghetto Jewish police, in Block B
19　Court
20　Prison
21　Housing Department, Social Services Department
22　German Labor Office

23 Jewish Labor Office
24 Jewish Labor Office – Gate Services; commodities warehouse;
    first aid station
25 First aid station in Small Ghetto
26 Clinic in Small Ghetto
27 Health services and hospital
28 Bath house
29 Lice removal clinic; Renovations Department; workshops; professional
    school – all in Block C.
30 Soup kitchen
31 Slobodka Yeshiva
32 School
33 Professional school
34 Children's house; carpentry workshop
35 Main ghetto workshops
36 Pottery workshop
37 Gardening facilities
38 Fire Station No. 1; bakeries
39 Fire Station No. 2 and Fire Department
40 Fire Station No. 3

Jewish Fighting Organization Bases
and Other Underground Sites

(circled on map)

41	No. 3 Kulvos St.	*Malina* (bunker), storeroom for rescued books
42	No. 23 Demokratu St.	*Malina*, training and weapons storeroom
43	No. 24 Gimbuto St.	Meeting point prior to liquidation
44	No. 11 Mildos St.	Apartment – Brit Zion meeting place
45	No. 7 Mildos St.	Eretz Yisrael Ha-Ovedet collective, *malina*
46	Block C	*Malina*, library
47	Aldonos St., pottery workshop	*Malina* that remained undamaged
48	No. 14 Ragucio St.	Apartment of Maria Leschinsky
49	Varnių St., in front of Gate v	Destroyed house, meeting point before departure
50	No. 34 Griniaus St.	*Malina* – Beitar
51	Vytenio St.	Site where Meck was hanged
52	Margio St.	*Malina*
53	Vegetable gardens, gardening facilities	*Malina* that remained undamaged
54	Vilya River bank	Meeting point for Organization activists
55	No. 5 Našlaičių St.	*Malina* – Irgun Brit Zion
56	No. 9 Griniaus St.	*Malina* – Beitar, weapons storeroom
57	No. 101 Kriščiukaičio St.	Stable, illegal school
58	No. 95 Kriščiukaičio St.	Site for secret training
59	No. 10 Vytenio	Meeting points prior to liquidation
60	Stulginskio St., inside pharmacy	Secret radio receiver
61	No. 5 Vygrių St.	*Malina* – Irgun Brit Zion command
62	No. 18 Bajoru St.	Hiding place of Haim Yellin
63	No. 8 Brolių St.	Apartment of Sukenik family (pioneer – Hashomer collective)
64	No. 4 Brolių St.	Site for regular military training, then meeting point prior to liquidation
65	No. 2 Brolių St.	Tunnel

66	No. 16–18 Puodžių St.	Secret apartment – Ulia
67	No. 27 Puodžių St	Secret training
68	No. 63 Linkuvos (Boroky) St.	Meeting point – Hashomer Hatzair
69	Koklių St.	*Malina* – Rabbis
70	Corner of Panerių St. and Dvaro St.	Apartment of Gail family (Irgun Brit Zion bloc)
71	No. 36 Ariogalos St. ("The Dead")	Secret apartment – Rivka Gordon
72	No. 24 Jesiboto St. (Hayeshiva)	Secret apartment
73	No. 18 Vežėju St. ("The Carters")	*Malina*, radio receiver
74	No. 10 Vidurinė St.	*Malina*
75	No. 8 or 10 Mėsininkų St. ("The Butchers")	*Malina* – Irgun Brit Zion
76	No. 5 Ariogalos St. ("The Dead")	Secret apartment – Rapopsky family (*Malina* for religious Jews)
77	No. 53 Jonavos St. (across the river)	Weapons storeroom of the ghetto underground in apartment of Pyotr Trofimov (see chapter 8)

Order of house numbers: from south to north, and from the river moving westward, with even numbers on the right side and odd numbers on the left.

Suggested Reading

Anonymous members of the Kovno Jewish Ghetto Police. Translated and edited by Samuel Schalkowsky. *The Clandestine History of the Kovno Jewish Ghetto Police*. Bloomington: Indiana University Press, 2014.

Eilati, Shalom. *Crossing the River*. Tuscaloosa: University of Alabama Press, 2008.

Levin, Dov. *Fighting Back: Lithuanian Jewry's Armed Resistance to the Nazis 1941–1945*. New York: Holmes and Meier, 1985.

Levin, Dov. *The Lesser of Two Evils. Eastern European Jewry Under the Soviet Rule: 1939–1941*. Philadelphia: The Jewish Publication Society, 1995.

Levin, Dov. *The Litvaks – A Short History of the Jews in Lithuania*. Jerusalem: Yad Vashem, 2000.

Levin, Dov. *Historian's Testimony – A Collection of Oral History Abstracts*. Jerusalem: Hebrew University of Jerusalem, 2013.

United States Holocaust Memorial Museum. *Hidden History of the Kovno Ghetto*. Boston: Little, Brown, and Co., 1997.

Bibliography

Files of testimonies

Files of testimonies on the Kovno Ghetto, stored in the Yad Vashem archives: 01/122; 03/633-638; M1/E105/676; M11/B28, B40, B42, B50, B55, B56, B60, B61, B81, B152; 016/44, 68, 109, 123, 124, 257; E/3-1, E/3-2, E/3-3, E/15-3, E/17, E/17A, 1M/1180, 1186.

Books

Apyvala, S. *Sakalai broleliai* [The brothers of the falcons]. Vilna: 1961.

Bilevičius, E. *Nemunas grįžta į savo vagą* [The Nieman returns to its course]. Vilna: 1961.

Cohen, Berel. *A yid in vold – bletlach fun a togbuch* [A Jew in the forest – pages from a diary]. New York: 1955.

Dallin, Alexander. *German Rule in Russia (1941–1945)*. London: 1957.

Dixon, C. and Otto Heilbrunn. *Communist Guerilla Warfare*. London: 1954.

Eglinis, M. *Mirties Fortuose* [In the forts of death]. Vilna: 1957.

Galpern, Dima (Dimitri), and Meir Yellin. *Partisaner fun Kovner geto* [Partisans from the Kovno Ghetto]. Moscow: 1948.

Gar, Josef. *In geloif fun chroba heiman* [In escaping from destroyed houses]. New York: 1952.

—————. *Umkum fun der Yiddisher Kovne* [The destruction of Jewish Kovno]. Munich: 1948.

Garfunkel, Leib. *Kovno ha-Yehudit be-hurbanah* [Jewish Kovno at the time of its destruction]. Jerusalem: 1959.

Gefen, M., H. Grossman, S. Holveski, Y. Segal, A. Kovner, and R. Korczak, eds. *Sefer ha-partizanim ha-yehudim* [Book of the Jewish partisans], vols. 1 and 2. Merhavia: Sifriyat Poalim, 1958.

Gelbart, Shmuel. *Das geto in flamen* [The ghetto in flames]. Munich: 1948.

Hitlerine Okupacija Lietuvoje [Hitler's occupation of Lithuania]. Vilna: 1959.

Kahanovitz, Moshe. *Milhemet ha-Partizanim ha-Yehudim be-Mizrah Eiropa* [The war of the Jewish partisans in Eastern Europe]. Tel Aviv: 1954.

Kaplan, Yisrael. *Dos folksmoyl in Nazi klem* [The nation in the Nazi vise]. Munich: 1949.

Kondratas, Z. *IX Fortas* [Ninth Fort]. Vilna: 1958.

Kurganovas, M. *Mirties akivaizdoje* [In the face of death]. Vilna: 1960.

Kutka. *Girioj aidi suviai* [Shots Echoing in the forest]. Vilna: 1958.

Lazer (Litai), Haim. *Hurban u-mered* [Destruction and revolt]. Tel Aviv: 1950.

———. *Yehudiyot be-shiabud: osef tziyurim* [Jewish women, enslaved]. Collection of paintings. Merhavia: 1945.

Lurie, Esther. *Edut haya: geto Kovno be-30 tziyurim* [Live evidence: the Kovno Ghetto in thirty pictures]. Tel Aviv: 5718/1958.

———. *Yehudiyot be-shiabud: osef tziyurim* [Jewish women, enslaved]. Collection of paintings. Merhavia: 1945.

Mačijauskas, J. *Už liaudies laimę* [The struggle for the people's happiness]. Vilna: 1957.

Mončiunskas, T. *Rūdninkų girios partizanai* [The partisans of the Rudniki Forest]. Vilna, 1959.

Oshry, Rabbi Ephraim. *Divrei Ephraim* [Words of Ephraim]. New York: 5720/1960.

———. *Hurban Lita* [The destruction of Lithuania]. New York-Montreal: 1951. Republished as *The Annihilation of Lithuanian Jewry*. New York: Judaica Press, 1996.

———. *Sefer she'elot U-teshuvot mi-ma'amakim* [Responsa from the Holocaust]. (New York: 5719/1959). Republished as *Responsa from the Holocaust*, trans. B. Goldman, Judaica Press: 2001.

Peretz (Perzikovitz), Aharon. *Ba-mahanot lo bachu; reshimos shel rofeh* [In the camps they didn't cry: a doctor's writings]. Tel Aviv: 1960.

———. *Dem goral antkegen; reshimos fun a daktar* [Towards fate: a doctor's writings]. Haifa: 1952.

Reitlinger, G. *The Final Solution*. London: 1953.

Shalitan, Levi. *Azoy zeinen mir geshtorbin* [This is how we died]. Munich: 1948.

Štaras, Povilas. *Drąsios širdys* [Brave hearts]. Vilna: 1958.

Sudarsky, Dr. M., Uriah Katzenelson, and Y. Kissin, eds. *Lita* [Lithuania]. New York: 1951.

Telpuchovski, B.C., ed. Otcherki Istorii Velikoi Otechestvenoi Voyni. Moscow: 1955.

Vicas, I. SS Tarnyboje [In the service of the SS]. Vilna: 1961.

Viršulis, A. Didvyrių kelias [In the path of heroes]. Vilna: 1959.

Journal Articles

"800 Yehudim humtu be-tahanat ha-kabaim be-Kovno" [Eight hundred Jews were killed in the Kovno fire station], as told by Kovno Jew Dovid P., who miraculously escaped and reached Moscow. Davar, 5272 (November 6, 1942).

"Al hurvot geto Kovno; mi-pi ed re'iya" [About the ruins of the Kovno Ghetto; from an eyewitness]. Davar, 5859 (October 24, 1944).

Altman, Eliyahu. "Di arbeter in di groysa geto-varstaten" [Workers in the large workshops of the ghetto]. Fun letztin churban, 8:58–63 (June 1948), Munich.

———. "Di fachshol in Kovner ghetto" [The trade school in the Kovno Ghetto]. Fun letztin churban, 9:23–36 (September, 1948).

———. "Elul 5701 in Kovner ghetto" [September 1941 in the Kovno Ghetto]. Unzer Veg, 50 (September 25, 1946), Munich.

Avi-Yoel, N[ahum]. "Ud mutzal mi-eish" [Embers saved from the fire], Shi'arim 153 (February 26, 1948).

Awi-Geto, J. "Far cwej jor in kowner geto" [Two years ago in the Kovno Ghetto] Landsberger Lager Cajtung 24 (April 2, 1946), Frankfurt-am-Main.

Bar-Levi (Brown-Levin), D.Z. [Dov-Zvie]: "Mi-neged le-fort ha-teshi'i" [Opposite the Ninth Fort]. Sefer ha-partizanim ha-yehudim [Book of the Jewish partisans]. Ha-Kibbutz Ha-Artzi Hashomer Hatzair. Merhavia: 1958, 1:197–257.

Ben-Eliezer, Rachi. "Kampas-bavaguneg in kovner ghetto" [Fighting organization in the Kovno Ghetto] Fun letztin churban 10:3–16 (December 1948).

Berman, Moshe. "Kovner geto shpitol" [The Kovno Ghetto hospital]. Fun letztin churban, 10:19–28 (December 1948).

"Be-tzel etz ha-teliya" [Memories of the Kovno Ghetto]. Ha-mashkif 2043 (November 2, 1945).

"Bi-netivei machteret – eiduyot mi-pi" [In the path of the underground – testimonies by]: Menachem Ganuni (Sadovsky); Malka Pugatzky-Smali; Baruch

Grodnick; Dov Levin; Zvie Brown; Michael Yitzhaki (Gelbtrunk); Penina Grodnick-Sukenik. *Yediot beit lohamei ha-geta'ot*, 20:89–95; 21:137–42.

Bonen, Z. "*Tzayeret ba-geto Kovna (Slabodka) u-ba-mahanot*" [Painter in the Kovno Ghetto (Slobodka) and in the camps]. *Dapim le-heker ha-Shoah ve-ha-mered*, 2:171–73 (Tel Aviv: 1952).

Borstein, Rahel. "*Vegin shreyber Michael Borstein*" [About the author Michael Borstein]. *Dene Keyt*, Tel Aviv: 1949.

Brick, Mottel. "*Fun geto tzum vald*" [From the ghetto to the forest]. *Fun letztin churban*, 10:16–19 (December 1948).

Brown, (Avraham) Zvie. "*Di shlacht oiyfen breg teych – zichronos fun Kovner geto 1941–1944*" [The battle on the riverside – memories of the Kovno Ghetto 1941–1944]. *Neyvalt*, Tel Aviv: May 19, 1950.

———. "*Ha-partisan ha-yehudi bi-tnuat ha-partizanim ha-sovyetit*" [The Jewish partisan in the Soviet partisan movement]. Yad Vashem, *Mehkarim be-parshiyot ha-Shoah ve-hagvura* (Jerusalem: 5720/1960), 4:169–89.

Brown, (Avraham) Zvie and Dov Levin. "*Al darkei ha-meri ha-yehudi u-meni'av*" [On the modes of Jewish revolt and their causes]. *Yediot Yad Vashem* 13:2–3 (April 1957).

———. "*Ha-meri shel yehudei Kovna*" [The revolt of the Kovno Jews]. *Yediot beit lohamei ha-geta'ot*, 9–10:16–19 (April 1955).

Cohen, Haim. "*Zikhronot me-avodoteinu be-meshekh ha-shanim ha-akhronot*" [Memories of our work over the last years]. *Nitzotz* 4 (September 16, 1945), Munich.

Don-Yichya, Shabtai. "*Mi-geto Kovna ad Tel Aviv – mipi ha-tzayeret Ester Lurie*" [From the Kovno Ghetto to Tel Aviv – from artist Esther Lurie]. *Hatzofeh* 2299 (July 24, 1945).

"*Ferter yortog fun der yidden-shkhita in Kaunus*" [The fourth anniversay of the massacre of the Jews in Kovno]. *Einikeit*, 124 (November 24, 1945).

Filateva T., Helemaa K.: *Svobudnaya Me Raz Paslovit Vas, Eto Deti Tvoi Rodina.* 80–98 (1958), Moscow.

Filc, Icchok. "*A tog in kovner geto*" [A day in the Kovno Ghetto]. *Aheim* 5 (March 21, 1946), Leipheim.

Gar, Josef. "*Akcje iber kinder, alte un inwalildn in kowner get*" [The *Aktion* of the children, the elderly, and the disabled persons in the Kovno Ghetto]. *Landsberger Lager Cajtung*, 10 (December 14, 1945).

———. *"Keitzad husal geto Kovno"* [How the Kovno Ghetto was liquidated]. *Shi'arim* 9 (October 1956).

Garfunkel, Leib. *"Ha-akziya ha-gedola ba-geto Kovno"* [The Great *Aktion* in the Kovno Ghetto]. *Davar* 6197 (December 7, 1945).

———. *"Ribbono shel olam! Hakol anu mohalim lokh, aval al yisurei ha-yeladim ha-ketanim – zichronot mi-geto Kovna"* [God in heaven! We forgive You for everything, but for the suffering of small children – memories of the Kovno Ghetto]. *Ha-mashkif* 2000 (September 12, 1945).

———. *"Teshuva la-bikoret"* [Response to critique]. *Yediot Yad Vashem* 21–23:24–26 (December 1959).

Gechtel, Haim. *"Zechtzen un einer"* [Sixteen and one]. *Dror*, the movement's newpaper in Germany, 12:11, Landsberg am Lech (April 30, 1947).

Goldberg, Ya'akov. *"Bletlach fun kovner Ältestenrat"* [Pages from Kovno's Ältesten-rat]. *Fun letztin churban*, 7:30–57 (May 1948).

Goldschmidt, Feivel. *"Di ramont-vershtaten in kovner geto"* [The inspection work-shops in the Kovno Ghetto]. *Fun letztin churban*, 8:62–64 (June 1948).

Golob (Tory), Avraham. *"Ha-briha min ha-fort ha-teshi'i, makom ha-hashmada mispar 2"* [The escape from the Ninth Fort, killing place number two]. *Yediot beit lohamei ha-geta'ot* 18–19:83–91 (April 1957).

Granowski, M. *"Der held mit der kamera"* [The hero with the camera]. *Dos fraje Wort* (December 12, 1945), Feldafing.

Greenberg, Zalmen. *"Heshvan 5702 be-Kovna"* [October–November, 1941 in Kovna], *Davar* 6471 (November 1, 1946).

Gringaus, Szmuel. *"Di agonie un der untergang fun der Jidiszer Kowne un Memel"* [The dying and disappearance of the Kovno and Memel communities]. *Jidisze Cajtung* 46 (November 8, 1946).

———. *"Dr. Rudolph Valsonok."* *Landsberger Lager Cajtung*, 13 (January 8, 1946).

———. *"The ghetto as an experiment of Jewish social organisation."* *Jewish Social Studies*, vol. 11, no. 1:3–20 (1949).

Gruenhoyz, Shmuel. *"Hurban Kovna"* [The destruction of Kovno]. *Fun Letzten Churban* 7(6–29); 8 (27–38).

Gurevitz, Y. *"Geto orchester"* [The ghetto's orchestra]. *Fun Letsten Churban* 9:52–58 (September 1948).

Gutman, Ephraim. *"15,000 Yehudim hushmedu be-Kovno lifnei knisat ha-rusim"*

[15,000 Jews were destroyed in Kovno before the Russians entered]. *Ha-mashkif* 1716 (October 17, 1944).

Gutman, Rivka. "*Persan Elchanan: Der religiezer leben in Kovner geto*" [Religious life in the Kovno Ghetto]. *Fun Letsten Churban* 9:36–51 (September 1948).

"*Ha-bitzur ha-teshi'i be-Kovna – kivram shel alfei yeladim Yehudim*" [The Ninth Fort in Kovno – the grave of thousands of Jewish children]. *Ha-boker*, 2753 (November 23, 1944).

"*Hashmadat Yehudei Kovno*" [The destruction of Kovno Jews]. Testimony of Ms. D.S.B. on April 26, 1946. *Bulletin of the Vaad Ha-Hatzalah of the Jewish Agency*. Jerusalem: December 1946, 3–15.

Ivri. "*11 Adar ba-mahane hesger*" [The 11th of Adar in a detention camp]. *Nitzotz* 11 (March 15, 1946).

———. "*Ba-leil ha-molad*" [On Christmas night]. *Nitzotz* 7 (December 31, 1945), Munich.

———. "*Hamesh shanim li-tnuat ha-ihud be-mahteret Lita*" [Five years to the Ichud movement in the Lithuanian underground]. *Nitzotz* 3 (November 2, 1945).

———. "*Mi-hektograph le-linotype*" [From hectograph to linotype]. *Nitzotz,* 13 (July 11, 1947).

K., Shabbtai. "*Ha-meshorer be-eretz ha-mavet*" [The poet in the land of death], third anniversary of the death of M. Borstein. *Nitzotz,* 7 (April 21, 1948).

Kaplan, Yisrael. "*Erodrom arbeit in Kovner geto*" [The work at the Kovno airfield]. *Fun Letsten Churban* 8:3–26 (June 1948).

———. "*Feder menshen in di Nazi negel*" [Writers in the Nazi grip]. *Unzer Veg* 62–63 (September 26, 1947).

———. "*Kovoner shul un lerershaft in umkum*" [Kovno's school and its teachers in their loss]. *Fun Letsten Hurban* 9:3–22 (September 1948).

———. "*Nitzotz,*" *Unzer Veg,* 20 (March 29, 1946).

———. "*Premdling un heftling*" (Michael Borstein). *Dos Vort,* 23 (April 4, 1947), Munich.

Kirilova, Irena. "*Ha-kurban ha-fashisti ha-aharon bi-Kovno – na'ar yehudi*" [The last Fascist victim in Kovno – a Jewish boy]. *Mishmar,* 342 (September 21, 1944).

Konyuchovsky, Leibel. "*A Ferd hot zikh oysgeglitsht: Zikhronot fun Kovoner geto*"

[A horse stumbled – memories from the Kovno Ghetto]. *N.O.H.M.* 3–4 (July 8, 1948), Munich.

———. *"Gut geshosen"* [Shoot your best]. *Dos Vort* 44–48 (September 5–19), Munich.

Koplevitz, Yitzhak. *"Me-zikhronotov shel yeled ba-geto Kovno"* [From the memories of a child in the Kovno Ghetto]. *Yediot beit lohamei ha-geta'ot* 21:133–36 (May 1959).

Kot, Dov. *"Tishkah yadi, tehshakh eini ha-ahat, im lo enkom"* [May my hand lose its cunning, may my one eye lose its sight if I do not avenge], letter from a Jewish partisan in Kovno. *Davar*, 6098 (August 25, 1945).

Kovner, Abba. *"Shlihutam shel ha-shomrim ha-partizanim"* [The mission of the Shomrim who were partisans]. *Sefer Hashomer Hatzair*, Merhavia: 1950, 641–43.

Krupavičius, M. *"Letuviu-Zydų santykiai ruduosios okupacijos metu"* [The relations between the Lithuanians and the Jews in the Nazi occupation period]. *Europos Lietuvis* 8:26–30 (June 28–August 9, 1956), London.

L.D. *"Bein meitzarim – ha-ken ba-geto Kovno"* [Within the straits – the cell in the Kovno Ghetto]. *Sefer Hashomer Hatzair*, Merhavia: 1950, 741–46.

Lerner, Aryeh. *Kocha shel omanut* [The power of art]. In the Kovno Ghetto, by Esther Lurie, an Israeli painter who was there at the time. *Davar*, 6127 (September 7, 1945).

Levin, Dov. *"Al gvurat yehudim be-sifrut Lita ha-sovyetit"* [Jewish heroism in the literature of Soviet Lithuania]. *Yediot Yad Vashem* 23–24 (May 1960).

———. *"Al tnuat he-mered ba-geto Kovno"* [The rebellion movement in the Kovno Ghetto]. *Yad le-Shoah ve-la-mered.* Jerusalem: 5713/1953, 58–59.

———. *"Drishat shalom me-hevrei Hashomer Hatzair be-Lita"* [Regards from the Hashomer Hatzair members in Lithuania]. *Mishmar*, 620 (August 20, 1945).

———. *"Ha-rotzchim be-nikyon kapeihem: nisyonot le-tihur ha-lita'im me-ashmat retzach ha-yehudim"* [The killers in their innocence: attempts to exonerate the Lithuanians from the charge of murdering the Jews]. *Yediot Yad Vashem* 15–16:6–7 (April 1958).

Levin (Kovna'i), Dov. *"Bi-metzudat ha-mavet shel Kovno"* [In Kovno's death fort]. *Yediot Yad Vashem* 19–20 (Jerusalem: 5719/1959).

Levin, Raphael. *"Froyen in arbeitz-einzatz fun Kovner geto"* [Women in forced labor in the Kovno Ghetto]. *Fun Letsten Churban* 8:39–49 (June 1948).

Lipson, Mordechai. *"Kovno – im hayedia be-itonut ha-Germanit ki Yehudei Kovno ne'enshu al ha-pishaim she-pashu biymei ha-shilton ha-Sovyeti"* [Kovno – following the report in the German press that Kovno Jews were punished for the crimes they committed under the Soviet regime]. *Hatzofe*, 1084 (July 27, 1941).

Lurie, Esther. *"Hagam shel medukaim"* [The festival of the oppressed], Rosh Hashana and Yom Kippur in the Kovno Ghetto in 1941, and in the labor camp in 1944. *Mishmar*, 636 (September 7, 1945).

———. *"Me-reshimoteha shel tzayeret"* [The impressions of a painter]. *Dapim le-heker ha-Shoah ve-ha-mered*, Tel Aviv: 5712/1952, 2:91–115.

Mahler, Elah. *"Ha-goya she-hetzila, ve-hayehudia she-nitzla – olot hadashot"* [The non-Jew who saved, and the Jew who was saved – New immigrants to Israel]. *Yediot Yad Vashem* 21–22:19–20 (December 1959).

Margolis, A. *"Hoveret zikaron ivrit le-gibor geto Kovno"* [A Hebrew memorial booklet for a Kovno Ghetto hero] (a letter from Moscow). *Davar*, 5895 (December 5, 1944).

Melamed, Avraham. *"Ba-machane be-germanya"* [In a German camp]. *Hatzofeh*, 2364 (October 10, 1945).

"Mot ha-kedoshim shel Rabi Elchanan Wasserman, Hy"d" [The martyr's death of Rabbi Elchanan Wasserman]. Details about the fates of Kovno's great rabbis. *Shi'arim*, 21 (June 7, 1945).

Nashmit, Sarah. *"Ha-tnua ha-partizanit ba-geto Kovno"* [The partisan movement in the Kovno Ghetto]. *Yediot beit lohamei ha-geta'ot* 20:82–88.

———. *"Le-ahrita shel yahadut Kovno"* [The end of Kovno Jewry]. *Yediot beit lohamei ha-geta'ot* 14–15:39–42 (April 1956).

———. *"Shtei derachim hayu la-getaot"* [The ghettos had two paths]. *Yediot Yad Vashem* 21-22:22–24 (December 1959).

Nementchik, Yitzhak (Nemenczik, Iccok). *"Der onhoyb"* [The beginning]. *Unzer Veg* 112 (August 1947).

———. *"Der zibeter fort"* [The seventh fort]. *Fun Letsten Churban* 7:58–70 (May 1948).

———. *"Dos geto-tojer"* [The ghetto gate]. *Jidisze Cajtung*, 42 (October 16, 1946).

———. "*In heiliken tog*" [On a holy day]. *Unzer Veg,* 123 (September 12, 1947).

———. "*Megilat Estland*" [The Estonia story]. *Landsberger Lager Cajtung,* 15 (January 25, 1946), 16 (February 5, 1946).

Nochimovsky, Yaakov. "*Meditzinisha onterzohogon biyam arbets-emet fun Kovner geto*" [Medical examinations in the Kovno Ghetto's labor office]. *Fun Letsten Churban* 10:28–37 (December 1948).

Olejski, Jakow. "*28 oktober, di grojse akcjein kowner geto*" [The Great *Aktion* in the Kovno Ghetto]. *Landsberger Lager Cajtung* 5 (November 12, 1945); 7 (November 22, 1945); 8 (December 2, 1945).

———. "*Di inteligentn akcje in kowner geto*" [The *Aktion* against the intelligentsia in the Kovno Ghetto]. *Landsberger Lager Cajtung* 10 (December 14, 1945); 13 (January 8, 1946); 14 (January 18, 1946).

———. "*Di likwidacje fun kowner geto*" [Liquidation of the Kovno Ghetto]. *Jidisze Cajtung,* 41 (October 9, 1946).

Oshry, Rabbi Ephraim. "*Al ha-moked, eikhah haya le-sreifat eish, hakham hamussar me-Slabodka Rav Avraham Grodzinski, Hashem yikom damo*" [Burnt at the stake: Lamenting the death by fire of the wise man of *mussar* (Jewish ethics), Rabbi Avraham Grodzinski, of Slabodka]. *Hatzofeh* 2759 (January 29, 1947).

———. "*Beis Ya'akov ba-geto Kovno*" [Beis Ya'akov in the Kovno Ghetto]. *Beis Ya'akov* 13:7 (Sivan 5720/June 1960).

———. "*Eichah nirtzachu rabbanei Lita*" [Lamenting the murder of the Lithuanian rabbis]. *Ha'aretz,* 7609 (September 12, 1944).

———. "*Ha-haim ha-ruhani'im ba-geto Kovna*" [Spiritual life in the Kovno Ghetto]. *Kol Yisrael* 16 (January 23, 1947).

———. "*Keitzad hishmidu et yaldei Yisrael be-Lita*" [How they murdered Jewish children in Lithuania]. *Kol Yisrael* 18 (February 6, 1947).

Person, Elhanan. "*Di bnei-yeshiva in Kovner geto*" [The yeshiva students in the Kovno Ghetto]. *Di yidisha shtime* 43 (November 21, 1947), Munich.

Peretz (Perzikovitz). "*Mitzad ha-mavet ba-geto Kovno*" [The death march in the Kovno Ghetto]; the fifth anniversary of the Great *Aktion*. *Hatzofeh,* 2693 (November 1, 1946).

Rabinovitz, S. "*Di kemper fun Kaunaser geto*" [The Kovno Ghetto fighters]. *Einikeit,* 627 (September 21, 1948).

Rabinowitz, Shulamit. "*Horim ba-golah la-banim ba-aretz*" [Parents in the

Diaspora to their children in Eretz Israel]. *Davar ha-poelet*, 11–12 (December 31, 1944).

———. *"Im hitrahesh ha-nes"* [If a miracle shall occur]. *Davar ha-poelet* 6–7:94–95 (August 28, 1945).

Rabinowitz, Y.A. *"Michal Peretz Borstein."* *Shnaton Davar* 5705/1945, 572–74.

Rochman, Yona. *"Mikhtav mi-Kovna"* [Letter from Kovno]. *Mishmar*, 486 (March 12, 1945).

Rosensweig, Eliezer. *"Keta mi-migilat ha-yesurim"* [A section from the saga of agony]. *Davar*, 6177 (November 7, 1945).

Rozin, Josef. *"Mi-geto Kovno le-ya'arot"* [From the Kovno Ghetto to the forests]. *Mishmar*, 999 (November 15, 1946).

S.L. *"Le-raglei tzeit nitzotz bi-dfus"* [On the occasion of the publication of Nitzotz]. *Nitzotz*, 48 (November 2, 1948), Munich.

"Sedutentit Lita'it mesaperet al geto Kovna" [A Lithuanian student talks about the Kovno Ghetto]. *Hatzofeh*, 2374 (October 22, 1945).

Segal, Eliyahu. *"Ha-psikhologia shel ha-hashmada: hamesh shanim le-aktziya ha-gedola ba-geto Kovno"* [The psychology of destruction: five years to the Great *Aktion* in the Kovno Ghetto]. *Ha-boker*, 3345 (November 1, 1946).

Segelson, Moshe. *"Di groysa varshtatan in Kovner geto"* [The large workshops of the Kovno Ghetto]. *Fun Letsten Churban* 8:50–57 (June 1948).

———. *"Di liquidatzie un evakuatzie Fun Kovner Ghetta,"* Landesburg (1945) (manuscript).

———. *"Ha-irgun ha-partizani ba-geto Kovno"* [The partisan organization in the Kovno Ghetto]. *Yediot beit lohamei ha-geta'ot* 22:99–108.

———. *"Meine zikhronot fun Kovno geto – 5 kapitalin"* [My memories of the Kovno Ghetto –five chapters]. Landsberg am Lech (August–December, 1945) (manuscript).

Shaus, L. *"Oyf di khurves fun kovoner geta"* [On the ruins of the Kovno Ghetto]. *Einikeit*, 93 (August 1944).

———. *"Avra ha-kos al yehudei Kovna"* [Misfortune afflicted the Kovno Jews]. *Mishmar*, 274 (July 2, 1944); 275 (July 3, 1944).

Shimeyte, Anna. *"A Brief zu Belashares zin in Eretz Yisrael"* [Letter to the Balosher children in Eretz Israel]. *Litvisher Yid* 7–8:17–19 (April–May 1946).

Shoys, A. *"Hurban Kovne"* [The destruction of Kovno]. *Der Litvisher Yid* 5–6 (March 1945).

Shtaras F.: *Ve Yedinom Stroyu. Sovyetski Partizani.* 630–70 (1960), Moscow.

Shuster, Zecharya. "*Kovoner Rav Shapira un zein zun Dr. H.N. Shapira dermordet fun di Nazis*" [The Kovno Rabbi Shapira and his son Dr. H.N. Shapiro were murdered by the Nazis]. *Litvisher Yid* 5–6:5–7 (June 1943), New York.

Šinkunaite, J. "*Aš komjaunole*" [I am a Komsomol member]. *Tiesa* 98 (April 25, 1958).

———. "*Didvyrių pedomis*" [In the footsteps of heroes]. *Tiesa* 79 (April 3, 1958), Vilna.

Slutsky, Yitzhak. "*Mikhtav mi-Kovno: tevah ayom be-Kovno u-va-sviva*" [Letter from Kovno: terrible massacre in Kovno and its environs]. *Davar,* 5858 (October 23, 1944).

Sterenberg, Yankev. "*Haim Yellin*" [Yiddish]. *Einikeit* 206 (September 13, 1945).

"*Toldot getan Kovna*" [Annals of the Kovno Ghetto]. *Bulletin Va'adat ha-Hatzalah* 6–14 (October [2] 1945).

Torchinsky, A. "*Arba shanim be-tofet ha-natzit*" [Four years in the Nazi hell]. *Davar,* 6092 (July 29, 1945).

Vershablowsky, Leon. "*Di shehitah in neintin fort*" [The massacre in the ninth fort]. *Tog* (May 27, 1947).

Yellin, Meir. "*Di fayerung fun October yomtov in Kovoner geto*" [October Revolution festivities in the Kovno Ghetto]. *Einikeit* 105–106 (November 8, 1944).

———. "*Haim Yellin, Tzum ershtan yortag fun zein heldishan toit*" [On the first anniversary of Haim Yellin hero's death]. *Litvisher Yid* (Journal of the Federation of American Jews of Lithuanian descent) 7–8:15–17 (April-May 1946), New York.

Yitzhaki (Gelbtrunk), Michael. "*Ba-gedud ha-partizani mavet la-kovshim*" [In the Death to the Occupiers partisan battalion]. *Yediot beit lohamei ha-geta'ot* 18–19:78–81 (April 1957).

———. "*Di festung fun toit*" [The death fort]. *Unzer Veg* 16 (January 18, 1945); 17 (January 25, 1945).

"*Za'akat misparim – hamisha luhot shel diagramot statistiyot she-hukhnu ba-geto Kovno be-shnat 1943*" ["The numbers shout" – five tables of statistical diagrams that were prepared in the Kovno Ghetto in 1943]. *Yediot beit lohamei ha-geta'ot* 21:142–44 (May 1959).

Zadok, Hirsch. *"Tzav'at 50,000 tvuchei Kovno"* [The last will and testament of the 50,000 Kovno slaughtered victims], a will in Yiddish on the title page of a book found in the basement of a destroyed house. *Ha'aretz* 7706 (January 9, 1945); *Ha-Boker* 2793, ibid.; *Ha-Tzofeh* 2135 (January 10, 1945).

Zedek, Baruch. *"'Nikmat dameinu tihiyehna matarat hayeikhem!' Be-mikhtav al zevaot Kovna nimseru devarav ha-achronim shel echad ha-korbanot."* ['May the goal of your life be to avenge our blood!' These last words of one of the victims appears in a letter about the atrocities of Kovno]. *Davar* 5899 (December 10, 1944).

Zilberis, E. *"Žūtbūtineje kovoje"* [An all-out war for survival]. *Kauno Tiesa* 135 (July 9, 1958), Kovno.

Zilberman, Ephraim. *"Gehaime post in Kovne geto"* [Secret mail service in the Kovno Ghetto]. *Fun Letsten Churban* 10:42–47 (December 1948).

About the Authors

PROFESSOR DOV LEVIN was born in 1925 into a traditional and Zionist family in Kovno, Lithuania. From kindergarten until the eleventh grade he was a student in schools where Hebrew was the language of instruction. As a teenager, he joined the youth movement Hashomer Hatzair. In 1940, when Lithuania became a Soviet republic and the use of Hebrew and Zionist activity were outlawed, Dov was forced to go to a school where the language of instruction was Yiddish. It was in this school that he completed his

1944

high school studies. During this time he joined the Zionist underground, which was active in the city of Kovno and continued to nurture Hebrew culture and the connection to the Land of Israel.

After the Nazis invaded Lithuania in June 1941, Dov was imprisoned together with his family in the Kovno Ghetto, which was established in a suburb of the city, Slobodka. In the ghetto Dov was a member of the anti-Nazi underground. He witnessed his father, Zvi Hirsch, his mother, Blume, and his twin sister, Batya, taken by the Nazis in the Estonia deportation in 1943. They did not survive. After this, Dov joined the Zionist "pioneering movements" collective at Mildos 7. In the framework of the underground organization, he escaped with others from the ghetto to fight as partisans; he reached the Rudniki Forests, where he joined the partisan battalion "Death to the Occupiers." After meeting up with the Red Army in June 1944, he was recruited into the security forces, which were locating collaborators with the Nazi enemy and murderers of Jews. At the same time he renewed his underground Zionist activity in the framework of "Bricha" (the organized flight of the surviving Jews in Europe to Palestine), and he set out himself for Eretz Yisrael, the Land of Israel.

Dov arrived in Eretz Yisrael (Palestine) in October 1945 and began his studies at the Hebrew University in Jerusalem. He also joined the Haganah and later fought in the War of Independence. In 1951, he completed his studies at the Hebrew University's School of Social Work. From 1951–1971 he served as the head of the Youth Section of the Social Work Department of the Jerusalem Municipality and also as the head of the Statistics and Sociology Department in the municipality. In 1954 Dov received his master's degree from the Hebrew University in sociology and Jewish history and during the years 1954–1958 also worked as a researcher in the Sociology Department.

During this period, with the help of his friend Zvie Brown, Dov began to document the activities of the Jewish partisans from Kovno. Dov would travel with a recording device to many places throughout Israel in order to interview survivors. He was one of the first researchers to correctly appreciate the importance of recording oral history as one of the primary sources for understanding the events of the twentieth century. He combined his awareness of being a participant in historical events with his experience as a social worker. He was one of the founders of the Oral History Division of the Avraham Harman Institute of Contemporary Jewry that was established in 1959 at the Hebrew University in Jerusalem. One of the most prolific interviewers that contributed to the collection of testimonies of the Oral History Division, he was chosen to be its director from 1985–2001 and continued to develop the principles and methods of documenting oral history while stringently upholding historical credibility. Today, Dov's recordings are kept in a special collection in the Division. In 2013 a catalogue of abstracts of these interviews was published, entitled "Historian's Testimony." Dov is the honorary president of the Israel Association for Oral Documentation.

Out of his documentation work grew Dov's academic research into the Jewish armed resistance against the Germans in the Baltic countries and the course of the Holocaust in those countries. In 1962 he published in Hebrew, together with Zvie Brown, his first book, *Toldoteha shel Machteret* (translated into English in the present volume: The Story of an Underground – the Resistance of the Jews of Kovno in the Second World War). This "monumental work" (as described by the US Holocaust Museum) is a detailed academic presentation of the story of the Kovno Ghetto and the escape to the forests by the members of the underground, including the authors themselves, to fight as partisans.

In 1966 Dov was a Fulbright Scholar at the University of Chicago. He received his PhD in 1971 from the Hebrew University in Jerusalem for his research and dissertation entitled "The Participation of the Lithuanian Jews in the War against the Germans in the Second World War" (Hebrew). For this work he was awarded the Yitzchak Sadeh Prize in Military History. The research was published as a book in 1974, *Lochamim Ve-Omdim Al-Nafsham*, and was the first comprehensive description of the organized resistance of the Jews of Lithuania against the Nazis. The book was later translated into English and published under the name *Fighting Back – Lithuanian Jewry's Armed Resistance to the Nazis*. Over the years Dov became one of the preeminent scholars in the world in the field of the history of the Jewish communities of Eastern Europe, particularly on the subject of the Jewish armed resistance to the Nazis in the Baltic countries. Dov Levin has published over 520 articles and sixteen books in Hebrew, English, Yiddish, Russian, and Lithuanian.

During the past twenty-five years, in addition to his research and writing, Dov also engaged in activities that brought his findings before the general public, both in Israel and throughout the world. He served as advisor to various documentary films and museums on the subject of the Holocaust. Perhaps the most important of these activities was when he served as an advisor to the exhibition on the Kovno Ghetto that was mounted by the US Holocaust Museum in Washington, DC, from 1997–1999. The book published by the museum on the occasion of the exhibition "Hidden History of the Kovno Ghetto" contains a chapter written by Dov. Another subject for which Dov advocated during the 1990s and until today was to raise public awareness of the efforts of the Lithuanian government and of other Baltic countries to "rehabilitate" those of their citizens who had collaborated with the Nazis.

As a young man, Dov Levin found his way in the midst of the inferno of the Holocaust to survive and fight. As a researcher, he tried always to discover and faithfully present the truth of a dark and difficult period in the history of the Jewish people. Nevertheless, he is blessed with a contagious sense of humor and an optimistic outlook on life. He is married to the artist Bilha (Deutsch) Levin and they live in Jerusalem. They have three children – Nitzana Borosh, Basmat Levin, and Tzvi Levin – and seven grandchildren.

PROFESSOR ZVIE A. BROWN (d. 1996) was born in 1920 in Warsaw, Poland, the youngest of eight children in a strictly religious family. In his youth he left religion and joined the socialist-Zionist youth movement Hashomer Hatzair. He arrived in Kovno during the Nazi conquest of Eastern Europe where he joined the underground in the ghetto and then fought as a partisan against the Nazis in the "Death to the Occupiers" battalion in the Rudniki Forests. He enlisted in the Red Army when it occupied Lithuania in 1944. Of his entire family, only two sisters survived.

1944

After the war, Zvie returned to his native Warsaw and worked as a newspaper editor. He began to study philosophy at Varoszlav and Lodz Universities. In 1950 he arrived in Israel and continued his studies at the Hebrew University, receiving his BA (1952), MA (1957), and PhD (1964). His doctoral thesis was entitled "The Contemporary Theory of Categories in Historical Perspective." In addition to serving as senior lecturer, he was a research fellow at Yale University (1965–1966) and guest lecturer at the University of St. Andrews in Scotland (1970–1971). He went on to teach philosophy at Hebrew University and from 1977–1980 served as chair of the philosophy department. His research encompassed philosophy as well as other fields, including the Holocaust.

Zvie authored, edited, and translated numerous books in Hebrew and English on philosophy, including: "On possibility and modal analysis" (1968), "On Shmuel Hugo Bergman's Philosophy" (1986), and "The Categories and the Principle of Coherence: Whitehead's Theory of Categories in Historical Perspective" (1987). In 1995 he published *"Am Lachud Batsvat"* (A People Trapped in a Vise), an analysis of various important issues of the Holocaust.

Zvie Brown died in 1996. He was married to Varda Esther (Goldberg) (d. 2010), and is the father of Moshe Brown and Urit Agami.

Index